11-6-00

D1090168

PC Ph.D.: INSIDE PC INTERFACING

MYKE PREDKO

McGraw-Hill

New York San Francisco Washington, D.C. Auckland Bogotá
Caracas Lisbon London Madrid Mexico City Milan
Montreal New Delhi San Juan Singapore
Sydney Tokyo Toronto

√

Library of Congress Cataloging-in-Publication Data

Predko, Michael.
    PC Ph.D.: inside PC interfacing / Myke Predko.
       p. cm.
    ISBN 0-07-134186-2 (alk. paper)
    1. Microcomputers. 2. Computer interfaces. I. Title.
    QA76.5.P716   1999
    004.16—dc21   99-35904
                                   CIP

McGraw-Hill

*A Division of The **McGraw·Hill** Companies*

1 2 3 4 5 6 7 8 9 0   DOC/DOC   9 0 9 8 7 6 5 4 3 2 1 0 9

P/N 0-07-134187-0
ISBN 0-07-134186-2

The sponsoring editor for this book was Scott Grillo, the editing supervisor was Peggy Lamb, and the production supervisor was Pamela Pelton. It was set in TimesNewRoman PS by Wanda Ditch through the services of Barry E. Brown (Broker—Editing, Design and Production).

Printed and bound by R.R. Donnelley & Sons Company.

This book is printed on recycled, acid-free paper containing a minimum of 50% recycled, de-inked iber.

McGraw-Hill books are available at special quantity discounts to use as premiums and sales promotions, or for use in corporate training programs. For more information, please write to the Director of Special Sales, McGraw-Hill, Inc. 11 West 19th Street, New York, NY 10011. Or contact your local bookstore.

CONTENTS

ACKNOWLEDGMENTS

When I did my first internship with IBM, it was in the summer of 1981. At the time, rumors abounded that IBM would be announcing a "Personal Computer" to compete with the "Apple II". While many of my co-workers thought that IBM had the right idea with the "big iron" and small computers was just a passing fad, IBM did announce, in August of 1981, the first "PC". In the almost twenty years since the first PC was shipped from the plant in Boca Raton, the IBM Personal Computer has become an integral part of our everyday lives.

I have watched the PC grow from just a fairly expensive game platform, word processor or a way to learn about electronics into an extremely cost effective business tool, communications medium and a basic part of many people's lives. This tranformation has been the result of literally millions of people's vision and work over the past two decades. I see no end to it as the next millenium approaches.

These improvements have been slow and steady, from the first PC, with a monochrome or color display and two diskette drives (and up to 256 KBytes of memory). Next came the first feature enhancements to the design, followed by the PC/AT with it's 80286. A fairly recent innovation is the "modem" and the worldwide networking abilities of the PC that we take for granted. Today, we work with PCs that have Graphical User Interfaces working with multi-tasking operating systems and memory sizes and raw processing power that was only available in "supercomputers" of a decade ago.

Over the years, I have encountered many people, in many companies, countries and circumstances who have been instrumental and unselfish in helping me and others learn about the intricacies of the PC and how to create our own applications. These people have also created on their own projects and products and have worked to make the PC into a faster, more capable and reliable tool that is easier to develop complex applications for. The fruits of their labors has been a product that is used and depended upon around the world and should be regarded as the greatest development project of the twentieth century.

I have literally spend several months trying to remember everybody who has given me information, hints or suggestions that has made my understanding of the PC better and has ultimately enriched this book. I can honestly say that I cold fill twenty pages trying to name everybody that I have been in contact with over the past twenty years and have learned something from. I wish I could provide a comprehensive list, but I fear that I could work for another six months exclusively trying to come up with all the names of people who have helped me and still miss some very important people.

What I want to do is say "thank you" to everyone that has put up with my questions, pointed out my mistakes and put ideas in my head that were always a lot better than anything I've been able to come up with on my own. I feel lucky to have been involved in a community that shares its ideas and helps out so freely. Part of the reason for creating this book is to return some of this knowledge and help to get others as excited about the PC and what you can do with it as I have been.

A special thank you goes to Ben Wirz for his encouragement and patience while I worked on the book. I appreciate the time you've spent listening to my ideas and making suggestions.

Without IBM and Celestica, I would not have been able to write this book. Thank you for exposing me to the latest and greatest in tools and equipment and putting up with me over the years and my hare-brained ideas for testers and applications.

During the production of this book, Kelly Ricci, the managing editor for this book was seriously injured. Her co-workers at Barry Brown's PRD Group rallied around and made sure this project and others being managed by Kelly were kept on schedule. I was very impressed with everyone's enthusiasm, even when problems were discovered in the text and graphics used in this book. Lana, Mark, Barry, Toya (and I'm sure I'm missing a few people) were instrumental in getting this book to the printers on time. Kelly, I hope you have a fast & complete recovery.

I also want to thank my editor at McGraw-Hill, Scott Grillo, for helping me develop the concept for this book along with the many other people who are involved in editing, production and sales at McGraw-Hill. Everyone I have talked to has been uniformly cheerful and, more importantly, helpful and always have had time to answer my questions and give me some encouraging words.

1998 was a busy year for business travel for me and I can't believe that an astounding twenty-five percent of this book was written either in airports or in economy class seating. A similar percentage was proofread under similar circumstances. There are two groups of people I want to acknowledge as a result of this. First, I want to thank the flight attendants that tried to make my life easier while working onboard the various flights. I appreciate your efforts to clean up after meals quickly to allow me to get back to work and answer my endless requests for ice water.

I also want to acknowledge the Scrooges in the airlines, despite their best efforts I did not become a bent-over arthritic with knuckles that drag on the ground. I hope that they use the new millenium as an opportunity to arrange connecting flights that are not at opposite ends of O'Hare and buy aircraft that don't having seating designed for lethargic smaller primates.

My children, Joel, Elliot and Marya did a lot to help me with this book (mostly by not wrecking any of the project prototypes I created and knowing to be quiet when dad's up in the "dungeon"). I know it's tough when I'm working on a book, but you have done a lot to make it easier for me. I owe you a trip to Disneyworld (which will be paid for using my "Air Miles").

As always, my biggest source of support is my wife, Patience. When the manuscript of this book was finally dropped off at FedEx (two months late), I know you were the happiest person on the planet. The effort you put in helping to proofread this book really lightened my load and made the frantic last weeks bearable. I know I was tough to deal with as the deadline came and past, but you really helped me get all the pieces together.

This book is a result of your endless love and encouragement. Thank you.

INTRODUCTION

When the IBM Personal Computer (PC) was first introduced in 1981, it was a marvel of simplicity, with only seven large-scale integrated circuits (not counting the memory chips) built into it. Of those seven, the disk controller and video controller were not part of the "central" printed circuit motherboard or "planar." Coupled with a very simple operating system and reasonably efficient expansion bus, an engineer could understand thoroughly and easily develop hardware interfaces for the original PC.

As time passed, the PC became more complex. In 1984, IBM introduced the PC/AT, which included a microprocessor that was capable of emulating the operating modes (including virtual machines with protected memory), which, up to then, was only available in mainframe architectures. Around the same time, Microsoft introduced *Windows*, which gave users a consistent, easy-to-learn interface and hid much of the operation of the PC hardware. These trends of increasing the complexity and sophistication of the hardware and simplifying the user interface has continued unabated to the point where the PC has become one of the complex, powerful, and easy-to-use computing systems ever available (Figure I-1).

Over the years, a number of ideas have been put forward. Some have become standards and others have languished and today are only used by a small number of users. As I write this

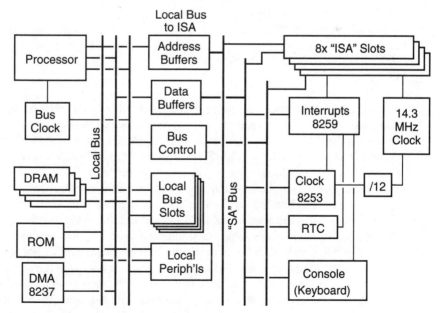

Modern PC Functional Block Diagram.

(early 1999), a modern PC consists of an Intel Pentium II or III processor-based motherboard running Microsoft Windows 98 or Windows NT (both of which are multitasking operating systems capable of taking full advantage of all the Pentium's 32-bit features). Interfaces can easily be designed for the ISA, PCI, and USB option busses, multiple serial ports, "Centronics" parallel printer ports, disk interface busses (including IDE and SCSI), and a user console, consisting of a graphic screen for output and a keyboard/mouse combination for input.

Many of these features have been available on the PC since the beginning. Creating applications that interface to external devices has become more complex. This is because of the increased sophistication of the PC's operating system and the unimaginable complexity of the modern hardware with Protect mode, caching, paging, and other features. This has driven the total number of transistors in a PC's motherboard logic from a couple of hundred thousand in the original PC to roughly 100 million on a modern motherboard.

Further complicating the task of creating a hardware interface to the PC is the legacy systems still in use in which many of the more-current interfaces are not available or the operating system is different from the 32-bit multitasking Windows "Win32" kernel. This book touches on many features, but, for the most part, it focuses on what I consider to be a standard system:

1 A Pentium-compatible processor with "MMX" technology.
2 32 MB (or more) of system memory
3 Diskette and hard disk drives
4 Windows 95/98/NT/2000 operating system
5 Super VGA color monitor
6 Mouse and keyboard
7 ISA expansion bus slots
8 PCI expansion bus slots
9 USB network connections
10 SoundBlaster audio I/O card
11 RS-232 serial ports
12 Centronics-compatible parallel ports
13 A game port

The IBM PC is presented as a system with a variety of hardware peripherals, controlled by operating-system software that can be used to control external devices and enhance the operation of the PC. The book first covers the architecture of the Intel PC processors and how they interface to the PC system. Understanding both architectures and how they interrelate is crucial to understanding how to add hardware to the PC.

Next is the operation of the MS-DOS operating system as an introduction to application programming the PC. The MS-DOS command-line interface is the basis of the operation of the PC. Included in this section are the BIOS and DOS interrupt interfaces to the PC.

Next, the different interfaces are presented in detail, starting with the standard interfaces (the ISA bus, the keyboard, RS-232 serial, and the Centronics parallel printer ports), followed by the USB bus interface. The explanations of the hardware include a number of demonstration projects to show you how these hardware devices can be used to interface with external devices. Along the way are some tricks and hardware interfacing ideas that you can use on your own.

The hardware projects presented are quite easy to replicate and they might seem deceptively simple. Although they are quite uncomplicated, this is not to say that they are simple or cannot teach you how the specific PC interface works. In each project, I try to point out important hints and explanations of what is actually happening and what should be done to prevent future problems.

In my previous books, many people created each sample application presented. I recommend this for you as well, although I do recommend that you only use them on an "experimental" PC (which is described in greater detail later in the book). Rather than expose your primary PC (or workstation) to homemade devices that are connected to motherboard power and signals, an outdated and cheap PC will provide many of the same capabilities and not expose you to the worry of damaging your primary work (or Internet surfing) tool.

The book does introduce the Windows *Win32* kernel operating systems (Windows 95, Windows 98, Windows/NT, and Windows 2000) and how software interfaces for the hardware are written. When presenting Windows, the concentration is on the Microsoft Visual Basic and Visual C++ tools for developing applications. Methods for creating Windows device drivers (DLLs, VxDs, and WDMs) are presented along with the Compuware tools that will make developing them quick and efficient.

When I was trying to decide which hardware interfaces to write about, I used Microsoft and Intel's PC/99 standard as a reference. This standard defines what features, both from a hardware and an operating-system software perspective, are going to be available in the future. If you read this standard, you will probably be surprised to see that the unique interfaces that are currently available (such as the keyboard ports and the ISA bus) are to be eliminated in favor of the Universal Serial Bus ("USB") and IEEE-1394 (known as *Firewire*). For this reason, I have added a fairly comprehensive section on the USB, incuding sample applications. As I write this, Firewire is not a standard feature on any PC (although it is being made available on Apple Macintoshes).

During the writing of this book, Microsoft announced that Windows NT 5.0 was renamed to Windows 2000; for this reason, I have minimized the references to Windows NT in the text. Windows 2000 is the next step in the evolution of Windows and, although it is derived from Windows NT (the current product that uses the full Win32 kernel), it is meant to be used in all Windows PCs, merging Windows 3.x/95/98/NT into one platform.

As I write this, the Linux movement has introduced version 2.2 as an alternative to Windows. I have not addressed Linux operating-system development in this book, but the hardware, BIOS, and processor information would be relevant for Linux hardware developers.

Additional Information and Resources

Although the purpose of this book is to introduce you to the basic PC architecture, operating-system software and interfaces, it is not a vehicle for teaching electrical engineering or computer science basics. It is assumed that you will have some experience in electronics, and assembly-language and high-level language programming techniques. Without a basic understanding of how computer processors work or having a basic understanding of digital and analog electronics, you might find this book to be confusing and difficult to understand.

Along with this, you should have a basic understanding of how to work with files in your PC, creating, editing, and processing. This book presents interfaces for the 16-bit (MS-DOS) interface, as well as the 32-bit Win32 (which consists of Windows 95, Windows 98, and Windows 2000) operating system.

If you are going to get the most out of this book, you should get a copy of an 8086 assembler and a high-level language to try out the example applications on your own, as well as create your own. Although this book presents Microsoft tools, other products (including freeware and shareware assemblers and compilers) are available, which can be used, too.

Included with this book is a CD-ROM that contains the source code used in the applications presented in this book. To aid in navigating around the CD-ROM, an HTML interface is included, which uses your PC's Internet browser.

I am a great believer in the Internet and its ability to help the engineer get technical information. For all of the products presented in this book, this is very true. Along with Web sites, where updated information can be found, I have also included information on list servers and user groups, along with information on contacting the part manufacturers directly.

This book provides a comprehensive introduction to the PC, a good understanding of the hardware used in the PC, and the ability to create custom hardware and software interfaces that will allow you to use your PC for much more than surfing the Web.

Conventions used in this book:

Hz	Hertz (cycles per second)
kHz	Kilohertz (thousands of cycles per second)
MHz	Megahertz (millions of cycles per second)
GHz	Gigahertz (billions of cycles per second)
bps	Bits per second
Kbps	Thousands of bits per second
mbps	Millions of bits per second
KB	1,024 bytes
MB	1,048,576 bytes
GB	1,073,741,824 bytes
Ω	ohms
k	1,000 ohms
μF	Microfarads
ms	Milliseconds
μs	Microseconds
0x0nn, $nn, 0nnh, and H'nn'	Hex numbers
0b0nnn, %nnn, 0nnnb, and B'nnn'	Binary number
nnn, 0nnnd, and .nnn	Decimal number

AND and &	Bitwise AND
OR and |	Bitwise OR
XOR and ^	Bitwise XOR
_Label	Negative active pin. In some manufacturer's data sheets, this is represented with a leading ! character or with a bar over the entire label.
[parameter]	The parameter is optional
parameter | parameter	One or another parameter can be used

Development Tools Used in This Book

When I created the application code for this book, I tried to use readily available tools. To this end, I have selected primarily Microsoft assemblers and compilers. Microsoft does support their tools quite well and, as described later in the book, it does provide low-cost "learning editions", complete with multimedia training CD-ROMs that will work with all the applications.

For the PC assembly-language code, I used Microsoft MASM version 6.11. This very complete assembler has many utilities to allow you to program assembly code in 8086 Real mode and 80286, 80386, and MMX Protect modes. A number of other tools are available from other vendors and as freeware (that will work with the examples), although you might have to chagne some directives.

Most of the MOS-DOS code is written in C. The compiler that I use is Microsoft C version 3.0 that I bought in 1987. The compiler itself does not support 80386 instructions or Protect mode, but it does produce excellent 16-bit MS-DOS code. Currently, a number of straight MS-DOS C compilers are available and I can recommend Hi-Tech's Pacific C shareware (referenced in Appendix B).

Most of the Windows applications are written in Microsoft's Visual Basic. All of the code has been tested on Versions 5.0 and 6.0. Visual Basic is a wonderful tool to introduce you to graphical user interface event-oriented programming and give you a few ideas about object-oriented programming at the same time.

Along with Visual Basic, I have also provided source for a number of applications and device drivers written in Microsoft's Visual C++. C++ is an object-oriented programming language; before attempting to create your own applications with it, you should look at the books referenced in Appendix B.

I reference the *Microsoft Software Developer's Toolkit (SDK)* and *Device Driver Toolkit (DDK)* in the book. These tools are available from Microsoft as part of the *Microsoft Developer's Network (MSDN)* "subscription" program. This program offers a number of options, each with varying levels of service and information.

To help make creating device drivers easier, I also use the Vireo software VtoolsD and Driver::Works. These excellent tools help take the mystery out of device-driver development and allow you to focus on the device-driver functions, rather than the syntax of the drivers themselves.

For almost all of the interface projects that use a microcontroller, I have used the Microchip PICMicro. This device family is extremely versatile and quite easy to program. I also use the Atmel AT89C2051, which is a 20-pin 8751-compatible microcontroller. If you are not familiar with these devices, you can find out more information and reference information from my Web page (given in Appendix B).

For the CY7C76xx USB microcontroller applications, I used the tool provided by Cypress in their USB Starter Kit. You can get more detail on these tools later in the book. For the PC, the operating system should be Windows 98 or Windows 2000. Windows 95 can be used as long as it is OSR 2.1 (or later) and has the WDM interface enabled.

If you were to buy all of the development tools presented in this book, it would cost somewhere on the order of $4500 retail. Before laying out more money for software than you probably spent on your PC, I suggest that you first read through this book and phase in the purchase of the software. As part of this, I suggest that you buy the Learning Editions of Visual Basic and Visual C++ first, both to get the multimedia training CD-ROMs, as well as to defray the cost. Buying all of the products that are listed in this book will result in an impressive (and intimidating) pile of documentation and about 20 CDs, none of which have a decent tune for you to listen to.

THE PC'S HARDWARE
AND SOFTWARE AND
HOW THEY WORK TOGETHER

HISTORICAL
PERSPECTIVE

Before I go through the PC's architectures and features, I would like to go through a historical perspective on the PC and where it has come from. I would never go so far as to say that the products of the past 20 years can be used to predict what the products of the next 20 (or 10 or even five) years into the future will be, but I think understanding it will help you to see why things are done in a certain way and help you to remember potential pitfalls and how to avoid them, or (as I always seem to be doing), climbing out of them.

In today's world of product lifecycles of less than six months, it might seem strange to start an introduction to a modern device's hardware architecture by first reviewing past products that are ancient by any reasonable measurement. Today's PCs are literally thousands of times more powerful and able to store millions of times more data than the first computer systems, but they do take a lot of what they are from their ancestors. Probably more than most other computer systems available on the market today.

I realize that many of the topics presented in this chapter are older than many of the people reading this book and probably don't seem that relevant to the devices of today. But, I always feel that understanding why things were done in the past is crucially important to understanding how modern devices work.

The history of the PC is really a history of the electronics industry over the past 20 years, with the ultimate goal of increasing a person's ability to carry out tasks and communicate with others more efficiently than they ever have before.

Before the PC

I hope you don't mind if I start with the environment before the PC at the beginning of home microcomputers, rather than with Hollerith and his punch cards. I want to describe the development of the microprocessor and systems that were created from them because from this era, the concept of the mass-marketed computer was developed and, concurrently many of the technologies that are currently being exploited were first being developed.

The first hobbyist/professional microcomputers that became available in the early 1970s were real behemoths in terms of size and power requirements by today's standards. As well, the user interface left lots to be desired with programming usually accomplished by a panel of switches (single pole, single throw) used to set the address and memory contents to be programmed.

To program these devices, the addresses and data for the address were set on the switches and programmed into the microcontroller's memory by pressing a button that stored the data into RAM. This sounds like it would take an unreasonably long time, but remember, microcomputers at the time had much less than one kilobyte of RAM available and it wasn't that big a chore.

Once the program had been entered into RAM, the microcomputer was reset and allowed to run the program.

What did the program do? Initially, they just flashed LEDs on the front panel of the box. As time went by, a number of projects were developed to add more memory (now counted in the kilobytes), teletypes, IBM Selectric typewriters (seriously, this was big), paper tape punches and readers, cassette recorders (for program storage), and the odd matrix keyboard and video modulator.

This era had a few problems. First, you definitely required a degree in electrical engineering to be able to program and use the microcomputer. To attach peripheral devices, you had to have the soul of a tinkerer to get many of the electromechanical devices listed above to work.

Making owning your own computer more difficult at the time was the need to be able to write assembler programs (there were no high-level languages) and hand assemble them (unless you worked for a large corporation that could afford to buy cross-assemblers for mainframes). This meant that after writing the application, you had to convert the assembler code that you had written into the bits that you programmed into the computer via the front-panel switches.

As the '70s progressed, the first hobbyist/hacker books became available and computer clubs began to spring up. Also, more and more surplus parts (including floppy diskette drives) became available, making more peripherals available to the user. This lead to a certain number of standards being accepted for microcomputers, resulting in more or less standard devices for users.

With the advent of floppy disks being available for microcomputers, the first standard operating systems ("CP/M" for 8080 and Z-80-based computers) and programming languages (such as Apple's/Microsoft's "BASIC") became popular and simplified the development of applications. With CP/M, for the first time, microcontroller users were able to transfer application code and expect code written on somebody else's machine to run on theirs without any modifications.

The first real integration of these standards was the Apple computer. The vision of the "two Steves" was to create a computer that a customer could buy at a store, take home, plug into the wall and TV, and start using.

The first Apple's, didn't quite hit this mark, but the Apple II became a big hit because of its integrated BASIC Interpreter and user friendly (for the time) disk interface.

Actually, there were a number of reasons why the Apple II was very successful, along with the improved software interface and this had to do with a number of very clever hardware features built into the microcomputer. These included a 40/80 column composite video output, 16K (expandable to 64K) DRAM interface (which was refreshed by using the DRAM as both microcontroller memory and video RAM and setting up the DRAM addressing to allow video RAM reads to refresh all of the memory in the computer) and a standard set of expansion card sockets that allowed additional hardware to be added very easily and consistently.

If you ever find a copy of an Apple II's schematics, I urge you to study them. If you are familiar with modern PCs schematics, you'll probably be amazed at how complex they seem (all the circuits, except for the microprocessor, are SSI or MSI TTL). The Apple II's circuit is actually very simple compared to modern PC designs because each box on the page doesn't represent 100,000 plus gates, each one represents 20 to 50 *transistors*.

Despite this, the Apple II was able to implement many of the features that we now expect in any PCs that we buy. These features include integrated video, disk access, and printer control. Also available was a suite of software development tools that allowed a system's programmer to interface personal applications with peripheral hardware. This was the real beginning of personal computing.

The Apple II was first introduced in 1977. In the following years, many other microcomputers tried to dethrone it. Many of these microcomputers were quite clever and tried to be better than the Apple II at different market segments. Some of these devices included the Radio Shack TRS-80, the Commodores and Ataris (both personal computers and home game machines), and the Sinclair ZX-80.

If you've never heard of the ZX-80, please bear with me while I reminisce a bit. The ZX-80 was Clive Sinclair's attempt at developing the simplest (and cheapest) computer possible. The ZX-80 was a home computer that only used three chips (a Z-80 microprocessor, a static RAM chip, and a custom chip that would now be called an *ASIC*), executed BASIC programs and displayed them on the screen of a TV. Most of the processing power of the Z-80 was devoted to creating composite video for the TV, but it could process its BASIC program during the vertical blanking interval. With this method of operation, the Z-80 was only available for running a program about 30% of the time, which made it far and away the slowest home computer available.

Today, I don't think anything like the ZX-80 could ever be sold seriously, the quality of the video output was horrendous, it's speed was worse than pathetic, it was hit or miss whether or not the cassette interface would save or load a program, and its power supply tended to burn itself out. But, for $30.00, there was nothing that competed. I was always amused by the extremes people enhanced their ZX-80s, adding real keyboards (the membrane keyboard that came with the unit was notoriously unreliable and difficult to use because it was only polled during vertical refresh periods), graphic video outputs, and disk drives were common upgrades that users put on their ZX-80s.

During this time, the CP/M operating system became available as an "open" product that many people could use and enhance. It was designed to run on the Intel 8080 and Zilog Z-80 line of microprocessors, which meant that the Apple II could not take advantage of the vast, free software library that was being developed. This disadvantage was actually nullified with the availability of many CP/M processor cards that could be added to the Apple II's expansion slots.

Despite this varied and aggressive competition, the Apple II remained king of the home and personal computers until the summer of 1981.

IBM's 5150

Where were you on August 2, 1981? (If you weren't born yet, don't bother telling me, it will just depress me.) On that day, IBM surprised the world by using the "Little Tramp" (Charlie Chaplin's trademark character) to announce a new personal computer, the IBM PC (IBM part number 5150). The product was met with mixed reviews, with its high-end price being a concern for many columnists. A major complaint about the IBM PC was the "boring" grey color.

The original IBM PC consisted of an Intel 8088 (the 8-bit external bus version of the 8086) processor running at 4.77 MHz, with 16 KB of RAM (up to 64 KB on the "motherboard" by adding memory chips), 64 KB of ROM (including a version of Microsoft's "GWBASIC"), a monochrome display (color, with a third party's screen, optional), a standard cassette interface for storing programs (diskette drives were optional) and five slots for system expansions and options. As meager as this system seems now, it was quite competitive to the other personal computer systems of the day in terms of processor power, storage and video display.

One term that you will hear a lot of, both in this book and outside it is the word *motherboard*. A true motherboard is completely passive; it just has a number of connectors. The PC main board, using IBM speak, is known as a *planar*. In some IBM documentation, you will still see the term *planar* used to reference what I will call the *motherboard* for the rest of the book.

The IBM offering broke "Big Blue" tradition in a number of areas; it was developed by a small team out of a Boca Raton lab, rather than through one of the big product labs with major marketing support, it used industry standards (such as using ASCII for communications, rather than EBCDIC) wherever possible. The design was "open," which allowed third parties to design products for it and application software was provided by external companies. All of these aspects, while being "standard" for the industry was very innovative for IBM (and you could probably argue that few of them have been repeated in products IBM has introduced since the PC).

Almost surprisingly, the PC very quickly became a hit and within a year was the top selling personal computer system in the world (displacing the Apple II). At the time, columnists accused IBM of using their marketing clout to force large customers to buy the product, but I feel that there are a number of reasons why the PC was adopted as a standard very quickly.

The first reason was the expandability of the IBM PC compared to its competitors. Most of the other personal computers of the day could claim some level of expandability, including optional disk drives, but the IBM PC offered up to 576 KB (which was later expanded to 640 KB) of memory (most other personal computers of the day could only handle up to 64 KB directly addressed memory), which meant much more complex programs were possible in the IBM PC.

This memory expandability was through the use of the Intel 8086 architecture in the processor. Although not providing full mainframe features, the 8086 did offer considerably more memory access, a richer instruction set, and integrated support chips than its contemporaries. All these factors helped make the design easier to implement and develop hardware and software applications for.

Even more attractive to customers was the "open" system of the IBM PC. By buying the IBM PC, you weren't locked into only buying a specific vendor's expansion options as you were with other personal computer makers. Although this turned into the explosion of "clones," it did provide customers with a lot of peripheral add-ons for the PC.

The Intel 8086 architecture allowed for up to 256 different interrupt sources, with any one of them being software generated. The IBM PC took advantage of that by making standard interrupt interfaces for accessing peripheral hardware inside the system. This was known as *BIOS (Basic Input/Output System)* and it gave programmers an easy and standard interface to access hardware. Part of BIOS was a simple disk interface, which allowed operating system programmers to relatively easily provide a file system for users.

But, the most compelling reason for customers to buy the IBM PC (in my mind) was the software. When IBM first released the PC, if optional disk drives were going to be purchased, the customer had a choice of three different operating systems, each one complete with development tools. This allowed customers to choose the best software and work with it.

Probably nobody remembers UCSD and CPM-86, but they were all offered along with PC-DOS, under the IBM logo. PC-DOS very quickly became the "standard," pushing its owners, a new company, Microsoft, to the top of the heap in terms of PC software vendors. PC-DOS (and Microsoft's MS-DOS, which was a relabeled version of PC-DOS with different cassette BASIC hooks) became successful because it had (as hard as it is to believe today) the simplest user interface of the three options.

Now, having said all this, I do have to say that the PC did have a few warts (which we still have to work with when developing software or hardware peripherals for PCs). The first was the decoding of only the first 1024 I/O addresses (up to 64 KB are available in the 8086 architecture). The feeling was that 1 KB was a lot of I/O addresses and decoding the entire 64 KB would add to the cost of the product, so only 1 KB unique I/O addresses are possible in the PC.

Another wart in an otherwise pretty good design was the use of edge-triggered interrupts, rather than level-triggered interrupts. *Edge triggered* means that when an interrupt is requested, the PC responds to it if interrupts are enabled when the interrupt request line transitions from one state to another. If interrupts are disabled while a transition comes in (such as when servicing a previous interrupt request), there is an opportunity for an interrupt request to be lost. Although some attempts have been made at changing this in the PCs standards, this is still something that hardware (and software) developers still have to contend with.

A concern at the time, because it almost turned into all out war, was use by IBM of interrupts for system tasks that were "reserved" by Intel. Now, there are two sides of the story, with IBM arguing that it didn't have any recourse because the operating system vendors were reserving interrupt vectors for their use (and not IBM's) and Intel could argue that they were designing products that used these vectors. The long and the short of it was, IBM designed the PC to use interrupt vectors for software functions that Intel later released hardware that used these vectors.

The last wart (pimple really) is that the standard I/O addresses are all located on byte addresses (as opposed to 16-bit word addresses). This is more of a concern for me because it did not take into account the possibility that the PC might be reprocessed in the future. Having a 16-bit I/O bus, or an eight-bit bus on one "side" of the data bus would have made implementing an 8086 (and the 80186, 80286, etc.) much easier than it turned out for later versions.

To be fair, all these problems that I have identified really are with the benefit of hindsight and the longevity and success of the PC in later years could not have been predicted. The real indicator of how good the PCs design is its longevity; no other personal computer system (and few products of any type) can demonstrate that it has been in continuous production for as long as the PC.

This, in itself, makes the original PC's design pretty spectacular.

The Clones

One of the greatest quotes about the IBM PC that I ever saw, was some wag proclaiming, "the best thing IBM did with the PC was to make it an open system. The worst thing that IBM ever did with the PC was to make it an open system." The very concept that made people look at and consider the PC in the first place turned into a major liability for IBM.

The PC was not IBM's first personal computer. The first IBM personal computer was the 5280, a rather large system that had a keyboard and an electroluminescent display and ran (ack!) APL. When this system was first introduced, it generated quite a media attention because it was the first computer for an individual user. Also during the 1970s, IBM increased the functionality of their typewriters (which caused them to be labelled as "word processors"), which were given many of the features of what would become known as "personal computers."

The problem with these computers (aside from only running APL programs, in the 5280's case) was that they were "closed" systems. You were provided with a user interface and some software. If you wanted anything additional, you had to order it from IBM. If you wanted something that wasn't available from IBM, you had to request IBM to develop it and hope that they would. It really wasn't a very satisfactory arrangement for the customer. With the PC, many companies created their own software products (including word processors, spreadsheets, communications programs, and programming tools) and created new peripherals for the PC (some specific to certain applications, others very general) and really improved personal computing, becoming standards in their own rights.

An excellent example of this was third parties providing fixed (hard) drives for the IBM PC. This spurred IBM to release the PC/XT, which had a 10-MB hard drive for faster program execution. Another example would be "mice." As professional graphics programs became available on the market, pointing devices were required for easier access to data on screens. These innovations help fuel the explosive growth of the PC and helped it find new applications that are easier for uses to operate.

Developing these products wasn't that hard because IBM had made available schematics and code listings for the PC, as well as fairly detailed documentation packages for the hardware and software. You might ask, how good was the documentation? Well, I still have my genuine IBM PC/XT, PC/AT, and PS/2 "technical references" and I find that I refer to them more than any other books. If you know of anybody who ever bought them when they first came out, chances are they're dog-eared, coffee stained, and worn out— but still considered irreplaceable.

Along with developing enhancements for the PC, a number of companies began to manufacture and sell copies of the PC, known as *clones*. The word *clone* is derived from the Greek word *klon*, which means *twig* and was first used to describe the process of creating an exact genetic duplicate of a living organism by taking a sample of its DNA and placing it in the cells of another.

As an aside, my first exposure to the word clone was in a 1972 edition of *Jimmy Olson, Superman's Pal*, in which Luthor uses cells taken from Olson by a corrupt dentist and uses them to create exact duplicates of Superman's friend which commit crimes and confound Superman. Superman eventually figures out what Luthor is up to and thwarts his plans by exchanging Olson's cells with those taken from a gorilla, the clone of which wrecks Luthor's laboratory and helps Superman capture Luthor.

Right from the beginning, "cloning" has always been perceived as something that invited illegal activities.

During the early '80s, the word *clone* was further sullied as it became synonymous with copies and knock offs of Apple IIs and IBM PCs. These copies ranged from exact duplicates of the PCs to redesigned systems that were capable of running the same software. These copies of the PCs were often (much) cheaper than IBM and Apple's products and caused their sales and market share to plummet almost overnight.

Apple's response to this was to develop the "Apple III," which was a business-specific computer, maintained some compatibility with the Apple II, but redesigned with new hardware (the recently introduced Programmable Array Logic chips) and not publishing the new system's specifications as they had with the Apple II. When this system failed to regain Apple's market share, Apple was forced to re-release redesigned versions of the Apple II and look for the next wave in personal computing (which resulted in the Lisa and Macintosh).

IBM was in a different position because the PC was based on the Intel microprocessor support chip set (for Interrupt handling, Timing and Direct Memory Access ("DMA"), whereas the hardware for these functions were provided as SSI logic. As well as being cheaper than IBM's product, many clones were also more powerful (either through the use of faster microprocessors or by using the 8086, 80186 or NEC 8088 compatible chips) and IBM appeared to be reluctant to change its course from the tried and true 4.77-MHz 8088.

IBM approached the problem from a different angle and studied the various clones and sued manufacturers for violating IBM patents and intellectual property. This resulted in the creation of the "IBM compatible PC" marketplace in which different manufacturers would vary parts of the original PC's design to escape the possibility of a lawsuit and gave an opening to some vendors to produce products that would make IBM-compatible PCs, but not violate any of IBM's proprietary information.

To help stem the loss of market share, IBM itself became a clone manufacturer and released its PCjr. To lower the cost of buying a PC, IBM integrated the video output of the PCjr, instead of relying on an adapter card for that function and had removed the DMA circuitry. The result was not a bad computer, although very slow when accessing a disk (every byte had to be processed by the 8088, rather than bypassing it using the DMA controller) and less capable all around than the PC. This reflected IBM's product philosophy at the time: if a product is to be cheaper than the current products, it had to be less capable.

Almost needless to say, the PCjr was an embarrassing failure for IBM.

Looking back over this period, a number of good things came from the onslaught of the clones. First, the PC "standard" was no longer under the control of any one company (although some people might argue this statement today) and the overall design was not fixed. After the PC was first released, most third-party products (hardware and software) relied on hardware characteristics of the "true blue" PC and would not run properly for third-party products. During this period, interfaces and methods of accessing were standardized. Much of the information presented in this book is a direct result of this period because methods of controlling application that wasn't vendor hardware specific were developed, resulting in a much more robust method of accessing hardware and running programs.

One good thing that I haven't talked about is the emergence of *PLD (Programmable Logic Devices)* and *ASIC (Application Specific Integrated Circuit)* and its effect on the PC "standard." The development of ASICs has meant that the PCs functions and hardware are available to anyone wanting to build a PC without violating copyright agreements with intellectual property owners. Today, part of the cost of an ASIC is used to pay the owners of the standard devices used in the chip. This has allowed PC vendors to create products that all meet a standard without having to look over their shoulders to see if a lawyer is pursuing them.

The last good thing about this period was that it created a competitive marketplace for PCs. By having multiple companies providing competing products, the PC has been improved immeasurably. Over the past 10 years, we have witnessed an incredible growth in speed and capabilities that has made owning a PC very similar to owning a beer (as "Archie Bunker" would say, "you never own it, you just rent it").

Despite the changes over the years in the PC, it has still remained largely compatible with the original PC's design.

The PC/AT

In the spring of 1984, the PC marketplace had become more and more fragmented because of different manufacturer's being sure they didn't encroach on IBM's intellectual property and used processors that were not 100% 8088 compatible or would run all programs written for the PC. (NEC was pushing the V20 and V30 chips as a higher-performance 8088 replacement and Intel had the 8018x enhanced microprocessors.)

I personally remember this as a time where leadership was needed because while a lot of manufacturer's said they were compatible, they really weren't.

IBM provided the needed leadership by announcing the "PC/AT" (Advanced Technology) computer. This PC provided a significant enhancement to the PC's operation by an Intel 80286 microprocessor running at 12 MHz (and offering three to four times the performance of the original 4.77-MHz PC 8088), eight 8-/16-bit expansion slots, a hard disk, up to 16 MB of memory and an enhanced graphic capability. The architecture is shown in Fig. 1-1.

Looking at this block diagram from a high level, it is actually very similar to the original PCs. This was deliberate to maintain compatibility, both in terms of hardware interfaces and software applications. In Fig. 1-1, many control and interrupt request-line data paths have been omitted for clarity.

To be facetious, I could summarize that just about everything in the PC/AT's design was doubled, the microprocessor has twice the data bus width and twice the hardware interrupt request and DMA channels. Along with this doubling, there were a number of additional features (most notably the battery-backed CMOS configuration information) added to the "baseline" design, as well.

The Enhanced Graphic Array that was offered with the PC/AT also gave the first standard interface that allowed reading and writing to the *video RAM (VRAM)* without worrying about the state of the CRT raster. (In the original *Color Graphic Adapter (CGA)*, if the screen contents were updated while the raster was drawing to the CRT, "snow" would appear on the screen because the same bus was used for reading VRAM data for the video display's data contents, as well as writing to it. These processor accesses were given precedence over the video output operations.) This allowed much faster updates to the screen and more complex applications (such as Windows).

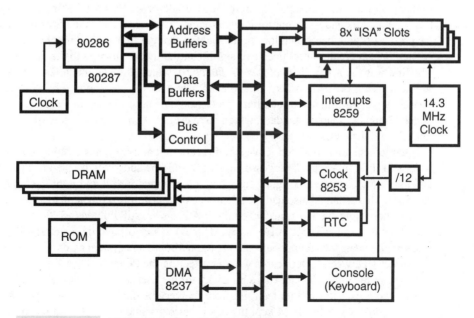

FIGURE 1-1   PC/AT functional block diagram.

When the PC/AT was introduced, other manufacturers quickly rushed to establish commonality with this design. The PC/AT architecture quickly became known as *ISA (Industry Standard Architecture)*.

Current PCs hardware interfaces are essentially unchanged from what was originally available in the PC/AT's and is what I focus on in this book.

In terms of software, the PC/AT originally worked with enhanced versions of the DOS Command Line interface, but with the EGA adapter, the first *Graphical User Interfaces (GUIs)* were possible.

The PC/AT provided the framework for today's PCs. As I show later in this chapter, most modern PCs still use the PC/AT's basic architecture (with a few improvements).

The PS/2

By the spring of 1987, IBM was looking to regain control of the PC marketplace and help redefine IBM's leadership position. When the PS/2s were introduced, IBM was only actively selling two different PCs, the venerable PC/AT and a simple laptop (the PC Convertible). Compared to other manufacturers, IBM's product line was quite slim and uninspired. The PS/2 line was a bold attempt to direct where the PC was going and to be sure that IBM was at the forefront of this new wave.

Many of you probably remember the PS/2 line as a failure for IBM. But, I'm including it because I feel that it was pivotal in bringing the PC into line with where we are today.

In my mind, the introduction of the PS/2 line was when, architecturally, personal computers became serious competitors to mini, mid-range and mainframe computers. With the introduction of the PS/2 lineup, IBM introduced 80386-based PCs for the first time (some of their competitors had some out for a few months). But, what made the PS/2 special wasn't the processors and their execution speeds, but the changes to how the PCs operated.

The PS/2 line really introduced two significant hardware changes to the PC "standard." The first was the *Microchannel Bus Architecture*, which allowed much faster peripherals to interact with the main processor and even take over the bus and use the PCs resources as if they were a primary or auxiliary processor. The second was the introduction of the Video Graphics Adapter standard, which gave users a totally new window (this pun is intended) into their PCs.

The microchannel architecture was the first attempt at developing a "Plug and Play" interface for PCs. In each adapter card, an ASIC could be addressed by the PC on power up and allow the computer to figure out what was plugged into it and boot the appropriate software. Microchannel also had the advantage of being able to run at up to a whopping 60 MHz (where eight-bit data transfers on the ISA bus were still limited to 720-ns cycle times and 16-bit data transfers ran at 160-ns cycle times), which offered the user a significant improvement in data throughput between the motherboard and system cards (as well as transfers directly between system cards without affecting the PC).

Although the microchannel was a bit tricky for the user to specify device locations, I always liked it. But it was doomed right from the very beginning, although only one major factor worked against it. IBM kept the bus proprietary and only released technical information to companies willing to sign a non-disclosure agreement with IBM. To make matters worse, to help keep the bus interface proprietary, IBM was reticent when releasing the "Plug and Play" interfaces, instead offering chips that they built and discouraging third parties from developing their own.

This strategy of making the bus proprietary was perceived as a tool for IBM to control the PC market and it backfired on them. Instead of solidifying the PC market on one bus, a number of other standards came out, which caused significant confusion in the marketplace. Some of these standards are still viable (most notably PCI and EISA), but consumers were battered by advertisements stating different manufacturer's computers were better because of a specific bus built into the PC. Most people didn't know what the bus wars were all about.

During this period (the late 1980s and early 1990s), the micro channel was further battered by the wide availability of cheap, high-performance ASICs. In previous PCs, the expansion bus was used to provide an interface for adapter cards that had disk controllers, extra memory, network connections, and video adapters. Looking at virtually any PC available on the market today, most of the logic required for these functions is built right into the motherboard. The need for very high-speed adapters for anything other than video graphics cards and network connections (often these functions are built onto motherboards as well) has really disappeared.

Why I consider the microchannel good and a positive occurrence in the history of the PC is that the micro channel bus signaled that the new, faster processors didn't have to be hobbled by the operation of the ISA bus. In fact, if you look at the architecture of most PCs, actually a number of busses are available in them.

In Fig. 1-2, I drew a box around the processor and its core components. These components run at the full processor speed. If other busses are used to interface with external devices, then data is passed through interface chips, which ensure that the timing impact to the PC's processor is minimal. This is actually the legacy of the microchannel; the changing of the PC standard to allow multiple busses of different types to run in one PC while allowing the processor to run at full speed.

The *Video Graphics Adapter (VGA)* and the *8415A Super VGA* were immediate successes with the PC consumer. The VGA could display a mixed text and graphics screen of up to 256 colors on a screen 640×480 pixels in size. I think nobody would disagree that this graphics standard is something that IBM got right.

The standard VGA interface was an enhancement to the color display adapters of the time. The big features made the creation of "Windows"-like programs include the ability to mix text and graphics on the same display, as well as be able to draw standard shapes very quickly in hardware, rather than devoting software to this task.

VGA and SVGA has been continually improved upon and today many "graphics accelerators" allow you to kill demons, shoot down MiGs, or display three-dimensional drawings much faster than ever before. The VGA standard, first introduced in the PS/2 was one of the first enhancements to the PC, which moved it beyond the realm of a personal computer and into that of workstations. Figure 1-3 shows some of the different display modes simultaneously available.

At the same time as the announcement of the PS/2, IBM also announced the existence of a multi-tasking operating system for 80286 PCs and beyond, which was called *OS/2*. This operating system, which was developed in conjunction with Microsoft was meant to be used in all personal computers (with 80286 and faster processors) which could perform many tasks at the same time, taking advantage of the multitasking features of the processors.

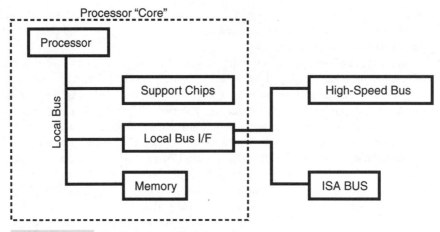

FIGURE 1-2 Multiple bus PC data paths.

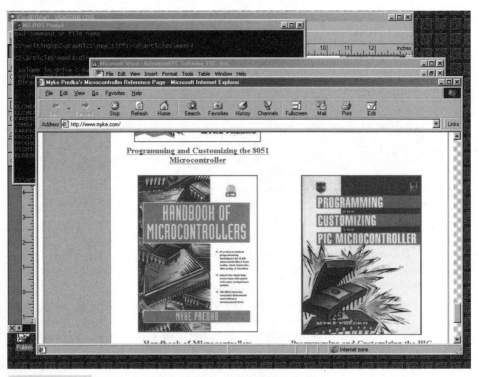

FIGURE 1-3 Example VGA mixed graphics and text.

At the same time, Microsoft did have a program called *Windows*, which was not much more of an interesting curiosity at the time. IBM's announcement spurred Microsoft to develop Windows into an user interface that did have some limited multitasking properties. Over time, this system has developed into the premier operating system for PCs and the one in which I focus on developing applications in this book.

Modern PCs

Since the PS/2, PCs have coalesced into a very homogeneous device, which are largely based on the PC/AT. Over the past 10 years or so, a number of new features have been tried until what I would consider a standard for a desktop PC has emerged:

- Intel "Pentium II/III" class processor
- 100+ MHz "Local Bus"
- 64+ MB of enhanced DRAM
- 4+ GB hard disk
- 8+ MB video RAM with a SVGA video accelerator
- 1+ free ISA (PC/AT) slots
- 2+ free PCI (local bus) slots
- Parallel, serial, and USB external device Interfaces

As you read this, I hope you haven't embarrassed you. My own system doesn't quite meet this standard either (but it was bought more than two years ago). To really stay current, you have to buy a PC every 18 to 24 months.

As I write this (mid-1999), these are the standards for PCs. As time goes on, I'm sure that new standards will develop and become a part of every PC.

Over the past 10 years, the PC/AT standard has changed a bit and most PCs would have a block diagram that looks something like Fig. 1-4.

The difference between this architecture and the PC/AT's is the two bus interfaces available. The local bus is a 66 MHz (or faster) bus that is driven directly by the processor. (As

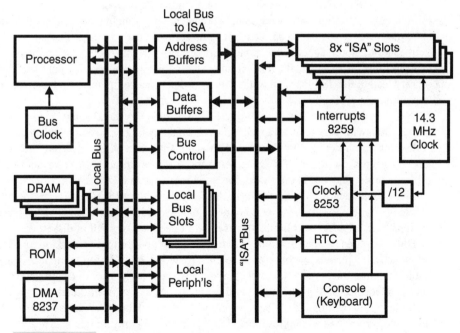

FIGURE 1-4   Modern PC functional block diagram.

a point of interest, this bus clock is multiplied within the processor by phase-locked loops to get the actual processor speed, thus a 200-MHz Pentium's local bus runs at 66 MHz, and the processor's PLL multiplies the clock three times to get the 200-MHz execution speed.) High-speed peripherals are typically put on this bus.

I have used the box labelled *Local Periph'ls* in Fig. 1-4 to include all the devices that are run at processor bus speeds. These devices include high speed disk accesses and the video drivers. In Fig. 1-4, I have referenced the DMA controller as an 8237; this is a bit of a misnomer. Although the DMA in modern PCs may have a command set and operation that is similar to the 8237, it is able to handle the full local bus access speeds and handle PCI bus "multi-mastering."

The modern PC typically has a number of "ISA" (PC/AT bus) slots, as well as a number of features that run at PC/AT speeds. These devices are typically the devices in which only a small amount of data are transferred.

Understanding how these devices interact and how to control them isn't that difficult, or rather I should say isn't that difficult in a DOS environment. As the PC's hardware became more sophisticated, so did the software. Now, understanding how GUI applications access hardware has become a major learning exercise. The advent of multitasking operating systems with protected device interfaces has meant that accessing hardware from software has gotten a lot more complex (and a lot less trivial).

LAPTOPS

It is truly amazing what is available today in laptop computers. When portable computers first came on the scene in the early 1980s, they were really complete PCs with a small screen, keyboard, and a full PC crammed into a barely luggable package. These computers didn't have internal batteries, they were simply computers you brought along and plugged into the wall of wherever you ended up. I remember an ad for an early portable that showed that the unit could be stored underneath a typical airline seat—with no room to spare for your feet!

And, for some reason that I'll never understand, they were incredibly popular. This popularity lead to the development of the laptop computer, a computer you could rest on your lap without crushing it.

The early laptops used very primitive LCD ("Liquid Crystal Display" technology) displays, often with very unusual aspect ratios and display modes. I remember Radio Shack's TRS-100 laptop with a 40-column by 4-row alphanumeric LCD. They often required the user to keep a multitude of diskettes on hand (there were no hard drives and only one diskette drive) and would only work for an hour or less on rechargeable batteries.

But, people kept on buying them (in the early days, the IRS-T00 was very popular because it was able to run for several hours on alkaline radio batteries and had several applications built in, which meant that the user didn't need pockets full of diskettes).

Today, laptops have changed from being a kind of poor sister to a desktop machine to a PC that can replace your desktop machine. At work, my desktop computer is a laptop plugged into a docking station, which allows my network connections, an SVGA screen and connects to a full-sized mouse and keyboard. Actually, from the user point of view, nothing would distinguish the laptop from a regular desktop PC, except that I can unlock the laptop from the docking station and take it home with me at night.

Laptops have helped improve the state of the PC art in several respects. The first is in high-performance ASICs. If you were to look at the motherboard of a typical laptop and compare it to the motherboard of a typical PC, you would be shocked at the incredibly small size of the laptop's board and the few components on it. Keeping the size down is important to push the size of the computer down (now, laptops are really not much bigger than a pad of 8.5" by 11" paper) and keeping the component count down is important to reduce power requirements.

The displays now available have become very impressive and compare very favorably to a CRT in terms of size, resolution, and brightness. As I write this, many high-end laptops are becoming larger in size because the screens are becoming larger. Most laptops also have an SVGA output, which allows either the laptop's display or a convenient CRT (or an overhead projector, if you're giving a pitch on the road) to be used without having to make any hardware or software settings or changes.

I'm always surprised to see that many laptops are used as the operator consoles for large computer and peripheral systems. A laptop as an operator's console is often ideal because they are relatively cheap, can run Windows interface code quickly and efficiently, and have many standard interfaces (such as RS-232 and USB) already built in.

Despite all these attributes and major companies using laptops for operator consoles that interface with their systems, I caution you against using them for your own interface projects. There are several reasons for this; the most significant one being that they typically don't work like regular PCs.

They don't work like regular PCs because their peripheral set is usually very limited (only one disk drive of a specific type, no peripheral busses, and power-saving features which restrict operations of some hardware to specific modes). This makes trying to develop interfaces for laptops very challenging and potentially fruitless if the design is changed.

With only a local processor bus, you will find that I/O timings on a laptop will be radically different than what you will see in a regular PC. Some methods of determining your peripheral I/O speeds are described later in the book, but for a laptop (which might not be available or later models will work differently), this is not a potentially high-yield exercise.

Now, standard parallel, serial, and maybe Ethernet ports are included on laptops, and these can be used as on a regular PC. But you have to be sure that no crucial, timing-specific I/O accesses cause problems when you move your application to and from a laptop.

One of the goals of this book is to provide you with a set of interfaces that will work across a wide range of PCs including laptops. For this reason, many of the applications in this book could be considered not very aggressive; instead of maximizing performance, I have concentrated on making the book's applications work reliably on a wide range of PCs and operating systems.

EMBEDDED PCS

One of the most interesting developments in the history of the PC is the creation of adapter cards that consist of a complete PC on a very small card format. These *embedded PCs*, as they are most commonly known generally consist of a PC-compatible microprocessor (386 or better), an ASIC (consisting of all the general PC functions including an I/O bus), SIMM memory, serial and parallel ports, a keyboard (and maybe mouse) port, and sometimes a VGA output. Often, these cards have a DOS emulator built in to allow booting the card and running regular programs.

Although I really won't go into great detail about this type of PC, you should be aware of their existence and think about using them in applications where a low-cost, rugged PC is required. They are ideally suited for applications where a PC is required to control manufacturing process controls and more than an eight-bit microcontroller is required. These cards can be programmed using standard PC development tools. The PC interfaces allow simple transfer of applications from the bench to the manufacturing floor.

A number of interesting features that define embedded PCs and help make potential uses much more obvious. The first feature is the availability of busses on the cards. These busses can consist of standard ISA, PCI, and PC/104 busses. Although the terms *ISA* and *PCI* should be familiar to you, this is probably the first time you've seen the term *PC/104*. PC/104 is a board form-factor (layout) bus and connector system designed for the high-noise industrial environment. The purpose of the bus and connector system is to provide a stable, expandable system (Fig. 1-5).

Often, you will see embedded PC processor cards with a multitude of connectors on them. These connectors can include keyboard, mouse, serial, and parallel interfaces, along with diskette, hard disk, and Ethernet connections. From these connectors, a full PC system can be run.

Actually, a system that probably runs on your PC at home can be built with integrated ISA and PCI cards. Often, these cards will be designed with card edge connectors for these interfaces, which allows the embedded PC card to be inserted into a passive backplane like an adapter card and drive the PC functions. I have heard of people creating a system where the processor is on an embedded card, so to upgrade the system when newer and faster processors become available, just the embedded PC card is replaced for significantly less cost and effort than replacing a motherboard.

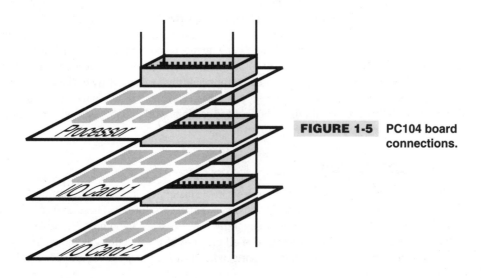

FIGURE 1-5   PC104 board connections.

Video output is an issue that the embedded PCs can often handle very easily. As you would probably expect, some devices are designed with VGA graphics on the board, but others are capable of driving graphic LCDs (usually monochrome) directly.

At the start of this subchapter, I mentioned that embedded PCs can have a built-in DOS emulator. This means that the DOS (or even Windows) functions are provided in a ROM/(E)EPROM that is built into the board. This interface can use the serial port for the console (keyboard and screen) functions or use an external keyboard and display. As you go through the book, the DOS functions are presented, showing what they can provide for an application. Having DOS built into the embedded PC means that applications written for a PC can be transferred directly to the embedded PC from a "real" PC with no changes to the software required.

If no (floppy or hard) disk is available to the embedded PC, often files are kept in battery-backed RAM or EEPROM to prevent the applications from being lost when power is removed. Using solid-state memory like this makes the embedded PC very rugged, as well as very miserly in terms of power consumption. An additional advantage of using on-board memory for application file storage is that reading from memory is a lot faster than accessing a disk.

Reading through this, you're probably thinking that a lot of options are available in the embedded PCs and many of these options are mutually exclusive (i.e., having an LCD driver in a system that is going to use RS-232 as the operator console) or necessary to start running the application (which can run from disk, EEPROM under DOS, or directly). To keep track of how the system is set up, configuration memory is implemented on the embedded PC boards. Understanding how to access and modify this information is vitally important to get a system up and running.

2

PC

ARCHITECTURE

In this chapter, I would like to introduce you to the PC's hardware and give you a "30,000-foot" view of the entire system. Some of the topics addressed will probably be of surprise to you because you would have thought these are issues that were lost in the mists of time, and advanced technology. But, these features, options and compromises have made a lasting impression on what to expect and design for when developing applications for today's PC.

One of the things that I would like to impress upon you is that the PC is an evolutionary piece of hardware that has not quite lost many of its original features and interfaces. In fact, many peripherals and software that were originally designed for use in the first PCs, will still run in today's systems. Even the highly operating systems that control modern PCs are able to run much of the software from the sophisticated early days.

Processor and Support Architecture "Core"

Over the years of working with different customers and their designs, I've found it most useful to understand how a card works from the inside (starting with the microprocessor) and working my way out. What I always look at first is the system's "core," which is the minimum hardware that is required to allow the microprocessor to run code.

In the PC, this "core" consists of the microprocessor, memory, the interrupt controller and a DMA controller (Fig. 2-1).

This set of hardware can run any program or interface with hardware attached to the local bus.

The next chapter focuses on the PC's processor, but for the purposes of this chapter, it is sufficient for you to understand that the processor outputs address and control signals and writes/reads data in 8-, 16-, and 32-bit data sizes.

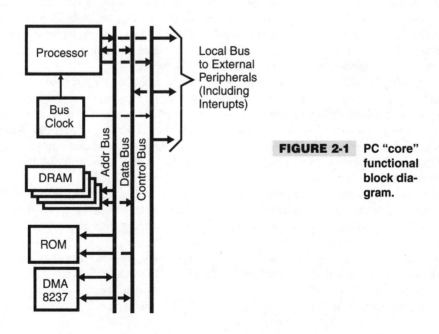

FIGURE 2-1 PC "core" functional block diagram.

I use the term *local memory* to describe all the memory that is accessed directly by the PC's processor. Although you might think of processor memory in terms of the megabytes that were advertised when you bought the PC, actually, three different types of memory are described in this chapter.

DMA (Direct Memory Access) consists of a hardware device that can be programmed to create addressing and control signals to move data between devices within the system without involving the processor. DMA is most typically used in the PC for moving data between local memory and the disk drives.

Interrupts are hardware events that require the PC's processor to stop what it is currently doing and respond to the external request. This request does not have to be responded to immediately, if at all, and it is up to the programmer's discretion to decide how to respond to the request.

Along with hardware interrupt requests are also *software interrupt* requests, which are fundamental to the operation of the PC. The later chapters explain how software interrupts are used within the PC.

In this section, I wanted to introduce how the processor interacts with the core elements from a high level. Later in this book, I will get into the nitty gritty of programming the DMA and interrupt controllers.

LOCAL MEMORY

The term *local memory* is kind of a loosely defined term that I use to describe memory on the PC's motherboard and not on external cards or subsystems. There are a number of different kinds of memory used on the motherboard, each with a different set of characteristic features.

The first type, *ROM (Read-Only Memory)* is only read when the PC first starts ("boots") up. Next, there is what I will call *main memory*, which is measured in megabytes (and was prominently advertised when you bought your PC). The PC's processor itself has cache memory, which is used to help speed the operation of the PC. Understanding how these different types of memory are used and what their characteristics are is important in understanding how your application executes. Understanding the different characteristics is important for predicting how your application will execute.

I would characterize *external memory*, as memory connected through one of the PC's busses. In the early days of the PC, adapter cards with memory on them was a very common means of increasing the amount of memory available to the PC's processor. Today, most motherboards can handle a large amount of memory in the form of *SIMMs (Single In-line Memory Modules)* or *DIMMs (Dual In-Line Memory Modules)* that can interface directly to the processor's bus. External memory might not be able to run at full bus speed, which lessens its usefulness in modern PCs.

Read-Only Memory, as the name implies, can only be read by the PC's processor and not written to. Typically, this memory is in the form of *EPROM (Electrically Programmable Read-Only Memory)* or "flash" in some special circumstances. This memory contains the code necessary to allow the PC to perform a self test (known as *POST, Power-On Self-Test*, or *POD, Power-On Diagnostics*, respectively), start up and load the operating system (boot) and provide a standard interface for devices on the motherboard (known as *BIOS*).

Flash is similar to EPROM, but can be electrically erased and reprogrammed while it is in circuit (such as on the PC's motherboard). The purpose of flash is to allow the manufacturer to update the PC's ROM code without having to take back the motherboards and replace chips. If you have flash on your motherboard, this should only be used for boot code and BIOS storage, it is not an area that can be used for storing data.

The PC generally has 64 KB of ROM on the motherboard (although some PCs might have up to 128 KB) starting at address 0x0F000:0x0000 (I will explain how addressing works in the following Intel 8086 processor architecture chapter).

Some adapter cards have ROM built into them, which provide specialized BIOS functions for the adapter hardware. This ROM is detected during the boot "scan" and "adds," this ROM to the PC's interface hardware. Adapter card ROM can be very useful when you are developing external hardware to the PC and I will go through how the ROM is wired to the ISA as an example application.

ROM has two primary characteristics. The first is that it never loses its programming—even when power is turned off. This is important because the code is used to self-test the PC and boot the PC's operating system. This ability to retain the programmed in data is known as *nonvolatility.*

RAM (Random-Access Memory) is known as *volatile* memory because its contents are lost when power is removed.

The other major characteristic of ROM is that it's slow. A relatively fast EPROM will have a 90-ns access time. This is a problem with modern PCs, which have a 133-MHz (7.5-ns period) local bus cycle time. When the processor is reading from the ROM, "wait states" are inserted so that the ROM has time to output the correct data. At the end of the wait states, the data is passed to the processor.

For example, if you had 150-ns ROMs (which require 10 CPU cycles to output valid data), the hardware within the PC would stop the processor for the nine extra cycles required to do the read.

Figure 2-2 shows a PC's bus operation when the PC is reading from cache memory (at full 66 MHz local bus clock speed), main memory (which has 50-ns access time DRAMs) and ROM (which, as I've said, has 150-ns access time). I use the label "L2" to describe this cache. This term will be explained later in this chapter.

These three reads require 14 local bus cycles, an average of 4.67 cycles per read. This means the effective speed of the PC's local bus is actually 14.3 MHz and not the 66 MHz of the local bus clock.

Obviously, things get much worse when the PC is executing totally out of ROM, the effective bus speed is reduced to 6.6 MHz. In this case, you would have a PC that would perform at roughly the same speed as an 8-MHz 286 PC/AT.

This speed is totally unacceptable. To improve it, upon power up, all modern PCs will copy the contents of the ROM into main memory and electrically "move" the block of

Bus Clock

| L2 | DRAM | ROM |

FIGURE 2-2 Cache/DRAM/ROM reading.

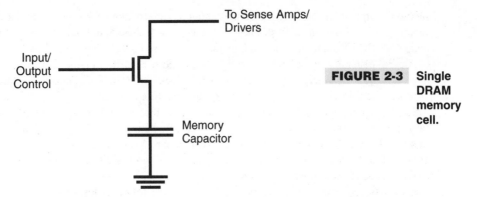

FIGURE 2-3 Single DRAM memory cell.

memory into the 0x0F000:0x00000 address that I described previously. Now, the BIOS will be read at main memory speeds.

In this example, moving the ROM into main memory will decrease the number of cycles required for the three reads to seven, which results in effectively doubling the execution speed of the PC.

Main memory is the region where the operating system and application programs typically operate; when you bought your PC, the advertised memory was probably a major consideration when you made the purchase.

This memory typically consists of *Dynamic Random Access Memory (DRAM)*. "Random Access Memory" simply means that you can read and write the memory at any time. *Dynamic* describes how the memory works.

You might have heard the term *single transistor memory cells* for descriptions of DRAM and that's actually a pretty good description of each cell (Fig. 2-3).

In this circuit, the transistor is used as a switch to allow a charge to be moved into or out of the capacitor. For a write, the transistor is turned on and a charge is either pushed into or pulled out of the capacitor. When the transistor is turned off, the charge is trapped in the capacitor and cannot change until the transistor is turned on again.

A DRAM read is accomplished by turning on the transistor and any charge that is in the capacitor will leak out and will be detected by a *sense amplifier*. The sense amp is an astable flip-flop that will amplify the charge and to the state of the capacitor. Before the transistor is turned on when writing to the cell, the sense amp will be set to a specific state to load the correct charge into the capacitor.

DRAM memory is characterized by how inexpensive and dense it is, as well as being moderately fast and requiring more support circuitry than *SRAM (Static Random-Access Memory)* or ROM.

Historically, DRAM has doubled in size every 18 months or so. My first computer was an Atari 300 that I bought in 1981 and only had 16 KB of DRAM using eight 16 KB by 1 chips. As I write this, it isn't unusual to buy PCs with 64 MB or more of DRAM with 64 MB chips (and 128 and 256 MB chips are on their way).

I remember thinking that as DRAM got larger, a PC could be implemented with only one DRAM chip. Instead of this prediction becoming true, PC operating systems and applications have become much more sophisticated and larger, meaning that as the memory size has increased, so have the requirements for it. Like it being impossible to be too rich, too thin, or too blond, it is also impossible to have too much memory or disk space in your PC.

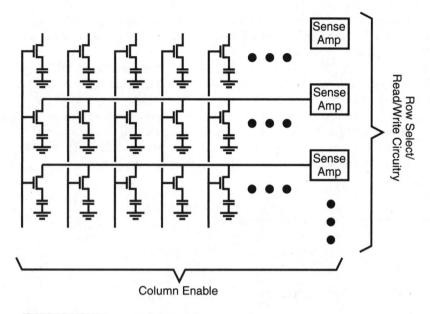

FIGURE 2-4   DRAM memory array.

In a DRAM memory chip, the cells are arranged in rows and columns (Fig. 2-4).

To address each cell within the chip, a row/column address for the element in the array has to be provided. Usually, to save pins on the DRAM chips, the row and column address lines are shared (multiplexed) together so that during a read or a write, first the row is selected and then the column.

The row is selected first so that if a write is occurring, the sense amp for the row can be set to the specific value. All the other sense amps are set in their astable state (the reason why is explained in a few paragraphs). When the column address is latched in, the transistors for the array row are turned on.

When the input/output control transistor is turned on, then the read/write occurs.

For the cells not being written to, the sense amp will not only read what the charge is in the capacitor, but it will also "refresh" it as well.

This is necessary in DRAM because the capacitor is actually a MOS transistor built into the chip, acting as a capacitor. Over time, any charge in this capacitor will leak away into the silicon substrate. By periodically "refreshing" the charge by performing a read (which will cause the sense amps to amplify the charge), the contents of the memory will never be lost.

Refreshing is typically done by enabling all the transistors in a column (without first specifying a row) and letting the sense amps do their thing. A read of an incrementing column address is usually implemented in the PCs DMA DRAM support hardware and is known as a *CAS (Column Address Strobe) Only Refresh*.

I'm giving this description of what's happening here so that you can see some of the challenges being experienced by both PC and DRAM designers.

As the memory gets more dense, the DRAM capacitors get smaller. As the capacitors get smaller, they hold less charge and a read might take longer to accomplish. As the chips get denser, more cells are on each row line, which means additional parasitic capacitance on each line (caused the input of the additional input/output control transistors) and more cells that need to be refreshed.

In the original PC, 5% of the computing bandwidth was lost because of DRAM refresh requirements. To overcome these potential deficiencies, PC designers have developed a few hardware features.

To speed up the access time, PC designers often interleave the memory. *Interleaving* means that adjacent addresses are located on different DRAM chips.

For example, if you were going to read a number of consecutive memory locations, a two-time interleave would be twice as fast as noninterleaved memory:

DRAM CYCLE	NON-INTERLEAVED	INTERLEAVED
0.5		
1.0	Address 1	Address 1
1.5		Address 2
2.0	Address 2	Address 3
2.5		Address 4
3.0	Address 3	Address 5
3.5		Address 6
4.0	Address 4	Address 7

To get around the refresh problem, designers can place DRAM in separate blocks, which are independently controlled and refreshed. As part of this, the DRAM controller keeps track of what's been recently read or written and skips over refreshing those column addresses.

To further reduce access time, *Synchronous Dynamic RAM (SDRAM)* was invented. This type of memory takes advantage of the fact that what mostly happens in a PC's main memory is that it is sequentially read (when a program is being executed). By providing a clock to the DRAM, along with internal synchronizing hardware, it will output data sequentially at this clock speed. If the data access does not consist of sequential reads, the SDRAM behaves like ordinary DRAM.

The big advantage of SDRAM is that its access times are typically in the 10-ns range, allowing full speed bus access without any wait states or refresh overhead because the sequential reads will refresh the DRAM cells automatically.

Now, if you were going back to the original memory-access timing diagram referenced to the bus clock, using ROM copied into SDRAM and using SDRAM, you can read a memory address each clock cycle.

Even with these hardware enhancements, the PC that will provide data from the bus at the local bus speed, not the speed of the processor. A processor that runs with a 233-MHz clock will require data 3.5 times faster than what the local bus memory can provide it at. At the example speed of 233 MHz, to provide data to the processor at its execution speed, 4.3-ns access time memory is required.

To get program and data into the processor at these speeds, a series of *cache* memory devices are used to store a small fraction of the total memory required to execute the current program. Two types of caches are available to the processor in Pentium PCs.

"Level 1" cache is on the processor chip itself. This cache is typically very small (8 to 16 KB) and it runs at the processor's speed (i.e., a 300-MHz Pentium will have an onboard cache with a 3.3-ns cycle time). Although a number of algorithms are used to predict which memory to load into caches, they generally revolve around the assumption that chances are, whatever you've most recently accessed, you'll access it again in the very near future because most code consists of loops.

For example, when a processor executes the code:

```
for ( i = 0; ( i < 0x040 ) && ( Array[ i ] != '\0' ); i++ )
                            // Erase "Tab" Chars from Array
    if ( Array[ i ] < 0x009 )   // Do we have a "Tab"?
    Array[ i ] = ' ';       // Yes, Convert to a Blank
```

Once all the code from the FOR statement to the semicolon is loaded into the Level 1 cache, the loop can proceed at full processor speed (whatever it is) without having to wait for data to be loaded through the local bus.

Level 2 cache is usually on the motherboard and runs at about twice the local bus speed and is usually measured in hundreds of kilobytes to megabytes. This cache usually holds a large fraction of the currently executing application and is a relatively fast source for the processor to reload its Level 1 cache.

The last important point to understand about caching is what happens when the processor must write to memory. Three primary strategies are used. The first is, when doing a write, initiate a wait for the write to complete to the slowest device that will have to store it (which is the DRAM).

The problem with this method is that literally hundreds of execution cycles could be lost waiting for the write to complete.

A more sophisticated way of doing a write from the processor is to write to the Level 1 cache and continue processing while other hardware on in the processor and on the motherboard writes the data to the Level 2 cache and DRAM. With this scheme, if multiple writes are requested or if the data written is read back, then the processor will have to hold until the previous write operation has completed. This is known as "write-through" cache.

To further improve upon the speed of execution, modern compilers look for opportunities to only use variables that don't have to be written back into DRAM. For the example code, "i" could be a processor register, which means that it is never written to cache and if it is not written to cache, then it never has to be stored back into DRAM.

A compiler could also notice that an automatic variable, while having to be stored in Level 2 cache, does not have to be stored in DRAM until the cache is "flushed" to make room for new data to be placed in it.

Understanding exactly how data is actually accessed by the processor at a given point is just about impossible because of the different memories the code could be located in and the algorithms and strategies used to load them. Although much of this is done by hardware on the motherboard and some of it performed within the operating system, means that understanding deterministically how the program executes and how long it will take to execute a section of code literally impossible.

Back in the old days (when we used a squirrel on a treadmill to power our PCs), it was quite reasonable to time how long a section of application code would take to run by examining the individual instructions of an application. But today, with sophisticated (and fast hardware) and multitasking operating systems, you cannot count on a program executing the same way with the same timing—even on the same PC.

Creating code that will provide external signals with specific timing, allowing consistent hardware access is an important aspect of this book. Later, I show how accesses of a specific length of time can be produced for a wide range of PCs.

INTERRUPTS

Many people shy away from interrupts in the PC. When I ask why interrupts are not considered for applications, it seems like interrupts fit in the category of things that are so difficult to understand that they're not worth it (and if they haven't understood them up to now, what's the point in learning then now?).

Further complicating this situation and making this argument seem more realistic is how the PC's interrupt structure has changed since the PC was first introduced. In 1981, when the PC was first released, the interrupt structure was quite simple, but, over the years, as new, more-complex processors with "Protect Mode" operating systems have become available, how interrupts in the PC's work has become much more complex and difficult to implement. Despite this, implementing interrupts in the PC is a necessity and really not all that hard to do (even in applications running under Microsoft "Windows").

Interrupts are kind of like statistics: you had to be able to answer the exam questions in school, but if now you can't figure out how many people are required for there to be a 50% chance of two people having the same birthday, you can go about your daily life quite happily. A lot of people think the same way about interrupts.

This is an unfortunate attitude to take because if you want to program MS-DOS applications, it is crucially important to understand how interrupts work and how they are used. If you're not sure about how interrupts work, you'll probably be dismayed to learn that two types are used in the PC: *hardware* and *software interrupts*. Hardware interrupts are signals from peripheral (or central) hardware, requesting that the program execution changes to deal with the hardware situation. Software interrupts are special instructions that jump program execution to an interrupt handler. I always think of software interrupts as being subroutine "calls" to addresses where you don't know where they are, but you do know they exist.

The first type of interrupt is the hardware interrupt. In your everyday life, this is analogous to working at your desk and being interrupted by somebody who needs your help.

You can make three typical responses to this interruption. The first way is to ignore the person and hope they go away. If the person is still there when you have finished your work, cleaned up, and have some time for them, then you can ask them to sit down so that you can help them with their problem. Another way you can respond is to ask them to sit down and wait for you to leave your work where you can come back to it easily. The last type of interrupt is when you are forced to drop everything and respond.

Deciding which course of action to take depends on the priority of the interrupt.

In the office interruption example, if somebody's asking for money for their kid's soccer team, I usually ignore them or throw wadded paper at them until they leave. Obviously, I don't do this very often (mostly because *I've* got kids that may be on a soccer team that needs money some day), but it is an option that I can execute when I have something more important to do (which is just about anything). Although this example may seem facetious, there are cases where we put off doing things until we have completed the task at hand.

For most other interruptions, I try to save what I am currently doing before responding to a person—this allows me to devote my full attention to the problem. In some cases (such as if the person coming into my office is smoldering), I drop everything and respond to the crisis. But, for the most part, I will take a moment and collect my thoughts and save what I'm doing before responding.

These three scenarios are identical to how hardware interrupts are handled within the PC. Not responding to interrupts at all, except when the application is ready to handle them, is known as *polling*. Using the office work example, you might not like interrupts and have discouraged them, but once an hour or so, you have to get up and and ask around ("poll") your co-workers if they need your help with anything.

This can be done in a PC as well. The problem with simply working through a program and then polling various inputs to see if an external event or input requires the processor's action is that while the mainline program is executing, multiple external events can occur without being responded to, or they wouldn't be responded to in a timely manner.

Polling is not usually performed in any application, although in parts of an application, it is crucial to process some data as quickly as possible. When doing this, interrupts can be turned off ("masked") to be sure the processing isn't interrupted, except for crucial events within the processor.

Interrupt events are handled by an interrupt handler, which is also known as an *interrupt service routine*. This book presents the framework for MS-DOS interrupt handlers, as well as the interrupt handler framework for working within 32-bit Windows operating systems.

The basic format of all PC interrupt handlers is:

1. If the event is not specific to this handler, jump to a previous (or the correct) handler.
2. If the handler is already executing, return.
3. Save the context information of the current program.
4. Reset the interrupt requesting hardware and re-enable the interrupts.
5. Process the interrupt request.
6. If other interrupt requests are pending, handle these.
7. Restore the context information and return execution to the appropriate code.

This probably seems more complex with a few subtleties than what you would do in the training system on which you learned assembly language programming. The reason for this additional complexity is the need for some other interrupts executing, which causes the current interrupt handler to be interrupted, and the possibility that execution will return to somewhere other than the code that was interrupted.

The first step in an interrupt handler is to determine whether or not the interrupt request is appropriate for this handler. This might seem unnecessary, but in the PC, multiple devices can have the same interrupt number. An example of this is the PC's serial ports; COM1 and COM3 request the same interrupt number. COM2 and COM4 also request the same number (different from COM1 and COM3). Properly sorting out which is the correct interrupt interrupt handler to respond to an interrupt can be difficult (and this is covered later in the book).

Before going on, a few terms and concepts need to be explained. The first is the interrupt number, which you might also see referenced as *level* in PC documentation. The PC can be interrupted by any one of 256 numbers, each number having a corresponding "vector." The *vector table* is located at the lowest (first) 1024 addresses of the PC processor's memory space. Each vector table element consists of a four-byte "long vector", which is the address of the interrupt handler. Along with creating the interrupt handler and loading it into memory, you also have to modify the interrupt vector table with the address of the handler. This is actually quite an easy process.

As I've mentioned, multiple interrupt handlers using the same vector are possible and the interrupt is known as a *shared interrupt*.

The standard PC has 15 possible hardware interrupt sources, each with its own (or shared) interrupt level. The interrupt sources consist of:

1. *Real-Time Clock (RTC)* and system timer interrupt
2. Keyboard and mouse
3. Diskette and hard drives
4. RS-232 serial communications
5. Printer
6. External interrupt sources

The reason why I use the term *standard PC*, is because an additional interrupt controller could be wired into the motherboard as well.

I check to see if the interrupt handler is already running because events might come in faster than the interrupt's handler has an ability to process them (this is true in cases where the interrupt handler is interrupt itself). Now, I can make the interrupt handler *re-entrant*, which means that it can execute multiple times, or simply set a flag. If set, the flag will return from the interrupt handler and the interrupt handler itself, upon finishing processing the current interrupt, will then check for additional interrupts and process them.

With this, I can model the interrupt handler as:

```
interrupt SomeInt() {          // Some Interrupt Handler
   if ( SomeInt ) {            // Is this the Appropriate Handler?
     Reset( Interrupt_Hardware ); // Yes, Reset the Interrupt Hardware
     if ( !SomeIntFlag ) {     // Is the handler Already Executing?
      push( Context_Registers ); // Save the Context Information
      while ( SomeIntPending ) { // If there is an Interrupt Waiting?
        SomeIntFlag = 1;        // Set the Interrupt Flag
        UnMask( Interrupts );   // Allow Interrupts to Execute
        // #### - Execute the Interrupt Handler
        SomeIntFlag = 0;        // Have Finished with the Interrupt
      }                         // Keep Handling Pending Interrupts
      pop( Context_Registers ); // Restore the context information
     }                         // Finished Executing Interrupt Handler
   }                           // Finished With "SomeInt"
} //    Return from Interrupt
```

This pseudo-C code demonstrates that there is a lot to do before actually handling the interrupt. This code will execute all the interrupt actions, listed above.

Looking at the C code, you might think that creating a re-entrant interrupt handler is simpler, but it actually isn't; when it executes, you might have the condition that the interrupts are handled in a different order, which might be a very big problem for some types of hardware.

Once the interrupt handler has determined that the source of the interrupt is the one that it is designed to process, the context registers are saved. The context registers consist of the central processor registers. To save them, they are "pushed" onto the stack.

With the context registers saved, I then reset the interrupting hardware, the PC's interrupt controller, and unmask the interrupt enable flag in the processor's status register. Resetting the hardware and unmasking interrupts will allow your interrupt handler to be interrupted. As I've shown, this is not a bad thing if you've planned your code to take care of this situation.

In this C code, it is assumed that the interrupt handler can simply check if it is the correct one to respond to the request. This might not be possible in your interrupt handler and you might have to save the context registers before doing this checking.

In this C code, notice that I have put in a WHILE statement to check to see if interrupt requests are pending for the handler to process. This WHILE statement will serialize the requests so that they are processed in the order in which they came in.

I haven't yet explained a number of hardware interrupts. These interrupts are used to help debug your application, notify you when a problem is encountered with the processor or application code, and handle hardware emergencies.

The debug interrupts basically consist of the breakpoint interrupt (number 3) and the single-step interrupt. These two interrupts are used in debuggers to allow the program to be single stepped through or stop at a specific location. In 386 and faster processors, additional features allow the processor to stop when a specific address or I/O port is accessed. When I debug my code, the only debug interrupt I explicitly use is the breakpoint instruction. The other interrupts are usually handled within the debugger that I am using.

Interrupts for processor problems like divide by zero or accessing memory outside of the currently defined "Protection Block" are also possible, although they are best avoided and handled by the operating system. This means that they should only be encountered during debug of your code. Developing handlers for processor fault interrupts is just too difficult.

Often processor errors are the basis for *General Protection Faults (GPFs)* in Windows.

The last type of interrupt is when a problem is detected within the PC. Known as "exception events", they could be a loss of power or a parity error within the memory. Loss of power is usually handled by the operating system working with an uninterruptible power supply.

Of more concern is the I/O channel check line, which is asserted when the PC detects a problem on one of its busses (it was originally just used for a parity error on the PC, which only had one channel). When this interrupt request is made, the whole system stops. In applications, typically ignore this interrupt and let the basic system deal with it. When developing hardware and software, I will handle these interrupts but I want to have the possibility of the requests to be eliminated.

Along with hardware interrupt requests, the PC can also process interrupts requested from the currently executing code. These are called *software interrupts*. Software Interrupts provide a mechanism for allowing the application code to call common subroutines (such as for hardware and operating system functions) without having to notify the application where the routines are.

To call a software interrupt (*call* is more of an appropriate term because software interrupts cannot be masked) the instruction:

```
int intNumber                        ; Call 'intNumber'
```

is used. Before the instruction is executed, the processor registers are loaded with the parameters to the call and after the instruction the returned parameters are read from the registers. For large volumes of data, the registers can contain a pointer to data.

Interrupts are a huge topic within the PC. I've really only scratched the surface in this section and told you what you can do. Explaining how they are actually implemented will take up a chapter of its own.

DMA

Direct Memory Access (DMA) is an important part of the PC's operation. DMA is used to transfer data between the PC's memory and peripheral devices, such as disk drives, without involving the PC's processor in the transfer. The DMA controller can be thought of as an auxiliary processor, used to transfer data between the PC's memory and peripherals without changing it in any way.

In a typical computer system, a DMA controller is added to the processor's busses (Fig. 2-5)

In this circuit, the DMA controller is programmed by the processor to respond to the different DMA requests.

When a request is made, the DMA controller responds by halting the processor and performs the transfer that has been programmed into it (Fig. 2-6).

In this sequence, the processor has set up the DMA controller to respond to a DMA request by reading from an I/O register address and then writing to a memory address.

When the DMA request is received by the DMA controller, the DMA controller requests that the PC processor "holds." The PC processor will stop executing when the current in-

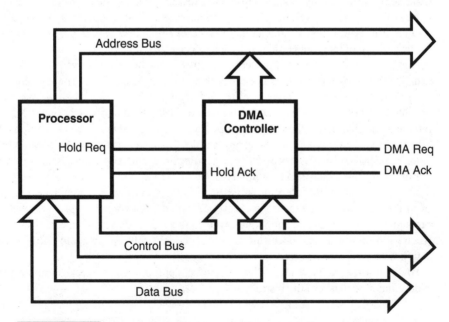

FIGURE 2-5   Direct memory access with processor.

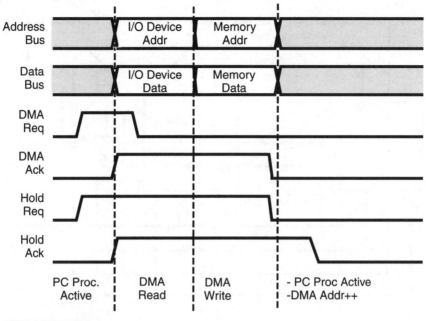

FIGURE 2-6   DMA I/O to memory operating waveform.

struction has completed executing and acknowledge that it is holding to the DMA controller. With the processor holding, the DMA controller takes over the processor's address and control busses and transfers the data between I/O space and memory. In doing the transfer, the data is read into and stored in the DMA controller, followed by the DMA controller starting the write sequence and then saving the byte that was read from the source device.

The requesting hardware should de-assert the DMA request line when the "DMA Ack" line becomes active. Leaving the line high could result in multiple, invalid DMA requests. With the transfer complete, the DMA controller releases ownership of the processor's busses and the PC processor can resume executing where it left off.

In concept, direct memory access operations seem pretty simple, but actually implementing them is another thing entirely.

In the PC, the DMA hardware subsystem is based on the Intel 8237A DMA controller chip. This chip is capable of tracking up to four DMA channels (and prioritizing and serializing them) and transferring eight bits of data from I/O to memory (and vice versa) with as many as 16 address bits.

A big limitation of the 8237A is only having 16 address bits for the transfers. This means that only a maximum of 64 KB can be transferred from the first 64 KB of memory. These are problems because with the PC, there has always been 1 MB or more of memory that is to be transferred.

In the original PC, to allow the DMA controller to access memory anywhere in the 1-MB memory area, a four-by-four register array was used, which increased the memory range that the DMA controller could access up to 20 bits (the same as the 8088), although it could only transfer up to 64 KB at a time. The four-by-four RAM was enabled by the DMA acknowledge (Fig. 2-7).

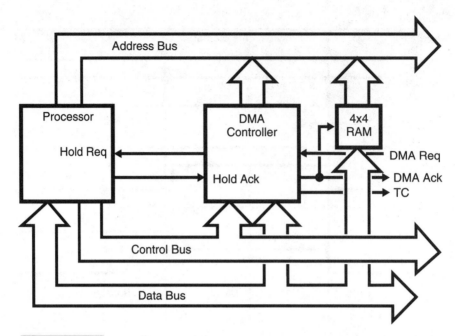

FIGURE 2-7 The PC's DMA block diagram.

For the PC/AT, this four-by-four array was increased to an eight-by-eight array so that the effective address was 24 bits (or 16 MB) for the two different DMA controllers. This has not changed for modern PCs, which means that DMA transfers is limited to the first 16 MB of memory. Today, this is a fraction of the total potential memory and means that the operating system might have to transfer memory after a DMA request to where it is required.

This scheme has two limitations. Memory-to-memory DMA transfers cannot be implemented in the PC because chances are that the source and destination are in different 64-KB address blocks. With a single upper four-bit memory channel memory, there is no way to transfer data between 64-KB address segments.

The other limitation is a lot more subtle and is an aspect of how the Intel processors used in the PC are architected. As is explained in more detail in the next chapter, each 64-KB segment in the PC's processor is separated to its adjacent ones by 16 bytes (one "paragraph"). Memory is allocated by MS-DOS and other operating systems by paragraph address and not 64-KB boundary. This means that if you use the MS-DOS memory allocate routines, you will be limiting the amount of memory available for the DMA transfer.

When the DMA controller is used for transferring data into and from memory, enough space must be allocated in both the MS-DOS memory allocation scheme and the 64-KB physical segment to allow the full transfer, otherwise the DMA address counter will roll over to zero and start reading from and writing to invalid memory.

With the idea of memory spaces, here's one concept that I haven't introduced yet: the ability of the DMA controller to increment an address pointer after every transfer. This is useful in something like a disk file read, where the data can be stored sequentially for easier processing.

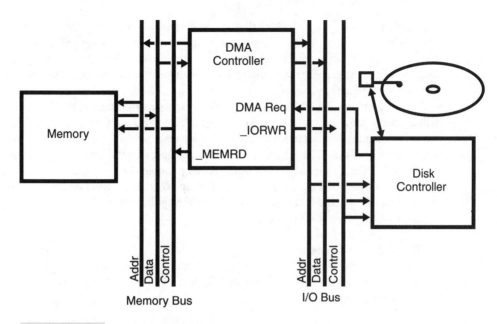

FIGURE 2-8   DMA/disk interface.

For a disk write, from memory to the disk controller hardware, you could think of the DMA as being the only processor in the PC and wired as shown in Fig. 2-8.

When the disk controller is notified that the disk is in position to have a byte written to it, it makes a request to the 8237A, which then takes over the I/O and memory busses of the PC to perform the memory read and then the I/O write. After the I/O write has occurred, the source address counter is incremented until the terminal count has been reached.

When terminal count (TC) is achieved, the DMA controller requests a hardware interrupt, which indicates that the data transfer has completed. For the disk drives in the PC, you might be surprised that the disk-request completion interrupt is actually a DMA terminal count. The disk hardware interrupt is requested when the disk has finished its read or write operation. If you trace through the PC's schematics, you'll find that the DMA "TC" line goes to the disk controller.

The interrupt controller can also be used to supply the signals to perform DRAM refresh. This is accomplished by using a timer channel output as the DMA Request line. By reading sequentially through the memory and not storing what is read, the main memory is refreshed using hardware already on the motherboard, along with circuitry that allows the DMA to take control of the bus.

This method of providing refresh to the dynamic RAM was first implemented in the PC and followed through in later computers. But, it might not be implemented in many modern PCs. Modern memory-control ASICs can track what's most recently been read, eliminating many of the unneeded refresh cycles carried out if the DMA approach is blindly followed.

How significant is this saving?

In the original PC, the overhead required for DMA totalled about five percent of the total processing bandwidth available. If the same scheme is used in a modern 200-MHz PC, 10 MHz of this bandwidth would be lost to refresh.

To try and quantify it, the cycles that would be lost to refresh are a loss of the computing power of two original PCs. This is one of the reasons why, when you look at PC performance comparisons, you'll see some very significant performance differences. By tracking the most-recent main memory reads and not refreshing those addresses, very significant performance improvements can be realized.

The cycle time of the DMA controller has not appreciably changed over the years (you will typically see a 160- to 720-ns cycle time). This has been a gating factor in increasing the speed of many devices (such as disks and networking cards). For example, if you have a disk drive with 1.25 MB per second maximum data-transfer speed, you will be running the PC's DMA controller at the maximum speed possible.

Some DMA channels are capable of transferring 16 bits at a time, but this increase is often not enough to make DMA attractive in modern applications.

To recap, the issues with DMA are:

- Slow data-transfer speed
- Terminal count interrupt is disk-completion interrupt
- Difficult to find good memory-transfer areas in a PC
- Limited memory access

For all of these reasons, I would recommend against ever designing an application to use DMA. Instead, a shared memory should be set up and the processor's data move instruction should be used. This will result in much simpler software development effort and a much easier hardware application to design.

As will be explained later in this book, the PCI bus uses a "Bus Mastering" scheme which allows data transfers at full PCI bus speeds without requiring the processor's involvement.

System Timer

The PC utilizes the Intel 8254 programmable timer for its system timer, as well as a part of the DRAM refresh circuit and speaker output. Other than using the speaker hardware, you'll probably be surprised to discover that I recommend that the timer should not be accessed at all, except to use the speaker timer for outputting a tone or for using it as software interval timer.

The 8254 consists of three timers, all driven by a 1.19-MHz clock (which is a 14.31818-MHz clock divided by 12). In the original PC, the 14.31818-MHz clock was used as a central systems clock and divided by 12 to get the 1.19-MHz clock. Each 8254 programmable timer channel takes the 1.19-MHz clock input and responds according to the mode in which it is operating.

Each channel can operate in six different modes. Because the timer is quite simple and you should only be accessing channel 2 (the speaker channel), I will go into more detail (sufficient to program the speaker) than for the other channels in the 8254.

The 8354 programmable timer, when used in the PC can be diagrammed as in Fig. 2-9.

The pins on the 8254 are quite simple. *Clock* is the input clock. *Gate* refers to an enable pin for the clock channel and *Out* is the output of the timer. The function of *Out* is defined by the 8254 operating mode.

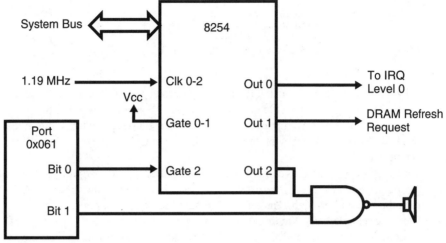

FIGURE 2-9 The PC's 8254 timer block diagram.

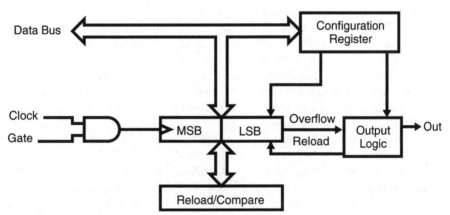

FIGURE 2-10 8254 channel block diagram.

Each channel of the 8254 could be modelled as in Fig. 2-10.

Four register addresses are used by the 8254. The first three registers are used for loading and reading the two eight-bit counter registers for each of the timer channels. The fourth address is the configuration register.

To control the operation of the three timer channels, the 8254 is internal to the 8254 and to specify how the channel timer registers are to be accessed, a control word is written to I/O address 0x0043. This control word is defined as:

```
Bits            Function
7-6             Channel to be used
5-4             Read/Write Load Type
                0 - Counter Latching
                1 - LSB Only
                2 - MSB Only
```

```
                  3 - LSB followed by MSB
   3-1            Mode Number (0-5 valid)
   0              0 - Divide by Hex
                  1 - Divide by Decimal (BCD)
```

Typically reading and writing the low byte followed by the high byte is typically used. The different modes provide quite a wide range of capabilities in the 8254.

Mode 0 causes an interrupt output on the channel output pin when the terminal count is reached. As you would expect, the PC's "Real Time Clock interrupt" is really a pulse that can be used for interrupts.

The 8254 can be used as a one shot in mode 2. After the *most-significant byte (MSB)* and *least-significant byte (LSB)* registers are loaded, Out is low, when the counter overflows, then the line will go high. The line will remain high for one cycle and then the count registers are reloaded with the initial value.

Mode 3 is similar to mode 2, except that a square wave is produced (half the period high, half the period low), rather than a pulse when the terminal count is reached.

Mode 2 is typically used for channels 0 and 1, where the timer has to produce a pulse. Mode 3 is most commonly used for the speaker.

The final two modes are used to output an edge after a specific delay has past. Mode 4 will output the pulse a set number of cycles after the channel registers are both loaded while mode 5 will wait for the channel's gate to become active before starting the count.

Although you can read channel 0 and 1 (to provide a fairly small granularity timer), you should never write to them. Channel 0 is used to provide the real-time clock information to the PC's operating system (as interrupt level 0). Channel 1 is used to initiate the DRAM refresh DMA read. Both these channels are set up by the PC's "POST" and their uninterrupted operation is crucial to the operation of the PC. Later, the book shows how the timer's channel 2 can be used to time fairly short (less than 100 μs) delays and the channel 0 real-time clock interrupt can be shared to provide additional functions. In performing the latter function, I will not change the operation of the clock interrupt.

Timer channel 0, which is used as the PC's real-time clock as it is running, typically executes in mode 2 with a reload value of zero. This essentially divides the incoming clock by 65,536. Dividing 1.19 MHz by 65,536 produces a pulse once every 18.207 ms, which is used by the real-time clock. This pulse is the basis of the PC's real-time clock and is why you will probably see documentation indicating that the PC's level 0 interrupt occurs 55 times per second (which is the reciprocal of 18.2 ms). The actual time value is calculated from counting the number of times that the level 0 interrupt has executed since the PC was initially loaded with a time value.

Channel 2 is used to output a tone on the PC's speaker. Mode 3 is the normal mode of operation, which outputs a square wave. Some funky applications (such as outputting speech from the PC's speaker) use other modes to create PWM outputs that actually output recognizable speech (as hard as it is to believe, it's true). As well, Channel 2 can be used as a delay timer for different-speed PCs.

The channel 2 frequency (in mode 3) output is determined by the formula:

Frequency out = 1.193 MHz/*Clock divisor*

To create basic musical notes, the following divisors are used:

NOTE	FREQUENCY	8254 DIVISOR
A	440 Hz	2,711 – 0x0A97
A#	466 Hz	2,560 – 0x0A00
B	494 Hz	2,415 – 0x09D2
Middle C	523 Hz	2,291 – 0x08E9
C#	554 Hz	2,154 – 0x086A
D	587 Hz	2,033 – 0x07F1
D#	622 Hz	1,918 – 0x077E
E	659 Hz	1,811 – 0x0713
F	698 Hz	1,709 – 0x06AD
F#	740 Hz	1,612 – 0x064C
G	784 Hz	1,522 – 0x05F2
G#	831 Hz	1,436 – 0x059C
A	880 Hz	1,356 – 0x054C
A#	932 Hz	1,280 – 0x0500
B	988 Hz	1,208 – 0x04B8
C	1047 Hz	1,140 – 0x0474

The error between the actual desired frequency and the actual frequency output is very low.

To output a tone (which is a value divisor), the following C code could be used:

```
outp( 0x061, inp( 0x061 ) & 0x0FC );  // Turn off Channel 2
                                       // Input/Speaker
outp( 0x043, 10110110B );              // Load Timer 2, Mode 3, LSB/MSB
outp( 0x042, Low( Value ));            // Load the LSB
outp( 0x042, High( Value ));           // Load the MSB
outp( 0x061, inp( 0x061 ) | 3 );       // Turn on the Speaker Output
```

This code will disable the speaker output, load channel 2 with the delay necessary to output the desired tone, and then enable the speaker's input clock gate and speaker output gate.

To end the "beep," simply execute the first line again:

```
outp( 0x061, inp( 0x061 ) & 0x0FC );
```

As I was preparing this section and trying out this code sequence, I accidentally entered the wrong value for address 0x043. I entered *0x056*, which caused my PC to completely lock up. Looking back at the control word register, this is a write to channel 1 which is the DRAM refresh DMA request.

This is a good warning about why you should never write to either channel 0 or 1.

Memory Mapping

One of the concepts I have introduced, but not gone into a lot of detail, is how hardware in the PC is mapped and addressed. In Appendix D, I go in a lot more detail about what is located at what memory or I/O address, but before being able to use it as a resource, you should have a good idea of how the PC accesses memory and resources.

When you were first introduced to microprocessors, you were probably told about two types of I/O addressing, memory mapped I/O and I/O space addressing. *Memory mapped I/O* means that the input/output control registers are accessible in the processor's memory address space (Fig. 2-11).

In this type of processor, care must be taken in developing programs to be sure that the I/O registers are read as program instructions or accidentally read or written as data.

In processors with I/O spaces as well as memory spaces, this is much less of a concern (Fig. 2-12).

The Intel processors have a separate memory and I/O space, although the same address and data busses are used. The two address spaces are kept separate by two different sets of read and write lines.

When the PC was first introduced, it used an Intel 8088, which could access as much as 1 MB of memory and 64 KB of I/O registers.

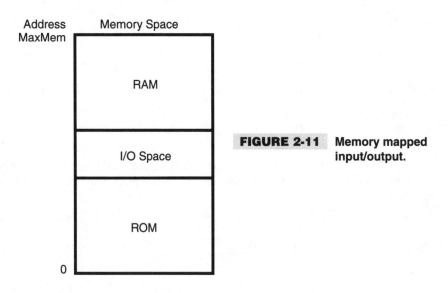

FIGURE 2-11   Memory mapped input/output.

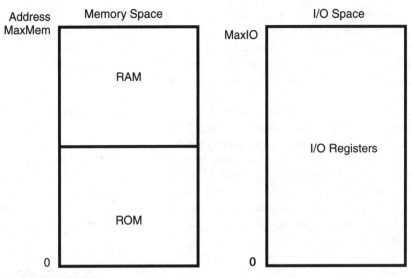

FIGURE 2-12   Separate memory mapped & I/O spaces.

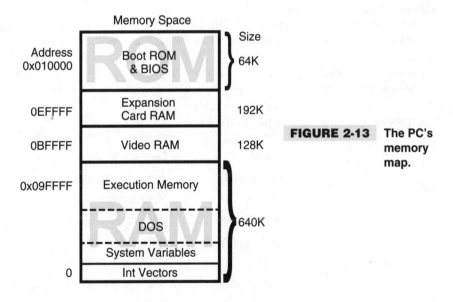

FIGURE 2-13   The PC's memory map.

In architecting the PC, IBM specified different addresses for the various memory and peripheral devices (Fig. 2-13). This provided space for not only programs to execute, but also for memory-mapped video, memory boot code, and BIOS, as well as some space left over for adapter card memory. As PC processors have become more sophisticated with larger memory spaces, this least-significant 1-MB memory area has stayed the same with extra RAM being placed above the 1-MB address. No "standard" peripherals have been located above the 1-MB address.

There are a few things to note about the memory area. The "Int Vectors" area of RAM is used to store pointers to interrupt handlers located elsewhere in memory. Each interrupt vector is a 32-bit address (the format of which is explained in the next chapter) and, as explained, there are up to 256 different interrupt sources. This means that the first 1 KB of RAM is used and is not available for program storage.

Above the interrupt vectors are the system variables. This memory space is used for storage of system information (such as the addresses of serial port, the keyboard state variable and keystroke buffer, the current time, etc.). The system variables can be useful to read by an application to get system information quickly.

I have provided a system variable map in Appendix D. The operating system variables are not included because they aren't publicly documented and different versions of different operating systems have this information located in different locations. Using operating system variables in an application is very risky because you are creating an application that will have to be re-compiled if the application is moved to a PC with a different version of the operating system.

The I/O space in the Intel microprocessors consist of a 16-bit address space. When IBM first created the PC, the assumption was that a 64-KB I/O space was much more than what would be required (after all, the PC itself was first shipped with 16 KB or 64 KB of RAM). So, only the least-significant 12 bits of the I/O address are decoded and the most significant four bits are ignored.

This decision has really haunted the PC over the past 10 years or so as the PC and its peripheral functions have become more and more complex and required more I/O space addresses.

For the PC/AT, the I/O address map was defined with address 0-0x0FF being decoded on the motherboard and addresses 0x0100 to 0x03FF available on the I/O slots.

REGISTER LOCATION	ADDRESS RANGE	DEVICE
Motherboard	0–0x01F	DMA controller 1
	0x020–0x03F	Interrupt controller 1
	0x040–0x05F	System timer
	0x060–0x06F	Keyboard interface
	0x070–0x07F	RTC, NMI mask
	0x080–0x09F	DMA page register
	0x0A0–0x0BF	Interrupt controller 2
	0x0C0–0x0DF	DMA controller 2
	0x0F0–0x0FF	Math Coprocessor
I/O slots	0x01F0–0x01F8	Hard Disk Controller
	0x0200–0x0207	Joystick I/O registers
	0x0278–0x027F	Printer port 2
	0x02E8–0x02EF	Serial port 4

REGISTER LOCATION	ADDRESS RANGE	DEVICE
	0x02F8–0x02FF	Serial port 2
	0x0360–0x036F	Reserved
	0x0378–0x037F	Printer port 1
	0x03C0–0x03CF	Reserved
	0x03D0–0x03DF	Color graphics adapter
	0x03E8–0x03EF	Serial port 3
	0x03F0–0x03F7	Diskette controller
	0x03F8–0x03FF	Serial port 1

From this, you're probably thinking there isn't a big problem, but with modern PCs and new standard devices, the 768 remaining addresses have been allocated to devices very quickly.

As described in the following section, configuring a PC system with hardware adapters could be a very complex issue, but features are now available to make it easier to properly configure a PC or at least detect when errors have been made in how adapters have been addressed.

Card Busses (ISA, EISA, and PCI)

Over the past 20 years, if you were to ask PC users if the bus interfaces in their PCs have been useful, you'd definitely get mixed reviews. The busses do provide a method of adding additional hardware features and functionality to the PC, but at the cost of a larger computer form factor (i.e., the size of the box), difficulty in integrating the additional hardware (and required software) into the PC, and higher actual costs of the PC (in the late 1980s, interface devices could increase the cost of owning a PC by up to 50%). Car companies would have gone out of business long ago if you had to upgrade and customize a car before it was usable in the same way that you have to set up a PC.

Fortunately, as digital electronics have improved, the requirements for expansion cards have been greatly reduced. Ten years ago, virtually all PCs required separate cards for the disk-control hardware, video logic and drivers, and memory upgrades. If these features were incorrectly installed, the PC wouldn't run and it might take hours to find the problem. Today, these features are integrated onto the mainboard (also known as the *motherboard*), allowing the system to run at some level, regardless of the user's best efforts to configure it incorrectly. Now, the busses are used to enhance the basic PC, rather than provide access to basic operating hardware within the PC.

This book provides an introduction to ISA, PCI, USB, and Firewire busses, and some practical experiments on how to create your own expansion devices.

I define a bus as having:

■ A method to control microprocessor to provide address bus hardware for both memory and I/O access.

■ The ability of the cards to request interrupt and DMA processing by the controlling microprocessor.

■ The ability to enhance the operation of the PC.

These characteristics differentiate a bus from a port and the hardware connected to them. A port device could be exemplified by a modem. By testing a modem device and its interface against the criteria I established, it is not a bus device because it cannot be addressed directly by the microprocessor and the interface via a bus device (the serial port hardware), and it cannot request interrupts or DMA from the microprocessor.

A modern PC usually has three primary busses, each one delineated by the access speed at which they are capable of running and the devices normally attached to them (Fig. 2-14). The three busses have evolved over time to provide data rates consistent for the needs of the different devices. You might consider that the problem is with cause and effect, but the busses and devices attached to them have sorted themselves out over the years.

The Pentium bus is a simple, high-speed bus, optimized for passing data between the CPU, memory, and peripherals. An interface to the rest of the system is provided by a "North Bridge" chip, which manages data flow among the Pentium, its caches, and the rest of the system. Memory on this bus is often very fast *SDRAM (Synchronous Dynamic Random Access Memory)*.

The Pentium Pro and Pentium II/III "Xeon" has a bus that can be shared amongst four processors. This ability is often used in high-performance *Symmetric Multi-Processing (SMP)* architected server systems.

The primary high speed interface is the *PCI (Personal Computer Interface)* bus. This bus is not only a staple of all modern PCs, but is also available on many other system architectures as well. This allows PCI bus cards to be used across a number of different systems and

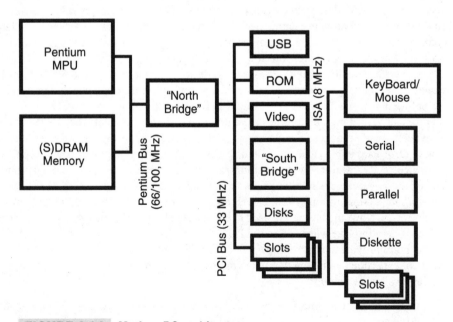

FIGURE 2-14 Modern PC architecture.

eliminates the need for designers and manufacturers to replicate their hardware for different platforms.

PCI runs with a bus access speed of 33 MHz, which means that up to 30 ns is available for reads and writes. PCI is somewhat of a hybrid bus with some internal features of the PC (notably video and hard-drive controllers) using the bus on the motherboard, as well as providing slots for expansion cards.

PCI is notoriously difficult to create expansion cards for. Along with the fairly high speed, it has complex data-transfer protocols, which generally require an ASIC to decode and process bus requests. For these reasons, other than just introducing PCI, I just concentrate on the two busses that are driven from PCI: the ISA bus and USB.

ISA's roots go back to the original IBM PC. It is an eight-bit bus that originally interfaced directly with the PC's Intel 8088 processor, which ran at 4.77 MHz. This processor clock speed gave the bus a 760-ns cycle time.

In 1984, with the introduction of the PC/AT, the ISA bus operation became formalized by virtually all PC manufacturers and was called the *Industry Standard Architecture*. Before this, a number of manufacturers created PCs with proprietary busses in the hopes that they could lock in customers to their PCs and bus adapters. As well as encompassing the original 8-bit PC standard, the bus size could be optionally increased to 16 bits and the access speed for 16-bit transfers were set at 125 ns (to accommodate an 8-MHz 80286). Today, this bus is used to provide an interface to slow-speed peripherals, such as the keyboard and mouse, as well as the serial and parallel ports. A detailed description of this bus and the different modes of operation (I/O byte read and write, ROM emulation/addition, interrupts and direct memory transfers, DMA) are provided later in the book.

The experiments presented use eight-bit data interfaces and do not take advantage of Plug'n'Play, a hardware/software feature that has become popular because it helps to avoid the need for the user to understand the addresses used by every device in the PC.

The other bus presented in this book is the USB, which is described in greater detail elsewhere in the book.

USB and Firewire are the cornerstone technologies for the "PC/9" standard from Intel and Microsoft. This proposal for a new PC standard avoids the requirements for parallel bus adapter cards all together and instead specifies a very comprehensive peripheral interface scheme that avoids many of the problems of today's PCI and ISA adapter cards.

PLUG 'N 'PLAY

One of the greatest productivity enhancements designed into modern PCs is the invention of "Plug 'n 'Play ("PnP") which allows a motherboard, during the PC's boot, to determine what kind of devices are connected to it. After the devices have been identified, the PnP functions configure them in such a way that their ROM, register and interrupt addresses do not conflict with any other devices in the system. I call this a productivity enhancement because, in the past, adding new hardware into a PC could result in hours, or even days of hair pulling because the new device would not co-exist peacefully with the other devices already installed in the PC.

Plug 'n 'Play was jointly developed by Intel and Microsoft as a method to allow automatic, unique addressing of devices within a PC. This was a daunting task because cards in the PC's ISA bus cannot be individually addressed and a read to a common address would result in all the devices with this addressing responding. The solution of the problem, on the ISA bus, was to provide a serial number ROM at the same I/O address and use "bus contention" to identify individual cards in the system.

Devices on other busses use different "Plug 'n 'Play" mechanisms.

"Bus contention" occurs when two or more devices drive a bus at the same time with different values. In a digital (binary) system, the actual value driven onto the bus is indeterminate. This is to say that the actual value read on the bus will not be the same value as all the different devices drove on it.

Normally, this is a bad thing, but in Plug 'n 'Play, this phenomenon is used to identify different devices by their unique serial numbers. This identification operation is carried out a bit at a time, with any mis-comparing devices dropping off the bus until the serial number read operation is initiated again. The serial number read operation is repeated until all devices in the system have been identified.

In the system, Plug 'n 'Play looks like Fig. 2-15 with the data comparators in each card comparing what is actually in the ROM to what is on the bus. This is done a bit at a time. When a bit miscompare happens within the device's comparator, the device stops responding to the Plug 'n 'Play serial requests until the operation is reset and started again.

Looking at the bus during a serial number read, the data will look like Fig. 2-16. When "Bit 3" is output, Card 2's "one" is lost due to Card 1 pulling the bus line low. From this point on, Card 2 does not respond to serial number requests until a PnP reset request appears on the bus, followed by the next serial number read.

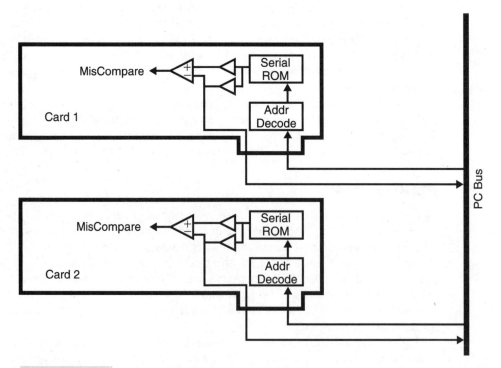

FIGURE 2-15   "Plug 'n 'Play" hardware block diagram.

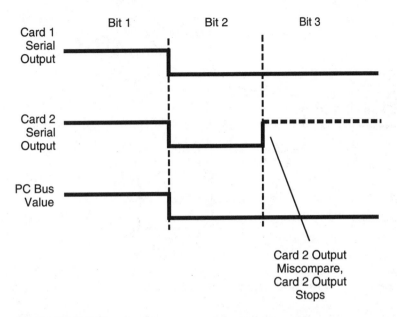

FIGURE 2-16   **"Plug 'n 'Play" hardware block diagram.**

Plug 'n 'Play is almost always implemented using a serial EEPROM and an ASIC to decode the PnP signals and commands. This level of complexity is very difficult to build with discrete logic. As well, the serial numbers must be "allocated" to avoid any chance of repeats. For these reasons, I will not pursue PnP designs in this book, but just give references to it.

USB

The *Universal Serial Bus (USB)* is a relatively new feature that has been added to PCs as standard equipment. Its purpose is to eliminate the need for ISA bus slots in the PC (along with having to open up the PC to install them and then configure them) and provide a common interface for the keyboard, mouse, and serial and parallel ports. USB is one of the cornerstones of Intel's and Microsoft's PC/99 standard, which describes a PC that will never have to be opened up by the user to add peripheral hardware.

USB, as the name suggests, is a serial protocol that allows up to 127 slave devices to be wired into the PC in what I call a *multiple star configuration* (as is shown in Fig. 2-17). To get multiple devices connected to a USB port, a *hub* is required. The hub allocates and passes data packets to different devices. Normally, a hub consists of its own USB connection that is "fanned out" to four (or eight) separate devices. The USB connection consists of four wires, which transports the data and provides 100 mA of current (at +5 V) to each USB peripheral.

USB is a very robust standard with hot plug/hot unplug (connecting and disconnecting devices while the host PC is running) allowed and safe from both the hardware and software perspectives. The USB devices are dynamically allocated and enumerated, which means that updating the config.sys file, setting addresses, loading software or other actions needed to configure the PC with the new device, are not required.

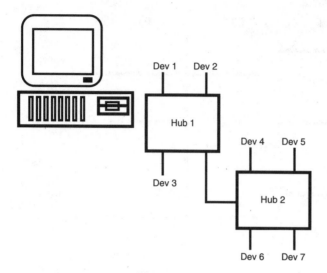

FIGURE 2-17   USB "Hub" and device architecture.

USB was developed in co-operation of over 250 companies with Compaq, Dell, IBM, Intel, Microsoft, NEC, and Northern Telecom being the primary sponsors. USB is designed for a wide range of peripherals (including telephone PBX interfaces) and will make configuring a PC much easier as the standard becomes more popular.

The vision of the PC/99 standard is to have a box with only three types of connectors for system power, peripherals (which is "USB") and high speed devices.

To show how USB connections are implemented, later in the book, I will present the Cypress CY7C6xx USB microcontroller.

FIREWIRE

Firewire was originally developed by Apple as a replacement for the SCSI bus used in Macintoshes. The Apple engineers felt that SCSI was not fast enough for real-time video applications mixed with other hardware-interface signals. Other problems with SCSI included bandwidth problems when multiple devices were placed on the bus and the short length possible using it. The solution was a very high-speed serial bus that not only could be used to link disk and video devices, but all the peripherals in a personal computer system. Apple gave their bus design to the IEEE standards committee as the IEEE-1394 bus standard. Today, this standard is most often known as *1394* or *Firewire*.

As I write this, Firewire has not made significant inroads into the PC market, although it has become quite accepted in the broadcast video industry as a relatively cheap way to handle video and audio data at better-than-broadcast quality. This is possible because of Firewire's very high data rates (currently at 200 MBps and growth to 1 GBps) and optimization designed for efficient passing of streaming data.

If you look over the Firewire and USB standards, you'll see that they have a number of features in common. These primarily center around usability with the features of Hot Plugging. Both standards are capable of providing a modest amount of power to the devices to which they are connected. Hubs are used in both cases to expand the number of ports.

The major difference in the two standards is in the speeds in which they pass data. USB is designed to run at up to 12 MBps while Firewire is designed to run at 200 MBps with 400 MBps and 1 GBps planned for the future. These speed ranges are used to differentiate the roles USB and Firewire will play in future PCs.

USB will most likely be used for low-speed, periodic data transfers, including keyboard, mouse, serial, and diskette interfaces. Firewire is better suited to handling video and in the future; you might see PCs without video adapters—digital video data will be sent to monitors directly and the monitor will convert the serial data into raster information internally. This will really allow the line between computers and TVs to blur with entertainment data (it can no longer be described as tunes or videos) being transferred between different devices within a household.

Another notable difference between USB and Firewire is that USB provides up to 100 mA per device. Firewire provides unregulated 8 to 40 Vdc at up to 1.5 A to connected devices. This also fits in with Firewire's use for taking data from a digital video camera or camcorder, which can be powered by the Firewire host.

This book does not present any practical information on interfacing Firewire devices directly to the PC in this book. As I write this, Firewire is very much in its infancy with few devices currently available outside the video broadcast industry. Over time, I'm sure development kits, similar to the Cypress USB kits, will be available to allow users to learn about and create their own Firewire applications.

You might be interested in the origins of the Firewire standard connector. Surprisingly enough (at least for me), it was from the Nintendo Game Boy. The next time somebody tells you that you are wasting your time with one of the "head-to-head" Mario Brothers games, you can honestly reply that you are helping to establish a robust connector technology for the digital broadcast industry.

Mass Storage

Using the term *mass storage*, I guess the time I spent working for IBM is really showing through. *Mass storage* is an IBM term for any device that stores information while the computer system is turned off. These devices include floppy disks, tape, hard disks, CD-ROMs, etc. For many of the other hardware features in the PC, I show you how to access them directly and even use them with a few tricks. This is not the case with the mass-storage devices because of the complexity in interfacing to them and the opportunity for inadvertently changing the media in such a way that it is no longer usable by the operating system.

The disk subsystems are probably the most-complex devices to successfully access directly from applications. As well, efficient and easy-to-use operating system interfaces are available to accessing the data. For these reasons, I avoid getting in the weeds of the hardware, registers, and BIOS. Instead, I rely on the operating system and high-level language interfaces to do all the dirty work.

In this book, I have included information concerning the architecture and operation of the disk subsystems in the PC to give you an idea of how data and programs are stored and how the disks work. I will also introduce you to some other mass-storage devices and how they are accessed.

The basic way to save and load data on the PC is to use the floppy disk drives. When the PC was first introduced, an audio cassette interface was provided (largely because contemporary PCs, such as the Apple II, used it) but it never worked very well and most PCs were quickly configured with a floppy disk and controller.

About five years ago, I was given the job to get a tester computer (an old IBM "System 1") that used a cassette recorder to load and store programs. The computer hadn't been powered up for six or seven years that and many people used the recorder for listening to audio tapes. Although the recorder did work, I had no idea of how to set it up. I spent two days with an oscilloscope, getting the volume and tone controls set in such a way that the data would be loaded reliably.

Actually, I never got it to load programs reliably, but I did get it to work once out of every two or three times, which seemed to be as good as it ever worked. Of course, a week after I got it running to this level, somebody used the recorder again to listen to their audio tapes while they worked. I was able to train a maintenance technician to set up the controls in just a few hours.

To end the story, I was able to justify getting rid of the old System 1 computer and replacing it with a PC because of the effort required to get the recorder to work reliably and the reliability of the PC's disk system. Once I had replaced the System 1 with a PC, the old computer and its peripherals were scrapped, except, of course, for the cassette recorder, which now just seems to be running on "AC/DC."

The floppy disk gets its name from how it is built. Unlike a hard disk, which uses a rigid plate, a floppy disk uses a plastic material that can be easily deformed (Fig. 2-18).

Each diskette has a number of tracks that go around the diameter of the diskette and contain a number of data sectors. Each sector consists of 512 data bytes, along with a CRC byte and other header information.

To determine the size of a disk and controller, the number of bytes per sector (512) is multiplied by the number of sectors per track which is multiplied by the number of tracks per disk side and then by the number of sides.

Disk size = 512 Bytes/Sector * n sectors/track * x tracks/side * y sides/disk

This formula can be applied to all disks, not just diskettes in the PC. Various PC diskette formats have been available over the years for PCs. The PC has always used a 512

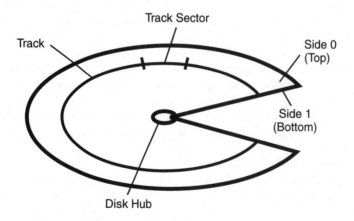

FIGURE 2-18   PC disk format.

byte/sector, although the diskette controller can be programmed to accept different sector sizes. If this is ever changed, then the diskette will become unreadable to the PC. Changing these parameters has been used by game manufacturers to "copy protect" the contents of diskettes.

The diskette formats that have been used over the years for the PC include:

DISK SIZE	SIDES	TRACKS/SIDE	SECTORS/TRACK	DATA SIZE	XFER SPEED
5.25	1	40	8	160 KB	250 KBps
5.25	2	40	9	360 KB	250 KBps
5.25	2	80	15	1.2 MB	500 KBps
3.5	2	80	9	720 KB	250 KBps
3.5	2	80	18	1.44 MB	500 KBps
3.5	2	80	36	2.88 MB	1000 KBps

As you can see, as the storage size goes up, the number of sectors per track increases, which increases the rate of incoming data. The transfer ("xfer") speed is the speed in which the data will be passed from the diskette to the controller; as the amount of data increases on each track, the transfer speed increases.

The 160-KB drive was first available on the PC. This was later superseded by the two-sided 360-KB drive. The PC/AT was introduced with a notoriously unreliable 1.2-MB diskette drive, which was often replaced with a 360-KB drive (the 1.2 MB drive could write to 360-KB drives, but few true 360-KB drives could read what was written). With the PS/2, the PC standard became firmly entrenched in the 3.5-inch diskette size, with the 1.44-MB capacity being the most common.

Each track has quite a bit of header information that is used by the disk controller as is shown in the table below.

OFFSET	SIZE	DESCRIPTION
0	80 Bytes	Index pulse gap
0x050	12 Bytes	Track synch pulse
0x05C	4 Bytes	Track index pulse
0x060	50 Bytes	Track gap

Each Sector has similar header information:

OFFSET	SIZE	DESCRIPTION
0	12 Bytes	Sector synch
0x000C	4 Bytes	Index address
0x0010	1 Byte	cylinder byte

OFFSET	SIZE	DESCRIPTION
0x0011	1 Byte	head byte
0x0012	1 Byte	sector number byte
0x0013	1 Byte	sector size (2 = 512 bytes)
0x0014	1 Byte	CRC
0x0015	22 Bytes	Sector gap
0x002B	12 Bytes	Sector synch
0x0037	4 Bytes	Data address
0x0038	512 Bytes	Sector data
0x0238	1 Byte	data CRC
0x0239	7 Bytes	Sector gap

I've included this information because it's important when you are looking at rated diskette capacities. With the extra track and sector overhead information, the actual storage available on the diskette is significantly less than the rated capacity.

For example, a 720-KB diskette actually has 832 KB stored on it, (and is described as a "1 MB unformatted capacity disk") more than 15 percent than you would expect. This is why when you look at a diskette's unformatted rated capacity, it is always greater than its formatted capacity. For 1.44-MB diskettes, the unformatted capacity is usually 2 MB.

Figure 2-19 shows the block diagram of the diskette subsystem and how it is built around the NEC 765 diskette controller chip.

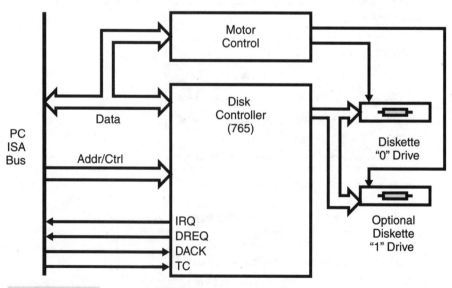

FIGURE 2-19   **PC diskette controller.**

The diskette drive's motor is controlled by a register that is not part of the 765. The reason for doing this was because when the 765 is finished reading or writing a sector, the diskette drive's motor is turned off immediately. In the PC, the motor's control is monitored in BIOS and the motor is turned off two seconds after the last access. The reason for doing this to to eliminate the delay required if multiple tracks are to be read by the PC and the motor has to spin up to speed for each sector read/write. This is why the diskette drive operation light stays on for a few moments after the diskette operation has completed.

The BIOS interface to the diskette controller is very straightforward, with the primary operations being read or write a sector, format a track, set the diskette type, or poll the diskette drive's status. As I indicated, calling the PC's BIOS, like reading or writing directly to the 765's registers (which also means the DMA and interrupt controllers because the diskette controller also accesses them), should be discouraged, but might be required in some circumstances.

These circumstances are pretty limited because, if you are going to write to a disk through BIOS, chances are you are going to destroy the MS-DOS file format information (formatting a track from BIOS means just that, file format information is saved within the 512 bytes of each sector). There are two cases where I would see creating an application where BIOS reads and writes would be used. The first case is an application where you would want to copy protect the contents of the diskette. By writing the application onto the diskette in your own format (for example, 256 bytes per sector) and providing your own reads and writes at disk addresses (sides, tracks, and sectors), MS-DOS would be unable to decode what is on the diskette and copy it.

The other application is developing an MS-DOSless PC boot disk. This will be gone through in more detail later in the book. But, for the most part, it is a pretty good way of creating simple applications that will load and execute very quickly.

The IDE hard disk subsystem of your PC is very similar to the diskette subsystem and uses the same BIOS (and MS-DOS) interfaces with just a few differences.

The first difference is the disk organization. Rather than having only one "platter" or disk, there can be multiple disks, each arranged in a similar format to the diskette (Fig. 2-20).

When specifying the disk side to read from or write to, a *head* is specified, which actually accesses one of the various disks. This allows much of the standard diskette BIOS interface to be used, although the number of tracks (known as *cylinders* in a hard disk because the same track is accessed on each disk side and graphically, it looks like a cylinder) per side is probably an unbelievably large value. The only difference is how the drives are accessed. For hard-disk drives, bit 7 of the disk number passed to the BIOS is set (for floppies, bit 7 is reset) this is the parameter that BIOS uses to determine whether it will access a diskette or a hard disk.

The standard hard-drive controller is the ST-506 that was first used in the PC/XT. Over the years, some effort has been made to keep commonality with this controller chip. But, there might be differences with the hardware. This is especially true for when SCSI and other mass-storage interfaces are used in the PC. Keeping the ST-506 interface allows new devices to be accessed by software using the same registers as the PC's BIOS is expecting, but you cannot depend on this.

For some disks, the hardware interface is completely different and the manufacturer has not attempted to have any commonality with the ST-506. In these cases, the manufacturer

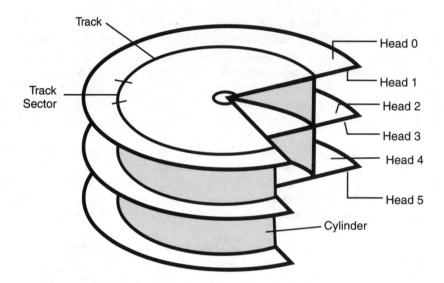

FIGURE 2-20 PC disk format.

will provide device drivers to allow applications and operating systems to interface with the hardware. BIOS overlays or interfaces aren't available for these interfaces.

I have included a description of BIOS interrupt 0x013 in the book. As I've noted, I do not recommend using the registers or BIOS interfaces to any mass storage devices because there is too big an opportunity for the devices to be put in an inoperative state, or for the information contained on them to be unreadable by MS-DOS. When you write your applications, play it safe and only access the disks through the high-level operating system interfaces.

When the PC/XT hardware was first available, a number of assumptions were made about the maximum size of the hard disk and what was possible. These assumptions have really haunted the PC world. If you remember back a few years, it was a big deal when the first IDE-equipped PCs were available with more than 504 MB of storage.

504 MB was the maximum size of an IDE disk that could be accessed by the PC's BIOS. The problem was caused by two incompatible standards used for the BIOS and the IDE (which had become the standard for the PC) drives.

When IBM created the hard-drive specifications for the PC/XT, nobody thought that the PC would be as successful as it was and certainly not as long-lived as it has turned out to be. As well, 15+ years ago, nobody could have anticipated how large in capacity small disk drives could become (as I write this, the first 30-GB SCSI drives are becoming available). Because of these assumptions, the disk BIOS was limited to 1024 cylinders per side, 256 heads, and 63 sectors per track. With 512 bytes per sector, this translates to a maximum of 8 GB of data on a hard disk drive.

The problem arose when the IDE disk interface specification was produced. The maximums were: 65,536 cylinders per side, 16 heads, and 255 sectors per track for a theoretical maximum of 130 GB.

The problem lay in how the two standards combined. The minimum values for each standard was the only way the drives could be interfaced:

	BIOS	IDE	PC MAXIMUM
Heads	256	16	16
Cylinders	1024	65,536	1024
Sectors	63	255	63

The resulting maximum size possible to interface to is defined as:

$$\text{Size} = 512 \text{ bytes/sector} \times 63 \text{ sectors/track} \times 1024 \text{ tracks/head} \times 16 \text{ heads/disk}$$
$$= 528,482,304 \text{ bytes}$$

To get around this restriction, the *Logical Block Addressing (LGA)* standard was created. This standard is used to virtually shuffle around the disk parameters so that a larger disk would be accessible by the standard BIOS parameters (i.e., a disk with 2048 cylinders would appear to the disk controller as having 1024 cylinders and twice the number of heads as it actually had).

As I write this, it is not uncommon to buy PCs with 4- to 6-GB hard drives, which means that in the near future the BIOS interface will become obsolete and all hard-disk interfaces will be through device drivers specific to the disk and controller hardware. This is a very good reason to avoid writing applications that access the disks through BIOS—soon the BIOS hard disk interface will be totally irrelevant.

The operating system itself track the files and space available on the disks and provide you with a pretty simple interface to the files. How to access MS-DOS is explained in more detail later in the book, but I did want to make a few comments.

The first is, avoid the DOS file commands that require the use of the *File Control Block (FCB)* structure. The FCB was first introduced in MS-DOS 2.0 and was rapidly superseded by a more-capable and easier interface. I'm amazed at the number of books on programming the PC still show the FCB structure, if you are looking at books on developing applications or teaching assembly language programming and find one that demonstrates file access with the FCB, look for another one.

The FCB disk I/O interfaces require each file to be referenced by a 41-byte data area. This data area is passed to MS-DOS when you want to carry out a disk operation.

The system introduced with MS-DOS 2.0 was a filename (with disk, subdirectory path, and extension information in a string) and handle-based interface. In this system, the filename (exactly the same as what you would use from the command line or from within a high-level language) is passed to the operating system with parameters for access (such as binary/text mode, read, write create a file, etc.). The operating system returns with a 16-bit file handle, which is used to reference the file in subsequent operations. When all file accesses are completed, the handle is closed.

The file commands (which are explained in greater detail later in the book) include:

- Opening the file
- Closing the file
- Reading data from the file
- Writing data from the file

- Moving to different places within the file
- Creating files
- Deleting files
- Creating/changing/deleting subdirectories
- Looking for files
- Change file-access modes (read only, etc.)

A big advantage of this system is that network files can be accessed exactly the same way as if the disk containing them was physically installed in the PC running the application.

This interface also allows you to access data on other devices as if it were located on a disk. This means that data on such diverse devices as RAMDisk and CD-ROMs can be read as if they were located in standard files (which, because of this interface, they are).

To interface to these nonstandard devices, device drivers have been created for them. I will go into greater detail on these software files (including how to create them) later in the book. You are probably familiar with such devices as writeable CD-ROMs and streaming tape. These devices are usually accessed using special applications written just for them, although, for some operating modes, the data on them is often readable using the file interface described previously.

Getting caught up in why you wouldn't use the BIOS interface for the hard disk, here's one reason why you might want to use it.

When the PC/AT first became available, the hard drive could be very easily damaged by shocks when it was powered down and the read/write head was resting on the disk's surface. At the time, hard disk drives were typically in glass houses, which kept them running continuously and the heads floating above the disk surface, rather than resting on it. Any slight shock on the table or desk the PC was sitting on could cause damage to the delicate read/write head of the disk surface itself.

With the PC/AT, it wasn't unusual to come to work in the morning, try to power your PC up, and discover that the hard disk was damaged and it wouldn't boot. To avoid continuously reformatting the hard disk drive and loading the operating system on again, many people kept their PC/ATs running continuously.

To help protect the PC/AT's disk drive, IBM shipped a program on the diskette that was used to configure the PC's RTC/CMOS that was used to park the heads. *Parking* means moving the head to a safe landing cylinder, devoid of data. Once the head was moved there, the PC's operator would be prompted to shut down the PC without carrying out any additional operations that would use the PC's hard drive. Now, with the head parked, if the PC was bumped, data on the hard drive wouldn't be lost.

Over time, disk-drive manufacturers changed their disk drives so that the heads were always over the landing cylinder or pad when the drive was not in use or moved there automatically when one PC was powered down. This prevented the head from contacting the disk surface when powering down. This feature is available on just about every hard disk drive currently available, which means that there really isn't any reason for your applications to attempt to access the hard-drive registers or BIOS.

DISK BUSSES

In this book, disk drives (of all types) are treated as black boxes and recommend that interfacing with them occurs via the operating system or high-level language APIs. What you might not realize is that the drives (and other devices) are connected to busses; some of these busses can do potentially more than just pass data to and from the processor. I don't show any examples on how to do this, nor do I go any deeper than what I'm going to present in this section for the simple reason that creating an IDE or SCSI device and its software driver is a major undertaking and should not be approached lightly.

A number of devices are ideally suited to these types of busses. The first is the floppy disk, up to two floppy disk drives can be attached in the PC system. The bus is very specific to the NEC 765 floppy-disk controller and is not suitable for any devices other than the standard floppy-disk drives discussed above.

The *Integrated Drive Electronics (IDE)* bus is most commonly known as a hard-drive and CD-ROM bus on the PC. This bus (and its descendent *EIDE*) are really decoded extensions of the PC's ISA or PCI bus. As many as two drives can be installed on each bus (with multiple busses per system).

The IDE bus decodes the I/O accesses from the processor and passes the I/O signals to the drive itself. For the primary IDE port, the following registers are used:

ADDRESS	REGISTER
0x03F6	Alternate status/device control
0x03F7	Drive address
0x01F0	Data port
0x01F1	Error register/precomp specifier
0x01F2	Low byte of sector count
0x01F3	High byte of sector count
0x01F4	Low byte of cylinder number
0x01F5	High byte of cylinder number
0x01F6	Drive/head specifier
0x01F7	Status/command

The data to and from these registers is passed via an 18-bit bus that is part of a 40-pin bus cable. Along with the data and address bits, the IDE bus also passes I/O read and write signals and interrupt requests.

What you might consider missing is a DMA interface to the host PC. This is where the *integrated* in *IDE* comes into play. Rather than pass data between the disk and the PC, as bytes become available or are needed (as is done with the floppy disk), the IDE buffers data between the PC and the disk.

To make a disk request, the buffer is set up initially using the buffer read/write commands and then a transfer is initiated by a separate command. When the disk transfer has completed, the IDE controller issues a hardware interrupt request to the host (Fig. 2-21).

Doing direct reads and writes to the buffer has some advantages. This is despite the disadvantages that each byte is really stored twice in memory and the transfer between the disk and the PC occurs twice and the processor is needed to transfer data, rather than using the DMA circuits to carry this out while the processor is idle. The biggest advantage is the

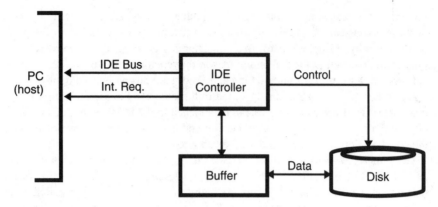

FIGURE 2-21 IDE disk subsystem block diagram.

simplified interface required for the PC and the operating system software. This is important for multitasking operating systems in which data can be transferred to a specific buffer without requiring additional system resources.

A nice feature of the IDE bus and standard is that device parameters can be read out directly in a manner similar to Plug'n'Play. Ten or more years ago, when a PC lost its Real-Time Clock/CMOS configuration information upon reboot (hopefully after replacement of the RTC/CMOS chip's battery) you would have to re-enter the disk parameters, including the number of heads, sectors per track, and tracks per cylinder. If you got any of these parameters wrong, then the PC wouldn't work and you could end up destroying (trashing) the contents of the drive. It wasn't unusual to see a PC's configuration information written on a "Post-It" note on the back of the system unit, in case of an RTC/CMOS problem.

Along with hard disks, popular IDE devices include CD-ROMs, ZIP drives, and streaming tape drives. These devices attach directly to the IDE bus and the device type and parameters (just like for hard drives) are read right out of ROM by the IDE bus when the system configures itself.

A periodically popular disk bus is the *Small Computer Serial Interface* (*SCSI*, usually pronounced *skuzzy*) bus. This bus typically runs much faster than the IDE bus (IDE transfers data at less than 10 MBps, but SCSI can run at 40 MBps) and it uses DMA instead of on disk buffering. As many as seven SCSI devices can be placed on a single SCSI bus.

SCSI is also better suited for external devices than IDE. On my PC's SCSI bus is a color scanner that can be placed as far as 15 feet away from the PC.

The drawbacks to SCSI include: a more-expensive PC and disk interface, a complex set-up procedure, and more-stringent wiring specification (including bus termination). These features make SCSI somewhat more difficult for a novice to add a bus device or recover from a system problem. SCSI is best suited for systems that have external devices or network servers, in which the high speed is a requirement and the extra skill required for configuration is available. I discussed SCSI as "periodically popular" because in the past, standard IDE devices have been able to match the size capabilities of the drives with a simpler hardware and software interface. SCSI will become the premier system when it offers capabilities unmatched by IDE.

Peripheral Devices

Even though I spend many pages describing processors, operating systems, and programming languages, the heart or meat of this book is in the peripheral I/O functions of the PC. The code and projects within the book are geared toward one concept: giving you the background information needed to develop hardware and software to interface with the various peripheral devices.

As I've stated elsewhere in the book, the PC "standard" is really in transition, with Intel and Microsoft trying to drive the PC architecture in a very specific direction via their "PC 99" standard. This standard will greatly simplify the end user's operation of the PC and will, potentially, make it easier for people like us to develop interfaces to the PC for our own nefarious purposes. Sometime in the future, you will see PCs that have no interface aside from USB or Firewire.

As I was writing out this book, I asked around about the PC 98 standard. The consensus that I received was that PCs with traditional interfaces will be available for a long time to come. The expectation is that USB (and Firewire) will become a very important aspect of the PC's operation and peripheral interface, but its introduction will be fairly slow, rather than revolutionizing the PC in a short time.

I really urge you to read through the subchapters that fall under this category; they really are the introductions to the body of the book and the interface circuits that I will present.

KEYBOARD AND MOUSE

The port used in PCs to interface with a keyboard was introduced by IBM for the PC/AT in 1984. This port allows the keyboard (or other devices wired in serial or parallel) to communicate with the PC. The use of the keyboard's protocol was expanded to include the mouse in 1987 with IBM's PS/2 line of computers. This freed up a serial port that previously had been used for the mouse in most systems.

The serial, bi-directional port used for the keyboard is quite simple. The communications protocol uses an 11-bit synchronous serial packet that is sent by either the keyboard/mouse or the PC. As is shown in Fig. 2-22, the packet transmitter is distinguished by whether or not the Start bit's high to low transition proceeds the clock's. The keyboard or mouse start data bit follows the clock bit's high to low transition. The Clock and Data lines are pulled up, which allows either the PC or the keyboard/mouse to take control of the bus (Fig. 2-21).

Adding peripherals to the keyboard or mouse port is actually quite simple, both from the perspective of hardware and software. The pulled-up bus and collision-detection features of the port allow devices to be added easily in parallel to the keyboard/mouse. In the PC, an 8051-compatible microcontroller is used to provide a PC register interface to the keyboard.

When developing peripherals that use the keyboard/mouse ports is in how the application works and the software it requires. The PC is not designed for nonconsole-related device

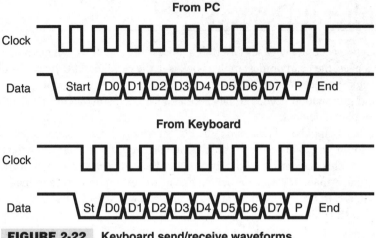

FIGURE 2-22 Keyboard send/receive waveforms.

I/O on these ports and using them as interfaces to arbitrary functions will result in substantial device driver development, so the new device can co-exist with the keyboard handlers. But, a lot of devices can use the port to provide keyboard and pointing-device functions and enhancements, such as bar code, magnetic strip readers, and devices designed for the handicapped to allow them to control the PC as if they were using a keyboard.

The original PC's keyboard port could only receive characters from the keyboard (reset was a separate line from the PC), although it used the same protocol. In 1987, when IBM introduced the PS/2 line of computers, a mouse port was added to the hardware standard. Both the keyboard and the mouse use substantially the same connector, but data is not sent from the PC to the mouse.

SERIAL INTERFACES

I always smile when I've assigned a new engineer the task of connecting a terminal, printer, modem, or other serial peripheral to a PC. The invariable reply is that they learned about serial interfaces in school and they won't have any problems setting up RS-232 connections between a PC and peripheral.

I know that they will be back in my office within a few hours, on the verge of tears because the PC and peripheral just sit there, they don't seem to be able to communicate with one another. Often, they will have bought a large supply of cables, gender changers, and breakout boxes, and can't seem to get data transferred. Even though they've talked to a number of people (that all claim to be experts) about it nothing seems to work.

Understanding how serial communication works is easy, implementing it is frustrating and hard. This is improving with the new high-speed networking protocols (USB and Firewire), but actually sitting down and getting the communication between two devices working is a pain. Much of the information that I present on RS-232 will seem obvious and well understood and the some of the projects quite pedestrian, but I urge you to work through them just so that you have an understanding of exactly what is happening.

THE PARALLEL (PRINTER) PORT

When hardware is to be interfaced with the PC, often the first method chosen is via the parallel (printer) port. If I was being introduced to the PC for the first time, I would probably look at this method first as well, but as I have learned more about the PC, using the parallel port would actually be one of the *last* methods that I would look at.

The parallel port is really the most difficult interface in the PC to use because it is really device (printer and PC) specific, has a limited number of I/O pins, and is quite difficult to time accurately. The only reason why I would see applications using a parallel port for interfacing is because electronically, it does not need a level translator and can connect directly to TTL/CMOS logic.

In the 1970s, the Centronics Corporation developed a 25-pin D-shell connector standard for wiring a computer to their printers. This pinout very quickly became a standard in the computer industry. Broadly put, this connector consisted of an 8-pin data-output port with strobe, two printer-control lines and five status lines from the printer (Fig. 2-23).

By the time the PC was being developed, this was the defacto industry standard and was chosen by IBM to help make the PC work with an industry standard. When the printer port for the PC was being developed, little thought was given to enhancing the port beyond the then-current standard level of functionality.

With the PC/AT, the 8-bit data-output circuitry was changed to allow data bits to be output and read back. This greatly improved the parallel port's usability, with respect to passing data back and forth from external hardware devices. This was designed to provide a two-way communication with PC-sized laser printers that were just becoming available and required much more sophisticated interfaces than the dot-matrix printers that were available up to that time.

This bidirectional capability in the PC/AT's parallel port allowed hardware to interface to the PC to be very easily designed. Further enhancing the ease in which devices could be designed to work with the parallel port was the standard timing provided by the PC/AT's ISA bus.

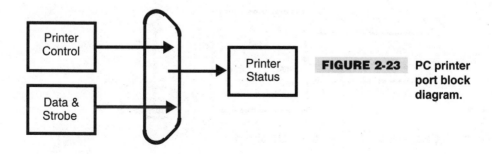

FIGURE 2-23 PC printer port block diagram.

The biggest problem today with interfacing to the parallel port is timing signals properly. Depending on the different PCs that I have experimented with, I have seen parallel-port interface timings that range from a 0.5 μs to less than 100 ns. This variability (especially toward the fast signals) has made using the parallel port much less desirable for creating a simple interface to the PC.

OTHER PERIPHERALS

One of the reasons why Intel and Microsoft want to simplify all the PC peripheral interfaces to one type is because of the many seemingly nonstandard devices available. With the availability of Windows/95, 98, and NT, this has improved a lot (I always remember loading the CD-ROMs for Wing Commander III and being awed by the literally hundreds of hardware options that had to be selected from for the game to work properly).

Most of these options were in the area of the joystick port, sound cards, and video. Adding any options to your system that falls under these categories can make your life unbelievably miserable and will probably render your PC unusable for a few days.

Despite this, a number of quite interesting things that can be done with the joystick and your sound card that can simplify a one-off project or give you some methods to transfer data to your PC without having to buy expensive equipment.

Joystick port While nominally designed for games, the PCs joystick port is actually an analog to digital precision sensor. "Reading" the resistance of the potentiometer in the joystick is accomplished by timing how long a RC network takes to charge/discharge. Looking at Fig. 2-24, the voltage on the capacitor is sensed as it is being charged or discharged through the resistor. This circuit follows a familiar negative exponent RC charge cycle.

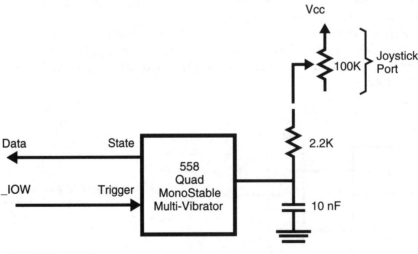

FIGURE 2-24 Joystick ADC circuit.

After waiting for the capacitor to charge with the driver set to a "high" or one output, the driver is set to a low logic level and the time for the charge in the capacitor to drop below the threshold voltage (usually 1.4 Volts) of the "Sense Input" is timed. You may expect the voltage rise/fall to be proportional to the current resistance of the potentiometer in the joystick.

Along with four potentiometer measuring circuits (for 2 "X-Y" joysticks), the PC's "Game" Port also has a number of digital inputs and can supply +5 Volts and Ground. This makes the Game Port surprisingly flexible for use in interfacing to external devices, both analog and digital.

Sound cards   One of the more-forgotten interfaces to the PC is the Soundblaster-compatible sound card. Originally, the PC came with just a timer-driven speaker, but this was improved with the different cards designed for creating sophisticated sound capabilities and speech synthesis (or at least recorded output). The Soundblaster, with its multiple voices and stereo output quickly became the defacto standard enhanced sound card for use in the PC for those of us scouring the Internet to download a .WAV file of Al Bundy's Ba-Woosh!

The Soundblaster was the first sound card to gain wide acceptance and this leadership was enhanced by other companies, which provided register compatible (clone) chip sets and game manufacturers reading and writing to the Soundblaster's registers, rather than using standard device drivers. Except for the motherboard and video RAM, the Soundblaster registers are the only absolute addresses that you will have to work with in PCs when you are developing applications.

As you will realize looking at Fig. 2-25, the Soundblaster is actually very complicated (it uses many of the same resources required by the disk subsystem). Typically, the sound card works with the file to be output stored in memory from a wave (.WAV) file. This file consists of a set of register commands that play a particular sound, noise, or tune.

The .WAV file's data can be loaded into the Soundblaster one of two ways. The most obvious way is for the processor to poll the command complete registers and load in new

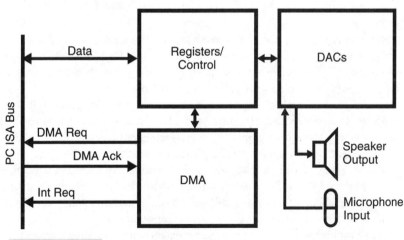

FIGURE 2-25   "SoundBlaster" block diagram.

commands when the previous ones have completed. The problem with this method is that it takes up a lot of processor cycles.

The most common way of passing a .WAV file to the Soundblaster is to use the PC's DMA resources to pass the data to the Soundblaster from memory. At the end of the .WAV file (or the data that has been loaded), an interrupt request is generated for the PC's processor to reload a file to provide additional music and sounds to the Soundblaster.

The Soundblaster also accepts audio level input, which can be recorded into memory using DMA. This input voltage sample is stored at a specific sample rate for later processing by the PC.

Configuration Information

Today, configuring your PC is largely an automatic operation. This is because of the ability of the PC to save the current configuration in nonvolatile RAM; on power up, the cards in each of the slots can be checked by Plug'n'Play hardware and code to see what's located in the PC. As well, disk drives and CD-ROM drives can be queried as to their type and parameters. This is quite a contrast to properly configuring the PC (even just a few years ago) because of the large amount of knowledge required to successfully get it working properly.

In the original PC, an Intel 8255 with DIP switches was read on boot and specified the PC's configuration. Along with this, each adapter card generally had a set of DIP switches for selecting where memory would appear in the PC's memory map, along with what interrupts and DMA channels would be used.

It was a nightmare.

The actual resource addresses and numbers weren't as firmly entrenched in convention as they are now and resources that were required for other hardware devices could be selected.

For example, I have an old (circa 1986) ISA token-ring network adapter card specification. The 16-KB shared RAM can be located from 08000h to 0E0000h and the interrupt levels can be 2, 3, 6, or 7.

Not properly setting the shared memory address switches could result in overlap (or "contention") between main memory or video RAM. Problems with the interrupt selected could result in the secondary serial port, diskette, or printer interrupts not working properly (because they would have to be shared with the token-ring card).

Unless you kept meticulous records of how a PC was configured and how the switches were set, it wasn't too big of a surprise if, after installing a new feature, the PC wouldn't boot or would stop working once the operating system was loaded. Often, it could take literally hours to get the system working with a new card.

Maybe it seems like I'm exaggerating the problem, but I seem to remember that if there was a problem with a PC after a card was added, I was generally the first person to get called. The upside of this was I still have a ton of documentation for old adapters that I can't bear to get rid of in case an old tester stops working.

These problems were relieved to some extent with four enhancements to the PC standard.

The first was the PC/AT's inclusion of the Motorola MC1461818 real-time clock and CMOS RAM chip. Along with a clock, this chip was used for providing nonvolatile memory, which stored much of the system's configuration information.

This actually made upgrading the PC much easier—especially with the strong resource conventions that were imposed by IBM with the introduction of the PC/AT. The CMOS memory tracked amount of memory accessible to the processor, as well as processor features, such as a numeric coprocessor.

In many ways, the CMOS RTC/RAM chip made things simpler, but it also made one thing more difficult. To set the clock and configuration in IBM's PC/AT, a special diskette was required. This diskette would write (early versions couldn't read back) the CMOS configuration. So, with the PC/AT, updating the configuration now required keeping a written copy of the PC's configuration and required you to keep the diskette in a safe place (I still have three kept in case of emergency). This continued on for the PS/2 (although the PS/2 could detect what the system was configured with and could store the CMOS update file on the hard drive).

The best solution to updating the CMOS RTC/RAM chip was to provide code in boot ROM that would provide a simple user interface allowing easy changing of the various parameters simply and intuitively. Pretty well all systems built after 1990 use this method.

As electronics became denser, motherboards began to have more and more function. These functions included video drivers, the serial and parallel ports and additional memory. These features had been previously provided on adapter cards. By putting these functions on the motherboard, the variability (once provided by being able to locate different standard resources at different addresses) was pretty much eliminated.

As an added bonus, these motherboards would not allow invalid addresses to be specified. Once an address was used on the motherboard, it would not be passed to any of the adapter busses. This latter feature meant that adapter cards set to the same address as hardware on the motherboard would not be accessed, making problems that would crash the PC much more remote.

The final enhancement to the PC that allowed easier configurations was Plug'n'Play (PnP). This hardware feature is coupled with code to determine how much memory plugged into the PC allows modern PCs to detect what type of hardware is present and configure the hardware to avoid conflicts or incorrect configurations.

The earliest system of auto configuration and checking was IBM's *MCA (Microchannel Architecture)* bus, which was made available with the PS/2s. During system boot, each slot would be polled and card-configuration registers would be checked against what was in the configuration CMOS memory. One of the problems with the IBM MCA bus was that when a new adapter card was discovered, special boot drivers had to be loaded from diskette.

The Plug'n'Play, invented by Microsoft, has pretty much eliminated all of the concerns of the other configuration systems. For a PC and adapters to be PnP compatible, a small serial PROM loaded with a 64-bit value must be located at bit zero of address 0x0203 and is read one bit at a time. As the PC's processor reads this address, each of the adapter cards outputs the 64-bit value, one bit at a time.

If one of the adapters detects a 0 on the bus when it was outputting a 1, then it stops outputting the data. Once an adapter has successfully output its 64-bit code, it no longer responds to read requests until the PC has gone through every one of the PnP adapters and has identified all of their 64-bit serial numbers.

The 64-bit PnP serial number consists of a manufacturer's code, a device code, and a unique device serial number. The serial number is used to allow multiple adapters to be plugged into the same machine and still have the operating system identify that there are more than one adapter of the same type and give each of them different addresses from the others.

Plug'n'Play has also been extended to such peripherals as hard disks and CD-ROMs. When your PC boots up, you might be surprised to see that the manufacturer and part number of the peripherals are identified during boot up. Along with this information, specific hardware information is also provided to eliminate the need for explicitly specifying the number of tracks, platters, and sectors that used to be required when installing new disk drives.

With Plug'n'Play, you can literally load your PC and start it up without worrying about the addresses and parameters that the peripheral devices have—they will be set up largely automatically.

Despite the radical advances in PnP technology, most PCs still use the MC146818 CMOS RTC and RAM chip. This chip has 50 bytes of RAM available to the host system and uses 14 bytes for the real-time clock function. These registers are addressed by writing the register address to I/O address 0x070 and then reading or writing address 0x071.

I do not recommend reading and writing to any of the memory locations directly in the MC146818 because, in many manufacturer's PCs, some or all of the memory has a checksum that is set during configuration write and checked during booting. Writing to a location that is protected by the checksum could result in your PC requiring a new configuration to be loaded into it the next time it is booted.

As well, for reading the time from the chip every second, the time address are updated once a second for 2 ms. During this period, the data is indeterminate and definitely incorrect.

There is a way around the time-reading problem. But the easiest way to avoid it all together is to use the BIOS interrupt 0x01A functions, which will allow reading and writing of the CMOS clock reliably without the once-per-second update problem or affecting the checksum value, which will cause problems when the PC is booted later.

Video Output

The *cathode-ray tube (CRT)* video display was first demonstrated in 1926. The cathode-ray tube used for the demonstration was very similar to what we are familiar with today in the TVs in our homes and the PC monitors on our desks. In this experiment, the video tube consisted of an electron gun (a hot element that had a high-tension voltage applied to it so that electrons would boil off) shooting electrons at a phosphor screen (which emits light when struck by electrons). This stream of electrons was guided by a series of magnetic coils to control where the phosphor screen was hit, resulting in an image. The first pictures that were sent were simply black shapes on a white background because the image quality was so poor. Although the actual hardware used in the 1926 demonstration is shockingly primitive, compared to modern PC displays or televisions, it does have all of the elements of its modern counterparts.

The first computer CRT display was the vector display, in which the X-Y deflection plates moved the electron beam to a desired location on the screen and then drew a line to the next location. This was repeated until the entire image was drawn on the screen (at which time the process started over). This was popular in early computers because only a modest amount of processing power and video output hardware was needed to draw simple graphics. Because of the way the vector displays operated, a complex image was often darker than and could flash more than a simple image which requires fewer vector strokes and could be refreshed more often. Vector displays enjoyed some popularity in early computer video displays (including video games), but really haven't been used for more than 10 years.

Today, a more-popular method of outputting data from a computer is to use a raster display, in which an electron beam is drawn across the cathode-ray tube in a regular, left-to-right, up-to-down, pattern. When some detail of the image is to be drawn on the screen, the intensity of the beam is increased when the beam passes a particular location on the screen, which causes the phosphors to glow more brightly (Fig. 2-26).

If you have an old black-and-white TV (or monochrome computer monitor), chances are that you can increase the brightness/contrast controls on a dark signal to see these different features.

If you are not familiar with video output, you're probably more than a bit intimidated and confused by the description of the operation of a raster display. You might also wonder about what the hardware looks like that is used to drive it.

Hopefully, I can put your mind at ease by saying that all raster computer output hardware consists of a shift register fed by data from a Video RAM (VRAM). In Fig. 2-27, the data to be output is read from the VRAM and then passed to a character generator, which converts the data from the Video RAM into a series of dots appropriate for the character. This series of dots is then shifted out to the video monitor.

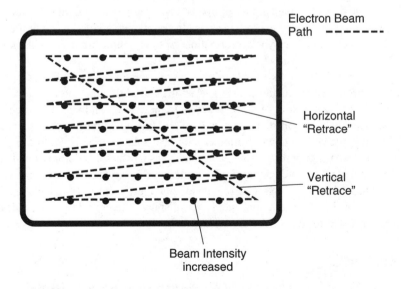

FIGURE 2-26 Video screen raster operation.

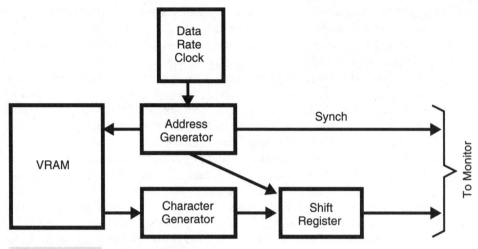

FIGURE 2-27 Video subsystem block diagram.

If graphical data is output, then the character generator is not needed in the circuit and the output from the VRAM is passed directly to the shift register. The shift register can also be connected to a *Digital Analog Converter (DAC)*, which converts the digital data into a series of analog voltages, which display different intensities of color on the display.

If you ever see a circuit for Don Lancaster's early TV typewriter, you might want to study it because it shows in excellent detail (i.e., using TTL chips) how a raster display driver is implemented.

The addresses for each byte's data to be transferred to the display are accomplished by using an address generator, which controls the operation of the display. The address generator divides the data rate (the number of pixels displayed per second on the screen) into character-sized chunks for shifting out, resets address counters when the end of the line is encountered, and also outputs Synch information for the monitor to properly display data on the screen.

The circuit in Fig. 2-28 shows an example address generator for an 80-character by 25-row display. This circuit resets the counters when the end of the line and field (end of the display) is reached. At the start of the line and field, horizontal and vertical synch information is sent to the monitor so that the new field will line up with the previous one.

That's all there really is to how a computer's raster display works. Now, I have simplified some aspects of the operation of the display (such as how color is output), but this subchapter does include the basic operation of a computer display used in just about all PCs and workstations. The following sections expand upon these concepts and include what is available in modern, high-resolution, windowed displays. Later in the book, I describe how data is formatted for display on the PC's screen.

MDA AND CGA

When the IBM PC was first announced, it was designed to be used with the IBM-designed *Monochrome Display Adapter (MDA)* or *Color Graphics Adapter (CGA)* cards that pro-

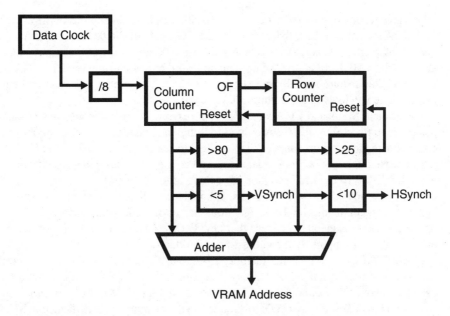

FIGURE 2-28   Video address generator block diagram.

vided video console output. These two adapters are extremely primitive compared to the SVGA adapter that is running on your PC, but they did provide the IBM PC with relatively advanced video capabilities.

The MDA could only output data in one format: 80 by 25 characters, which could be optionally emphasized (made brighter) or underlined. Each character and its parameters were set in VRAM in a 16-bit word mapped to the display output. With the IBM-provided screen, the characters were quite crisp and easy to read.

The MDA provided text data in the same format as the IBM word processors of the time. Limited graphics could be presented using special characters that were built into the Enhanced IBM character set (which was really an 8-bit version of the ASCII standard with the upper 128 characters designated for non-ASCII characters and simple graphics). Using this character set, boxes around text and special characters could be displayed, but arbitrary graphics could not be.

The CGA gave color graphics to the PC, but at the price of resolution. Were as the MDA provided 640 × 400 pixel output, the CGA could only provide 640 × 200 pixels. At this resolution, only two colors (black and white) were available. This meant that for creating graphics, quite a bit of skill was needed to be sure that everything was proportioned correctly (i.e., circles were actually round) and was identifiable. This lack of vertical resolution made it very difficult to use the screen in text mode for a long period of time.

In both the MDA and CGA, processor access to VRAM was given priority. This meant that unless the screen was in a Retrace mode, any characters read or written from the memory would be passed to the output shift registers and "snow" would be displayed on the screen. With VRAM updates and reads only occurring during retraces, the operation of the PC seemed very slow, often much slower than competing machines in certain applications.

One nice feature of how IBM architected the PC was in setting up the VRAM addresses. The MDA started at address 0x0B0000 and the CGA at 0x0B8000. This meant that the two display adapters could co-exist together in the same PC and many of the original PCs were set up with an MDA for code development and word processing and used the CGA just for graphics. This feature is really not required in today's graphical user interface environment, where windows can be minimized or restored easily.

The original MDA and CGA were far from perfect. Many clone versions output composite video (the MDA and CGA only output digital signal levels), allowing inexpensive composite video monitors (and TVs) to be used instead of the expensive IBM TTL monitors. The Hercules monochrome adapter was a very popular add-on because it would work with the IBM MDA TTL monitor to output high-quality alphanumerics and CGA-compatible graphics. These clone cards, although providing enhanced features to the PC, helped to cement the display BIOS functions as part of the PC standard. As with any add-ons, there was considerable concern that new BIOS functions would make it difficult for other vendors to support IBM and third-party products.

Video RAM (VRAM) has the memory from 0x0A0000 to 0x0C7FFF allocated for its use. This was prescient because it allowed enough space for updated adapters and it is still used for today's SVGA and AGP adapters. Some BIOSes, follow IBM's original lead and write *Power-On Self-Test (POST)* information to the memory areas dedicated to MDA and CGA—even if no devices are present.

I am mentioning this because you may discover the ASCII message "xxx RAM Ok" in your shared RAM instead of the nulls or blanks you may expect.

EGA

The *Enhanced Graphics Adapter (EGA)* was introduced with the PC/AT in 1984 as a replacement for the MDA and CGA. The improvements put into the EGA allowed the PC to be used for serious word processing and graphics applications using the same screen, instead of a separate color and monochrome screen, required by the original PC to carry out this function.

The EGA's main advantages included dual-ported VRAM and the ability to display up to 400 lines of video raster data in character mode (resulting in an 8- by 14-pixel character box) with as many as 16 colors. Graphically, the resolution was increased to 640 by 400 pixels, with as many as 16 colors taken from multiple palettes. The increased resolution made characters much easier to read and actually brought the character resolution up the MDA's level.

Personally, the biggest improvement was the addition of the dual-ported memory. This meant that the VRAM could be updated at any time without any snow appearing on the screen. This snow was a problem with the MDA and CGA if the video RAM was updated at other than when a horizontal or vertical retrace was occurring.

The MDA/CGA video BIOS did support the retrace operation. But this meant that the MDA/CGA screen could only be updated one character per line, which translated to an update speed of about 12,000 characters per second (more than 0.1 second to update the entire screen). The EGA's dual-ported memory meant that screen updates could occur as fast as the processor could write to the ISA bus (on the order of 1 MBps).

As the PC's BIOS included code for the MDA and CGA, a ROM with the EGA's BIOS commands was included on the EGA card. Also, it had a number of smaller features, which improved the capabilities of the EGA. These included the ability to scroll the display by a set number of pixels. At work, I created an "Earthquake" TSR that could be put onto a victim's PC and would periodically shake the screen for a few seconds. When a customer service representative (repairman) was called in, we would disable the program so there wasn't any problem to be seen and turn it back on after the repairman had left.

The Enhanced Graphics Adapter quickly became a standard for the PCs and opened the doors to the first Graphical User Interfaces (GUIs), such as the initial versions of Microsoft Windows.

(SUPER) VIDEO GRAPHICS ARRAY

Like the other popular video standards, the Video Graphics Array (VGA) was introduced by IBM with the announcement of a new PC line. The VGA standard was introduced as an enhanced EGA with the PS/2 line of personal computers. Unlike the MDA, CGA, and EGA, IBM is not the ultimate source on what is and what isn't VGA compatible. Over the years, many improvements and enhancements have been made to the VGA standard by other companies. Today, VGA and SVGA is a low-level compatibility standard for many manufacturers that provide video hardware that provides remarkable video capabilities for the PC.

The big departure for the VGA over previous standards was its ability to display both text and graphic Windows over a graphic background. As I was writing this, I decided the best way to illustrate this ability by taking a screen shot of the PC as I am writing this (see Fig. 2-29). This screen shows an MS-DOS window, a Corel Draw window, and an Internet Explorer window all displayed at the same time. The source information for each of these windows is located in different areas of video RAM and the VGA processor brings them together and clips them appropriately without a significant investment in software.

The hardware features devoted to displaying multiple windows in hardware obviously made the development of Microsoft Windows much easier. Moving a window or giving a specific one focus simply consists of changing the VGA window display registers.

Super VGA is a renaming of the IBM "8514/A" video specification. This video hardware and software standard was an enhancement by IBM to the original VGA specification. The 8514/A was an enhancement to the default screen resolution (which was 640-×-400 pixels) and provide a hardware mechanism to draw basic shapes (squares, circles, triangles, etc.) on the display without the microprocessor having to write individual pixels to VRAM. The 8514/A was designed strictly for IBM's *Microchannel Architecture (MCA)*, but has been ported to ISA and PCI as the "Super VGA".

In the more than 10 years since VGA and 8514/A have been introduced, several new video adapters, which are based on these standards, have come forward with the most recent being Intel's AGP. Several other manufacturers also provide custom hardware and drivers for games, digital video, and other high-resolution applications.

This book does not show how to write to the VGA (and beyond) hardware. Instead, I rely on Windows and development-language APIs to provide an interface to the hardware. By doing this, I will not have to worry about correctly interfacing to the different VGA hardware that different PCs use. This might seem like a bit of a divergence from how I work with the 80 × 25 text-display applications, in which I will write directly to VRAM, but in these applications, writing directly to Video RAM is the most efficient, fastest way of updating the display.

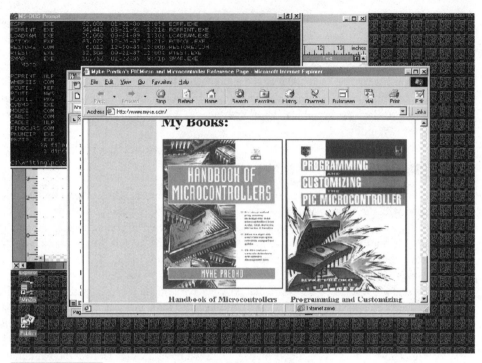

FIGURE 2-29   Example VGA mixed graphics and text.

For the VGA, which will primarily be used with Windows applications, finding the actual VRAM of a specific window is not possible over the wide range of VGA hardware available.

PC Power Supply

One of the more-overlooked or taken-for-granted features of the PC is the power supply. Understanding what this supply's capabilities are crucial when you are planning on connecting applications to the PC. Taking advantage of the PC's power supply could mean that your application will be cheaper and simpler.

Most PC power supplies deliver ±5 V and ±12 V, with some also providing +3 V for Pentium operation or +48 V unfiltered DC for distributed power applications.

If available, the Pentium and distributed power sources should not be used because for the Pentium supply, the voltage is crucial (to millivolts, for some Pentiums that I have seen) and any additional load or noise could result in the PC running unreliably or not at all. The 48-V distributed power supply should be avoided simply because when I say it's unfiltered, I mean it. The +48 V could be simply rectified AC, with the RMS average being 48 V.

With digital logic, +5 V is the primary logic supply. This is also true in the PC, where typically 90 percent of the power draw in the system is +5 V. This can be supplied at 40 or more amps of current, meaning that the power supply could be used as an arc welder, if you're not careful!

The +12-V supply is provided for disk drive power, as well as one of the two RS-232 reference voltages. To run the disk drives, up to three amps of current will be sourced by the supply at +12 V.

The two negative supplies probably seem unusual and not that useful (especially considering that they are only capable of sourcing a few hundred mA). The −12 V is used as the second RS-232 reference voltage, but −5 V is not used. The −5-V supply was added to the original PC's supply because some types of DRAMs available at the time required −5 V to provide a greater amount of charge to the DRAM memory cells. I have never seen an application that has used −5 V, but it's there if you need it.

Three ways are available to get +5 V power from the PC to your application. They are: have an adapter card take it from the bus slots, use a disk-drive power connector as a power source, or access it through a keyboard/mouse port.

The bus slots will provide a great deal of current, but at risk to your motherboard, in the case of a short, or if an unreasonable amount of current is drawn. For high-current applications, I recommend that a disk power connector be used instead of getting the power through the bus slots. In this case, if too much current is drawn, the power supply will crowbar (shut down) from over current, rather than burn a hole in your motherboard.

The power connectors to the motherboard are known as *P8* and *P9* or *PS8* and *PS9*. They are wired as:

CONNECTOR	PIN	POWER/SIGNAL
P8	1	Power good
	2	+5 VDC
	3	+12 VDC
	4	−12 VDC
	5	Ground
	6	Ground
P9	1	Ground
	2	Ground
	3	−5 VDC
	4	+5 VDC
	5	+5 VDC
	6	+5 VDC

Disk power is supplied by a 4-pin PWB connector wired as:

PIN	POWER
1	+12 VDC
2	Ground
3	Ground
4	+5 VDC

Of course, for any high-current application, a fast-blow fuse should be put in line to protect the application.

Actually, most PC keyboard ports include an inline fuse on the power line to the mouse or keyboard to prevent damage to the motherboard (or keyboard/mouse) if something is added to the port and excessive current is drawn. Hardware connected to these ports should never require more than 500 mA total current (including the keyboard/mouse).

PC power supplies are typically pretty complex switching power supplies. Because of this, I have a few comments.

The first is, PC power supplies require a minimum load (about 5 A) to work properly. This means that if you want to use a PC power supply as a bench supply, you're going to have to add a 1-Ω ballast resistor for the power supply to work properly.

The power supply can take a significant amount of time to provide a stable power output because it is a switching supply. The positive active Power Good signal coming from the supply will indicate when the power output is stable and usable. The Power Good line is used as the PC's Reset line.

As a final word of caution, do not modify a PC power supply to try to fix it if it breaks. The energies inside the power supply's capacitors could kill, burn, or cause a fire—even if the power supply has been left unplugged. As well, modifications or repairs could make the power supply unsafe during operation. If you require specific voltages, buy a properly certified bench supply with overcurrent protection. If the PC's power supply breaks down, send it to a certified repair center for repairs, or buy a new one.

PC power supplies have gone through the same cost pressures as the other components inside of the PC's cabinet. This means that precautions taken in early PC supplies might not be present in modern ones and opening one could expose you to unnecessary risk.

PERSONAL
COMPUTER
PROCESSORS

It shouldn't surprise you that the heart of the PC is the processor. I've introduced you to the different devices that provide interfaces to a PC, which are all controlled by the PC's processor using standard hardware and software interfaces, many of which have been available since 1981. This has meant that the Pentium processor, used in modern PCs running complex multi-tasking applications must have the same I/O capabilities of the original 8088, along with the capability to emulate the 8086 processor for instruction execution. I believe that this requirement has hampered the efforts to develop the PC's processors to the same performance levels as what has been achieved in workstation *RISC (Reduced Instruction Set Computers)* processors.

This enforced commonality, although restricting the PC's performance from achieving the theoretical maximum number crunching speed, has kept the PC as the primary workstation used in engineering and business for most of the past 20 years.

This means that before you can truly understand how the PC works, you must have a good understanding of how the processor works and executes programs and instructions. I realize that it is most likely that you will never program a PC in assembly language (and it's probably best that you don't), but I believe that it's crucial for you to understand how your PC's processor operates. You should have a strong understanding of how instructions are processed, data is addressed and improved processors (starting with the 80386), have changed the way in which applications execute.

This chapter provides a background into the PC, starting with the 8086/8088 (the first processors used in the IBM PC) and move up into the high-performance Pentium III processors of today.

The Intel 8086

When the PC first came out, it used a 16-bit Intel 8088 microprocessor. This device consists of an Intel 8086 processor core with an 8-bit data bus. When the processor was selected for the PC, much of the PC's design had already been built around the Intel 8085 (an 8-bit processor). Using the 8088 gave IBM the opportunity to use a 16-bit processor in their system at a time when most of their competitors only had 8-bit processors.

This was rather fortuitous because it meant the PC would not only be competitive to its contemporaries, but also had an upgrade path to more capable processors that Intel had in design. The basic 8086 processor core has been enhanced in the later processors, but the same basic registers and instruction set is still available in even the latest Pentium class microprocessor.

This has made learning to program the PC a growth experience instead of one where application developers have to continually learn to use a new system. Actually, this book is laid out in such a way that, as you go through it, you will first learn about the 8086 and the MS-DOS operating system and go on to develop Windows applications for Pentium-processored PCs.

Using the 8088 resulted in about a 30-percent performance loss over an 8086 running at the same clock speed. This was because of the need for the 8088 to take two memory cycles to read a 16-bit instruction or data value (or variable), whereas the 8086 could perform the operation in one memory cycle.

After reading the preceding paragraph, the 30-percent performance degradation probably seems surprising and a 50-percent degradation would probably seem to make more sense.

The reason for the better-than-expected 8088 performance is because of the way instructions are implemented in the 8086. An instruction can be one, two, three or five bytes

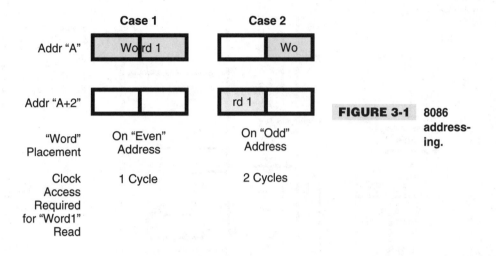

FIGURE 3-1 8086 addressing.

long. Because the instructions are not all on a word (even address) boundary, the 8086 often requires two memory cycles to read 16-bits out of memory, the same as what the 8088 requires.

Looking at Fig. 3-1, Case 1 has the word (16-bit data) on an even address (address bit 0 is reset) and the entire word can be read in one cycle. In Case 2, two reads are required because the word is split across two even addresses. For both the 8086 and 8088, the 16-bit word read in Case 2 requires the same number of cycles. When this is averaged out over application code and data, the performance of an 8088 works out to approximately 30 percent less than the 8086.

Because the processor core is the same in either the 8086 or the 8088, I tend to think of the PC's processor as just an 8086, which it actually is. As I work through this chapter and the book, you'll see me reference the 8086 almost exclusively because the instruction execution is the same across all PC microprocessors, except in the case of Protect mode and numeric co-processor instructions, which were introduced with the 8087, 80286 and 80386. When I use the term *8086*, I'm really talking about all the microprocessors that have been used in IBM compatible PCs when they are working in 16-bit Real mode.

In both the 8086 and 8088, the processor core gets instructions and data from a *Bus Interface Unit (BIU)*, which controls the access to the memory and I/O busses. More importantly, the BIU reads ahead instructions to help speed up the operation of the PC. *Reading ahead* means that while the PC's processor is executing an instruction, the BIU is reading the next one, or storing the next one while data is being read or written. This feature allows the 8086 (8088) to run more efficiently without any unused bus cycles because the processor is processing data.

8086 ARCHITECTURE

The 8086 architecture follows the design set out by the 8080. A central core of 16-bit registers is used to manipulate data. This means that it can manipulate data in the range of

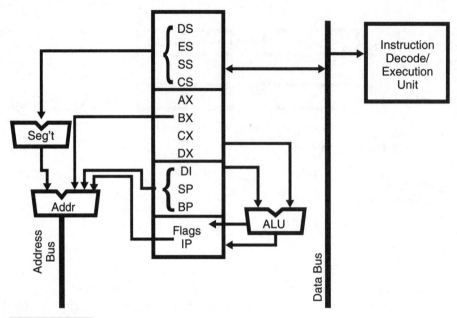

FIGURE 3-2   8086 processor architecture.

zero to 65,536 (or –32,768 to +32,767) within a 65,536-byte (64 KB) address space. This perspective might seem somewhat limited—especially if you have a Windows/98 Pentium II running a 2-MB Excel spreadsheet that is doing financial calculations for you.

I am starting with this limited perspective on the PC's processor because this is really all the original PC was. As time progressed, the capabilities of the PC grew out of this humble architecture to the processing behemoths we are familiar with.

The actual architecture can be modeled with Fig. 3-2.

The first four registers (DS, ES, SS, and CS) are the Segment registers, which are used to specify the 64-KB segment that the data or code is located in, in the 8086's 1-MB memory space. Later, this chapter includes a lot more about these registers and how they work. This section ignores them and focuses on the 16-bit data registers.

Like the 8080, Intel has defined default functions for the 8086's different registers. AX, BX, CX, and DX can all be broken up into 8-bit registers, known as *AH* (the high 8-bits of the AX register), *AL* (the low 8-bits of the AX register), *BH*, *BL*, *CH*, *CL*, *DH*, and *DL*. These registers can be the source or destination of arithmetic and bit instructions.

AX is normally used as a general-purpose arithmetic register with DX used as well for 32 bit values (such as the result of 16-bit multiplication). BX is a general-purpose index register, which (along with DI, SI, and BP), provides the ability to index data within various 64-KB segments. These index registers are used not only to index data in arrays, but also to provide pointers to subroutine parameters and strings. The next few sections go through these registers as well.

The Flags register (described in greater detail in the next sub-chapter) contains the processor's execution status and results from previous arithmetic operations. This register is not directly accessible, but the bits stored in it can be used to change the execution of the application.

The original 8086 (which includes the 8088, 80186 and 80188) only runs in Real mode. This mode consists of 1 MB of memory distributed in a number of 64-KB segments.

As time has gone on, the 8086 has been superseded with the 80286, 80386, 80486, and Pentium processors. These processors can also support much more than the 1 MB of memory of the 8086 using Protect mode. Later, this chapter introduces you to the 32-bit Protect mode (which is used by the 80386 and later processors), which not only provides access to larger amounts of memory, but protects memory allocated to one program from affecting another.

The flags register   The 8086's flags register provides the status information after all arithmetic instructions and two interrupt control bits. The flag bits might be somewhat confusing and functions between bits might seem redundant, but they actually are quite easy to understand and useful in applications.

The flags register is defined as having the bits:

BIT	DEFINITION
15–12	Ignored
11	OF - Overflow Flag
10	DF - Direction Flag
9	IF - Interrupt Mask Flag
8	TF - Single Step Interrupt Trap Mask Flag
7	SF - Sign Flag
6	ZF - Zero Flag
5	0
4	AF - Auxiliary (Nybble) Carry Flag
3	0
2	PF - Parity Flag
1	1
0	CF - Carry Flag

I have ignored the upper four bits because these bits are unused in the 8086 and used for controlling protect mode in the 80286 (and faster) processors. These four bits should never be altered when accessing the flags register.

If you are creating contents of a flag register for an interrupt handler or new process, I would have to suggest that you copy in the current flags register using something like the sequence:

```
pushf              ;  Put the Flags on the Stack
pop    AX          ;  Load AX with the Flags
and    AX, 0x0F002  ;  Clear All the Bits Except for Top 4 and Bit 1
or     AX, NewFlags ;  Load in the New Flags Value
```

At the end of the sequence, the value in AX can be saved and used as the new flags register.

The different flags can be broken up into three major categories: string operations, interrupts, and arithmetic. The string operation flag is the *direction flag (DF)*, which specified how the index registers are updated at the end of the string instruction. If the flag is reset, then the index registers will be incremented. When the DF is set, the index registers will be decremented. Normally, this flag is reset for most applications (the index registers are incremented at the end of the string instructions). Before using the flag, you should always set it to the value needed to carry out the data movement. Afterward, it is not a bad idea to be sure that the flag is reset by default. For some early versions of MS-DOS, this operation is not carried out and the assumption that the flag is reset is made. This led to the system crashing unpredictably during interrupts, and the problem was very hard to debug.

As far as I know, this is not a problem with MS-DOS versions 3.2 (and later). But, in the interests of avoiding any potential problems, I suggest that you always leave the DF flag reset. If you set it, you might want to consider having interrupts masked while the flag is set so that any operating system interrupt does not use it inadvertently in this state.

The interrupt flag bits are used to control the operation of the PC with respect to masking interrupts (IF bit) or halting after each instruction has completed executing (TF). The Interrupt Flag (IF) bit is used to "mask" or prevent interrupts from taking control of the 8086 during specific instances. The *Trap Flag (TF)* causes the 8086 to jump to an interrupt service routine (or handler) after the instruction following the one that enabled it has finished executing. The TF bit and interrupt is normally used by debuggers to help find code errors; it allows you to single step through a program.

Ideally, neither flag should be changed from within an application. If you have code, which is crucially timed and cannot be interrupted, instead of masking all the interrupts by resetting the IF bit, I suggest that you come up with another interface. Masking interrupts is potentially very dangerous with errant code locking up the PC—even with a debugger active or missing real-time clock interrupts. The same comment goes for the single-step TF bit; handling the single-step interrupt is best suited for debuggers and not for use within applications.

The arithmetic flags are the ones you will probably be most concerned about and use most often. Although you will typically only directly access one of them in your applications, the others will be often accessed to control program execution.

After an arithmetic operation, such as addition, the *Zero Flag (ZF)*, *Carry Flag (CF)*, *Auxiliary Carry Flag (AF)*, *Overflow Flag (OF)*, *Sign Flag (SF)*, and *Parity Flag (PF)* will be updated according to the results of the operation. Not all instructions will update all the different flags; bitwise and logical operations will only affect the zero, sign, and parity flags. Understanding how the different flags work will help you to understand how to correctly branch based on the results of an instruction.

The most basic flag is the zero flag (ZF) and it is set when the results of an operation are equal to zero. If the result is larger than the destination word size, but what is to be stored in the destination is zero, the zero flag will be set. This definition probably seems somewhat different from what you've been given before, but there are some reasons for this rather precise explanation of how the zero flag works.

To show what I mean about the zero flag being set: if the result being placed in the definition is zero, we could be adding 0x0A6 to 0x05A together and storing the result (0x0100) into an 8-bit destination register. The register will be loaded with 0x000—even though this is not the complete result. Along with being loaded with 0x000, the zero flag will be set.

In this example, along with the zero flag being set, the carry flag (CF) also shows you that the result is greater than 255 (or 0x0FF, which is the maximum value which can be stored in an 8-bit register). The carry flag indicates when the result goes beyond the destination and should affect higher-order bytes or words. Carry is set in addition or subtraction when the result is outside the limits of what the destination can represent.

If you were carrying out 32-bit addition in the 8086, the carry flag from the addition operation of the lower 16-bits would be used with the addition of the upper 16-bits to complete the 32-bit addition.

This can be shown in the statement:

$$A = B + C$$

where the three variables are all 32 bits (doublewords) in size. To carry out the operation, the following instructions would be used:

```
mov    AX, B              ; Add the Lower 16 Bits
add    AX, C
mov    A, AX
mov    AX, B+2            ; Add the Upper 16 Bits with Carry
adc    AX, C+2
mov    A+2, AX
```

In this instruction sequence, the AX register is loaded with the lower 16-bits of B and then added to the lower 16-bits of C and the result is stored in the lower 16-bits of A. During this instruction, the carry flag is set if the result was greater than 0x0FFFF. Next, the upper 16-bits are summed together with the carry incrementing the result, if it was set. The add and subtract with carry instructions allow you to operate on numeric variables that are greater than 16 bits in size.

Notice that the flags are not changed during "mov" (move) instructions in the 8086. This is different than in some other microprocessors, but it allows data to be transferred within and without the processor without affecting the flag information of previous operations.

The carry flag is unusual in that it is the flag most often used for passing single-bit parameters (such as pass/fail data) between routines and APIs. The reason for this is that carry is only affected by addition and subtraction instructions along with the clc and stc instructions (which explicitly reset and set carry). No other instructions can change the carry flag's value.

The auxiliary carry flag performs the same function as carry, but with the lower four bits (also known as a *nybble*) of the addition/subtraction result. This instruction is primarily used for single-digit processing and, like the carry flag, is only affected by the addition and subtraction instructions.

The overflow flag (OF) is used to indicate when the result of an addition or subtraction is outside the two's complement range for the destination. This might be confusing the first time that you see it because you probably thought that it was the carry that indicated when the result of an arithmetic operation result was outside the destination's range was provided by the carry flag. In some cases, with two's complement numbers (which the 8086 handles implicitly), the carry flag might not indicate whether or not the result is outside the range of the destination.

To illustrate this, the example of what happens when −47 is added to −57 as two 8-bit numbers:

```
-47 + -57 = 0x0D1 + 0x0C7
          = 0x0198
```

In this case, the carry flag will be set and the result (0x098) will be stored in the destination. 0x098 translates to −104 decimal (which is the result expected).

Even though the carry flag is set, the overflow flag should not be set because the result is not outside the two's complement range of the destination. If −47 were added to this result (−104), we would get the result:

```
-47 + -104 = 0x0D1 + 0x098
           = 0x0169
```

This also has the carry flag set, but the result is outside of the two's complement range for the destination. The expected result is −151, which is less than the minimum value that can be stored in an 8-bit two's complement number (which is −128). In this case, the result that is stored in the destination 0x069 represents a positive number in an 8-bit two's complement variable, so an *overflow* has taken place and the OF bit in the flags register will be set.

In the previous example, the overflow flag was actually the final authority on the validity of the value of a two's complement result. The final arbiter of the sign of the two's complement result is stored in the "sign flag". Depending on how you have been taught two's complement negative numbers work in a computer processor, you might think that the sign flag is just a parroting or the most significant bit of the result. Although this is true for many processors, it is not quite true in the 8086.

In the 8086, the sign flag is actually the value of the bit above the most significant bit of the result of the addition/subtraction operation. For an 8-bit result, the sign bit is actually the ninth bit; for a 16-bit result, the sign bit is actually the 17th bit. This bit might seem to be the carry flag, but in some cases, they are different.

For example, if you were to add 100 to 91, the result would be 191, which is 0x0BF, the two's complement representation of −65. In the 8086, even though bit seven of the result is set (which indicates a negative result), the sign flag would be reset, indicating a positive result. Later in the chapter, I will present conditional jumps and point out that the sign flag instructions (jump on less than and jump on greater than) should be used, rather than the jump on carry when determining whether or not the result of an addition or subtraction operation is positive or negative.

The last flag is the parity flag (PF); after an arithmetic operation (or data test instruction), it will be set with the odd parity of the result. This can provide a single-bit error-detection capability in some situations. Chances are you will program the PC in assembly language without ever using the parity flag bit. I believe that the parity flag bit was originally implemented in the 8086 to allow parity information to be passed to devices that cannot generate the information themselves and needed the bit to send along with a data byte. All modern devices that I have seen (including the 8250 used for PC serial communications) create their own parity information and don't require the system's processor or software to generate it explicitly.

20-bit addressing   The most confusing aspect of the Intel 8086's architecture is the 20-bit addressing scheme. This is unfortunate because it gives quite a bit of flexibility and protection between data and code in an application. Before beginning any assembly language-software projects in this book, I suggest that you read through and understand the sections dealing with the 8086's segmentation, registers, and addressing.

When the IBM PC first came available, IBM proudly proclaimed that up to 576 KB of memory could be accessed (640 KB addressing became possible with the PC/XT), many people were surprised because IBM advertised that the PC used a 16-bit processor (with an 8-bit data bus). Sixteen address bits can only access up to 64 KB (65,536) of memory. There was quite a bit of confusion trying to understand how the PC was able to access 576 KB, as well as a full 1 MB, including video and boot ROM.

Previous microprocessors used full 64-KB segments with up to four bits added to the top of the address to provide 16 64-KB pages (Fig. 3-3).

In this scheme, any address within a selected 64-KB block could be accessed. Problems arise with this method when code and data blocks do not fit neatly into 64-KB pages.

For example, if an application had 36 KB of code, 48 KB of data, and 30 KB of stack, it would require three 64-KB pages, each one separate because no two data structures can exist in a 64 KB page (because the sum of their sizes is greater than 64 KB). 192 KB of memory is required.

Today, this doesn't seem like a lot of memory (more like a fraction of an obsolete chip), but in the late 1970s, when the 8086 was being designed, this would be horrendously wasteful. Sixteen kilobit DRAM chips had just become available and, in terms of chips, if the 114 KB of the application was stored in 192 KB, then 39 memory chips would be required that wouldn't be used (which was unthinkable with 64 KB of memory costing approximately $1000). Put another way, this application would be less than 60-percent efficient with the memory required.

Intel's solution to the problem is actually quite inspired. Rather than having the segment index address use only four bits of the 20-bit address, they designed the 8086 with 16-bit

Memory

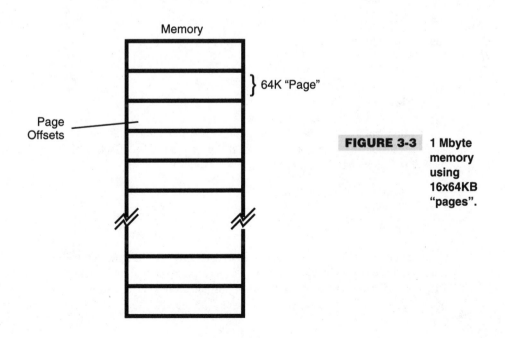

64K "Page"

Page
Offsets

FIGURE 3-3 1 Mbyte
memory
using
16x64KB
"pages".

segment registers which were combined with the offset within the segment to produce the 20-bit address.

The 16-bit segment address was actually shifted up four bits in the combination to get the actual address. By shifting the segment address up by four bits, it meant that the segmentation had a granularity of 16 bytes (i.e., the difference between one segment and it being incremented was 16 bytes). This 16 bytes space is known as a *paragraph* in the 8086. By increasing the segment location granularity by increasing the number of bits used for locating them, the potential memory space lost between segments was quite minimal. Using the example above, the 8086 could store this application with only a maximum of 32 bytes of wasted space between the segments to give a well over 99-percent memory-usage efficiency.

This scheme is often represented as showing the physical address being the sum of the offset within the segment added to the segment register shifted to the left by four bits:

```
Address = ( Segment << 4 ) + Offset
```

or:

```
Segment << 4    xxxx0
Offset        +  yyyy
--------        ------
Address         zzzzz
```

when addresses are usually presented in the 8086, they are in the format:

```
Segment:Offset
```

So, for offset 0x01234 in segment 0x0FE07, the address would be represented as:

```
0x0FE07:0x01234
```

and would be the actual address in the memory map:

```
  Segment << 4    0x0FE070
+ Offset          0x001234
  -------         --------
  Address         0x0FF2A4
```

It is important to remember that the address is a maximum of 20 digits. This can lead to some confusion in certain circumstances. For example, the offset 0x01234 in Segment 0x0FF00 actually has the address:

```
  Segment << 4    0x0FF000
+ Offset          0x001234
  -------         --------
  Address         0x000234
```

And not 0x0100234 (which is above the 1-MB address limit), as you might expect. Fortunately, this is not a big concern in the PC because in the 0x0F000 segment, motherboard BIOS ROM is located there, with no opportunity for you to create an application that places code over this boundary. It is an issue with the 80286 and later processors that have

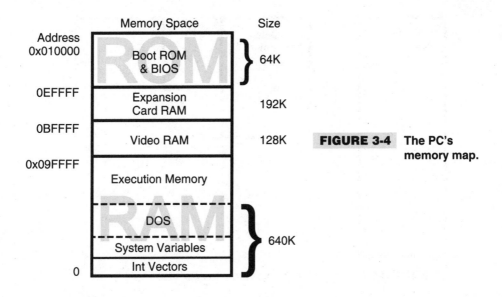

FIGURE 3-4   The PC's memory map.

more than 20 address lines. In the PC/AT and later systems, address bit 20 can be masked by built-in hardware to prevent reads and writes to memory above the 1-MB boundary.

The Segment:Offset format of listing the address is not only is it appropriate for the 20-bit addresses in the 8086, but it can also be used for Protect mode addresses used in the 80286 (and faster) processors.

Segment registers   The 8086 has four segment registers, which are used to separate different types of data. The purpose of these registers is to provide a convenient method to access different segments in an application. The multiple-segment registers means that data can be transferred between segments directly without temporarily storing the data in processor registers. The segment registers provide the upper 16-bits of a 20-bit data address, as described in the previous section.

The *Code Segment (CS)* register is used with the *Instruction Pointer (IP)* to load the next instruction to execute. The *Data Segment (DS)* register points to the current variable area used by the application. The *Stack Segment (SS)* register is used to point to the current data stack area. The stack is used to save the code segment and instruction pointer during sub-routines and interrupts along with a context information or parameters. The final segment register is the *Extra Segment (ES)* register, which is normally used to point to different segments during data-transfer operations.

Figure 3-5 shows different memory segments for each segment register for an application. This is an ideal case and, as is described in the next section, different segment arrangements are used to provide different options in applications.

Normally, one of three specific segment registers is used by default for different instructions and operations. The CS register is used when instructions are being fetched for execution. The SS register is used to save or retrieve data from the stack. The DS register

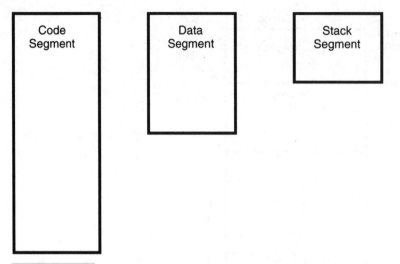

FIGURE 3-5   8086 application segment registers.

is primarily used for passing variables between the processor and memory. The "Extra Segment" ("ES") register is used to move data between segments pointed to by the other three segment registers and an arbitrary location in memory. As is described later in this chapter, the default segment register usage can be overridden by specifying a segment register to be used in your assembly language source code.

Allocating (and overriding) the segments and registers in the 8086 is really not that hard to understand once you begin to work with the processor. Later, this chapter shows how to transfer data between segments and describes different executable application segment models.

Indexed addressing   The 8086 has four registers that can be used for indexed addressing. When the 8086 was designed, each register was given a function to perform in applications; the function determines which register to use and which default segment register is used. Three indexed addressing modes are available in the 8086: no offset, offset, and string.

No offset indexed addressing is just what's implied: no offset is applied to offset provided by the index register. To indicate that indexed addressing is to be used, the index register is enclosed in square brackets.

```
mov   AX, BX                    ; AX = BX
```

This instruction loads the AX register with the current contents of the BX, but:

```
mov    AX, [BX]                 ; AX = [DS:BX]
```

loads AX with the 16-bit word pointed by the *Data Segment (DS)* and BX registers.

If the data is located in another segment, then the *Extra Segment (ES)* register can be used to point to the correct address using segment overrides (which are described later in this chapter). For example, if the data to load in AX was located at the address pointed to by ES and BX, the instruction used would be:

```
mov     AX, ES:[BX]           ; AX = [ES:BX]
```

Further enhancing the indexed addressing, a constant offset from the index register can be included as well:

```
mov     AX, ES:[BX + 2]       ; AX = [ES:(BX + 2)]
```

This will load AX with the word at two bytes (one word) above the address pointed to be ES:BX.

One other index register and a constant can be added to the index register to give very complete control over the address to be accessed:

```
mov     AX, ES:[BX + SI + 4] ; AX = [ES:(BX + SI + 4 )]
```

Using this level of complexity, nested structures and arrays within a segment can be accessed directly using one instruction without having to save the index registers and generate the final address in software before loading an index register with them.

In Microsoft MASM, data structures can be defined for use with the indexed addressing. A very common structure that I use all the time is the *FarPtr (Far Pointer)*, which defines how two words are combined to form a 32-bit data address in the 8086:

```
FarPtr STRUCT
   PtrOff dw ?
   PtrSeg dw ?
FarPtr ENDS
```

The PtrOff and PtrSeg elements are used to access the individual data addresses within a 32-bit variable. Although they can be used as constants added to the index, they are normally used in a different format:

```
Mov  DX, [BX].PtrOff      ; Load ES:DX with the Pointer to the String
Mov  AX, [BX].PtrSeg      ; Pointed to by DS:BX
Mov  ES, AX
```

Structure elements are added to the index with a dot (.) outside of the square parenthesis, instead of a plus sign (+) within the square parenthesis.

The BX register should be the first index register used when accessing indexed data. DI and SI are the string index registers, as is explained in the following paragraphs (and later in the chapter). The BP register is the Base Pointer, which is used to save the stack pointer at a function's entry point for accessing passed input parameters.

The default segment registers for the four index registers are:

Index Register	Segment Register	Function
BX	DS	General Purpose Index Register
DI	DS/ES	General Purpose Index Register/String Destination Index
SI	DS	General Purpose Index Register/String Source Index
BP	SS	Function Parameter Pointer

The 8086 is capable of processing string data easily using the *Source Index (SI)* and *Destination Index (DI)* registers and the string instructions (described later). These instructions perform the data-movement operation and then increment or decrement the index registers so that they're pointing to the next character address in a string. Note that DI can work with either DS or ES as its default. DS is the default when DI is used as outside of String instructions and ES is the default for DI in string instructions.

8086 INSTRUCTION SET

My original intention for this section (and those following it) was to give you all the information necessary to not only write assembler, but figure out the correct instructions and how to calculate the appropriate Op Codes (which are the bits and bytes the processor executes). As I have gone through the instructions, I'm realizing that this goal is virtually impossible and keep this book under a couple of thousand pages. The problem lies in all the different permutations and combinations available for each instruction. Even simple additions can have up to eight different operating modes, the number of which expands exponentially when register combinations are included. In the interests of keeping the book's size reasonable and not over focussed on 8086 assembly language, I have provided an explanation of the instructions in the following table. The following section describes the operation of different types of instructions and how they interact with the processor hardware.

When you go through the instruction table, you'll notice that most instructions do not have only one way of working and many have options based on the input parameters.

Going back to the addition instruction, you can add the contents of two registers together, a constant to a register, a constant to an index address, etc. Most instructions are two bytes (16 bits) long with the most-significant byte being the instruction type and the least-significant byte is used to specify the addressing mode used. To simplify the number of options, Intel created the Instruction ModRegR/M format for 8086 instructions. The ModRegR/M is used (along with bits in the instruction) to specify the addressing mode used in the instructions.

The most-significant two bits of the ModRegR/M byte are the operating mode of the instruction. These two bits select whether the source and destination are registers or memory locations.

'Mod' Bits	Function
00	Destination is not written
01	Eight Bits of Data are stored as 16-bits of Data (the Sign is Extended)
10	Sixteen Bits of Data are Stored in Low Byte/High Byte Format
11	Destination are Registers/Not Memory

The data size is selected by the data-size bit (w) of the instruction byte. This is the least-significant bit of the byte and when reset, indicates that a byte is used for the operation. When the data-size bit is set, a 16-bit word is used for the operation. With the data-size bit, the Reg (Register) specification is used to select an 8-bit or 16-bit register in the instruction.

```
'Reg' Bits   Eight Bit (w=0)   Sixteen Bit (w=1)   Segment Register
000          AL                AX                  ES
001          CL                CX                  CS
010          DL                DX                  SS
011          BL                BX                  DS
100          AH                SP
101          CH                BP
110          DH                SI
111          BH                DI
```

If the mode has selected two registers, then the R/M bits define a register, using the previous table. If the Mode Selected is for external memory, then the bits are defined as:

```
'R/M' Bits   'Mod' Bits   Address          Default Segment
000                       [BX]+[SI]+Disp   DS
001                       [BX]+[DI]+Disp   DS
010                       [BP]+[SI]+Disp   SS
011                       [BP]+[DI]+Disp   SS
100                       [SI]+Disp        DS
101                       [DI]+Disp        ES
110          == 00        Memory Save      DS
110          != 00        [BP]+Disp        SS
111                       [BX]+Disp        DS
```

Most of these instructions use one of the four index registers with their default segment registers.

I've probably given you a headache with all the information in this section. The purpose of this was not to overwhelm you, but give you an idea of what the various combinations are and how they work.

This information is taken from the default instruction format that is:

```
Instruction  Destination, Source
```

where the Destination may also be part of the operation. For example, in:

```
Add          Sum, BX
```

The instruction executes as:

```
Sum = Sum + BX
```

with Sum not only being the final destination, but one of the parameters to the add instruction.

When I look at the instructions and tools (such as debuggers with integrated assemblers), I don't see any reason for you to know how the bits and bytes are actually produced, so in the following instruction table, I have left out the actual encoding. This information can be found in Intel datasheets or other books that are specific to PC assembly-language programming.

```
Instruction   Operation                   Operation/Comments
AAA           If (( AL & 00Fh ) > 9 )     Used after Adding two
              AL = ( AL _ 6 ) & 00Fh      BCD Bytes together to
              AH = AH + 1                 convert the result back
              AF = 1                      to BCD.
              CF = 1
```

AAD	AL = (AH * 010h) + AL AH = 0	Adjust AL before dividing two unpacked values.
AAM	AH = AL / 10 AL = AL mod 10	Create an Unpacked Decimal Value.
AAS	if (((AL & 00Fh) > 9) | (AF == 1)) AL = AL - 6 AH = AH - 1 AF = 1 CF = 1 AL = AL & 00Fh	Use after subtracting two BCD Values to make sure result is in BCD Format.
ADC Dest, Source	Dest = Dest + Source + CF ZF = (Dest + Source + CF) == 0 CF = (Dest + Source + CF) > Size AF = ((Dest & 00Fh) + (Source & 00Fh) + CF) > 00Fh OF = Set if 2's Complement Changed SF = 2's Complement Sign PF = Destination Parity	Add Two Values together with the Carry Flag. Carry Flag is set if the Result is Greater than the data's Size.
ADD Dest, Source	Dest = Dest + Source ZF = (Dest + Source) == 0 CF = (Dest + Source) > Size AF = ((Dest & 00Fh) + (Source & 00Fh)) > 00Fh OF = Set if 2's Complement Changed SF = 2's Complement Sign PF = Destination Parity	Add Two Values together. The Carry Flag is set if the Result is Greater than the Data's size.
AND Dest, Source	Dest = Dest & Source ZF = (Dest & Source) == 0 CF = 0 OF = 0 SF = 2's Complement Sign PF = Destination Parity	"AND" together two Values.
CALL Label	Stack = Current [CS:]IP SP = SP - 2|4 [CS:]IP = Label	Save the Current Execution Address and jump to the new Address at "Label." The Address at "Label" can be Either inside or outside the Current code segment.

CBW	if (AL < 080h)
	AH = 0
	Else
	AH = 0FFh
		Convert the value in AL to a 16-bit signed value in AX.

CLC	CF = 0	Clear the Carry Flag
CLD	DF = 0	Clear the "Direction" Flag. When the Direction Flag is Reset, string Operations Increment.
CLI	IF = 0	Mask Interrupts.

```
CMC                 CF = CF ^ 1                          Complement the Carry
                                                         Flag.

CMP Dest, Source    ZF = ( Dest - Source ) == 0          Subtract two values and
                    CF = ( Dest - Source ) < 0           set the Processor Flags
                    AF = (( Dest & 00Fh ) -              appropriately.
                    ( Source & 00Fh )) < 0
                    OF = ( Dest - Source ) < -Size
                    SF = ( Dest - Source ) < 0
                    PF = Parity of ( Dest - Source )

CMPS[B/W] [Dest,Source]                                  String Compare. See
                    ZF = ( Dest - Source ) == 0          "String Operations"
                    CF = ( Dest - Source ) < 0           later in this chapter.
                    AF = (( Dest & 00Fh ) -
                    ( Source & 00Fh )) < 0
                    OF = ( Dest - Source ) < -Size
                    SF = ( Dest - Source ) < 0
                    PF = Parity of ( Dest - Source )

CWD                 if ( AX < 08000h )                   Convert the Word to a
                      DX = 0                             Signed Double Word.
                    Else
                      DX = 0FFFFh

DAA                 if ((AL & 00Fh ) > 9) | (AF == 1))   Correct Result of BCD
                      AL = AL - 6                        Addition.
                      AF = 1
                    If ((AL > 09Fh) | (CF == 1))
                      AL = AL - 060h
                      CF = 1

DEC Dest            Dest = Dest - 1                      Subtract One from the
                    ZF = ( Dest - 1 ) == 0              Destination without
                    OF = ( Dest - 1 ) < -Size           affecting the Carry
                    SF = ( Dest - 1 ) < 0               Flags.
                    PF = Parity of ( Dest - 1 )

DIV Divisor         AX = AX / Divisor                    Divide AX by the
                    CF = Undefined                       Specified Value. Note
                    ZF = Undefined                       that the Flag Bits will
                    AF = Undefined                       be changed to Unknown
                    SF = Undefined                       values.
                    OF = Undefined
                    PF = Undefined

HLT                 N/A                                  Stop the Processor
                                                         until "Reset" is cycled
                                                         or an Interrupt Request
                                                         is Received.

IDIV Source         AX = AX / Source                     Execute a Signed
                                                         Division.
                    CF = Undefined                       Note that the Flag Bits
                    ZF = Undefined                       will be changed to
                    AF = Undefined                       Unknown Values.
                    SF = Undefined
                    OF = Undefined
                    PF = Undefined

IMUL Source         AX = AX * Source                     Execute a Signed
                    CF = ( AX * Source ) > Size          Multiply. Note that
                    OF = ( AX * Source ) > Size          some of the Flag Bits
                    ZF = Undefined                       are changed to Unknown
                    AF = Undefined                       Values.
```

```
                       SF = Undefined
                       OF = Undefined
                       PF = Undefined

IN Dest, Port          Dest = [Port]                    Read the eight or
                                                        16 Bit I/O Port
                                                        Address into AL or AX.


INC Dest               Dest = Dest + 1                  Add One to the
                       ZF = ( Dest + 1 ) == 0           Destination without
                       OF = ( Dest + 1 ) > Size         affecting the Carry
                       SF = ( Dest + 1 ) < 0            Flags.
                       PF = Parity of ( Dest + 1 )

INS[B|W] [Dest]        Dest = Port[DX]                  String Port Read
                       [DX = DX + 1]                    Operation. See String
                                                        Operations later in
                                                        this chapter.

INT Number             Stack = Flags                    Execute a Software
                       Stack - 2 = IP                   Interrupt and jump to a
                       Stack - 4 = CS                   handler.
                       Stack = Stack - 6
                       CS:IP = [0:Number * 4]

INTO                   if ( OF == 1 )                   Execute the Overflow
                          Stack = Flags                 Result Interrupt
                          Stack + 2 = IP                Handler if appropriate.
                          Stack + 4 = CS
                          Stack = Stack + 6
                          CS:IP = [0:040h]

IRET                   CS = Stack + 2                   Return from an
                       IP = Stack + 4                   Interrupt Handler.
                       Flags = Stack + 6
                       Stack = Stack + 6

J(Cond) Label   if ( Cond == True )                     If the Specified
                          [CS:]IP = Label               Condition is true then
                                                        jump to the specified
                                                        address. See "Jumping
                                                        and Conditional
                                                        Branching" later in
                                                        this Chapter.

JMP Label              [CS:]IP = Label                  Change Execution to the
                                                        Address at "Label."
                                                        "Label" can be inside or
                                                        external to The current
                                                        Code Segment. See
                                                        "Jumping and
                                                        Conditional Branching"
                                                        later in this Chapter.

LAHF                   AH = SF/ZF/X/AF/X/PF/X/CF        Load the AH Register
                                                        with The Arithmetic
                                                        Result Flags.

LDS Reg, Variable      DS = [Variable + 2]              Load DS:Reg with the 32
                       Reg = [Variable]                 bit Pointer in
                                                        "Variable."
```

LEA Reg, Label	Reg = Offset(Label)	Load the Register with the Offset of the Label. This Method will ensure a Register is loaded with a Constant, rather than the Contents of the Address at "Constant."
LES Reg, Variable	ES = [Variable + 2] Reg = [Variable]	Load ES:Reg with the 32 bit Pointer in "Variable."
LODS[B|W] [Source] 	AX = DS:SI SI = SI + (-1 ** DF)	Load AL/AX with the Value Pointed to by DS:SI. See "String Operations" later in this Chapter.
LOOP Label and	if (--CX != 0) Goto LABEL	Use CX as a Counter Loop until CX is equal to zero. If CX is Initially equal to Zero, immediately fall through loop.
LOOPE Label	if ((--CX != 0) && (ZF == 1)) Goto Label	Use CX as a Counter and Loop until CX while Equal to Zero. If CX is initially equal to Zero, immediately fall through loop.
LOOPNE Label	if ((--CX != 0) && (ZF == 1)) Goto Label	Use CX as a Counter and Loop until CX is Equal to Zero. If CX is initially equal to Zero, immediately fall Through loop.
MOV Dest, Source	Dest = Source	Move Data from the "Source" Register or Memory (which Can be an indexed address) to the "Dest"ination Register or Memory (which Can be an indexed address).
MOVS[B|W] [Dest, Source] 	[ES:DI] = [DS:SI] SI = SI + (-1 ** DF) DI = DI + (-1 ** DF)	Do a String Move from DS:SI To ES:DI. See "String Operations" later in this Chapter.
MUL Source	AX = AX * Source CF = (AX * Source) > 0FFFFh OF = CF	Multiply AX by the specified Multiplier.
NEG Dest > Size	Dest = (Dest ^ 0[FF]FFh) + 1 CF = ((Dest ^ 0[FF]FFh) + 1) > Size AF = (((Dest & 00Fh)^ 00Fh) + 1) OF = CF	Perform a Two's Complement on the Specified Value.

```
                        ZF = ((Dest ^ O[FF]FFh) + 1) == 0
                        SF = ((Dest ^ O[FF]FFh) + 1) < 0
                        OF = ((Dest ^ O[FF]FFh) + 1) > Size
                        PF = Parity of ((Dest ^ O[FF]FFh) + 1)

NOT Dest                Dest = Dest ^ O[FF]FFh                 Do a Bitwise Complement
                        CF = 0                                 of the Specified Value.
                        AF = 0
                        OF = 0
                        ZF = ( Dest ^ O[FF]FFh ) == 0
                        SF = ( Dest ^ O[FF]FFh ) < 0
                        OF = 0
                        PF = Parity of ( Dest ^ O[FF]FFh )

OR Dest, Source          Dest = Dest | Source                  "OR" together two
                        ZF = ( Dest | Source ) == 0            Values.
                        CF = 0
                        OF = 0
                        SF = 2's Complement Sign
                        PF = Destination Parity

OUT Port, Source        [Port] = Source                       Output the Contents of
                                                               the Source Register (AL
                                                               or AX) To the Specified
                                                               Port I/O Address.

OUTS [Port, Source]                                            See "String Operations"
                        [Port] = Source                        later this Chapter.

POP Dest                Dest = Stack + 2                       Store the Top of the
                        Stack = Stack + 2                      Stack Into the
                                                               "Dest"ination and Move
                                                               the Stack Pointer up by
                                                               two.

POPA                    DI = Stack + 2                         Pop all the Register
                        SI = Stack + 4                         values off the Stack.
                        BP = Stack + 6
                        SP = Stack + 8
                        BX = Stack + 10
                        DX = Stack + 12
                        CX = Stack + 14
                        AX = Stack + 16
                        Stack = Stack + 16

POPF                    Flags = Stack + 2                      Restore the Flags
                        Stack = Stack + 2                      Register from the
                                                               Stack.

PUSH Source             Stack = Source                         Push the Source Value
                        Stack = Stack - 2                      onto the Stack and Move
                                                               the Stack Pointer Down.

PUSHA                   Stack = AX                             Push all the Registers
                        Stack - 2 = CX                         onto the Stack.
                        Stack - 4 = DX
                        Stack - 6 = BX
                        Stack - 8 = SP
                        Stack - 10 = BP
                        Stack - 12 = SI
                        Stack - 14 = DI
                        Stack = Stack - 16
```

PUSHF	Stack = Flags Stack = Stack - 2	Push the Contents of the Flags Register onto the Stack.
RCL Dest, 1|CL	Dest = (Dest << 1) + CF CF = Dest >> Size	Rotate the Destination once or CL times through The Carry Flag. The Operation Explanation shows The Operation for "1" or "CL" Equals to "1" times.
RCR Dest, 1|CL	Dest = (Dest >> 1) + (CF << Size) CF = Dest & 1	Rotate the Destination once or CL times through the Carry Flag. The Operation Explanation shows the Operation for "1" or "CL" Equals to "1" times.
RET [Number]	[CS:]IP = Stack Stack = Stack + 2|4 [Stack = Stack + Number]	Restore [CS:]IP to the value on the Stack. If a "Number" is Specified, Increment the Stack that value.
ROL Dest, 1|CL	Dest = Dest << 1	Rotate the Destination once or CL times. The Operation Explanation shows the Operation for "1" or "CL" Equals to "1" times.
ROR Dest, 1|CL	Dest = Dest >> 1	Rotate the Destination once or CL times. The Operation Explanation shows the Operation for "1" or "CL" Equals to "1" times.
SAHF	Flags = AH	Store the Contents of AH Into the Arithmetic Results Of the Flags Register.
SAL|SHL Dest, 1|CL	Dest = Dest << 1	Shift the Destination once or CL times. The Operation Explanation shows the Operation for "1" or "CL" Equals to "1" times.
SAR Dest, 1|CL	Dest = Dest >> 1	Shift the Destination once or CL times. The Operation Explanation shows the Operation for "1" or "CL" Equals to "1" times.
SBB Dest, Source	Dest = Dest - Source - CF ZF = (Dest - Source - CF) == 0 CF = (Dest - Source - CF) > Size	Subtract Two Values together with the Carry Flag. The Carry Flag

	AF = ((Dest & 00Fh) - (Source & 00Fh) - CF) > 00Fh OF = Set if 2's Complement Changed SF = 2's Complement Sign PF = Destination Parity	is set if the Result is less than the data's Size.
SCAS[B|W] [Dest]	if [Dest] == AX|AL ZF = 1	Scan through the Data List to Find a Matching Value. See "String Operations" Later in this Chapter.
SHR Dest, 1|CL	Dest = Dest >> 1	Shift the Destination once or CL times. The Operation Explanation shows The Operation for "1" or "CL" Equals to "1" times.
STC	CF = 1	Set the Carry Flag
STD	DF = 1	Set the Direction Flag. When the Direction Flag is Set, the index registers will be decremented. Normally, this flag is left Reset or "Cleared."
STI	IF = 1	Unmask Interrupts.
STOS[B|W] [Dest]	[Dest] = AL|AX	Save the Data in AL\AX at the Destination Address. See "String Operations" Later in this Chapter.
SUB Dest, Source	Dest = Dest - Source ZF = (Dest - Source) == 0 CF = (Dest - Source) > Size AF = ((Dest & 00Fh) - (Source & 00Fh)) > 00Fh OF = Set if 2's Complement Changed SF = 2's Complement Sign PF = Destination Parity	Subtract Two Values together without the Carry Flag. The Carry Flag is set if the Result is less than the data's Size.
TEST Dest, Source	ZF = (Dest & Source) == 0 CF = 0 OF = 0 SF = 2's Complement Sign PF = Destination Parity	Logically "AND" The Dest to the Source to find out if the result is equal to zero.
WAIT		Stop Execution until an Interrupt Request is Received. This instruction is different from "HLT" because the Processor clock is not Stopped.
XCHG Dest, Source	Temp = Source Source = Dest Dest = Temp	Exchange the Two Values. The Operation of the Instruction

		shown is how it would be implemented in Software.
XLAT	AL = [BX + AL]	Do a Table Look Up.
XOR Dest, Source	Dest = Dest ^ Source ZF = (Dest ^ Source) == 0 CF = 0 OF = 0 SF = 2's Complement Sign PF = Destination Parity	Exclusive "OR" ("XOR") together two Values.

ADDRESSING MODES

The arithmetic instructions have four basic addressing modes that can be used with the ADD, ADC, AND, MOV, OR, SUB, SBB, and XOR instructions. These four modes allow one or two input parameters to be loaded into the ALU, optionally processed and then stored in a destination parameter.

The basic arithmetic instruction format is:

```
Instruction   Destination, Source
```

where the Destination can also be the first parameter of an operation. For example, in the instruction:

```
Sub   Var1, BX
```

The code executes as:

```
Var1 = Var1 - BX
```

If you want to process two input variables and put the result into a third location, then you will have to use an intermediate register to temporarily store the operations result before saving it in the final destination. For the statement:

```
Var2 = Var1 - BX
```

The code required would be:

```
mov   AX, Var1
sub   AX, BX
mov   Var2, AX
```

The four addressing modes are Immediate, Register, Variable, and Indexed.

Immediate addressing is when an immediate value is used instead of the contents of a register or memory location:

```
mov   AX, 77
```

This instruction will load the AX register with the value 77. Immediate differs from the other addressing modes because it cannot be used as a destination.

This value can be either binary decimal or hex, depending on the default radix used in the source file. This is a subtle, but important, point and one that is sure to trip you up when you start writing assembly language (and some high-level language) applications. I normally set the default radix to decimal (because that's what I naturally think in) and explicitly identify hex and binary values.

The fastest way to access data is retrieving it from and storing it to one of the processor registers. When registers are used as the source and destination for data in instructions, it is known as *register addressing*.

```
mov   AX, BX
```

is an example of register addressing, where the contents of the BX register are stored in the AX register.

As well as being the fastest method of accessing data, register addressing can be used for other functions. The most often used is loading a register with zero, by XORing the contents of the register with itself:

```
Xor   AX, AX                ; "mov AX, 0"
```

You will often see this done in compiled programs because it executes quickly and requires the fewest numbers of bytes to carry out one operation.

Variable addressing uses an address that was declared using a db, dw, dd, or dt directive. Normally, this variable is located in the current data segment (if it's not, then you should use the Segment Overrides, explained in the next section).

The db, dw, dd, and dt directives define a variable as being a byte, word (16 bits), double word (32 bits), and 10 bytes, respectively. The variable can also be part of a structure or an explicit offset within an array to be accessed. The address to access is specified within the structure element or the offset from the array's first address.

To access an offset within an array, the offset is simply added to the variable name in the instruction:

```
mov   AX, Array + 7
```

This offset is in bytes, so to get the correct offset into an array; the element number is multiplied by the size of the array elements. For an array of 16-bit words, the offset used has to be the element number multiplied by two.

Another form of variable addressing is to specify the address explicitly in the instruction, instead of using a variable. To do this, the address is put inside square brackets ([and]), otherwise, the address will be assumed to be an immediate value.

At other times, you will want to load a register with a variable's address. This is accomplished by using the *lea (Load Effective Address)* instruction. If you look through the *Intel Data Sheets*, you will see that this instruction doesn't actually exist; it is a construct of most assemblers, which substitute in a "mov Reg, Immediate" instruction, where Immediate is the offset label in the data segment. The mov instruction could be used, but using "lea" avoids any potential confusion about what is being loaded.

Sometimes in assembly-language programming with explicit variables or memory addresses, the size of the data will be ambiguous to the assembler and it won't be able to determine whether or not you want to use 8 or 16 bits of data. To avoid potential problems, it is a good idea to put the term:

```
WORD PTR
```

or

```
BYTE PTR
```

into the instruction. For example:

```
mov   AH, BYTE PTR [77]
```

will load the byte at DS:77 into AH.

One of the most useful programming constructs is the array. Array programming allows a large number of variables to be addressed, without each one having to be individually named and can be easily accessed using arithmetic data within the application, rather than explicit labels. Indexed addressing in the PC has a lot more options than you are probably used to when you've worked with other microprocessors. Four different index registers can be used in 10 different ways. Earlier in the chapter, I showed the different index modes and in a following section, I show the String Operations modes.

My biggest piece of advice for using indexed addressing in your assembly-language programming is to keep it simple. You can work with multiple indexes and displacements, but for your initial efforts, at least, just use the BX register as an index, along with DI and SI for String Operations.

Segment register overrides   When you develop 8086 application code, chances are that you will have to change the default segment register used in some specific instructions. This is actually quite easy to do. The best part is that it will make sense when you see it in the code.

Just to recap, if you are accessing a variable in a standard instruction, such as:

```
mov   AX, Variable
```

the *Data Segment (DS)* register will be used. For code information, the *Code Segment (CS)* register will be used and for stack information, the *Stack Segment (SS)* register is used.

For indexed and string data accesses, different segment registers are used by default:

Register	Index	String
BX	DS	
BP	SS	
SP	SS	
DI	DS	ES
SI	DS	DS

The data-segment register should normally never be updated and always be pointing to the application's variable segment. As a rule, I never change the stack segment from what was provided by the application. This leaves only the extra segment register for accessing memory in segments other than in the defaults. I hope I don't have to explain why the code-segment register cannot be set to another segment and used for data. To access data in another segment, the ES register is loaded with the new segment using the code:

```
mov   AX,   New_Segment
mov   ES,   AX
```

And the "ES:" override is used when a variable or data in the new segment is to be accessed. The instruction will look like:

```
mov    AX, ES:[BX]
```

where the table element pointed to by BX in the ES segment will be loaded into AX.

The segment override is not limited to ES, any of the four segment registers (CS, DS, ES, and SS) can be used. The only caveat is that the CS or SS should never be changed. Normally, I keep the data segment pointing to the appropriate current data segment in the application and only change it for string data moves and then restore it when the operation requiring the change has finished.

The override is placed in front of the address parameter of the instruction and cannot be placed in front of constants. I realize that this should be obvious, but I've ended up scratching my head, wondering why I have a syntax error from an assembler when I have inadvertently put an override on a constant that has a similar name to a variable.

Only one override can be used per instruction. If you are using a mov instruction that passes data from one memory location to another, one of the two variables must be in the data segment.

If you are interested in the bits and bytes, the segment overrides are actually single-byte instructions that are placed in front of the instruction bytes. In some assemblers (most notably the one in debug.com), the override must be placed before the instruction and not the variable's address or index.

The overrides and their codes are:

Register Override	Code
CS:	0x02E
DS:	0x03E
ES:	0x026
SS:	0x036

String operations   One of the features of the 8086 that I have always liked is the string data instructions and repeat prefixes. These instructions allow very fast data movement, comparison, or scanning. In the 8086 (and virtually all other processors), a *string* is defined as a series of bytes (normally ASCII characters) that are placed together in memory in some kind of order. Normally, this order is an increasing address to provide text strings. In many processors, operating on strings can only be accomplished by doing repeated reads and writes with index registers on the individual bytes. The 8086 has some powerful features, which makes operating on strings quite easy and efficient.

The string instructions movs, cmps, and scans each can operate in three modes. The first uses explicitly defined data areas pointed to the data and extra-segment registers (DS and ES, respectively).

The instruction:

```
movs dest, source
```

will move the byte at DS:Source to the location pointed to by ES:Dest. Placing the source address in the SI index register and the destination address in the DI index register can eliminate the need for the source and destination parameter. Now, the movs instruction (in the movsb or movsw form) executes as:

```
[ES:DI] = [DS:SI]
DI = DI + ( -1 ** DF )
SI = SI + ( -1 ** DF )
```

where *DF* is the direction flag (in the Flags register) and is used to specify whether the registers get incremented or decremented at the end of the string instruction.

Normally, the DF flag is reset, which causes DI and SI to be incremented. I have seen a number of references that state that the bit should always be left in this state, but I've found a few cases in applications, over the years, where this hasn't been true. Before running a string operation, be sure that the DF flag is in the correct state. As I indicated earlier in this chapter, the DF flag must always be left reset for subsequent string operations.

During string operations, interrupts do not have to be disabled for fear that the DF flag will be changed because, during an interrupt, the flags register is saved on the stack along with the CS and IP registers. Upon return, even if DF was changed within the interrupt handler. The flag will be restored to the correct value.

The ES:DI and DS:SI pairs are the preferred way of accessing string data because they allow the string instructions to work with the repeat prefixes. One of the biggest problems new assembly-language programmers have with the string instructions is remembering which segment is paired with which index. I always remember that the two Ds (DS and DI) never go together.

The repeat prefixes are used to repeat the string instruction, decrementing CX at the same time and, optionally, as long as the zero flag is not set. The repeat prefixes allow repeated data movements and operations to require only one instruction to execute.

To move 10 bytes from SourceVar to DestVar, the following code could be used:

```
push DS                    ; ES = DS for Variables
pop ES
lea DI, DestVar            ; Point to the Variables
lea SI, SourceVar

mov CX, 10                 ; Moving 10 bytes

cld                        ; Reset the DF so the Indexes Increment

rep movsb                  ; Move the 10 bytes
```

The movsb instruction moves data one byte at a time and could be sped up if the movsw instruction was used (which moves one word or two bytes, at a time). If movsw is used, then CX would initially be loaded with five because two bytes are moved instead of one.

Cmps, cmpsb, and cmpsw are used to compare data and set the status flags appropriately. The repe or repne prefixes can be used with this instruction to provide a fast-string compare operation:

```
push DS                    ; ES = DS for Variables
pop ES

lea DI, FirstString        ; Point to the Variables
lea SI, SecondString

mov CX, StringSize         ; Get the Number of Bytes to Compare

cld                        ; Reset the DF so the Indexes Increment
```

```
    repe cmpsb                      ; Compare the Two Strings

    jl First_LT                     ; Jump if First is less than second
```

In this code snippet, the repe instruction causes the cmpsb to repeatedly execute while the zero flag is set.

Scans, scansb, and scansw are used to scan through a string for a null character. This can be used to find the length of an ASCIIZ strings (which is an ASCII string terminated with a 0x000 character):

```
    push DS                         ; ES = DS for Variables
    pop ES

    lea DI, ASCIIZString            ; Point to the String

    mov CX, StringSize              ; Get the Number of Bytes to Compare

    cld                             ; Reset the DF so the Indexes Increment

    repne scansb

    mov AX, DI                      ; Find the Position of the Zero in the
    sub AX, ASCIIZString            ; ASCIIZ String
```

With the string operations, watch for a few things. The first is if CX is equal to zero when the prefix and string instruction are first encountered, the string instruction will not execute. This is important to know because this is not true in the NEC V20 and V30 chips, which were introduced in the early 1980s as sped-up compatible 8086 and 8088s. In this case, the V20 or V30 would execute the string operation 64k times until CX was decremented back to zero. It's more important to be aware of how the Intel parts work; I don't know of any divergence in any other 8086-compatible (or higher) processors, but you should know what to expect if a count of zero is experienced.

When you look over the instructions, you'll see that I haven't included the lods and stos instructions in this discussion. These instructions load or store data from memory to the AL or AX (for the word versions) registers. The reason why I don't include them as primary string operations is because they aren't useful with the repeat prefixes. But, when coupled with the loop instructions, some quite useful operations can be performed.

The following code uses *lods* and *stos* to convert the lower-case characters in a string to upper case:

```
    push DS                         ; ES = DS for Variables
    pop ES

    lea DI, ASCIIZString            ; Point to the String
    lea SI, ASCIIZString

    mov CX, StringSize              ; Get the Number of Bytes to Compare

    cld                             ; Reset the DF so the Indexes Increment

    ls_Loop:                        ; Come Back Here for Each Byte

    Lodsb                           ; Load AL with String Byte
```

```
    Add AL, 255-'z'              ; Do the lower to upper conversion
    Add AL, 'z'-'a'+1
    Jc Skip
    Add AL, ' '                  ; Lower Case, make Upper
    Skip:
    Add AL, 'A'
    Stosb                        ; Save the Contents of AL back into the
String

    Loop ls_Loop
```

The loop instructions (loop, loope, loopz, loopne, and loopnz) work similarly to the repeat prefixes; if CX is not equal to zero (and the optional condition is true), then CX is decremented and a jump to the label is executed.

Jumping and conditional branching   Jumping to different locations within the 8086 memory map can be done a variety of different ways. The different jumps reflect how the memory models (i.e., segments) work within the 8086. The information in this section is also relevant to the subroutine call explanation, contained within the next section.

Nonconditional jumping can work two different ways, with either an offset (positive or negative) added to the current instruction pointer or changing the instruction pointer and optionally the code segment register to a new value. Both these methods have advantages in different situations.

For a short jump, an 8-bit signed value is added to the Instruction Pointer as a Relative address. The 8-bit offset is available to use to the minimum amount of code space (only two bytes per instruction with the offset) and can jump −126 to +129 bytes from the address of the instruction. The short, unconditional jump has the bit pattern:

```
    0x0E9 Offset
```

Later in this section, I'll show short, conditional jumps.

To describe offsets, Intel defines them as from the address of the next instruction; I tend to think of it as from the current instruction and add two to the values. This makes it easier for me to visualize the range (because I care primarily about the current instruction). So, where Intel would consider the short, signed jump to be from −128 to +127 from the next instruction, I tend to think of it as being from −126 to +129 relative to the current.

Although this seems simpler, it can be a bit more confusing when you are hand assembling. To show what I mean, if the instruction pointer was currently at 0x01234 and I wanted to jump to an address that was 40 bytes before (or negative), I would use the offset of −42 because the address is of the next instruction. This means that the actual code that I would use is:

```
    0x0E9 -42 (Decimal)
    0x0E9 0x0D6 (Hex)
```

When jumps or calls to addresses in other segments are made, both the CS and IP registers are written with an explicit value from the instruction (either part of the instruction or from a variable pointer). The actual address can either be made part of the instruction or be read from a variable. This type of jump is known as a *long* or *intersegment jump* and is to an explicit address within the code segment.

I have described absolute versus relative addressing elsewhere in this chapter, but it's worth noting that intersegment jumps are the only case where absolute addressing should be used in a program. As well, the actual address should be calculated by the assembler and not by you.

For a variable, the data is stored in four bytes or two (16 bit) words with the new instruction pointer first and followed by the new CS value. This is known as a *double word* and a variable storing this data could be coded as:

```
Pointer DD 0x012345678
```

If a jmp pointer instruction was executed, CS would be loaded with 0x01234 and the instruction pointer with 0x05678. I find this somewhat confusing, so I tend to declare the variable as:

```
Pointer DW 0x05678        ; Offset
        DW 0x01234        ; Segment
```

which allows me to see how the variable is set up immediately and use the FarPtr structure that I defined earlier in the chapter.

This format in C terms is known as a *far pointer*. Later in the book, I will explain more about pointers and how they are actually implemented, but I wanted to note that this four-byte construct is used in high-level languages and something I work with in C all the time.

Conditional jumps check the state of the flag register and do a short relative jump if the condition is true. The following table lists the different jumps, their op codes, and conditions, which cause the jumps.

INSTRUCTION	OP CODE	CONDITION	FLAGS	COMPLEMENT
ja, jbne	0x077	> 0	CF = 0 & ZF = 0	jbe
jae, jnc, jnb	0x073	>= 0	CF = 0	jb
jb, jnae, jc	0x072	< 0	CF = 1	jae
jbe, jna	0x076	<= 0	CF = 1 | ZF = 0	ja
je, jz	0x074	== 0	ZF = 1	jnz
jg, jnle	0x07F	> 0	ZF = 0 & SF = 0	jle
jge, jnl	0x07D	>= 0	SF = 0	jl
jl, jnge	0x07C	< 0	(SF ^ OF) = 1	jge
jle, jng	0x07E	<= 0	((SF^OF)|ZF)=1	jg
jne, jnz	0x075	!= 0	ZF = 0	jz
jno	0x071	No Overflow	OF = 0	jo
jnp, jpo	0x07B	Odd Parity	PF = 0	jp
jns	0x079	>= 0	SF = 0	js

INSTRUCTION	OP CODE	CONDITION	FLAGS	COMPLEMENT
jno	0x070	Overflow	OF = 1	jno
jp, jpe	0x07A	Even Parity	PF = 1	jnp
js	0x078	< 0	SF = 1	jns
jcxz	0x0E3	CX = 0	N/A	

These instructions are pretty straightforward with a simple letter convention of the conditions:

LETTER	CONDITION
n	Not—complement next letter
g	Greater than
l	Less than
e	Equals to
b	Below
a	Above
o	Overflow
p	Parity
s	Sign

There's really no need to memorize or keep a list of conditional jump instructions handy. Actually, for the entire 8086 instruction set, you really don't have to memorize anything at all; the instructions are very straightforward.

When I'm working with conditional jump instructions, I usually go through what I want, rather than what I think I need. For example, a jump on greater than (jg) is better than a jump on no carry (jnc) because even though jnc seems to work the same way as the jg instruction, jg also takes into account overflows and two's complement negative results.

The preceding instruction table included the complement of the conditional jump instruction. The reason for this is that these instructions are short jumps and, as indicated, can only jump −126 or +129 bytes from the current instruction. To give additional flexibility, a long conditional jump uses the complement to jump over the actual jump to label.

Many assembly-language programmers will create an include file of macros, such as:

```
ljz MACRO FarLabel
  local SkipLabel
  jnz SkipLabel
  jmp  FarLabel                ; If Zero flag Set, Jump to FarLabel
SkipLabel:
  ENDM
```

When the macrocode is encountered, if the zero flag is not set, the jnz instruction will cause execution to jump over the long jump to the specified address. When the zero flag is set, execution will fall through the jnz instruction and jump to FarLabel. The usual convention for this type of macro is to place a small L in front of the actual conditional jump instruction that you want to execute.

Subroutines   Like most computer processors, the 8086 is capable of jumping to subroutines with the return address saved on a stack in memory. The call and ret (return) instructions are extremely flexible and give you a similar amount of flexibility in programming. I won't spend a lot of time explaining how subroutines work in the 8086, except that, for the most part, they work as you would expect in a processor. When the call instruction is encountered, the address of the next instruction is pushed on the stack before the label on variable address (like the jmp instruction) is used as the new execution address.

The return (ret) instruction pops the saved return address off the stack and stores it into the instruction pointer and, optionally, the CS registers.

The caveat in the previous sentence is what you have to watch. In the jmp instruction, if you jumped to an address in a new segment, which would cause a change in the CS register, there is no concern with keeping track of the return address. This isn't true with the call instruction, where two or four bytes are pushed onto the stack, depending on whether or not the call was intrasegment (within the same segment) or intersegment (to an address in another segment).

The easiest way around this is to only use one type of call. For simplicity, I try to use long (intersegment) calls only. This means that a subroutine located anywhere in memory can be accessed without concern as to whether or not a short (just IP) or far (CS and IP) ret instructions are required.

The type of subroutine (far or short) is defined as part of the subroutine definition. In my code, you will see:

```
SubRtn PROC FAR
   :                        ; Subroutine Code
  ret                       ; Return to Caller
SubRtn ENDP
```

used throughout my code. This will force any short calls to long calls and the "ret" instruction to a "far ret".

Later, the book covers software interrupts, but I wanted to point out a feature of the ret instruction that is its ability to be used as an interrupt return. Ret before loading CS:IP from the stack can increment the stack a specified number. In a software-interrupt handler, if two bytes are skipped, then the contents of the flags register is not popped off, the stack and simple parameters can be returned to the caller through the flags register.

In many BIOS functions, you will see the code:

```
stc                        ; Return Fail to Caller
ret 2                      ; Return to Caller
```

This snippet of code will set the carry flag, indicating that an error occurred in the software interrupt BIOS function and restore the CS and IP without restoring the flags register.

The "ret n" instruction should really only be used for this purpose and not a way to reset the stack pointer for data parameters passed on the stack (although this is often used for this purpose in Pascal implementations). An incorrect value could cause the application to crash; from experience, I have to tell you that this is one of the toughest bugs to find.

Parameter passing   If you've done any assembly-language programming before, you'll know that passing data (or parameters) to and from subroutines is needed to get useful information between the two routines. This is also true in the 8086's case that can call subroutines explicitly or use the addresses of system wide resource routines.

Parameters can be passed three different ways in the 8086: with registers, common variables, or using the stack.

Using the processor's registers is the most common method for assembly-language programming. Unfortunately, no convention is used to pass data, but as a rough proposal that matches many of the BIOS and MS-DOS APIs, you could use:

```
AH = Function Number
AL = Error Code
Carry = Set on Error
CX = Counter
ES:DI = Pointer to Destination
DS:BX = Index to Source/Destination Data
```

When registers are modified to pass parameters note that the DS, SP, BS, and SS registers should never be used or modified within the subroutine. These registers are usually crucial to the operation of high-level languages (and the operation of any application) and indiscriminately changing these values can lead to application failures later, which will require you to step through the application, looking for invalid register changes. This can be quite difficult to do and can be avoided by simply not modifying these registers, unless you understand exactly what you are doing.

Data can also be passed using common variables. For the variables to be common, they have to be known to both routines (during assembly) with a common segment. If these routines are in different files, then you will have to be sure that the parameter's label is available to both routines as PUBLIC and EXTRN.

Passing parameters using common variables is an acceptable way to share data between routines. I would recommend using one of the other two methods outlined in this section because the requirement for using a common variable makes the routines less portable and requires more work to use later in different applications.

The last type of parameter passing is to use the hardware features built into the 8086. In the caller, the parameters to pass are pushed onto the stack. Upon entry, the base pointer (which uses the SS register as its default segment) is set to the stack pointer (SP register) value before the call statement.

The caller would then have pushed the parameters onto the stack in a previously agreed upon order.

This can be hard to visualize, so I'll use the code:

```
push Var1
push Var2
call Rtn
add  SP, 4 ; Restore the Stack Pointer
```

to show how calls to Rtn are implemented with Var1 and Var2 pushed onto the stack.

After executing the call instruction, the stack will be set up with:

```
SP+6    Var1
SP+4    Var2
SP+2    Return Segment
SP      Return Offset
```

To load the parameters, the start of the subroutine would be:

```
Rtn   PROC FAR

  Mov   BP, SP         ; Point to the Passed Variables
  Add   BP, 4

  Mov   AX, [BP + 2]   ; Get "Var1"
  Mov   RtnVar1, AX

  Mov   AX, [BP]       ; Get "Var2"
  Mov   RtnVar2, AX

  :                    ; Subroutine Code
```

These variables do not have to be stored in variables specific to Rtn. In Rtn, Var1 and Var2 could be accessed using indexed addressing with the BP register as it is set up here.

Chapter 13 expands upon this method as a way to interface assembler with C. Along with C, this method is used to pass parameters between Pascal, although in a different order.

I really don't say it elsewhere, but the secret to successful assembly-language programming is to use standard blocks of code (at least standard for you) for such mundane things as passing parameters and concentrating on how the algorithm is implemented.

ABSOLUTE VERSUS RELATIVE ADDRESSING

Many new assembly-language programmers fall into the trap of wanting to specify absolute addresses in their applications. Often this is done within the current code or data segments or as an absolute 20-bit address within the PC. The reason for doing this really comes from habits gained while working with other microprocessors. When programming the 8086 in the PC environment, there are very few absolutes when addressing is concerned.

In fact, you can probably do all of your programming without ever needing to use absolute addressing. For interfacing, you won't be quite so lucky, but in only three cases absolute addresses should be used:

■ Interrupt Vector Table
■ System Variables
■ Video RAM

All other addresses (including application variable addresses) should be high-level language and assembler generated.

Variable address offsets (within a segment) should not be specified in the source because it takes away your flexibility in adding or taking away variables, as well as using the segment with other modules. If the offsets within the data segment are explicitly set in the source code, then modifications requiring changing the number of variables required will result in wasted space or a lot of effort to work through the source to make the space required as compact as possible. Virtually all assemblers are excellent at allocating variable memory, based on the variable's size. This feature should be exploited.

If you are creating code to be used in a ROM that will be placed on a hardware adapter, you might be tempted to set explicit addresses. This should also be discouraged because it limits the use of the ROM to very specific applications and PCs. ROM code is written to be relocatable because it can be set to different addresses within different PCs. In this case, you might have application code pass variable segment information (the code segment is implicitly known because it has been loaded into the CS register) to the application upon reset or initialization. In the example applications, I will show how relative addressing can be used for accessing variables which may be in arbitrary locations in memory.

Another case where you might be tempted in using absolute addresses is when creating patch-code areas in your application. In some schools of thought, space is explicitly allocated using the org statement that specifies a specific address, along with specific addresses to reference them. In the application, jumps to labels at these org statements are used to jump around patch code space, which has been left to fix an application from a debugger. I like to avoid this technique as much as possible because patch code is difficult to document and remember the changes made to get the application working properly. As well, you might find that your source code goes beyond the address set for the end of a patch-code area. This results in problems with the assembler trying to resolve which code (the current code, the code after the org statement, or the code meant to be located before it) is to be used in the application.

Code changes and additions made in the source code are much easier to follow and, when marked with comments, easy to identify.

Ideally, you will never attempt to set an absolute address within your application. As noted at the start of this section, in some instances, absolute addressing is needed to access system resources, but this is the only case where it should be done. Just because code has been loaded once (or a thousand) times in a PC and absolute addresses don't cause a problem, it doesn't mean that they never will. As well, even if two PCs seem to be configured in exactly the same way, you cannot depend on an application being loaded at the same address between the two. Avoiding absolute addressing within an application will save you hours of grief later when something is changed, loaded, or not loaded and the application refuses to behave the same way that it has for years.

The 8087 and Floating Point Computing

When I first started programming and worked with BASIC and Fortran, I created many of the usual first programs, such as simulating a satellite orbiting around the Earth. When I first got into microprocessor programming, I was dismayed to find that real numbers were very rarely used and difficult to work with. At the time, real numbers were usually implemented in software with general-purpose conversion and arithmetic operations written and stored in libraries or in ROM. The operations often took a large amount of CPU resources and time to calculate values.

When the PC first came out, hardware support was built in for the Intel *8086 Floating-Point Unit (FPU)*, which was given the chip identifier *8087*. This device, when it became available in 1983, gave the PC a fast way to handle 80-bit IEEE floating-point real numbers. The 8087 was very popular with engineers, accountants, and other real number crunchers because it increased the speed of floating-point operations by up to a factor of four.

The 8087 is actually an auxiliary processor to the 8086 and 8088. In the application, code, and instructions that run on the 8087 are recognized and ignored by the 8086 processor. If no 8087 or FPU is installed and an 8087 instruction is encountered, an exception interrupt is generated by the 8086 processor.

The 80-bit number is a binary representation of the mantissa and exponent of a floating-point number that is in the format:

$$\text{(Sign) Mantissa} \times 2 ** \text{ (Exponent Sign) Exponent}$$

The Mantissa is multiplied by the signed exponent to get values less than or greater than one.

The data formats supported by the 8087 are:

DATA FORMAT	DATA RANGE	DATA SIZE
Word	$\pm$ 32 KB	2 Bytes
Double word	$\pm$ 4.3 GB	4 Bytes
Long word	$\pm$ 9.2 (10^{18})	8 Bytes
Packed BCD	$\pm 10^{17}$	8 Bytes
Single precision real	$\pm 10^{38}$ to $\pm 10^{-38}$	3 Bytes
Double precision real	$\pm 10^{308}$ to $\pm 10^{-308}$	8 Bytes
Extended precision real	$\pm 10^{4932}$ to $\pm 10^{-4932}$	10 Bytes

This gives you a lot of flexibility to work with a wide range of numbers in different applications. All the number formats can be processed together with the final result being in the most accurate format (i.e., a word and single precision combined together will have a result as a single precision number).

The 8087 processor has a stack with its own 16-bit status register (Fig. 3-6). Data is pushed onto the stack and operations consist of either the two top stack elements or the top element and another, arbitrarily positioned, element.

The FPU Status Word records the result of the operation and is defined as:

BIT	FUNCTION
15	"B" - FPU Busy
8-10, 14	FPU Condition Code
11-13	Top of Stack Pointer
7	"ES" - Error Summary Bit
6	"SF" - Stack Fault Bit
5	"PE" - Precision Exception
4	"UE" - Underflow Exception
3	"OE" - Overflow Exception
2	"ZE" - Zero Divide Exception
1	"DE" - Denormalized Exception
0	"IE" - Invalid Operation

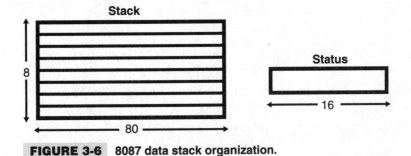

FIGURE 3-6 **8087 data stack organization.**

This book contains only an introduction to the 8087, its capabilities, and the kind of data spaces used. For any applications that require operations on real numbers, I highly recommend a high-level language that supports 8087 operations, instead of assembly language. For basic floating-point operations, it is not difficult to work with the 8087 in assembler. Difficulties arise when you start working with arbitrary values (which could cause exceptions) and use results in comparisons and program branching. I recommend that you just avoid the hassles of learning the 8087 and program in a language that makes the operations transparent to you.

8087 INSTRUCTION SET

The following table of 8087 instructions is provided to give you an idea of what's possible. I suggest that if you are going to do any kind of significant floating-point operations that you get an Intel 8087 reference.

INSTRUCTION	DESCRIPTION
F2MX1	Calculate 2**Stack Top - 1
FABS	Find the absolute value of the stack top
FADD	Pop the top two stack elements, add them together, and push the result onto the stack
FADDP	Pop the top two stack elements, add them together and store the result
FBLD	Push packed BCD onto the stack
FBSTP	Pop packed BCD from the stack
FCHS	Toggle the sign bit in the top stack element
FCLEX	Clear the 8087's exception flags
FCOM	Compare the top two stack elements and store the result of the operation in the 8087's flag register
FCOMP	Complement the top stack element
FCOMPP	Pop the top two stack elements, compare them and store the result of the operation in the 8087's flag register
FDECSTP	Decrement the 8087's stack pointer
FDISI	Disable 8087 interrupts
FDIV	Pop the top two stack elements, divide the second from the first and push the result back onto the stack
FDIVP	Pop the top two stack elements, divide the second from the first and store the result in memory
FDIVRP	Pop the top two stack elements, divide the first from the second and push the result back onto the stack
FENI	Enable 8087 interrupts
FFREE	Change the 8087's destination flag to empty
FIADD	Pop the top stack element, add an integer to it and push the result onto the Stack
FICOM	Compare the top stack element to an Integer and save the result in the 8087's flag register
FICOMP	Pop the top stack element, compare it to an Integer and save the result in the 8087's flag register
FIDIV	Pop the top stack element, divide it by an integer and push the result onto the stack
FIDIVR	Pop the top stack element, divide it into an Integer and push the result onto the stack
FILD	Push an integer onto the stack

INSTRUCTION	DESCRIPTION
FIMUL	Pop the top stack element, multiply it by an integer and push the result onto the stack
FINCSTP	Increment the 8087's stack pointer
FINIT	Initialize the 8087
FINITI	Initialize the 8087
FIST	Save the top stack element as an integer
FISTP	Pop the top stack element and store it as an integer
FISUB	Pop the top stack element, subtract an integer from it and push the result onto the stack
FISUBR	Pop the top stack element, subtract it from an integer and push the result onto the stack
FLD	Push a real variable onto the stack
FLD1	Push 1 onto the stack
FLDCW	Load a user-specified 8087 control word
FLDENV	Load a user-specified 8087 environment variable
FLDL2E	Convert the top stack element to its natural logarithm
FLDL2T	Convert the top stack element to its base-ten logarithm
FLDLG2	Convert the top stack element to its base-two logarithm
FLDPI	Push PI onto the stack
FLDZ	Push zero onto the Stack
FMUL	Pop the top two stack elements, multiply them together, and push the result onto the stack
FMULP	Pop the top two stack elements, multiply them together, and save the result in memory
FNCLEX	Clear the 8087's status word
FNDISI	Disable the interrupt mask
FNENI	Enable the interrupt mask
FNOP	NOP
FNRSTOR	Restore the state information
FNSAVE	Save the state information
FNSTCW	Save the control word
FNSTEN	Save the environment information
FNSTSW	Save the status word
FPATAN	Convert the top stack element to its ARCTAN

INSTRUCTION	DESCRIPTION
FPREM	Pop the top two stack elements, divide the second into the first and push the remainder onto the stack
FPTAN	Convert the top stack element to its TANGENT
FRNDINT	Convert the top stack element to an integer
FRSTOR	Restore the state information
FSCALE	Multiply or divide the top stack element by the power of 2
FSQRT	Convert the top stack element to its square root
FSAVE	Save the state information
FST	Store the real value
FSTEN	Save the environment information
FSTCW	Save the control word
FSTP	Pop the real top of stack element
FSTPSP	Move the real element to the top of stack and pop
FSTST	Move the specified stack element to the top of the stack
FSTSW	Save the status word
FSUB	Pop the top two stack elements, subtract the second from the first and push the result onto the stack
FSUBP	Pop the top two stack elements, subtract the second from the first and store the result in memory
FSUBR	Pop the top two stack elements, subtract the first from the second and push the result onto the stack
FSUBRP	Pop the top two stack elements, subtract the first from the second and store the result in memory
FTST	Compare the top stack element to zero and store the result in the stack flag
FWAIT	Cause the processor to wait for the floating point unit to complete the current instruction
FXAM	Examine the top of stack
FXCH	Exchange the top stack element with another in the stack
FXTRACT	Extract and save in memory the top stack element's exponent
FYL2X	Convert the top stack element to its base-two logarithm and multiply by the second stack element
FYL2XP1	Increment the top stack element, convert the result to its base-two logarithm and multiply by the second stack element

The Intel 80386 and 80486

After the 8088, the first significant enhancement to the PC's processor was the 80386 (most often known simply as *386*). The 80386 gave the PC the capability to run multiple tasks, including multiple real mode (ability to run 8086 code directly) and protected mode (using 32-bit data and new instructions) tasks. The 80386 first became available in the spring of 1987 and quickly established itself as a standard for PCs and its capabilities were crucial for sophisticated operating systems, such as Windows, to be possible. The 80386 also offered significant performance gains to PC users over their previous equipment.

The previous paragraph may be controversial because many people probably would think that the 80286 (as used in the PC/AT) was the first significant enhancement to the PC and its architecture. I would say that it was and it wasn't. The 80286, with its 16-bit data path and 24-MB memory access was an enhancement to the PC, but was not sufficient to significantly change the way personal computers worked. The Protect mode features of the 80286 were quite difficult to work with (including having to reset the PC's processor to get out of it and return to Real mode) and did not provide an easy upgrade path for users working with 8088 PCs.

The 80386 did not have this last deficiency, being able to run in 8086 Real mode, 80286 Protect mode, and its own 32-bit Protect mode. This feature made the 80386 attractive for new operating systems that not only provided their own interface, but also an MS-DOS compatible one as well. Without these features, the multitasking operating systems that we enjoy on our PCs would not have been possible. The 80386 provided the path for the PC to move from a desktop toy, to the workstation/server that is now competing with RISC-based machines on their own turf. It is important to note that the operating modes and features, first introduced with the 80386, are still available in the Pentium PCs of today and that the new operating systems (Windows 95 or 98) can run on an 80386 (although I would imagine painfully slowly).

This is why I consider the 80386 to be the first significant enhancement to the PC. The 80286 provided an evolutionary half step, but did not change the way personal computers were used.

When the 386 first came out, its cost was very high. To help attract customers to it, Intel developed the 80386SX, which, to the 80386, was analogous of the 8088 to the 8086. The 386SX had a 16-bit external databus (and 20-four bit addressing), which allowed it to be used in PC/AT-like systems very easily.

This microprocessor was very popular and when Intel came out with the 80486, an enhancement to the 80386, an SX version was also made available, which also had a 16-bit bus to provide a lower-cost version of the processor. As I was writing this book, this tradition has continued with Intel introducing the Celeron processor, which is a feature-, complexity-, and cost-reduced version of the Pentium II microprocessor.

The 80486 (not surprisingly known as the *486*) provided a quantum leap in performance to the 80386 and was able to run at double the speed of the 386 and had the numeric coprocessor built in. Many versions of the 486 were introduced, each running faster than the previous version, leading to today's price/performance wars.

MULTITASKING, 32-BIT INSTRUCTIONS AND PROTECT MODE

The title of this section probably seems overwhelming in its scope and could be the title for a book all by itself. Many books have been written on these subjects and most of them are pretty weighty tomes. In comparison, aside from this introduction, not much deal detail is provided on how 32-bit data, addresses, and Protect mode work in the 80386 (and faster) processors. This section can be thought of as an introduction to Windows at a low level and how Windows applications execute.

Protect mode was first introduced in the 80286 and was enhanced in the 80386 to provide direct access to 32-bit data and address space [giving a maximum word value and address size of 4.3 GB (4,294,967,296 bytes)]. This 32-bit mode has been used in all processors since the 80386 and is often referred to as the *Flat Memory Model* because it allows you to develop and run applications that run in a single 32-bit segment, which does not require any segment registers.

Protect mode is actually a generic term for a number of features and operating modes of the processors, which work together to allow Windows (and other multitasking operating system) applications to run in such a way that they are completely separate from other applications. This means that resources and errors unique to individual applications will not affect other applications.

The 80386 boots up in what is known as *Real mode*, in which it emulates the operation of an 8086. This Real mode is not to be confused with the 8086 Emulation mode; when an 80386 (or faster) processor boots up in Real mode, it can only access up to 1 MB of memory, 16 bits at a time. To get the advanced features of the 80386 (such as 32-bit data and addressing, and segment protection), the processor must be put into Protect mode.

The basis for Protect mode is the protection ring operation built into the processor (Fig. 3-7). The hardware access given to code is dependent on the ring in which the code executes. These rings or privilege levels are specified in a code or data-segment descriptor. There are three types of descriptors (Fig. 3-8).

These descriptors are used to define how the processor and applications run. The descriptors consist of the size limits for the segments, as well as their starting addresses in physical memory and their privilege (ring) level.

Each descriptor is given a privilege level that specifies what level of hardware the segment can access and be accessed by. For example, code running at privilege level (ring) 2 can access data at privilege levels 2 or 3. An error is generated if accesses to rings 0 or 1 are attempted. An access can be a data read or write or a jump to.

To access segments at higher privilege levels, a *gate descriptor* is used. This descriptor provides an entry point to a procedure along with a check of the current execution level. The gate descriptor points to a code-segment descriptor with a procedure entry point (Fig. 3-9).

When the processor is running, it is loaded up with *descriptor tables*, which are used for the operating system (the Global Descriptor Table) and individual applications (which are known as *tasks* or *processes*). Within the applications, you might have multiple subtasks, which are known as *threads*. This is the basis for multitasking in Windows and other Protect mode operating systems.

In the data segment descriptors, data is protected in a variety of ways and can be accessed differently by various tasks. For example, in a voting machine, a data segment

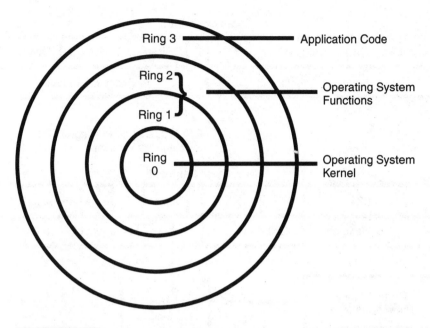

FIGURE 3-7   Protect mode execution "rings".

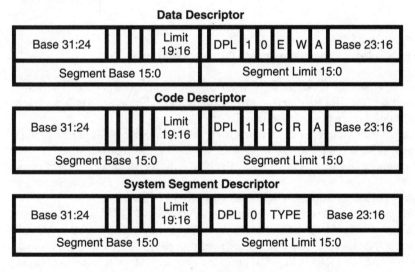

Data Descriptor

Base 31:24				Limit 19:16	DPL	1	0	E	W	A	Base 23:16
Segment Base 15:0				Segment Limit 15:0							

Code Descriptor

Base 31:24				Limit 19:16	DPL	1	1	C	R	A	Base 23:16
Segment Base 15:0				Segment Limit 15:0							

System Segment Descriptor

Base 31:24				Limit 19:16	DPL	0	TYPE		Base 23:16
Segment Base 15:0				Segment Limit 15:0					

A - Access
C - Conforming
DPL - Descriptor Privilege Level
E - Expand-Down
Limit - Segment Limit
R - Readable
W - Writeable

FIGURE 3-8   Protect mode descriptors.

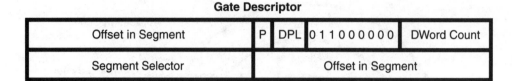

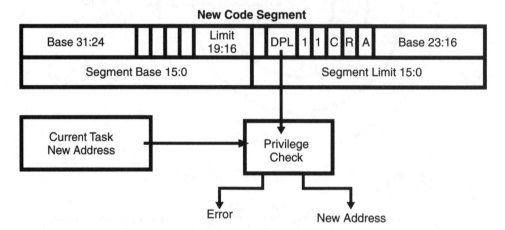

FIGURE 3-9 Protect mode gate DT call operation.

might be write only to the voting high-level application interface tasks. The purpose of this is to protect the data from prying eyes with diskettes. The actual votes are tabulated by a Ring 0 task, which processes the results.

The segments can operate in four different modes. Sixteen bit, 32 bit, emulated 8086 (known as *Virtual 8086* or *V86*), and Real mode. The 16-bit protect mode is used to maintain compatibility with the 80286, which could only access up to 16 MB of memory (only 16 bits wide) and uses a 16-bit segment (a maximum size of 64 KB). Sixteen-bit Protect mode was used by Microsoft Windows versions 3.11 (and earlier).

Thirty-two bit mode consists of segments as large as 4.3 GB in size. These segments can be shared between the CS, DS, and SS registers, giving you a 32-bit processor that is able to access 4.3 GB in one contiguous segment (the flat memory model). This mode is used within Windows 95, 98, and NT to provide a simpler method to access an application.

In all of the Protect-mode segments, if an application and operating system require more memory than is available to the processor, then individual segments can be stored elsewhere and brought in through the use of Virtual memory of V/M. This feature is used in Windows 95, 98, and NT and Linux as the performance improvement you get when you add more memory to the PC. V/M is not trivial to work with and is really an OS-only level function.

The two 8086 emulation modes run slightly differently, but both can be used to access I/O registers. The Emulated Protect mode 8086 will run anywhere in memory and its I/O access is determined by the operating system (usually allowing accesses to devices that other Protect-mode tasks haven't accessed yet). In Windows, multiple MS-DOS prompts (emulated Protect-mode 8086s) can be run simultaneously (although Windows controls I/O access).

The Real-mode 8086 runs at Ring 0 privilege and is used in Windows to store Windows file and video drivers (also known as *MS-DOS*). In Windows, the I/O device drivers execute in this Real-mode 8086.

This basic description of Protect mode probably seems very cursory—at least in comparison to the description of other aspects of the PCS processor. But to properly explain Protect mode, with its different options and segmentation models, would probably take up as much space again as the rest of the book and is really not important to understanding how to interface hardware to your PC either under MS-DOS or Windows.

32-BIT INSTRUCTION SET

The register architecture used in 32-bit mode is not very much different from what you are used to with the 16-bit 8086. The major difference is the extension of the 16-bit registers to 32 bits. In 32-bit Protect mode, a flat model memory space is used, eliminating many of the issues with addressing data using the segment registers (Fig. 3-10).

The registers can be accessed as either their original 8- or 16-bit incarnations or as 32-bit values. The lower 16 bits can be addressed directly, but the upper 16 bits must be shifted down from the registers.

In the 32-bit protected mode (executing in Ring 3) used by Windows, the processor runs with only three segment registers (known as "selectors") a code segment (pointed to by CS), a data segment (pointed to by DS), and a stack segment (pointed to by SS). The ES segment register is still available, but because the program is set up with full 32-bit ad-

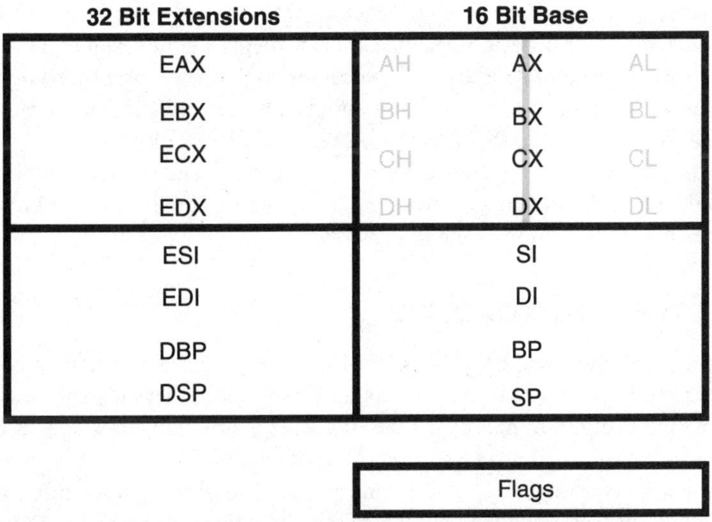

32 Bit Extensions	16 Bit Base		
EAX	AH	AX	AL
EBX	BH	BX	BL
ECX	CH	CX	CL
EDX	DH	DX	DL
ESI		SI	
EDI		DI	
DBP		BP	
DSP		SP	

	Flags	

FIGURE 3-10   80386 32-bit processor architecture.

dressed segments and cannot access memory outside of these defined memory areas, its use, except for string transfers (in which it has the same value as DS) is limited.

Even with this caveat on the segment registers, you will not have to expend any effort trying to figure out how to work the segment registers, they are effectively unused. The only issue that you might have is that read tables should be declared as initialized variables in the data segment, rather than in the code segment.

The flags register's bits, in 32-bit mode, is only 16 bits wide and the arithmetic result flags (i.e., Zero, Carry, Auxiliary Carry, etc.) all have the same bit positions in the register.

In the previous section, I explained how Intel created what is effectively a register superset of the 8086's register and segment modes in the 32-bit flat address model. This leverages the knowledge gained from the 8086 and actually makes addressing within the 8086 (and faster processors) easier than what was possible in the 8086.

This tradition continues with the 32-bit instructions; the instructions available in 32-bit mode are largely identical (with some additions) to the 8086's instruction set. The major difference is that the instructions can address data as 8-, 16-, or 32-bit sizes.

Although there is some commonality in the op codes generated for 16-bit 8086 instructions and 32-bit 80386+ instructions, there are major differences in most op codes. You cannot simply take an 8086 object code file and expect it to run without any problems in a processor running in 32-bit mode. Unexpected instructions will execute and the application will not run correctly.

This is an important point; it means that you have to use an assembler or compiler that produces native 32-bit instructions.

The Pentium and the Need for Speed

You would have had to be lost in a jungle for the past 10 years not to know that the driving forces for PCs has been to speed up the processors. They are now performing almost as fast as RISC workstations. These performance improvements are the result of a lot of work to change the processor and motherboard chip designs so that very high speed busses and enhanced instructions can be used while maintaining commonality with the Legacy PC requirements (640 KB Real mode, ISA bus and diskette, and VGA displays).

The typical modern PC is architected as shown in Fig. 3-11. The purpose of this book is not to go into detail on the Pentium system, but it explains a number of the new features and how they affect the operation of the interfaces.

ARCHITECTURE AND CACHES

What really separates the Pentium processors from the previous i86 family of microprocessors is its use of internal caches for data and instructions. These small, high-speed memories allow the Pentium to operate at the 500-MHz instruction clock speeds enjoyed today.

A *processor cache* is a very fast local memory that is used to retrieve often-used instructions and data, instead of relying on the relatively slow main memory. Figure 3-12 shows the block diagram of a cache. If the requested instruction is in the cache

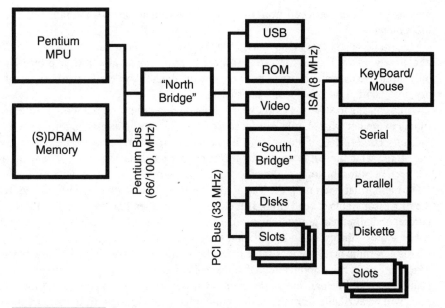

FIGURE 3-11 Modern pc architecture.

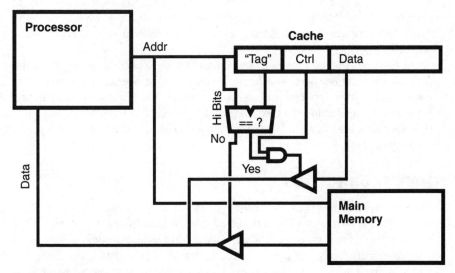

FIGURE 3-12 Inten "Pentium" cache operation.

memory, then it is retrieved from there. If it is not, then the instruction is retrieved from main memory.

Modern PCs can run with up to a 600-MHz processor, but main memory moves along at a relatively pokey 100 or 133 MHz. If there were no cache, a 600-MHz processor would only be able to execute instructions at the rate in which they were fetched from main memory, instead of at the processor's internal speed.

Using a cache to store the next expected instruction requires a number of different algorithms to predict what should be saved in cache. The most common algorithm is the *Least Recently Used (LRU)*; if a new word is encountered, then it is read in from main memory and, at the same time, it is written by the processor into cache memory. The word that has not been used for the longest period of time is overwritten by this new word.

During normal operation, the Tag RAM address value is compared to the address that the processor wants to read from. If there is a match, then that address Tag RAM counter is reset and all others are incremented. This means that when there isn't a matching Tag RAM address, the cache address with the highest counter is replaced.

This algorithm is relatively simple to implement, is quite fast, and takes advantage of the characteristic of most applications that the execution tends to stay in small loops. With execution staying in small loops, the cache will be infrequently updated and most instructions will be available from the cache without having to retrieve from main memory.

The Pentium has two caches. The L1 cache is essentially the high-speed cache, as described previously. This cache is usually only several kilobytes in size. The other cache, known as *L2*, performs a similar task, but is much larger (512 KB for the Pentium II) and somewhat slower. Its purpose is to provide cached memory while the main memory SDRAM is resetting its read address, which takes an enormous amount of time, from the processor's perspective.

The good news about caches is that you don't have to know anything about them, other than what is described here. The Pentium's cache and its operation is totally internal to the device (as far as the application designer is concerned) and is largely transparent to the operation of the application. To take the most advantage of the built-in caches, you must design your software to stay in fairly small loops and use a central set of variables, which are not written to often.

MMX TECHNOLOGY

My first exposure to MMX technology was a list of 57 instructions in *PC Week*, with a very brief explanation that it was designed to provide additional high-speed graphics support for the Pentium processor. When I looked at the instructions, it appeared that they were new instructions, designed to speed up the transfer of data using the full 64-bit bus width available in Pentium processors. This appeared to be a worthwhile goal because if data could be transferred 64 bits at a time, then I would expect to see an eight-fold increase in speed over 8-bit data movements.

It appeared to be a worthwhile improvement to the Pentium, although I felt that MMX was just an enhancement to the instruction set. I looked at Intel's advertisements about MMX technology as being more of a marketing gimmick than an actual improvement to the breed. In my research for this book, I very quickly realized that MMX technology is more than just adding additional instructions to the Pentium's microcode. MMX is the ac-

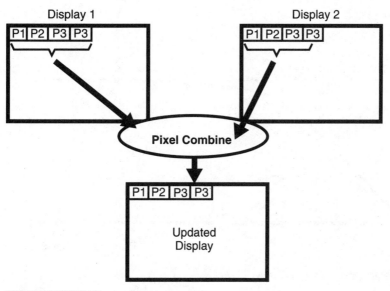

FIGURE 3-13   MMX screen update.

tual addition of another parallel processor to the Pentium's central and floating-point processing units. This parallel processing allows very fast data transformations to be carried out on multiple data points (in packed data format), while the other processors were working on other aspects of the application.

A typical application for MMX would be updating a graphics display in real time. In MPEG data-compression schemes, the next screen is coded as changes to the previous one.

To create the next frame, the pixels in the previous frame (Display 1 in Fig. 3-13) are combined with the new data (Display 2 in Fig. 3-13). With MMX technology, retrieving multiple pixels (usually four) from the first frame and processing them to the new value using pixel information for the next frame can execute in one instruction. When this operation has completed, all of the pixels are to be written to the display memory at the same time. Rather than repeating this operation once for each pixel, multiple pixels are processed at the same time, resulting in a significant improvement in data throughput.

MMX technology can also be used with real-time audio processing, as well as other forms of *digital signal processing (DSP)*. In this book, an obvious application would be to work with the Frame Grabber or a SoundBlaster Digital Oscilloscope and compress the received data, based on adjacent values. Another possibly useful MMX application is decompressing Web data, to allow PCs to present data faster than is currently possible.

I have not yet worked with MMX, so everything I have to say is pretty theoretical—and this is mirrored in the real world, with very few applications as yet taking advantage of it using standard modems. I can say, however, that I do consider it to be an essential part to any PC.

One comment from Intel caught my eye. MMX is the most significant enhancement to Intel architecture since the Intel 386 processor, which extended the architecture to 32 bits. Like the 80386 32-bit mode, MMX has not been immediately taken advantage of, but I expect in a few years, MMX technology will be crucial to the operation of all PCs.

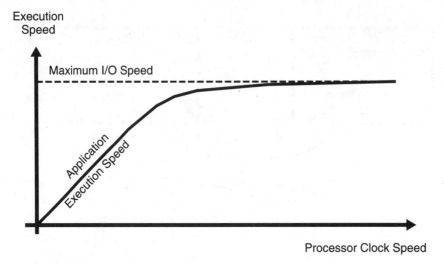

FIGURE 3-14 PC maximum performance chart.

THE PENTIUM PRO

After the Pentium was first introduced, it became obvious that although processors could be run at higher and higher speeds, their dependency on main memory and I/O would keep the actual execution speed of the applications limited to a maximum speed. Looking at the relationship between processor speed and actual execution speed can be modeled when the maximum memory fetch and I/O speed is taken into account, as shown in Fig. 3-14.

This asymptotic relationship shows that as the speed of the microprocessor is increased, the actual execution speed of the application will plateau at the maximum speed that data can be accessed in the PC's hardware.

To break this barrier, Intel designed the Pentium Pro with some innovative architectural features. When you read Intel's literature about the Pentium Pro, you'll find that the microprocessor is capable of twice the throughput of the standard Pentium. This is a result of architectural changes to how the Pentium Pro executes instructions and stores data.

In a regular Pentium microprocessor, if the instruction sequence:

```
mov    AX, Variable
add    BX, AX
inc    CX
sub    DX, SI
```

was encountered and *Variable* was not in instruction cache memory, then the processor would wait until *Variable* was loaded from memory and then execute the mov and following three instructions even though the last two are not dependent on *Variable* or any of the registers that it is loaded into.

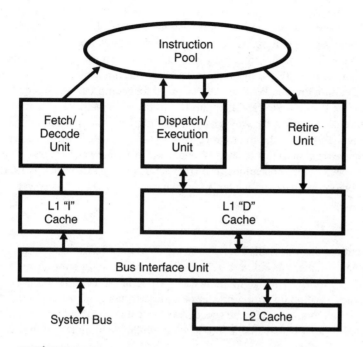

FIGURE 3-15   Pentium "Pro" block diagram.

In the Pentium Pro, instructions are loaded into a pool and executed when the prerequisite information required for the instruction is available. This is done in a fairly complex processor architecture (known to Intel as *micro-architecture*) as shown in Fig. 3-15.

The Fetch/Decode unit loads and looks at the instructions in the pool and determines which can be executed, according to what data is available in registers and the L1 data cache. The Dispatch/Execution unit performs the instructions or partial instructions that do have the available resources. When the instruction operations are complete, the Retire unit stores the results and removes the instruction from the pool.

Using the previous example code, the Pentium Pro could execute the instructions in the following order:

```
inc    CX
sub    DX, SI
mov    AX, Variable
add    BX, AX
```

This allows instructions that are not dependent on data that is not available to execute first and then execute the data-dependent instructions when the data should have been fetched from memory.

Along with the changes to its micro-architecture, the Pentium Pro is also designed for simple parallel processor operation. Multiple microprocessors can be wired to the same memory and I/O bus in parallel without any special considerations for the multiple devices. This feature, along with the dynamic instruction execution of the micro-architecture, makes the Pentium Pro and Pentium "Xeon" ideal for multiprocessor servers.

The changes to the Pentium Pro (and Pentium II introduced in the next section) over the 80x86 architecture do not affect the way that you should plan your application code. The changes are designed to allow the microprocessors to take advantage of the faster clock speeds and minimize the impact that the relative increases in memory and I/O response have on the execution speed of the applications. The architecture changes are primarily needed to operate system authors, to give them the tools to make the PC run as efficiently as possible.

THE PENTIUM II

Although the Pentium Pro was really designed to be the most efficient for multiprocessor, high-speed server systems, the Pentium II was designed for high-performance desktop PCs. The Pentium II took advantage of what was learned in the Pentium Pro's development and operation to come up with a processor that performs at up to 50 percent faster than the Pentium Pro running at the same speed. As I write this, the Pentium II is the faster 8086-compatible PC processor available today (although the Pentium III will be available by the second half of 1999).

The major difference between the Pentium II and the Pentium Pro is the Pentium II's dual bus architecture (Fig. 3-16). This enhancement to the Pentium micro-architecture moves the

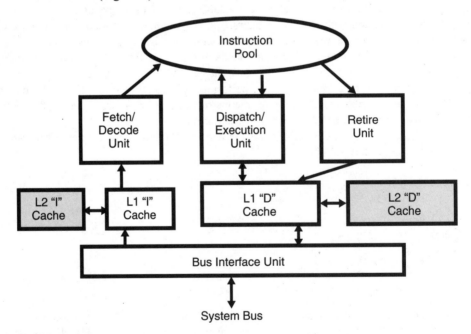

FIGURE 3-16   **Pentium II block diagram.**

L2 cache data from having to go through the Bus Interface Unit to its own address and data busses. This means that the L2 cache can be accessed while the Bus Interface Unit is accessing memory from the system without having to wait for any previous accesses to complete.

To further improve the performance of the Pentium II, Intel designed the microprocessor with multiple *Arithmetic Logic Units (ALUs)*, which allows multiple instructions to execute at the same time, as long as their input and output parameters are not used in more than one instruction.

Other Processors

As I write this, the AMD K6-2 Processor is a very popular low-cost Pentium clone for PC compatibles. This chip is available in many current systems as a cheaper alternative to the true Pentium II. Because the PC processor market is so lucrative, AMD is not and has not been the only second source supplier of processors for PCs. Intel can also be considered, with their own low-cost compatible chips, the Celeron line.

For the most part, these replacement chips work exactly the same as the Intel parts they're designed to replace and offer improvements in speed, cost, or capabilities. The decision on which type of processor to use in your PC should be an informed one. At the start of this paragraph, I noted that, for the most part, the replacement chips work exactly the same.

There can be some significant differences.

This ideal situation can be very hard to achieve in real life. If you are developing a product, you will probably want to try out prototypes in a variety of different processors and support chip sets to be sure that you're not getting calls from angry customers later. One way that will help you avoid these potential problems is to use standard development tools (such as brand-name compilers) and keep the amount of assembly-language programming to an absolute minimum. Another point with development tools is to be sure that you have compiled your code in the latest level and run it on the latest versions of operating systems. If you're wondering just how likely this type of problem is, you can rest assured that it is pretty unlikely. Modern third-party chips are designed with a high degree of commonality and with proper coding techniques the dangers of having problems are very small.

PERSONAL

COMPUTER

SOFTWARE

In a lot of ways, this book will seem more like a programming primer for the PC than a book on interfacing hardware to one. Because the PC is such a powerful system and the software and hardware has grown so much in complexity, to be able to interface hardware to the PC, you must be familiar with the processor, operating systems, and system hardware interfaces.

This is really the basis of "systems programming" for the PC. Much of the information presented in this book is available in other books and even in MS-DOS and Microsoft Windows operating manuals. The difference between this book and the others is that I provide you with an understanding of how all the pieces fit together. This will enable you to choose the best method of interfacing hardware to the PC.

Firmware Versus Software

The PC operates as a mix of firmware and software. These two elements complement each other to provide a workstation that has a strong set of basic functions, along with customizable application and user specific features. When designing your applications understanding the issues between firmware and software are important to enable you to make the correct decisions on how to best interface additional hardware to the system.

Firmware refers to code that is burned into ROM chips on the PC's motherboard and adapter cards. It is typically written for 16-bit Real mode and provides access to the input/output (I/O) devices built into the PC. Firmware typically comes in two flavors in the PC; POST and BIOS.

POST (Power On Self Test) is run at system boot to first test the PC's hardware and then set it in a state ready for an operating system to load. The POST operation is pretty cursory and, in many ways, is primarily responsible for putting hardware into a "known state" to facilitate operating system boot. The tests are somewhat simple for two reasons. The first is that the tests have to run quickly (nobody likes waiting a long time for their PC to boot) and the second is that often additional devices must be connected or be known good to complete the test.

POST is normally written in a manner that works from the inside out. First, the processor is tested, followed by the immediate devices attached to it (memory and address decode), followed by the timer, interrupt controller, DMA controller, etc., with each device being tested dependent on devices already tested as much as possible. Often, for a complete test to be run on the "inside" devices, the "outside" ones that will provide stimulus for the tests are either not present or have not yet been tested to guarantee their correct operation. In many cases, such as with diskette drives, the only way to provide the testing signals is to run them as they would in the system. This results in a "catch 22:" the only way being able to completely test the PC is to use parts of it that have already passed a test.

The *BASIC Input/Output System (BIOS)* is a set of routines available within the system that provide a standard interface between the operating system and application software to the hardware within the PC. The BIOS functions, which can be considered to be *APIs (Application Programming Interfaces)*, are normally accessible by software interrupts. This mechanism is explained later in the book.

If you're familiar with early IBM PCs, you'll know that one BASIC interpreter (known as *Cassette BASIC*) was loaded into ROM and would execute if no operating system was available. This program doesn't fit into the POST or BIOS categories and really belongs in the software operating system category because it executes user applications and loads and saves the applications (to an audio cassette tape). I realize that this statement really has no reference up to this point; it will make more sense as you read through the book.

What might be surprising is that both the POST and BIOS can be enhanced or changed when new hardware is placed in the system. This is accomplished by adding new ROMs into the PC's memory map or running software designed to run and load the new routines. The details on how this is accomplished is presented later in the book.

Software is always loaded into the PC (usually from disk) and is often specific to the PC that it will run on, the features connected to and loaded in it, and the operator. I tend to break the term *software* into three categories: operating system, tools, and applications.

Operating systems are used to provide an interface to the user with the ability to load and execute tools and applications, as well as manage system resources. MS-DOS is a very rudimentary example of an operating system capable of providing these functions; the latest versions of Microsoft Windows are very good examples of what an operating system's capabilities can be.

When the PC first came out, one of the marketing ploys was to compare the performance of a PC's processor to a mainframe (just for your information, the first PC was approximately as powerful as a 1968 System/360). The operating system was never compared because MS-DOS was at the level of sophistication of what a 1950s vintage computer would have. Windows 98 and NT offer almost all of the features (and certainly all of the features in terms of networking) as mainframes. This is a big reason why modern operating systems take so long to load (for example, I have worked on UNIX server systems where the operating system load requires 45 minutes or more).

I define a *tool* as any program that converts data in one form to another. Another differentiator is in how it executes, a tool essentially executes in the "Input -> Processing -> Output" model of basic data processing. A good example would be a compiler that takes source code and turns it into a binary object file.

Applications are programs that perform some kind of task for the user. An example application could be a Web browser, which interfaces with the user to look up information. I define *applications* as "event-driven programs," which do not follow the "Input -> Processing -> Output" model of tools and spends much of its time waiting for external input before responding and processing information.

Under these definitions, it's important to note that I consider an editor (used by an user to input data into the computer and save it on disk) as an application. This is somewhat of an unusual definition because most people would consider it to be a tool. I categorize programs in this way so that I can work out a set of requirements when I am about to start developing an application.

INTERRUPT INTERFACES

The software interrupt is very important within the PC system. As is explained in the next section, the software interrupts provide the *Basic Input/Output System* (*BIOS*) and operating-system *Application Program Interfaces* (*APIs*). These interfaces are typically set up in the same manner, with the AH register having the specified function, while the other registers are used for input and output parameters.

Proper set up of the hardware interrupt and their interfaces to applications is crucial for proper operation of the PC and the applications. Hardware interrupts, other than the disk subsystem, DMA, timer, keyboard, and mouse software interrupts are not a crucial part of the BIOS and MS-DOS. These interrupts do not have BIOS or OS resources dedicated to handling them, other than to mask any inadvertent occurrences.

Typically, hardware interrupts are handled within device drivers, which provide an interface via the operating system to not only the interrupt, but to the low-level hardware using the file interface of the operating system.

Operating Systems

I've defined an operating system as a program that manages system resources, allows applications to execute, and provides an interface to the user to control the operation of a computer. This definition holds up very well when applied to most PC operating systems (including MS-DOS and Windows).

In this book, I am primarily concerned with creating applications that can interface with hardware. To do this, an understanding of how resources are managed and interfaced is crucial. Working through the hardware, I'll show you resources that are shared (requiring definite strategies for accessing) and how to interface with high-level languages (normally through the use of device drivers or library routines).

Writing software that interfaces with hardware in the PC, whether to the built-in devices or to devices you've designed is known systems programming, although in this book, it is called *application programming*.

The operating system provides a number of routines that can be called from the application, known as *Application Programming Interfaces (APIs)*. This book explains how to call BIOS (firmware), MS-DOS, and Windows APIs to allow your application to access all of the PC's resources in the most efficient manner.

MULTITASKING OPERATING SYSTEMS

Multitasking operating systems (which I tend to simply call *multitaskers*) can be thought of as a superset of the operating system description that I gave in the last section. Chances are that you already know what a multitasker is and how it works. But, to be sure that there is no confusion, I define a *multitasker* as an operating system that executes multiple applications and programs in "time slices" of varying intervals (Fig. 4-1).

These different tasks execute for a set period of time or until they request a resource that is not available or needs some time to come on line. When the task can no longer run, the processor is switched to another task to operate. Multitaskers tend to be very efficient with the CPU resource because it is always executing application code.

With each of these execution intervals ("time slices") occurring quite a few times per second, it can give Windows (and other multitasking operating systems) the appearance of running multiple applications at the same time.

Applications in multitaskers are normally known as *processes*. These processes can communicate to the operating system via a communications protocol that accesses the operating system device drivers and kernel. This communications capability also allows processes of different priorities (and, hence, different protection levels) to communicate with one another, as well as small processes within the applications (known as *threads*).

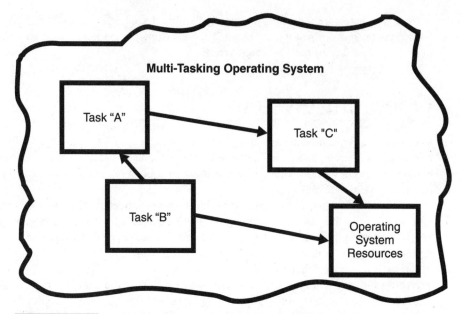

FIGURE 4-1   Multi-tasking operating system application.

This communication ensures that resources, such as the disk, are not swamped with conflicting requests.

One of the nice features of Windows is that it will provide an environment for your applications that "seem" like they are the only applications running in the PC. This extends to preventing the application from overwriting memory and resources devoted to other applications. This is a feature of the Protect mode, mentioned in Chapter 3. It actually gets better because Windows will "hide" the Protect mode realities of the operating system from you. Interfacing tasks to each other and to resources is done through APIs.

In the single-tasking operating system, only one task can be accessing resources. In a multitasker, multiple tasks can try to access the same resource simultaneously. This means that the resource requests must be arbitrated by the operating system.

A good example of this problem is having two tasks try to access the hard-disk controller at the same time.

Task A could be executing:

```
open file "123.txt"
jump to fileEnd
write contents of VarA to file
```

While Task B is executing (on an already open file):

```
read file contents into VarB
jump to File Start
```

If these commands aren't arbitrated by the operating system, then, chances are, one or the other is going to read from or write to the wrong file and file offset.

Now, you might think that you are smart and point out that MS-DOS allocates specific handles each time that a file is opened, avoiding such a problem. To some extent, this system avoids some of the problems, but MS-DOS has one big problem. What happens if a new command is sent before the previous one has finished? This is MS-DOS' notorious *nonreentrancy* problem. File-system requests will cause the PC to crash.

This situation could be shown in the previous example. If Task A was executing the open file and waiting for a BIOS interrupt to indicate that data had been read, processor control would be given to Task B, which first sends the command to read data, resulting in a locked-up PC and a potentially trashed disk. Thus, a successful multitasker must be able to arbitrate these requests and prevent these types of problems from occurring.

The modern 32-bit Windows incarnations don't have these problems with the file system because of the design of the file system device drivers. Windows device drivers are covered later in the book. Without tracking these issues, you might experience similar problems when you attempt to develop your own applications.

A very important feature of multitasking operating systems is the ability of tasks to communicate with one another. This is performed by the use of "messages," which copy a data area from one task to another. This feature can help you to create simple applications that would be nearly impossible in a single-tasking environment.

Windows will really keep you from getting your hands dirty in learning how to interface with the innards of the Protect-mode processor, but you will still need to understand how hardware resources are accessed. This is really a mechanical task.

Graphical User Interfaces (GUIs)

If I had to attribute one feature that has contributed to the success of the PC, I would have to choose the *Graphical User Interface (GUI)*. This concept's origins date back to the 1970s, with Xerox PARC as a more-intuitive method of interfacing with a computer. Through the 1980s, the GUI was introduced to the masses by Apple in the Lisa and then the Macintosh computers. In the late 1980s, Microsoft introduced Windows, which brought the GUI to the PC world (Fig. 4-2).

This book focuses on Windows, and shows how hardware interfaces can use the Windows interface and standard development tools to provide an easy-to-work-with user interface.

Many people know me as a "Windows hater" because I always felt that Windows applications tended to be slower for arbitrary tasks, difficult to debug, and unnecessarily large. These perceptions are largely untrue with the modern development tools (specifically the latest Microsoft Visual Toolkit). Windows applications can be developed very quickly and efficiently, and excellent debugging tools have become available in recent years.

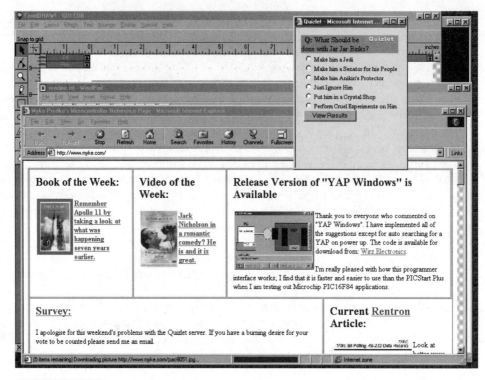

FIGURE 4-2 Microsoft "Windows" graphical user interface.

PERSONAL

COMPUTER

DEVICE

ADDRESSING

CONTENTS AT A GLANCE

PC Memory Map
FINDING AVAILABLE MEMORY
MEMORY APPLICATION

The PCI/ISA Busses
I/O SPACE AND BUS

Interrupt Allocation

Protect-Mode Hardware Features

If you've been working with and setting up PCs for any length of time, you will know that the biggest issue with adding new features to the PC is the difficulty in defining what is available for use by devices that you want to install. For most commercial devices, this issue has been largely eliminated by the introduction of Plug'n'Play. For your own ISA bus adapter designs that will not have designed-in Plug'n'Play, you will have to identify memory and I/O addresses, as well as interrupt numbers, that can be used safely without affecting any other devices in the system.

This is not a trivial task, especially with unbelievably wide variety of different options that a PC can have. This chapter describes the issues of identifying available addresses by searching the system and using established PC address conventions (many of which are listed in the appendices). Along with understanding the address availability issues, this chapter will help you to understand the differences in device timing that might cause an application to behave inconsistently between different PCs or addresses.

This book cannot contain a comprehensive list of the addresses used by different devices. I am just trying to give you an idea of how to look for available address resources and design your applications to work with a user-specified address.

PC Memory Map

As I've said elsewhere, in modern PCs, the only memory area that is really available to you for developing memory-mapped hardware interfaces is in the first 1 MB. This is not a major inconvenience, but more of a design point that you should be aware of.

The first 1 MB of memory really follows the conventions established for the original PC (Fig. 5-1).

The RAM area should be quickly recognized as the area of the operating and applications reside under MS-DOS (and Windows). This memory should always be loaded up with 640 KB and at least 550 KB of it available for applications (with interrupt vectors, system variables, and the MS-DOS kernel taking up no more than 90 KB).

The video RAM area (VRAM) probably seems quite large, but this space is needed to accommodate the different SVGA memory and addressing options.

The BIOS areas I've reserved probably seem unreasonably large at 128 KB, but many modern PCs use this entire area to accommodate built-in SVGA, SCSI, and networking BIOS. This area is often shadowed with SDRAM, in which the contents of the BIOS ROMs are copied into faster RAM.

After taking away these dedicated areas, only 96 KB is left for adapter RAM and ROM. The next two sections show you how to determine what is available. Later, the book shows more information about accessing this memory in ISA hardware and adapter cards.

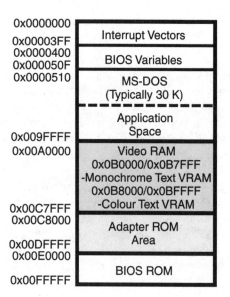

FIGURE 5-1   **PC/8088 memory map.**

FINDING AVAILABLE MEMORY

When you are installing an ISA adapter that uses memory resources for ROM or RAM into a PC, you will have to find a location in the PC's memory space that has the required space. This can often be a real challenge, which is why I have written the program in the next section; it uses techniques that I use to figure out where memory has been used and what is available.

Before going too far, it's time to explain the location of this memory. When the PC/AT (which largely defines modern PCs) was first designed, the PC's bus was upgraded (and ended up being called the *ISA bus*) to address the entire 16-MB 80286 memory address space. Before I started writing this, I looked in the newspaper to see what was offered in terms of memory for a "typical" PC. I found that most PCs today are shipped with 64 MB of memory. Looking at the "memory map" that I've provided in the previous section, all the ISA addressable memory (16 MB) is accessible by the PC's processor above 1 MB is going to be allocated to DRAM. This means that the only place your adapter's memory can be placed is in the 96 KB available between 0x0C8000 and 0x0DFFFF.

In many ways, this is good because it means that the amount of memory you have to look through is actually quite small; knowing how the data is stored makes figuring out what is used is quite simple. You should first look for RAM, followed by ROM.

To check for RAM, I suggest that you check each location from 0x0C8000 to 0x0DFFFF using the following algorithm for each byte.

1 Set the current address to 0x0C8000.
2 Save the contents of the current byte.
3 Write 0x0AA to the current byte.
4 Write 0x055 to 0x0F000:0.
5 Read and compare the contents of the current byte to 0x0AA.
6 If miscompare, go to 12.
7 Compare is good, write 0x055 to the current byte.
8 Write 0x0AA to 0x0F000:0
9 Read and compare the contents of the current byte to 0x055.
10 If miscompare, go to 12.
11 Restore the contents of the current byte.
12 Increment the current byte counter.
13 If the current byte counter is not equal to 0x0E0000, go to 2.

This algorithm will test for RAM memory by setting and resetting each bit, but not ultimately changing the original contents. You might want to disable interrupts between Steps 2 and 12 to ensure that the changed value isn't inadvertently used during an interrupt.

The reason why I write to the current address and then 0x0F000:0 is to ensure that the bus has a different value from what I expect to read. The ISA bus is notorious for allowing a previously read value to "float" on the bus. The second write ensures that if there isn't a RAM (or ROM) at the current address, the bus will have a different floating value.

Reading ROM is accomplished by knowing how the boot ROMs are inserted into the memory space. As you look on in the book, you'll discover that ROMs start with the pattern 0x055, 0x0AA, and then the number of 512-byte blocks that the ROM uses.

The algorithm used to search from ROM is much simpler:

1 Set the current address to 0x0C8000.
2 Read the current address and compare to 0x055.
3 If miscompare, go to 10.
4 Read the current address plus one and compare to 0x0AA.
5 If miscompare, go to 10.
6 Read the current address plus two and multiply by 512.
7 Mark the current address to the current address plus the result of Step 6 as ROM.
8 Add the current address and the result of Step 6 to get a new current address.
9 Go to 11.
10 Add 512 to the current address to get a new current address for testing.
11 If current address is less than 0x0E0000, go to 2.

MEMORY APPLICATION

The first example application in this book is the "memory" program that will search the PC's memory from 0x0A0000 to 0x0F0000 and indicate where RAM and ROM is located in the PC. The application itself is quite simple and I was able to complete it in a day. It does not access any file systems and is written entirely in C. When I ran it, I did find some interesting results and learned a bit more about how PC operating system works.

```
// MEMORY.C - Find What has been Plugged into the PC
//
// This Program is used to find unused memory in the PC, by looking
//  for RAM and ROM in the C8000 to DFFFF Memory Area. Memory that
//  is found is identified and Displayed on the Screen.
//
//  Myke Predko
//
//  Started: 98.10.16
//  Updated: xx.xx.xx
//

//  Include Files
#include <stdio.h>
#include <dos.h>
#include <asmprocs.h>

// Defines
#define KEYINT 0x016          // Codes for Reading a Character
#define KEYREAD 0x000

// Global Variables

// External Routines
// Subroutines
int MemCheck( unsigned long Addr, int far * Size ) // Look at Memory
{                                    // at Specified Addr/Determine Type
```

```c
char far * TestAddr;              // Pointer to the Test Address

long i;
int j;
char Temp;                        // Saved Value for RAM
long ROMSize;
int retvalue = 0;                 // Assume Nothing There

    ( long ) TestAddr = Addr;
    if (( TestAddr[ 0 ] == 0x055 ) && (( TestAddr[ 1 ] & 0xOFF )
                                                    == 0x0AA )) {

    ROMSize = TestAddr[ 2 ] * 512L; // Look for ROM

    for ( i = j = 0; i < ROMSize; i++ ) // Get CheckSum
      j += TestAddr[ i ];

    if (( j & 0xOFF ) == 0 ) { // Have Some ROM
      *Size = ROMSize / 512;
      retvalue = 2;
    } // endif
} // endif

if ( retvalue == 0 ) {        // Check for RAM
    Temp = TestAddr[ 0 ];
    CLI();                        // Disable Interrupts
    TestAddr[ 0 ] = TestAddr[ 0 ] ^ 0xOFF;
    if ((( Temp ^ 0xOFF ) & 0xOFF ) == TestAddr[ 0 ]) {
      TestAddr[ 0 ] = Temp;       // If Change, put back
      STI();                      // Turn Interrupts Back On
      retvalue = 1;
    } // endif
    STI();                        // Turn Interrupts Back On
  } // endif

  return retvalue;

} // MemCheck

// Mainline
main(argc, argv, envp)
 int argc;
 char *argv[];
 char *envp;
{
long i;
int j, k;

union REGS regs;

  printf( "Memory Check: +0x0400 +0x0800 +0x0C00 +0x1000 +0x1400 +0x1800
+0x1C00" );

  i = 0x0A0000L; // Start Reading
  while ( i < 0x0F0000L ) { // Loop to the End
    if (( i & 0x1FFFL ) == 0 )    // Start New Line?
      printf( "\n0x0%5lX ", i );
    if (( i & 0x03FFL ) == 0 )
```

```
            printf( " " );                    // Space Out Columns
        switch ( MemCheck( i < 12, &j ))
          {
            case 1:                           // RAM Found
              printf( "%c%c%c", 177, 177, 177 );
              i += 0x00200L;                  // Increment the Address
              break;
            case 2:                           // ROM Found
              for ( k = 0; k < j; k++ )    {
                printf( "%c%c%c", 219, 219, 219 );
                i += 0x00200L;              // Increment the Address
                if ((( i & 0x1FFFL )  == 0 ) && ( k < ( j - 1 )))
                  printf( "\n0x0%51X      ", i );
                if ((( i & 0x03FFL )  == 0 ) && ( k < ( j - 1 )))
                  printf( " " );            // Space Out Columns
              } // endfor
              break;
            default:                          // Nothing Found, Skip Over
              printf( " " );
              i += 0x00200L;                  // Increment the Address
          } // endswitch
        } // endwhile
      regs.h.ah = KEYREAD;                    // Wait for a Keystroke Before Ending
      int86( KEYINT, &regs, &regs );

      printf( "\n" );                          // Put in a New Line

} // end LIFE
```

The code itself checks each 512-byte boundary from the memory range by looking for first 0x055, then 0x0AA, and then for the checksum of zero for a built-in ROM. If no ROM is found, the current value is saved and then complemented to see if it actually consists of RAM. After the check is performed, blanks are written to the screen for neither ROM nor RAM, crosshatch characters for RAM and solid characters for ROM.

Each line of the application indicates the status of the 8192 bytes starting at the address in the left-hand column of the output. Each of the eight columns to the right of this value actually consists of two columns, with each one representing a block of 512 bytes. This was done to show how memory was actually set in the case of a small ROM. As you will see, when you run this application, chances are that the actual data will probably consist of the entire memory space allocated.

When you run this program, I suggest that you first enter:

```
Mode 80,50
```

Which will put the MS-DOS screen/window in to a 50 line by 80-character mode. This will be useful because the output is 40 lines long and a standard 25-line display will end up scrolling over the initial results. The program runs very quickly; don't be surprised if it completes in less than one second.

When I ran the program to test it, I got a number of very surprising results, as is shown in (Fig. 5-2). The program was run for my Windows '98 PC from the MS-DOS prompt window and shows that everything from 0x0A0000 to 0x0F0000 is RAM, except for the 32 KB from 0x0C0000 to 0x0C8000. When I tried this on a number of different PCs running the Win32 kernel, I got the same result which confused me.

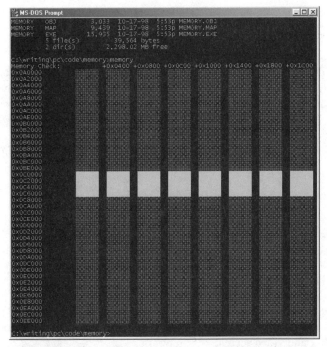

FIGURE 5-2   "Memory" executing in Windows/98

I then rebooted the PCs to execute in just MS-DOS mode and found that there was only RAM at 0x0B8000 to 0x0C0000 and ROM at 0x0C0000 to 0x0C8000. For video memory, this was in line with what I expected, but what I found was that network and SCSI adapter ROM was not showing up. Nobody could explain what was happening until I pulled open a machine and noticed that the adapter cards did not have jumpers or switches on them.

The lack of jumpers or switches meant that they were Plug'n'Play and were not "inserted" or "enumerated" into the system by MS-DOS (the version I used for the test was 5.01) and they did not have the ROM/RAM address decoders operating.

Going back to the unexpectedly large amount of RAM found in Windows (as shown in Fig. 5-2). I can only deduce that when Windows creates Protect mode "Emulated 8086s" for the MS-DOS prompt, rather than provide a window into the ISA busses expansion addresses (0x0A0000 to 0x0DFFFF) or BIOS ROM (0x0E0000 to 0x0FFFFF), Windows provides a simulated ROM for special functions and gives almost a full megabyte of RAM.

With this extra RAM, the question is what can be done with it. I would have to respond with an emphatic "nothing." Some of this RAM is memory mapped to the video display (i.e., you can write directly to it as if it were Video RAM in an MS-DOS system), which makes its operation a bit unpredictable. If you use this RAM in your application, then, in later versions of Windows, you might discover that it is no longer available, it cannot be used in MS-DOS applications because this RAM memory is simply not available.

The PCI/ISA Busses

The form of hardware interfacing to the PC you are probably most familiar with is the card bus. Your Pentium PC probably has four types of card busses: ISA, PCI, memory, and video. This book only addresses the first two. The memory card bus is really Pentium support chipset and motherboard specific, with different pinouts, speeds, and devices used in different situations. The modern video bus is *AGP (Advanced Graphics Processor)*; the design of adapters for this bus is beyond the scope of this book and is very device specific.

The *PCI (Peripheral Control Interface)* and ISA busses meet my definitions of a bus, which include:

1 System power
2 Power up and reset signals
3 Processor memory access
4 Processor I/O port access
5 Interrupt request hardware
6 DMA request and acknowledge hardware

Each of these features allows a very wide variety of adapter cards to be plugged into the slots. These features were used in the original PC and PC/AT to provide the standard I/O interfaces (such as disk and video access).

The ISA bus was introduced with the PC/AT as a 16-bit enhancement to the PC's 8-bit I/O bus. The term *ISA (Industry Standard Architecture)* came about when the PC/AT and "clone" manufacturers wanted to provide a system that was compatible with IBM's (I presume that "Industry Standard Architecture" is more palatable than "IBM PC/AT compatible" to IBM's competitors).

The ISA bus itself provides an 8- or 16-bit interface to the processor's I/O and memory busses, but with a number of caveats. The big one is that only a subset of the total I/O and memory addresses are available on the bus. If you look at Appendix D, you'll see that only I/O addresses 0x0100 to 0x03FF and memory addresses 0x0C8000 to 0x0DFFFF are available on the bus. To make matters worse, of these addresses, only certain of these addresses are available to your own applications because many of the available addresses are already allocated to system resources, such as the disk controllers and the video drivers.

The ISA bus is best characterized as a cleaned-up 8086 bus, with the built-in addresses filtered out. This filtering is important because, for high-speed accesses (such as memory), no wait states are required when bus devices are not being accessed. When a bus device is accessed, "wait states" are inserted to allow the bus device the specification time to respond. The problem is that during an ISA bus access, literally hundreds of CPU clock cycles can occur (especially in Pentium III PCs).

One interesting aspect of the ISA bus is the difference in data speeds between the 8- and 16-bit transfers. Eight-bit transfers normally occur at the PC's 760-ns cycle time, but 16-bit transfers are only given 160 ns to complete. This difference often trips up engineers, who think that they can double the data-transfer speeds by going from 8 to 16 bits. They find out that the transfers are almost five times faster in 16-bit mode. The actual speed up is about nine and a half times.

ISA is a good general-purpose bus, but even at 160 ns per word, it cannot transfer data quickly enough for some devices and the number of wait states added to the processor is prohibitive. Such devices as disks, video, and networking require a faster bus to keep up with the speed improvements to the processor. Over the past 15 years or so, a number of different busses have been introduced to eliminate this bottleneck. The apparent victor is PCI, which can transfer data at up to 66 MBps.

PCI, from a high-level overview, has many of the same features as ISA, but actually uses a very complex protocol to determine card parameters and provide initial reads and writes. The PCI bus is introduced in this book, but the intricacies of actually interfacing to the bus are not included because of the need for a specially designed ASIC for the purpose.

I/O SPACE AND BUS

Along with the memory space, the 8086 family of microprocessors has a separate 64-KB I/O space, which provides registers to control the hardware. As you would expect, many of the individual addresses have been allocated, leaving only a few available for user-defined interfaces. Knowing which register addresses are available and how they are accessed can be challenging in a modern PC. This is a major advantage of the serial busses being installed in PCs, such as USB and Firewire.

When IBM first designed the PC, the full 64-KB was thought to be overkill, with many times more registers than a small computer would ever require. As well, the digital electronics of time were largely restricted to TTL chips, which used a lot of chips (needing more board space and cost) to implement additional decoding functions. In this light, decoding all 16 address bits was deemed as wasteful. The result was when the PC I/O space was specified; the top six bits of the address space were ignored.

This gave the PC 1024 actual I/O register addresses. At the time, this seemed like a lot, not a restriction. Even four years later, when the PC/AT was introduced, the 1024 addresses were not seen as too few.

As another restriction, the 8086 is capable of addressing I/O registers as 16- or 8-bit values. This was not an issue with the original 8088 (which is only capable of 8 bits at a time), but when the PC/AT was designed, multiplexing the 16-bit data bus of the 80286 to 8 bits created a separate I/O bus. This 8-bit bus has continued to today.

As I write this, the PC was first released more than 17 years ago and technology has changed, resulting in the original 1024 addresses being insufficient. But, to remain compatible with previous versions of the PC, we are still stuck with just 1024 8-bit port I/O addresses.

In many modern implementations of the PC, the addresses above 0x03FF (1023 decimal) are used for advanced functions. These functions or addresses should not be used by your applications. To avoid possible conflicts, I recommend that the most significant six bits of the I/O space be decoded and compared against zero to be sure that there are no conflicts with any possible devices located in the 63 KB addresses above the "defined" 1,024.

In Appendix E, I have outlined the common I/O addresses, along with special hardware addresses that have been added over the years. When you look at the addresses, it is important to remember that addresses 0x0000 to 0x0100 are for devices on the motherboard and might not be available on any of the busses.

The I/O space addresses can be blocked out, as shown:

ADDRESS	DEVICE
0000h-001Fh	DMA controller 1
0020h-003Fh	Interrupt controller 1
0040h-005Fh	Timer
0060h-006Fh	Keyboard interface
0070h-007Fh	CMOS/Real-time clock
0080h	MFG_PORT register
0081h-009Fh	DMA page registers
00A0h-00BFh	Interrupt controller 2
00C0h-00DFh	DMA controller 2
00E0h-00EFh	Reserved
00F0h-00FFh	Numeric copocessor
0100h-01EFh	Reserved/used in the PS/2
01F0h-01FFh	Hard disk controller
0200h-0207h	Joystick interface
0208h-0277h	Undefined in PC specification
0278h-027Fh	Parallel port 2 (LPT2)
0280h-02E7h	Undefined in PC specification
02E8h-02EFh	Serial Port 3 (COM3)
02F0h-02F7h	Undefined in PC specification
02F8h-02FFh	Serial Port 2 (COM2)
0300h-031Fh	Prototype card
0320h-035Fh	Undefined in PC specification
0360h-036Fh	Reserved
0370h-0377h	Undefined in PC specification
0378h-037Fh	Parallel port 1 (LPT1)
0380h-038Fh	SDLC communications control
0390h-039Fh	Undefined in PC specification
03A0h-03AFh	Bisynchronous serial communications controller
03B0h-03BFh	Monochrome display adapter/Integrated LPT1 Printer Port
03C0h-03CFh	Reserved
03D0h-03DFh	Color graphics adapter

ADDRESS	DEVICE
03E0h-03EFh	Undefined in PC specification
03F0h-03F7h	Diskette controller
03F8h-03FFh	Serial port 1 (COM1)

These registers can be addressed with the not decoded bits set. For example, serial port 1 should "show up" at addresses 0x03F8, 0x07F8, 0x0BF8, 0x0FF8, 0x013F8, etc. Accessing registers by setting upper address bits is not recommended because, in some chipsets, these addresses might be used by the system.

The motherboard hardware is located below I/O space address 0x0100. The reason for this is to allow the motherboard registers to be accessed using the Direct, In, and Out instructions, which do not require DX to be set with the actual address. Being able to use the direct I/O instructions allows much faster access to the motherboard and system-specific instructions.

It is important to remember that the I/O addresses are all 8 bits wide. Sixteen-bit I/O port In and Out instructions must not be used because they will be changed in the PC's hardware to two 8-bit accesses. Even if you were to design an adapter that could use 16-bit I/O transfers (other than DMA) on the ISA bus, you will probably find that the actual accesses will be converted to two 8-bit transfers.

Interrupt Allocation

A type of resource that is often overlooked in the PC is interrupts (hardware interrupt requests, as well as BIOS-like API requests). Like memory, this resource is often overlooked and not planned for appropriately. Interrupts in the PC also have a reputation for being difficult to work with and fully allocated, which might make people ask, "Why bother to use interrupts?"

Interrupts, once the issues regarding the difficulty in using them is overcome, can actually improve your application and make it easier to write. Later in the book is a comprehensive explanation of how interrupts work and how to write their "handlers."

Once you understand and can work with interrupts, you will discover that basically none are available in the PC. Part of being able to apply interrupts in the PC is understanding what is available and how they can be shared. Hardware Interrupts are normally "shared" with standard device interrupts; for software interrupts, the Multiplex interrupt is used to provide new BIOS functions within the PC without using already allocated interrupt interfaces.

Protect-Mode Hardware Features

When the PC/AT first came out, IBM wanted to take advantage of the 80286's Protect mode to allow the development of multitasking RTOS; the 80286 initially booted up in Real (8086 compatible) mode and then could be placed in 16-bit Protect mode.

A problem with the 80286 was that it could not be taken out of Protect mode from software. The solution was to use address bit 20 as a request for initiating a reset. When the hardware was set, a write to an address above the 1-MB boundary would cause the motherboard to reset the 80286 and restart in Real mode.

Before the reset was initiated by the keyboard controller, a four-byte area is set to an expected value (0x0FF00AA55) and this is checked in BIOS. During POST, if this value is found, then the hardware initialization is ignored and the code jumps directly to a vector set in another location in memory. By using these features (although I'm reluctant to describe them as such), Protect-mode programs could execute from MS-DOS and return to Windows.

You may be aware that the 80286 could be "tricked" out of protect mode by what is know as a "triple fault inerrupt." This is an invalid instruction which does not have a defined error handler. When the instruction is executed, it wll cause an internal error (invalid instruction) followed by two more errors due to a missing handler and an exceed error limit. At the end of the three errors, the processor resets and returns to real mode. This trick was not known when the PC/AT was being designed and the hardware implementation was used instead.

In the 80386 (and faster) processors, this feature, although it is usually built into the motherboard's hardware, is not required to return the processor to Real mode. If you look at a number of applications, you will probably be surprised to see that it is actually used instead of the software methods because it is easier to implement.

PC
INTERFACE
SOFTWARE

6

BASIC

ASSEMBLER

PROGRAMMING

This book has focused on assembler programming, instead of specific high-level language programming thus far to explain the operation of the PC. Chances are, you are not planning to do any assembler programming for the rest of your life (which, all in all, is not a bad plan). I find that the actual bits and byte accesses and paths can be most easily visualized with assembler code.

Another reason is one of the things I am famous for: my debugging of applications in assembler. Normally, I write my applications in C, but I am able to predict what I expect to see in the assembler code and I can usually find the problem quite quickly. This is especially useful when I'm working with pointers in C. This probably sounds more than a bit strange; but it is how I am most efficient when debugging an application.

Regardless of the plans you have for the future, if you are going to be doing any type of systems level programming, you are going to have to be able to write some assembler code. I realize that most high-level languages give you the capability of accessing specific I/O registers and interrupt vectors, but to get exactly what you want out of an application, driver or understand what your high level code is doing to the hardware.

Assembler Directives

Directives are statements in a source file that are only recognized by the assembler or compiler as instructions to it. These directives indicate which processor is active, how the segment is arranged, and many other options.

The following list is used for Microsoft Macro Assembler (MASM) 6.11, but many other PC assemblers use the same directives or similar ones with the same method of operation.

DIRECTIVE	FUNCTION
.186	Enable 80186 instruction assembly.
.286	Enable basic 80286 and 80287 instruction assembly.
.286p	Enable all 80286 and 80287 instruction assembly, including Protect mode.
.287	Enable 80287 numeric coprocessor instruction assembly.
.386	Enable Nonprotect mode 80386 and 80387 instruction assembly.
.386p	Enable all 80386 and 80287 instruction assembly, including Protect-mode instructions.
.387	Enable 80387 numeric coprocessor instruction assembly.
.486	Enable 80486 instruction assembly.
.486p	Enable 80486 instruction assembly, including Protect-mode instructions.
.8086	Default/enable 8086 and 8087 instruction assembly.
.8087	Enable 8087 instruction assembly.
ALIGN	Aligns the next variable or instruction in the listing file on the boundary specified after the Align statement (usually "2" or "4").
.ALPHA	Order the segments alphabetically.
ASSUME	Enables checking on segment registers. If a variable is outside of the current segment, an error will be produced by the assembler.
.BREAK	Stops executing within a conditional assembly .WHILE or .REPEAT Loop.

DIRECTIVE	FUNCTION
BYTE	Reserve a set number of bytes in memory that is optionally initialized.
CATSTR	Concatenate text items.
.CODE	Indicates the start of the code segment when used with the .MODEL directive. The code segment name is specified after the .CODE directive.
COMM	Create a communal variable of different data types.
COMMENT	Place a comment in the source. The most common single character for this function is the semicolon (;).
.CONST	When used with the .MODEL directive, a read-only segment is defined.
.CONTINUE	Jumps to the specified label from within a .WHILE or .REPEAT loop.
.CREF	Enables the listing to provide a label address cross reference.
.DATA	When used with the .MODEL directive, a data segment (read and write) is defined.
.DOSSEG	Orders segments according to MS-DOS conventions, code, segments not in DGROUP, DGROUP segments, and stack segments.
DB	Define byte.
DD	Define double word.
DQ	Define quad word (8 bytes).
DT	Define 10 bytes.
DW	Define word.
DWORD	Reserve a set number of double words in memory that is optionally Initialized.
ECHO	Displays message during assembly. Same as %OUT.
.ELSE	Marks the end of a conditional block with start of complement condition block.
.ELSEIF	Combines .ELSE and .IF into one statement.
.ELSEIF2	ELSE/IF evaluated on every assembly path.
.ENDIF	Mark the end of the conditional assembly block.
ENDM	Indicate the end of the macro definition.
ENDP	Indicate the end of a subroutine.
ENDS	Indicate the end of data to be stored in a segment.
.ENDW	Indicate the end of a .WHILE loop.

DIRECTIVE	FUNCTION
EQU	Specify that a label is to be replaced with a constant.
.ERR	Force an error from the source (conditional code).
.ERRB	This directive is passed a string. If the string is blank, then force an error.
.ERRDEF	Force an error if a label is already defined.
.ERRDIF	Compare two strings and force an error if they are different.
.ERRE	Evaluate an expression and force an error if the result is equal to zero.
.ERRIDN	Compare two strings and force an error if they are the same.
.ERRNB	Force an error if a string is not blank.
.EFFNDEF	Force an error if the label is not defined.
.ERRNZ	Evaluate an expression and force an error is it is not equal to zero.
EVEN	Aligns the next variable or instruction onto an even byte.
.EXIT	Generates terminate code; the application execution will return to command.com.
EXITM	Stops macro expansion.
EXTERN	Specify that a label is external to the current file (also EXTRN).
EXTERNDEF	Similar to EXTERN, but is used to make defines in the file PUBLIC.
.FARDATA	When used with .MODEL a far data segment for initialized data is created.
FOR	Repeat a block of code for a number of arguments. Same as IRP.
FORC	Repeat a block of code, once for each character in a string. Same as IRPC.
GOTO	Transfers conditional assembly to a new location.
GROUP	Add the specified segments to the name of a specified group.
.IF	Assemble the following statements if the condition is true.
IF2	IF evaluated through each assembler pass.
IFB	Assemble code if string is blank.
IFDEF	Assemble code if label is defined.
IFDIF	Compare two strings and assemble if different.
IFE	Evaluate expression and assemble if result is equal to zero.
IFIDN	Compare two strings and assemble if the same.

DIRECTIVE	FUNCTION
IFNB	Assemble following code if condition is not equal to zero.
IFNDEF	Assemble code if label is not defined.
INCLUDE	Insert a Source Code File in the Source File Text.
INSTR	Search a string for an occurrence of a second string and return the starting position.
INVOKE	Call the assembly procedure.
LABEL	Create a new label at the current address.
.LALL	Starts listing of macro expansion statements. Same as .LISTMACROALL.
.LFCOND	Starts listing of statements in false conditional assembly blocks. Same as .LISTIF.
.LIST	Default. Starts listing of statements. Same as .LISTALL.
.LISTMACRO	Start listing of macro expansion statements. Same as .XALL.
LOCAL	Used within a macro to specify a label that is only used within the current macro.
MACRO	Define a block of code that will replace a keyword.
.MODEL	Initializes the program memory model, high-level language types and stack type. Valid memory types are: TINY, SMALL, COMPACT, MEDIUM, LARGE, HUGE, or FLAT. Valid language types are: C, BASIC, FORTRAN, PASCAL, SYSCALL, and STDCALL. Valid stack types are: NEARSTACK and FARSTACK.
.NO87	Force an error if a numeric coprocessor instruction is encountered.
.NOCREF	Do not produce a label address cross reference. Same as .XCREF.
.NOLIST	Turn off file listing. Same as .XLIST.
.NOLISTIF	Turn off file listing if the condition's result is equal to zero. Same as .SFCOND.
OPTION	Used to enable/disable assembler features.
ORG	Set the address of the code to the specified address.
PAGE	Force a listing page break.
POPCONTEXT	Restore the context register information.
PROC	Define a subroutine.
PUBLIC	Define a label to be accessible in external source files.
PURGE	Delete the specified macros from memory.

DIRECTIVE	FUNCTION
PUSHCONTEXT	Save the current context register information.
QWORD	Allocate and optionally initialize an 8-byte block.
.RADIX	Set the radix used by the assembler (2, 10, and 16 valid). The default is 16 (Hex).
REAL4	Allocate four bytes for a real variable.
REAL8	Allocate eight bytes for a real variable.
REAL10	Allocate 10 bytes for a real variable.
RECORD	Declare a data structure with the given bit definitions.
.REPEAT	Repeat a block of code until the condition is false. Same as REPT.
.SALL	Turn off macro expansion listing. Same as .NOLISTMACRO.
SBYTE	Allocate and initialize a signed byte.
SDWORD	Allocate and initialize a signed double word.
SEGMENT	Define a segment to be used for code or data.
.SEQ	Order segments sequentially.
SIZESTR	Return the size of the string.
.STACK	When used with .MODEL defines a stack segment.
.STARTUP	Generates .EXE start-up code.
STRUC	Define a data structure. Same as STRUCT.
SUBSTR	Return the specified substring.
SUBTITLE	Define a subtitle for the listing. Same as SUBTTL.
SWORD	Allocate and initialize a signed word.
TBYTE	Allocate and initialize 10 bytes of memory.
TEXTEQU	Assign a string to a label.
.TFCOND	Toggles listing of false conditional blocks.
TITLE	Defines a title for the program listing. TYPEDEF defines a new type of data structure.
UNION	Defines multiple data structures that can use the same block of memory.
.UNTIL	Condition statement for .REPEAT.
.UNTILCXZ	Used with .REPEAT and will return to .REPEAT directive until CX is equal to zero.
.WHILE	Repeat conditional code operation until the condition is false.
WORD	Allocate and initialize a word.

8086 Segment Allocation

The segmented architecture of the PC provides a fairly low level of protection for code and the data against invalid writes. To take advantage of these features, you must plan out how the data and code segments are to be arranged. The Section MS-DOS Command-Line Programming describes the different types of executable files and how the segments are arranged. This covers the mechanics of declaring segments in assembler.

Before any variables can be declared or code written, the segment that it is going to be located in must be declared using the Segment directive. A segment can be combined with others as *external, local,* or *public* and is defined to start on a paragraph (16 byte) default boundary.

A segment is defined as:

```
SegName    SEGMENT (alignment) (combine) [`class´]
:
SegName    ENDS
```

The *Alignment* option determines whether or not the segment starts at the next *byte, word,* or *paragraph* from the previous segment. Normally the Paragraph default is best because the segment registers cannot access data on byte or word boundaries.

The *Combine* option allows you to define where the segment is to be located and if it is to be shared with other segments.

COMBINE TYPE	DESCRIPTION
AT 0x0####	Specify a location where the segment will physically reside. This type cannot be used with code, but with data, such as video RAM or BIOS system variables.
PUBLIC	The segment in the current object file is added to the segments in other files that have been given the same segment name.
COMMON	All segments that have this segment name share the same memory area. The segment's size is not a function of the sum of the sizes used in each of the object files, as PUBLIC uses.
STACK	Define a stack segment.

The *class* is used to group segment types together and can be *code, data,* or *stack.*

Along with the segment command, the *Assume* directive is used to indicate to the assembler how the registers are initially set up. The format for this command is:

```
ASSUME CS:CodeSegName [, . .]
```

To Set CS to CodeSeg and DS to DataSeg, the assume statement for the procedure is:

```
ASSUME CS:CodeSeg, DS:DataSeg
```

What I really haven't answered is how the segments should be used. You could go to such extremes as a code segment per subroutine, with its own data segment or one segment for all the code and data in the application.

In MS-DOS, other than in the case of a .COM application, you are really open to however you want to structure the program. I always use the "large" model (which uses an intersegment call) and "far" pointers, so this is not a significant issue for me. Personally, I like to set up an AsmCode and an AsmData segment for all of my assembly-language routines. This eliminates the need to figure out multiple, appropriate segment names and it offers some protection from invalid code overwriting a routine's code and data.

Defining Variables

Once the segment to be used for storing variables has been defined, the variables are declared using the *define byte* (*DB,* eight bits), *define word* (*DW,* 16 bits), *define doubleword* (*DD,* 32 bits), *define quadword* (*DQ,* 64 bits), and *define tenbytes* (*DT,* 80 bits). Each of these different types of data can be used with the STRUC directive to create any type of data structure required for the different instructions or applications.

The basic format for defining a variable is:

```
Label D? [n dup(] [init | ?] [)]
```

Where *D?* is the DB, DW, DD, DQ, or DT directives. In this definition/declaration statement, a variable can be defined with a label and given an arbitrary number of bytes or initialized with a value or string.

For example:

```
VarA DW 77
```

Allocates two bytes (16 bits) for *VarA* and initializes the memory to 0x0004D (77 decimal).

```
VarB db 77 dup ( ? )
```

Allocates 77 bytes of memory to the label *VarB,* but does not specify an initial value for the 77 bytes.

The *dup* directive repeats the number times you want the data type. The argument before *dup* specifies how many times the type is to be used and *dup's* argument is the initial value. Note that in the previous sentence I use the term *type* instead of variable. Arrays of structures can be repeated along with the D? types.

The definitions are very straightforward with the only thing to watch for is the DD instruction that can be used for a pointer and 32 bits of data. Normally, the initial value is stored in offset/segment order (which is the default for 32 bit pointers in the 8086).

The DQ and DT variable definitions are best suited for 8087 floating-point unit variables.

Strings can easily be defined by placing ASCII text in a single quote. Additional characters and strings can be concatenated using a comma.

For example:

```
String DB "This is an ASCIIZ String", 0
```

To place single quotes (´) into the text, the ASCII value 0x02C must be used. In the previous example, if I wanted to place "ASCIIZ" in single quotes, I would have to use the initialization:

```
String DB "This is an", 02Ch, "ASCIIZ", 02Ch, "String", 0
```

The STRUC directive allows variable declarations to be grouped together in a structure, similar to what is available in C or Pascal. The format of STRUC can be used to declare a 32-bit pointer. I use this declaration so often that I normally place it in all of my assembly-language source files:

```
FarPtr STRUC
PtrOff DW ?
PtrSeg DW ?
FarPtr ENDS
```

When a structure is defined, initial values for the elements in the structure can be initialized or left as "?".

Variable in this format are defined using the format:

```
struc_Variable struc_name [:Initial Values]
```

The initial values can be set if the initial values in the structure are left to "?".

Source Code Formatting

Well-written assembly language code is difficult to read (at best) and can be totally cryptic (at worst). When writing assembly-language code for the PC, I recommend a few conventions to make your assembly code easier to read and faster to write and debug.

What really helps with assembler source files is to lay them out consistently and group functional blocks together. When I create the code, I create "chapters" or "sections" to the code in the following order:

1 Header and revision information
2 Publics and Externals
3 Constants
4 Macros
5 Structures
6 Segment information
7 Variables
8 Mainline
9 Subroutines
10 Closing information

The header/revision information that I use generally takes the form:

```
title 'FileName - Single Line Description. . .'
;
```

```
;  Filename
;
;  Revision Number : #.##
;  Revision Date: ##/##/##
;
;  Myke Predko
;
;  Description of File Contents/Description of Subroutines
;
;  Linking Information
;
;  Revision History:
;
page
```

The *title* will be placed on the first line of all subsequent pages in the listing file. I like putting in the filename on the top of each page so that complete page sets can be recreated later if they are mixed up (which happens occasionally—especially when you live in a house with three children who are constantly looking for paper to draw on). Also, a *Subtitle* directive places information after the title, but I don't tend to use it because it becomes active *after* the page it is on, which isn't useful because many of the sections are only one page long.

At the top of the title, I include commented file and revision information, the author, along with a detailed file description and comments on how this file is to be linked with others.

The linking information is probably the most crucial information in this section. *Linking files* is the operation of concatenating object data together into a final executable file. The object files are generated from the source files from an assembler program.

As described elsewhere in the book, a number of different executable formats have different addressing and segmentation options. This means that the constituent object files of an executable application must be compatible in these two areas.

I also like to list the changes made to the source in the first section of the code. Marking changes in the actual source can be confusing and reduce its already limited readability.

Publics and *Externals* are subroutine and function labels that are located in the file and are accessed by external routines. They are also routines in other files that are accessed by the routines in the current file. Although publics and externals can be variables located elsewhere in the application, I like to limit them to functions and subroutines and then pass variables as parameters, rather than relying on "global" variables.

The terms *publics* and *externals* can be confusing; I always remember how to use each one by noting that I am making internal labels *public*. When I want to access something outside of the file, it is *external*.

Very often, I place the needed constants and macros in files that are included at assembly time. This saves me from having to update all the local copies of the values when I update one file with new information. A central declaration file allows me to look for data without moving from the current location in the source file that I am working on.

Structures are not really useful in assembler, except in very limited cases (such as for defining the 4-byte pointer structure shown elsewhere). If you are going to use complex data structures in your application, I would definitely recommend writing it in a high-level language, rather than assembler.

All the information that follows is actual code and data, so segments are required. Ideally, each file would have one segment for the routines and place all the required variables into a common segment, so DS does not have to changed when accessing data in different source files. PC-application memory and segmentation models are described later in the book.

I format my code based on a "2-1-3" tab count. Labels are placed on the first column of a line, instructions two tabs over. Instruction parameters are one tab from the instruction and comments are three tabs from the parameters.

```
Label:      Ins. Parameters     ; Comments
```

Using eight columns per tab, this works out to at least 48 columns, which fits on an assembler listing file nicely and allows reasonable label and variable lengths.

When I do rep instructions, I normally place the *rep* at the *Ins*. Position and the instruction at the parameter tab location:

```
rep    movsb
```

This format is the least ambiguous for me because people often put the repeat a few columns over from the left edge, which can be confusing with labels and assembler directives.

When I use comments, I try to make them meaningful and explain, in high-level terms, what the relevant assembler code is doing. For example, if I wanted to decrement an index and jump if the result is equal to zero, I would use the code:

```
dec    Index
jz     Label
```

I feel that it is totally unaccepable and wasteful to simply repeat what the instructions are doing:

```
dec    Index                    ; Decrement "Index"
jz     Label                    ; If Zero Flag Set, Jump to
                                 ; "Label"
```

This is not telling the reader anything useful. Instead, I feel that it is important to put in comments that state, from a high level, what is happening.

One very common way to document assembler application code is to use high-level language statements:

```
dec    Index                    ; if ( --Index==. )
jz     Label                    ;    goto Label
```

Although this is a bit clearer, it still does not explain what is happening in the application. This code is explaining how a C compiler would convert the statements in the comments into the assembler instructions.

The best comments for the instructions explain what the code is doing in relation to the application:

```
dec    Index                    ; Point to the Previous
jz     label                    ; Element and Stop if at
                                 ; the Start of the Table
```

If you have to look at the code years down the road, you'll be happy you spent the extra effort putting in meaningful comments that explain exactly what is happening.

White space (blank lines) is useful to help distinguish between blocks of code. For example:

```
      or    BX, BX              ;  If At Array Start
      jnz   Skip                ;     Increment the Counter
      inc   AX
      jnz   Skip
      inc   DX
Skip:
```

Is easier to read and understand as:

```
      or    BX, BX              ;  If At Array Start
      jnz   Skip                ;     Increment the Counter

      inc   AX
      jnz   Skip
      inc   DX
Skip:
```

With the functional blocks exposed with appropriate comments, I find it much easier to see what the assembler code is doing.

I always run out of label names in assembler. Useful ones include *end*, *loop*, *skip*, and *delay*. Note that *end* is an assembler directive and *loop* is actually an 8086 instruction.

To use and help differentiate these labels, I will put the subroutine acronym in from of these standards.

Instead of:

```
GetChar:                          ;  Get a Character from the
                                  ;     Input Device
   :
                  jnz   End
   :
End:
                  Ret             ;  Return to Caller
```

which prevents *end* from being used anywhere else in the application, I would use:

```
GetChar:              ;  Get a Character from the
                      ;     Input Device

   :
                  jnz   GC_End
   :
GC_END
                  Ret             ;  Return to Caller
```

In the second case, *end* is not only restricted to the end of the assembler file (in the first case, you would get a syntax error if you were to assemble that code) and it can be used in other subroutines. Using the acronym of the subroutine name with a label service two purposes. The first is the basic label can be repeated or used if it were impossible before. The second is, that misplaced labels (i.e., inadvertent jumping between subroutines) can be easily found.

Floating Point Programming

In this chapter, I will recommend that you avoid three types of assembly-language programming. Floating-point programming is the first; the other two are MMX and Protect mode. I don't feel it is reasonable to write floating-point code when high-level languages can create the code for you at least as efficiently as if you were going to do it yourself. By using a high-level language, you will avoid the hassles of working with the instructions and their peculiarities.

Having said this, you can work with the floating-point instruction set, built into the processor quite reasonably and in the process, learn something about compilers. So, don't skip onto the next section, I promise that something here is quite useful in everyday programming.

When you use floating-point instructions, always use them in a block of code that carries out a complete operation and do not execute a conditional jump based on the results of operations. If you are going to use the results of a floating-point operation to base a test, convert the result to a word or double word, and carry out a compare on that. If you follow this rule, you will find that your code is a lot easier to write.

The floating-point processor is a stack-based machine, which means that parameters to be operated upon have to be loaded onto the stack before executing.

For the example statement:

$$A = B + C$$

The floating-point instructions to execute the code would be:

```
fld    B           ; Push "B"
fld    C           ; Push "C"
fadd               ; Add the Two Elements on the Top of the Stack
fst    A           ; Pop the Result off the Stack
```

The first two instructions push B and C onto the floating-point processor's stack. *fadd* pops the top two elements off the stack, adds them together and pushes the result onto the stack. *Fst* pops the result and stores it in A.

More-complex high-level statements can be carried out this way as well:

$$A = B + [C * (D - E)]$$

Can be simply coded by pushing the statement parameters onto the stack in the order of highest priority:

```
fld    D
fld    E
fsub               ; D - E
fld    C
fmul               ; C * ( D - E )
fld    B
fadd               ; B + ( C * ( D - E ))
fst    A
```

This is exactly how a high-level language converts a statement into a usable form for the processor. The highest-priority operations are pushed onto a stack (which could be the processor's general-purpose registers, in the case of the 8086) and then popped off and operated upon. At the end of the series of instructions, the result is popped off the stack and stored.

Older HP calculators worked in this mode, which was known as *Reverse Polish Notation*. The reference to the calculator is useful because this is the best way to use the floating-point processor. The operation could be expanded to include conditional operations, but I shy away from them because, to be sure that they are complete, you have to poll the floating-point processor's status word's bit 15 (the busy flag) until you can safely use the arithmetic result flags. The reason for this is that the floating-point processor is separate from the core processor. Its instructions do not necessarily complete before the standard processor begins to execute after reading in the floating-point instruction. I realize that this relegates the floating-point unit to just being a number cruncher, but when you are writing in assembler, this is the best use for it.

Real-Mode Programming

With the different processor modes described, Real mode, 16-bit Protect mode, and Flat 32-bit Protect mode, I have to explain that Real mode is the 16-bit 8086-compatible operating mode that the PC's processor first boots up in. Real mode (MS-DOS) software cannot run in full Windows, except within the emulated MS-DOS prompt window.

In this book, I give MS-DOS Real-mode applications primarily written in C, but they could be ported to assembler with very few changes (other than the assembly-language code will be very complex). This is not true for Windows Protect mode applications, which should never be written in assembler because of the complexity of accessing the Windows APIs.

Protect-Mode Programming

When I was writing this book and thought about protect-mode programming in assembler, I remembered my experiences in doing it in 1989 for a PC memory card test and I realized that I could write this whole section using only one word: "don't."

Protect-mode programming in assembler can be very hard to get running. However, you won't have the most basic problem that I had in 1989—the unavailability of working 80386 assemblers. You will have the issue of not having any working debuggers or other tools unless you buy them specific to your needs (or modify your needs to what is available). If you want to use interrupts, you're going to have to develop your own device drivers to handle I/O interrupts and work out how you are going to return to Real mode (for MS-DOS).

Hopefully, I have scared you off from ever wanting to create an assembly-language Protect-mode application (or any Protect-mode application from MS-DOS or any other Real-mode operating system). I created an application that jumps from Real-mode MS-DOS to a Protect-mode "flat" 32-bit memory area and it took me two weeks of 16-hour days to get it running. There has to be some compelling reason to run in Real mode (for me, the requirement was to test memory 32 bits at a time in the memory above the 1-MB region at a time when there was no "native" operating system support yet). If you want to do it just to learn the most possible about the 80386 (and higher) processors, then I would suggest that you are better off becoming an expert at Windows interfacing.

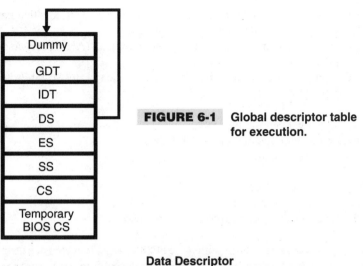

FIGURE 6-1 Global descriptor table for execution.

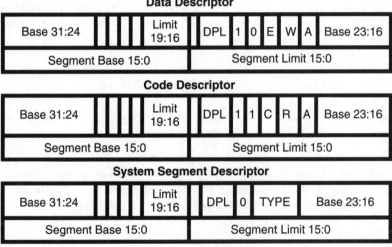

A - Access
C - Conforming
DPL - Descriptor Privilege Level
E - Expand-Down
Limit - Segment Limit
R - Readable
W - Writeable

FIGURE 6-2 Protect mode descriptors.

If you are going to work in 16-bit Protect mode, then you can use the BIOS interrupt 015h system services with AH = 089h to start the application running after creating a global descriptor table that is in the format of Fig. 6-1.

Each descriptor table entry is 8 bytes long. The dummy descriptor table is 8 bytes of zeros. The GDT is simply a pointer to the table itself. The format for the other descriptors is defined as in Fig. 6-2.

The IDT is the interrupt descriptor table. It points to a series of vectors that handle the primary interrupt controller (at I/O address 0x020) output.

With this GDT built, you can execute the BIOS interrupt 015h (AH = 089h) and execute in 80286 (16 bit) Protect mode.

You can also execute the following steps in your own code to enter 16-bit Protect mode without the BIOS function:

- Save the SS:LP in the DS descriptor table.
- Save the Real-mode return address at 0x040:0x0067
- Set the CMOS shut-down bit.
- Build the GDT.
- Enable A20 on the address bus.
- Set the Protect-mode bit in the processor's MSW register.
- Jump to clear the prefetch queue/Protect-mode address.

To exit from the 80286 Protect mode, either the 80286's reset is cycled or a "triple fault" interrupt. In this code, loading the IDT with an invalid (zero) limit will cause the processor to request an interrupt 8, which is invalid, followed by (an invalid instruction which fails again), and the processor resets.

The code to do this is:

```
Real286    dw    0, 0, 0 ; Six Zero Words
Skip:

lidt       Real286      ; Set limit Pointer to zero
mov        eax.cro      ; Execute invalid
```

I have not explained this operation in complete detail because of the few 80286-processored machines out there. Of greater interest is 80386 machines, on which Protect mode is to be run. I want to go into more detail about the 80386 and its 32-bit "flat memory model" Protect mode. To enter 80386 Protect mode, the following steps are taken:

- Build the GDT.
- Enable A20 on the address bus.
- Enable Protect mode in the processor-controller register.
- Jump to clear the prefetch queue.

The global descriptor table is the same 64 bytes long; each element can be defined as:

```
DescTable Struc
Seglimit          DW ?
SegBaseLow        DW ?
SegBaseMid        DB ?
DTAcc             DW ?
SegBasHi          DB ?
DesctTable ENDS
```

For the DTAcc word, you can use the value 0x00093 for both code and data. This will give you a 32-bit addressed segment that is 32 bits wide.

To enable A20 to use the processor's value, the keyboard controller has to have 0x0DF written at I/O address 0x0064.

To enable Protect mode, the processor's CR0 or MSW must have bit zero set and then a jump is made to clear the prefetch queue.

To return from 80386 Protect mode, the sequence of instructions that must be executed are:

```
Real386     DW 03FFh        ; Restore the Real Modes Interrupt Table

   :

   mov      EAX, CR0

   LIDT     Real386         ; Reset the Interrupt Table

   and      AL, 0x0FE       ; Turn off Protect Mode Bit

   mov      CR0, EAX

   jmp      RealAddr        ; Jump to the Real Address
```

I realize that this doesn't look that difficult to do, but I have to emphasize that jumping from Real mode to Protect mode and back again successfully is one of the most masochistic things you can ever do.

If you insist on working with Protect mode from MS-DOS, then I have a few recommendations:

■ Have an assembler that supports 808386 instructions.
■ Get a copy of an Intel *Programmer's Reference* and *Operating System Reference* manuals.
■ Do not use 80286 (16 bit) mode.
■ Set up the full (4.3 GB) memory spaces accessible for both data and memory.
■ Run the Protect-mode program from Ring 0.
■ Don't get clever. Avoid BIOS interfaces, interrupt handlers, and virtual memory.
■ Understand how upper memory is mapped for EMM, MS-DOS, and other drivers, and avoid that area of memory.

Even with this, expect to spend several weeks, full time, creating your first working Protect-mode application. As one hint, if all you are doing is transferring data between upper memory and the first 1 MB of Real mode, I highly recommend that you use BIOS interrupt 015h, AH = 087h (block move), instead of writing the code yourself. It will save you days of frustration writing the code yourself (and probably a good fraction of your hair).

Macros and Conditional Code

Depending on how much experience you have with writing assembly-language code for the 8086, you might not have been exposed to macros or conditional code before. These tools can make your coding easier by keeping the number of keystrokes needed for a file to a minimum (which will also keep the opportunities for error at a minimum) and allow you to provide assembly options in your code to allow you to support and select multiple processors, hardware, or capabilities. Macros and conditional code is not only available in assembly language. Many high-level languages, such as C and C++, also have this capability.

A macro is similar to a subroutine, except when it is invoked, instead of "calling" the code, the code is copied directly into the source. Macros are useful when operations have to be repeated and the keystrokes required for the code is tedious or makes the code harder to read.

A classic 8086 example of a macro is creating a "long" conditional jump. If you want to jump on zero conditionally to an address label that is more than 127 bytes after the next instruction (or more than 128 bytes before the next instruction), you will have to write the code:

```
    jnz    Skip           ; If Zero Flag Reset, Skip over
    jmp    Label          ; Long Jump
Skip:
```

This is not terrible for one or two instances in a small routine, but in a large program with lots of conditional jumps, it can be tedious to repeat.

The solution is to put these three lines of code into a macro and each time the macro is invoked, the code replaces the macro. The macro that I normally use for this case is:

```
ljz macro Label
local Skip          ; Define Local Label
  jnz Skip          ; If zero flag reset, skip over
  jmp Label         ; long jump
Skip:
endm
```

When the code:

```
ljz     Label
```

Is encountered, then the *jnz Skip/jmp Label/Skip:* sequence is inserted in the source from the macro.

In the macro statement, besides the macro name, a single parameter is used to pass the address to jump to from the macro's *jmp* instruction. The parameter string is substituted, unchanged, for *Label* in the macro.

For the parameter and code, I find it best to think of a macro as a small program. The directives are instructions to the macroprocessor and the 8086 instructions (or high-level language statements) are print statements (with the destination of the prints being the source code itself). The macro parameters are variables that affect the operation of the macro program.

Following the *macro* statement in the *ljz* macro is a dummy label declaration. The dummy label (specified by the local directive) is used as a label that is only accessed inside the macro code. This allows multiple macro invocations to use their own labels without being confused with the same label in other invocations (or labels in the "mainline" code).

The end of the macro is marked by the *endm* directive. Once the *endm* directive is encountered, the macro is stored in memory; each time the macro's label is encountered, it is replaced with the macro code. That's all there is to writing a macro; they really are just a way to simply put repeating code into a program.

Macros and mainline code can be enhanced by adding conditional assembly/compile code statements. Conditional code is used to select what code will be processed, based on conditions within the program. These conditions can be numeric values, defines, or errors.

The format of conditional code is pretty simple with it following a structured programming if/else/endif format.

The *ljz* macro is not necessarily the most efficient way of doing the jump on zero flag set in all cases. In some cases, the label is less than the -128 or +127 limit needed for "small" jumps and, in the interests in saving space, you would like the macro to put in the two instruction code or a simple short conditional jump, based on what is appropriate. For this requirement, I can update the macro to the following:

```
ljz macro Label
local Skip          ; Define Local Label
 .if ( Label < $ ) & (( $ - Label ) < 126 )
  jz  Label         ; Can do the Short Jump
 else
  jnz Skip          ; If zero flag reset, skip over
  jmp Label         ; long jump
Skip:
 .endif
endm
```

In this macro, the destination address is checked to see if it is before the current address and if it is before and less than 126 bytes away, I will put in a simple jz instruction.

I did not include a forward check because, when this code is executed, label addresses above (greater than) the current address are not known and the value cannot be evaluated properly. In Microsoft assemblers, if I were to put in the forward check, there is a good chance that a "Phase Error" would be flagged. This error indicates that as the code was assembled, the size changed, which means that label addresses changed as well, and the actual code produced could be in error.

In this case, the phase error could happen if the first time the code was executed, the Label address returned by the code was less than 125 bytes away from the current address. When the second pass of the assembler executed, the Label address was more than 125 bytes away from the current address. In this case, the first pass would be sized for the jz instruction (which requires two bytes) and, in the second pass, the code would be sized for the jnz/jmp instructions, which can be five or seven bytes long. Phase errors are to be avoided with a passion; they are just about impossible to find and correct in large programs. To avoid them in your source, you should only write your code in such a way that conditional code can never execute differently in each assembler pass.

Macros and conditional code should only be used within small pieces of code. When I first started working full time, I was charged with the task of maintaining an RTOS that was built entirely out of macros and conditional code. By putting all the source code in macros, it was impossible to figure out exactly what the source code looked like. I had an absolute devil of a time trying to understand how the code worked, although I became particularly adept at figuring out what compiler statements produced what kind of assembly-language code. This is probably the main reason why I am very comfortable debugging applications from assembly-language code.

This was a total misuse of the macro and conditional code capabilities of the high-level language. Small macros are best for providing functions that you can easily forget to do, or you might have to go back and correct syntax errors or instruction limitations (such as the *jz* and *ljz* situation described in this section).

Assembler Versus High-Level Languages

I do want to say emphatically that I feel that high-level languages should be primarily used for writing PC applications, including those that interface with external hardware.

For people that know me, this statement will probably be a surprise. At the university, I wrote an 8086 RTOS totally in assembler and got the course's professor angry with me because I demonstrated that I could update the code for a significant design change quicker than most of the rest of the class could in C. At IBM and Celestica, I am famous for debugging all my C code by setting the CodeView display for assembler, rather than using native C. So, the question is, why do I devote so much space in this book to the 8086 native instructions and architecture, if I feel that high-level languages, which really don't require this information, are superior?

The answer lies in what this book is about: PC interfacing. If I was going to write a book about programming the PC, I would probably describe only the high-level languages and operating system interfaces. Because I am writing about interfacing to hardware, then a fairly complete understanding of how the PC's microprocessor works, along with an understanding of how to write assembler, is required.

If you are writing applications that you hope one day somebody else will maintain, then high-level language is the only way to go. Large assembly-language applications and routines are just about impossible to follow if you are coming back to them after a period of time or if you are looking at somebody else's code. To minimize the problems with maintaining code, I believe that the assembler must be kept to an absolute minimum and really only used for interrupt handlers, to provide small, tight code.

Two arguments I often hear for writing applications only in assembler are the speed increases and application-size decreases experienced with assembler. A great example of this was when I worked at IBM and we ordered a compiler for a PC-based tester. The consultant who created the compiler insisted upon writing the entire application in assembler and we had nothing but trouble with it. Internally, we created a document to explain how to get around the known problems and we refused to pay the full agreed-to fee until the identified problems were fixed. We ended up hounding the consultant for so long with our problems that he closed up shop and started a new business elsewhere because he was unable to support the application in such a way that he would make any money.

The reason why the consultant insisted on assembler was because it would run much faster than the same application written in a high-level language. Philosophically, he felt that high-level languages, written in a structured format, were unnecessarily wasteful of memory and took a long time to run. As well, he felt that compilers could not produce code that could compete with what he could produce.

My counter arguments were that as time goes on, PCs will get faster processors and more memory, so this speed element is really irrelevant and modern compilers (even circa 1990, when this program was being created), produced code that rivaled that of most experienced assembly-language coders. To be fair, the compiler we received was astonishingly fast, which was largely because of the consultant's refusal to use subroutines. Instead, he repeated routines using macros, which gave a significant penalty in the ultimate program size, but maximized the execution speed.

The final result wasn't worth it. The compiler was all but unusable unless you had our document to explain how the source had to be coded to prevent the compiling PC from crashing. One of my favorites was the need for the source code to have a comment on an empty line after an "if" statement or the PC would lock up.

I consider myself to be an expert 8086 assembly-language programmer. I have created many assembly-language-only applications, but now I only write in C because of the performance and capability improvements of modern PCs and compilers. When I first started writing PC applications, the 8088 running at 4.77 MHz was the norm with very poor compilers. Microsoft's original Pascal compiler produced executable code that ran at about the same speed as GW-BASIC and was virtually impossible to follow in a debugger from the assembler-language code produced. When the PC was fairly new, it did make sense to write applications in assembler, but today, with fast processors accessing large, flat memory spaces in protect mode "processes" and fast, efficient compilers, it doesn't make sense to write in assembler.

7

INTERRUPT
PROGRAMMING

Understanding how interrupts are implemented in the PC is crucial to any advanced hardware-interfacing application. As the PC has become more complex over the years, the operation of interrupts has become more sophisticated and crucial to the correct operation of the entire unit. Unfortunately, interrupts in the PC have a reputation for being very difficult to implement and many programmers and engineers shy away from implementing them in their applications, if at all possible.

This chapter introduces you to the PC's interrupt subsystem and its operation, and provides some code and procedures needed to successfully implement handlers of your own.

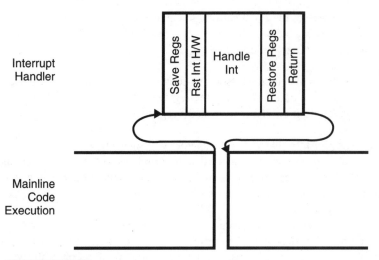

FIGURE 7-1   Interrupt execution.

Interrupt Execution

Interrupts are one aspect of computer operations that are very analogous to our everyday lives. Just as the computer has to handle external asynchronous and unplanned events, humans (and all animals) must be able to do this as well.

The most basic of interrupts is the hardware interrupt. A good example is driving your car to work and then seeing a fire truck approaching from behind. In North America, you are required to stop and let the fire truck pass. After it has gone by, you resume your journey, arriving just a few moments later than you would have without the interruption.

This is an example of an interrupt (the fire truck) and after the interrupt has completed, the mainline task resumes. This can be modeled as Fig. 7-1.

A hardware interrupt is known as an *interrupt request*. This is an accurate term because an interrupt is actually a request. The processor can choose to ignore the request instead of responding to it immediately. In the fire truck example, this is analogous to not stopping immediately and going a few yards further because you don't feel it is safe to stop where you are.

Not responding to an interrupt immediately is known as *masking the interrupts*. Masking interrupts in the PC is potentially dangerous for long periods of time because not responding to interrupts could result in problems with execution and information lost by not servicing the interrupt requests in a timely manner.

The subroutine used to respond to an interrupt is known as an *interrupt handler* or *interrupt service routine*. A handler, in the PC, normally takes the form:

1 Save the context registers
2 Reset the interrupt requesting hardware
3 Reset the interrupt controller
4 Enable interrupts

5 Execute the response to the event causing the interrupt

6 Restore the context registers

7 Return execution to the mainline

The context registers are the processor's various internal registers that are used during software execution. You could save only the registers changed in the handler using specific push instructions, but I prefer to save all the registers using individual "pushes" or the "pusha" instruction.

Saving only the registers changed in the handler will save a few bytes and execution cycles, but also leaves open the opportunity that later updates to the interrupt handler code will result in the few pushes and pops in the code to not include the newly accessed and changed registers. I recommend that you avoid this potential problem and save all the registers as a matter of course.

Because pushing and popping registers is a potentially dangerous operation (i.e., having a different number of pushes and pops) or restoring the registers in the wrong order will trash the application at least and cause the system to lock up at worst, I always save the registers in what I call the *SAIS format*.

SAIS is an acronym that I invented for *Stack, Arithmetic, Index, and Segment*. I use it as a check to be sure that I haven't missed any of the registers. I also use this mnemonic to remember how the registers are saved in assembler routines that are linked to C applications.

The order of pushing is:

```
BP          - Stack" Register

AX          - "Arithmetic" Registers
BX
CX
DX



DI          - "Index" Registers
SI



DS          - "Segment" Registers
ES
```

When each register group is saved, note that I always save the registers in alphabetical order. That way, I can always easily remember the order in which they are saved.

Popping the registers off the stack is done in the opposite order.

This order is not the same as what is used in the pusha/popa (push/pop all) instructions. I tend to ignore these instructions because the original 8088/8086 did not have the instructions and I just use my own. Today, all PCs that your application is likely to run on will have these two instructions and you would probably be better off using them, instead of explicitly doing the pushes and pops, as I do.

Once the context information is saved, you can now reset the requesting hardware and save any information that is specific to it.

It is important to do this immediately following saving the context information because the next step, resetting the interrupt controller will allow any following interrupt requests to halt the current handler and you could lose the information gained when the original interrupt occurs.

When executing the interrupt response, it is important to keep it short and fast. This is for three reasons. The first is to be sure that the interrupt handler has completed before the next interrupt comes in. If another interrupt occurs while the handler is still executing, then you will have to write the code in such a way that no data is lost in either interrupt handler.

This is known as a *re-entrant interrupt handler.* Believe me, you don't want to write one—before attempting to do so, you must design your application to potentially receive data in differing orders (because you might have more than two interrupts to handle), as well as different sets of variables.

The second reason for keeping the interrupt handlers short and fast is because the time spent executing the handler is time not spent executing the mainline. Short interrupt handlers will prevent the perception that your mainline code is slow and inefficiently written.

The third reason, as I will go into later in this chapter is that interrupts are *edgetriggered* and long responses to interrupt requests can mean missing subsequent requests.

Along with hardware interrupts, the 8086 architecture supports the use of software interrupts. These interrupts and their handlers are invoked by the *int xx* instruction (where *xx* is the interrupt number). Software interrupts cannot be masked and might not access any hardware. The software interrupt handler has a similar structure to that of the hardware interrupt.

The primary purpose of the software interrupt is to provide a system-wide subroutine interface that does not require a method for applications to "look up" the actual function addresses. The PC's BIOS, MS-DOS operating system, and some peripheral APIs use software interrupts to provide a simple interface to the PC's hardware and operating system functions.

INTERRUPT TABLE

The *interrupt table* in the 8086 is a memory area reserved for the 256 interrupt vectors needed for each interrupt available within the 8086.

The vectors themselves are pointers to the various interrupt handlers. This table is located at the start of the processor's memory (at address 0x00000:0x00000). Each vector consists of a four-byte "far pointer," with the first word (two bytes or 16 bits) as the offset to the interrupt handler and the second word as the interrupt handler's code segment.

The address of each vector can be simply found by multiplying the interrupt number by four. For example, the vector for the MS-DOS function interrupt (021h) is at 0x00000:0x00084. Don't worry about learning how to calculate the vector's address (i.e., multiplying a hex number by four), instead let the programming language do it for you:

```
mov    BX, 0
mov    ES, BX

mov    BX, IntNum * 4        ; ES:BX points to the Interrupt Vector
```

256 vectors are available within the 8086. These vectors are broken into a number of groups, according to function.

The following table groups the interrupt numbers by function:

INTERRUPT	FUNCTION
0 - 7	Processor interrupts/print screen
8 - F	Hardware I/O interrupts—interrupt controller 1
10 - 1A	BIOS functions
1B	*Ctrl-Break* exit vector
1C	Interrupt 8 "shadow"
1D - 1F	Parameter tables
20 - 3F	MS-DOS function interrupts
40 - 57	BIOS interrupt extensions
58 - 6F	NetBIOS function interrupts
70 - 77	Hardware interrupts—interrupt controller 2
78 - 7F	Unused
80 - F0	Used by built-in BASIC ("GWBASIC")
F1 - FF	Reserved for System Boot

Appendix F shows the actual usage of each interrupt vector.

From this list, you can see that there aren't a lot of vectors available for enhancements to the system. You could say that the short-sightedness of the original PC design has really squandered the 256 vectors, but this actually has not been a terrible thing. Most of the BIOS extensions have been defined for specific functions and are available to help you with your standard device interfacing needs.

Even though interrupt vectors 0F1h to 0FFh are not defined, they cannot be used by your application. The memory taken up by these vectors is used as temporary stack space during POST. I realize that the UCSD system identified these vectors for the system use, but, to stay safe, I recommend that you do not use them for your own application,

It is important to note that the PC really doesn't support additional interrupt controllers. Although interrupt controller 1 is quite full, controller 2 does have five unallocated sources that can be used for your applications.

Software Interrupts

One of the most powerful features of the 8086 is the software interrupt instruction. This feature allows system-level subroutines to be placed anywhere in memory without any application being given the address of the subroutine. This is taken advantage of in the PC as the mechanism to interface with the BIOS and operating-system functions.

The use of software interrupts greatly enhances the operation of the PC in several ways. Most significant is in loading an executable file. If software interrupts were not available or not used, then the loader would have to look up all instances of BIOS/operating system calls and replace the code with the addresses of the operation. Another way of doing this would be to put BIOS/operating system labels at a standard location in memory and, from this location, jump to the actual subroutines. The software interrupt table is simpler, uses less memory space, and allows handlers to be easily relocated.

The input parameters to a software interrupt normally consist of the interrupt number itself, along with the contents of the processor's registers. By convention, AH (the upper half of the AX register) contains the function within the software interrupt handler to execute.

For example, the code:

```
mov   AH, 9
lea   DX, String

int   021h
```

Will execute a subroutine within MS-DOS that will print the string pointed to by DS:DX until it encounters a $ character. Returned parameters are placed in the processor registers, with the Carry flag often used as an error indicator (when set, an error occurred).

Appendix F lists the interrupt numbers and their usage in the PC. Appendix G and Appendix H list the software interrupt functions for BIOS and MS-DOS. In the next few chapters, I will go through the BIOS and MS-DOS interrupt functions and explain how they work.

Not a lot of interrupts are available for you to provide your own software interrupt functions (or BIOS), but you can "share" an existing BIOS vector, as is described later in the chapter.

Hardware Interrupts

The PC's interrupt hardware follows a very straightforward path within the PC. The hardware itself is designed following Intel's *Reference Designs* almost to the letter. As described later in the book, multiple interrupt sources are possible, but they cannot be present on the same ISA *Interrupt Request* (*IRQ*) pin. The PC/AT interrupt-allocation standard is actually quite comprehensive; a modification to the interrupt controllers is not required.

The basic interrupt circuit can be blocked out as in Fig. 7-2. The interrupt request is a positive active edge on the interrupt pin. The pull down (which is not always present on older motherboards) is used to ensure that no request is being made by default. To request an interrupt, this line is driven high.

If the interrupt channel is unmasked in the 8259 controller and it is the highest-priority pending interrupt, the interrupt controller will make the Int pin to the processor active. If interrupts are not masked in the processor (i.e., the IF bit is set), then the current instruction is completed and the processor makes the *IntA* (*Interrupt Acknowledge*) line active. When the interrupt controller receives the active IntA line, it drives the number of the interrupt onto the low eight bits of the processor's bus. These eight bits are multiplied by four and used as the address to read the interrupt vector from.

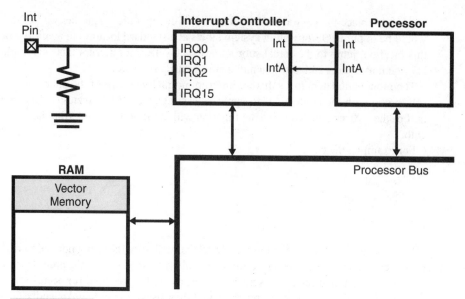

FIGURE 7-2   Interrupt circuit with I/O pin.

With the interrupt vector, the processor saves the basic context registers (the CS, IP, and Flags registers) and jumps to the vector address and executes the interrupt handler. During this operation, the IF bit of the Flags register is reset, not allowing nested interrupt requests to execute.

When the processor is able to accept interrupts again, the processor writes a 0x020-byte value to the interrupt controller, requesting the interrrupt to reset it and turn off the pending interrupt request. At this time, new interrupts can be requested and processed from the original interrupt's handler.

Allowing interrupts within a handler is somewhat of an advanced operation. Elsewhere, the chapter describes creating interrupt handlers that are able to execute repeatedly or at unexpected and potentially invalid times.

INTERRUPT CONTROLLER

The PC uses the Intel 8259A as its interrupt controller. Even though the age of this chip is approaching 25 years, and it was originally designed for the 8080/8085, it has provided excellent service for the PC and looks like its design will be used for at least another 20 years. As I've gone through how interrupts work, you've probably wondered where the "vectors" came from, along with some of the other hardware features, well, here is the source. This section is really no more than an introduction to the 8259A, but sufficient information is contained here for you to understand how it works and use its functions for interrupts in your application.

The 8086 was designed to use the 8259A, which means that it interfaces seamlessly to the device and can access its different modes, including cascading, which allows multiple 8259As to be wired together to provide as many as 64 interrupt sources for the processor. Today, most of the 8259A's features are embedded in ASICs (which is why I discuss its

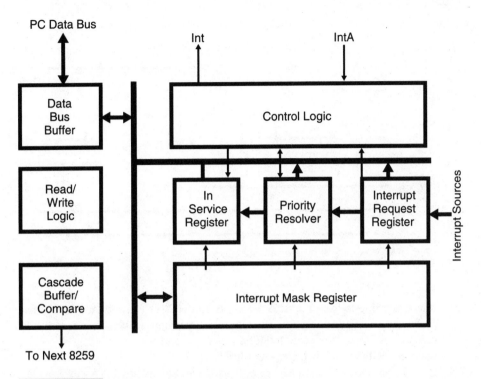

FIGURE 7-3   8259 interrupt controller block diagram.

"functions" & "design" rather than the actual device), but the function of the interrupt controller is identical to the operation of the PC/ATs two 8259As.

The 8259A (Fig. 7-3) is a sped-up version of the 8259 (the "A" part can run with a 5-MHz bus speed), which was first designed in the mid-1970s. The device is designed for use with Intel microprocessors of this vintage. The device can take in eight interrupt sources and request interrupts of the processor, with different interrupt sources given different priorities. The 8259A can run in three different modes (which are defined by the priority levels given to each of the eight interrupt sources). The 8259 design, although being older than many people reading this book, is quite versatile and well suited to the 8086 (and faster) processors.

In Fig. 7-4, the interrupt source transitions from "Low" to "High" which requests the interrupt. The interrupt request is checked inside the 8259A and the Int pin to the processor is made active. When the processor is able to accept the interrupt, the IntA pin is driven active and the interrupt number (output by the 8259A) is read from the data bus. When the IntA pin becomes active, the 8259A disables the Int pin and is ready to request a new interrupt. This sequence of events can take anywhere from less than 1 µs to tens of seconds (because of masking the interrupts within the processor).

When the interrupt has finished processing, the processor will write an *End Of Interrupt (EOI)* byte (equal to 0x020) to the 8259A to indicate that the interrupt has been processed.

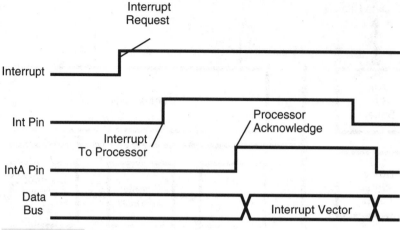

FIGURE 7-4   8259 interrupt operation.

Interrupt requests from the 8259A can be "nested" (i.e., inside an interrupt handler, the processor's IF flag can be set, allowing new interrupts while the current handler is processing). As long as execution within interrupt handlers is not changed, the 8259A will track the EOIs for the different interrupt instances.

When the PC/AT was introduced, it used two cascaded 8259As to provide the same number of interrupts as the PC along with the PC/AT's *real-time clock (RTC)* and six additional interrupts for the 16-bit-wide ISA bus. Figure 7-5 does not show the cascade bits, which are driven from the master 8259A to the cascaded slave 8259A to indicate that the IntA request is meant for the slave.

In the PC's master (primary) 8259A, the following interrupt sources and numbers have been allocated:

INTERRUPT NUMBER	LEVEL	DESCRIPTION
0x008	IRQ0	8254 clock
0x009	IRQ1	Keyboard
N/A		Slave (Reserved)
0x00B	IRQ3	Com2
0x00C	IRQ4	Com1
0x00D	IRQ5	Hard disk/LPT2
0x00E	IRQ6	Floppy disk
0x00F	IRQ7	LPT

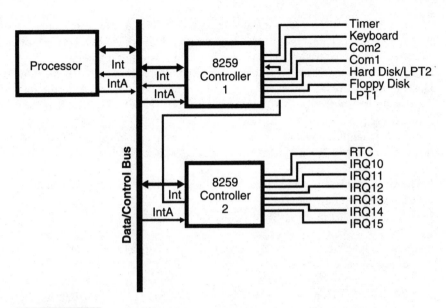

FIGURE 7-5   The PC's interrupt block diagram.

The *interrupt number* is the number for the interrupt source output from the 8259A when the IntA pin is asserted. The *interrupt level* (also referenced as *IRQn*, where *n* is the level) is an arbitrary value given to the interrupt by IBM when it designed the PC. Personally, I prefer working with the interrupt number, but most documentation will still reference the interrupt level, so I keep this convention in this book.

The slave (secondary) 8259A uses the following interrupt source and number allocations:

INTERRUPT NUMBER	"LEVEL"	DESCRIPTION
0x070	IRQ8	Real-time clock
N/A		Redirected to keyboard
0x072	IRQ10	ISA pin D3
0x073	IRQ11	ISA pin D4
0x074	IRQ12	ISA pin D5
0x075	IRQ13	Numeric coprocessor
0x076	IRQ14	ISA pin D7
0x077	IRQ15	ISA pin D6

In the secondary 8259A, the interrupt sources are primarily available on the 16-bit extension for the ISA bus. These pins are not allocated and can be used by user-defined hardware.

In the 8259A, only two registers are actually available. At the base address (0x020 for the primary 8259A and at 0x0A0 for the secondary 8259A), the EOI byte is written to the status register. At the base address plus one is the mask register address.

The mask register bits are set if specific interrupt sources are used to invoke interrupt requests to the processor. The mask register bits correspond to the bit of the request (i.e., Com1 is bit four of the primary 8259A) and must be set before interrupts requests can be passed to the processor.

Inside the mainline code, to unmask the interrupt request and allow requests to interrupt the processor, the following instruction sequence is followed:

1 The vector address is set to the address of the handler. (This is shown in the "Interrupt Capturing" section).
2 The mask register bit for the interrupt is set.

To disable interrupts, the mask-register bit is simply reset (although the vector address can be reset to the original address).

Inside the interrupt handler, after the hardware requesting the interrupt has been reset, the EOI byte is written to the 8259A's control register (address 0x020 for the primary 8259A and 0x0A0 for the secondary 8259A). Ideally, the EOI byte should be written to as early as possible in the handler. This will allow nested interrupts to work without fear that interrupts will be lost.

This is really all that's required to know about the 8259As in a PC to be able to successfully use hardware interrupts. I have glossed over quite a bit of what is actually going on in the 8259A, but I should point out that POST has set up the 8259As in the correct state and they should not be changed. As well, in most modern PCs, the 8259A's function is provided by ASICs, but actual 8259As (or even their logic designs) are not provided in the ASICs and the initialization sequence for the actual hardware (if there is any) is different from the original 8259As.

As I read this over, there may be one aspect of PC interrupts that I haven't explained adequately and that is the catching of interrupt requests while the IF flag is reset. If interrupts are masked within the processor, then any requests that come in are saved in the 8L59A and presented to the processor in priority order when the IF flag is set.

SECONDARY INTERRUPT CONTROLLER

The second 8259A interrupt controller is "daisy chained" to the primary interrupt controller in the PC. The major difference between the two 8259A comes in the area of register addressing. Although the primary 8259A's register addresses are 0x020 and 0x021, the secondary 8259A is at 0x0A0 and 0x0A1. Interrupt requests from the secondary 8259A are passed to the primary interrupt controller and recognized as external interrupt controller requests before being passed onto the processor (Fig. 7-6).

Like the primary 8259A, to reset an interrupt in the secondary 8259A is accomplished by writing a 0x020 byte to the control address (which is 0x0A0 in the secondary 8259A), followed by writing 0x020 to the primary 8259A's control address (0x020). This is required because the secondary 8259A is daisy chained to the primary 8259A and interrupt requests affect the operation of this interrupt controller, as well.

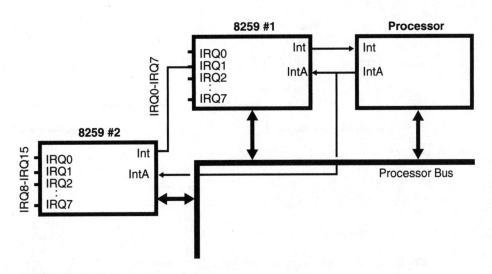

FIGURE 7-6 Interrupt architecture with the processor.

In C, this would be accomplished by:

```
outp ( 0x0A0, 0x020 );    // Reset Secondary 8259A
outp ( 0x020, 0x020 );    // Reset the Primary 8259A
```

Address 0x0A1 is the "mask register" for the secondary 8259A.

The secondary 8259A's interrupt vectors start at number 0x070 and are allocated as:

IRQ REQUEST	INTERRUPT REQUESTER	VECTOR ADDRESS
IRQ8	CMOS/RTC Clock Interrupt	0x00000:0x001C0
IRQ9	Redirect to Interrupt 010h	0x00000:0x001C4
IRQ10	Not Used	0x00000:0x001C8
IRQ11	Not Used	0x00000:0x001CC
IRQ12	Not Used	0x00000:0x001D0
IRQ13	Floating Point Coprocessor	0x00000:0x001D4
IRQ14	Hard Disk Controller	0x00000:0x001D8
IRQ15	Not Used	0x00000:0x001DC

In the *PC/AT Technical Reference Manual*, IRQs 10, 11, 12, and 15 are marked as *reserved*, but I have marked them as *not used* because they have not been assigned by specific hardware.

EDGE VERSUS LEVEL-ACTIVATED INTERRUPTS

If you have read critiques of the original IBM PC, one of the biggest ones that you will see is that it was designed with positive active edge-triggered hardware interrupts, rather than

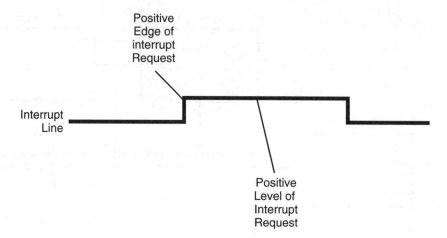

FIGURE 7-7 Edge versus level triggered interrupts.

negative level-triggered hardware interrupts. This design decision was kept in the PC/AT and affects how devices that generate PC hardware interrupts operate. As you read through this chapter, you'll find that I structure my interrupt handlers a bit differently from what you've probably been taught in school or might have used with other systems.

An *edge-triggered interrupt* is when an interrupt is requested of one of the PCs two 8259As and the 8259A responds on the leading edge of the signal from the interrupting hardware. A *level-triggered interrupt* is when one of the 8259A requests an interrupt of the PC any time the requesting line is active. The difference can be seen graphically in Fig. 7-7.

Normally in a PC, when the leading edge of the interrupt request is received by the 8259A interrupt controller, the 8259A passes the request on to the processor only once. If the 8259A was programmed with level-triggered interrupts and the interrupt was active at any time that the interrupt bit in the 8259As mask register was enabled, an interrupt request would be passed to the PC's processor.

The level-triggered interrupt has the advantage that any time the interrupt request line is active, an interrupt request will be passed to the processor. This avoids the problem of a missed request edge or an edge that is masked by a previous interrupt request. This is most likely to happen with multiple interrupts on the same line.

The next two sections describe how to create code that provides two separate interrupt functions on the same request line, but this section comments about providing multiple interrupt sources on the same line.

Normally, when devices are to have multiple interrupt sources on the same line, a negatively active line (usually edge triggered for the reasons described previously) is used. When the PC was first designed, shared interrupts were not felt to be an issue (the original PC had only five adapter card slots and two unused interrupt-request lines). As the PC became more complex, this became more of a problem.

Normally, tri-state buffers control interrupt-request lines. When the interrupt code is active, the buffer is enabled. To provide multiple devices, I prefer making the tri-state buffer output enable line the interrupt-request line, with the buffer's input pulled high. This is shown in Fig. 7-8.

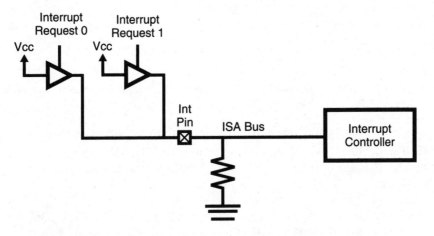

FIGURE 7-8 **Multiple interrupt request circuit.**

With this circuit, when the interrupt is being requested by the adapter hardware, the tri-state buffer's output is enabled and the line is pulled high. By using this circuit in all of the interrupt-requesting adapters on the line and keeping the interrupt handler's response time to resetting the interrupt-requesting hardware (turning off the interrupt request) very short, you can implement multiple interrupt resources on an interrupt pin.

Now, this doesn't mean that you have completely eliminated the opportunity for any requests to be missed, but it does greatly minimize it. The only way to completely eliminate the opportunity for any missed interrupts is to only place one interrupt source on each interrupt-request line.

This method also avoid the opportunity for bus contention because multiple devices can only drive the bus one way (with a high).

Interrupt Capturing

You probably now feel like you know everything there is to know about PC interrupts and are ready to start writing interrupt handlers. To a large extent you are, but you should be asking yourself one question:

"How do I put the interrupt vector pointing to the handler into the Vector Table?"

The most obvious way to do this is by writing some code to change the default vector over to point to the new handler routine.

The code could be:

```
xor    BX, BX
mov    ES, BX
mov    BX, IntNum * 4        ; ES:BX Points to the Vector Address

lea    AX, IntHndler         ; CS:AX Points to the Handler

cli                          ; Disable Interrupts
```

```
mov    ES:[BX+2], CS          ; Put the Address in CS:AX at ES:BX
mov    ES:[BX], AX

sti
```

This isn't too bad. Interrupts are masked when the vector is written to, in case an interrupt request is made while the vector update is only half done (i.e., the CS register contents have been written, but not the AX).

The problem with this code is that it is assumed that the application runs as long as the PC does because if the application stops before the PC is shut down, then the vector will remain pointing at the memory where the handler was when the application was loaded into memory.

This could be a problem when a new program is loaded into the PC at the memory location where the vector is pointing. If an interrupt request comes in, then invalid code will be executed, potentially locking up the PC.

When this happens, because the reason for the problem is a previously loaded program leaving the PC in an incorrect state, finding and debugging the problem will be just about impossible. This type of problem will cause the PC to behave strangely, sporadically and the problems will not necessarily behave in any kind of repeatable fashion.

This seems to be the number one problem made by new engineers and programmers creating their first program with an interrupt handler.

To prevent this, the original vector should be saved in a 4-byte variable before the vector is changed. When the application ends, the vector will be restored to the original value. This will eliminate any chance for errors caused by invalid interrupts after the application has stopped running.

This might not sound correct because the interrupt controller will still be set to request an interrupt when the hardware request becomes available. When the PC powers up, unused interrupt vectors are always set to "D11". "D11" is a label inside BIOS that contains an interrupt handler, which determines which interrupt made the request (by reading the interrupt controller registers) and then masks this interrupt from having any subsequent requests acknowledged. If this label is referenced by the vector, then the request will only be processed once.

Although explicit code can be used to read from and write to the interrupt vector table, I recommend that the MS-DOS system APIs "GetVector" and "SetVector" be used instead. The reason is a bit subtle, although very important to understand. Most debuggers (including CodeView) track the changes to the interrupt vector table. If a program is ended without restoring the interrupt vectors, if the debugger has recorded the change, it can restore the interrupt vector table based on what it was before execution. If the vector table is written to explicitly, then the debugger can't track the changes and restore them before returning to the command line.

Interrupt Sharing

Capturing Interrupts is only half of the story when implementing hardware interrupt handlers in a PC. Often, you will have to share the interrupt vectors with other devices and handlers. A classic example of this is the serial port interrupt vectors; in the PC definition, four standard serial ports can be installed in the system: COM1, COM2, COM3, and COM4. The COM1 and COM3, and COM2 and COM4 pairs each share a single interrupt handler. Understanding how to share interrupts will ensure that your application works properly and you are not getting calls from your customers demanding to understand why your product is causing another application to fail in (or worse, crash) their PC.

Sharing interrupts consists of creating an interrupt handler that is specific to a hardware interrupt source. This handler tests the hardware specific to it to see if it has requested the interrupt. If it has, then the interrupt is serviced, as was shown in the previous section. If the hardware didn't request an interrupt, then the previous interrupt service routine is executed.

The vector is set up the same as I showed earlier, but the handler is blocked out slightly differently:

1 Save context registers.
2 If the hardware reset by this handler did not request the interrupt:
   A Restore the context registers.
   B Jump to the previous interrupt handler for this interrupt number.
3 Reset the requesting interrupt hardware.
4 Reset the interrupt handler.
5 Re-enable interrupts in the PC.
6 Execute the interrupt response.
7 Restore the context registers.
8 Return to code executing before the interrupt occurred.

Watch for a few things. The first is that some other interrupt handlers do not share interrupt sources. These applications should be loaded and executed before an application that can share interrupts.

This is a bit tricky because there isn't a standard for sharing interrupts. At one point, various suggestions were made regarding placing the original interrupt vector somewhere where programs could pick them up to allow shuffling of the vectors, such as placing the storage for the previous vector in the four bytes before the start of the vector:

```
OldIntVector dd      ?         ; Location of the Original Vector


IntVector:                     ; Location of New Interrupt Vector
:                              ; Code follows
```

If a "midstream" handler was going to take itself out of the vector chain, with all handlers using some kind of standard way of storing the downstream vector, it could search for the immediately upstream handler and redirect its "OldIntVector" variable to the handler that was downstream before removing itself from memory.

These efforts were never really accepted and the most common way of creating handlers that can share vectors is to create a small "terminate and stay resident" handler or "device driver" that would always stay in memory, although it could be shut off by the mainline application code. During debugging, it wouldn't be unusual to have five or six of these handlers in memory; each one loaded every time that the application debug was started.

If you look through the default vectors, you will see that some of the Interrupt Controller 1 and many of the Interrupt Controller 2 vectors point to "D11". "D11" is a default interrupt handler that masks the requesting interrupt in the controller so that future interrupt requests will be ignored.

D11 came from the original IBM PC's BIOS code; it was the label that executed these functions. The label is still used as the reference to this routine. The D11 interrupt handler should never execute because it will mask interrupts without your knowledge, which will cause your application to hang on subsequent interrupts (the request will never be acknowledged).

For this reason, you must always be sure to test for every possible interrupt occurrence in an application and make sure they will be responded to correctly. Unexpected interrupt sources can be masked in hardware and be ignored in software. But if they are missed and execute D11, your application will stop receiving those interrupt requests.

Handler Skeleton

When adding a hardware interrupt handler to an application, I often will copy in the following skeleton and "flesh" it out for the application:

```
Inthandlerxx PROC FAR

pusha                   ; Save all the Potentially Changed Registers
push DS
push ES

; #### - Reset the Interrupt Requesting Hardware

mov   AL, 020h          ; Reset the Interrupt Controller
out   020h, AL          ; 020h - Interrupt Controller 1
                        ; 0A0h - Interrupt Controller 2
sti                     ; Allow Nested Interrupts

; #### - Process the Interrupt Request

pop   ES                ; Restore the Processor Registers
pop   DS
popa

iret

Inthandlrxx ENDP
```

In this code, after saving all the processor context registers, I reset the interrupting hardware (saving any important information first). If this was a serial data read interrupt handler, I would save the byte received before resetting the serial port interrupt request hardware.

Next, the interrupt controller is reset and made ready to receive the next interrupt. If the next interrupt is requested while execution is still in this handler, after the sti instruction, execution will jump to the new handler (which is now known as a *nested interrupt handler*).

Notice that I put in the marker for the I/O space address for resetting Interrupt Controller 1 or Interrupt Controller 2. Which controller that should be reset is known implicitly by the interrupt number being serviced.

Lastly, the registers are restored and execution returns to the instruction after the one where the interrupt request was acknowledged.

A modification to this code is required for shared interrupts:

```
Inthandlerxx PROC FAR

pusha                   ; Save all the Potentially Changed Registers
push DS
push ES

; #### - Check the Requesting Hardware; did it request this Interrupt?

pop    ES               ; Not this Interrupt, Jump to the Saved Vector
pop    DS
popa

jmp CS:OldIntHandler

SInthandlerxx:          ; This was the Handler Requesting the Interrupt
                        ; - Service the Interrupt

; #### - Reset the Interrupt Requesting Hardware

mov    AL, 020h         ; Reset the Interrupt Controller
out    020h, AL         ; 020h - Interrupt Controller 1
                        ; 0A0h - Interrupt Controller 2
sti                     ; Allow Nested Interrupts

; #### - Process the Interrupt Request

pop    ES               ; Restore the Processor Registers
pop    DS
popa

iret

Inthandlrxx ENDP
```

In this handler, before resetting the hardware, I check it to see if it requested the interrupt. If it didn't, I restore the context registers and jump to the previous handler (to which I've saved the address as "Old Int Handler" in the current code segment). Otherwise, I process the interrupt in exactly the same way as I did above.

Passing Parameters to Interrupt Handlers

Earlier in the chapter, I presented the problem of how to pass information between an application mainline and its interrupt handlers. At first blush, this probably doesn't seem like that big a problem; just define a variable that is common to both the mainline code and interrupt handler that both can access when they are "linked" together. But, also in this chapter, I noted that for shared interrupts, you might wish to make the interrupt handler a *TSR* (*Terminate and Stay Resident*) program, which is external to the application mainline and would not be removed from memory so that an interrupt handler chain would not be broken.

In the latter case, I like to set up my own BIOS software interrupt handler for facilitating the passing of parameters between the mainline and interrupt handler. As I pointed out earlier, free interrupts are not always available or safely usable. In these cases, I add my BIOS functions to the one that seems most relevant, but make the request numbers start with bit seven set. The request number is placed in the AH register of the processor. Most BIOS functions do not have over 127 routines in them, so starting my BIOS functions at 128 (0x080) is not going to conflict with other functions. If handler code is not available for a given AH value, then by convention, the BIOS software interrupt handler returns with the carry flag set.

The new BIOS interrupt handler will take advantage of what was presented in the "Interrupt Sharing" section and be written to look for bit seven of AH to be set. If it's not, it will jump to the original BIOS interrupt handler:

```
BSInthandlerxx PROC FAR

test   AH, 080h              ; Check for Bit 7 of AH Set
jnz    BSInthandlerxx_Start

jmp    CS:OldIntxx           ; It wasn't, Jump to the Original BIOS

; #### - Bit 7 of AH was set, Process "My" BIOS Interrupt Handler

BSInthandlerxx ENDP
```

Earlier, I showed how a serial string interrupt handler could be implemented. Using this BIOS interface, I could create the following functions for the interrupt handler:

AH	FUNCTION
080h	Enable/disable interrupt request hardware
081h	Use buffer pointed to by DS:DX
082h	Return current string receive status

Later, the book presents more about the system BIOS. What I wanted to do here was present how software interrupts can be used to provide a parameter interface between a mainline application and its interrupt handler.

Application Debug Interrupts

To make your applications easier to debug, Intel, when designing the 8086, provided three interrupt sources that have little usefulness in application execution, but they can make finding problems in applications easier. These interrupts are often captured and used within debugger and monitor programs and allow program execution to be halted in different circumstances and allow you to examine the register contents and data of the current application.

One word of caution on using these interrupts. Be sure that they are cleared out of your application before you release it. Failure to remove the interrupt instructions or hardware requests could result in the application stopping or the PC or operating system recognizing an invalid error.

Handlers for these interrupts should not be put into the application because they can affect the operation of the debugger and its ability to provide these functions to you for application debug.

NMI (IOCHK) INTERRUPT

Probably the most useful interrupt available for debugging is one you've never seen in use before this requires remarkably simple hardware to utilize it and is supported by most debuggers that I have worked with under virtually all operating conditions. This is the *NMI* (*Non-Maskable Interrupt*) interrupt or *Interrupt 2* in the 8086.

You're probably wondering why you haven't heard of this interrupt before and why it isn't advertised as a resource and I can't really think of a good reason why this is the case.

I should really modify that: I can't think of a good reason why it hasn't become more popular.

In the PC, the NMI is connected to the "–IOCHCHK" pin of the ISA bus. When this pin is pulled down, an NMI interrupt request is passed to the processor and the code pointed to by the Int 02h vector is executed. For the NMI to execute, neither the processor nor the interrupt controller have to be initialized in any way; this is at the heart of the term *NMI*. *Non-maskable* means that it will execute regardless of how the hardware is executing.

The PC's NMI interrupt is normally used to indicate that a parity error has occurred in a memory read. Traditionally, PC memory is nine bits wide, with the ninth bit used to store the parity information of the other eight bits. When a parity error occurs, the NMI interrupt is requested and the PC locks up with a parity error message.

This feature was crucial in early PCs with ISA memory adapter cards and fairly unreliable and primitive memory (Don't forget that the first PCs were available with 16Kx1 DRAMs and failures were often blamed on Alpha particles from trace radioactive elements in the memory chip's plastic encapsulant breaking down). To prevent the errors from affecting the operation of the application, the parity compare circuitry was connected to the 8086's NMI through some masking circuitry (which meant that in the PC, the non-maskable interrupt is actually maskable).

In modern PCs, with much more reliable memory that is usually on the motherboard (eliminating the chance for data to be corrupted by EMI) and error-corrected memory, this requirement has largely gone away. -IOCHCHK of the ISA Bus (pin A1) makes the NMI request available for use in debugging applications.

To add a manual control to -IOCHCHK, a momentarily on pushbutton switch is connected between the A1 (-IOCHCHK) and B1 (ground) pins of the ISA bus (Fig. 7-9).

This interface is dead simple to wire and will provide you with a method of halting your application's execution and returning to a debugger. Later, when presenting the debug card, I'll show how the -IOCHCHK switch is implemented.

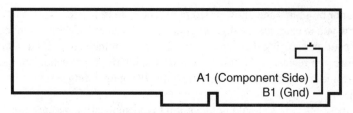

FIGURE 7-9   NMI debug interrupt.

If you add this switch, be sure that you don't press it when you are not debugging an application or it will cause your PC to lock up with a memory error. As well, do not change the masking hardware for the NMI; although it is possible to mask the interrupt request, I really don't recommend doing it.

BREAKPOINT INTERRUPT

A very useful instruction in the 8086 is the breakpoint interrupt request. This single-byte instruction (code *0x0CC*) is usually used to replace the first byte of the instruction where you want the execution to stop. The breakpoint interrupt request is interrupt number three in the interrupt vector table.

Most debuggers will provide breakpoint set, reset, and list functions. These functions replace the first byte of the instruction where you want to stop with *0x0CC*, restore the first byte of the breakpoint and list the currently set breakpoint addresses.

MS-DOS's debug.com does not have these features and will have to be implemented manually when you are debugging a program (i.e., putting in *0x0CC* for the first byte of the instruction where you want to stop, after recording the instruction's original first byte).

The only caution on using breakpoints is not to set them in code areas that will be copied into different areas of memory. If code with breakpoints is copied to another location in memory and executed, the breakpoint interrupt will stop execution, but the debugger will not have a reference to the original code.

When you're developing code and want to set an explicit breakpoint, you could add the subroutine:

```
Breakpoint PROC FAR
int   3                          ; Stop Execution
ret
Breakpoint ENDP
```

to your code. If you are running in a high-level language, this can be written in assembler and then executed as a function.

I typically place this code in an application when it's difficult to find the proper reference point from the debugger after the program is loaded. When I say "difficult," I mean that the breakpoint you want to insert is within a nested subroutine that is not visible when the debugger first starts to execute.

If you add this code, I must caution you to be sure that you track all references where it is used; before releasing the application, clear them all out of the source. A good way of doing this is to keep breakpoint in its own object file; when you are ready to release the code, link the application *without* this object file. All the remaining references to this code will be identified by the linker for you.

This is important to do because, although I have seen some versions of MS-DOS ignore this interrupt, other versions will flag an error and stop execution.

SINGLE-STEP INTERRUPT

The last debug interrupt should not be accessible or initiated by you. This interrupt is used by a debugger to allow a program to be single stepped by a user or run in an "animate" fashion to allow the user to observe how the code executes. This feature is really only used in a debugger. Creating the code to process the interrupts is difficult and will interfere with the operation of any debuggers that you want to use.

Single-step mode is initiated by setting the *Trap Flag (TF)* of the flags register with the PC's interrupts masked (by resetting the IF bit) and is followed by an iret instruction. After the iret instruction is executed, which should return execution to the instruction to be single stepped, the instruction is executed and control is returned to the interrupt 01h handler. Interrupt 01 cannot be masked from within the application, which is why you can single step through an application—even when it masks the interrupts.

In 8086s, note that instructions that update a segment register do not execute the single-step interrupt. The reason for this is based on the feature of the 8086, whereby if a segment register is updated, an interrupt request is ignored until after the next instruction has executed. The reason for doing this is to allow segments and index registers to be set up without an interrupt, causing problems with the pointer half loaded. This feature was not passed along to later versions of the i86 architecture (in these cases, you should disable interrupts before updating a segment register and index).

THE
PC BOOT
PROCESS

To successfully interface hardware to the PC, you must have a clear idea of how the PC powers up ("boots"). Understanding this in terms of identifying and setting up hardware resources, allocating interrupt vectors, and loading the operating system will help you decide on the best strategy to develop your hardware interfacing application with. As part of this process, the PC will look for devices attached to busses to interface with. By using this hardware scan, your hardware devices can be loaded and set up into the PC without the user having to run any special software. It will make your software development effort easier, both in terms of deciding how to do it and actually implementing it.

Hardware Boot

The hardware boot process has remained quite static since the PC was first introduced. I wouldn't be surprised to discover that much of the original PC's boot code is still used in modern systems. The process is important to go through because you should be aware of some features. You will want to take advantage of them when you create your own hardware-interfacing application.

The information contained here should be correct for your PC, although for some different systems (most notably laptops), there might be some deviations. These deviations will be caused primarily by differences in motherboard hardware. If you do have differences in the boot operation of a particular PC, you should be able to identify the differences and map them out fairly easily with the aid of the appropriate technical reference, the motherboard's set up routine and the "Memory" program presented earlier in the book.

POST OPERATION

Power On Self-Test (POST) is the first code that your PC executes when power is applied and the Power Good signal in the power supply is asserted. The name is somewhat misleading because, as well as testing the hardware within the PC's motherboard, POST also initializes the system and leaves the processor, motherboard, and peripherals ready for operating system and application load. I suspect the reason why the term *POST* is used for all of these operations is that somebody likes this acronym.

The execution of the POST uses a "center-out" philosophy; the code is written so that it tests the PC's processor first, followed by the ROM memory, interrupt controller, DMA, DRAM Memory (which needs DMA for refresh), and so on. The idea behind this order is to test and initialize hardware only after the circuits that it is dependent upon have already been tested.

What is of significant importance in POST is the ability to recognize that the PC's hardware has been set up to load the operating system and run applications when POST has completed. As POST executes, the timer, interrupt controller, DMA controller, etc. are left in a state ready to begin operating as a PC under MS-DOS or Windows.

MFG_PORT and POST codes   While POST is executing, a POST test number is written to an I/O port that normally only has hardware connected to it during the board's manufacturing test process. This port is written with a POST test number and if an error is detected during the POST's execution, the PC goes into a *hard loop* (a loop with interrupts disabled) until the processor is reset. The last value to be written to the "MFG_PORT" address is assumed to be the failing POST test.

This port is known as *MFG_PORT* and it resides at I/O space address 0x080. A typical circuit that provides the "MFG_PORT" readout function could be as simple as Fig. 8-1.

A more-sophisticated MFG_PORT display circuit is built into the ISA prototyping card that is presented later in the book.

The MFG_PORT codes generally follow what was specified for the PC/AT, but if your PC uses a BIOS that is different from IBM's, they might have some different codes than the table listed.

Along with the MFG_PORT, some BIOS's also use a set number of beeps from the PC's speaker of different durations. More than once I've called a bunch of people around to listen to the beeps from a failing motherboard to determine what the failure code is. I've also put on a digital storage oscilloscope with a one or two second per graticule sweep speed to see if I could capture the length of the beeps for an easy readout. This is not a very efficient way to figure out the error code; you should really build a little ISA card based on the circuit in Fig. 8-1.

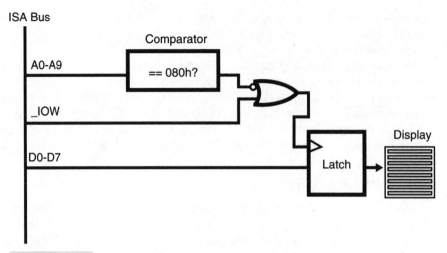

FIGURE 8-1   "MFG_PORT" decode and display circuitry.

The PC/AT POST codes are listed in the following table. As I mentioned, these codes should really provide no more than a reference for you to choose codes in any adapters that you design and want to use the MFG_PORT for displaying your own POST error codes. As well as using the MFG_PORT mechanism, if you are running a POST of your own from an adapter's bus ROM, you might wish to avoid the MFG_PORT altogether and display the failure information on the PC's display. Speaking as a test engineer, using both methods to write failure information would be preferable because it would give the manufacturing site the greatest amount of flexibility in structuring its test.

CODE	TEST
001h	Processor read/write test
002h	CMOS shutdown byte test
003h	CMOS checksum test
004h	Timer all bits set test
005h	Timer all bits Reset test
006h	DMA channel 0 initialize register
007h	DMA channel 1 initialize register
008h	DMA page register read/write test
009h	DRAM refresh test
00Ah-00Dh	Keyboard controller and configuration jumper test
00Eh	Base 64-KB read/write test
00Fh	Base 64-KB parity check test

CODE	TEST
011h	Read switch settings
012h	Protected-mode register test
013h	Initialize interrupt controllers test
014h	Initialize temporary interrupt vectors
015h	Initialize BIOS API vectors
016h	Verify CMOS shutdown capability test
017h	Set defective CMOS batter flag test
018h-01Ah	Set CMOS checksum test
01Bh-01Ch	Protected mode test
01Dh-01Fh	One-MB memory size determine
020h	Shutdown PC from Protected mode
021h	Real-mode stack check test
022h	Enable video output
023h-024h	Video adapter test
025h-028h	Interrupt controller test
029h	Timer interrupt test
02Ah-02Ch	Timer checkout
02Dh	Run keyboard controller delay test
02Eh-031h	Full memory test
033h	Address line 16 to 23 test
034h	Return to Real mode
035h-038h	Keyboard presence test
039h	Keyboard buffer test
03Ah	8042 RAM test
03Ch	Diskette adapter initialization
03Dh	Diskette hardware test
03Eh	Initialize hard disk
03Bh	Optional ROM presence "scan"
03Fh	Initialize printer
040h	Enable floating point coprocessor
041h	Look for ROM at address 0x0E000:0
042h	Enable NMI request hardware
043h	Enable NMI request interrupt

Looking through these codes, you should notice that they are not necessarily in ascending order (in some cases, such as memory test, you will see the values cycle between codes). I have provided a list of codes as they run in chronological order to give you an idea of the steps that the PC takes to boot up.

As I proof-read this, I realized that I have not emphasized that the MFG-Port is only accessible through a system's ISA port. For systems to comply with the latest versions of the Intel/Microsoft "PC/99" specification, the ISA bus is not included on the motherboard. In these cases, the "Post Test" information is not available through this port. Instead other interfaces are used. This is usually documented in the PC motherboard specifications.

Interrupt set up   An important aspect of POST is the set up of interrupts. The functions of these interrupts are documented in Appendix G, but a number of comments should be made with respect to the PC's boot process and the vector set up.

The interrupt vectors are stored in RAM. As pointed out in the previous chapter, these vectors point to the interrupt handler locations. These vectors point to BIOS and MS-DOS APIs, default hardware interrupt-request handlers and adapter hardware interrupt handlers.

With the vectors are all stored in RAM, they can be very easily changed in an application. For example, you would probably expect that the BIOS and interrupt vectors are all pointing to addresses within the 64-KB BIOS ROM segment, starting at address 0x0F0000. If you look at where they actually are pointed to in your PC (using a debugger), you'll find that they can be in all kinds of different locations.

For example, in my laptop (running Windows 3.1), I looked at a few of the BIOS interrupt addresses and discovered that a number of them pointed to unexpected segments:

```
Int 08h        0x02CAC:0x00000      Real Time Clock Interrupt
Int 14h        0x00EA8:0x008F4      Serial Port BIOS
Int 15h        0x02C6E:0x00000      System Services
Int 18h        0x0F000:0x0F2DC      Cassette BASIC Start interface
```

Of these four vectors, only one is actually pointing to the ROM segment; actually, I would have expected only one of these to be redirected. The one I would have expected was the real-time clock interrupt because the clock is used for task switching.

These redirections are made by the operating system and device drivers to provide enhanced features and monitor the status of the hardware. This monitoring is done to ensure that the non-re-entrant APIs are not given new requests before previous ones have completed.

CMOS/RTC CONFIGURATION

On every PC motherboard since the first PC/AT is a battery backed-up CMOS real-time clock and memory chip. This chip was first put on the PC/AT as a means to track the time while the PC is shut down and save configuration information. Using the chip avoids the need to reset the time on power-up, as well as record how much memory is available in the system and what kind of disks are installed. Today, this chip serves essentially the same purpose and has been enhanced to record such diverse parameters as what types of keyboards, power-up password, video, and network hardware should be accessed and how. Although Plug 'n 'Play will confirm many of the options, the CMOS/RTC chip (as it is known) contains a lot of crucial hardware configuration information needed to properly setup and boot the PC.

In the original PC/AT, a Motorola MC146818 real-time clock chip with RAM was used to provide this function. This chip provides 32 bytes of RAM and RTC function registers. This chip is still used in many PCs and a number of applications have been written using different MC146818 RAM registers for saving data between power up sessions. I want to discourage you from thinking about doing this in your own applications. Different BIOSs use different registers in the CMOS/RTC chip and you might overwrite data that is needed at bootup. Even worse, different memory locations have a checksum applied to them to allow POST to see if the data has been corrupted.

In many systems, chips other than the Motorola MC146818 are used. These chips have different function registers addresses and operation. The actual addresses used in these devices are much different than in the MC146818. Writing to these registers could result in the PC not recognizing the confiuration in format on boot up.

Some standard BIOS interrupt APIs can be used to write and read to the CMOS/RTC chip, but they should not be used in case of incompatibilities between PCs. Instead, if you need nonvolatile storage of information, you should add your own battery backed-up RAM or EEPROM memory or simply save the information in a file on the PC's hard disk.

PLUG 'N 'PLAY

At this point of the PC's boot, all of the standard motherboard devices are initialized and ready for the operating system. The adapters (serial ports, parallel ports, network adapters, etc.) have not been set up by the system. In older systems (and adapter cards), the addresses for ROM, RAM, I/O ports, and interrupts were set manually by the user with jumpers and switches. In modern systems, Plug 'n 'Play, as described in Chapter 2, set the adapter card addresses.

Few practical considerations for Plug 'n 'Play are worth noting. First, Plug 'n 'Play will attempt to locate standard devices at the initial default addresses. This can cause problems if you have some non-Plug 'n 'Play cards at the initial default addresses. The PC motherboard will not recognize the non-Plug 'n 'Play cards; setting the Plug 'n 'Play devices at the same address will cause serious problems when the PC is operating. To avoid this problem, non-Plug 'n 'Play hardware should be located at secondary or unused addresses.

This problem is further complicated by many motherboards with integrated I/O ports. The ports themselves are set up with Plug 'n 'Play, hardware built in.

The conflict between Plug 'n 'Play, and non-Plug 'n 'Play hardware is the primary reason why many people refer to *Plug 'n 'Play,* as *Plug 'n 'Pray.*

Finding out which addresses Plug n´ Play, will choose can be done empirically by seeing what addresses are used without any adapters installed. This can be done within the Setup screen of most BIOSs. For example, to see the setup screen in AMI BIOS, the Delete key is pressed during system boot. Often, the Plug 'n 'Play, devices can have secondary addresses selected; this information is recorded in the RTC/CMOS and will be used each time the PC boots.

Ideally, Plug 'n 'Play, and non-Plug 'n 'Play adapter cards should not be mixed in the same system.

As indicated earlier in the book, Plug 'n 'Play, can be an operating system or a BIOS construct. It is also available on virtually all the busses built into modern PCs. When I introduced Plug n´ Play, earlier in the book, I showed how it worked for the ISA bus and devices that are used with it. Plug 'n 'Play, is also implemented on IDE, PCI, SCSI, USB, and Firewire busses. Each bus Plug 'n 'Play, protocol works somewhat differently and can execute during firmware boot (as does the ISA) or after the operating system is loaded.

The important simularity is the use of a serially accessed serial number ROM that is used to uniquely identify each device from any others like it in the system.

BUS ROM

When the PC reaches this point, the motherboard and standard hardware have been initialized and supporting resources (memory and interrupt handlers) have been set up for them. The PC will now begin to look through the PCI and ISA slots, looking at adapter cards and executing their on-board ROM.

This search for bus adapter cards' ROM is known as a *scan* and how the ROM is recognized is explained in Chapter 12. When a ROM is recognized, execution is passed to the code on the ROM for initializing the adapter hardware and any system resources needed to support it.

Typically, an adapter's ROM code will carry out the same functions as the motherboard's POST, but for the adapter card. The ROM should test the function of the hardware, set up the interrupt and DMA resources and initialize hardware.

At this point, the PC is ready to boot so the ROM may take over the PC and boot it from there. This is often done in diskless PCs that load the operating system from a local-area network card.

The ROM can also be used to run a completely unique PC application that does not need the operating system. This method of booting is often done in embedded PCs, which can be run as a completely solid-state device, which can run PC applications and does not have the fragility or complexity of disk-drive systems.

Later in the book, I will pesent some applications which take advantage of these features.

OS Boot

When the PC has completed its hardware boot, it is then ready to start up the operating system. This operating system start up (boot) normally consists of first checking for a LAN and then the disk drives (floppy drive A; followed by hard disk C) for a boot program in sector 1, track 0 of side 0 of the disk. Once it has found a boot source, the operating system will be loaded into RAM, first with the boot sector, which will initiate the loading of the entire operating system. If no boot source is found, the PC might start executing Cassette BASIC, a graphic that will prompt you for a diskette or simply sit there and let you figure out what's wrong.

I am going to break up the operating system boot into two parts. The first is the MS-DOS boot with the 8086 running in Real mode (or a Protect-mode version to provide the LIM Extended Memory Manager). MS-DOS boot does little more than prepare the memory to be allocated to applications. Operation of the MS-DOS Prompt in Windows provides the ability to execute MS-DOS applications, but you might find some problems when working with advanced video modes (i.e., you can't have two copies of MS-DOS "Doom" running under two invocations of the MS-DOS Prompt window of Windows).

The Windows boot itself builds upon the MS-DOS boot and extends it with increased hardware accesses and more-sophisticated hardware operating modes. After MS-DOS has loaded,

Windows takes over and places the processor in Protect Mode, ready to load and execute applications. It is presented as more of a "black box," but I wanted to give you more of an idea of the complexity of what Windows has to do to provide the GUI multi-tasking operation.

MS-DOS BOOT

The MS-DOS boot operation is relatively simple with the file system and command.com (the user interface) put into memory starting at address 0x0050:0x010 (the memory below this is used for the interrupt vectors and system variables). With this load complete, the required device drivers are loaded and memory is prepared to be allocated by applications. Once this has been completed, command.com executes autoexec.bat and prompts the user for a command.

That is just about all there is to MS-DOS. I tend to think of MS-DOS as a file-system BIOS that is set up after POST has completed and this is really not an unfair characterization. Advanced processor features, other than what is required for the LIM Extended Memory Manager, are not used by MS-DOS. If they are to be accessed by user programs, the processor must be returned to its original state before the application can return control to "command.com" (the command line user interface used by MS-DOS). MS-DOS really provides a computer system that is ripe for plunder.

A good example of this is running a text console application in video Page 2. If control is returned without setting the default video output back to Page 0, you'll find that the first time you enter a command, the screen will scroll up and you will have lost control of MS-DOS.

For this reason, I've always felt MS-DOS was not suitable in a professional environment. Errant applications can very easily overwrite other applications, the operating system, or "command.com", with the end result being that the PC is no longer able to operate.

For this bad news, there is some good news. When a program has trashed the system, MS-DOS does reboot relatively quickly.

WINDOWS BOOT

The best way to describe the Microsoft Windows boot operation is to think of it as protect-mode overlay to MS-DOS. Windows will use MS-DOS standard disk interfaces (although in Ring 0) and provide an operating system "kernel" to run applications in Protect mode with MS-DOS being used as a device driver. Windows loads after MS-DOS and sets up the console and memory resources as it requires.

This statement isn't 100-percent accurate. Windows 3.x/95/98 all load in the manner described, but Windows NT/2000 are full operating systems with their own built-in file systems and video drivers. They do not rely on MS-DOS and run in a much more "integrated" environment. As I write this, Windows 95/98 are the predominant operating systems available and, as such, I will concentrate on describing their operation.

In the Windows boot operation, along with the disk system being set up as a series of virtual device drivers interfacing the MS-DOS functions, the serial and parallel input/output ports and standard device drivers make other hardware interfaces accessible as well. Once this operation is complete, the start-up applications are executed and control is passed to the user.

When you look at Windows and see that it requires several hundred megabytes of disk space, you're probably thinking that I'm missing something. From a high level, no, I am not; the boot process is actually quite simple to conceptualize.

9

THE
BIOS
INTERFACE

When I'm programming applications for the PC, I like to think of a hierarchy of interfaces available to the application. This hierarchy allows me to select the appropriate interface for the application to access hardware or communicate with the user (Fig. 9-1).

As you go up this hierarchy chart, the interfaces become simpler and more general. Thus, the functions are able to work across a wider variety of hardware using the same application interfaces (which are often known as *APIs, Application Programming Interfaces*).

The BIOS interrupt interface provides the most basic standard interface for the hardware and the I/O functions are only suitable for MS-DOS command-line user interfaces. BIOS provides a standard interface for the console devices, disk subsystems, and processor operation.

Along with the standard interfaces, you might wish to develop BIOS interfaces of your own for unique hardware designs to simplify the application software effort required for the final application.

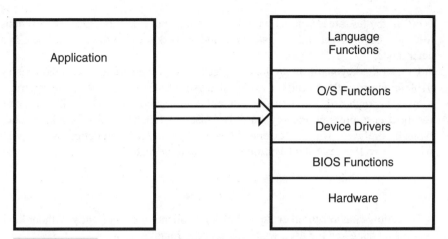

FIGURE 9-1   **Application resources interface.**

BIOS Interrupt Interface

The BIOS software interrupt interface differs from the MS-DOS interrupt interface because it provides a direct hardware interface to the PC's hardware (keyboard, mouse, serial port, parallel port, etc.). These interrupt interfaces should only be accessed by applications in specific instances that are explained later in this chapter.

The BIOS interfaces follow the convention of using the AH register to specify the function of the software interrupt. For example, in the keyboard interface, a wait for the next key, the buffer status or the *Shift/Alt/Ctrl* status can be checked using the keyboard BIOS services (interrupt 16h) with different values of AH. For example, AH = 0 waits for an unread keystroke to be stored in the buffer, AH = 1 returns the status of the buffer, and AH = 2 returns the state of the keyboard control (including *Shift, Ctrl, Alt,* etc.). I have included a list of the BIOS APIs in Appendix H.

If you are going to access BIOS services, be sure that you understand exactly how they work. Some BIOS APIs might not work exactly as expected. A good example of this is the serial port BIOS API. Sending a character requires the handshaking lines to be configured appropriately between the PC and the device to which it is attempting to communicate. If the handshaking lines are not held appropriately, the API will wait a certain amount of time and then stop without sending the character. The same is also true for read; a character can come in, but if the handshaking lines are not correctly set up, the character will not be returned to the API's caller.

Console Interfacing

When I work with the console in MS-DOS applications, I generally avoid developing the interface using MS-DOS API interrupt functions and use the BIOS functions directly. This is one of the few areas where I would suggest this, but I do it because BIOS functions allow the most efficient and consistent method of working with the PC's console in a character mode.

To read the keyboard, I can generally get by with the extended keyboard read (AH = 010h for interrupt 016h) and the extended keystroke status (AH = 011h for interrupt 016h) to read the keyboard. The first function either returns the first unread keystroke or waits for the user to press on the keyboard. Because this function waits for a keystroke, I will typically preface it with the extended keystroke status check function, which will return with the zero flag reset if a keystroke is waiting to be read:

```
if ( ExtendedKeystrokeStatus() != 0 )
   Keystroke = ExtendedKeyboardRead();
```

This allows me to run other aspects of the application concurrently without having the processor "hang" on the user, waiting for a keystroke.

This snippet can be modified to clear the keyboard buffer:

```
while ( ExtendedKeystrokeStatus() != 0 )
   ExtendedKeyboardRead();
```

In this snippet, while the extended keystroke status API is not zero (indicating that keystrokes are in the PC's buffer), a character is read from the buffer until the buffer is empty. This code can be used at the start of an application to be sure that extra keystrokes do not affect the operation of the application.

I use the extended keyboard commands because they work consistently for all keys on different keyboards. Using the standard keyboard read and keystroke status commands, the full 12-function key states, as well as some other keys, will not be read or recognized. In Microsoft Windows PCs, the Windows Function Request Key (the key labeled with the "Flying Windows" logo between the *Ctrl* and *Alt* keys) press information is not available on any systems through BIOS or any APIs because it is devoted to the operating system.

The video BIOS interrupt (010h) is also very simply accessed with the Set Mode (AH = 000h), Set Cursor Type (AH = 001h), Set Cursor Position (AH = 002h), and Select Active Display (AH = 005h) being the only APIs normally used in both character and graphics modes. To write data to the screen, I normally do direct writes to the VRAM, as shown in the next section.

Notice that if I am writing an application in MS-DOS, I normally only run in character (alphanumeric, A/N) mode (usually mode 3: 80 by 25 characters in 16 colors) and stay away from the graphics modes. If I want to have graphics in my application, I will go with a Windows application and development environment, which provides a device-independent set of graphics APIs.

The BIOS commands that I use allow me to specify different display pages and move the cursor around on the pages. Pages, in video terms, are essentially separate video RAM "screens" that can be displayed instead of writing over the current page. The MS-DOS prompt normally uses page 0, but the CodeView debugger uses page 1, leaving six other pages for your application's use.

To move the cursor and set its type, I use the BIOS APIs built in for the function. When I do the *set cursor* type command, I work with the values:

CURSOR TOP LINE	CURSOR BOTTOM LINE	CURSOR TYPE
(CH)	(CL)	
000h	00Bh	"Block"
00Ah	00Bh	Normal
008h	00Bh	"Insert"
02Bh	00Dh	None

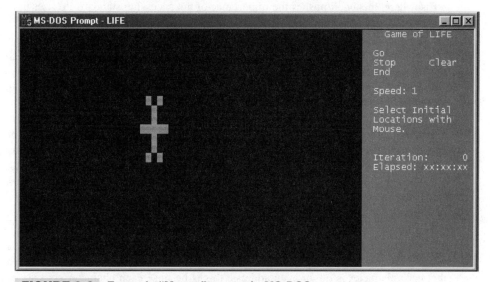

FIGURE 9-2   Example "Mouse" screen in MS-DOS.

The final console device that I work with is the mouse. This might seem surprising because the mouse is usually associated with Windows GUIs and not text-mode console applications, but the mouse can be used effectively within an MS-DOS character-mode screen, both on its own or being displayed in a Windows MS-DOS prompt window (Fig. 9-2).

For the mouse, I use the Mouse Reset (AH = 000h), Show Cursor (AH = 001h), and Get Button Status and Position (AH = 003h) APIs. I continually poll the Get Button Status and Position API. When the left button (normally) is pressed, I read the current position. This is shown later in the book in the Game of Life application.

This is not the same as how Windows provides the mouse information in event-driven programming languages, such Visual Basic and Visual C++, where the routines are called when they are clicked. In my MS-DOS mouse routines, I have to manually check the position to see if the mouse is over any clickable "control" locations on the screen.

ACCESSING VIDEO RAM DIRECTLY

How often do you see an MS-DOS application where the screen updating is done in the wink of an eye, but others seem to take forever to update? In the MS-DOS prompt of Windows, this difference can be even more pronounced because characters in the MS-DOS prompt window often have to be created from individual graphics elements. As well as wanting to create a similar application, you might also want to put different colors on the screen at different locations on the screen. When you look at the MS-DOS APIs, you will probably end up with the conclusion that it is impossible.

If you've gone through this, then it should be obvious that there is a different way of writing to the display—writing directly to the *Video RAM (VRAM)*. This section shows how a combination of BIOS calls and direct VRAM writes can be used in MS-DOS to create a fast, useful display.

Elsewhere, this book pushes the importance of not accessing standard PC user interface hardware directly. But for fast MS-DOS video display updates, you will have to write to the hardware directly. This is not necessarily bad because, in all modern PCs, the VRAM is located at the same addresses in the Real-mode address space. With dual-ported VRAM, no flashes or "snow" are on the display.

I concentrate on the "alpha-numeric" ("A/N") or Character modes available in the VGA BIOS. These are modes 0 through 3; each one provides two bytes for each character, one for the Extended ASCII character code and one for the color attributes of the character. The methods shown here can also be used to write "pixel" information for graphics in the other modes. To simplify what I'm showing you and make it the most applicable, I have created the code for Mode 3, which can have up to 16 colors displayed on the screen and 80 by 25 characters in eight different "pages" (one of which can be shown at any one time). This mode is the most useful for general-purpose character displaying.

The screen itself is set up on 4-KB boundaries for each page in the 0x0B8000 segment. Offset zero of each 4-KB boundary is the top left corner of the display.

In Fig. 9-3, I have shown the offset for the initial characters on the display page. Notice that each character is on an even address; this is because each character consists of two bytes. The first byte is the extended ASCII character and the second byte is the foreground (character) color with the background color and is known as the "color byte."

The extended ASCII character set, listed in Appendix C, is a mapping of the character generator ROM and does map the standard ASCII character set very faithfully. Although the ASCII control characters (codes 0x01F and lower) and their operations are not supported, just character representations are given. If you were writing a program that received characters and displayed them on the screen, you would be responsible for handling characters like Backspace, Carriage Return, and Tab in the application.

The color byte is defined as:

BIT	COLOR/FUNCTION
7	Foreground blink
6	Background red
5	Background green
4	Background blue

BIT	COLOR/FUNCTION
3	Foreground high intensity ("HI")
2	Foreground red
1	Foreground green
0	Foreground blue

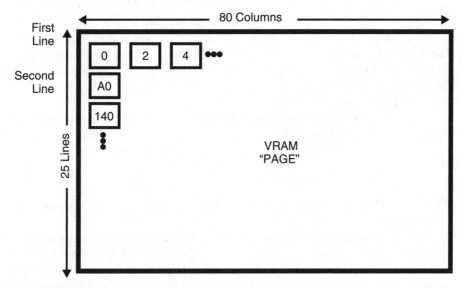

FIGURE 9-3 Video RAM addressing layout.

These basic colors can be combined into:

HI	RED	GREEN	BLUE	COLOR
			X	Blue
		X		Green
	X	X		Cyan
	X			Red
	X		X	Magenta
	X	X		Brown
	X	X	X	Light grey
X				Dark grey
X			X	Light blue
X		X		Light green
X	X	X		Light cyan

HI	RED	GREEN	BLUE	COLOR
X	X			Light red
X	X		X	Light magenta
X	X	X		Yellow
X	X	X	X	White

Because the background only has three RGB bits, only the first eight colors in the table can be used for the background. The HI bit is used with the foreground colors and it provides a range of colors that stand out from the background. As a general rule, you should always pick foreground colors that have the HI bit on (except for light gray, which has the three-color guns on).

If you've ever done any HTML programming, you'll have been exposed to the idea that you should never use Blink. This is also true for the foreground blink bit in the color attribute byte. The only time it should be set is for crucial messages, such as:

```
Reactor Meltdown in 2 Minutes
```

because it is really obnoxious. If you use it often in an application, don't be surprised if lots of angry people complain.

I have used the blinking bit to indicate that a link is up, but in this case, I used a very dull color combination (red against green) that really doesn't offend the same way that a blinking yellow message on a blue background would. This probably wasn't the best use of the blink attribute. Instead, each time I check the link, I should have XORed the byte contents to give the impression of the blinking attribute, but actually display the results from the ping operation.

When I am writing to the VRAM in C, I normally set up a pointer to type *pixel*:

```
struct Pixel
{
 char character;
 char color;
};

Pixel far * Screen;
```

After these declarations, I can initialize *Screen* to point to the VRAM page in memory:

```
(ulong) Screen = (ulong) ( 0x0B8000000L + ( ActivePage * 0x010000 ));
```

This initializes *Screen* to point to the VRAM page in memory. With it set up, I can write to the video memory as simply as:

```
Screen[( Row * 80 ) + Column ].character = 'A';
```

This line of code will store the ASCII A code at the specified row and column on the screen. *Row* and *Column* are zero based at the top left-hand corner) and end at 79 and 24 (decimal), respectively.

When I set up the *Screen* address, I also specify a nonzero and nonpage-one specification. Normally for MS-DOS C programs, I use CodeView for debugging. CodeView's display uses page 1 and I like to return to page 0 (the default MS-DOS command line page) with the original information text just as I left it. Rather than having a blank screen or one partially filled with the application, I normally use page 2 for my application.

One problem occurs with page 2: if you return to MS-DOS with the page active, you'll find that the commands no longer work and you'll have to reboot. For application development and debugging, I set *Activepage* to *zero* and before I release the code, I set it to *two*.

To control which page is active (and its mode), as well as the cursor location and type, I use the standard video BIOS APIs. These APIs run very quickly and allow you to ignore the differences between different display drivers and adapter hardware that your application might encounter.

When to Use BIOS Functions

Deciding when to use BIOS calls in applications is actually pretty simple. As a general rule: they should never be used, except in a few specific instances.

Accessing the BIOS functions from within the application essentially bypasses the operating system and could place the PC in a state in which the operating system cannot recover. An excellent example of this is changing the disk interface using BIOS interrupt 013h APIs instead of the operating system disk functions. By doing this, the disk subsystem will not be in the state expected by the operating system and reading and writing of files might no longer be possible.

For console (display, keyboard, and mouse) operations, you will use a combination of direct I/O and BIOS calls. The combination that I recommend optimizes application execution size & development effort.

Often, when starting up a new application or input screen, you will want to clear the keyboard buffer before processing any user input. The easiest way to do this is only using BIOS calls. The C pseudocode for a buffer clear that executes a key read while the buffer is not empty is:

```
While ( KeyStatus() == Not_Empty )
  KeyRead();
```

Which would be coded in assembler as:

```
KeyClearLoop:                   ; Loop Here until Buffer is Reset
  MovAH, KEYSTATUS              ; If the Buffer is Empty, Exit the Loop
  IntKEYINT
  Jz KeyClearDone

  MovAH, KEYREAD               ; Keystroke in the Buffer, Read it
  IntKEYINT                    ; to Clear it out

  JmpKeyClearLoop

KeyClearDone:
```

This function seems to be rare in high-level languages and can be very useful.

The video BIOS functions do work fairly well with MS-DOS, although they are quite limited in what can be accomplished. As I described earlier in the chapter, I often just set the video mode in BIOS and then write directly to VRAM by passing the high-level language, MS-DOS, and BIOS APIs all together. This gives me much faster screen updates because the operating system overhead is completely avoided.

If you are going to work with the BIOS APIs, you should be wary of one commonly used set. The BIOS serial interface APIs use hardware handshaking that cannot be disabled. This means that three-wire RS-232 connections or interrupts from the serial port cannot be implemented using the BIOS serial interface APIs. I typically bypass the BIOS functions all together in this case and write my own serial interfaces using direct UART device reads and writes.

System Variables

Appendix F lists the system variables that are stored in segment 0x040 and are normally used by BIOS to control the operation of the PC. Great care when writing to this area is required. If you don't completely understand what you are writing to and what it controls, you could end up locking up your PC (or worse).

To avoid any potential problems with the PC, I never write to these variables and only read a few of them back. Instead, I use the MS-DOS and BIOS functions responsible for accessing them.

I do read a few system variables because they make some application functions easier to implement.

In several applications, I have read the Break Key State byte (at address 0x00040:0x00071) and polled bit seven of the byte. When bit seven is set, the *Ctrl-Break* key sequence is being pressed. Many times polling for *Ctrl-Break* is easier to implement than using the *Ctrl-Break* interrupt vector available in the application's PSP.

The best way to understand which key modifiers (*Shift*, *Alt*, and *Ctrl*) are being pressed is to read the keyboard state flag at address 0x00040:0x00017. The keys set the following bits:

BIT	FUNCTION
7	*Insert* mode active
6	*Caps Lock* mode active
5	*Num Lock* mode active
4	*Scroll Lock* mode active
3	*Alt* key pressed
2	*Ctrl* key pressed
1	*Left Shift* key pressed
0	*Right Shift* key pressed

These flags can be useful in using the different keys as controls in your application or if you are editing text, indicating the actual key sequence.

The last variable I regularly access is the counter used for the PC's 8254 timer-based real-time clock. These four bytes start at address 0x00040:0x0006C. This counter keeps track of the number of 18.2-ms clock ticks that have occurred since the midnight of the day the PC was started (with the next double word, at 0x00040:0x00070, being incremented for each day the PC has been executing since the first day).

The Multiplex Interrupt

If you've ever written system code for the PC, you might be a bit surprised to see that I include the Multiplex interrupt in the BIOS interrupt APIs. I have done this because the Multiplex interrupt provides a method of adding an arbitrary number of BIOS interfaces without looking for unused interrupts or trying to establish your own standard. The Multiplex software interrupt is the primary user interface for device drivers.

The Multiplex interrupt consists of a number of software interrupt handlers sharing the interrupt or chained together, with each one testing the contents of AL for its number and processing the command in AH if its (process) number matches the contents of AL.

The process number is determined when the process interrupt handler is loaded into the chain. Often, a number will have to be tried before a valid one (one that just returns an error for the GetInstalledState API). MS-DOS has reserved a number of process numbers that you must be careful not to use. These process numbers are generally installed portions of functions, such as *Print* (AL = Process Number 1).

Although the Multiplex interrupt operation is described in greater detail in Appendix I, there are a few comments I wanted to make here. The first is, the Multiplex interrupt is used by a lot of different applications as a method of providing a consistent interrupt interface. For this reason, when they are used, you will have to be sure that it can distinguish between MS-DOS and Windows operation.

A big issue for Multiplex interrupts is determining the appropriate process number that should be used. In different MS-DOS versions, I have seen different reserved ranges. The safest range to use seems to be 0x00C to 0x0EF.

MS-DOS

Along with needing a good understanding of the 8086/8036 processor, BIOS, and hardware, to develop hardware interfaces to the PC, you must also have a good understanding of how MS-DOS works. Programs are presented in this chapter, designed for executing from the MS-DOS command line exclusively. After the hardware interfaces are thoroughly covered, Visual Basic interfaces for Windows are included.

I realize that you probably already have a pretty good understanding of how to use MS-DOS, but I want to go through some information that might not seem obvious, but is important to understand before you can begin to develop your own applications. The information in this chapter is meant to complement, not replace, the standard MS-DOS usage information and it might help you to understand how MS-DOS actually works.

The DOS Program Segment Prefix (PSP)

One of the most useful and generally unknown MS-DOS resources available is the *Program Segment Prefix (PSP)*. When a program is loaded and executed on a PC, this 256-byte block of memory is set up at the very start of the memory allocated to the application and provides information useful to executing the application. This is not an application resource or feature that you have to know backwards and forwards, but just knowing that it exists can make your programming much easier and help you to understand why some things are done the way they are in the PC.

From the PSP, the Environmental Information block can be found and accessed by the application. This block of information contains the file-system path information and system specifications. For many applications that require loading and processing information or using temporary files, understanding how the Environment block is laid out can make the effort much easier.

The PSP block, could be modelled as a structure with data at types:

ADDRESS	LENGTH	DESCRIPTION
0	2 bytes	CD 20 - Interrupt 0x020 request
2	Word	Top of memory (normally 9FFF)
4	1 byte	Reserved
5	5 bytes	Long call to DOS
A	Double word	Int 22 - Terminate address
E	Double word	Int 23 - *Ctrl-Break* exit address
12	Double word	Int 24 - Crucial error exit address
16	22 bytes	Reserved
2C	Word	Segment address of Environment block
2E	34 bytes	Reserved
50	2 bytes	CD 21 - Interrupt 0x021 request
52	10 bytes	Reserved
5C	16 bytes	FCB block 1/argument 1
6C	16 bytes	FCB block 2/argument 2
7C	4 bytes	Reserved
80	1 byte	Parameter length
81	127 bytes	Command-line parameters

To show what this looks like for an actual program, Fig. 10-1 shows the actual PSP contents of a program loaded into "debug."

Looking at this screen shot and comparing it to the address table above, you should start seeing a few of the features. Notice that the "reserved" bytes can essentially have random data, not all zeros or 0x0FFs, as you might expect. Even with the "reserved" title, you should be sure that you never write to these addresses and you should never count on them being the same value among PCs, operating systems, or even applications.

Next, notice the two interfaces to the operating system at offsets 0 and 0x050 of the PSP block. Interrupt 0x020 is the DOS program terminate and can be accessed by a simple jump to address zero.

```
jmp    0                  ; End the Program
```

Using Interrupt 20 is not a recommended way to terminate a program. Instead, Interrupt 21 functions 0x04C (terminate a process) or 0x031 (terminate a process, but stay resident) are recommended because they can return an error code that can be queried during a batch program's execution.

At offset 0x050, the operating system interrupt request is made by a call instruction:

```
call 0x050   ; Do an Operating system Function
```

When I began to understand the workings of MS-DOS, I always wondered about the purpose of these instructions in the PSP. It was confusing because doing the jump or call to these offsets actually took more bytes than simply executing the interrupt instructions.

The reason for doing it is for high-level languages that do not have a direct interface to the 8086 software interrupts as part of the language. If you review most languages for the PC (BASIC, Pascal, and C), you'll find this to be true. In high-level languages, the operating system functions can be accessed by declaring a label at these addresses and then jumping to or calling these labels. Without this interface, high-level languages would have to provide an assembly-language interface to the operating-system functions, which would reduce their portability between processors and operating systems.

The three double words starting at offset 0x00A in the PSP are pointers to DOS-execution extension interrupts. The handlers for these interrupts use these addresses to jump to when different conditions are encountered and the application can redirect these addresses (vectors) to handlers specific to the application. This gives the application additional control over its execution.

If you are going to add features to these handlers, then I recommend doing it in the following manner.

First, the original address is saved in a four-byte variable and then replaced using the code:

```
les    DI, PSPIntVector      ; Read the Original Vector
mov    PSPIntVector_Old, DI  ; Save the Original Vector
mov    AX, ES
mov    PSPIntVector_Old + 2, AX
mov    AX, CS                ; Set the New Vector
mov    PSPIntVector + 2, AX
```

```
mov    AX, NewPSPIntVector
mov    PSPIntVector, AX
```

It is not crucial to disable interrupts during this code because the vectors are only accessed by an application operating system call. Because you have control over the application, you know that no operating system call will be made while the PSP interrupt vector is in the process of being changed.

The actual handler code (starting at label *NewPSPIntVector*) can end with a simple *iret* instruction. This is possible because no registers have been pushed onto the stack at this point of execution. If you are going to change any registers (other than the flags register), you will have to push them onto the stack.

The handler code could look like:

```
NewPSPIntVector:                          ; New Handler Code

  push         AX                         ; Save the Changed Registers

  :                                       ; Execute the Interrupt Handler

  pop AX                                  ; Restore the Changed Registers

  iret/jmp PSPIntVector_Old               ; Return or Jump to Original Address
```

For the terminate address at offset 0x00A, I highly recommend that you don't attempt to capture the execution. The reason is that when the vector is active, that's when the program terminates. The application should have control over its own termination; if it doesn't, then there is the chance that the termination command will execute when something crucial is happening in the application. If this happens, there is a chance the PC will be left in an invalid state (i.e., with a file open or corrupted, and no way to correct the problem).

It really comes down to poor coding practice and it should be ignored.

The next vector, *Ctrl-Break* (MS-DOS interrupt 0x023) at offset 0x00E will indicate that the *Ctrl-Break* key sequence has been pressed when the next operating-system interrupt is requested. This interrupt vector is only executed if the Break function is enabled (using Int 21 Function 0x033).

When I've used this function, I generally have this code set a flag and then jumped to the original vector using code, such as:

```
NewInt23Vector:              ; New Interrupt 23 Vector

  mov CS:BreakSet, 1         ; Indicate "Break" Key Sequence

  jmp CS:Int23Vector_Old     ; Jump to the Original code
```

In the mainline, I poll BreakSet and respond when it is no longer zero. This fits in with my philosophy that interrupt handlers should execute as quickly as possible to minimize the impact on the operation of the operating system and application.

The final vector, at address 0x012 is the MS-DOS crucial error handler (interrupt 0x024). If the vector at this address is executed, then some error (usually a disk error) occurred and the application code has to work with it.

When the vector address is jumped to, AH bit 7 is reset if a disk error occurred. If bit 7 of AH is set, then some other error was encountered. The DOS error number can be read out of the lower eight bits of DI and are defined as:

ERROR NUMBER	ERROR TYPE
0	Attempted to write to write-protected disk
1	Unknown drive unit selected
2	Drive not ready
3	Unknown command
4	CRC data error on read
5	Bad request structure
6	Seek error (going beyond file end)
7	Unknown media (no table description)
8	Sector on disk not found (file corrupted)
9	Printer out of paper
A	Data write fault
B	Data read fault
C	General device failure

Several of these errors can be corrected within the program and execution returned without problems.

For example, writing to a write-protected diskette could result because the application prompted the user to make the diskette writeable and then commanded DOS to retry the operation.

Returning control to DOS is simply accomplished by setting the AL to a command value and then executing an Iret command. The commands are defined as:

AL COMMAND VALUE	OPERATION
0	Ignore the error
1	Retry the failing DOS command
2	Terminate the program
3	Return error to failing DOS request code

Telling MS-DOS to ignore the error can be very dangerous and a complete understanding of the error is required. What if the failure occurred because the drive wasn't ready (which usually means that a diskette is not in it)?

In this case, the ignore would be indicating to MS-DOS that the error was invalid and that a diskette was actually in the drive. Later operations could operate as if the file was opened correctly and could result in invalid data being processed by the application or data not be saved.

The best operation is to fix the problem (such as requesting the user to remove the write protection on a diskette) and the returning to the DOS command with a retry. The other options could result in corrupted disk data.

The stack, upon entry into the Interrupt 24 handler is set up as:

IP	First three bytes required for "iret"
CS	
Flags	
AX	Registers when failing DOS request made
BX	
CX	
DX	
SI	
DI	
BP	
DS	
ES	
IP	
CS	
Flags	

So, rather than return control to DOS, the first three registers could be popped off the stack (because they are not required by the application), the registers reloaded from the stack, the error condition noted, and then an iret instruction executed to return to the address of the caller.

As you might expect, this is a dangerous operation that requires considerable effort in handling the error correctly in the application. When it comes right down to it, I have to recommend that the critical error interrupt is left alone and instead, errors should be processed through the standard DOS features of looking for the set carry flag at an MS-DOS function return and requesting extended error information from MS-DOS if an error is detected.

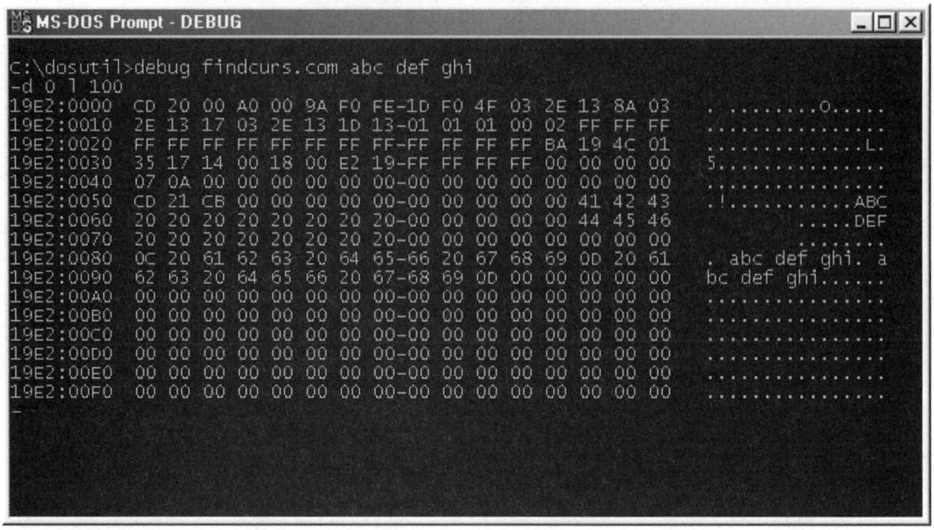

FIGURE 10-1 Actual PSP data.

File Control Blocks (FCBs) should really be avoided as a method of interfacing to the disk system. But, to maintain compatibility for applications written before the advent of MS-DOS 2.0 (when the handle-based interface was created), the PSP contains two 16-byte areas for saving FCB information at 0x05C and 0x06C.

Along with being used for the MS-DOS 1.x file interface, the two FCBs in the PSP are also used to store the first two command-line parameters. This can be seen in Fig. 10-1, with the first two parameters, *abc* and *def* saved in uppercase, starting at address 0x05D and 0x06D, respectively.

The entire command-line parameters are stored at address 0x081, with the byte at address 0x080 being the number of characters input. Multiple blanks between command-line parameters are reduced to a single blank in the PSP to make parsing the data easier.

If you look at the screen shot of the actual PSP (Fig. 10-1), you'll see that the command-line parameters are repeated. This is not something you can count on. The actual command-line parameters can be a maximum of 127 bytes, which means that if you have a set of parameters that are longer than 63 bytes, then a second set after the first set of parameters will be corrupted.

As can be seen in the screen shot, the first character at 0x081 is a blank, with a leading blank before each separate parameter. The end of the parameter string can either be found by adding the contents of 0x080 to the constant 0x081 or by reading through the string and trying to find the first carriage return (0x00D) after address 0x081. In this case, the carriage-return character is at address 0x08D, which is the sum of the contents of 0x080 and the constant 0x081 (which is the start of the command line parameter buffer).

If you program in C and specify the main parameters of *argc*, *argv* then the C compiler will create an array (*argv*), which points to each different parameter, starting at element one (element zero is the first being the program invocation) and a count of elements (in *argc*), so you know which is the last command-line parameter in the array.

Reading through and parsing the command-line parameters is quite simple, regardless of the language in which you are programming.

The last feature of the PSP is the segment of the Environment block. The Environment block contains the information needed to execute applications from the MS-DOS command line. The next section covers the Environment block's information and how it is used during COMMAND.COM and application execution.

The PSP might look like an area that can be used for variables or to move code into to save space. This is especially true for "Terminate and Stay Resident Programs," which you might want to make as small as possible to allow other larger applications to execute.

I have to caution you against writing anything into the memory reserved for the PSP because the PSP block's data will be accessed by the operating system. This could result in your PC having intermittent problems or not run at all.

The PSP itself only takes up 256 bytes and, in modern PCs, this is a minuscule fraction of the total memory available. It might seem like something of a waste to leave the PSP unused, but save yourself a difficult debug later (potentially much later, in the case of an operating system upgrade) and just read from the PSP at defined addresses and don't write to it in any way.

Environment Information

Along with the PSP, the executing application also has a user-defined block of memory that contains information needed for program execution. This includes file-path information needed to search standard subdirectories, as well as operating parameters needed by applications to correctly execute in the PC. Using the environment information can give your application's execution a professional "feel" and make it easier for the user to run.

Unlike the PSP, the environment information is in a series of ASCIIZ strings with headers. This means that each block of information is prefaced by an identifier and the end is noted by a "null" (0x000 or '\0') character.

This can be seen in Fig. 10-2, which is the Environment block for my PC. The address for the Environment block uses the segment defined at the PSP's offset 0x02C. Within this segment, the Environment block is at offset zero. The end of the block is defined by two ASCII null characters (one to end the identifier and one to indicate the end of the block).

In Fig. 10-2, the different identifiers can be seen quite clearly. Breaking the Environment block up, I could write out the PC's environment information as:

```
TMP=C:\WINDOWS\TEMP
TEMP=C:\WINDOWS\TEMP
PROMPT=$p$g
winbootdir=C:\WINDOWS
COMSPEC=C:\WINDOS\COMMAND.COM
PATH=C:\WINDOWS;C:\WINDOWS\COMMAND;C:\DOSUTIL;C:\BAT;C:\IBMC2\BIN;
     C:\MASM\BIN;C:\E3;C:\MPLAB;C:\PKZ;
INCLUDE=C:\ASM\ASMPROCS;C:\ASM\MYKEMACS;
windir=C:\WINDOWS
BLASTER=A220 I5 D1
CMDLINE=debug findcurs.com
```

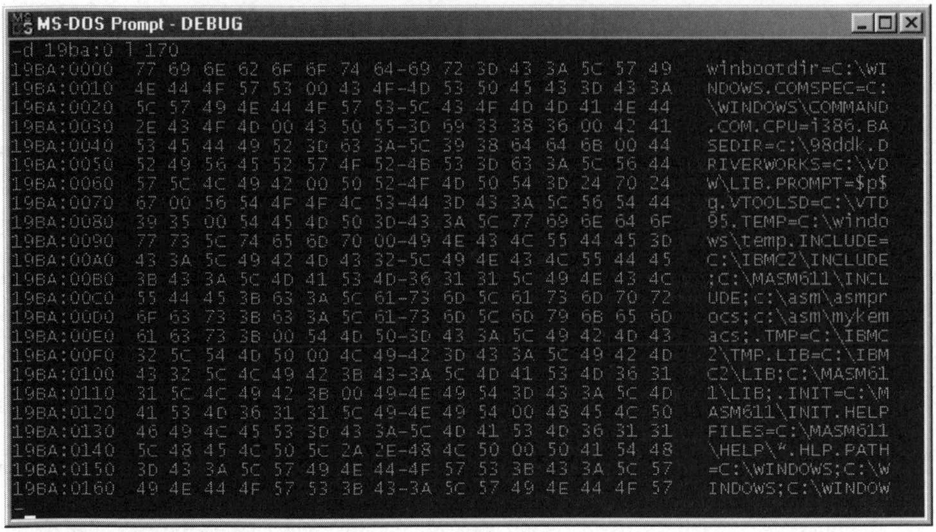

```
MS-DOS Prompt - DEBUG                                                    _□×
-d 19ba:0 1 170
19BA:0000   77 69 6E 62 6F 6F 74 64-69 72 3D 43 3A 5C 57 49   winbootdir=C:\WI
19BA:0010   4E 44 4F 57 53 00 43 4F-4D 53 50 45 43 3D 43 3A   NDOWS.COMSPEC=C:
19BA:0020   5C 57 49 4E 44 4F 57 53-5C 43 4F 4D 4D 41 4E 44   \WINDOWS\COMMAND
19BA:0030   2E 43 4F 4D 00 43 50 55-3D 69 33 38 36 00 42 41   .COM.CPU=i386.BA
19BA:0040   53 45 44 49 52 3D 63 3A-5C 39 38 64 64 6B 00 44   SEDIR=c:\98ddk.D
19BA:0050   52 49 56 45 52 57 4F 52-4B 53 3D 63 3A 5C 56 44   RIVERWORKS=c:\VD
19BA:0060   57 5C 4C 49 42 00 50 52-4F 4D 50 54 3D 24 70 24   W\LIB.PROMPT=$p$
19BA:0070   67 00 56 54 4F 4F 4C 53-44 3D 43 3A 5C 56 54 44   g.VTOOLSD=C:\VTD
19BA:0080   39 35 00 54 45 4D 50 3D-43 3A 5C 77 69 6E 64 6F   95.TEMP=C:\windo
19BA:0090   77 73 5C 74 65 6D 70 00-49 4E 43 4C 55 44 45 3D   ws\temp.INCLUDE=
19BA:00A0   43 3A 5C 49 42 4D 43 32-5C 49 4E 43 4C 55 44 45   C:\IBMC2\INCLUDE
19BA:00B0   3B 43 3A 5C 4D 41 53 4D-36 31 31 5C 49 4E 43 4C   ;C:\MASM611\INCL
19BA:00C0   55 44 45 3B 63 3A 5C 61-73 6D 5C 61 73 6D 70 72   UDE;c:\asm\asmpr
19BA:00D0   6F 63 73 3B 63 3A 5C 61-73 6D 5C 6D 79 6B 65 6D   ocs;c:\asm\mykem
19BA:00E0   61 63 73 3B 00 54 4D 50-3D 43 3A 5C 49 42 4D 43   acs;.TMP=C:\IBMC
19BA:00F0   32 5C 54 4D 50 00 4C 49-42 3D 43 3A 5C 49 42 4D   2\TMP.LIB=C:\IBM
19BA:0100   43 32 5C 4C 49 42 3B 43-3A 5C 4D 41 53 4D 36 31   C2\LIB;C:\MASM61
19BA:0110   31 5C 4C 49 42 3B 00 49-4E 49 54 3D 43 3A 5C 4D   1\LIB;.INIT=C:\M
19BA:0120   41 53 4D 36 31 31 5C 49-4E 49 54 00 48 45 4C 50   ASM611\INIT.HELP
19BA:0130   46 49 4C 45 53 3D 43 3A-5C 4D 41 53 4D 36 31 31   FILES=C:\MASM611
19BA:0140   5C 48 45 4C 50 5C 2A 2E-48 4C 50 00 50 41 54 48   \HELP\*.HLP.PATH
19BA:0150   3D 43 3A 5C 57 49 4E 44-4F 57 53 3B 43 3A 5C 57   =C:\WINDOWS;C:\W
19BA:0160   49 4E 44 4F 57 53 3B 43-3A 5C 57 49 4E 44 4F 57   INDOWS;C:\WINDOW
```

FIGURE 10-2   Actual PC environment data space.

Most of the information contained within the Environment block is path information. The TMP, TEMP, PATH, and INCLUDE identifiers contain information that is used to find files in specific categories easily. TMP and TEMP are file directories used for temporary storage of files needed for the operation of compilers and data-processing applications. INCLUDE is used by compilers and assemblers for loading in definition files and linking in standard libraries.

PATH lists the directories that contain the most-used executable files. It is searched by COMMAND.COM when a statement is made from the MS-DOS command line, which is not built into COMMAND.COM and is not an executable located within the current directory.

Notice that for multiple subdirectories in one category (i.e., PATH and INCLUDE), each different subdirectory is delineated by the use of a semicolon. If you have created an application that takes advantage of this path information, by knowing the individual subdirectories end in either a semicolon or a null character, you can easily copy them into strings and append file names for searches.

The file identifier blocks can be updated either from the command line (i.e., "SET PATH = ...") or in a batch file. Because the update operations append the new information directly to the end of the old, it's important to be sure that every subdirectory identifier ends with a semicolon to ensure that appended paths will be interpreted correctly.

The remaining information is used to specify the operating mode of the PC. PROMPT governs how the user will be prompted by the system in the MS-DOS command line. pg is most commonly used; it specifies that before user input can be processed the current subdirectory, is displayed followed by a ">" character to prompt the user to enter a command.

The "*winbootdir* and *windir* parameters specify where the MS-DOS command line will start execution and where the Windows operational code and programs are located. These indentifiers must never be modified from the command line, batch, or applications (*winbootdir* can be changed, however, by the Properties pull down in the "MS-DOS Prompt" dialog box of Microsoft "Windows"). If these parameters are changed, then the operation of the PC might become erratic or it might stop working completely.

Going further, none of the environment information should ever be modified in memory by an application. The Environment block that is pointed to by the PSP in your application is global to the entire PC. Incorrect changes to this information could cause problems with other applications or even the PC's operation.

The COMSPEC identifier indicates the data input interface used by MS-DOS. This should always be COMMAND.COM (or SHELL.EXE, if you run with the simple GUI created with some of the later versions of DOS) unless you want to create your own interface. For some versions of MS-DOS, you might want to add some parameters to COMMAND.COM's operation; these are explained in MS-DOS manuals and are added to the Environment block by modifying the autoexec.bat file.

CMDLINE is used to indicate what the current program's execution is. This parameter can be a bit unpredictable; in the case shown in Fig. 10-2, the indicator is showing that the current program is debug (correct) and debug was executed with parameter FIND-CURS.COM (incorrect). I never access this identifier because of the opportunity for the information contained within it to be incorrect. Instead, I rely the implicit knowledge of what program is running and the PSP to look up the command line parameters.

The final parameter is the BLASTER identifier, which is used to specify the operating conditions of the sound card in the PC. Other hardware installed in a PC could use the Environment block and its parameters, such as this one to specify how it is set up and allow applications to access them appropriately.

DOS Interrupt Interface

The DOS interrupt interface is similar to the BIOS interrupt interfaces; specific processor registers are set with specific values and then a software interrupt is invoked. The primary MS-DOS interrupt interface is interrupt 0x021, although a number of other interrupts have been allocated to MS-DOS to provide additional functions.

Appendix E includes the different MS-DOS interrupt interfaces. This chapter introduces some of the most commonly used MS-DOS functions and how they are used in applications.

CONSOLE INTERFACING

If you've read through the book up to this point, you'll probably have a good idea of what I'm going to say about console interfacing using MS-DOS. If you guessed that I would say that it shouldn't be done, you'd be just about completely correct. Writing directly to VRAM and accessing the keyboard and mouse from the BIOS APIs is a much more efficient and faster way to develop applications. It allows data filtering and processing that would have to be repeated if the MS-DOS functions were used.

But, if you are just beginning to write assembler applications for the PC, then I would recommend using them instead of the BIOS routines because they do not require any parameters or special knowledge, other than the PC's extended keystrokes (listed in Appendix D).

Interrupt 021h AH = 01h is the console input with echo and displays each keystroke as ASCII characters and returns when Enter or a function key is pressed.

The function keys return 0x000 or 0x0E0 as their ASCII character in the two bytes returned, so a second MS-DOS read is required to get the scan code as a second byte.

Reading a character and returning its value could be coded as:

```
        mov CharExt, OFFh       ;  Assume an ASCII Character
        mov AH, 1
        int 021h
        mov CharRead, AL        ;  Save the Return Keystroke


        cmp AL, 0E0h            ;  Is the Keystroke Extended?
        jz Get Extend
        cmp AL, 000h
        jnz HaveChar            ;  If it is Not 0x000 or 0x0E0 it is Not
                                ;  Extended
Get Extend:                     ;  Get the Extended Keystroke
        mov CharExt, 0
        mov AH, 1               ;  Read the Next Character
        int 021h
        mov CharRead, AL


    HaveChar:                   ;  "CharRead" has the Return Character
```

To further simplify input, you can use MS-DOS API AH = 00Ah, which places a string from the keyboard into a user specified buffer. The buffer address, which is passed to the MS-DOS API, has its first byte loaded with the maximum number of characters and the second byte will return with the number of characters written into the buffer. MS-DOS API AH = 00Ah buffered keyboard input will allow some editing inside the function by using the Backspace key and overwriting the erroneous data.

A single byte can be output to the display using the MS-DOS API AH = 2 (write character) or the MS-DOS API AH = 9 (write string ending with a "$" character) will output a string of data.

These APIs are very easy to work with.

The issue with the MS-DOS console APIs that I don't like is the inability to move the screen pointer to different locations (other than the line start or next line) and you cannot write characters in different colors. This is possible with the ANSI.SYS device driver, but this interface is slow and cumbersome when compared to accessing VRAM directly.

With the APIs described in this section, the PC just behaves like a monochrome Teletype, which makes for a good beginner's interface, but gets old and difficult to work with very quickly—especially in light of what is possible.

Practical Graphics Programming

For some of your MS-DOS applications, you might want to take advantage of the VGA hardware in your PC and create a graphical display. I discourage this as much as possible because the graphics hardware in a PC can be slow, difficult to work with, and nonstandard for high-resolution applications in MS-DOS. I really don't recommend using it and instead recommend that you develop the application under Windows using Visual Basic, where these problems are virtually unknown. If you do insist on using graphics in MS-DOS, a few suggestions can help you out.

Saying that PC graphics tends to be slow is probably surprising (and infuriating if you've dropped several hundred dollars on an ultra-fast 3-D graphics adapter card). The reason for the problems with the speed is how the hardware operates at a basic level. For all of my programming, I stick with the basic VGA capabilities and avoid the enhanced features.

The reason why I avoid the advanced features is because they are not standard across all devices and documentation and libraries are not necessarily available, unless you are willing to sign an *Non-Disclosure Agreement* (*NDA*) or buy a developer's kit. These solutions can be very expensive and take a great deal of time if you have to get a lawyer involved. As well, you might have the situation where you have designed your application to take advantage of a specific adapter's hardware, only to find that in the future, the functions or even the card itself is no longer available.

This leaves you with the basic VGA specification that is up to 640 by 400 pixels with each pixel having at least 256 different color combinations (different hardware implementation can move this into literally billions of different colors). These colors are selected from a look-up table, which outputs to a *Digital Analog Converter* (*DAC*) to output the correct voltage levels for the displays RGB CRT guns (Fig. 10-3).

To draw something on the screen, the DAC table (known as the *palette*) has to be loaded with the appropriate value and the pixels in the VRAM have to be updated appropriately.

The basic VGA mode (mode 013h), which I recommend that you use, is a 320-by-200 pixel display. Each pixel can select between 256 colors, requiring one byte per pixel. To update each pixel on the screen, at PCI data rates (33 MHz), would take a minimum of:

```
Full Update = 320 x 200 x 30 nsec
            = 1.9 msec
```

This does not include palette updates or processing, which will add significantly to the time required to do a full update. For example, adding 1 usec per pixel for processing increases the total display update time to 66 ms, which would give a maximum frame rate of 15 frames per second (in contrast, movies are normally 24 frames per second and TV is 30 frames per second).

Even a 1-µs per pixel calculation speed is very optimistic and the actual graphic animation speed would probably be two to five frames per second. This is why nonaccelerated games are so slow and why, after a game is written, the designers will spend literally months working through the application, looking for opportunities to speed it up. Nobody wants an F-16 flight simulator that crawls through the sky.

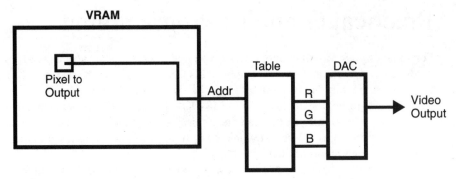

FIGURE 10-3   Graphic output hardware.

Because each pixel has to be written individually, developing shapes and Polygon transformations, along with screen clipping all has to be done in software which makes the application very complex and "bulky". Libraries might be available for the compiler you are using to provide many of these functions, but you will probably find that they don't interface well with what you want to do and probably seem quite slow.

Now, you might take exception to my characterization that MS-DOS graphics are nonstandard, but I am referring to being able to display standard graphic files (such as .JPG, .GIF, etc.). There could be libraries written to handle these file types, and they could interface with your compiler. Chances are, they will be slow because they have to work in a variety of systems.

Graphic statements are also not standard across different implementations of C or BASIC. This means that code that works very well in one compiler might not in others. Different hardware also has different interfaces, which is why I tend to stick with the basic VGA standard.

With this background, I'm going to say that for your MS-DOS PC applications, the screen should remain static and only well-supported modes used. As I indicated, I recommend *Video Mode 013h*, which gives you a 320-by-200 display (which is 40 by 25 characters in Text mode) with 256 colors out of a palette of 16 million.

Each pixel in the display is represented as a byte that can select from 256 colors loaded into the palette's Table register. This might seem limited, but run graphic4.exe from the Graphics subdirectory on the CD-ROM. This program provides a scrolling graphic display that runs in real time. Also on the screen is a text message that has its foreground and background changing color continuously (Fig. 10-4).

After watching the program (to end it, press any key), take a look at the source file, all 205 lines of it.

This is not a very complex application and, to give the impression of movement, "color palette rotation" is used. The palette is originally loaded with black going to white, black going to red, black going to green, and black going to blue. Each of these operations occur in 64 steps (to make up the 256 palette table entries).

When this program runs, I simply wait for the 55-ms system timer to increment its counters and then shift the palette table entries by one. By rotating the 256 palette entries, it gives the appearance of changing every VRAM byte on the display once every 55 ms.

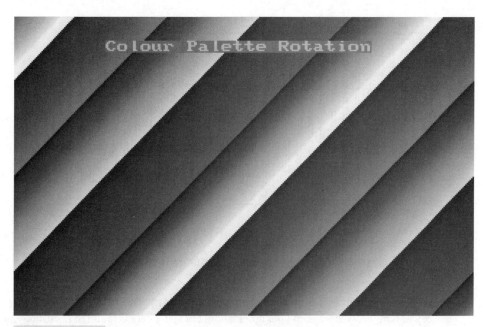

FIGURE 10-4   Graphics output color rotation in mode 013h.

This technique of changing the palette settings instead of VRAM can be very power-ful in a variety of situations. For example, later in the book I will present some exam-ples of how Visual Basic can create bar-graph displays. In the Visual Basic examples, the PC's display actually gets written to with new VRAM values to implement the function. In an MS-DOS VGA graphic display, setting up a bar graph in which each bar written to VRAM is given a different palette entry can simulate this same function (Fig. 10-5).

In this case, to display Full, all I have to do is load all 32-palette entries with a nonblack value. To show half full, the pallet entries for Bar 0x000 to 0x00F have to be set to a non-black value (with the remaining 16 set to a black value).

The color palette register updates can execute very quickly and do not require any changes to the pixels on the screen. They will allow you to give the impression of move-ment without having to actually write to VRAM.

This is what I meant when I said that it is best to leave the display static. Instead of changing the VRAM contents, the palette can be changed very quickly and more easily. This method, using video mode 013h with the palette table is fully supported in BIOS and is a very effective tool to create impressive animated graphic displays.

MEMORY ALLOCATION

Before you begin writing complex applications in MS-DOS, you have to realize that mem-ory is a resource in the traditional meaning of the word. Blocks of it can be allocated, re-sized, or freed using the MS-DOS allocate memory (AH = 048h), free allocated memory

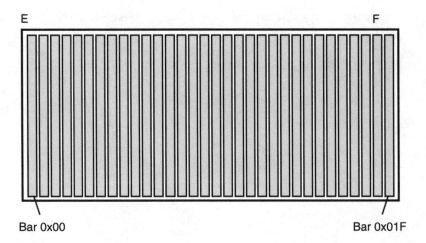

Bar 0x00   Bar 0x01F

FIGURE 10-5   **Gauge using color palette for display.**

(AH = 49h), and resize allocated memory (AH = 4Ah). The APIs allow you to use memory as temporary storage in your application, but some care is required to ensure you don't end up with undetectable errors or errors, which will cause MS-DOS to fail.

In MS-DOS, memory is normally set up as in Fig. 10-6. This shows that after the application is loaded into the available memory, all of the remaining memory above the application can be used by the application.

When MS-DOS loads an application, all of the available memory is allocated to it. Many high-level languages free the unneeded memory before your code begins to execute. If you are writing an application in assembler, one of first things you should do is to resize the

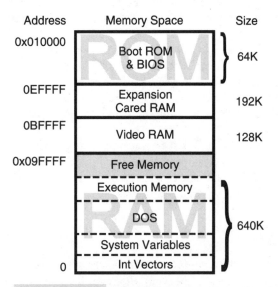

FIGURE 10-6   **The PC's memory map showing free memory.**

memory allocated for the application to just what's required. This will give you the rest of the memory to be dynamically allocated by the application.

You might be wondering why allocating memory from MS-DOS is even required, many high-level languages have a built-in heap space, from which the application can allocated memory. The problems with the heaps are that they are of limited size (normally 32 KB, to avoid integer bit 15 negation inconsistencies) and are also used by library routines to process data. When large amounts of data are needed in an application, it is much safer and more efficient to use the memory unused by BIOS, MS-DOS, or the application.

Each memory block is the allocated size, rounded up to the next paragraph boundary and headed by a single paragraph (16 bytes), which is used by MS-DOS to indicate the status of the memory block.

The paragraph header is in the format:

OFFSET	SIZE	DESCRIPTION
0	Byte	0x05A if the last block in memory (to 0x09FFFF), 0x04D if not
1	Word	PSP segment address of block owner
3	Word	Size of blocks in paragraphs
5	3 bytes	Reserved
8	8 bytes	ASCII string of block owner

These header blocks can be manipulated in software, but it is much easier to allow MS-DOS to do it for you via the APIs listed.

To allocate (or resize) a segment of memory, the number of paragraphs required is passed to the MS-DOS memory-function APIs. I use the following formula to determine the amount of paragraphs needed for a specific number of bytes.

```
Paragraphs = ( Bytes + 15 ) / 16
```

This formula will round up to the next required paragraph and then divide down by the paragraph size to specify the actual number required.

As many blocks as are required can be allocated, although I try to keep the number small. The problems with allocating many blocks include keeping them straight and trying to avoid memory fragmentation.

For example, in your PC application, you might have 320 KB available and an application initially allocates nine blocks of 32 KB each. Later in the application, the second and fifth blocks of memory are freed. The problem arises when you want to allocate a single block of 40 KB (Fig. 10-7).

First, you would try to allocate a single block of 40 KB, but this will fail because no single block of this size is available. In this case, you would have to move the data in one of the blocks adjacent to a free block into the other free block to make a total free space of 64 KB. This works, but will take some effort, both in terms of moving the data, as well as ensuring that the pointers to the moved data are also changed.

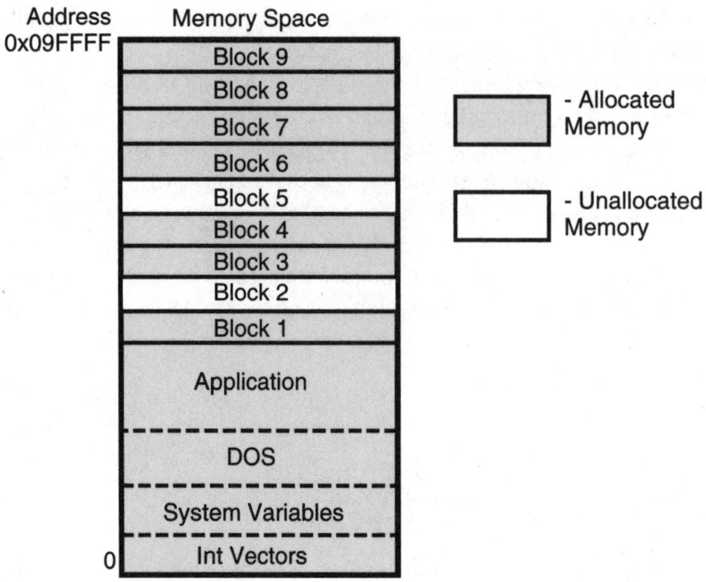

Address   Memory Space
0x09FFFF

| Block 9 |
| Block 8 |
| Block 7 |
| Block 6 |
| Block 5 |
| Block 4 |
| Block 3 |
| Block 2 |
| Block 1 |
| Application |
| DOS |
| System Variables |
| Int Vectors |

- Allocated Memory

- Unallocated Memory

FIGURE 10-7 **Memory allocation problem.**

Even when the application ends, the allocated blocks will still be in place in memory and will not be available to any subsequent applications. Forgetting to free allocated memory blocks is a common error that can result in a lot of head scratching later when an application is being run repeatedly and stops after the second or third perfectly run execution.

When allocating memory using the MS-DOS APIs, remember to check the carry flag status. If it is set, the returned value is not a segment of newly allocated memory, but the maximum number of paragraphs available. Writing to the number of paragraphs available as an address instead of a valid segment will trash your application just as surely as if you wrote data randomly into the PC's memory. This is a common problem for people writing their first memory allocation applications and it can seem like something totally unreasonable is happening.

Another common mistake is to write data beyond the size of the block that has been allocated. When this happens, often the header paragraph of the next block is overwritten and its data is lost. This problem usually presents itself as the:

```
Unable to load Command.Com
```

Failure, which has little to do with the actual error. If you don't know the cause, it will be just about impossible to find.

When memory has been allocated successfully, the Memory Allocate API returns the starting segment address of the newly allocated block and the carry flag will be reset. The initial offset within the block's starting segment is 0x00000, which means that the header is in the previous paragraph (address Block Start - 1:0x00000).

In a high-level language, I use the segment returned from the Memory Allocate API to create a far pointer to the segment and simply reset the offset and use it as a normal pointer to an array of bytes. This concept is explored in more detail in the C/C++ description.

LIM EXPANDED MEMORY SPECIFICATION

A few years after the PC first became available, it became obvious that the 640 KB in MS-DOS was insufficient to run large PC applications (with one of the most notable problems with very large spreadsheets). Lotus, Intel, and Microsoft worked together to create a specification to add additional memory to the 1-MB 8086 memory area.

The *LIM standard* (as it became known) was very successful. I always credited this success to the three companies that were involved and the foresight that they showed. Microsoft implemented the standard in MS-DOS and it can still be used today as *EMM*; it can store MS-DOS functions outside of the 640-KB area to free up the space for applications. Intel was able to work with the function to allow it to be implemented in the 80386 microprocessor and Lotus implemented the standard in their popular "1-2-3" software to ensure that it was optimized for applications.

In my first PC, it was much cheaper and faster for me to buy a LIM-compatible memory card with 256 KB of DRAM, load it up with the contents of a boot diskette, and run from there, rather than buy a hard drive or even a second diskette drive.

The LIM specification essentially took a portion of the 8086's memory and used it as a memory-mapped window into a much larger memory space (Fig. 10-8).

The maximum 32 MB of expanded memory is broken up into 2048 16-KB "pages". As many as 12 of any of these pages could be accessed through the memory-mapped "page frame".

When the standard was originally released, the expanded memory was an ISA bus card that had hardware used to select which page would show up in the different frames. In the

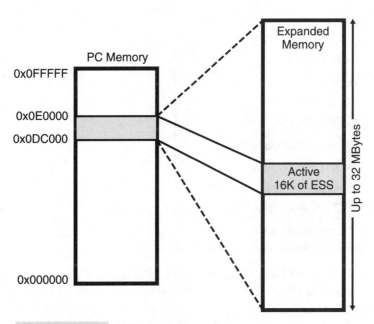

FIGURE 10-8   LIMS frame operation.

80386, it was possible to set up a LIM expanded memory manager (EMM) totally in software and the code was added to MS-DOS 3.0. This code interfaced to Intel's XMAMS.SYS device driver and allowed programs that use extended memory to have EMM co-exist with it. For several years, in the late 1980s and early 1990s, EMS, EMM, and XMAMS drivers would be loaded into the system, each given specific memory areas to operate from. This made setting up PCs much more technically challenging for the operator than they are today.

It is important to note that when XMAMS.SYS is enabled, the PC's processor is actually running in Protect Mode. The LIM EMS Protect mode has created a "virtual" 8086 Real-mode session with one major discontinuity in the first 1 MB to provide the window into the LIM EMS page frame and the pages that it logically displays.

Even without the shift from MS-DOS to Windows, LIM EMS was doomed with the 80386. LIM EMS is a very slow way to access large amounts of memory. In many MS-DOS programs that required more than the 640 KB available, the processor is run in 32-bit "flat model" Protect mode with the entire memory space available to the application.

FILE CONTROL BLOCKS VERSUS THE HANDLE-BASED INTERFACE

I am always amazed at the number of modern applications that have been written to use the MS-DOS file-control block APIs, instead of the handle-based APIs, which are really much easier to work with. Microsoft first introduced the file-handle APIs with MS-DOS version 2.0, which was first released in 1983. The only reason that I can presume it is still popular is because many beginner assembly-language programming books were written with only the File-Control Block APIs referenced.

A file-control block is a small block of memory reserved in the PSP for file I/O. The block is in the format:

OFFSET	DATA FIELD
000h	Drive Number (0 = A, 1 = B. .)
001h	File Name (8 Bytes)
009h	File Extension (3 Bytes)
00Ch	Current Active Block (Word)
00Eh	Record Size (Word)
010h	MS-DOS File Size (Double Word)
014h	MS-DOS File Data (Double Word)
018h	Reserved (8 Bytes)

The MS-DOS and Reserved fields are set up by MS-DOS and should not be accessed by the application code. The MS-DOS FCB APIs reference one or the other FCBs when accessing the files.

The problems with this interface is that the FCBs in the PSP must be written to (a potentially dangerous operation), subdirectory path information is not available with the filename, and you must keep track of the file manually. The lack of subdirectory information that makes keeping track of what is happening very difficult. A secondary problem is that the extra long file names of the *High-Performance File System* (*HPFS*) are not supported.

The file-handle APIs work much more simply, only requiring the file's drive, subdirectory and file name, and extension. The HPFS long file names are supported in these APIs. After a file is opened, a 16-bit handle is returned that is used to reference the specific file. Under the file-handle APIs, the maximum number of files that can be opened at any time is limited by the number of files specified in the config.sys file of the PC.

For the file-handle APIs, the file name is in the form of an ASCIIZ string. This is simply an ASCII character string that is ended with an ASCII null (0x000) character. The filename string is in the same format as you would use from the MS-DOS command line.

An assembler variable containing the ASCIIZ string for the command.com file in a Windows system would be defined as:

```
CmdFile DB "C:\Windows\command.com", 0
```

The file-handle-based API interface fits in very well with high-level language interfaces. For example, to read the first 10 bytes of a file into a buffer in C, the code:

```
Handle = open ( FileName, Options );
read ( Handle, Buffer, 10 );
close ( Handle );
```

would be used, which, when converted into assembler would be:

```
mov AH, 03Dh              ; Open the File
mov AL, Options
push DS                   ; DS:DX Points to the FileName
lds DX, FileName
int 021h

mov BX, AX                ; Save the File Handle in BX
                          ;  - where it is used.
mov AH, 03Fh              ; Read the first 10 Bytes
lds DX, Buffer            ; DS:DX Points to the Buffer
mov CX, 10
int 021h

mov AH, 03Eh              ; Close the File
int 021h

pop DS                    ; Restore the Data Segment
```

Every time the file is read or written to, an internal MS-DOS pointer is moved to the new location. The pointer can be moved with the *lseek* file-pointer move API.

Files can be created (which automatically opens them and returns a handle) or deleted with this the file-handle API interface. If you are writing beyond the end of the current file, the file simply becomes larger. In this case, you could run the risk of going beyond the size available on the target disk. *Write* always returns the number of bytes actually written. If you run out of space, this value will be less than the expected number.

Later in the book (especially in the sections devoted to OSless booting, you can see some good examples of how the file-handle APIs work and are used.

MULTIPROCESSING IN MS-DOS

I wrote this at the same time as when I was writing "Protect Mode" in Chapter 6 and I felt that I should do everything I could to steer you away from trying to create multitasking applications in MS-DOS. Before getting too flippant and just putting in something like "don't!", I realized that there are some things I should explain about why you shouldn't attempt to create multiprocessing applications in MS-DOS.

I consider *multiprocessing* to be an extension of *multitasking*, in which independently triggered events cause a special handling code to execute. These events can be timers or external hardware, and the code is usually part of a device driver or MS-DOS "Terminate and Stay Resident" ("TSR") application. Multitasking operating environments are normally not available in MS-DOS and multiprocessing avoids this issue by placing the extra handlers outside of the currently executing application.

MS-DOS is not re-entrant; if while it is processing one request, another comes along, the second request will cause the first or second to fail, the disk contents to become damaged, or the whole PC to lock up. A real-life example of this would be having a TSR sharing the timer tick interrupt (Int 008h) and this TSR had to access the disk periodically, you could get into the situation in Fig. 10-9.

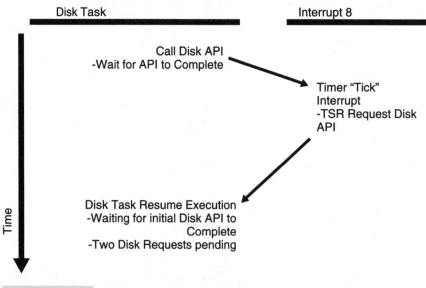

FIGURE 10-9   Disk task waiting for timer Int to complete.

When the timer time-interrupt handler invoked the MS-DOS disk API, MS-DOS is not able to serialize the two requests. The second request will cause MS-DOS to change the variables required for the first request with obviously disastrous results.

As a potential work around, you might want to capture all Interrupt 021h and BIOS disk requests and provide the serialization yourself. This will work, but will make your application much more complex because now it requires a state to skip interrupt requests for some period of time until the command has completed.

Some readers may remember Sidekick, which was a TSR application that provided many of the functions of the Windows desktop and was available from a hot-key sequence. Sidekick had some specific routines and features to avoid using the MS-DOS APIs when the "foreground" application used them. Despite the efforts placed in the TSR to avoid interfering with the executing application, Sidekick had a number of problems and could cause the PC to lock up.

I highly recommend that you avoid these issues and do not attempt to carry out any multiprocessing under MS-DOS, instead your application should be able to handle all external events required of the PC or a multitasking operating system, such as Windows, should be used.

THE COMMAND LINE AND COMMAND.COM

You will probably be surprised to discover that MS-DOS command line processing is not a part of the operating system. Instead, it is a program (called *command.com*) that takes user input, carries out some basic file operations (such as copy and delete) and executes applications. In some versions of MS-DOS, you might have the option of the "shell.exe", which provides a rudimentary GUI. In either case, the front-end program provides the user interface and allows application and utility execution.

Command.com not only loads and executes applications (ending in *.com* or *.exe*), but it also executes batch files (which ends in *.bat*). Only one file at a time can be executed from command.com, although these programs can load and execute other *.com* or *.exe* files using MS-DOS APIs.

A copy of command.com is required for each disk or diskette from which the PC is to boot MS-DOS. It is normally copied onto the disk with the "/s" (add "system files") parameter when the disk is formatted. Simply copying it on to a diskette without the boot files will not create a "boot diskette". A number of "hidden" files are also required.

AUTOEXEC.BAT

The AUTOEXEC.BAT file is primarily responsible for how the user will interface with the MS-DOS command-line program (COMMAND.COM). Along with path information, AUTOEXEC.BAT specifies the operating conditions of the PC and will run any programs needed during execution (a common program to be run is MOUSE.COM, which provides the mouse interface for the PC). AUTOEXEC.BAT does affect the operation of Windows by specifying the path information used by some applications (such as compilers and linkers) when they are looking for a file to use.

The AUTOEXEC.BAT file is not used by the operating system. Instead, it is only accessed when the MS-DOS command-line interface is started.

The most crucial function of AUTOEXEC.BAT is its specifying of path information for the system's environment. This information is used to search for a specific file is standard directories without making the user or an application responsible for loading the file to search through the whole hard drive to find the correct files.

The AUTOEXEC.BAT file is executed by the COMMAND.COM program, after it has been loaded by the operating system. This is after MS-DOS has booted and the information and programs in CONFIG.SYS have been loaded. This is important to remember because, for some applications, certain drivers and programs have to be loaded and executed before others.

Enhanced batch-file functions (such as conditional jumping) can be run from AUTOEXEC.BAT, but it's not recommended. AUTOEXEC.BAT should just be used to set the operating parameters of the system.

I don't go into a lot of detail about either AUTOEXEC.BAT or CONFIG.SYS and the programs that are normally loaded from them. A number of excellent books are dedicated to how your PC should be set up and how to create the initialization programs.

CONFIG.SYS

The CONFIG.SYS file is used to specify resources available within the operation of the PC. It differs from the AUTOEXEC.BAT file because the parameters do not directly affect how the PC appears to operate to the user. The file parameters (which are known as *device drivers*) are executed from COMMAND.COM and load new capabilities in terms of BIOS and file-system functions for the PC.

Many of the features available (e.g., extended memory) are specific to certain applications and hardware. These options are documented by their authors, along with their operating parameters.

You should be aware of two parameters: "Files" and "Buffers". These parameters provide resources for the applications to execute. *Buffers* specifies the number of file temporary data areas for file-system transfers. *Files* specifies the number of files that can be open at any one time.

```
FILES = 20
BUFFERS = 30
```

are good defaults to use in MS-DOS systems. Ten should be added to each parameter for Windows 95/98 systems.

MS-DOS

COMMAND-LINE

PROGRAMMING

Later, the book presents instructions on how to write software-control applications for Microsoft Windows 95/98. Before going through this, it is important to know how programs are formatted and executed within the PC. This chapter presents the different types of application software files; their uses and a couple of example applications, including an MS-DOS version of "The Game of Life".

Much of the information presented in this chapter (and the one following) is available in other books (and might be more comprehensive), but my focus is on the practical aspects of interfacing the user to the hardware. These practical aspects not only consist of focusing on how the software executes, but how to properly interpret data coming in and display it to the user.

Batch Files and Interpreters

Batch files are an interesting construct within MS-DOS. They are similar to script files in Unix and other operating systems because they can execute command-line statements, as well as provide some logic to the operations. As I go through the different capabilities of batch files, I think you will be impressed at what is possible and will see some opportunities for your own application programming.

Batch files are primarily used in three different application types. AUTOEXEC.BAT, covered elsewhere in the book, is used to specify the operating parameters of the PC (both for the MS-DOS command line and Windows). The second use is to simplify the operation of common commands that have many different parameters to remember to use (and key in) known as "wrappers". The final use is to actually create applications from batch files.

In all three different applications, batch files execute MS-DOS applications in the source as the function of the application. In AUTOEXEC.BAT, these statements are used to specify the operating characteristics (such as the search subdirectory *paths*) and load any TSRs that enhance the PC's operation. The MS-DOS statement execution is the batch-file program output.

To change the current operating subdirectory within a batch file, the *cd* statement is used. If the current subdirectory is changed, the batch file will still continue to execute because it was loaded into memory before the *cd* statement was executed and does not have to be reloaded during execution.

The normal execution invocation format for batch files is:

```
BatchFileName [Parameter [, Parameter .. ]]
```

The parameters are passed to the batch-file program and can be accessed as *%1*, *%2*, etc., for the *Parameters* (*%0* does exist as the filename of the batch file itself). These values are used within the batch-file source and when the source file is executed (from COMMAND.COM); the parameters are substituted for the values.

For example, a batch file (called *cbackup.bat*) that copies a C source file into a .BAK (backup) file could be:

```
copy %1.c %1.BAK
```

Invoking this batch file is accomplished by entering:

```
cbackup C_Source
```

Where *C_Source.c* is the source file to save as a .BAK file. This batch file could be useful to run before an editor in which the source code is modified by an editor. Expanding on this, editbak.bat, which saves the current source as a .BAK file before allowing the user to modify it could be:

```
copy %1.c %1.BAK
edit %1.c
```

Simplifying the operation of applications using batch files is often referred to as *wrappers* and is used when many different parameters are available for an MS-DOS application file. I normally keep a number of these in my \bat subdirectory for simplifying assembling, compiling, and linking.

To create more-complex applications, the batch-file processor built into COM-MAND.COM has a number of statements, along with string variables, that it can use to execute more-complex applications.

These statements (which can be in upper, lower, or mixed case) are:

STATEMENT	DESCRIPTION
call	Call a batch file as a subroutine. At the end of the called batch file, execution is returned to the calling batch file.
echo	Display text (no variables) or turn the echoing of each batch file line on or off.
For	Not a traditional FOR statement—used to repeat an operation within a set, rather than using a variable.
goto	Change execution to a label.
if [not] ERRORLEVEL	Compare the current ERRORLEVEL value to a constant and execute conditionally.
if [not] exist	Execute conditionally if file exists.
if parm1 == parm2	Compare parameters and execute conditionally.
rem	Comment follows for the rest of the line.
shift	Move accessible window of command line parameters "down." Initially only *%0* to *%9* is available, after executing *shift*, *%1* becomes *%0*, *%2*, becomes *%1*, etc.

String variables are defined as environment strings and use the *set* command. To set a variable value, you could use:

```
set Variable=ValueString
```

Numerical variables cannot be defined, only strings. These strings can be modified by new *set* statements either to change the string, concatenate a string to the end of it, or delete it all together.

To delete a variable, which is important at the end of a batch file to free up the environment space used, by the variable, the *set* statement is used with no *ValueString* specified.

```
set Variable=
```

Concatenating strings onto the current variable use the format you are probably familiar with from AUTOEXEC.BAT and adding subdirectories to the *path* environment variable:

```
set Variable=%Variable%NewString
```

Because batch file variables are implemented as environment variables, there is the opportunity for batch-file variables to cause problems with variables needed in the system. To avoid this problem, batch-file variables should never contain the following substrings:

```
inc   path   com   temp   tmp   win   blaster prompt net
```

Numerical variables cannot be used within batch files. Some applications use strings as the numeric values and process them in complex batch-file subroutines or in small applications, but you really are best off not using them at all. The following paragraphs show how concatenating characters on a string can be used as a counter in batch files.

So far, I've shown the % character in a few places. % is the "escape" character in batch files. It is used to specify the start of a constant string or, when it encloses a string, it used to specify the variable value, rather than the variable name.

The other special character used in batch files is the @ ("at") symbol, which is used at the start of the line to suppress outputting of the entire line. For debugging batch files, you can suppress the outputting of some lines by placing an @ character as the first statement.

For many complex batch files, you will see the first line:

```
@echo off
```

which suppresses all data output throughout the batch file (the "echo off" statement) and prevents the *echo off* statement from being displayed.

Labels within batch files are labels with a colon (:) at the start of the line with no blanks in between the colon and the label. An example of a valid batch file label is:

```
:label
```

Labels can be any alphanumeric string that starts with a character. There are no reserved label names, as you will get in other languages.

The IF statement (in its three different incarnations) executes in the format:

```
if [Condition is True] Statement
```

Where *Statement* is executed if the condition or test is true. The *Exist* condition returns true if the file specified exists. Strings can also be compared.

ERRORLEVEL is interesting because it contains a numeric value that can be set by an executable program when it returns to the command line (the MS-DOS program-terminate APIs allow this value to be returned). Normally, if everything is working correctly, *ERRORLEVEL* is set to zero; if there is a failure, it is set to −1. Other values are used as parameters.

The FOR statement in batch files merits some attention because it does not work as you would most likely expect. FOR is used in the format:

```
For %%VariableName in (set) do Statement
```

A typical example using FOR could be:

```
for %%a in (*.lst) do delete %%a
```

which deletes all the *.lst* files in the current subdirectory.

A single statement can be repeated multiple times using the FOR statement, such as:

```
for %%a in (! ! ! ! ! !) do Statement
```

in which *Statement* is executed six times. FOR cannot be used to execute multiple statements repeatedly. To do this, I use the template batch file:

```
@echo off
rem FOR_LOOP, Show how a 'FOR' Loop Can be Simulated in a Batch File
```

```
set target=
if %1! == 0! set target=
if %1! == 1! set target=!
if %1! == 2! set target=!!
if %1! == 3! set target=!!!
if %1! == 4! set target=!!!!
if %1! == 5! set target=!!!!!
if %1! == 6! set target=!!!!!!
if %1! == 7! set target=!!!!!!!
if %1! == 8! set target=!!!!!!!!
if %1! == 9! set target=!!!!!!!!!
set count=
:loop
if %count%! == %target%! goto end
set count=%count%!
echo %count%
rem #### - Put Code in the FOR_LOOP Here
goto loop
:end
echo %target% Done
set target=
set count=
```

In this file, the first parameter (*%1*) is used to load a variable with a string with a set number of *!* characters, based on the value of the first parameter. *Count* is cleared and then each iteration has a *!* character concatenated onto it and compared to *target* (the string of *!*s that is equal in size to the first parameter). When the two variables match, then the batch file "falls out" of the loop.

One important aspect of this batch file to note is that it clears the two variables (*count* and *target*) at the end and frees up the environment space that they use.

Over the years, I have seen some incredibly complex batch-file applications that rival that of any Assembly, BASIC, or C program that I have ever seen. Even though I have just spent several pages showing you how flexible and powerful the batch-file processor in COMMAND.COM is, I would have to recommend that you keep your batch files fairly simple and use the tricks I've shown when it makes the most sense. These cases include simplifying the user operation of an application with lots of parameters or running MS-DOS applications with different specified files. These "wrapper" applications are easy to write and do make your life easier.

Any other applications should be written in a high-level language and converted into an executable file. The reason for this is because of the environment space used by the batch-file application (which might not be sufficient for the application and called MS-DOS applications to execute), the difficulty in creating complex applications, and the relatively slow speed of execution at which the batch files run.

"Tiny" (.COM) Memory Model Programs

When you first begin assembly-language programming for the PC, I highly recommend that you only write "Tiny" or ".COM" programs initially. These programs avoid the issue of how to handle the segment registers and allows you to think of the PC as a simple 16-bit computer with 64 KB of memory. From this perspective, it's actually quite easy to understand how to program the 8086.

Later, this chapter explains the different execution program memory models used in MS-DOS executable files (.EXE) and how their names have come about. I am only noting this because a compact model would seem to make sense if its executable file was ended in .COM (or at least more sense than having Tiny executable file names end in .COM). .COM was originally paired with what was known as the *compact executable memory model*, but as more complex definitions came about, the *compact* label seemed to make more sense for describing a different executable-file memory model (which ends in .EXE).

The previous two paragraphs could appear to be quite an overwhelming and frightening statement, depending on some people's background and previous experiences. To clarify, here's more about how the PC works. To understand .COM applications, you should think back to when you worked on microcontrollers or eight-bit microprocessor trainers. In these systems, along with the application, you probably also had to create the interfaces for different hardware that can be addressed by the processor. At the very least, a BIOS ROM was included in the system that took space away from the total memory that was available for the application.

If this is what came to mind when I introduced .COM programming, you probably got a sinking feeling because, looking at your PC, to add your own I/O, you would have to develop your own file system (that could read and write to DOS formatted files on diskette, fixed disks, and CD-ROMs), video drivers, network interfaces, keyboard and mouse interfaces, and video drivers. Coupled with a 64-KB limitation, you're probably thinking that it would be impossible to write a meaningful application.

And you'd be right. The complexity of modern PCs has really made it impossible for these functions to be stored in a very small space (although, with the first IBM PCs, the BIOS and operating system did require less than 32 KB) and it would be really inefficient to have the application programmer develop this code (and really invalidate the previous two chapters on the built-in BIOS and MS-DOS).

Applications always take up a fraction of the total memory available in a PC. After being loaded into memory, an application has all the remaining memory allocated to it (this is commented on more elsewhere in this chapter), and can access the system resources using the BIOS and OS API interfaces and interrupts.

I usually think of the PC's memory map, with an application as in Fig. 11-1. The application program (including .COM files) executes from memory and uses the resources available in the PC.

The .COM executable file contains the program code and variables within a single 64-KB segment. This means that all code and data can be accessed directly without having to set up different segment values or execute far calls and gotos. Obviously, accessing the PC, BIOS, or operating-system resources require making these changes to some extent, although with the interrupt interface, this is virtually eliminated, except when you want to access system variables in segment 0x040 (Fig. 11-2).

When the application is created, you have to decide where to place the features in the code. This is dictated by the .COM program being loaded directly into the PC's memory with the PSP being placed in the first 256 bytes of the program and execution starting at address 0x0100.

PC Memory Space

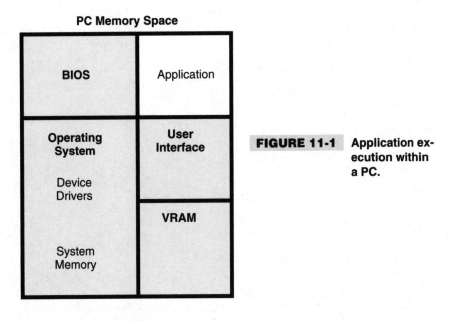

FIGURE 11-1   Application execution within a PC.

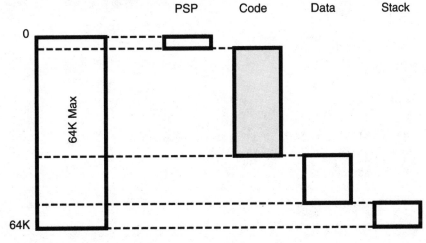

FIGURE 11-2   "Tiny" memory model.

To make developing a .COM program easier, I typically use the assembly-language template:

```
PAGE ,132
TITLE FileName - File Description
;
; FileName - File Description
;
; This Program is assembled and linked into a .COM format executable.
;
```

```
;
; Written By: Myke Predko
;
;
; Version x.xx
;
; Started: xx.xx.xx
; Updated: xx.xx.xx
;
;
; Conventions:
; lower case - assembler mnemonics, macro names
; Mixed Case - Variable Names, Program Labels, And Structures
; UPPER CASE - CONSTANTS AND ASSEMBLER KEYWORDS
;
; Chapters:
; Chapter 1 - Header
; Chapter 2 - Start
; Chapter 3 - Structures
; Chapter 4 - Macros
; Chapter 5 - Constants
; Chapter 6 - Mainline Code
; Chapter 7 - Subroutines
; Chapter 8 - Variables and Messages

PAGE +
 .model tiny
 .stack
 .code
ProgSeg SEGMENT PARA PUBLIC 'CODE'
 ASSUME CS:ProgSeg, DS:ProgSeg, ES:ProgSeg, SS:ProgSeg
 ORG 100H

PAGE +
subtitle Program Structures
;
PtrFmt STRUC ; Format of a Pointer to Memory
PtrOff dw ? ; Offset to the Pointer
PtrSeg dw ? ; Segment of the Pointer
PtrFmt ENDS

PAGE +
subtitle Program Macros
;

PAGE +
subtitle Program Constants
;
DOSINT = 21h ; DOS Interrupt Vector
DOSPrt = 09h ; Print String Operation
DOSEnd = 4Ch ; Stop Execution
DOSSet = 4Ah ; Re-Allocate Memory

PAGE +
subtitle Mainline
Mainline PROC NEAR
;
```

```
PAGE +
subtitle Subroutines
;

PAGE +
subtitle Program Variables and Messages
;

Mainline ENDP
ProgSeg ENDS
 END Start ; End of Program
```

This might be a bit hard to understand, so I'll basically go through the program line by line.

After the program header, I tell the assembler to assume that only one segment used and each of the segment registers should use it. When a .COM program begins executing, the operating system sets all four of the segment registers to the current program segment. With this done, you don't even have to worry about the segment registers with which the program executes (and you are essentially working with a 16-bit processor with all the "standard" interface resources available).

The application execution starts at address 0x0100 and no code can be placed from 0x0000 to 0x00FF. As noted, the program's PSP is loaded into this space when the application is loaded before execution. When the program is assembled, linked, and converted into binary form, this memory is not loaded with anything, although the linker will not place 256 bytes of space in the .COM file. This might make it confusing in circumstances when you are trying to figure out within the program how large it actually is.

With the segment defined and space reserved for the PSP, the mainline can begin to execute. This is probably not all that obvious in the code because after the *org 100h* statement, I put in the program structures, macros, and constants. None of these instructions should take up any memory, so the address at the Mainline label will be 0x0100 and the application can begin executing from there.

I usually put subroutines after the mainline and follow it up with variables. There is no real reason for this order, other than it eliminates a jump from 0x0100 to the start of the mainline. In the next section, when I talk about TSR programs, there are some pretty definite rules about where subroutines and functions are to be placed in the code.

Any time that an executable program is loaded into MS-DOS (or the Windows MS-DOS command line), all of the memory up to the 640-KB boundary (Address 0x09FFF:0x000F) is allocated to the running program. This is also true for .COM programs, even though they are only a maximum of 64-KB in size. For many applications that execute and then end, this is not a problem. For programs that "terminate and stay resident" or use the DOS APIs to allocate buffers, the memory allocated will have to be resized.

If I am going to allocate memory in the program, I always resize the allocated memory to just the required size of the code and variables as one of the first operations that I execute. To do this, I take advantage of the built-in DOS code for allocating/deallocating memory (and not having to write it myself).

The next section shows some code to determine from within the program how to reallocate the program's memory.

The actual file type that is loaded for a .COM file is different from an .EXE. As noted, a .COM file is in exactly the format that it is written in, with no indirection possible. Older tools cannot produce linked files in this format (although newer ones, such as the Linker that comes with Microsoft MASM 6.11, which I used for this book, can). In these cases, a program called *EXE2BIN* was used to convert the .EXE format produced by the linker into .COM format.

To convert a .EXE file to a .COM file, it can only have one segment (and each of the segment registers assumed to use it as I've shown in the template) and it cannot be larger than 64 KB. The process for the conversion is really tool specific and rather than try to go through every possible tool and list how it's done (with the chances are I will miss the tool that you are using), I'm going to recommend that you read through the documentation for the tools that you are using and learn how to create .COM programs from there.

.COM programs have no separate data or stack areas defined. As noted, when a .COM program executes, all segment registers point to the program's execution segment. This means that areas have to be set aside within the "code" segment for variables and, what's often forgotten, the stack.

When a .COM program begins to execute, the Stack Pointer register (SP) is initialized to the end of the 64K segment. If you look at the value in a debugger, you'll see that it's set to 0x0FFFE. If the program memory allocation is resized to the end of the program code and variables to allow the program to allocate memory and the stack pointer is not pointing to a new area within the segment, then there is a chance that your program execution will cause the PC to crash or corrupt its own data when new memory areas are allocated.

To avoid this possibility, create a data area within the variable block for the stack, and before resizing the program, which should be done from the mainline to avoid missing subroutine "return links," move the stack pointer to the end (highest address) of this area. With this done, it's now safe to execute a DOS SetBlock and free up the unused space.

Determining the minimum size of the stack should take into account the lowest level of nested subroutines, along with all of the possible data pushed onto the stack. Added to this should be 30 or so bytes to allow interrupts to process anywhere in the system (including at the bottom of the nested subroutines). Normally, I run with a 1-KB stack, which is adequate for virtually all .COM applications, unless recursive subroutines are used in the application.

In the template file, you should notice that I've put in a number of constants and a structure. These constants are pretty well always used in my assembly-language programming, so to avoid having to look them up, I simply added them to the template.

The structure is the pointer structure that I described earlier in the book:

```
PtrFmt STRUC ; Format of a Pointer to Memory
PtrOff dw ? ; Offset to the Pointer
PtrSeg dw ? ; Segment of the Pointer
PtrFmt ENDS
```

This structure will allow simple access of the segment and offset in any four-byte pointer in an application.

For example, with the pointer defined:

```
Ptr     dd      0            ; Define a Pointer
```

To save the contents of AX into the segment word, the following code is used:

```
mov     Ptr.PtrSeg, AX        ; Load the Pointer Segment
```

To avoid confusion, in all of the PC programming (including .COM executables) I only use *far* pointers, which consist of four bytes, a word containing the offset, followed by a word containing the segment. This is the format used within MS-DOS for pointers within data blocks and is the most common format for *far* pointers used in MS-DOS high-level language compilers.

.COM programs are a bit of an anachronistic beast because of the advent of fast processors, large memories, sophisticated operating systems, and available programming tools. Practically speaking, you will probably never have to develop applications in the .COM format. Although, if you're old enough, you might remember the revolutionary Borland Turbo Pascal products, which, after compiling the source code, produced code in the .COM format.

Turbo Pascal was revolutionary because it showed that a compiler could be made very simply for the PC (which meant cheaply for the customer) at a time when most compilers on the market were trying to emulate their mainframe cousins and provide access to all of the possible features in the PC. The developers of Turbo Pascal realized that the .COM executable program layout gave them a great deal of flexibility with a simple environment to develop executable code.

TERMINATE AND STAY RESIDENT PROGRAMS

One of the more interesting developments of the 1980s PC world was the proliferation of *Terminate and Stay Resident (TSR) applications* that were written for PCs. These programs developed into a remarkable array of "subapplications" that people loaded into their PCs to add to the overall capabilities of the PC. In many ways, this really was an indication that PC users wanted to be able to do more than one thing in their PCs (which probably accelerated the introduction of GUIs in PC operating systems).

The most famous of the TSR program was called *SideKick* by Borland, which would "pop up" and give you a calculator, calendar, address book (which would dial your modem, saving you to do it manually), along with a number of other functions. Sidekick was followed by a host of other applications that would do their best to obscure what was already on the PC's screen.

These screen helpers, although being interesting, really distracted from the primary purpose of the TSR program capability of MS-DOS, which is to provide a method of to enhance a PC and provide resources for all applications, instead of features for just one. The next section includes what I feel is an appropriate use for a TSR.

I have included TSR applications in the .COM executable file section because this is really where they belong. In the original PCs, it wasn't unusual to have PCs with 256 KB or 512 KB of memory, so enhancing programs (such as Sidekick and FindCurs, in the next chapter) were written to use as little space as possible. Although the .COM format helped with this space requirement, most applications were also written in assembly language to really keep the memory requirements to a minimum.

As a side benefit, the .COM applications could simply load the DS and ES segment registers with the contents of the CS register, which simplified the operation of the TSR and sped it up.

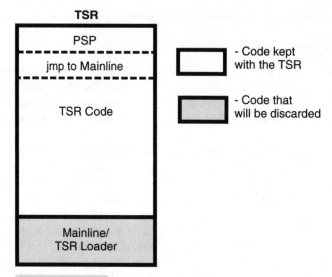

FIGURE 11-3 TSR organization.

I find it is best to think of a TSR program graphically, as in Fig. 11-3:

As a .COM, execution will start at address 0x0100 (after the PSP that the operating system sets up for it). In a TSR, the first instruction is to jump to the mainline code, where hardware is initialized, interrupt handlers are set, and variables are initialized. When the application is ready to run on its own, execution can return to COMMAND.COM, with the code needed to run the application left in memory.

To create a TSR, I have created the template:

```
PAGE ,132
TITLE FileName - File Description
;
; FileName - File Description
;
; This Program is assembled and linked into a Terminate-and-Stay-
Resident
; (TSR) .COM format executable.
;
;
; Written By: Myke Predko
;
;
; Version x.xx
;
; Started: xx.xx.xx
; Updated: xx.xx.xx
;
;
; Conventions:
; lower case - assembler mnemonics, macro names
; Mixed Case - Variable Names, Program Labels, And Structures
; UPPER CASE - CONSTANTS AND ASSEMBLER KEYWORDS
;
;
```

```
; Chapters: (TSR Format)
; Chapter 1 - Header
; Chapter 2 - Start (Jump to Init)
; Chapter 3 - Structures
; Chapter 4 - Macros
; Chapter 5 - Constants
; Chapter 6 - Variables
; Chapter 7 - TSR Interrupt Handlers
; Chapter 8 - TSR Subroutines
; Chapter 10 - Mainline Code (Setup Program and go TSR)
; Chapter 11 - Messages

PAGE +
 .model tiny
 .stack
 .code
ProgSeg SEGMENT PARA PUBLIC 'CODE'
 ASSUME CS:ProgSeg, DS:ProgSeg, ES:ProgSeg, SS:ProgSeg
 ORG 100H
Start: jmp Mainline ; Jump to the Program Initialize
 nop ; Put Variables on Word Boundary

PAGE +
subtitle Program Structures
;
PtrFmt STRUC ; Format of a Pointer to Memory
PtrOff dw ? ; Offset to the Pointer
PtrSeg dw ? ; Segment of the Pointer
PtrFmt ENDS

PAGE +
subtitle Program Macros
;

PAGE +
subtitle Program Constants
;
DOSINT = 21h ; DOS Interrupt Vector
DOSPrt = 09h ; Print String Operation
DOSTSR = 31h ; DOS Terminate and Stay Resident

PAGE +
subtitle Program Variables
;

PAGE +
subtitle Interrupt Handlers
;

PAGE +
subtitle TSR Subroutines
;

PAGE +
subtitle Mainline - Setup Program and go TSR
Mainline PROC NEAR
;

; Everything Done - Now Terminate and Stay Resident
 mov ah, DOSPrt ; Print Message
 lea dx, TSRMsg
```

```
        int DOSINT
        lea ax, Mainline ; Get Code Size needed in Paragraphs
        add ax, 15 ; Goto Next Highest Paragraph
        mov cx, 4
        shr ax, cl
        mov dx, ax
        mov ah, DOSTSR
        mov al, 0
        int DOSINT

    PAGE +
    subtitle Initialization Messages
    TSRMsg db 0Dh, 0Ah, 'TSR Template - Version x.xx'
     db 0Dh, 0Ah, 0Dh, 0Ah, 'Written by Myke Predko - xx.xx.xx'
     db 0Dh, 0Ah, '$'

    Mainline ENDP
    ProgSeg ENDS
     END Start ; End of Program
```

This template, once the code is loaded into it, is assembled into a .COM program and will execute as a TSR. The MS-DOS TSR API (Interrupt 21h AH = 031h) is a regular application terminate (including returning an error code to the command line), but does not free up all the memory of an application. This memory left over is the TSR code.

In the template, memory is defined to be left behind as everything before the *Mainline* label. This means that I may have to duplicate variables and subroutines if it results in smaller code saved with the TSR.

Defining the memory to leave is done in "paragraphs," the specification of which I have described elsewhere in the book. To determine how many paragraphs to save, I use the calculation:

```
    TSR Size = ( "Mainline" + 15 ) / 16
```

I have included this section on TSR programs out of nostalgia more than anything else. TSRs can be a lot of fun to write and in some cases are exactly what the doctor ordered. Today, with Protect-mode Windows operating systems and memory shipped with PCs in the 128-MB range and more, the requirement for them has really disappeared, except in very specific circumstances, such as embedded PCs, which run MS-DOS out of a ROM, instead of a disk.

FINDCURS: THE WORLD'S SMALLEST USEFUL APPLICATION

Okay, I admit to more than a bit of hyperbole with coming up with the title of this section. Other applications might well be smaller than this one (which takes up only 123 bytes) and they could be more useful, but FindCurs has a special place in my heart. It was the first assembly-language application that I wrote that I felt took advantage of all the APIs and features available in the PC. This application does reads and writes to RAM, has an interrupt handler, uses BIOS and MS-DOS APIs, and accesses BIOS and system variables.

I originally wrote the application in 1986 when I got an IBM PC Convertible. This was one of the first true laptops and it had a very primitive (by today's standards) monochrome

LCD display. Because the contrast was very low on the display, I wanted to create a program that would help me find the cursor. This was actually a significant problem with early laptops.

The TSR is very simple. When both Shift keys were pressed, the cursor would be updated with a value that would cause it to take up the entire character box where it was located. When one of the two shift keys was released, the cursor parameters are returned to their original value.

The Shift key status byte in the BIOS system variable segment (0x040) is polled each time that the 55-ms interval RTC interrupt (int 0x008) is requested. I used this interrupt instead of the keyboard interrupt so that I wouldn't have to try to interpret the commands coming in from the keyboard or interface with the buffer directly. I could have simply polled the Shift key status byte at the end of the keyboard interrupt, but checking 18 times a second via the RTC interrupt seemed simpler.

FindCurs' interrupt handler can be described in C pseudo-code as:

```
int Int0x0008()                    // Put up a 'Block' Cursor if both
                                   // Shift Keys Pressed
{

 OrigInt0x0C();                    // Call' the original Interrupt
                                   //0x00C
// Handler
  If ((( ShiftStateVariable & 3 ) | keyVal ) == 3 ) {
    OriginalCursor = ReadCursorValue();
    SetCursorValue( Block );  // Both Shift Keys Pressed, Set 'BlocK'
// Cursor
    keyVal = 4;               // Mark that 'Block' is Active
  } else
    if (( keyVal == 4 ) && ( ShiftStatVariable & 3 ) != 3 )) {
      SetCursorValue( OriginalCursor );
      keyVal = 0;             // Restore the Cursor to Original Value
  }
} // End Int0x0008
```

This code was what was left in the PC as the TSR code (along with the application's PSP).

To capture the interrupt handler, the vector is first read from memory and then the Int0x00C handler's address is written there. In FindCurs, I used explicit reads and writes to the vector segment (0x00000) and offset (0x00024) to save the original handler's address and set the new handler's address. If I were to write this application today, I would use the DOS interrupt APIs AH = 025h and AH = 035h (read and change interrupt handler vectors) instead.

The "set up" code for the interrupt handler and TSR address is:

```
Mainline PROC NEAR

  xor AX, AX ; Point to the Interrupt Vector Table
  mov DS, AX

  les BX, DS:020h ; Save Interrupt 0x008 Vector
  mov CS:Orig0x008.PtrOff, BX
  mov CS:Orig0x008.PtrSeg, ES

  cli ; Now, Set the New Vector
```

```
lea AX, Int0x08
mov DS:024h, AX
mov DS:026h, CS
sti

; Everything Done - Now Terminate and Stay Resident
lea AX, Mainline ; Get Code Size needed in Paragraphs
add AX, 15
mov CL, 4
shr AX, CL
mov DX, AX
mov AX, ( DOSTSR * 256 )
int DOSINT
```

This application is ideal for TSRs because it is simple (it doesn't carry out any complex tasks, which makes it appropriate for assembler) and it performs a task that enhanced the PC/MS-DOS.

Executable (.EXE) Programs

The primary format for executable applications is .EXE. This file type is normally produced by MS-DOS linkers and can be used by all versions of MS-DOS and Microsoft Windows.

When planning this book, I debated how much I would describe this file format and finally decided not to go through the actual information because it is different for different execution environments. Although an .exe file is quite straightforward when a simple program with only a code and data segment is used, it becomes very complex when such issues as CodeView debugger source information is included in the file or it is destined to execute under Windows (which means that Protect-mode segments have to be added to the .EXE file).

These different formats are specified within the .EXE's header block. This block (and the code and data segments that are linked to it) is created by the "linker."

OFFSET	SIZE	DESCRIPTION
0x000	Word	Always 0x04D5A: .EXE file signature
0x002	Word	Length of file mod 512 bytes
0x004	Word	Length of file, including header in 512 byte Blocks
0x006	Word	Number of relocation table items
0x008	Word	Size of header in paragraphs
0x00A	Word	Minimum number of paragraphs to load the program
0x00C	Word	Maximum number of paragraphs to load the program
0x00E	Word	Displacement of stack segment in module in paragraphs
0x010	Word	Contents of the stack pointer at execution entry

OFFSET	SIZE	DESCRIPTION
0x012	Word	Two's complement checksum of the .EXE file
0x014	Word	Contents of the instruction pointer at execution entry
0x016	Word	Displacement of code module relative to start of program
0x018	Word	Offset to the first relocation item in file
0x01A	Word	Overlay number
0x01C	Word	Variable RESERVED space
Variable	Word	Relocation table
Variable	Word	Variable RESERVED space
Variable	Word	Program and data segments
Variable	Variable	Stack segment

When the .EXE is loaded into the PC's memory, the header and associated information is processed by the operating system to correctly load the application.

You should only be concerned with how the application is loaded. When MS-DOS loads the application, the PC's memory is updated with the PSP, code, and data segments. An example of how this is done is shown in Fig. 11-4.

In Fig. 11-4, you should never forget one thing. When an executable is loaded, all of the free memory is devoted to the application. Most high-level languages produce code that will resize the memory used to the actual size of the application; the remaining memory can be allocated by the application for data structures.

It is important to note that how the application is loaded is largely up to the operating system and this is why I shy away from precisely defining how the .EXE is formatted.

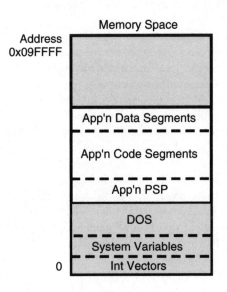

FIGURE 11-4   .EXE installation organization in memory.

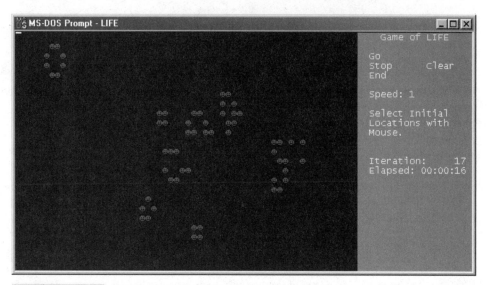

FIGURE 11-5   Game of Life executing.

.EXE formatting and loading is best left up to compilers/linkers, and MS-DOS and Windows and the operations that they perform are best treated as "black boxes."

THE GAME OF LIFE

To show how an executable file can be created for MS-DOS, I wanted to use an example that would show how code is linked together, how subroutines are used, how to create a console interface and how an MS-DOS event-driven program should execute. I wanted to do a game because I knew this would give a pretty good example of how these diverse elements worked together (Fig. 11-5).

The game I chose is an example of chaos theory, showing how a seemingly random series of events could be demonstrated using a computer and a very structured set of rules. The "Game of Life" was invented in the 1960s by a Cambridge mathematician, John Conway, as a way to model how populations of individuals interact.

Using three simple rules, the development of a population could be observed. The rules are based entirely on how the eight array points around a central one are currently populated. This is shown in Fig. 11-6 and shows how a, b, and c to h surround the X square. The number of populated surrounding squares is totaled to determine whether or not the central square is to be populated or left empty.

Each square in the matrix is tested for three rules before being updated. The actual "world" for the individuals is normally represented on a two-dimensional screen, as is shown in Fig. 11-5, but it's actually a lot more complex than that. The "world" is really a doughnut-shaped "toroid" (shown in Fig. 11-6) with the top folded over to the bottom and the two sides connected to one another. The reason for this shape was to avoid having to figure out how to model the edges.

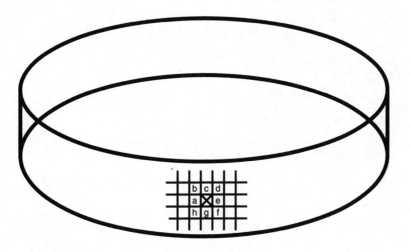

FIGURE 11-6   *Game of Life "Toroid".*

These rules for the individuals in each square are:

1. A new individual will be created if three of the neighboring squares (or cells) are populated.

2. An individual will die if four or more of the neighboring squares are populated or if less than two of the neighboring squares are populated.

3. An individual will survive the generation (*iteration*, as I have called it in my program) if two or three of the neighboring squares are populated.

Chances are, you've at least seen the "Game of Life" on a PC.

When I created the "Game of Life" program for this book, I had some ideas about how I wanted it to work. My requirements were for it to run in an 80-by-25 character MS-DOS text screen that allowed a mouse to set the initial conditions and allow the mouse to either be used to control the operation or rely on the keyboard. For console updating, I wanted the program to interface only with the video RAM directly. An important aspect of the program, for me, was that I could do everything from Microsoft C without having to resort to assembler. The program that I have included in the book took me an evening to write and I'm pretty pleased with the results; I achieved virtually all my goals.

The user interface uses event-driven programming techniques that are described in greater detail later in the book. These techniques are important to use with this application because I wanted to have an interface that would work consistently, regardless of whether or not the application (The Game of Life) was operating.

This interface consists of:

```
int flag = 0;
int runflag = 0;

while ( flag == 0 ) {          // Run Until 'End'
```

```
 if ( runflag != 0 ) {
// #### - Run the Game of Life
 } // endif

 if ( Left Button Pressed )
   if ( Mouse == "End" )
   flag = 1;                        // If Mouse Indicates End Program
 else {
// #### - Process the Mouse at the Current Position
 } // endif

 if ( Keystroke Pending )
   switch( Keystroke ) {
     case 'G':                      // Start the Program Executing
       runflag = 1;
       break;
     case 'S':                      // Stop the Program from Executing
       runflag = 0;
       break;
     default:
// #### - Handle the Other Keystrokes
   } // endswitch

 } // endwhile
```

If you look through the source code (LIFE.C), you will recognize this pattern (it is expanded upon when describing event-driven programming). This code reflects the simplicity of the actual application. The application will only accept keystrokes for:

1 Start
2 Stop
3 End (return to the MS-DOS command line)
4 Clear the field
5 Set the speed in iterations (generations) per second

For setting the position of the different individuals before the game was started, I use the "mouse" to select Stop, Start, End, and Clear. For the most part, the mouse can be used to control all operations of the application.

When you look at the initialization code, you'll notice that I make the hardware cursor invisible and don't allow any keyboard input, other than ASCII characters. I completely ignore function keys and cursor movement keys. For this application and my design point (I didn't think it would be efficient to expect the user to move the cursor to different points on the "world" to set up the initial conditions), this simple keyboard input was appropriate.

When I initialized the screen, you should notice that I first set up page 2 with the screen that I am going to use. This screen is broken into two parts: the left 60 columns are the "world" and I load that with ASCII "nulls" (0x000) with a color attribute of red on black. The happy faces (IBM extended ASCII character 0x002) are displayed in red. The right 20 columns makes up the control information for the application. I put the key instructions in yellow (which doesn't show up in Fig. 11-5) to make them more noticeable to the user.

All the screen writes are accomplished using straight C with the "Screen" pointer, pointing to the structure as shown earlier in the book regarding console interfacing:

```
struct pixel // Value to Put on the Screen
{
 char character; // The Character
 char color; // Color Attributes
};
```

The application's display executes on Page 2 was chosen so that the program could change the look of the screen without affecting the operation of page 0, which is used by COMMAND.COM. When you run the program, you'll notice that after you end that the same screen settings you had before "life" was executed will be returned. Rather than save the entire page's contents, I simply made a different page active for the game.

I chose page 2 because CodeView, the debugger I used with Microsoft C, uses Page 1 to display its information. By choosing Page 2 for the screen, I could still use CodeView to debug the application.

You will probably be surprised to see that I was able to use the mouse easily in the application (only three mouse BIOS interrupt API functions are required for the application). Using MOUSE.COM and the int 33h APIs as specified by Microsoft (and implemented by other mouse vendors) does work very well within the MS-DOS environment. If you have started up an MS-DOS prompt window in Windows, you'll see that the regular mouse is overlaid on the application's MS-DOS prompt dialog box. If a full screen is used for the application, a square block (sometimes surrounded by another block) is used to show where the mouse currently is.

Like the keyboard, the mouse functions for this application are also quite simple, with only the left button used to select "individuals" or application controls. In the Execute loop, I poll the left button; when it is pressed, I check its position. The position itself is returned at 8 "mickeys" to the character. To get the actual position, I divide these values by 8. Zero-zero is in the upper left-hand corner of the display screen, which works nicely with the normal operation of the display.

Where I did fail in meeting my objectives for the program was in the area of polling the keyboard BIOS to see if a keystroke was waiting to be processed. I was unable to get the MS-DOS and BIOS interrupt APIs to work within the C code, so I had to create two small assembly-language subroutines to check the keyboard buffer status and read the keyboard buffer using the BIOS APIs. The problem that I had with executing these software interrupts was in the use of the Zero flag for returning the status and the version of Microsoft C that I was using did not handle this very well.

If you've ever tried "The Game of Life" before, you'll know that it is very addictive and I'm warning you that you can spend many hours trying different initial positions of the individuals to see what happens. I found that if I could keep a nonrepeating pattern going for more than one thousand iterations, I was doing very well. If you are interested in learning more about "The Game of Life", textbooks and Web sites include excellent explanations of the program and interesting initial patterns, including "gliders" or "R-pentomino," that you can try.

I can immodestly say that I am very pleased with this application and I think that I have created something that is quite good, considering that it is only about 550 lines long. Note that this application is linked to my assembly language functions ("asmprocs") to provide MS-DOS APIs. The application as it stands, does show how to provide a sophisticated user interface, as well as accessing APIs and hardware from a high-level language in MS-DOS without using graphics.

Device Drivers

I have never found device drivers in MS-DOS to be useful, except to provide new mass data transfer device interfaces in a PC. *Mass data transfer* is my term for the class of devices that move data blocks at a time and the transfer to an application is initiated by the application. Appropriate devices for MS-DOS device drivers include diskettes, hard files, printers, CD-ROMS, and scanners.

Simple I/O is normally inappropriate for device drivers because of the extra overhead of the device driver. In these cases, in and out instructions/functions should just be used. Device drivers are appropriate if the data streams have to be buffered or processed (using a modem for file I/O could make using device drivers necessary) or if the application is going to be ported to a 16-bit version of Windows (Windows 3.1 and earlier). For the most part, I/O device drivers are not required for MS-DOS applications.

Device drivers are used like a file from your application. This means that you will "open" the device driver and claim a handle and perform reads, writes, "lseeks" exactly as if you were working with a regular file device. Often, the "writes" of devices are strings (or blocks) used to control the device.

Device driver files are generally ended in .SYS and are loaded when CONFIG.SYS is executed. When loaded, they link to the multiplex interrupt; when the device name is opened, the multiplex interrupt is accessed and the device driver's handler responds to requests.

I have not included a substantial amount of information on the MS-DOS device drivers because the need for them is really going away. Windows' popularity has changed the requirements for interfacing devices from MS-DOS to Windows—even for low-volume applications, such as manufacturing and engineering control environments, which traditionally have primarily used PCs running applications written in QBASIC or Turbo Pascal. Today, they are written in Visual Basic, Visual C++, LabView, or Java, and require DLLs, VxDs, and WDMs, which are described later in the book.

12

RUNNING

WITHOUT AN

OPERATING

SYSTEM

CONTENTS AT A GLANCE

ROM Extensions

Operating Systemless
Diskette Operations

LOADING AND RUNNING AN
APPLICATION FROM DISK

When you first saw this chapter, you probably felt that there was nothing very special about using a PC without an operating system. Diskless PCs that can load applications from a network have been available for many years. Recently, efforts have been made toward creating a "network computer" that downloads the applications to be used off a small network. These computers, although certainly avoid the need for loading and maintaining and operating system and application on a local disk, still require operating-system functions for executing applications, loading and storing data, and providing I/O functions. This chapter is an introduction to the concept of using a PC with nothing more than BIOS available.

This idea might seem quite radical—especially in light of your experiences and what I have written so far, but when working with embedded PC processors (which are 386s or 486s with some ROM and I/O), the additional licensing cost and extra RAM required for a ROM-based version of MS-DOS might make the project unaffordable.

To avoid these problems, there are two methods of taking control of the PC's processor before MS-DOS has a chance to boot. The first method is to take control of the PC instead of MS-DOS using a built-in ROM. The second method, which is shown in this chapter shows how applications can be loaded into a PC from disk without an operating system.

When developing OSless applications, a different philosophy has to be used than you would normally use for developing applications. Your code will definitely have to be simpler and cannot have as complex I/O as you would have in a normal PC application. Actually, your applications should only focus upon the hardware that is required and the user interface limited to simple console I/O, RS-232, or keyboard and a basic display (such as an LCD).

ROM Extensions

After POST has done its test of the PC's hardware and set up the default interrupt handlers into the interrupt table, it then scans through the ROM memory area (from 0x0C8000 to 0x0E0000) for ROM, which will be executed and normally provides new BIOS functions to the PC. This BIOS is normally stored in a ROM built into an adapter card. By placing the ROM on the card, there shouldn't be any issues with having to track a diskette for the code needed to use the adapter.

The format of the data on the ROM is:

OFFSET	VALUE
0	055h
1	0AAh
2	Length of ROM in 512-byte blocks
3	ROM scan entry point
:	

The ROM area is scanned in 2-KB blocks for the 055AAh data pattern. When it's found, the next byte is read in and multiplied by 512 to get the ROM size. A *4* in this byte would mean that the ROM is 2-KB long. Using this method, a ROM of up to 128 KB long can be supported.

When the ROM has been detected and the size has been read, then each byte (starting at offset zero) is read and summed. If the least-significant byte of the ROM byte sum is equal to zero, then execution will start occurring in the segment, starting at offset three using a "far call" instruction.

At this point, the ROM has control of the PC. With this control, you might wish to run your application without loading MS-DOS or Windows. Of course, you will be limited to only having the BIOS functions available, but, in this case, you can completely ignore the disk subsystems, which will make your application reasonably easy to write.

Operating Systemless Diskette Operations

The title of this section probably seems like an oxymoron. You're probably only familiar with diskette operation with a diskette formatted by MS-DOS. By setting up a diskette with head 0, track 0, and sector 1 with a program to load and execute, you can run an application directly from a floppy drive without being encumbered by an operating system. In doing this, you are loading an application with its own operating system from diskette and it can be as simple or complex as you want it to be.

After the PC has run POST, software interrupt 019h is invoked, which loads the first sector on either a floppy disk, a hard disk, or a network adapter. For PCs, the default (which might be an option in CMOS/RTC memory) is to first check the A: diskette drive. If a diskette is present, one 512-byte sector at head 0, track 0, and sector 1 is read into memory and executed. The sector at head 0, track 0, and sector 1 is known as the boot sector of the diskette.

If the diskette is strictly a data diskette, this sector is loaded with a data pattern between offset 0x002 and 0x03D, which indicates to the PC's interrupt 019h code that the diskette cannot be used for booting. If this pattern is not present, then execution jumps to the first address and executes from there.

With this basic description, I decided to see if I could come up with my own diskettes, which could be loaded with a loader and application. When you look at the "boot" subdirectory of the CD-ROM, you will probably be surprised at the number of small programs that I wrote for this application. These programs were used to test assumptions and display what is going on with the boot process.

My first challenge was to come up with a way of creating programs that could be loaded onto the diskette. I decided to go with assembler because I knew that I would be setting up all the segment registers and addresses. Figuring out how the addresses were set up was the most difficult part of this exercise.

When I wrote my applications, I wrote them to execute in binary (.BIN) format. This is really the same as the Tiny (.COM) model, except that the code begins at address 0x00000 and not 0x00100.

After assembling the code, I used a straight link (with no options) and then converted the .EXE file to binary format using "Exe2bin". "Exe2bin" is an old MS-DOS utility that converts .EXE files into straight code without any segment information, headers, or stack information. It can also be used to convert .EXE's into .COM files as well.

Exe2bin was available in MS-DOS up to version 5.00. Newer versions of MS-DOS do not include this utility, but the latest linking programs from Microsoft provide a binary output option.

With the process of developing the applications in place, I decided to see if I could load and execute my own application from diskette. To do this, I wrote BOOT1.ASM, which simply consists of an application to write an *A* on the PC's display and then go into an endless loop.

```
ALLPROCS SEGMENT                    ; Segment for Everything
         ASSUME CS:ALLPROCS, DS:ALLPROCS, ES:ALLPROCS, SS:ALLPROCS

PAGE+
; Constants
VIDINT   EQU 010h ; BIOS Video Interrupt
READCURS EQU 003h ; Read the Cursor Position
MOVECURS EQU 002h ; Set the Cursor Position
VIDWRITE EQU 009h ; Write Attribute/Byte at Cursor

PAGE+
; Structures
```

```
PAGE+
;  Macros


PAGE+
;  _GETKEY - Return the First Character in the Keyboard Buffer
 org 0                             ; Start at Address 0
START:
  mov AH, VIDWRITE ; Write a Character
  mov AL, 'A'
  mov BH, 0 ; Page 0
  mov BL, 7 ; Grey on Black
  mov CX, 1 ; 1 Character
  int VIDINT

Endless:     ; End and Just Loop
  jmp SHORT Endless

ALLPROCS ENDS
          END     START
```

To load this on a diskette, I created the program *Bootmkr*, which read in the specified file and then writes it (if it is less than 512 bytes in size) on the diskette at head 0, track 0 and sector 1.

```
// BootMkr - Put the File 'boot1.bin' onto the Boot Sector
//
// This Program Loads the Specified binary file (or 'boot1.bin' by
//  default) and then loads the file onto the boot sector of diskette
//  in 'A'.
//
// Myke Predko
// 98.11.18
//

// Defines
#include <stdio.h>
#include <dos.h>
#include <asmprocs.h>
#include <fcntl.h>
#include <sys\types.h>
#include <sys\stat.h>
#include <io.h>

#define DiskInt 0x013   // Diskette Interrupt
#define DiskReset 0     // Reset the Drive Subsystem
#define DiskStatus 1    // Get Status of Previous Operation
#define DiskRead 2      // Read the Sectors in Memory
#define DiskWrite 3     // Write to the Disk Sector

// Global Variables
char Buffer[ 512 ];     // Data Buffer

// Subroutines


// Mainline
main(argc, argv, envp)
  int argc;
  char *argv[];
```

```
    char *envp;
{

struct SREGS sregs;      // BIOS Variables
union REGS regs;

int i, j;

int handle;              // File Handling Variables
long handle_size;

char far * SourceFile;   // File to Load onto the Diskette

  if ( argc == 1 )
    SourceFile = "boot1.bin";
   else                  // Else, Use Specified File
    SourceFile = argv[ 1 ];


  if (( handle = open( SourceFile, O_RDONLY | O_BINARY )) == -1 )
    printf( "Unable to Find File \'%s\'\n', SourceFile );
    else {               // Read/Load the File

  if (( handle_size = lseek( handle, 0L, SEEK_END )) > 512L ) {
    printf( 'File Too Lange to Process\N' );
    close( handle );
    } else {             // Put the File on the Diskette

    lseek( handle, 0L, SEEK_SET );
    read( handle, Buffer, handle_size & 0x0FFFF );
    close( handle );     // Read the Binary File
    for ( i = handle_size; i 512; i++ )
      Buffer[ i ] = 0x090;

    printf( 'Offset 0 1 2 3 4 5 6 7 8 9 A B C D E F 0 1 ..' );
     for ( i = 0; i 16; i++ ) { // Display What was Read
       printf( ' %3X ', i * 32 );
       for ( j = 0; j < 32; j++ ) { // Display Each Line
         printf( "%2X", Buffer[( i * 32 ) + j ] & 0x0FF );
         if (( j & 0x007 ) == 7 )
           printf( " " );
       } // endfor
       printf( "\n" );
     } // endfor

    regs.h.ah = DiskReset; // Reset Disk Drive A
    regs.h.dl = 0;
    int86( DiskInt, &regs, &regs );

    if ( regs.h.ah != 0 )
      printf( 'Error Writing to Diskette\n' );
      else {                      // Write File onto the Boot Sector

      regs.h.ah = DiskWrite; // Write the First Sector
      regs.h.dl = 0;         // of Disk A
      regs.h.dh = 0;         // Head 0
      regs.h.ch = 0;         // Track 0
      regs.h.cl = 1;         // Sector 1
      regs.h.al = 1;         // Only 1 Sector
      regs.x.bx = GETOFF( &Buffer[ 0 ]);
```

```
            sregs.es = GETSEG( &Buffer[ 0 ]);
            int86x( DiskInt, &regs, &regs, &sregs );

         if ( regs.h.ah != 0 )
            printf( "Error Writing to Diskette\n" );

        } // endif
      } // endif
    } // endif

  } // End BootMkr
```

I have included this code to show how BIOS interrupts can be handled in C. I've said it elsewhere in the book, but I want to make it clear that you should not use the disk BIOS operations unless you are writing to specific areas of the disk and know exactly what you are doing. This application falls under this criteria.

Errors in specifying the wrong track (or, worse, disk) could result in a damaged hardfile, which you might not be able to recover from without reformatting and loading your operating system and applications again. When using these routines, I ensure that I only write to a diskette by checking that bit seven of disk specification (in DL) is reset when it is passed to the BIOS routines.

With *Boot1* ready and *Bootmkr, I* formatted a diskette and ran Bootmkr to put the BOOT1.BIN file at the diskette's boot sector. Next, the diskette was taken to my experimental PC (which is described later in the book) and it is booted with this diskette in its drive.

To my amazement, the program worked the first time I tried it, with an "A" displayed in the upper left corner of the PC's monitor.

My ultimate goal for this exercise was to create a utility that I could use to load. .COM applications onto a diskette and load and execute them without requiring an operating system. From Boot1, I realized that I would have to understand where the boot sector was loaded into memory and figure out how to jump to specific addresses from here.

To do this, I created *Boot2*, which displays the initial CS:IP of the application, along with the stack pointer information. The code can be shown as the C pseudo-code:

```
Main ()                        //   'Boot2' Code
{

START:                         //   Label at the Start of the Application

char far * StartPtr;
char far * StackPtr;

  StartPtr = START;            //   Point to the First Address loaded in.
  StackPtr = SS:SP;            //   Get the initial Stack Pointer

  printf ( 'CS:IP = %p\n', StartPtr );
  printf ( 'SS:SP = %p\n', StackPtr );

  while ( 1 == 1 );            //   Loop forever

} // End Boot2
```

To convert this to assembler and have it run correctly took me almost a full day because of the difficulty in figuring out where the application was placed in memory and then figure out where variables were located. Only relative addressing was used to avoid the problem of knowing the actual address of labels with segments.

To help debug the code (and try out new things), I originally created .COM programs from the binary file (the difference being that the *org 0100h* statement in the .COM program, compared to the *org 0* statement in the binary file). But, I found that the most useful way of debugging the code was to load it at an arbitrary address. Creating *"Exectest"* and making it into a .COM did this:

```
PAGE+
ALLPROCS SEGMENT                      ; Segment for Everything
         ASSUME  CS:ALLPROCS, DS:ALLPROCS, ES:ALLPROCS, SS:ALLPROCS


PAGE+
; Constants
DISKINT   EQU     013h               ; Diskette Interrupt
DISKRST   EQU     000h               ; Reset Disk Sub-System
DISKREAD  EQU     002h               ; Read the Diskette


VIDINT    EQU     010h               ; BIOS Video Interrupt
READCURS  EQU     003h               ; Read the Cursor Position
MOVECURS  EQU     002h               ; Set the Cursor Position
VIDWRITE  EQU     009h               ; Write Attribute/Byte at Cursor


PAGE+
; Structures
PtrFmt  STRUC                        ; Pointer Structure Format
PtrOff  dw       ?                   ; Offset
PtrSeg  dw       ?                   ; Segment
PtrFmt  ENDS


PAGE+
; Macros


PAGE+
; _GETKEY - Return the First Character in the Keyboard Buffer
 org 0100h                           ; Start at Address 0100h for .COM
START:

    mov    AH, DISKRST               ; Reset the Disk Sub-System
    mov    DL, 0
    int    DISKINT

    mov    AH, DISKREAD              ; READ the Application from the
    mov    DL, 0                     ;   Diskette
    mov    DH, 0                     ; Head 0
    mov    CH, 0                     ; Track 0
    mov    CL, 1                     ; Sector 1 (Boot Sector)
    mov    AL, 1                     ; Read in First 8,7104 Bytes
    mov    BX, 0200h                 ; Point Past Currently Loaded Code
    int    DISKINT

    jmp    TestStart

 org 0200h

TestStart:
```

```
PAGE+
; Variables

ALLPROCS ENDS
        END       START
```

This code loads the boot code at the next 0x0100-byte boundary, then jumps to the first address to start executing. When the boot code begins executing, it is at address 0x0200 of the .COM segment.

Now, if you're expecting to hear I had a problem with memory allocation, I should point out that once executable files are loaded into a PC, they are allocated all of the available memory in the PC. This means that data can be loaded or stored without fear of trashing memory-allocation blocks.

With "Exectest", I was able to debug "Boot2" and understand exactly how it works. The problem was, I didn't believe what I was seeing.

When I ran the application, the following information was displayed:

```
CS:IP = 0000:07C0
SS:SP = 0000:03FA
```

I was more than a bit concerned about the segments of zero and couldn't understand why I wasn't getting what I considered a valid stack offset. With a stack segment of zero and an offset of 0x03FA, the stack was inside the interrupt vector table.

This caused a lot of head scratching, but then I noticed that vectors 0x0F1 to 0x0FF (addresses 0x00000:0x03C4 to 0x00000:003FF) are classifed as *unused*. Well, they are really used during boot. More warnings in PC documentation should be made to indicate that these vectors should never be used by devices as their BIOS or hardware interrupt vectors, (especially these setup by boot ROMS).

Part of the work done to convincing myself that the values were correct was by creating BOOT3.ASM. This program uses the display routines from Boot2 and displays the contents of the interrupt vector space and by pushing data onto the stack (and into the vector table).

It was surprising to me to discover that the 512 bytes available to the boot sector cannot carry out very substantial functions. As is shown in the next section, it is more than enough to load and execute an application; extrapolating this, I can see where it would be very useful in loading an operating system from disk.

LOADING AND RUNNING AN APPLICATION FROM DISK

With the ability to load and execute programs from a diskette, I wanted to see if I could create a loader process that would allow me to easily develop OSless applications while capitalizing on the investments I made in learning how the PC boot process works. I decided to create an application that would load a .COM file from disk along with a "loader" program that would set it up and run it without the need for an operating system.

To do this, I created *Bootmkr2*, which puts a LOAD.ASM into the boot sector of a diskette with a .COM application on the following sectors of the track. For a 3.5" 1.44-MB diskette with 512 byte sectors and 18 sectors per track, this meant the .COM application could be up to 8704 bytes long. It could be longer if I was willing to use other tracks on the diskette (and write the code to support it).

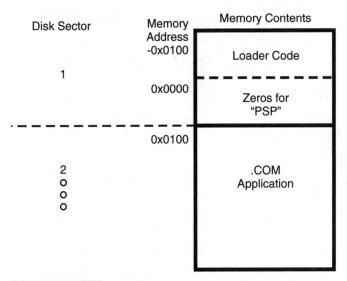

FIGURE 12-1   "Operating Systemless" disk format.

When this program was loaded onto disk, Bootmkr2 would store it in the format shown in Fig. 12-1. Once LOAD.ASM was copied from the boot sector into memory and executed, it would copy the remaining 17 sectors of the track into memory immediately following its address.

The code to do this is:

```
PAGE+
ALLPROCS SEGMENT                       ; Segment for Everything
         ASSUME  CS:ALLPROCS,  DS:ALLPROCS,  ES:ALLPROCS,  SS:ALLPROCS


PAGE+
; Constants
DISKINT   EQU      013h        ; Diskette Interrupt
DISKRST   EQU      000h        ; Reset Disk Sub-System
DISKREAD  EQU      002h        ; Read the Diskette

VIDINT    EQU      010h        ; BIOS Video Interrupt
READCURS  EQU      003h        ; Read the Cursor Position
MOVECURS  EQU      002h        ; Set the Cursor Position
VIDWRITE  EQU      009h        ; Write Attribute/Byte at Cursor


PAGE+
; Structures
PtrFmt   STRUC                 ; Pointer Structure Format
PtrOff   dw        ?           ; Offset
PtrSeg   dw        ?           ; Segment
PtrFmt   ENDS


PAGE+
; Macros


PAGE+
; LOAD - Load the Application into the PC's Memory
```

```
        org  0                          ; Start at Address 0
START:

     call  GetAddr                      ; Get the Actual Starting Address
IPValue:                                ; Actual IP Value
     mov  AX, SI
     lea  BX, IPValue
     sub  AX, BX
     add  AX, 00100h                    ; Move 512 Bytes Up
     mov  ES, AX                        ; Save the Segment Start for Later
     shr  AX, 1                         ; Shift down by 4 to Get the Correct
Paragraph
     shr  AX, 1
     shr  AX, 1
     shr  AX, 1
     mov  BX, CS
     add  AX, BX                        ; Make Sure Correct for Debugging
     mov  DS, AX
     mov  SS, AX
     add  AX, 010h                      ; Point to the Save Address for the
     mov  ES, AX                        ;  Read
     mov  SP, 0FFFEh                     ; Setup the Stack Pointer

     mov  AH, DISKRST                    ; Reset the Disk Sub-System
     mov  DL, 0
     int  DISKINT

     mov  AH, DISKREAD                   ; READ the Application from the
     mov  DL, 0                          ; Diskett
     mov  DH, 0                          ; Head 0
     mov  CH, 0                          ; Track 0
     mov  CL, 2                          ; Sector 2 (After Boot)
     mov AL, 17                          ; Read in .COM's First 8704 Bytes
     mov BX, 0000h                       ; Point Past Currently Loaded Code
     int DISKINT

     call GetAddr
     add  SI, JumpAddr - $         ; Update the Jump Address
     mov  WORD PTR CS: [SI], 0100h
     mov  WORD PTR CS: [SI + 2], DS

     xor  AX, AX                         ; Clear all the Registers
     xor  BX, BX
     xor  CX, CX
     xor  DX, DX

     xor  DI, DI
     xor  SI, SI
     xor  BP, BP

     push DS                             ; Setup ES
     pop  ES

     db   0EAh                           ; Jump to the Code
JumpAddr:
     dd   0                              ; Address for the Instruction

     PAGE+
```

```
; Subroutines
GetAddr:                        ; Get the Address of the Call

  pop  SI

  push SI

  ret

PAGE+
; Variables

ALLPROCS ENDS
        END       START
```

From the disk, the application would be copied directly into the memory following the boot sector using the BIOS disk-interrupt APIs. The boot-sector code is responsible for loading the code and calculating the segment starting address and then jump to this new segment at address 0x0100.

To accomplish this reasonably simply, the boot sector was designed to be broken up into two halves of 256 bytes each. The first half is the loader code (shown previously), which loads in the application and executes the .COM application. As can be seen in Fig. 12-1, this loader code cannot be accessed by the .COM application (I store it at address 0x0100) with the following 256 bytes of the sector (which are all loaded with zeros) as the PSP of the application.

From this point, the application .COM file is loaded into memory directly and starts executing at offset 0x0100. As you look through the LOAD.ASM code, you'll notice that to carry out the jump to the .COM code, I use self-modifying code to set the address of an intersegment jump instruction.

In many people's eyes, this is one of the worst programming sins I could commit, but this was the most effective way I could set the address in a variable. The problem with this method was I would be stuck with jumping with a variable and not knowing at what offset the variable was located. I would probably have had to write over the address of the variable in the jump statement.

As I write this, (about two months after developing the code), I realize that there is a better easier way. Instead of using the self-modifying code, I could have pushed the starting address onto the stack and then used a subroutine *ret* instruction to return to the starting address.

This code would be:

```
push     DS
mov      AX, 0100h
push     AX               ; Start Address DS:0100h on the Stack
xor      AX, AX           ; Restore AX to Zero
ret                       ; Pop Start Address off the Stack and
                          ;  put in CS:IP
```

I realize that 8.5 KB of application space is not very much (especially with virtually 640 KB available in the PC and up to 1.44 MB on the diskette) and you can modify the LOAD.ASM and Bootmkr2 code to load in larger applications. If you are going to stick with the .COM application file format, I have to caution you that LOAD.ASM should never become larger than 256 bytes or you will have to come up with a new way to load the code and the PSP information. As it stands now, LOAD.BIN only takes up 103 bytes, so increasing the size for larger applications does not appear to be a significant problem looming on the horizon.

MS-DOS
PROGRAMMING
LANGUAGES AND
APPLICATION
DEVELOPMENT
TOOLS

Over the years, a plethora of programming languages and development tools have become available for the PC. This wide variety is a result of the PC being the first device to legitimize small-systems programming. Some of the languages are experiments that people have tried and used to become successful. Others were their author's favorites, which became successful as PC implementations. Currently, a wide variety of languages are both excellent and not that expensive. The languages for which I present code for this book are chosen for their universality and the ease in which compilers are available. Along with the languages, understanding how modules of different devices are linked together and understanding what types of capabilities are available for debuggers is useful. The chapter is rounded out with a brief introduction to editors and the kind of features you should be looking for.

Other than the Borland "Turbo" products, MS-DOS does not have the sophisticated *Integrated Development Environments (IDEs)* that are available for Windows development tools. This means that you are free to choose the editor, compiler, linker, and debugger that works best for you.

Batch Files

When I first started seriously learning how to interface with the PC, I was amazed at what was capable with batch-file programming. Today, people usually think of batch-file programs as parameter set-ups (such as AUTOEXEC.BAT) or a "wrapper" (i.e., putting the appropriate compiler parameters in a batch file to make compiling easier). Looking beyond this, batch files are actually source files to the built-in interpreter in MS-DOS's COMMAND.COM with a reasonably powerful set of functions available.

In Chapter 10, I described batch programming in quite a bit of detail. This chapter focuses on creating simple input/output applications that interface with the user using the batch-file interpreter. For these functions, I will concentrate on passing data—either through the command-line invocation or through the MS-DOS ERRORLEVEL variable.

With the small I/O applications given here, as well as the information contained in Chapter 10, you could develop some very complex batch-file applications. I strongly suggest that you don't do this because of the complexity of some of the batch interpreter operations (i.e., it cannot process integers) and the slowness in which it operates.

Simple applications, however, have not really been explored and I think that some useful tools could be developed.

The ERRORLEVEL value can be used to pass data from programs. For example, the user could be prompted to enter *Y* or *N* using the program:

```
//    BATY_N - Wait for the User To Input "Y" or "n"
//
//    This Program doesn't take any input parameters.
//
//    This program returns:
//     0x000 - If "Y" or "y" Entered
//     0x001 - If "N" or "n" Entered
//     0x0FF - For Anything Else
//
//    Myke Predko
//
//    98.10.31
//

//    Defines

//    Includes
#include <stdio.h>
#include <stdlib.h>
#include <dos.h>
#include <asmprocs.h>
```

```
//    Global Variables

//    External Routines

//    Subroutines

//    Mainline
main (argc, argv, envp)     // Define with the Input parameters
    int argc;
    char *argv [];
    char *envp;
{

union REGS regs;

    while ( GETKEYSTAT () ! = 0 )  // Clear the Keyboard Buffer
      GETKEY ();

    switch ( GETKEY() & 0x0FF )     // Process the User Input
      {
        case 'Y':    // "Y"es
        case 'y':
          regs.h.al = 0;
          break;
        case 'N':                   // "No"o
        case 'n':
          regs.h.al = 1;
          break;
        default:                    // Everything Else
          regs.h.al = 0x0FF;
      } /* endswitch */

    regs.h.ah = 0x04C;        // End with The ErrorLevel as the
    intdos ( &regs, &regs );// Contents of the Register

} // End BATRead
```

This could be extended to interfacing to hardware within the PC. To write to a register in the PC, the following C program could be used:

```
// BATWrite - Write to a Register in the PC
//
// This Program takes the Input Parameters:
//
// batwrite addr Value
//
// And Writes them to the Specified Port.
//
// Myke Predko
//
// 98.10.27
//

// Defines
```

```
// Includes
#include <stdio.h>
#include <stdlib.h>

// Global Variables

// External Routines

// Subroutines

// Mainline
main (argc, argv, envp)          // Define with the Input parameters
  int argc;
  char *argv [];
  char *envp;
{

  outp( atoi( argv[ 1 ]), atoi( argv[ 2 ]));

} // End BATWrite
```

To write a value to a register, use the command-line instruction:

```
batwrite  addr  value
```

Remembering that "addr" and "value" are in decimal:
Reading a register could be accomplished with a similar program:

```
// BATRead - Read from a Register in the PC
//
// This Program takes the Input Parameters:
//
// batread addr
//
// And returns the data read to the MS-DOS "ErrorLevel"
//
// Myke Predko
//
// 98.10.27
//

// Defines

// Includes
#include <stdio.h>
#include <stdlib.h>
#include <dos.h>

// Global Variables

// External Routines

// Subroutines

// Mainline
main (argc, argv, envp)          // Define with the Input parameters
```

```
    int argc;
    char *argv [];
    char *envp;
{

union REGS regs;

    regs.h.al = inp ( atoi( argv[ 1 ]));

    regs.h.ah = 0x04C;              // End with The ErrorLevel as the
    intdos ( &regs, &regs );       // Contents of the Register

} // End BATRead
```

This program is invoked similarly to the BATWrite with:

```
batread addr
```

When the program returns, the ERRORLVL variable in MS-DOS is set to the contents of the register.

When the PC was first introduced, batch files were very predominate in many commercial applications and were often very complex. I would argue that they were needlessly complex.

Today, most batch files are quite simple. Many are "wrappers", which carry out a complex single function for a user. For example, when I want to compile a C source, I use the COCCOMP.BAT file:

```
del %1.obj
CL -Zi -c -AL -Fs /Gs %1.c
```

Which first deletes the object file produced by the compiler (because if the compilation fails, the object file isn't updated) and then compiles the source with the numerous options that I normally use.

If you are a new PC user, I would suggest that you should have the ability to develop simple wrappers (because they can really make your life easier). Going on from this, you should be able to develop batch files with some of the conditional statements that I have presented in this chapter and in Chapter 10. This level of knowledge will provide you with the ability to create simple applications quickly that can be used to test out hardware.

Assembler

So far, this book has provided a lot of information on 8086 assembler. For this section, I wanted to concentrate on where it is best used. High-level languages offer a lot of advantages over assembly-language programming, although, in some situations, you may want to use assembler.

The primary situation where assembler should be used is for an interrupt handler. With the edge-triggered environment of the PC and the potential problems for missed interrupt requests, having interrupt handlers that reset the interrupt controller and process the interrupt as quickly as possible is imperative. This is hard to do in a high-level language, which saves registers and carry out hardware accesses "its own way."

After the interrupt is acknowledged and reset, you could call a high-level language function to process the data from the interrupt, but this requires that the DS, BP, and other registers are set up properly within the assembler interrupt routine to call the C code. Figuring out what is required is actually a pain and I tend to keep all the code in assembler. If I want to retrieve data for processing, I will create my own BIOS interrupt handler and return the data to the high-level language from there.

Other than this one case, I would suggest that you avoid assembler whenever possible. Most modern high-level languages have register I/O along with interrupt interfaces either built-in or in callable libraries.

BASIC

BASIC is the granddaddy of all high-level PC programming languages; its roots go back to the hand-assembled version created by Steve Wozniak almost 25 years ago for the Apple II. This original BASIC was distributed on a cassette tape. For many people (myself included), it was their first introduction to programming. Over the years, BASIC has been greatly modified and improved, but the points that make it useful for beginners have been left alone.

When the IBM PC was first introduced, an expanded version of Microsoft's BASIC-80 (for use with the Intel 8080 microprocessor) was burned into ROM. This version was called *Cassette BASIC* by IBM because if the PC booted into BASIC, it meant that it didn't find a diskette-based operating system and the only way to get data in and out of the ROM BASIC was by using an audio cassette player. Microsoft shipped this BASIC (which they called *GW BASIC*) with the first versions of MS-DOS. This section focuses on GW BASIC and introduces some of its features.

GW (which stands for *Gee Whiz*) BASIC was remarkably full featured with some reasonably sophisticated file- and data-handling capabilities and some rudimentary debugging features. The application program is interpreted, which means that its execution is actually pretty slow. Despite this, many useful programs were written in GW BASIC, including quite a few early games.

I mention games because they typically require the most from a programming language and hardware platform in terms of speed and graphics.

GW BASIC application code is stored in a "tokenized" format. This means that the source would be converted into a series of symbols for the program to execute quicker (fewer "parsing" operations required) and load in less time because tokenized code is smaller that source code. If you compared a GW BASIC tokenized .BAS file to an ASCII source file, you'll find that the .BAS file is about 30 percent smaller.

One interesting aspect of GW BASIC was the user interface. The screen is nominally broken up into lines. Each time *Enter* is pressed, the line the cursor was on would be processed. If you wanted to do a calculation, perhaps to find the area of a circle 2.5 inches across, you could use GW BASIC as a calculator by simply typing in:

```
PRINT ( 2.5 * 2.5 ) * 3.14; " Square Inches"
```

To indicate the line was part of the application, an integer number was put at the start:

```
100 PRINT (2.5 * 2.5 ) * 3.14; " Square Inches"
```

This quasi-full-screen interface was quite effective for program entry and editing. To change a line, all you would have to do is list it, move the cursor to what you wanted to change, update it, and then press *Enter*.

Because each line was numbered, adding and deleting lines was quite simple (it was recommended that you separate each line by a count of 10 to allow new lines to be inserted between them). Alphanumeric labels were not supported, which meant that you tended to do a lot of jumping back and forth between gotos and the destinations.

Of course, if you forgot to separate each line by 10, or if you added nine lines between two lines (and still wanted to do more), you could command GW BASIC to renumber everything (including the goto references). The only problem with doing this would be if you grouped specific functions by line number, the renumber operation would put everything consecutively.

One nice feature of GW BASIC is the *in* and *out* instructions, which allow direct access to the PC's I/O registers. In the original PC, incorrect or casual use of the *out* instruction could result in the PC locking up, while the worst this could do would be to require that the PC is rebooted, this level of access could cause serious problems in a Windows system.

Compiled code could be BLOADed into memory and executed. This was a carry-over from the Apple II's BASIC and operation and was the only way to run object code in the Apple II. This interface was really quite cumbersome and didn't catch on; most applications were compiled into a .COM or .EXE program and executed directly from the command line.

I could go on with different aspects of BASIC that I felt were restrictive, but the biggest problem was the maximum code size of 64 KB (maximum data size was 32 KB). This made the creation of highly complex applications just about impossible.

Despite the limitations, GW BASIC was an excellent introduction to programming and it has never left the mainstream of PC application development. Very shortly after the deficiencies with GW BASIC became apparent, compilers became available, which advertised that GW BASIC could be used for debug and the compiler could be used to create executable files that were faster, small, and kept the source code private. Later BASICs (such as Quick BASIC) worked at eliminating these deficiencies.

BASIC language will probably always be around to program PCs. For the Windows applications presented later in this book, I use Visual Basic, which is an event-driven programming language dedicated to opening up the realm of Windows application programming to people that don't want to spend the time learning the Windows operating-system APIs. Visual Basic provides many of the advantages to the beginning Windows programmer that GW BASIC gave to the beginning MS-DOS programmer.

Pascal

Pascal is a bit of a funny language that I don't really consider to be optimal for systems programming use. Personally, I have never really liked it because the use of statement ends (semicolons) is inconsistent and something that I always get wrong and have to recompile and re-edit often. Pascal became a popular tool because of Borland's "Turbo Pascal". This inexpensive compiler produced application code that executed quickly. Pascal is very well-suited to tool development for the PC; you'll discover that many compilers and assemblers are written in Pascal.

I don't like Pascal for systems programming because of how parameters are passed at the assembly-language level. The 8086 is designed to pass parameters on the stack and use the BP register as the offset to the parameters. Pascal passes the parameters in the reverse order in which they are placed in the source. This means that, unlike C (which puts its parameters in order), you cannot make functions that operate on an arbitrary number of parameters (such as C's *printf* function) and keeping track of the parameters in assembler is more difficult than in C.

The MS-DOS versions of Borland's Turbo Pascal did have a number of features to make writing systems applications that accessed hardware quite reasonably, as well as an interrupt function type. The interrupt function provided a function type that could be pointed to from the 8086's interrupt vector table. When the interrupt was invoked, this function type would first save all the registers and set up the DS and SS segment registers before allowing the code to execute. At the end of the function, the registers would be restored and an *iret* instruction was executed.

Turbo Pascal also contained an IDE, although early versions had no source-level debugger. The code produced was in .COM format and could be reasonably easily debugged using DEBUG.COM.

A version of Turbo Pascal was produced to develop Windows applications, but this version never really caught on. Visual Basic and C++ became the primary methods to develop Windows applications. As this book went to press, early versions of Borland's Pascal and C compilers have become available on their website, free of charge for down loading. I recommand you down load a copy of each compiler for use with developing your own applications.

C/C++

By far the most popular language for writing PC systems applications is in C. C is often described unfairly as "structured assembly language." I say unfairly because C is a universal language, written for virtually all the processors in existence and I think it's a credit to the designers of the 8086 that the processor architecture meshes so well with the code required for C and C++ statements.

I could probably write a book the same size as this one on C and C++ application development for the PC. C is an incredibly rich language with many features built in to make it easier for both low-level and high-level interfaces. These features include built-in pointers, structures, libraries, macros, and conditionally compiled statements along with assembly-language interfaces. These features, when properly leveraged make your development and resulting code much faster and more efficient.

This chapter focuses on using C when interfacing with hardware added to the PC. This book does not contain an introduction or a primer to the language and, as I work through the examples, I try to keep the advanced functions to a minimum. But, I will expect that you have some familiarity with the language.

Before describing the features of C that are important for systems programming, here is some information on code formatting. All the C code in this book is written in the conventional format with conditionally executing statements indented after the IF, WHILE, and SWITCH statements that started them. I tend to avoid the *do/until* function in C simply because I find it confusing to provide the "negative condition" test that is required.

The standard *if* code format can be shown as:

```
if ( A == B ) {

  printf( "\"A\" is equal to \"B\"\n" );

  SoundAlarm();

} // endif
```

When I first started programming, I was taught PL/1 and PL/S (two internal IBM languages) in the traditional way (from a big guy who would hit me with a stick each time I deviated from "acceptable" code formatting). Because the IBM way of acceptable code formatting was drilled into me, I coded in C for many years like:

```
if ( A == B )
  {
    printf( "\"A\" is equal to \"B\"\n" );

    SoundAlarm();

  } // endif
```

This method is really not a major divergence from the conventional C format, but it was enough for some people to say that my code was harder to read than it should have been. Over time, I have been forcing myself to follow the traditional C conventions and I suggest you do as well.

C has a wonderful feature where statements can be placed within other statements. Included in this are the pre- and post-increment and decrement operations that allow you to avoid having to key in repeatedly.

For example, instead of:

```
i = i + 1;
```

the statement

```
i++;
```

will work just as well.

These compound statements allow for terrific abuses in C and are the reason why, when I was learning it, I described C as the "APL of the 1980s." If you don't know what APL is, trust me when I say that the people who liked it were the ones that used to race each other doing math problems on slide rules.

You might see a way to compress many statements, such as:

```
A = F( i, j );
```

```
K = K + A;

if ( k > 17 ) {

  printf( "Finished\n" );

  Ret = 1;

} // endif
```

into:

```
if (( K += ( A = F( i, j ))) > 17 ) printf( "Finished\n", Ret = 1 );
```

Which is functionally equivalent, but just about impossible to read and figure out what is actually happening. There's a lot of truth to the cliché that C was developed as a language for professors to scribble out lines to prove their mental superiority. The difference between you and a professor is that they will never have to support the code they write (they get students to do that for them). Even saving 75 percent of the possible keystrokes will become insignificant five years down the line when you are trying to figure out what the combined line is doing. Make it easy on yourself in the future and work to make your code easily readable and understandable.

When you first learned C, you probably had a hard time understanding pointers. People who understand, like, and use pointers fall into one of the uncomplimentary categories of people, usually "nerds" or "keeners." Pointers are also currently out of favor because *Java* doesn't use them.

Unfortunately, pointers are a basic part of C programming and you have to understand them to at least a basic level. Fortunately, this basic level is ideal for systems programming and can allow you to efficiently move data around in a PC, as well as work with the MS-DOS and BIOS APIs. The next few paragraphs show everything that I think you need to know about pointers in PC C programming.

First, you should know is that "far" pointers use the same format as 32-bit pointers in the 8086. "Short" or "huge" pointers are generally compiler constructs that do have advantages in terms of data space, but will cause more complex code to be generated, as well as potential problems understanding where they are actually pointing in absolute memory. Short or huge are much more difficult to work with when you want to do something funky, such as accessing VRAM from C. For these reasons I only work with *far* pointers.

Data pointed to can be very easily accessed as a single-dimensional array of bytes in C. For example, if you wanted to find the third byte in a string and print it out, the following C code is all that is required:

```
char far * StringPtr;

char String[ 45 ] = "I've Seen All Good People Turn Their Heads..";

  StringPtr = &String[ 0 ];

printf( "The Third Character of \"String\" is: \"%c\"\n",
  StringPtr[ 2 ]);
```

The first line defines a pointer named *StringPtr* to type *char*. The next line creates a pointer ("String") to a single-dimensional array 45 bytes long that has been initialized to a line from an old song. In the third line, the pointer to the initialized array is passed to StringPtr. The last line is used to output the third character of the initialized array to the PC's display.

In this code, a pointer is used both to point to data, as well as provide a label into an array element. After seeing this code, you're probably wondering about the difference between a string, an array or characters, and a pointer to a string. There really is no difference at all.

This point is important because it means that you can store data from a file into a buffer, point to the buffer, and index into the buffer using the same pointer that was set up when the buffer was initially created and the memory for the buffer allocated.

Being able to understand and use this complexity of pointers is all I think anybody should be capable of when developing a C application. This level of knowledge will allow you to access buffers (as single-dimensional arrays), as well as keep track of where the buffers are in memory.

To be honest, I still create data structures and unions, and link lists or link them together using pointers (just as you remember from your nightmare assignments at school). This makes the actual code very ugly, but I do it out of necessity when they provide the most efficient solution.

Instead of linked lists, I'll often create buffers full of ASCIIZ strings with the end of the strings marked by a *Null* character at the end of the last ASCIIZ string. Depending on the size of the data, this is a very simple and reasonably fast way to implement arrays of strings.

I would use a structure/union for this application if the data was not all man-readable text and if each record was the same size. Other than this limited case, I look for solutions to creating data sets other than structures and unions using pointed to strings.

When you buy a C or C++ compiler, you'll probably get a thick book (or a CD-ROM) detailing all of the library functions available for your use. Even before you dive into the language and try to understand it, go through this manual and try to understand what these libraries can do for you. I did not do this and ended up creating the ASMPROCS library that I have included with this book. As I became more sophisticated with C, I found out that I had rewritten many of the functions commonly available in standard C libraries.

When you go through a set of library functions, pay particular attention to memory allocation, hardware access, interrupt APIs (for BIOS and MS-DOS), and the file-system I/O. In many C compilers, memory allocation is only from the "heap" and not system memory. As indicated in the next chapter, I use the MS-DOS memory APIs instead of those built in. This gives me more memory to work with and doesn't affect the application's operation if I end up allocating much of the available space.

Normally, C libraries allow you simple access to the system hardware and APIs. The inp and outp functions allow you to access I/O hardware in the PC. If there are options for writing interrupt handlers in the compiler, avoid them because often the generic set ups will cause you a lot of problems. These problems include not setting up the data segment and pointer access properly and not saving all the registers that are required in the interrupt handler. Interrupt handlers are generally best written in assembler (which also helps you keep them short and fast).

Look for file-system APIs that provide as similar direct access to the MS-DOS file system as possible. The standard C f-file functions (fopen, fread, etc.) do not work exactly the same way as the MS-DOS APIs. You'll find it easier in the long run to work with just one system and always working with the operating-system APIs will reduce the ambiguity when doing assembler or working with other languages.

Macros and conditional code should be used sparingly to enhance the operation of the application. Try not to fall into the trap of using the same source for multiple applications (which deviates "only a little"). Instead, macros and conditional code should just be used to enhance or simplify operations where you have to write out the same code repeatedly.

C generally has a wonderful assembly-language interface that allows assembly language to be interfaced with it quite easily. Later, this chapter shows how assembly language can be written to interface directly with C.

Some C compilers allow assembly-language statements to be inserted directly into the source code. I recommend that you avoid this and place assembly-language functions in their own source files to help people reading your code. I know that for myself, nothing is more disconcerting that encountering code that looks like:

```
for ( i = 0; i < 77; i++ ) {

  printf( "i = \"%i\" for data ", i );

  mov   AH, DOSPRT
  mov   BX, i
  mov   DL, Table[ BX ]
  int   DOSINT

  printf( "/n" );

} // endfor
```

Even with well-commented code, I have difficulty maintaining the "thread" of what's supposed to be happening and I find myself asking questions like I would for the code:

1 What is the purpose of DOSPRT and DOSINT? This will send me scrambling for an MS-DOS technical reference and the included *.h* files.
2 Why is the table entry loaded and output using 8086-native instructions when "printf" should be able to carry out the same function?
3 The *mov BX, i* and *mov DL*, Table[BX] instructions use DS by default. Are both *i* and *Table* in the current DS? How do I know this?

In the beginning of the 1990s, some language vendors (notably Microsoft and Borland) began to ship C++ compilers to replace their C compiler lines. C++ is an object-oriented programming enhancement to C in which data and code is combined into "objects" of specific "classes." The purpose of C++ is to simplify the effort required to develop code for similar objects and provide a mechanism for easily sharing code across applications.

C++ (pronounced "See Plus Plus") never caught on with MS-DOS programming the same way it has for Windows programming, but it still is an interesting enhancement and understanding how *object-orientated programming (OOP)* works will help you structure and format your own applications.

A classic example of an object is a wheel. A wheel "class" can be made up of different "methods," which are used to describe how the object exists and provides and interface to change it. For the wheel, the methods could describe:

1 The wheel's diameter.
2 The wheel's depth.
3 The wheel's axle size.
4 The wheel's inflation pressure.

These methods can be modified for different types of wheel objects (such as a truck tire or a bicycle wheel) and provide "derived" classes that have many of the same methods, properties, and attributes, but differ where appropriate.

Later, when describing Visual C++, this book provides programming examples of C++ classes and objects and how they are used.

It is important to remember that C++ is a superset or C. Traditional C programs can be compiled using C++ compilers without any problems.

Linking Object Files

After a source file is compiled or assembled, it must be linked with other compiled/assembled source files and libraries into an executable file. Chapter 11 presented the concept of executable files (.EXE) and linking.

An object file is essentially all of the 8086 instructions created from a source file by the compiler or assembler. I say *essentially* because it is not in a format that will allow the code to be executed. Along with the code are references to labels and information that has to be linked to the other files. Along with the executable information, most object files include information needed to run a source-code debugger.

For MS-DOS executables, a number of options are available that will affect how your program is set up and runs. I mentioned the binary output (.COM) format, but you should be aware of a number of other options.

The first option is the ability to produce *hooks* in the file for a source code debugger. I normally leave the full debugging options until I am ready to release the code. These hooks can add as much as 20 percent to the final size of the application.

An interesting option in Microsoft MS-DOS linkers is the ability to selectively load code during program execution only when the subroutines used in them are required. To use this option, the object files to be linked have to be specified in a definition (.DEF) file. For my PICLite compiler, I use the definition file:

```
Piclite global memmgmt error +
(pass1 pass1c)+
(pass2 pass2b pass2c)+
(pass3 pass3c pass3f getconst)+
(pass4 pass4d pass4fb pass4fa pass4fl pass4fi getvar)+
(pass5 pass5a pass5b pass5c pass5k)+
```

```
(pass6 pass6g pass6get)+
(pass7 pass7get)+
(makeasm)+
c:\asm\asmprocs\asmprocs
piclite
piclite/map
llibce;
```

In this file, the main programs and routines that must always be present are outside the parentheses. The groups of object files inside the parentheses are only loaded when one of them is called. By using this feature, no more than 200 KB of memory is used by the program at any time, leaving space for the debugger and temporary data buffers.

The three last lines of the file are linker specific and specify the executable filename, the map filename, and the library to use. The + character at the end of each line is used to indicate that the object file-specification lines are continued onto the next line.

The other options that you should be aware of include the ability to compress the final .EXE file, where to place the executable (in regular or "high," above 1-MB Memory), and where to look for libraries and setting segment and stack sizes. These options are language and linker specific.

I should point out that these options are not an issue for linking Windows executable files from a development system. Appropriate "make" files are generally created automatically before the linking operation by the development system.

LINKING ASSEMBLER TO C/C++

This section is really an extension to "Parameter Passing" in Chapter 3. It expands upon the introduction that the 8086's stack is normally used for saving parameters. C (and Pascal) use this method for passing parameters. It works quite well and is very easy to set up for assembly-language programming.

For a C function call:

```
X = subroutine( A, B, C );
```

If you were to look at the assembler, you would see that the compiler converted the statement into:

```
push        C                       ; Push the Parameters onto the Stack
push        B
push        A
call        subroutine
add         SP, 6
mov         X, AX                   ; Save the Returned Value
```

This code pushes the parameters onto the stack in their reverse order, calls the subroutine and resets the stack to the value before the function call statement and saves the return parameter.

In the subroutine, reading the passed parameters is accomplished by:

```
Subroutine:
    push        BP              ; Save the Base Pointer on the Stack
    mov         BP, SP          ; and use it to point to the input
                                ; parameters
```

```
    mov       AX, [BP+6]
    mov       sbrtnA, AX
    mov       AX, [BP+8]
    mov       sbrtnB, AX
    mov       AX, [BP+10]
    mov       sbrtnC, AX

    :                          ; Execute the Subroutine Code

    mov       AX, Result       ; Load AX with the Result

    pop       BP               ; Restore the Base Pointer to
                               ;   the original value
    ret
```

First, the BP register is saved on the stack and then set with the current stack pointer value. Variables start at the new base pointer value plus six. Six is added to one stack pointer because the first four bytes are the return code segment and instruction points, followed by the "BP" register contents. The stack contents follow in the stack segment after these six bytes.

From this point, the parameters can be read or even used as local variables. The variables are accessed in ascending order to correspond to the parameter order in the high-level C statement.

The parameters are put onto the stack in backward order for reasons other than it makes it more intuitive to interface from assembler. C can have functions with parameter lists that are not fully defined; *printf* is a good example.

In these functions, the number of parameters is defined by the first parameter (in *printf*, the number of parameters can be found in the specified output string) and, as the parameter types are read in, then the individual data values are loaded in by the assembler routine.

Returning data is passed in the AX register for 8- and 16-bit data values; 32-bit and pointer data is returned in DX:AX.

Earlier in the book, I stated that I only used FAR pointers, far calls and large memory models because they simplified how applications are written. Also, it is easier to write applications that better interface with assembler, as well. Using 32-bit pointers and far calls eliminates any wrong choices to be made in how data and subroutines are accessed.

I don't recommend calling C subroutines from assembler. The object code for C might require specific register set ups (especially for DS) that are difficult to figure out or set up from within assembler. If you do want to call C functions from assembler, I recommend that you run the compiler with an Assembler Generation option to see exactly how the code works for very small applications. An ideal application for this purpose would be:

```
int Increment( int I )
{
   return i + 1
}

main()
{
int i;
   i = Increment( i );
)
```

As well, in the C routine, you should only use automatic variables and parameters that are totally stack based. "Global" variables may use difficult to find segments.

ASMPROCS

As I started writing "serious" applications for the PC in Microsoft C, I found that the standard functions were not always perfect for my needs. This was especially true for BIOS/MS-DOS APIs, which pass parameter information in the Flags register. To get around these problems, I created my own assembly-language library functions in the file *AsmProcs*.

I have included AsmProces on the CD-ROM for your use. To get an idea of what is available, here is the AsmProcs.h file, which includes the prototypes for including in the C source files:

```
/*  Calling Subroutines - The Format and Explanations...

    Started: 02/08/89        Myke Predko
    Updated: 93.04.16
    Updated: 96.02.15 - Got Rid of "STRINGLEN" and Used "strlen" in
                        C Libraries. MAP
           97.01.03 - Added "CLI()" & "STI()" Instructions

                                                                  */

int GETKEY();                  /*  Return Keyboard Key Character  */
int GETKEYSTAT();              /*  Return Key or Zero (no Key)    */
int GETROW();                  /*  Return the Cursor Row          */
int GETCOL();                  /*  Return the Cursor Column       */
GOTOXY( int Row, int Column );/*  Move Cursor to Specified loc'n */
SCREENCLEAR();                 /*  Clear the Screen               */
long int GETMEMAVAIL();        /*  Return Amount of RAM Available */
void far *GETMEM( long int MemSize );  /*  Allocate Specified RAM*/
        FREEMEM( void far *FreePtr );  /*  Free Allocated RAM     */
        RESIZE( void far *ResizePtr, long int MemSize );
                               /*  Resize Specified Memory Block  */
    int GETSEG( void far * Ptr );  /*  Return Pointer Values      */
    int GETOFF( void far * Ptr );
        DECASCII( char far *StringPtr, int Value );
                       /*  Int to ASCII                           */
    int STRSUBCMP( char far *SuperStr, char far *SubString );
                       /*  like C "strcmp" Function               */
    int STRSUBCMPI( char far *SuperStr, char far *SubString );
                       /*  like C "STRSUBCMP", but Case           */
                       /*  Insensitive                            */
long int MINIMUML( long int Value1, long int Value2 );
                       /*  Return Minimum Value                   */
        BREAKPOINT();          /*  Simply Execute a X'CC' Instruct*/
        CLI();                 /*  Execute a "CLI" Instruction    */
        STI();                 /*  Execute an "STI" Instruction   */
    int STRINGSEARCH( char far *SuperStr, char far *SubString );
                       /*  Search Super for Sub                   */
                       /*  If Found, Return Offset                */
                       /*  If NOT Found, Return -1                */
        BLOCKMOVE( char far *Dest, char far *Source, int Count );
                       /*  Move the String...                     */
long int SHORTTOLONG( int i );/*  Convert from 16 Bit to 32 Bit  */
```

```
HEXBYTE( char far * String, long int Value );
                        /*  Convert Integer to 2 byte Strg */
int ASCIIINT( char far * String );
                        /*  Return First Two Bytes as INT  */
```

If you are very familiar with C, you'll realize that about 50 percent of the functions in AsmProcs can be implemented using standard C library functions (including data-type conversion-language features) or interrupt APIs directly instead of my functions. My normal excuse for this is that many of these functions were written as I was learning C and I wasn't very well versed in what was possible.

This statement isn't quite accurate; I developed this code because I felt I could create code that could carry out library functions more efficiently than C could provide. This feeling was based on the "generality" of the standard C library functions and the appearance (when I disassembled them) that they were written in a high-level language instead of assembly. An important issue for me was that I had to use large amounts of memory; the built in "heap" was not sufficient for my needs.

For the half of these functions that can't be recreated using standard C library functions [which includes the keyboard, memory allocation, interrupt control ("CLI"/"STI") and breakpoint setting], the functions presented here are indispensible.

For the MS-DOS memory-allocation functions, you should note that they work with *bytes*, rather than *paragraphs* and access memory outside of the application and its "heap." These functions carry out the byte-size to paragraph-size conversion using the formula:

$$Paragraph\ requirements = (Byte\ requirements + 15)/16$$

Which means that you don't have to worry about the number of paragraphs in your application.

The BREAKPOINT function simply executes an int 3 (which has an opcode of 0x0CC) instruction and is useful for very large applications in which you want to have set breakpoints and don't want to work through a source-code debugger finding a particular file and line. It is important to be sure that you remove all occurrences of BREAKPOINT( ) before releasing your application because, depending on the version of MS-DOS, your application might hang at unexpected times.

To remove the breakpoint after the application is compiled and you've lost all of the source code, look for the data pattern: 0x0CC 0x0CB, which is int 03h followed by an intersegment return. Using a bit/byte editor, convert the 0x0CC to 0x090, which is the nop instruction.

I suggest that you at least look through the AsmProcs source because it contains some good examples of how parameters are passed between C functions and assembler code. This is one of the primary reasons why I have kept this code around for so many years; when I have to develop assembly-language functions, I copy this file into a new one and rewrite the functions, "stealing" the parameter handling interface that is required.

MAKE FILES

In one of the previous sections, I showed a .DEF file that I use to link together the object files of an application. Although this type of file cuts down on a lot of repetitive typing, another tool that is available with most high-level languages and linkers is called a *make utility*. This program completes the assembly, compiling, and linking of an application with options and conditional executing of MS-DOS command-line statements.

In its most basic form, a make utility uses a script file for a set of commands used to list the elements needed to create an application. In it, the source files are checked to see if the source files' MS-DOS file dates are later than the MS-DOS file dates of the object files. If they are, the files are assembled or compiled. The utility then links together all the object files into a new executable file if any of the resulting object files have MS-DOS file dates later than the current executables.

A make script file could be in the format:

```
CCOMP: C_SOURCE

ASM: ASM_SOURCE

LINK: APPLICATION, C_SOURCE + ASM_SOURCE, STD_LIBRARY;
```

In which it combines C_SOURCE and ASM_SOURCE along with a standard library to create APPLICATION.EXE.

Many make utilities have a simple if/then/else capability that allow you to create applications with different options. This could be used to create an application with or without the source-code debugger hooks. With this feature, I have seen make files seem as complex as the applications that they are compiling and linking.

In some development tools, notably Borland MS-DOS and Borland/Microsoft Windows IDEs, make files are automatically generated. In these cases, you will be prompted to add additional object files, rather than editing the file directly yourself. In these cases, I recommend that you let the IDE update the make file and maintain it for you. You should avoid editing the make file manually. Many IDE-specific make files contain special characters or commands and are not documented.

Debuggers

Choosing a debugger to work with an application is less of a personal choice and more of an exercise in learning what comes with (or works with) the compiler that you have chosen. Because of the time needed to debug an application, I might suggest only choosing compilers that are part of an *IDE (Integrated Development Environment)*, which includes an integral debugger.

In suggesting this, I am not getting kickbacks for IDE Developers; chances are that you will spend more time with the debugger than you will with the editor. I feel that it is crucial to work with a debugger that can step through the application's source code and show you exactly what is happening and be able to relate the errors back to the source directly.

DEBUG.COM

Every copy of MS-DOS and Windows is shipped with a simple debugger called, appropriately enough, DEBUG.COM. I am always amazed that this program is still being

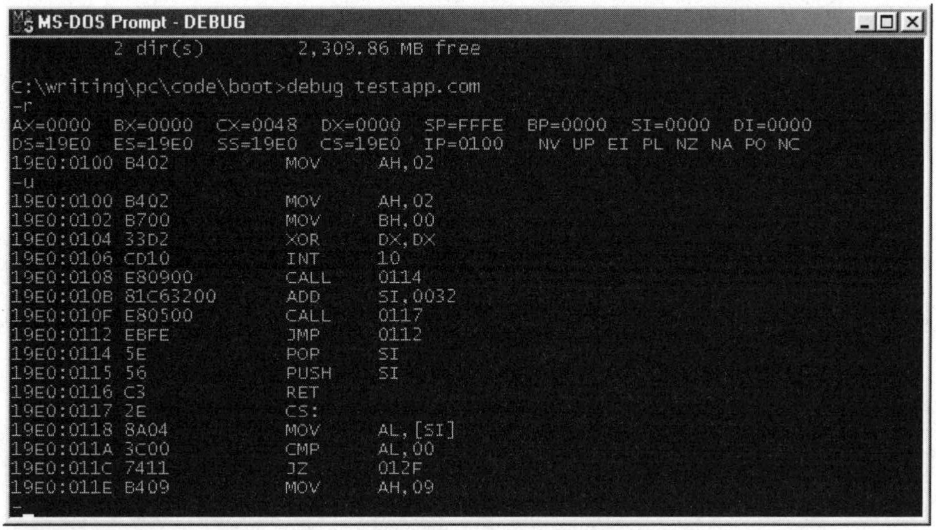

FIGURE 13-1 "Debug.com" register and program display.

shipped—I tend to think that it is still there because of inertia, nobody wants to be bothered removing the program from the installation package.

This little application is exceedingly useful for providing you with a window into your PC, as well as the applications that you create. DEBUG.COM can help you to understand how hardware works inside the PC and can be used for you to debug your hardware interfaces. With this send up, I hope you aren't expecting something as easy to use as Lotus 1-2-3 or BASIC, but you get a tool that will help you with your application development.

DEBUG.COM is a complete debugger, although it does not provide any symbolic information. This limits the usefulness quite a bit for substantial application development. Instead, DEBUG.COM is a good introduction to the PC's hardware and its interfacing.

DEBUG.COM runs off the current register information for the program being executed (Fig. 13-1). This information displays the current register contents, along with the disassembled instruction at the current CS:IP. Note that all assembly/disassembly operations cannot use labels or variables.

When invoking the program, the format:

```
debug [filename.ext]
```

is used where FILENAME.EXT is the application to be debugged.

I have included DEBUG.COM's command set because I have found it difficult to find documentation on how to use the program. Parameters in square brackets ("[" and "]") are optional. All constants are in hex.

Command	Parameters	Operation
A	[Address]	This command initiates a simple command line assembler at either CS:IP or the specified address. Instructions are entered in the standard Intel format with the

		square bracket convention used for variables (no brackets for constants). The only directives available are "db" and "dw" which are used to store data bytes in space provided. To end, press "Enter" on a blank line.
C	First [Range] Second	Data at address "First" is compared to data at address "Second" for "Range" bytes. The command stops at the end of the range or the first mismatch. "Range" has to have an "L" before the value. Up to 64K can be compared.
D	[address] [range]	Dump the data as bytes and hex at the specified address or the last address "D" displayed. Up to 64K can be displayed, with the default being 128 Bytes.
E	address [list]	Change the contents of memory at "address" with either the specified "list" or debug will prompt you to key in new values. After a new value, the "Space Bar" is pressed to increment to the next address. Press "Enter" to end the function.
F	address range value	Fill the memory starting at "address" for "range" (starting with "L") with "value." Multiple bytes in "value" will be placed in memory repeatedly.
G	[[CS:]address]	Starting executing at the current CS:IP value or the specified address. Execution will end when an "int 3" instruction is encountered, but not by the "Break" key sequence.
H	First Second	Add and subtract the two hex numbers ("First" and "Second") and displays the sum and the difference.
I	Port	Reads and displays the current contents of the specified "Port" register.
L	[Addr [Drive Sec Sec]]	This loads in either the file (specified by the "N" Command) or the disk sectors to the optional address ("Addr"). Loading from sectors explicitly is not recommended.

M	First range Second	Move the contents of memory starting at "First" to "Second" for "range" (which starts with "L").
N	[D:][path]filename.ext	Set the current contents of the debugger's memory to a specific filename.
O	Port Value	Write "Value" to the I/O "Port" Register.
P	[[=NewCS:]address]	If at a "call" instruction, entering this command will execute through the subroutine and stop at the instruction after the "call" instruction. If a specific address is to be used, then the "address" with, optionally, "NewCS" specified. For a new address in a segment different than the current "CS", then the address has to start with an "=" character.
Q		Exit debug.COM.
R	Register	Display and change the processor register. The flag register can only be accessed by bits which are defined as:

OV - Overflow Set
NV - Overflow Reset
DN - Direction Down
UP - Direction Up
EI - Interrupts Enabled
DI - Interrupts Disabled
NG - Negative Sign
PL - Positive Sign
ZR - Zero Flag Set
NZ - Zero Flag Reset
AC - Aux. Carry Set
NA - Aux. Carry Reset
PE - Even Parity
PO - Odd Parity
CY - Carry
NC - No Carry
These flag register values are also used in "CodeView."

| S | address range list | Search memory starting at "address" for "range" bytes for "list." Execution stops at a match or range end. "range" must start with an "L." |
| T | [[=NewCS:]addr] [count] | Single step through one or "count" instructions. If no "addr"ess specified, then execute from the current CS:IP. If a new "CS" is specified, then an |

		"=" character must precede the new value.
U	[address] [range]	Dissasemble the code at CS:IP or "address" to the end of the screen or for "range" (which is not preceded with an "L") bytes.
W	[addr [drive sec sec]]	Save the data used by debug onto disk. The filename.ext should be set by the "N" command. Saving to explicit drives and sectors is not recommended. The number of bytes to save is specified as a thirty-two bit number in CX and BX. The start of the write takes place at CS:IP. Ideally, the "W" command should be executed with no parameters and CS:IP and CX:BX used with the correct values.

CODEVIEW

An excellent example of a source code-level debugger is Microsoft's CodeView. This application takes the output of a CodeView-enabled compiler and linker to allow you to monitor the execution of the application—either line by line or with specific breakpoints (Fig. 13-2).

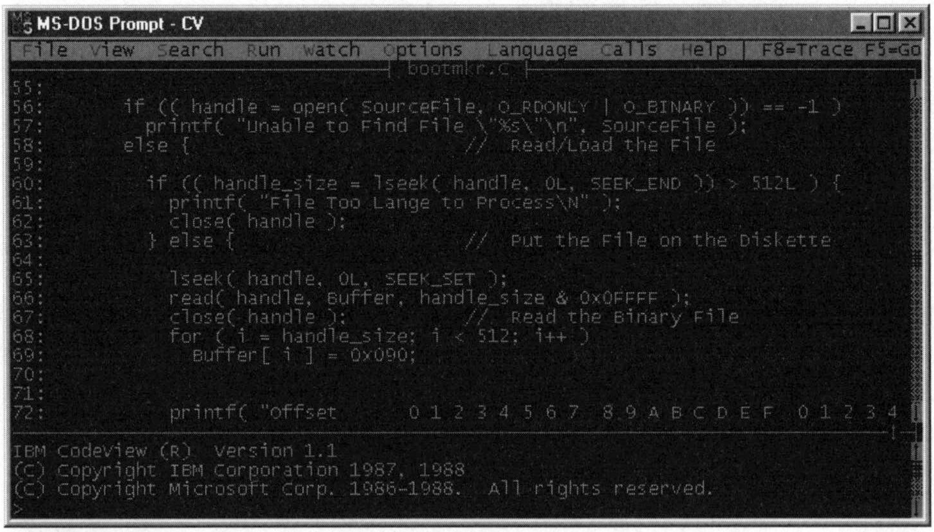

FIGURE 13-2   Codeview main operating "window".

CodeView is not the only tool available, but it is one of the most popular and familiar. Many of the commands introduced with DEBUG.COM are used for this application with the addition of breakpoints stopping after subroutine execution and viewing code three different ways (high-level language source, high-level language source with assembler and just straight assembly). These three different views are why I often say I debug programs in assembly. When I'm looking at C applications (particularly with pointers) and a line isn't working the way I expect, I can view the assembler code that was produced to see how the compiler did the conversion. Usually looking at the conversion, I can figure out what semantically is wrong with the line.

This method of debug is especially useful for pointer or conditional operations. The latter might seem surprising, but one of the biggest errors I make in C is:

```
if ( i = Const )
```

when I want:

```
if ( i == Const )
```

If this error is made, the first line is interpreted by the C compiler as:

```
i = Const;
if ( i != 0 )
```

I can usually see this problem very quickly from CodeView when I see that the assembler produced is:

```
mov     i, Const
mov     AX, i
or      AX, AX
jnz     ..
```

When I expect something like:

```
mov     AX, i
cmp     AX, Const
jnz     ..
```

Now, being able to predict the assembly code produced by a compiler is a reflection of the many years I've spent writing C code for the 8086 and knowing exactly how it works and what to expect. Even if you are fairly new to programming, if your code isn't working properly, you might want to drop into one of the assembly-language views and step through it to view the problem from another perspective.

CodeView set many of the standards used by Windows Visual Toolkit IDE debuggers. If you are familiar with CodeView, you will be able to work with the Visual Basic and Visual C++ debuggers very easily.

Using a source-code debugger is something of a learning process. Although it is interesting to watch your code execute, you should learn how to think through the code and figure out where to stop the execution before the problem and step through it to recognize where the failing code is executing. As you work with it, you will learn how to do this with multiple loop iterations without requiring a lot of time (or keystrokes) to stop at a specific statement after an arbitrary number of iterations.

CodeView works on Source code one line at a time. Earlier in the chapter, I showed that the code:

```
A = F( i, j );

K = K + A;

if ( k > 17 ) {

  printf( "Finished\n" );

  Ret = 1;

} // endif
```

could be "compressed" into:

```
if (( K += ( A = F( i, j ))) > 17 ) printf( "Finished\n", Ret = 1 );
```

If this was to be debugged using CodeView, the line would be executed in a single step and you would not be able to tell how it executed, unless you were to display the native instructions and step through them. A much better way of understanding what is happening is to use the expanded format of the statement and step through each line. This will make your debugging much easier because in the compressed form, the only way you will be able to figure out what is happening is if you display the assembly-language code and execute it instruction by instruction.

CodeView for MS-DOS is not Protect-mode aware and you'll have to remember that disabling interrupts or trashing the operating-system memory will cause problems for CodeView and continued execution. Two features that I would like to see in CodeView (if it is ever going to be enhanced) is the ability to run in extended memory and not take up any space in the 640-KB MS-DOS memory as well as the ability to repeat instructions. CodeView typically uses at least 320 KB that cannot be used by the application or for allocated memory. When you are developing large applications, you will have to plan for CodeView's space requirements; this typically means that code must be linked as a series of loadable routines, instead of one large one, as I showed for "PICLite" earlier in the chapter.

Editors

Choosing an editor is really up to you. Don't be surprised if you ask for some recommendations and end up being flooded with different editors to try. I believe that it's important to pick one that seems right for you and will help you to develop applications efficiently. Instead of suggesting a number of editors for you to try, here are some important features to look for.

First consideration is whether or not it is Windows- or command-line-based program. Windows-based programs are probably very familiar to you; you can interact with the Windows clipboard, allowing easy cut and pasting of code between applications. With a Windows editor, you usually can change the font to one that you consider to be the most readable.

An MS-DOS command-line editor doesn't have these advantages and might not use the mouse (or, if it does, it might be an ugly square character). What an MS-DOS editor does offer is fast screen updating, which can be useful for large files. It can also offer more highlighting options to make seeing constructs or errors more easily.

How the file is handled, either as a string of text or as a series of lines is important. Text editors, such as those used with your e-mail system, use paragraphs as a set of lines that end with ASCII carriage-return/line-feed characters. This text is displayed to the end of the line. If it goes beyond it, the line wraps around to the next line. Line editors work on a line-by-line basis and often make working with software source code (and data) easier. In the past, I have programmed exclusively with a line editor, but because the editors shipped with *Integrated Development Environments (IDEs)* provide a text editor, I have started to use text editors exclusively.

An important feature is the control keys; do you want to pull-down operations and features, or do you like entering *Ctrl* and *Alt* key combinations? I know quite a few people who still use early 1980s editors (such as *XyWrite*) because they like the *Ctrl* key functions built in to the editors.

A very important feature for an editor is to call up other applications that will use the source code without having to save the source or leave the editor. Your first thought might be that this feature is useful for documenting programs, something like Microsoft Word could be started that would aid in the documentation of the application, but I want to use an editor that I can initiate compilers, simulators, and the application itself. In many cases, this means that the editor is part of a do-it-yourself IDE.

Along with the ability to initiate compilers and simulators, I feel that source-code interfaces to these programs are really important. I like having an interface to the compiler output so that syntax errors are highlighted in the editor and in the simulator, I like watching the source code execute, not the compiled assembler. These features are usually only available in the more-sophisticated IDEs (although with the following programmable editor, I was able to highlight syntax errors after compiling a source file).

You might want an editor with programmable features. This might sound like user-definable *Ctrl/Alt* keystroke sequences, but it can often go much further than that. For many years, I used an editor tailored to C program development. This editor was programmed in REXX and provided implicit code updates. An example of this was when IF was entered in uncommented text, the editor would put in the code:

```
if () {
} else {
} // endif
```

If you are looking for an editor for your code development, the only real advice I can give is: look for an IDE for the language in which you want to program. If one is not available, then look at as many editors with user-programmable features as you can find.

Many of the features presented in this section are used to save keystrokes and make application development easier. The best way to save time in your application development is: think of how the application is going to work and how you are going to create the source code before you put your fingers to the keyboard. Often, problems arise because the operators started using the tools before they were ready.

Before starting any project, think through exactly what you want to do. You'll find that you can have the most feature-poor, difficult-to-use, and quirky editor and the code development will still go very quickly and efficiently.

PRACTICAL

PC

PROGRAMMING

CONTENTS AT A GLANCE

Before jumping into programming interfaces for the PC, I have a few comments and suggestions. The purpose of this chapter is to give you some background in the programming techniques that you will need for developing your own applications.

The examples are written in pretty generic C code. This is on purpose because I feel that this language best illustrates how algorithms execute and can be easily ported to other languages. For the system level code (such as getting keystrokes, outputting console data, or accessing disk information), I use the standard C functions wherever possible, although I point out situations where more direct forms of interfacing might be more appropriate.

Parsing Command-Line Parameters

MS-DOS command-line programs have always had the ability to specify how the application is going to work. The execution parameters are specified when the program is loaded and executed and often have the reputation for being complex and nonintuitive with few conventions in place. This section is an introduction to the concept of using command-line parameters and how to make it easier for users to work with your applications.

When an MS-DOS command line application is started, a statement like:

```
My_App Source.fyl /Dest.fyl -options
```

is used to describe the format of its invocation. As I have indicated elsewhere, SOURCE.FYL, /DEST.FYL, and -options are the command-line parameters that are saved in the application's *Program Segment Prefix (PSP)*. The parameters are stored in the PSP, starting at offset 0x081 (the byte at address 0x080 is loaded with the length of the string stored starting at 0x081). The data loaded in is the string of command-line parameters, character by character, except that multiple blanks between parameters are replaced with a single blank character.

In assembly-level programming, you will have to check address 0x080 for a value not equal to zero and then read through each parameter until a blank or the end of the string is processed.

A typical subroutine to process the parameters is:

```
ReadParm:                       ; ES - Has the PSP Segment Already

   xor   BX, BX                 ; BX is the index into the parameter string

RP_Check:                       ; Are we at the Specified Parameter?
   or    CX, CX                 ; If CX = 0 then ES:BX Points to the Start of the
   jz    RP_Have                ;  Specified Parameter

RP_Loop:                        ; Read through the parameter to it's end
   cmp   BL, ES:[ 081h ]        ; At the end of the parameters?
   jz    RP_End                 ; Yes, Return to the Caller

   mov   AL, BYTE PTR ES:[ BX + 081h ]

   inc   BX                     ; Point to the next Character

   cmp   AL, ' '                ; Was a Blank Encountered?
   jnz   RP_Loop

   dec   CX                     ; Yes, Decrement the Count

   jmp   RP_Check

RP_Have:                        ; Have the Parameter

   clz                          ; Reset Zero to Indicate that the Parameter is
                                ;  pointed to by ES:BX
RP_End:                         ; ES:BX Points to the Specified Parameter if the
                                ;  Zero Flag is Reset
```

This routine does go through the first parameters to find a specific parameter, but this is not a major inefficiency. Upon return from this routine, if the zero flag is set, then the parameter isn't present, else ES:BX+0x081 points to the starting address of the parameter.

The C language passes the parameters directly to the application in two standard variables and is available at the "main" (start of program statement). The standard format is:

```
main( argc, argv, env )              // Application Start Point
{

}  // End main
```

The *argc* variable is an integer count of the number of parameters passed with the application. This value is never less than 1, with *1* indicating that there are no parameters. The *argv* variable is an array of string pointers with an indeterminate number of elements. The first pointer in the array points to the application's filename, but each parameter is pointed to by an index.

To read the elements, the code:

```
for ( i = 1; i < argc; i++ ) {

    :                                // Process the Arguments

}  // endfor
```

can be used with *i* being the *argv* index.

In the previous main statement, three parameters are actually passed to it. The *env* parameter is a pointer to the MS-DOS environment information. Each entry in the environment is separated with an ASCII null character (0x000) and the end of the string is noted by two null characters.

Specifying the different parameter types should follow some kind of convention. This will make life a bit easier for your customers (and for you). The conventions that I am talking about is a preceding character used to denote the type of parameter that is being passed to the application. Note that I indicated the "proceeding character" in the singular. You could use multiple characters (i.e., *input=filename.ext*), but this requires more parsing by the application (more work for you) and more keystrokes by the user (more work for the customer). Having something as simple as a slash symbol to denote an output file makes the parameters simpler for the user to use and understand.

The conventions that I use and suggest for MS-DOS command-line file parameters are:

- Nothing for input files
- A slash (/) for output files
- A dash (-) for application-specific parameters
- A question mark (?) for outputting help data. This should also be a single *h* or an *h* preceded by a slash or dash.

If a help character is recognized, then all other parameters should be ignored and the program help information is displayed without executing the application. The typical help information could be:

```
Application Name

Author/Owning Company

Version/Revision Number

My_App Input.fyl /output.fyl -options

OPTIONS:

-A - First Option
-B - Second Option
 :
```

Sometimes, I use "unlikely" characters to provide functions I don't necessarily want the user to experiment with. "Unlikely" characters include ".", ",", "~", "^", "|", and "+". These characters maybe embedded in filenames, but seldom used on their own. When I created the "PICLite" compiler, I used . to stop the deletion of the temporary compiler file so that I could look at how the compiler worked in different cases for debugging.

As pointed out in Chapter 18, the input parameters should not be ordered. I find that it is confusing when parameters are ordered because other users don't necessarily follow the order that I would use intuitively. By using the preceding characters, the type of parameter should be easily identified by the application, no matter where it resides. Ordering parameters might be required for some applications, but, if at all possible, they should be avoided.

I/O Interface Code

Most of the remainder of this book presents information specific to how to interface hardware to the PC and how to write application code to work with it. Before going on, here are some terms and concepts that are important to help you to successfully carry out the integration of hardware to the PC without being overwhelmed with debugging problems. I don't pretend to have all the answers for each and every different case, but you should get some ideas for when you approach a project or a problem.

Interfacing in the PC is carried out through the I/O registers or the DMA subsystem. I/O registers should only be eight bits wide to avoid timing problems associated with the simulated two byte I/O executed because the I/O bus is only eight bits wide. DMA transfers should also only be between eight-bit I/O registers and memory. Sixteen-bit I/O reads, writes, and DMA transfers are possible in the PC, but they should be avoided because they can be somewhat less than optimal in some situations and generally are always more complex.

When writing to hardware, it will always be carried out as a register write. This might be surprising because you might have to create an arbitrary waveform, such as that in Fig. 14-1.

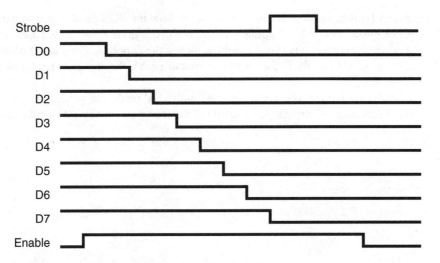

FIGURE 14-1 Arbitrary wave form from a PC.

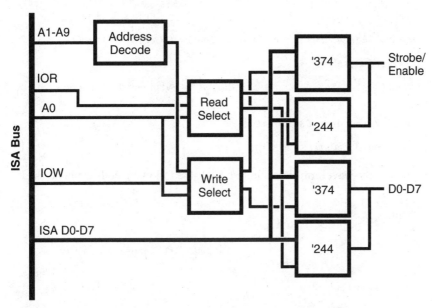

FIGURE 14-2 Circuit to generate the arbitrary wave form.

To output this, the output bits are given I/O port addresses. Ideally, the bits should have a read-back capability that can be used to make the circuit more general. This read back can be used to read and write or to check the current output and whether or not there is a "stuck bit" (either a blown driver or the pin is overdriven to high or low). A circuit that could produce this waveform and has these capabilities could be like the one shown in Fig. 14-2.

This circuit (which, incidentally is very similar to how the PC's parallel port is wired) decodes ISA bus-address bits A1 through A9 to get a two address range, which uses A0 to select between the control bits (Strobe and Enable) or the data bits. The outputs of these select units are used to strobe in the data for output or enable the drivers to read back the bits.

In your application code, you could either do individual reads and writes, or create bit and port I/O functions. To drive signals out of the ISA bus, you could create the functions:

```
Strobe( int Value )        //  Output the Value to the Strobe
{

  if ( Value == 0 )         //  Make the Bit Low?
    outp( BaseAddr + Ctrl, inp( BaseAddr + Ctrl ) & !Strobe );
  else                      //  Make the Bit High
    outp( BaseAddr + Ctrl, inp( BaseAddr + Ctrl ) | Strobe );

}  //  End Strobe

Enable( int Value )        //  Output the Value to the Enable Bit
{

  if ( Value == 0 )         //  Make the Bit Low?
    outp( BaseAddr + Ctrl, inp( BaseAddr + Ctrl ) & !Enable );
  else                      //  Make the Bit High
    outp( BaseAddr + Ctrl, inp( BaseAddr + Ctrl ) | Enable );

}  //  End Strobe

DataOut( int Value )       //  Output a Byte to the Data Port
{

  outp( BaseAddr + Data, Value );

}  //  End DataOut
```

To produce the waveform shown in Fig. 14-1, the following code could be used:

```
Strobe( 0 );               //  Set up the Initial Conditions
Enable( 0 );
DataOut( 0x0FF );
BitDlay();                 // Make Sure there is a Constant Delay
                           //    between Bit Transitions.

Enable( 1 );
BitDlay();

DataOut( 0x0FE );
BitDlay();

DataOut( 0x0FC );
BitDlay();

DataOut( 0x0F8 );
BitDlay();

DataOut( 0x0F0 );
BitDlay();
DataOut( 0x0E0 );
BitDlay();
```

```
DataOut( 0x0C0 );
BitDlay();

DataOut( 0x080 );
BitDlay();

DataOut( 0x000 );
BitDlay();

Strobe( 1 );                    //  Drive the Strobe
BitDlay();
BitDlay();
Strobe( 0 );
BitDlay();

Enable( 0 );                    //  Deselect the Device
```

The BitDlay functions are used to provide a constant delay between the bit transitions. Later, the book shows how these delays are generated across a wide range of PC hardware.

The waveform code could also be placed in a function to make your mainline code easier to read:

```
WriteData( int Value )          //  Write the Data to the Port
{

    Enable( 1 );                //  Enable the Device
    BitDlay();

    Dataout( Value );           //  Output the Value
    BitDlay();

    Strobe( 1 );                //  Strobe the Value
    BitDlay();
    BitDlay();
    Strobe( 0 );
    BitDlay();

    Enable( 0 );                //  Deselect the Device

}  //  End WriteData
```

Now, in the mainline, the WriteData function can be invoked, which makes the hardware interface function appear as if it were part of the language.

In the Strobe and Enable routines, notice that I use the actual bit values as defines, for example, if *Strobe* was bit 0 and *Enable* was bit 1, I would define them as:

```
#define Strobe 1                //  Bit 0
#define Enable 2                //  Bit 1
```

And this way, I don't have to play around with figuring out what is the correct bit pattern for the different bits. In the parallel-port chapters, later in the book, I continue this method of defining bits, as well as showing how these functions work for negatively active I/O bits.

If you are sending data in streams to some I/O ports and handshaking is used, it is a good idea to put handshaking before the register I/O. By placing the handshaking polling before any code that accesses the register, the time needed to wait for the next write to be valid can be reduced by the execution of the other instructions in the application leading up to the I/O write. Placing the Wait behind will not have the same advantages and will require a Wait after the last character sent (which really isn't necessary).

If feedback registers are not available, then you will have to record the current state of the bits before they are used. For Fig. 14-2, if the '245's were not present in the circuit, global variables would have to be included in the application to track what the ports are outputting. The write to the strobe register would become:

```
Strobe( int Value )                    //  Output the Value to the Strobe
{                                      //   - With No Feedback Register

  if ( Value == 0 )                    //  Make the Bit Low?
    outp( BaseAddr + Ctrl, Ctrl_Var = Ctrl_Var & !Strobe );
  else                                 //  Make the Bit High
    outp( BaseAddr + Ctrl, Ctrl_Var = Ctrl_Var | Strobe );

} // End Strobe
```

This is not a tremendous inconvenience, but something to be wary of.

Reading from the I/O ports is generally very straightforward and I normally use a '244 or '245 eight-bit buffer to enable the data being passed back to the processor. The feedback circuit in Fig. 14-2 is a good example of this.

Having gone through all this, you'll probably be annoyed when I say that the best hardware interface is one that you don't have to write in the application. Ideally, it should be a device driver or BIOS API that has been created specifically for the hardware. This will give you the opportunity to re-use the hardware or port it to another operating system with a minimum of fuss.

Memory Organization

When you work with large amounts of data, having a good strategy to organize how memory is used in an application is crucial. Poor choices in how data is stored can make the application larger, more complex, and significantly slower than an application that has good memory organization strategies. There aren't a lot of rules for creating memory and variable data areas in MS-DOS, but the ones that I have come up with can be worth their weight in gold.

First, be sure that all of your variables are in the same data segment. Often variables will be placed in a module (file or subroutine) specific code or data segment. This can be a big problem with new assembly-language programmers. If multiple data segments are used, the overhead needed to handle the multiple segments (DS and ES register loads and keeping what each segment register has at a given time) can become mind-numbingly complex. It can be almost impossible to know which data segments are being pointed to and whether or not you have to change a segment register.

In MS-DOS, many assembly-language programmers use the current code segment for variables. The most obvious problem with this is that incorrect execution could trash memory or code. Also, by doing this, the code cannot be easily ported to a Protect-mode environment.

When handling large amounts of data, I only work with it in the size of "chunks" that are best suited to the processor. In the 8086, I feel that this is 32,768 (32 KB) bytes. I prefer 32 KB to a full segment (64 KB) because the full 15-bit data space can be accessed by *int*-type variables without worry about two's complement negative numbers. I usually forget to declare variables that will be indexed memory arrays as "unsigned" and end up trying to figure out why my indexed addressing doesn't work.

If I'm going to be working with data that is transferred to or from external devices, then I will allocate the memory from the operating system, rather than declare it in the program. Declaring large amounts of variable space can cause problems with some high-level language's heap space.

To access memory, the MS-DOS int 021h functions 0x048 (allocate memory), 0x049 (free allocated memory), or 0x04A (resize allocated memory) are used. Each of these APIs accesses MS-DOS memory from the pool of left-over memory.

At the start of each memory block, a 16-byte (one "paragraph") header is used to describe the information for the block. This block is defined as:

OFFSET	SIZE	DESCRIPTION
0	Byte	0x05A if last block, 0x04D if not
1	Word	PSP segment address of owning process
3	Word	Size of block in paragraphs
5	3 bytes	Reserved
8	8 bytes	ASCII string of owning process

Blocks of memory can be explicitly defined, but it really is much easier to simply use the predefined MS-DOS APIs.

A 32-KB block size is also good because it is small enough that if there are fragmentation issues with memory (i.e., many small blocks available, but no large ones), a free 32-KB block can consist of the fragments available. Larger sizes are less likely to be available as contiguous blocks of memory and in the MS-DOS Real mode; there is no way to concatenate multiple blocks together into one contiguous block of memory.

Reading and Writing File Data

A section on how to efficiently read data from a file might seem somewhat unusual in a book about interfacing hardware to a computer, but in some instances, you have to read a relatively large amount of data to process or download into an external device. Having a plan on how to do it beforehand and knowing some of the pitfalls can save you lots of time waiting for the application to read data or avoid untold grief when something doesn't work as expected.

I can't tell you how many times I've helped out somebody who has created data read code like:

```
    :
char Buffer[ 20000 ];              // Define a buffer to store data
```

```
        :

    ReadRtn()
    {

      handle = open( "FileName.Ext", Parameters );

      FileSize = read( handle, Buffer, 20000 );

          :                                    //  Process the Code

      close( handle );

    }  //  End ReadRtn
```

This code is used because the programmer has specified the format of the data and knows exactly how large the file is going to be. These assumptions rely on the base assumption that nothing is ever going to change.

This code has the advantage that the entire file is loaded into an array and data can be processed anywhere without concern as to whether or not sections of the file has to be reloaded.

The base assumption is really what separates novice programmers from experienced application designers.

Anybody making this assumption usually finds that the file is not the size they expected, data is not where they want it to be, and it is not in the format for which they have planned. To make matters worse, the file could be ended with a special character that affects the total size and operation of the application. If the file size grows, it might require more space than is available in the PC or can be easily addressed using the standard data types.

This results in the program from being changed from above, where the programmer is sure about everything, to where nothing is for sure:

```
        :
    char character;                       //  Character Read from the File
        :

    ReadRtn()
    {

      handle = open( "FileName.Ext", Parameters );

      while ( read( handle, character, 1 ) != 0 )
        switch ( character ) { //  Process the file a Byte at a Time
          case 0x000:          //  Handle the Null Character

              :                //  Process each different Byte Value

        } // endswitch

      close( handle );

    }  //  End ReadRtn
```

In this code, each character is individually read and processed. If it is affected (or affects) surrounding data bytes, the data is saved in unique strings or arrays.

To be fair, this code can easily handle (or be changed to handle) every case that comes up, but will take much longer to execute. I often find the programmer ending up spending a lot of time (for a long time) maintaining this style of code, fixing and tweaking until the source becomes unmanageable and they feel stuck.

A major problem with this type of programming is that data cannot be accessed randomly. It might have a number of *lseek* function calls, resulting in reloads at different locations.

These problems are really a result of lack of planning. By developing a few rules, I can usually come up with an input data format and read routine that will run quite quickly and avoid many potential problems that I have pointed out in the previous two examples.

If you are new to application programming, you are probably surprised that I would indicate that you have to come up with a format for the input file, but spending a few minutes here will simplify the work required later to debug the application. This format should be designed in such a way that it can be created and read by an ASCII character editor, data records can be easily defined, and locations within the code can be quickly identified.

The file definition I usually use is a two ASCII byte representation for each data byte with a Carriage Return/Line Feed (ASCII characters 0x00D and 0x00A) used to define the end of each data record. This source is "man-readable" and can be created, edited, or checked using a simple PC text editor.

If I had a file with hex bytes used for test data, which is sent in blocks of eight, the file could be defined in C as:

```
char * line1 = "0001020304050607\r\n";
char * line2 = "08090A0B0C0D0E0F\r\n";
char * line3 = "1011121314151617\r\n";
char * line4 = "18191A1B1C1D1E1F\r\n";
```

If the file data was C source code and only valid ASCII display characters were used, I could use a single byte to define each data byte:

```
char * line1 = "  if ( i > 7 )\r\n";
char * line2 = "    printf( \"i is too large\\n\" );\r\n";
```

The important feature of either case is that the data can never be ASCII control characters. If control characters (other than the Carriage Return/Line Feed at the end of each record line) are encountered, then the input file is in error.

As I read each record to get the record's length, I just read through to the line-feed character:

```
for ( i = 0; linex[ i++ ] != '\n'; );
```

This FOR statement will allow me to find the end of the current record (and the start of the next) very easily and very quickly.

This probably makes a lot of sense for applications that require input from man-readable text, but not as much sense for binary data. In the first example, the 32 bytes could have been loaded into an array directly from the input file and then sent to the hardware (assuming that processing occurs after every eight bytes) using the code:

```
for ( i = 0; i < 4; i++ ) {
  for ( j = 0; j < 8; j++ )
```

```
    send( Buffer[( i * 8 ) + j ]);//  Send Each individual Byte
  Process();                        //   Process the eight byte block
}
```

I would argue that the code required for my format is not much more complicated and can really be used in a very similar format once the file is loaded in:

```
for ( i = 0; i < 4; i++ ) {
  for ( j = 0; j < 8; j++ )
    send( GetHex( &Buffer[( i * 10 ) + ( j * 2 )]);
  Process();
}
```

Using my format, the same basic layout of the code can be used, the difference is that the data will be loaded from the file image loaded into buffer and that allowances will have to be made for the carriage return/line feed at the end of each line.

The advantages over the marginally few additional cycles needed to execute this code really make this format of storing and loading data much more efficient. The biggest advantage is the fewer CPU cycles required from you to develop and monitor the data files and the status of their processing. If straight data bytes were used, then you would have to create a program to generate the data. Using the ASCII format, a straight PC ASCII editor can be used and the data can be monitored easily, without having to write a translator to read the files.

Some editors can create arbitrary eight-bit ASCII codes (using an *Alt* key, keypad selection); all editors can produce files in straight ASCII format. Using this format will lessen the requirements for specific tools to be used.

If raw eight-bit data is used, then an editor might not be able to display it correctly (this is also true for typing a file from the command line to look at its contents). Any bytes with a value less than 0x020 (32 decimal or an ASCII blank character) will be interpreted as an ASCII control character and not necessarily displayed as extended ASCII symbols. In the ASCII format, the record-ending carriage-return/line-feed and file-end characters are the only ASCII control characters used.

Two comments regarding this file format. In the MS-DOS "Edit" program (along with at least one other editor), sometimes an ASCII control character (usually a backspace (0x008)) will be put into a file when you're working on it. This character may or may not show up as a missing character in a line when you type it out (the Backspace might be deleting an extra character) and will not show in the editor. But when you try to operate on this file, you will find unexpected errors; the only way to fix the problem is to delete the line and enter it in again.

The second comment is more of a be careful statement: be sure, whenever possible, to avoid putting in the string *AT* (with any upper- and lower-case combination of *AT*) in your source files. I realize that this will restrict your vocabulary somewhat in the files (I try to remember to use @ instead of *at* in my source-code comments), but this string is used by Hayes-compatible modems as the command string. If you are sending a file via modem with this string in it, you might inadvertently change the modem settings and screw up your file transfer.

This problem can also be avoided by only sending data via modem using a binary format or PKZIPping them up first (so that the *at* is essentially scrambled). The biggest reason for always using this data format is to handle files easily that are larger than the buffer that they're going to be put into.

Most PC high-level languages cannot handle buffers greater than 64 KB and the integer word size is usually 16 bits. In C, *int* (an integer data type) is a signed value (from -32768 to +32767). I make my buffers a maximum of 32,768 (32 KB, 0x08000) bytes long.

Also remember that the buffer's memory should be allocated from the operating system, rather than defined as part of the application. Allocating the memory will result in a smaller final executable file size and avoid potential heap problems.

When processing data files, I assume that the files are greater than 32 KB (and their size is not a multiple of 32 KB) and use the following code to process them:

```
handle = open( "Path\FileName.Ext", Parameters );


FileSize = lseek( handle, End );;);
lseek( handle, Start ););          // Find the Size of the file
FileProc = 0;                      // Nothing from the File Processed

while ( FileProc < FileSize ) {  // Process the File
    lseek (handle, Start, File Proc);

    read( handle, Buffer, minimum( 32767, FileSize - FileProc ));
                                   // Read in to Buffer Size

    if ( minimum( 32767, FileSize - FileProc ) == 32767 ) {
      for ( i = 32767; Buffer[ i ] != '\n'; i-- );
      Buffer[ ++i ] = '\0';         // Terminate the File
    } else                          // Terminate the String in the Buffer
      if ( Buffer[( FileSize - FileProc ) - 1 ] == 0x01A )
        Buffer[( FileSize - FileProc ) - 1 ] = '\0';
      else                          // Exclude FileEnd Character
        Buffer[ FileSize - FileProc ] = \0';

    i = 0;  LFlag = 0;
    while (( Buffer[ i ] != '\0' ) && ( LFlag == 0 )) {
                                   // Loop through the Buffer

       :                           // Process the File Data

    } // endwhile

    FileProc += i;                 // Update the File Processed Counter

} // endwhile

close( handle );                   // Finished Reading/Processing File
```

In this code, after the file is opened, the size is found by moving the DOS pointer to its end (and saving the offset). Once this is done, the pointer is moved back to the start of the file so that data can be read in "buffer"-sized increments. Using this method, the file can be of any size.

At the end of each read function, I find the end of the last line and place a null character (0x000, '\0') after its line-feed (0x00A, '\n') character so that I have marked the last record to process. By doing this, reloading is simple, moving the file pointer to the line after the last processed and does not involve figuring out how to re-assemble a partially loaded line.

When the last bit of code has been loaded, notice that I check for a 0x01A character at the end of the file. In many early MS-DOS systems (and editors), this character was used to mark the end of the file. Despite the fact that it hasn't been required for more than 15 years (since the introduction of MS-DOS 2.0), this character is still put in by many editors and is used by many programs. Personally, I don't bother with it because many editors and programs don't use it or add it to the end of a file, and I can never see myself using DOS 1.x ever again.

In the previous code, if the 0x01A character is at the end of the file, I simply write over it with a null character.

As I process the data, I accommodate multiple lines of data for different data types.

For example, if you were implementing an interpreter and you were looking for the code:

```
while( condition )          // Execute while "condition" is true

    :

wend
```

which has to be in the same 32-KB block (to simplify execution), I would check to see if the buffer is loaded with both statements using the code:

```
if ( strncmp( &Buffer[ i + 2 ], "while(", 6 ) == 0 ) {

  for ( j = i; ( Buffer[ j ] != '\0' ) &&
           ( strncmp( &Buffer[ j + 2 ], "wend\r", 5 ) != 0 ); )
    for ( ; Buffer[ j++ ] != '\n'; );      // Look for "wend" Stmt

  if ( Buffer[ j ] == '\0' ) {

    FileProc += i;           // Reload the Buffer from "while"
    lseek( handle, Start, FileProc );
    read( handle, Buffer, minimum( 32767, FileSize - FileProc ));
                             // Read in to Buffer Size
    if ( minimum( 32767, FileSize - FileProc ) == 32767 ) {
      for ( i = 32767; Buffer[ i ] != '\n'; i-- );
      Buffer[ ++i ] = '\0'; // Terminate the File
    } else                   // Terminate the String in the Buffer
      if ( Buffer[( FileSize - FileProc ) - 1 ] == 0x01A )
        Buffer[( FileSize - FileProc ) - 1 ] = '\0';
      else                   // Exclude FileEnd Character
        Buffer[ FileSize - FileProc ] = \0';


    for ( j = i = 0; ( Buffer[ j ] != '\0' ) &&
             ( strncmp( &Buffer[ j + 2 ], "wend\r", 5 ) != 0 ); )
      for ( ; Buffer[ j++ ] != '\n'; );   // Look for "wend" Stmt

  } // endif

  if ( strncmp( &Buffer[ j + 2 ], "wend\r", 5 ) != 0 ) {

    :                                    // No "wend", Report Error

    LFlag = 1;                           // Stop Executing Code
```

```
} else {
    :                                    // Execute "while" loop
} // endif
```

If the whole *while* to *wend* is not in the current buffer contents, then the code will reload the buffer from the file starting at the line that contains the WHILE statement and look for the *wend*. If *wend* isn't there after the reload, then an error is processed.

After each line is processed, *i* is incremented to the start of the next record (line) of the data file using the code:

```
for ( ; Buffer[ i++ ] != '\n'; );
```

This code will stop when the end of the record is encountered (at *'\n'* or line feed) and then increment the index once more (which causes it to point to the next line). This code can be put into a *LineEnd* macro (or *define* in C), which makes your coding much easier.

When processing data, it is easier to work through the code sequentially than it is to read at random. Even in the *WHILE/wend* example, notice that even though I move the DOS file pointer back, I still process the data sequentially.

Sorting and Formatting Data

Every few months, I have to sort an array of data. The reasons can consist of sorting quality results (producing "parettos" of data) or organizing and listing data in a specific order. The requirements are normally for this work to be done quickly. I was going to add "with a minimum of overhead," but this is really not necessary to state because most sorting algorithms require very small amounts of memory to operate. The most important resource to conserve is the number of cycles required for the sort, to minimize the amount of time that the user has to wait for the sort to complete.

When I talk about sorting data, I'm usually talking about sorting data that fits in memory. For Windows programming, this isn't a big issue, with up to 4.3 GB of virtual memory available for an application. It is, however, an issue for MS-DOS, where data should be on the order of tens (and, in rare cases, hundreds) of kilobytes. If the data is too large to be stored in memory, I use the "Sort" utility that comes with MS-DOS.

Normally, data is in the form of records, with the data to be sorted is just a small portion of the total record. For example, in a quality record:

```
Column 0   34   78                        79
         QUANCOMPDESCRIPTION               *
```

Only QUANtity, COMPonent, or DESCRIPTION of the failure is to be sorted. But not all three of these items ("fields") are to be sorted at the same time. The sort routine will have to move the entire record, based on the field that is sorted. This means that to maximize the sort execution speed, the number of record moves must be minimized.

The primary sort algorithm that I use is "QuickSort". Now, half of the people reading this are wondering what it is and the other half are groaning because they remember QuickSort as being difficult to understand and implement. What you're probably most familiar with (and have used in the past is BubbleSort), which is very easy to understand and implement. QuickSort does require more code and a better understanding of what is happening, but the performance gains will more than make up for the extra difficulty in implementing the algorithm.

The BubbleSort algorithm is very simple. It just runs through the array of data for each element and moves the current largest element to the end of the array. This is repeated once for each element in the array that needs to be sorted. The algorithm can be written as:

```
for ( i = 0; i < Size; i++ )
  for ( j = 0; j < i, j++ )
    if ( Ele[ j ] > Ele[ j + 1 ])
      Swap( Ele[ j ], Ele[ j + 1 ]);     //  Swap the position of the
                                          //  current two elements
```

Although it is exceedingly simple and frugal on memory resources, it has a major drawback in terms of performance. The time required to execute the algorithm is proportional to the square of the number of elements (known as an *order* n-*squared algorithm*). You can see this by the nested FOR statement, the inner loop executing through each element in the array for every single value of the outer loop, which runs once for each element in the array.

You should have also noticed that in the inner loop, I decrease it by the number of the outer loop (this value skips over already sorted elements). By doing this, I will actually decrease the number of iterations required by 50 percent, but it does not remove the order n-squared nature of the sort algorithm.

This is why I work mostly with QuickSort. QuickSort repeatedly breaks the array down into halves, one half less than the mean of the whole group and one half greater. Before starting the sort, I first find the mean of the entire array using code such as:

```
Average = 0;
for ( i = 0; i < Size; i++ )
  Average += Ele[ i ];
Average = Average / Size;
```

The sort routine itself then divides the list into an upper and lower half, then calls itself recursively to sort through the two halves:

```
Sort( ArrayType far * Array, int Start, int End, int mean )
{                             //  Use "QuickSort" to Sort the "Array"

int i = Start;
int j = End;

int LowMean = 0;
int LowTotal = 0;

int HighMean = 0;
int HighTotal = 0;
  while ( i != j )        (   // Work from the Ends Until they meet
```

```
    while ( Array[ i ] < mean ) {    //   Find the First Element Equal to or
                                     //   Greater than the Mean
        LowMean += Array[ i ];       //   Save the Average as it is worked
                                          through
        LowTotal++;
        i++;
    }

  while ( Array[ j ] > mean ) {      //   Find the First Element Equal to or
                                     //    Less than the Mean
        HighMean += Array[ j ];
        HighTotal++;
        J--;
    }

   if ( i != j )   //  Swap if Possible
      Swap( Array[ i ], Array[ j ]);

  }  //  endwhile
  if (( i - Start ) > 1 )            //  Sort the Low Values
     Sort( Array, Start, i, LowMean / LowTotal );
  else                              //  If only a few Elements, Manually
                                        Sort
     if (( i - Start ) == 1 )             //  If two are present
        if ( Array[ Start ] > Array[ i ])
           Swap( Array[ i ], Array[ Start ]);

  If (( End - j ) > 1 )             //  Sort the High Values
     Sort( Array, j, End, High Mean / HighTotal );
  else                         //  else, Sort the Values manually
     if (( End - j ) == 1 )            //  If two are present
        if ( Array[ j ] > Array[ End ])
           Swap( Array[ j ], Array[ End ]);

}  //  End Sort
```

Despite being much more complex than the BubbleSort, QuickSort will execute much faster with large arrays of data. Figure 14-3 shows the performance difference between the BubbleSort and QuickSort running in an 8051 microcontroller.

With just a few elements, the BubbleSort is more efficient than the QuickSort, but this advantage is very quickly lost as the array size increases.

The reason for the QuickSort's flatter curve as the number of elements increases is the method in which it works. The array is broken up into two equal chunks each time the algorithm executes. This happens base-two logarithm times for the size of the array. If, in each sort invocation, all of the array elements are checked (and can be potentially moved), the execution would be on the order of the number of array elements multiplied by the base-2 logarithm of the number of array elements. This makes QuickSort an *order* n-*log*-n sort algorithm that is as good as you can get for a sorting algorithm. Other *order* n-*log*-n data-sorting algorithms are also available, but I have found QuickSort is the best for working on arrays loaded into memory.

User Interfacing

Everybody's got an opinion about creating user interfaces and how they should work. Having a well-thought-out user interface really is the most significant factor in the differ-

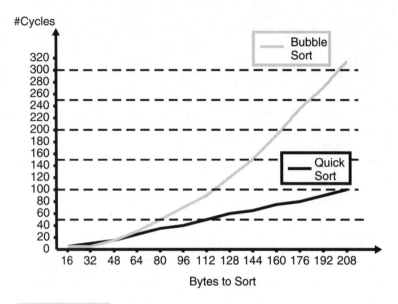

FIGURE 14-3   **8051 sorting comparison.**

ence between successful PC applications and ones that are not well accepted by their users. This section is intended to make you think about copying the standard Windows and interconnect interfaces because these are what users are most familiar with and will be the most productive with.

A well-designed application provides all the information needed by the user in a simple, easy-to-read and respond-to format. Unneeded or missing data is frustrating to users and will cause them to be annoyed with the application—even if it is working properly. The same goes if the user has to access multiple dialog boxes or screens to enter data.

To get an idea of what's possible, try as many applications as possible. You will definitely see some things you like and some things that will leave you scratching your head, wondering why anybody would think the interface was useful.

A great example of the latter is a Windows simulator that I once downloaded from the Internet. The simulator was a PC simulation of an old computer. The front panel (which was the computer's primary interface) was faithfully reproduced with graphics of switches that flipped up and down and knobs that turned. As beautiful as it looked, I had a very hard time learning how to operate the simulated computer because the arcane terms used on the simulated system display meant nothing to me. This visually stunning program, which somebody spent hundred of hours on, went into my Recycle Bin after 15 frustrating minutes.

One of the best places to get an idea of how things can be done well is the Internet. As Web browser capabilities become more and more sophisticated, some beautiful interfaces have been developed that follow PC conventions and put interesting slants on how to work with a computer.

For MS-DOS, chances are you are going to have simple menus that the operator responds to by entering a selection:

```
1. Load
2. Run
3. Edit
4. Quit

Enter Selection: ___
```

The big question for me is, does a single selection key (such as "1", "2", "3," or "4" in the example above) execute the function or is the selection plus enter work best? Normally I use a selection plus enter, which gives the user the opportunity to backspace over the selection if they made a mistake.

Many people feel that this is less than optimal (especially if they aren't touch typists) and would like just a single keystroke.

I have tried to figure out how to decide which to use. What I have come up with seems to meet the requirements of both camps. I feel most comfortable with using a single keystroke when another menu is going to be presented. Going up and down the menus with only one keystroke seems appropriate, but when there is an execution function or ending the program, I require the keystroke plus *Enter*. In this case, where a crucial operation is requested, the user will have a chance to change the entry before the system executes it.

In terms of *Ctrl*, *Alt*, and function keys, I try to avoid them unless they provide a "standard" function. For function keys, I normally follow the CodeView conventions when I'm creating a debugger. Otherwise, I try to keep their use to a minimum because their use requires the user's fingers to leave the keyboard, which can be annoying for touch-typists.

The "standard" functions include:

```
"Ctrl_N" - Create a new file
"Ctrl_O" - Open an existing file
"Ctrl_S" - Save the current file
"Ctrl_R" - Run the application
"Ctrl_C" - Also "Ctrl_Break". Stop the executing application
"Ctrl_X" - Return to the MS-DOS command line
```

Despite all that I've written, two points sum up creating interfaces. The first is, don't be creative. Use the conventions that have been established by the PC community. These conventions might not be the best for your application, but they are what your users know.

Second, ask other people what they think and listen naively to their comments. They might not know what you're trying to do, but they're the ones stuck with what you create. Part of this is responding to suggestions positively after the application has been out for a while. It is a lot easier to fix your application's human interface than it is to fix your customer's perception of your interface to other humans.

Formatting Data Output

I realize that many books have been written and courses taught on how to display output data to a user, but I feel that a few points should be made when interfacing with external devices. Much of this follows on the previous sections, but few issues are important to making the data easy for the user to understand.

The first rule is: be sure that the numbering base system is obvious. If the user saw the data *10* coming from an ISA card, how would they know if it's binary, decimal, or hex? Even it is obvious to you, indicate what is by using one of the established assembly-language conventions:

```
Hex:     0x0##, $##, h'##', 0##h
Binary:  0b0########, %########, b'########'
Decimal: .###, d'###'
```

I realize that adding these characters will make the display more cluttered (which is the next point), but they do make the data easier to read.

I have not included octal (base or radix 8), but this value is really not used that much in modern programming. It was more of a fixture during the 1960s and 1970s, as well as being the base used with C used with VAX processors. This radix selection is really not that popular (especially now) and octal is actually quite difficult to convert mentally into the other value systems.

A cluttered screen is hard to read. Ideally, only two or three data values should be given per line with columns of data ideal. Tables should be displayed with each entry taking the same amount of space, with some spaces between adjacent columns.

One exception to this is a debugger screen. To get a full 32 bytes of hex data on each line, each byte is concatenated with the previous and following bytes. This format has been used for a long time and has become a convention.

If you are displaying data on a screen, make sure you don't go crazy with colors. Try to keep the number of colors used to a minimum, with the ideal being two. The foreground (which is the character itself) should be white or gray and the background should be blue or black. For highlighted characters, yellow is always good. Avoid red or green, not only because they are not as bright as white or yellow, but also because colorblind people (like me) have a very hard time telling them apart or distinguishing them from a non-black background.

In your text displays, always be sure to use blanks (ASCII 0x020) to space rather, than tabs (ASCII 0x009). Different editors will display text with tabs differently in different situations. If you've ever done your own Web page, you'll know that sometimes you'll have created a page with embedded tabs for a specific browser, only to find that when you see it on another browser, it looks terrible.

For graphics, it's always a good idea to put a background grid or "graticules" to show where the data is. Computer printers and displays might distort output, making it hard to see everything in the proper perspective.

EVENT-DRIVEN

PROGRAMMING

One of the biggest conceptual challenges you will have when creating Microsoft "Windows" PC applications is to get out of the mode of traditional "Input-Process-Output" programming model and start thinking about event-driven programming. *Event-driven programming* is a $10 way of saying that the application waits for an external event and responds to it. In concept, it's easy to understand, but many people have difficulty working through it.

When you were first taught programming, you were probably given the model shown in Fig. 15-1 and told that it was the basis for all programming. This should have been a bit of a puzzle because you cannot see how this works in programs like my Tic-Tac-Toe game (Fig. 15-2), which takes input continuously and processes it according to what is requested.

In the Tic-Tac-Toe game, the input is made repeatedly after data output and the game can be reset or ended at any time (not just at the end of the game). When you look at the source code a bit later, you'll see no clear termination at the end of a "mainline". This application clearly does not fit into the model given in Fig. 15-1.

It does, however, fit into the event-driven programming model. In this case, the software waits for an external event (such as a mouse click on a "button") and responds according to the current conditions (which includes past input and output), displays the results, and then waits for the next input event. This is the basis for Windows programming, as well as

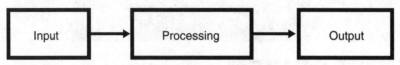

FIGURE 15-1   Traditional programming model.

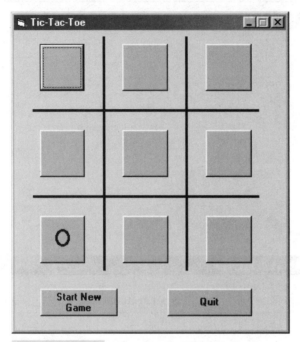

FIGURE 15-2   Visual basic "Tic-Tac-Toe".

a number of other applications you're probably familiar with, including MS-DOS games and device-control programs that might not use the traditional Windows interface, but still use an event-driven model.

Taking the input-processing-output model diagram, I modified it to show how event-driven programming works (see Fig. 15-3). The most important difference between the models is that the application ends, based on the commands from the user and not from completing output operations.

The User Interface

Ideally, for an event-driven application, an appropriate external event can interrupt the application to be processed. These events include keystrokes, mouse clicks (and movements), timer countdowns, and hardware interrupts. Most Windows programming languages provide simple interfaces for these events, but MS-DOS applications have to handle a wide variety of inputs and filter all of them out, except for the ones you want to process.

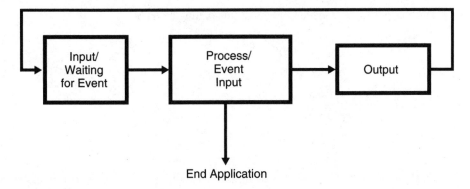

Input/
Waiting
for Event

Process/
Event
Input

Output

End Application

FIGURE 15-3   **"Event Driven Programming" model.**

For example, to handle control keystrokes in the primary interface, you could use the code:

```
retvalue = 0
while ( retvalue == 0 )
  switch( GetKey()) {
    case Ctrl_X:              // End Program
      quit();
      retvalue = -1;
      break;
    case Ctrl_O:
      retvalue = FileOpen();
      break;
    case Ctrl_N:
      retvalue = FileCreate();
      break;
    case Ctrl_S:
      retvalue = FileSave();
      break;
    case Ctrl_R:
      retvalue = App_Run();
      break;
    other:;                    //  Handle the other Characters
  } // endswitch
```

For Windows-development environments, such as Visual Basic and Visual C++, this "switch" operation is actually executed within the command processor, along with the code for interpreting the mouse position when one of the buttons is "clicked" or keyboard button is pressed.

This interface works quite well, although, for multitasking applications, instead of using a GetKey API, which will wait for a keystroke to be pressed, the keyboard buffer should be polled. If nothing is waiting to be processed, then another task should execute for a few milliseconds.

When I describe the keyboard and mouse ports, I note that the mouse transmits its position to the PC motherboard 20 times each second. This frequency provides apparently "seamless" movement to the user. For processing keystrokes, this is a good general rule; poll the keyboard buffer once every 50 ms for keystrokes and process them in a timely fashion.

The changes to the code to implement this polling could be:

```
retvalue = 0
while ( retvalue == 0 ) {

    retvalue = ExecApp();           //  Execute Application Operation Code
                                    //  Code Executes for 50 msecs
    if ( GetKeyStatus() != 0 )      //  Poll the Keyboard Buffer
      switch( GetKey()) {           //  KeyPresent, Process it
        case Ctrl_X:                //  End Program
          :
      }  //  endswitch
  }  //  endwhile
```

The problem with this method is that the application must be broken into small pieces to execute for a small amount of time before returning to the caller to poll the input device.

Notice that the valid requests have changed so that it can be stopped or ended. After these requests are processed, the original code is used.

The best way to carry this out is to interrupt the application periodically using a timer and a state variable. This allows just a single input routine with the state variable, indicating what inputs can be used. The input routine as an interrupt handler becomes:

```
retvalue = 0;  StopState = 1;

   :

int InputRtn()               //  Input Interrupt Handler
{

  if ( keyState() != 0 )     //  Key Waiting
    switch( GetKey()) {       //  Process the Key
      case Ctrl_X:            //  End the Application
        retvalue = -1;
        StopApAPIC();         //  Notify O/S to Free Application
        break;               //    Interrupt
      case Ctrl_O:
        If ( StopState == 1 )
          retvalue = FileOpen();
        break;
      case Ctrl_N:
        if ( StopState == 1 )
          retvalue = FileCreate();
        break;
      case Ctrl_S:
        if ( StopState == 1 )
          retvalue = FileSave();
        break;
      case Ctrl_R:
        if ( StopState == 1 ) {
          StopState = 0;
          RunApAPIC();                  //  Run the Application
        }  //  endif
        break;
      case Ctrl_C:                      //  Break (Stop) Execution
        if ( StopState == 0 )
          StopState = 1;
        Break;
      other:;                           //  Handle other characters
    }  //  endswitch

}  End InputRtn
```

This interrupt handler, with the appropriate APIs, will allow the code to select whether or not to load or save files, execute, stop, or end the application. This code can be used with the interrupt 008h (timer) vector to handle external events or even be shared with the keyboard interrupt (0x009) to handle the keystrokes as they are input.

The problem with this code is it is actually much simpler than what is required in a real application. In a real application, along with keyboard interrupts, you will also need mouse, timer, and hardware interrupt handlers, as well as the handler written for the complete set of keyboard codes and respond appropriately under all conditions. The actual code to provide this capability is quite simple to design, but it becomes very complex with the number of different cases that will have to be supported. Although it is possible to write this for MS-DOS, I would recommend that you create these applications in Visual Basic or Visual C++ and let the development tools worry about the code that is going to execute for each noncrucial event and set up for the specific ones.

The event code itself should be very short routines that just execute the desired function. As I present Visual Basic, you'll see how to create event handlers that do little more than just start actions and update buttons or start executing applications.

System Resources

Incorrect accessing of systems resources (memory, files, display, interface hardware, etc.) in event-driven programming can be the cause of some very difficult to find and diagnose problems, and could result in some unexpected responses from your application. In Windows development languages (such as Visual Basic), many of the issues described are not a problem because they automatically provide the required functions that make event-driven programming easy to implement.

When I use the term *resources*, I am describing hardware or data within the PC that is accessed through the operating system, BIOS, or directly, and might be required by multiple applications (tasks), dialog boxes, or threads (which I'll collectively call *applications*). Multiple requests for a resource can cause problems with the application's execution.

These problems can range from a file's contents being required or a digital thermometer being accessed by multiple programs. These multiple accesses can cause data discrepancies or actual invalid writes to devices.

An example of this could be a file that contains operational information for multiple programs in running in the PC. A problem could arise in two programs that are attempting to read and write independently of each other.

Assuming that the file is left open and the handle is available to both programs, the first *PGM A* might attempt to the file:

```
LSEEK( handle, End, 0 );
WRITE( handle, PGMA_Buffer, PGMA_BufferSize );
```

And "PGM B" will read from the file:

```
LSEEK( handle, Start, PGMB_Offset );
READ( handle, PGMB_Buffer, PGMB_BufferSize );
```

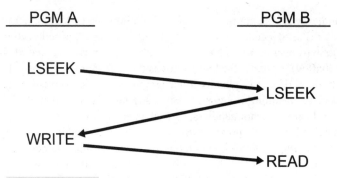

FIGURE 15-4   **Shared resource disk access.**

Unless these two operations can be executed completely separately from each other, problems will occur. Elsewhere in the book, I have described the problems when the DOS requests are not serialized and requests overrun each other. In this section, it is assumed that the serialization of the requests is executed by the operating system, but the requests themselves are not serialized to provide a consistent operation for the two programs.

For the case where PGM B executes its LSEEK after PGM A's, the data that will be written to the file in PGMA will put at the location PGM B "wants" to read from. After the PGM A write has completed, PGM B will execute again and read from the current file pointer location (which is the correct offset, but with PGMA_BufferSize added to it). This can be seen graphically in Fig. 15-4.

The net result will be a trashed file and wrong information read into the PGMB_Buffer. The root cause of these two errors will be very hard to find and debug.

The usual solution to this problem is to use a *semaphore flag* to serialize the requests by only allowing one program to have access to the resource at a time. A semaphore is a flag that is assigned to a resource and can be requested by programs to indicate they have control over resources. If the semaphore is free, the program can access the resource. If the semaphore is not free, then the program must wait for it to be freed by its owner.

By changing PGM A to:

```
While ( Status( Semaphore ) == Reserved );      // Wait for the
                              //  Semaphore to be freed
Allocate( Semaphore );    //  Allocate it for the Application

LSEEK( handle, End, 0 );

WRITE( handle, PGMA_Buffer, PGMA_BufferSize );

Free( Semaphore );       //  Finished with the Resource
```

And PGM B to:

```
While ( Status( Semaphore ) == Reserved );      //  Wait for the
                                  //  Semaphore to be
                                  //  freed
Allocate( Semaphore );    //  Allocate it for the Application

LSEEK( handle, Start, PGMB_Offset );
```

```
READ( handle, PGMB_Buffer, PGMB_BufferSize );

Free( Semaphore );        // Finished with the Resource
```

The opportunity for the problem presented is eliminated.

Semaphores can be operating-system resources or they can just be a global variable that can be accessed by both programs. Normally, when a semaphore is tested and allocated, interrupts are disabled to prevent an interrupt handler from disturbing the natural flow of the operation. Actually, in this code, the WHILE statement wouldn't even be present; the Allocate function would simply not return until the program had the semaphore allocated to it.

Multiple programs accessing a resource, such as an I/O port, should be avoided altogether (especially with semaphores) because some data crucially required by a program might not be readable in a timely fashion. This is true of applications that must record data from a sensor.

After going through all this, you probably feel like managing system resources in an event-driven application is a lot of work. The answer I would give is "yes and no."

"Yes", it is difficult in an MS-DOS application environment because most of the interfacing and serialization must be provided within the application and it cannot take advantage of any resources built into the operating system. It can also be difficult to understand exactly why the semaphores and resource allocation is required. You might have to work through a few applications to really understand what is required. Device drivers could be created that provide all the necessary functions and avoid the serialization issues altogether.

The answer is "no" when the application is going to be written for Windows. The serialization and resource access-control functions are built into the operating system and Windows-development tools (such as Visual Basic and Visual C++). This makes application development much easier.

The concept of event-driven programming is where I see a natural boundary for the choice between MS-DOS command-line and Windows dialog box-based applications. For multiple operation input or multiple-task applications, you should only consider Windows.

At this point of the book, you will see a change in the sample code from MS-DOS to Windows. I have given you all of the information that I have for MS-DOS; now I want to focus almost exclusively on Windows.

MICROSOFT
WINDOWS

Where I characterized MS-DOS as just a file system added to BIOS, Microsoft 32-bit kernel Windows is much more substantial. Each application running under Windows 95/98/NT is executing under a Virtual Machine with just enough memory allocated to it for the application code and required data memory. Another difference between Windows and MS-DOS is Windows' shielding of the hardware resources in the PC; an application cannot access any registers or specific memory in the PC directly. In Windows, if an application is going to interface with hardware, then operating-system links and specialized device drivers must be used with it.

None of this is actually a bad thing; programming the application is easier because the application is running in a 32-bit Protect-mode flat memory model *Virtual Machine (VM) session*. If a program executes incorrectly, Windows will notify the user of the problem and clear out the failing application. If an application attempts to access resources that are not allocated to it, the operating system flags an "access violation" and prevents invalid accesses. These invalid accesses could cause problems from the perspective of the other applications and the entire system.

This book includes information concerning the *Win32 kernel*. The kernel is the task-control program responsible for how applications execute and which resources they can access. The operating systems described includes Windows 95, Windows 98, and Windows NT. Windows 3.1 uses a 16-bit kernel and does not provide the same level of resource/application protection as the Win32 kernel operating systems. If you try to apply what is written here to Windows NT, note that I focus on Version 5.0 (which has been renamed to *Windows 2000*) and its WDMs, which are also shared with Windows 98.

One day on the Internet, I found a great analogy of the different PC operating systems available to commercial air traffic. The article wasn't very complementary, highlighting the faults of the different operating systems, rather than their strengths, but it did highlight the reasons to consider the different operating systems.

MS-DOS was described as the Wright brothers' airplane; it did fly, but it hit the ground a lot and often needed repairs and upgrades. Windows 3.1 is a great-looking airplane that you can get on with everything working properly and every once in a while blows up in flight. Windows 95 (and the other Win32 kernel operating systems) is like an airplane where various parts fall off, but it will stay together well enough for you to get safely on the ground. This description of the various operating systems illustrates why I feel that modern applications should be written for the Win32 Kernel; if a problem develops with an application, you will be able to recovery gracefully without having to reboot your PC (or worse, reload its hard file).

The Windows Graphical User Interface

Despite the fact that Windows interfaces are designed to be specific and custom to the application, they are really very standard beats with common methods and features for inputting and displaying data between the PC and the user. Deviations from these conventions will make the application more difficult for users—even if the deviations make the application simple to work with.

The Menu in Fig. 16-1 follows the basic conventions that are needed for Visual C++ applications. Fortunately, most Windows development tools can develop code that follows these conventions by default.

The top line (*Application Name* and *Dialog Control Buttons*) is primarily used by the application to globally control the application. The square box in the top left corner allows basic operation of the application. This box can either be accessed by the mouse or by the *Alt* key from within the application. The three boxes in the top right corner allow the user to minimize, maximize ("restore"), and end the application. The application's name should be identified along this line as well.

When I develop a Windows application, I generally do it for a specific size with the Maximize button disabled to avoid an application that looks peculiar when it is taking up the whole screen. This problem is shown in Fig. 16-2.

I like my applications to be usable on a 640-by-400 or an 800-by-600 VGA display. This is usually large enough for most applications. Most modern PCs operate with 1024 by 768

Application
Name

"Pull Downs"

Application Control
ToolBar

Dialog
Control
Buttons

Menu
Information
Area

Status
Line

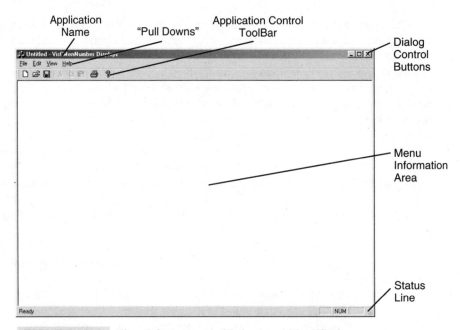

FIGURE 16-1   Visual C++ menu with features identified.

FIGURE 16-2   "Maximizing" a dialog box.

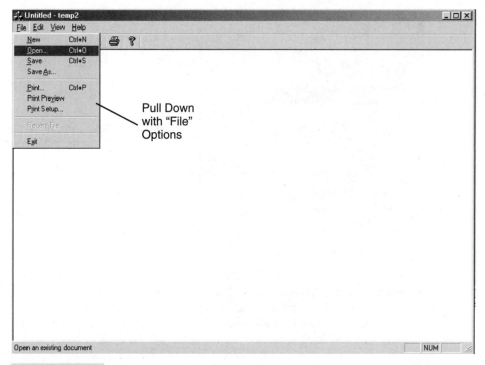

FIGURE 16-3 Visual C++ menu "file" pull down active.

or more pixels, but by designing for the smaller screen sizes, I don't have to worry about my applications not being able to be fully displayed on older PCs.

Pull downs are used to provide access to the basic functions of the application and can be accessed either via the keyboard or the mouse (although the mouse is more traditional). Most development tools, such as Visual C++, allow you to specify *Ctrl* key sequences to execute the application directly from the keyboard without having to move your hands. Figure 16-3 shows the Visual C++ file pull-down selections.

Help information can range from a complete tutorial and reference for the application or it can simply be a pointer to the program version and author. One of the more interesting implementations that I have recently seen has been to connect to an Internet site for help information stored in the .HTML format. From this site, the help information is continually kept active and accurate. When you work with the Visual Development Suite, you'll see that the Microsoft Web site provides errata and additional examples to enhance the basic Help information for the development tools.

The next line of Fig. 16-1 is the *Application Control Toolbar*. This line provides a number of designer specified icons that are used to provide mouse-based controls that should be available in the pull downs. On this line, the left-most three are New File, Open File, and Save File. These icon-based buttons are known as *controls*; once clicked, they perform an operation from the source code.

Straight dialog boxes provide nothing, but a control interface to the application, and the Menu application type provides a large area that can be clicked on or used to display in-

FIGURE 16-4 Adding a dialog box to "make sure".

formation from the application. For most applications that interface with hardware, I use a dialog-box interface that is described in greater detail later in the book.

In the middle of the menu is a large controller area for data input and output. This area in a menu can be selected by the mouse or keyboard data can entered manually by the user. For menus, canned controls cannot be put in, although for a dialog box, this is possible.

For applications that can run for more than just a couple of seconds, you should put in a Stop request. This request could be part of a Run/Stop button or a separate Stop button, but it should be present and respond quickly after being "pressed" by the user.

Windows applications can also spawn subdialogs. These dialog boxes can be modal or nonmodal. *Modal* means that for the application to continue executing, the open, spawned subdialog boxes must have their operations completed. The classic example of this is the Are You Sure dialog box brought up when Quit has been selected from a primary dialog box (Fig. 16-4).

In this case, you can't go back to the original Dialog box and select another option unless No is clicked first. Clicking on the parent dialog box can test modality. If the "focus" of Windows does not move to the parent dialog box (and the subdialog box hidden), then the subdialog box is modal.

This is a brief introduction to how to structure your Windows applications. Many references are available with more complete instructions. This section is intended to give you an idea of how your applications should be structured to give users a familiar dialog-box framework to work from and to introduce you to some of the terms that are used with Windows and the dialog-box interfaces.

Win16 versus Win32

When Windows NT was introduced, for server PC applications, a real schism developed between PCs running Windows 3.x (the then-standard Windows operating system), and the win32 kernel of Windows NT. Windows 3.x used a 16-bit operating system capable of running on 80286 PCs. Windows NT accessed all of the Protect mode features of the 80386 (and faster) processors and could not be run on 8086 or 80286 processors. The newer, more complex operating system did provide the ability to run the 16-bit operating system's code. It also provided protection for the hardware and crucial software resources (such as the operating system), which isn't available in the 16-bit kernel.

The 16-bit kernel was originally designed for the 80286 and used many of the same features as the straight 8086, including 16-bit addressed (64-KB sized) segments for the applications. The 16-bit Windows applications are very similar to MS-DOS applications that access Windows APIs for accessing MS-DOS. One of the advantages of the win16 kernel was that MS-DOS device drivers could be used without modification.

The win16 kernel's two biggest problems were that it was not a true multitasker and often crashed unpredictably. Applications could run in the background, but if the file system was accessed by a background task, Windows would block the task until it was made the foreground task. This was done to avoid the opportunity for calling the MS-DOS file system re-entrantly and causing it to fail.

Application failures in Windows 3.x would cause everything running in the PC to fail through a *General Protection Fault (GPF)*. This was caused by the win16 kernel's inability to properly identify the failing component and isolate it. I always found this problem to be infuriating when I was developing applications for Windows 3.x. I always looked forward to an operating system that would not cause a problem with the entire system when one element failed.

The Win32 kernel, on the other hand, works with the 80386 "flat" 32-bit Protect mode memory model that can access up to 4.3 GB of memory for an application. This large amount of memory is normally loaded as *Virtual Machine (V/M)*, which is used if the operating system cannot devote enough memory resources to the application. In the win32 kernel, the Virtual Machine hardware built into the processor is used to load/save portions of the applications. This feature makes the code quite easy to develop (with not having to access segmentation information).

The biggest advantage of the win32 kernel is the full multitasking provided to the applications. The MS-DOS interface is serialized (or more accurately, as is shown later in the book, "virtualized") within the kernel to be sure that background requests do not "stomp" over foreground requests and visa-versa. This full multitasker also allows messaging between application threads and failure encapsulation to avoid taking down the entire PC if one application fails. Although you may be familiar with the "Blue Screen of Death" which indicates the system is corrupted. This seems to be more of an operating system problem than application and as Win32 becomes more robust is becoming less prevelent.

Win32 is the superior kernel and with the introduction of Windows 98, Microsoft has established a migration path for Windows workstation and server users to a common operating system known as *Windows 2000* (it was formerly known as *Windows NT 5.0*). This operating system resolves some of the issues with the Windows NT platform, namely the difficulty to interface with hardware from the application software and the Windows 95/98 issues because they do not have the networking and multi-processor capabilities of Windows NT. As part of this migration, Windows 98 has included the ability to execute .WDM device drivers that will be the primary format for device drivers in Windows 2000.

The Win32 kernel tends to execute applications faster than the 16-bit Windows kernel for two reasons. The first is that most modern PCs are designed with 32-bit data busses, which allows the instructions to be loaded in their native format of 32 bits wide, instead of the 80286's use of the eight-bit base from the 8086.

The second reason why the Win32 kernel executes applications faster than the Win16 kernel is the use of a "flat" 32-bit application process space, which can be accessed directly from within the application. The 16-bit 80286 Protect mode can only have *selectors* (equivalent to 8086 *pages*), which are 64 KB in size. Because the APIs are greater than 64 KB in size, multiple selector loads are required for Win16, whereas Win32 provides a "virtualized" copy of the APIs in each process, eliminating the need to reload data from the PC's hard drive.

The Windows applications in this book focus on the win32 kernel and present device drivers for both the VxD (Windows 95) and .WDM (Windows 98 and Windows 2000). The reason is to provide you with information that will be useful for the longest period of time while still recognizing the legacy device drivers and development tools currently available.

WIN.INI and Windows Registry

If you are at all familiar with Windows 3.x, you will be familiar with the WIN.INI file. This file contains the resource and set-up information used when Windows boots. Although I won't go through each line of the file and explain what it is doing, I do describe some aspects of the file format and how it can be useful for your own applications. The end of this section shows the Windows Registry (used for Windows) using the Win32 kernel and the differences involved there.

If you type out the WIN.INI file from an MS-DOS Prompt window, you will see a file that consists of parameter names, followed by an equals sign and then the parameters:

```
[windows]
load=C:\GLIDE\XPOINT.EXE
run=
NullPort=None
device=HP LaserJet 6L PCL,PCL5EMS3,LPT1:

[Desktop]
Wallpaper=C:\WINDOWS\TILES.BMP
TileWallpaper=1
WallpaperStyle=0
Pattern=174 77 239 255 8 77 174 77

[intl]
iCountry=1
ICurrDigits=2
iCurrency=0
iDate=0
iDigits=2
iLZero=1
iMeasure=1
iNegCurr=0
iTime=0
iTLZero=0
s1159=AM
s2359=PM
sCountry=United States
sCurrency=$
```

```
sDate=/
sDecimal=.
sLanguage=enu
sList=,
sLongDate=dddd, MMMM dd, yyyy
sShortDate=M/d/yy
sThousand=,
sTime=:

[Fonts]

[FontSubstitutes]
Helv=MS Sans Serif
Tms Rmn=MS Serif
```

This information is about 10 percent of the WIN.INI file in one of my PCs. I just wanted to give you an idea of the information and format of the file. The file goes on for a number of pages, listing all the different characteristics of my PC when it executes.

This file was first introduced with Windows 1.0 and has since been reused by other versions and applications. The reasons for the usefulness mirrors my comments in Chapter 14; the files are "man-readable," are delimited by ASCII carriage-return/line-feed characters, and can be very easily edited outside of the application.

All of these advantages leads me to suggest that you follow this format when you are creating parameter information for your own applications. This will allow you (or the application's users) to change the parameters outside of the application easily.

Inside the application, when it first powers up, the .INI file should be loaded in and processed. Ideally, the .INI file should be in something like the System Programs subdirectory (folder) that is present in all Windows PCs. If you were really clever, to make it easier on the user, you should have this file automatically created with defaults if the program boots up and its .INI file is not present.

After loading the .INI file, it should be stored in memory and resaved each time that the default/power-up information is changed. This can be useful if your PC (or, more likely, application) crashes during execution. Saving the current status information will allow you to return to where the problem occurred quickly. This is useful for you because you can look through to find the problem; for the users, it avoids the need for them to retrace their steps to get back to where the problem occurred.

To handle the .INI file in the application, its maximum possible space should be allocated. This will allow the file to grow or shrink, according to the new requirements of the application and user. Keeping the file in RAM will minimize the processing time for reading/writing.

A routine for reading a parameter could be:

```
Char far * Read_ini( char far * Parm )
{                              //  Return to Parameters Pointed to by 'Parm'

int  I = 0;

  while( strncmp( &iniFile[ I ], Parm, strlen( Parm )) != 0 )
    while ( iniFile[ I++ ] != '\n' );

  while ( iniFile[ I ] != '=' );
```

```
        return &iniFile[ ++I ];   //  Return a Pointer to the Parameters

  }  //  End Read_ini
```

In this routine, notice that the search code first checks the start of the line for the passed parameter. If it doesn't match, the line is read past the end of the line-feed character at the end of the line. This is a fast way to read through text that is ended with carriage-return/line-feed characters. Actually, it can be used for any string data that has each record ended with a definite character.

WRITE_INI would use the same search algorithm, but once the correct parameter is found, everything up to that point is written back to the file, then the new parameter is saved, followed by everything following it. With this completed, the .INI file buffer would be reloaded from the file. Carrying out the write in this order eliminates the need to move strings in memory and only takes marginally more time.

In PCs that run the Win32 kernel and operating system (Windows 98/NT/2000), WIN.INI does not exist. Instead, the hardware information is recorded in the Windows registry. This tool allows you to look at the actual hardware configuration of the PC and how it is configured. The Windows registry information is used by Plug'n'Play during operating system boot to determine the correct location for the hardware. In Fig. 16-5, you can see the interrupt specification for my PC.

The information contained in the registry is really specific to the user with each entry called a *key*, which consists of a number of different access methods. For example, the key access parameters for a key include:

NAME	KEY ACCESS
Class	Optional object class name
Security descriptor	Used in Windows/NT
Last write time	Optional record of last time key changed
Values	Optional parameter information stored with the key

Accessing the registry information really goes beyond the scope of this book, but if you are creating Plug'n'Play hardware, understanding how a PC is configured by looking at the Registry windows is crucial to checking the operation of the device. To bring up the registry display dialog box, you have to click on Programs from the Start bar, followed by Accessories, and then System Tools. From System Tools, simply click on System Information.

Installation Programs

I'm sure that when you've loaded some Windows applications, you've discovered the vendor has included a very impressive application program. This program will guide you through the installation of the application, both in terms of placing the application into a folder (subdirectory) and desktop group, but also for the actual operating options. This tool

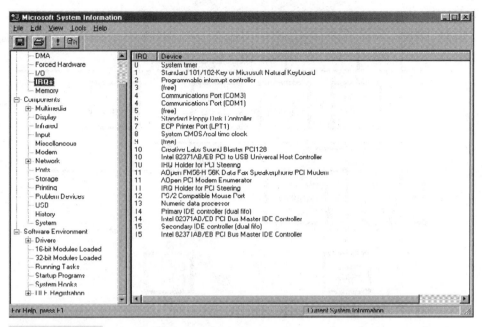

FIGURE 16-5 Microsoft Windows/98 "registry".

(usually named SETUP.EXE or INSTALL.EXE, by convention) can really simplify installing the application. Tools to develop *setup.exe* are included in Visual Basic & Visual C++ and are used to package one application up with the accessory device drivers.

Using these tools to create the *setup.exe* for an application is a good idea for distributing one program to users which may not have Visual Basic or Visual C++ installed and do not have the necessary device drivers to execute the applications.

Windows Applications

When you create Windows applications, I find it best to design the dialog boxes and menus, followed by their execution before starting with the operating-system APIs and hardware-interface device drivers. It is very easy to get bogged down in the details of interfaces or file I/O and discover things don't work the way you want them to.

I generally envision a Windows application development project to look like that in Fig. 16-6.

This is essentially a top-down approach to application development. First the high level is done, getting the look and feel of the application designed, followed by working down through the various subdialogs and device drivers.

With Visual Basic and Visual C++, the dialog creation is largely automated with a great-looking application (that doesn't do anything) produced by the graphical Dialog Box and Menu development tools. This is why I've specified Phase 3, which is the dialog code development. I recommend that you focus on only using the high-level languages (especially

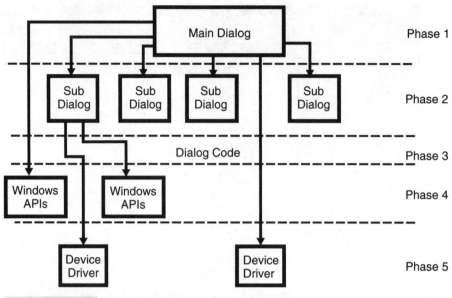

FIGURE 16-6 Windows application design.

at the beginning of your career developing Windows applications), which will interface to the Windows APIs for you.

WINDOWS APIs

Like MS-DOS, the Microsoft Windows operating systems have a horrendous number of APIs available for basic I/O and interface functions. These APIs control the loading and displaying of applications, their dialogs, file systems, messaging across threads, and access to miscellaneous functions. These APIs are accessed as labels and interrupts in the application. For this book, knowing these APIs is really not necessary to develop hardware interfaces and device drivers to your PC, but I did want to make a few comments about how Windows APIs are implemented and used in applications.

As you develop your skills with Windows programming, you can begin to expand the operating systems functionality of your applications. These enhanced functions are generally provided within the Visual Basic and Visual C++ languages. This is why I feel that programmers really do not have to be exposed to the low-level interface functions built into Windows. Incorrect use of these APIs can have more dire consequences than incorrect use of MS-DOS APIs, where only one application is affected. In Windows, incorrect API usage can affect all of the executing applications and any network connections that are currently active. Incorrect usage can also result in the "Blue Screen of Death" which is the same as the PC locking up.

To avoid these potential disasters, I have focussed in my own application development to just using the built-in language features and avoided accessing the Windows APIs all together. This is in contrast to my almost continual avoiding of the built-in MS-DOS C APIs and, instead, working with the MS-DOS APIs almost exclusively. Using Windows libraries to provide advanced functions is well documented in Walter Oney's *Windows Systems Programming*.

DEVICE DRIVERS

Up to this point in the book, I have concentrated on MS-DOS programming, in which hardware can be accessed directly. Within MS-DOS, the need for device drivers is more of an abstract concept, with hardware able to be accessed directly within an application. This is possible because MS-DOS runs in Real mode and not Protect mode, such as Microsoft Windows. As I begin to focus on Windows application development, you will see that I will lessen the importance of the application code and focus more on the need for device drivers within Windows.

Along with providing an interface for applications to interface with hardware, Windows device drivers also are responsible for providing an interface between the Protect mode application and Real mode. This interface is necessary because the Windows application (process) runs in the least-privileged ring of the operating system. Applications running in this ring cannot access hardware or respond to interrupt requests directly. This is shown in Fig. 16-7.

Along with the need for a device driver to provide an interface between the physical hardware and the Protect mode application, device drivers also have to virtualize the hardware access. This concept is a bit hard to understand—especially in comparison to serializing access. Elsewhere in the book, I showed the importance of serializing hardware requests as ensuring that different processes or threads didn't get mixed up in their requests.

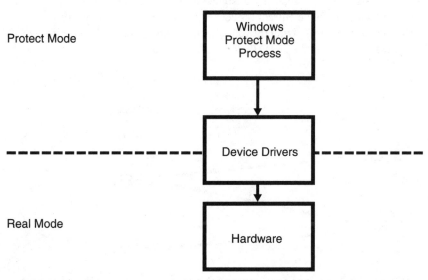

FIGURE 16-7   Windows application/device driver operation.

The example I used was two separate programs (which are processes or threads) accessing the disk subsystem. The code for each of the tasks executes:

```
PGM A                          PGM B

LSEEK Write Position           LSEEK Read Position

Write PGMA Data Buffer         Read Disk into PGMB Data Buffer
```

If the code was to execute (Fig. 16-8), the data would be written to the wrong location on disk and the wrong data would be read. Both programs would fail and the actual cause, if you are not familiar with how multitasking operating systems operate, would be very hard to diagnose.

The problem with serializing hardware accesses like this is that the application code is actually more complex because the application programmer has to understand which semaphores are used for which resource and how the semaphores are used. Ideally, the semaphores should be allocated for a very short period of time to prevent other tasks from waiting excessively. More importantly, the semaphore allocation has to be very short to keep the operating system from accessing the disk for such important operations as caching, paging, and application start up.

In Microsoft Windows, hardware accesses go far beyond simple semaphores with the accesses being "virtualized." Each application that runs under Windows is given its own "virtual machine," which gives the application the appearance that it is the only application running under a processor. This avoids the need for the application programmer to understand how serialization and semaphores work, but it makes the operating system and device drivers much more complex.

To allow successful access to hardware for multiple applications (as well as the operating functions), device drivers are designed to track everything that is accessing them and respond according to the current request status passed by the device driver.

For the need for virtualizing the requests, the primary form of device driver in Microsoft Windows is known as the *VxD (Virtual x Driver)*, shown in Fig. 16-9.

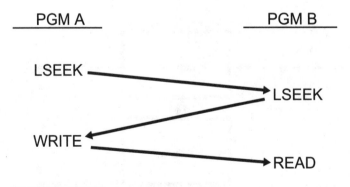

FIGURE 16-8   Shared resource disk access.

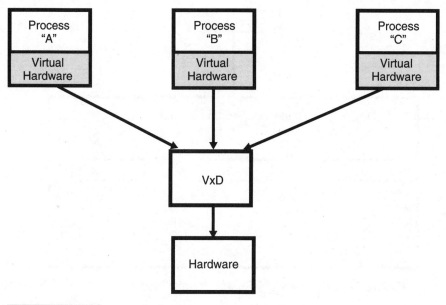

FIGURE 16-9 VxD operation.

Along with the VxD, Windows also uses *Dynamic Link Device Driver Libraries (DLLs)* and, more recently, *Windows Device Models (WDMs)*, each of which serve somewhat different purposes and operating systems.

USER, GDI, AND KERNEL

Windows uses three core DLLs to provide the console and operating-system interfaces to applications. These three DLLs are known as USER, GDI, and KERNEL, and provide dialog-box operations, basic graphics, and operation APIs, respectively. I feel like calling these device drivers *DLLs* to be a bit of a misnomer because they are loaded with the operating system and are only unloaded at shutdown. Personally, I like to think of these three files as *operating-system device drivers*.

The first DLL, USER32 (the "32" indicates that it is designed for the Win32 operating system) maintains the dialog boxes displayed on the PC's console. The primary operations controlled by USER32 is creating, moving, resizing, and destroying the dialog boxes. Unless you are going to be writing assembly-language Windows dialog-box applications (which I highly discourage), you will never have to access the APIs associated with this DLL.

GDI32 is used to control images on the PC's console and provide basic drawing functions. The GDI32 APIs will be accessed if you are creating a graphic display program. Many of the APIs provided in this DLL are "overridden" by high-performance graphic cards. The purpose of overriding the APIs is to provide a fast data path to the graphic card and its graphic-generating hardware, rather than having the PC's software generate the graphics.

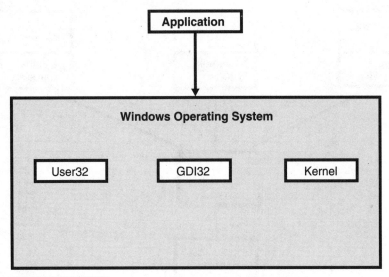

FIGURE 16-10   "User", "GDI" and "Kernel" operation.

The last DLL is the KERNEL32 interface. This DLL provides the APIs for application memory management, file I/O, and application loading and execution. In high-level languages, the APIs associated with KERNEL32 are generally accessed through the use of such functions as Open, Read, Allocate, etc., and are invisible to the programmer.

Current versions of the Windows operating system have USER16, GDI16, and KERNEL16 DLLs that provide backward compatibility for Win16 applications. These DLLs rely on "thunks" (which are described in the next section) to provide the required functions, rather than convert the 16-bit device driver APIs to operate within the 32-bit Win32 environment. Like other backward-compatibility features built into Windows, the USER16, GDI16, and KERNEL16 DLLs will be available for the foreseeable future, but applications should be developed for the Win32 operating systems to ensure maximum life and Microsoft operating-system support.

THUNKING

As you learn more about Windows systems programming, you are going to encounter the term *Thunks*. A *thunk* is a device driver that converts 32-bit API calls from an application to 16-bit device drivers and visa-versa. The primary use for thunks is to allow an application that is designed for one Windows operating-system type (Win16 or Win32) to work with device drivers or operating-system APIs without having to port the application over the other operating-system type.

The two types of thunks are: *generic thunks*, used by Win16 applications to call Win32 operating-system APIs, and *flat thunks*, which work in the opposite direction and are primarily used by Win32 applications to access Win16 device drivers. Flat thunks are primarily used in Windows 95/98/NT/2000 to allow 16-bit applications to execute.

In this book, it is assumed that all applications will be run under Win32 operating systems and will be compiled for Win32 operation. This assumption really eliminates the need for understanding thunks and I recommend that, as you develop your own applications, you stick to this convention.

You might find it interesting to discover that Win16 applications run slower than native Win32 applications in the current Windows operating systems. For this reason (and the obvious one that learning how thunks operate and how they are programmed is more work), I recommend that you only develop your applications and device drivers for the Win32 operating systems.

DOS Protect-Mode Interface

When Microsoft Windows first became available, the format for application code was left as the 16-bit MS-DOS format. Protect-mode Windows applications executed DOS Protect-Mode Interface APIs to begin executing from Real (actually Virtual 8086) mode to Windows Protect mode. This allowed Windows to execute both MS-DOS- and Windows-specific applications from the desktop and only require Windows application loader and executor. For the initial 16-bit versions of Windows (version 3.x), this worked quite well.

The reason why it worked well was that Protect-mode applications, even if they were running in 80386 (or faster) processors, still used the 16-bit 80286 Protect mode and instruction set. This operating mode allows 16 bit, essentially, 8086 code to run without modifications in Protect mode. Obviously, in Windows 95/98/NT/2000, where code executes in the native 80386 32-bit mode, using the DPMI will not give you the ability to execute 32-bit 80386 Windows Protect-mode applications from the MS-DOS Prompt.

The DPMI APIs primarily use interrupts 02Fh and 031h, which are listed in Appendix J. The primary interface is interrupt 02Fh, AX equal to 01687h, which puts the application into Windows Protect mode. If DPMI is present and the application can execute in 16-bit Protect mode, then AX, upon return, is equal to zero.

Typical code for changing the execution of an MS-DOS application from Real mode to Protect mode is:

```
    mov AX, 01687h          ;  Put the Application into Protect Mode
    int 2Fh

    or  AX, AX              ;  Was Zero Returned from the API?
    jz  Execute_Protect

;   #### - Put in "No DPMI" Error Message

    mov AH, 4Ch             ;  End the Application
    mov AL, -1
    int 21h

    Execute_Protect:        ;  Now Executing in Protect Mode
```

Notice that if the DPMI is not present or cannot execute for some reason, AX is not equal to zero. After an error message is displayed, I use the standard interrupt 21h MS-DOS API to end the application (AH = 4Ch). I did this to point out that all the interrupt 21h APIs are available from MS-DOS programs running in Protect mode from DPMI.

As in this example, the typical way to end a DPMI Protect-mode application is to set AH equal to 4Ch and execute an *int 21h* instruction.

Just a comment on DPMI for future (i.e., Windows 2000) versions of Windows; I can see that the DPMI interface will continue to be supported in the near future, but as time goes on, I would expect that the DPMI APIs to be taken out. For this reason, I would suggest that applications that are written with DPMI should be ported over to the Win32 interface, where they will run faster and support will be available for the foreseeable future.

WINDOWS

PROGRAMMING

LANGUAGES

AND

DEVELOPMENT

TOOLS

CONTENTS AT A GLANCE

Visual Basic	LabView
Visual C++	Microsoft DDK
Java	Other Languages and Development Tools

If you were to look at MS-DOS development tools and languages, I wouldn't be surprised if you discovered that literally thousands of different assemblers, compilers, and linkers are available from a wide variety of companies. Looking at Windows tools, you'll find only two or three major vendors and only a handful of development environments, all based around high-level languages. Despite the limited quantity of tools, the quality is uniformly excellent with most tools being part of an *IDE (Integrated Development Environment)*, which contains an editor, compiler, linker, and full-screen, source-code debugger.

This chapter introduces some of the most popular Windows-development tools and, later in the book, I will work through a number of examples using these tools. It is important to note that these languages generally cannot interface with hardware in the PC except through specially written device drivers, which are presented later in the book.

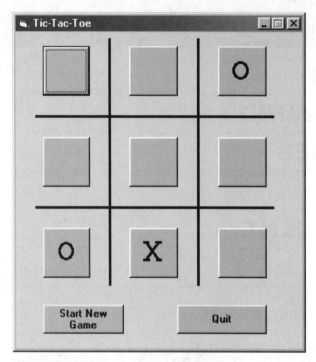

FIGURE 17-1   Visual Basic "Tic-Tac-Toe".

Visual Basic

Microsoft's Visual Basic is, hands down, the most popular Windows application development tool and, in many ways, has assumed the same position for Windows software development as Microsoft's GW-BASIC had for MS-DOS. Visual Basic is a remarkably easy tool to work with. I found that after an hour's familiarization, I was able to develop my own application (a tic-tac-toe game), shown in Fig. 17-1.

Visual Basic works the way that I would want a Windows development language to work; the actual window (also known as a "form" in Visual Basic) is created and then the various features have code added. This makes Visual Basic very fun to play around with and try out "what if" things.

The language is very simple and is a super-set of GW-BASIC. Included with the "Learning Edition" is an interactive multimedia CD-ROM that you can work through, with the end result being a pretty good knowledge of Visual Basic. It took me about four half-days to complete, but, as you can see from Fig. 17-1, you will be more productive shortly after opening the box.

Visual Basic does not offer all the capabilities of (Visual) C++ or other high-level languages and it is somewhat expensive (the Learning Edition is about $100 U.S. and the Professional Edition is almost $500 U.S.), but it is the best introduction to Windows programming that I've seen.

Visual C++

Visual C++ has a reputation for being difficult to learn and it is richly deserved. Microsoft's Visual C++ has emerged as the premier systems-development language for Windows, with its wide range of capabilities to efficiently control how Windows applications operate and provide a rich language with powerful data-processing capabilities. C++ of any kind is not a language for beginners, although its capabilities become very attractive as you become more familiar with creating Windows applications.

C++ is an *object-orientated programming (OOP) language. Object orientated* is a way of defining data and subroutines so that they merge into objects. I find that if you write well-structured C code, you will not have significant problems in creating and understanding OOP applications.

Visual C++ is part of Microsoft's complete Visual Development tools and they provide an *Integrated Development Environment (IDE)* for C++ programming, which allows easy and automatic cross-referencing of objects, classes, variables, functions, and dialog boxes and their controls. Provided in the IDE is a source code editor, along with a number of different graphic editors for the different graphics elements used with Visual C++. Later in the book, I will describe the "MicroSoft Foundation Classes" ("MFC") which are used to simplify the operation of developing C++ Windows applications. When specifying the application initially, a program called *AppWizard* will guide you through the selection of dialog boxes, basic objects, and resources for use in the application.

I started my basic Windows programming by the tortured route of Borland's Turbo Pascal for Windows, Borland's C++ for Windows, Visual C++, and then Visual Basic. Obviously, there was no plan in what I was doing and it took years to get to the point I am now at where I can develop my own applications and device drivers reasonably efficiently. I don't recommend this path to anyone else; instead, if you are learning from the beginning, I recommend starting with Visual Basic and only moving to Visual C++ if you need more capabilities in your applications or want to develop device drivers.

This really isn't a vote of confidence for Visual C++, but I think it is a realistic, easy-to-learn path that will give you a better chance of successfully developing Windows graphical applications without giving up in frustration. Starting with Visual C++, unless you have large amounts of support and a gun to your head, is just about impossible to become successful in a reasonable length of time. By starting with a development tool, such as Visual Basic, first, you will learn many of the concepts for working with dialog box controls and Windows interfaces that can be applied to your Visual C++ applications as you begin learning the language, object-orientated programming, and the tool with its wizards.

Java

The Java programming language and operating environment was developed a few years ago by Sun as an alternative to the myriad of programming languages that are available for different PCs, workstations, and mainframes, as well as the different operating systems available on them. If you read the Java advertisements, you're probably wondering why everyone isn't running straight to Java. Java is a compiled language that produces "tokens" that can be run under any system that has the Java operating system ported to it. The tokens are advertised as being able to run on anything from mainframes to PCs to embedded devices, such as cellular phones and *Personal Digital Assistants (PDAs)*.

As a language, Java is similar to C, with one important difference; Java does not have the capability to use pointers. For the thousands of people who hated learning how to use pointers in their C and Pascal classes, this is probably a big reason to go to Java without reservation. I realize that I'm simplifying the language considerably, but I wanted to get across the idea that Java is not harder to learn than C, although I would characterize it as being "different" and requiring the same amount of effort to learn.

Currently, Java is very popular for providing enhanced display and console capabilities (often games) to Web pages, but has not really caught on as a development tool for overall applications. This includes hardware access, with very few texts information on interfacing Java to hardware.

This is a very important point because as I go through the Java literature, I don't see any tools advertised for designing hardware device drivers. This is unfortunate because, with the PCI and USB busses, I would have thought that Java would be an ideal way for vendors to create hardware interface devices that can be used in a variety of systems.

To be fair, as I write this book, the entire computer industry is trying to figure out how to be sure that all computer systems (including banking, air traffic control, networking, databases, etc.) will be working at 12:01 AM January first, 2000. Java started off with a lot of enthusiasm in the 1995 and 1996 time frame, but has since lost momentum because of the industry focus on the "Y2K bug."

It will be interesting to see what will happen in the new millennium with regards to Java. The year 2000 might well usher in a new era in computing, one that is standardized across the industry. As part of this new era, I hope that the Java standard will be extended to include embedded device-driver development tools, device-driver toolkits, and standard interfaces for busses, such as USB and Firewire.

LabView

The visual Windows programming environments described previously are actually quite easy to work with and efficient, compared to standard MS-DOS assembler and C editor, compiler, and linker combinations. Despite the GUI easy-to-use interface, when you get right down to it, the visual tools are front ends to quite traditional high-level languages, with assignment statements, conditional execution, and API interfacing. Even though these tools are part of the "Visual Toolkit" by Microsoft, they really do not provide a graphical programming environment and still require a high level of knowledge in traditional programming techniques.

National Instruments' LabView application development environment is designed specifically to develop hardware-interface applications for the PC and other workstations. Instead of using traditional programming languages, LabView allows the user to graphically create an application with a front-panel dialog box that is used to provide a user interface to the module (or instrument) that is being created.

LabView itself was developed about 10 years ago as a tool to allow simplified interfacing to National Instruments products. National Instruments provides a variety of different bus controllers (for GPIB, among other types of instrument busses) and ISA and PCI adapter cards with different interfacing features. LabView was first created as a simple programming tool to allow engineers that aren't very familiar with conventional programming, to create applications very quickly with a minimum of training. Over time, new device drivers have been added for the PC's serial, parallel, and USB bus, as well as high-level instruments that have been written for devices, such as power supplies, digitizing oscilloscopes, and DMMs. Today, LabView has a very substantial range of instruments available and a wide user base. LabView is available for the Macintosh and Sun Sparc workstations, allowing software to be ported very easily between applications.

The "instrument" itself is the application or subroutines used in the application. Simple instruments can be nested into more-complex instruments to provide a high-level top-down function quite easily. Within the instrument, different blocks are selected and connected together by the user, such as designing an electrical circuit in a "schematic capture" program.

Figure 17-2 shows part of an *ESS (Environmental Stress Screening)* control instrument used in Celestica to show a virtual instrument and its associated front panel. This is actually quite complex, with a program event sequencer, a FOR loop and a WHILE loop built into the instrument.

Many programmers, such as LabView's ease-of-code development (this really is a full-featured programming language)—especially with the ease in which instruments can be shared between applications. Adding instruments is very straightforward with type checking done automatically when the instrument is "wired" into the application.

To create a LabView application, the user drags functions onto the Block Diagram dialog box. Figure 17-3 shows how to create a simple instrument that will add two user-specified integers together. The DBL inputs and outputs have been connected together with an adder.

If a data output is split to multiple inputs (a "branched path"), the application can run with a modest multitasking capability. I say "modest" because a handful of independent operations can be occurring at the same time. As the number of independent operations increases, the execution performance of LabView drops almost exponentially.

Multiple outputs into a single input is obviously not allowed unless an instrument or operation box conditions or serializes them.

On the front panel, user input and output controls automatically appear and provide the user with a simple means of inputting the values to be summed together (Fig. 17-4). The result is displayed on the control on the right side of the Front Panel dialog box.

LabView is an excellent tool for general engineering and scientific applications with instruments and interfaces that are available. LabView has problems if new bus interfaces

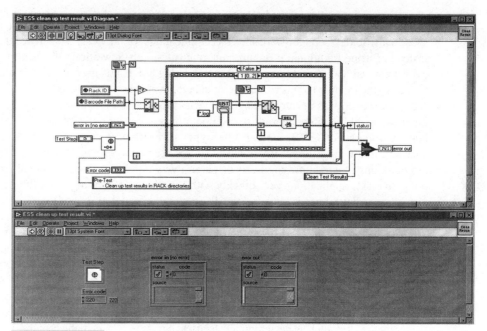

FIGURE 17-2   Complex "Labview" application.

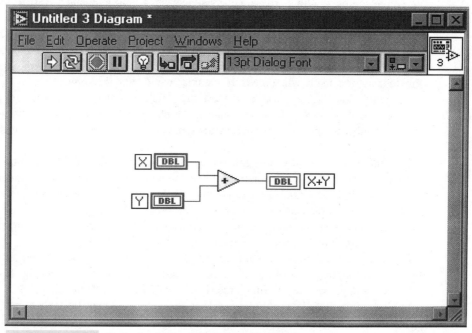

FIGURE 17-3   "Labview" block diagram display.

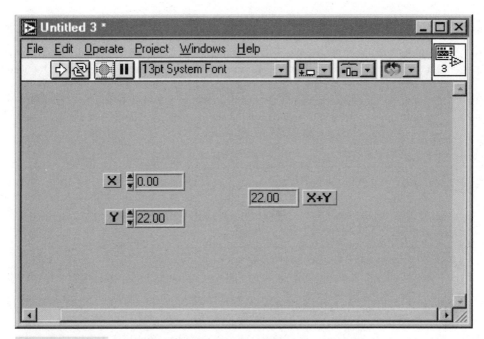

FIGURE 17-4   "Labview" front panel dialog box.

are required for an application/computer. Like creating a Windows device driver, a LabView device driver requires quite a bit of specialized knowledge, although through National Instruments and user groups, finding a device driver for a specific bus or device is actually quite easy.

Other than this limited introduction, I won't be using LabView for interfacing devices to the PC. LabView is primarily designed for applications that use bussed, commercially available hardware that already has low-level instruments device drivers written for it. For an application this type of environment, I would recommend using LabView over traditional high-level language-development environments.

Microsoft DDK

The Microsoft DDK is a set of Visual C++ classes, utilities, and example applications that are used to develop device drivers under Windows. *DDK* is an acronym for *Device Driver Kit* and different ones are available for the different Windows operating systems. The Microsoft *SDK (Software Development Kit)* is a set of classes, utilities, and example applications for creating Windows applications using the Visual Toolkit. To get the Microsoft DDKs and SDKs, you will have to subscribe to the *Microsoft Developer Network (MSDN)*, which will send CD-ROMs with the necessary software on a regular basis. Subscribing to the MSDN will keep you up to date on what is happening with Microsoft Windows products.

Information for subscribing to the MSDN can be found at:

http://msdn.microsoft.com/subscriptions/default.asp

This site will allow you to download application resources, as well as subscribe to the MSDN. This site updates the MSDN CD-ROMs that come with your Visual Tools, and includes Microsoft sample applications and updated documents. As a subscriber, you will also be able to get Microsoft Press books and the *Microsoft Developer Journal* at reduced prices.

The MSDN subscription should not be confused with registering Professional or Enterprise Visual Basic or Visual C++ and receiving the MSDN Library CD-ROM with the product. The Library CD-ROM is a subset of what is available as an MSDN Subscriber.

As I write this, the CD-ROM set contains:

1 Windows 95 DDK with documentation, tools, and samples for Windows 95 device drivers and virtual drivers
2 Windows 95 Far East DDK with support for developing applications in the Far East
3 Windows NT 4.0 DDK with documentation, tools, and samples for Windows 95 device drivers and virtual drivers
4 Windows NT 4.0 Hardware Compatibility Test (HCT) for PCs
5 Windows NT 4.0 Far East DDK
6 Windows 98 DDK with support for documentation, tools, and samples for Windows 98 WDM device driver tools
7 PC 98 Hardware Compatibility Test

To access the data on the CD-ROMs, a help utility (Fig. 17-5) is used. This utility allows searching for specific information on any of the MSDN tools and the COM/OLE application/database interfaces. This utility is constantly updated to allow more efficient access to the help data and code examples. This data is also available on the Internet; in fact, you

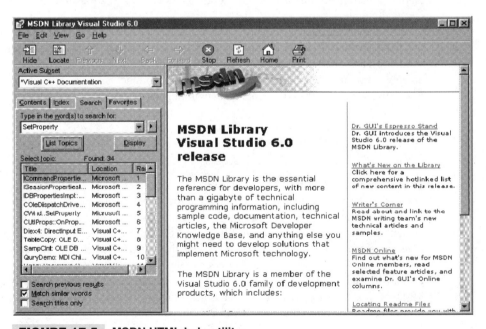

FIGURE 17-5   MSDN HTML help utility.

might find updates to the Internet information after you receive one set of CD-ROMs and before you receive the next.

There are three levels of an MSDN subscription. The lowest (and least costly) is the Library subscription, which only provides you with the current set of CD-ROMs. The next level up is the Professional subscription, which includes access to the latest operating systems (for application testing), SDKs/DDKs, incidental help, and the CD-ROMS. The Professional subscription provides you with all of the Visual Studio development tools, BackOffice Test Platform, Office Developer, FrontPage (for Web Page Development), Project, and everything provided with the Professional subscription.

The price for the subscription is quite high (anywhere from $200 to $2400 U.S., as I write this), but you will get a lot of useful information, as well as a set number of problems ("incidents") for which you can call (with an 1-800 number) Microsoft. If you are going to develop device drivers using VtoolsD, the MSDN subscription is not required, but, when developing WDMs with *Driver::Works*, you will need the subscription.

Other Languages and Development Tools

I've mentioned everything in this section elsewhere in the book, but I felt it was important to re-iterate the points in one place as a reference. I think this is important because developing Microsoft Windows applications is not trivial. If you don't have the correct tools, you could really be in a lot of trouble.

The compiler itself should be for an accepted Windows-development high-level language. This means the language is really limited to BASIC, C++, and Java. Other languages, no matter how good they look, will have problems when you are looking for support.

Ease of use is very important. For example, if you wanted a program that just put up a dialog box with a message and buttons for the user to end (Fig. 17-6) actually requires more than 1000 lines of C++ and requires 22 KB of memory! In Visual Basic and Visual C++, the user is protected from this level of complexity and guided through the dialog box development process.

As part of this, the development system should handle the make files, as well as low-level interfaces so that you don't have to. In MS-DOS, I would not consider this an issue, but with the extreme complexity of Windows Applications, I consider it a necessity.

A source level debugger is absolutely crucial for successfully developing applications. The ability to patch code is not as useful as it is in an MS-DOS debugger (and ever there, I frown upon it), but the ability to set break points and look at and update variables is very useful. Visual Basic has a good example of what I would consider to be an appropriate debugger built into the code.

As part of the previous points, the compiler, editor, and debugger should be part of an Windows application integrated development environment (as is demonstrated in Visual Basic and Visual C++). Again, Windows is too complex for someone to mix and match tools. A well-designed, integrated development environment will simplify your application development and help you to efficiently debug your application.

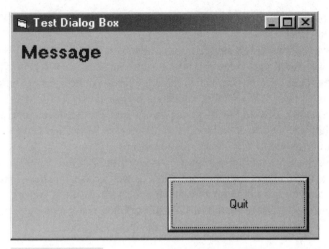

FIGURE 17-6   Example dialog box created in Visual C++.

PROGRAMMING

FOR

ERRORS

One area of programming that I find has been neglected in courses and text books is the concept of handling errors and working with humans (which many programmers characterize as an unstable input device just waiting to pass invalid data to their project programs). Over the years, I have tried to come up with a set of rules that I can uniformly apply to my applications, although I feel like I still have a lot to learn. I have seen applications that have wonderful error-reporting mechanisms, don't miss anything, and provide good pointers to where the problem lies. On the other end of the spectrum, I have seen many applications that either just stop (and maybe lock up the system) or continue blindly on, as if there aren't any problems. I tend to give up on the latter types the quickest.

It is impossible to list every different type of error. By spending some time during application design and initial coding, you can anticipate different errors and look for ways to either fix the problem within software or notify the user as to the nature of the problem and what they can do to help resolve it. This extra work also has the added benefit of helping you when a problem arises during application debug. Spending a few minutes (and a few lines of code) can pay off in large dividends when something stops working and you have no idea of what the problem is.

I have tried to list the major classes of errors that I plan for when I am creating an application, as well as the philosophy behind the code put in place to avoid the problems. Trying to anticipate problems before you have them will save you time later when debugging and soothing angry customers. This chapter is an introduction to thinking about what kind of problems you can encounter and how to plan to avoid them. Having a good level of error checking and user feedback will always be regarded as a positive feature and will help in the users' satisfaction of your product.

Inadvertent Application/PC Crashes/Resets

The biggest error to plan for when designing your application is: what happens if the PC loses power, another application causes the PC to crash, or your processor misses a few beats. Any one of these incidents will cause your application to stop running and any data created up to that point to be lost. Designing your application to "survive" these catastrophic system failures is quite simple and does not require a significant amount of extra work in the design of the application.

I could probably write four or five pages listing all the possible causes for the application to stop running (ranging from mice putting a nest on top of your nice warm hard drive to terrorist actions). It is much easier just to say that you have to plan for events that will cause the application to either stop working or be unable to properly access the files in the system.

For some reason, often when I have system-wide problems, other people's applications will seem to continue to execute (especially if they are not paged onto disk), but I cannot access file information. For me, this is the primary problem that I have to deal with and, depending on the fail mechanism, an open file could be corrupted when a problem occurs.

The solution to this problem is quite simple, never have an open file unless absolutely necessary and only keep it open for the shortest period of time. This means that when a data transfer is required, the file is opened, saved in memory, and closed in the shortest period of time. For large files that are opened repeatedly to read small pieces indvidually, the current file pointer must be tracked and used to *lseek* to the correct location in the file.

The code for a typical transfer will look like:

```
handle = open( FileName, options );

lseek( handle, CurrentPointer );          // Move to the Current
                                          //   Location
read( handle, Buffer, BufferSize );       // Read the Data that is
                                          //   required
close( handle );

CurrentPointer += BufferSize;             // Update the Pointer to the
                                          //   next location to Read
                                          //   From
```

Opening a file, moving the file pointer, transferring data, and then closing the file probably seems like it will really slow down the system. In modern systems, this series of operations really isn't a significant time adder, compared to just leaving the file open. This statement is because, in part, to the high speed and efficiency of modern hard drives. As well, in the Windows operating systems, file data tends to be buffered in blocks that are convenient for the operating system; the blocks are only freed up when other processes require the memory resource. This means that file data must be already available in memory when reads are about to occur. Write operations execute when the file system is able to transfer the data to disk. This can happen some time after the Write API has been invoked in the application. Often, writes occur after the file Close operation.

For applications that generate data asynchronously and unpredictably (i.e., from user input), updating the buffer file must be updated after some set number of events or incoming data bytes. For many editors, I see automatic updates once every 1024 keystrokes, which seems like a pretty good general rule. Looking at the logic behind this, namely that if the assumption is made that the average typist can type at an effective rate of 10 words per minute, then the file would be updated once every three minutes assuming 5 characters per word.

This rule can be used for other types of data and, if it is saved at this rate, then only a maximum of three minutes of data is lost in the event of a catastrophic failure.

Application operating configuration data should be stored in a file and only read upon application initialization and only written to when the user has changed default settings. Otherwise, the configuration data should just be stored in memory. The reason is to minimize the opportunity for the configuration data to be corrupted and the retyping that the user will have to do to get the system "back where they wanted it." I personally hate systems that lose default paths and other configuration information when the system crashes and I have to enter it in again.

For file operations, I typically don't check for possible error codes from the Open, Lseek, Read, or Write APIs. For the application to execute properly at the point where data is being read, checks of whether or not files can be opened and accessed will already have been made. If a catastrophic error has occurred and the file system no longer works, chances are that the Open statement will not return or will return an invalid file handle, which will cause the operating system to notify the user directly.

After a catastrophic failure, you should check to see if any files were "damaged," which really means that sector pointers were lost. In the MS-DOS and Windows file systems, the sector pointers are doubly linked lists used to connect the various parts of a file. During some failures, a sector can be written with incorrect data and that will cause the file information to be lost.

For a fully fault-tolerant application, you should probably put checksums or CRCs in any data files that are used in the application and then check these values each time the file is opened to be sure that the file has not been corrupted in any way. This really isn't that hard to write and only adds a small incremental delay to the operation of the computer.

For most applications, this is not required. This is not to say that after a catastrophic failure, I would not recommend that you check over the system with a "chkdsk" or "scandisk" utility to ensure there aren't any issues with any of the files (especially operating-system files). Other than this, no precautions or remedies must be taken with regard to catastrophic system failures.

When I wrote my notes for this section, I added the idea that after a catastrophic error, the application should end "gracefully" and restore all captured interrupts and resources and use a proper *terminate* statement to end execution. This is really not necessary because, with a catastrophic error, these resources are not available. Chances are that the operating system is unable to process any APIs or commands.

The hard drive in the laptop that I used for e-mail "ate" itself as I was working on this book. I know that "ate" isn't the technical term, but if you heard the grinding noises it made you'd have to come to the conclusion that digestion was somehow involved. This reminded me of the importance of backing up your work.

For my books, I use a "CD-R" (write-once CD-ROM recording drive) to back up all the text, graphics, and application software. I religiously do this once a month to be sure that if I do have a hard drive failure, I can recreate most of what I had quite easily. This is a relatively inexpensive and fast process and it gives me great piece of mind when I turn off the machine or go away for a business trip.

For your own application development, I recommend that you follow a backup process as well. If you are just starting out, then you might only want to use diskettes, which are pretty cheap. As you develop larger applications, you might want to use a CD-R or streaming tape drive. Although not especially cheap, they certainly are a lot cheaper than if you were to lose all your work.

As part of this, be sure to keep the original diskettes and CD-ROMs of your operating system, development tools, and applications that you use on your PC in a safe place (along with your own development backup). If the catastrophic failure you experience is something like a trashed hard drive, you can recreate the PC relatively easily and quickly.

Processing User Input

After I graduated from the university, I was put on a tester development project with the task of developing its user interface. Like most new graduates, I concentrated on the technical aspects of what I was doing (interfacing directly with VRAM to provide very fast screen updates and keeping a certain number of screen "pages" in memory to avoid having to save and reload data from disk), rather than on how the users (manufacturing technicians) were going to use the tester. In many ways, this was an eye-opening experience for me and I learned some very important rules about application development. Like the book *All I Really Need to Know I Learned in Kindergarten*, this first experience taught me rules about user interfacing that I continue to reflect upon and use in my current applications.

The first rule was: only one person should develop the user interface. My part of the project was to create a set of tools that allowed other engineers (responsible for specific hardware devices used in the tester) to design their own interface "pages." Four or five people developed these pages. Although each engineer was technically excellent and had some very good ideas, each page was completely different and did not follow any kind of consistent theme.

When the tester was first released to the manufacturing floor, the technicians had a lot of problems trying to keep the operation straight and could not develop a rhythm for using the tester and bouncing between the pages. The number one complaint that we got about the tester when it first became available was that the same keystrokes did different things on different pages.

This really taught me the importance of keeping everything consistent. We were amazed at the source of the complaints; in some areas, the tester barely worked or would crash in the middle of a product debugging session. Compared to the problems with the user interface, these were considered minor by our customers.

I ended up rewriting most of the interfaces to give a consistent look and feel to the pages. As I released the updated pages and menus, the complaints about the tester shifted from how interface was executed to the execution instability problems that we considered to be much more serious.

The interface was designed in 1985 and used a text display with the function buttons (*F1* through *F10*) for operational input. Even by standards of the day, it wasn't considered very attractive or user-friendly, but once the pages were rewritten to have the same format and established function-key operating conventions, all of the complaints about the user interface ended.

This is why, when I develop Windows applications, I try to be sure that the established conventions are followed and don't stray from them too much. The Windows dialog box conventions have been honed over the past 10 years into a reasonably efficient interface with which users are comfortable.

Another problem with the tester and the users was with free-form input. The user provides free-form input when the interface provides a prompt for them. This input is often used to specify options, rather than click off items in a menu.

From the MS-DOS prompt, this is often the only way to input operating parameters and data into an application. For many applications, this can result in some very complex operations. For example, here are the options available for PKZIP from the Command Line to control its execution:

```
Usage:  PKZIP [options] zipfile [@list] [files...]

 -a              Add files
 -b[drive]       create temp zipfile on alternative drive
 -d              Delete files
 -e[x,n,f,s,0]   use [eXtra|Normal (default)|Fast|Super fast|NO
                 compression]
 -f              Freshen files
 -l              display software License agreement
 -m[f,u]         Move files [with Freshen | with Update]
 -u              Update files
 -p|P            store Pathnames|p=recursed into|P=specified & recursed
into
 -r              Recurse subdirectories
 -s[pwd]         Scramble with password [If no pwd is given, prompt for
                 pwd]
 -v[b][r][m][t][c] View .ZIP [Brief][Reverse][More][Technical][Comment]
                 sort by
   [d,e,n,o,p,s] [Date|Extension|Name|natural
                 Order(default)|Percentage|Size]
 -&[f|l|u|       Span disks [Format|format Low density|Unconditional
    ul|w|v]      format|Unconditional Low density|Wipe disk|enable dos
                 [s[drive]]     Verify|Back up entire disk w/ subdirs
                 (-rp)
```

This list was taken from one (there is another) screen of command-line options available for the application. These options are pretty complex for a user (not to mention remember).

When we put in this type of option list, nobody could use the system properly. The fix (the one that I would recommend) was creating operating parameter set-up pages that were recorded for each operator. By doing this, the system was customized to each operator and did not require the operators keeping a "cheat sheet" of the different parameters to be able to use the tester.

With the free-form operating parameters, data and commands were mixed in together with the parameters. Once the operating parameters were removed and the commands were initiated by function keys, the operator input error rate dropped drastically.

But there was still a very significant "noise" level of problems that included incorrect data sequences and values. Placing the input fields for specific data variables at specific locations on the page and then filtering the data so that it could only be entered into a specific format (e.g., hex) minimized this problem. Once the data was entered, the values were checked to ensure that they were valid.

To show what kind of improvements can be gained from forcing a user to use a standard format with specific entry fields, I looked at a memory test application. If the application was to run from the MS-DOS command line, the input parameters would probably look something like:

```
Usage:  memtest Pattern Start:Address End:Address

"Pattern" Values:
 -0            Load 0s
 -1            Load 1s
 -a            Data = Address
 -p            Pseudo-Random
```

By following the rules I developed over the tester application and using a Visual Basic Dialog box, this application interface could be as shown in Fig. 18-1, which is a lot easier to understand for the user and, surprisingly enough, easier to program.

The reason why it is easier to program is that Visual Basic provides a dialog box editor that provides the EITHER-OR function for the pattern values and provides user specified "Start" and "End" addresses at specific locations in the string.

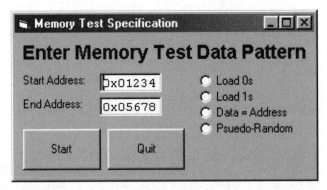

FIGURE 18-1 Application options using a dialog box.

When you are working with a free-floating input string, you will find that the users will tend to think of the order of how the data should go in differently from you. In the tester example, we set specific orders for data entry, which caused problems with users forgetting the order or other orders being more natural for them. By allowing any arbitrary order (which required some indication, i.e., the *Start:* and *End:* in the previous above), the user input error rate was reduced.

But parsing the input and figuring out how the data should be formatted made the application code much more difficult. In the Visual Basic example, the only real input processing is to check the Start and End addresses to ensure that they are within valid limits.

A free-form text input line also has the issue of trying to process all the input from the user. This means that you must come up with a way of prefacing each parameter for a specific operation and to have it distinguished from other ones. In the previous example, I used the prefacing strings *Start:*, *End:* and - to identify which parameter is being input. These prefacing strings have to be parsed; if an unexpected parameter is encountered, an error message must be generated. It really is easier for both you as the programmer and the user to have a dialog box with specific input controls and eliminated the opportunity for the user to input bad data.

The last bit of knowledge I gained from the tester operators was that people will look for shortcuts and tend to reference operations by the keystrokes used to initiate the operation. If shortcuts are not present in the system and fairly lengthy key sequences are needed to move between applications, you can bet that the users will be requesting control-key sequences to move to often-used pages quickly. In the tester example, we were able to eliminate the need for control-key sequences by placing all execution screens one function keystroke away from a base menu and then having a function key access all of the base menus. This meant that no matter where you were in the application, any other page was only two function-key presses away.

It is important to remember that users see your applications differently from you. In the tester example, running the tester in Sort mode was simply referred to as *F5*. Debug mode was *F4/F5* and the Actual/Expected Data Comparison page was *F4/F6*. I made a small reference for answering technician questions and allowed me to translate what they were saying into the actual pages. This was not a necessarily bad thing, but it added an unnecessary level of complexity that can be avoided in Windows GUI applications.

File Input/Output

Using files for loading data for an application or using them for configuration information can make your applications quite a bit simpler. In some applications, you will probably want to use file data for passing along to hardware or using as a command set. Earlier, the book described the format of file data that should be used ("man-readable" ASCII), but this chapter describes what to do if there is an error or if the file is in an invalid format.

File operations are pretty simple. If you are not working with a database, your operations consist of: creating, opening, closing, reading, writing, and moving the file pointer. Not a lot can go wrong with this and you can easily check for problems and alert the user to their nature. As will become evident as I describe these problems, you really won't be able to fix the problems from within your application, but you should get a pretty good idea of what they are.

Creating a file just about always works. The only time it will fail is when the disk is unavailable to the application. The causes of this can be no diskette in the drive, a disk that is totally full (more likely with a diskette than a hard drive) or a network disk to which the application does not have "write authority." In either case, if the handle returned from the Create API indicates that the operation is impossible, an error message should be passed to the user and the program ends (after restoring any changed hardware, freeing any allocated memory, and closing any open files).

Opening a file is making an existing file's contents available to an application for reading or writing. If a failure is returned from the API, then chances are that the problem consists of the file not being available on the disk. The Open API might also flag a file that has its permissions set to Read Only and an attempt made to open with the intention of writing to it. This error might not exist in all versions of Windows and MS-DOS and might not even be flagged during a write to a read-only file.

To rectify the problem with a file that cannot be found, the user could be prompted to select the correct disk/subdirectory for the file. In MS-DOS, I tend to avoid this because it is a lot of work to come up with a way for the user to list possible files and select the correct one. In Windows Visual Development tools, the job of providing this interface is much less onerous; built-in dialog boxes will perform this in a standard method for the application.

When reading data from a file, the only error that you can get is if you attempt to read more data than is available in the file from the current file pointer. This is found by checking the byte counter returned at the end of the API and is not flagged by the operating system. To avoid this problem, I always keep track of how much I have available to read from the file and don't go over this limit.

You might have one subtle problem when reading (and writing) file data and that is how end-of-line conditions are stored in the file. Traditional applications indicate an end-of-line condition by putting a carriage-return (0x00D) and line-feed (0x00A) character at the end of the line's text.

This convention is really not held by all applications and you might find that file-line ends just consist of a single carriage return or line feed. Depending on how the file is opened, you might discover that files that use the carriage-return/line-feed convention have the line-feed character filtered out by the parameters used in the application.

To avoid these problems, I always write my files with a carriage return/line feed at the end of each line and when I read them back, I don't count on anything being true. The code I normally use to find the next character after the end of a line is:

```
while (( Buffer[ i ] != 0x00D ) && ( Buffer[ i ] != 0x00A )) {
    :                                   // Process Line Data
}

if ( Buffer[ i ] == 0x00D )             // "Carriage Return" At Line
                                        //  End
    if ( Buffer[ i + 1 ] == 0x00A )     // Followed by a "Line Feed"
        i += 2;                         // Skip Two Characters
    else
        i++;                            // Else, Just "Carriage Re
                                        //  turn"
else                                    // Else, "Line Feed" at Line
                                        //  End
```

```
    if ( Buffer[ i + 1 ] == 0x00D )      //  Followed by a "Carriage
                                         //  Return"
        i += 2;                          //  Skip Two Characters
    else
        i++;                             //  Else, Just "Line Feed"
```

This code finds the position of the start of the next line in the buffer that has been loaded by file reads in any of the different cases listed.

Another possible error that you can encounter when reading files is determining the end of the file. When MS-DOS was first introduced, a file end was indicated by an MS-DOS specific file-end character (0x01A). Some applications (even if they're written today) still use this convention to indicate the end of a file.

This can cause problems when you are processing a file and before you come to the end of the file, you discover that after a line-end character (set), you might have a character that you don't know how to handle.

To avoid this problem, when I am reading in data, I allocate a buffer that is at least one character larger than I need. Then check the last character read in. If it is the 0x01A character, I overwrite it with a null (0x000) character. If no 0x01A character is at the end of the file, I put the null character at the byte beyond the end of the file. This character is used to indicate the end of the input file in the buffer. Using it makes processing a file much easier (you simply read through it until you encounter the null at the end of the buffer).

Writing to a file really only has one potential problem when you are unable to write the buffer into the file. The cause of this problem is a file that cannot be written to. The most-common reason for this error is a full disk (which will most often happen when writing to a diskette). This error can be discovered by checking the number of bytes written to the file against the number expected.

To be honest, when reading and writing file data, I don't bother checking how many bytes are actually transferred because I already know how much I am going to transfer. With modern hard drives (with many GB available), there really isn't much danger of running out of space. I realize that it is possible to go too far with diskettes, but these problems are also pretty rare and problems show up in other areas. The reason for the problem is usually pretty easy to find by doing a *dir* on the disk and discovering "0 Bytes Free."

Processing a file should be kept as simple as possible. For example, in my previous books on microcontrollers, I have created programmers that convert user programs to IHXM8S format object files that have to be transferred to the device to be programmed. The file looks like:

```
:100000001030850086018316083085008601831232
:100010003A203A203A203A20303086000515051162
:100020003A2005150511422005150511422038308E4
:1000300029200C30292001302920413034208510D11
:100040001F2885192128613034200508103A8500C1
:100050001F288510860005150511FC390319322863
:10006000422033283A200800851486000515051122
:100070004220080004308C001830013E03188C0B1D
:100080003D28080001308C00E030013E03188C0B45
:0400900045280800F7
:02400E00F93F78
:00000001FF
```

At the end of each line, there is normally a carriage-return/line-feed combination. I say "normally" because for one programmer, I relied on the Windows terminal emulator utility "HyperTerminal" to transmit the file to the programmer. After releasing the application, I discovered that in some versions of HyperTerminal (as is provided with Windows 98) the line-feed character is discarded and just a carriage-return character is sent to the programmer. This is an example of why I never count on getting a carriage return w/line feed at the end of a line.

When processing data files, I have to determine whether the format is correct. I generally treat free-format files as a user-input line and parse them using similar rules as to what was just described. For specific-format lines, such as those in the previous file, I try to make my checking as simple as possible.

For the file shown, I know that a colon is always in the first column of the line. As well, the number of bytes on the line is in the next two characters and the address the data is to be programmed into is located in the following four characters. The next two bytes are used to indicate whether or not the line is data (0) or the end of file (1). Next, the data is inserted into the line with the last two characters being a checksum of the data in the entire line.

Despite all of this specific information that will clearly tell me whether or not the data is good, the only checking that I do is to see if the first byte of each line is a colon (:). In any case, having a leading colon as the starting character in a file is quite unusual; it really indicates that the file is an object file, not any other type.

I realize that applications might use a colon at the start of a line to indicate the start of data or labels, but I felt that the chances of this were quite remote because the object file would be located in a subdirectory with source and list files. Getting a file that has colons as the line-start character was very unlikely for this application.

What also makes this method reasonable to use is the slow data rate that the information is sent to the device to be programmed (1200 bps). At this speed, correct data is a given for short data lengths using properly shielded cabling. Deciding what level of checking you should do is really application dependent. For the programmer application described here, if I was sending the data at 19,200 bps over long-distance phone cabling, I would definitely want to have at least the checksum test and an acknowledge protocol built in. The processing and data checking/verifying depends on the quality of the data link, as well as the format of the data, relative to other files used in the system.

Hardware

Problems with hardware can cause a great amount of difficulty for you and your users. These problems can consist of anything from stuck single bits or the hardware interface not responding. I am appalled at the number of hardware-interface applications that either don't detect some gross errors as missing hardware or have no built-in features to help the application detect whether or not there is a problem. These applications can be frustrating for users to work with and will probably be poorly reviewed.

This book describes a lot about how hardware is interfaced to the PC, but I really don't spend a lot of time describing what can be done to identify errors and allow them to be fixed quickly. This topic is near and dear to my heart as a test engineer. Much of my career has been creating debugging processes for products that do not pass back an acceptable amount of information for efficient debugging. This chapter is intended to make some suggestions for designers to make their products better for their customers and the poor people that have to build them.

The biggest problem that I see with products that interface to the PC is a lack of "feedback" built into the interfaces. When I say "feedback," I mean a hardware method to determine whether or not the device is even connected to the PC and that the interface is working. Figure 18-2 shows a simple interface circuit that allows a PC to write to an external device. Instead of just passing the data in one direction to the device, I have added an input buffer, which can read back the output latch's data for the PC to check to be sure that it is coming out properly.

The typical code that I would use to test the interface would be something like:

```
int IF_Test()                    //  Test the Example Interface
{

int retvalue = 0;                //  Assume the Interface is Good

  IFOut( 0x0AA );                //  Write the First Pattern
  IFLatch();                     //  Latch it into the "Output"

  IFOut( 0x055 );                //  Put out a different Pattern to
                                 //  clear
                                 //  the Interface
  if ( IFIn() != 0x0AA )         //  Read the Value stored in the
                                 //  Latch
    retvalue = -1;               //  Mismatch - Error
  else {                         //  No Mismatch, check the complement

    IFOut( 0x055 );              //  Write the Complement
    IFLatch();

    IFOut( 0x0AA );              //  Put out a different Pattern to
                                 //  clear
                                 //   the Interface
    if ( IFIn() != 0x055 )       //  Is there a Mismatch?
      retvalue = -1;             //  Yes, Flag the Error

  }

  return retvalue;               //  Return the IF_Test Error Value

} //  End IF_Test
```

In this code, a bit pattern is output to the latch and latched in to write to the device. Next, I output the complement to ensure that the value is not held in the interface bus capacitively (as might happen if no interface and device are connected to the PC's bus). With this invalid value possibly being held on the PC interface pins, I then read back the output latch's contents through the input buffer. If what is returned is not what was output, then I flag it as an interface error.

This might seem like a very simple solution to the problem, but it really is all that is needed to avoid 90 percent of all the interface problems that you and your customers will encounter. Despite its simplicity, feedback registers are only rarely available in many interface devices; without it, the software will attempt to blindly send data to the device without knowing whether or not it is being received properly.

Looking at this circuit, you might feel that it is not valid for all conditions because it is external to the device. In modern digital electronics, most adapters are built from ASICs or microcontrollers, in which this feedback function can be added in very simply. I have found over the years that if the chip works well enough for this function to work, there is an almost-100-percent chance that it will work for all other functions.

Also, in the example code, I have assumed that the interface is eight parallel bits. As you go through this book, you will discover that very few (just the parallel port and ISA bus) work in this mode. Most other interfaces are serial or require a transmission protocol. In these cases, a "ping" function must be added to allow the application to test the interface periodically. In the keyboard interface, the *ping* is when the PC sends a 0x0EE byte to the keyboard and expects a 0x0EE back.

For a serial interface, any value is acceptable as long as each interface line (data and clock) is toggled high to low and back again.

The IF_Test function provided is okay for knowing whether or not the interface to the adapter device is working; I would be comfortable shipping a product with this level of problem detection. It is not, however, acceptable for debugging the interface. For debugging, the IF_Test should return the bits that are in error.

For the 0x0AA test, the error test should be:

```
if ( IFIn() != 0x0AA )
   return IFIn() ^ 0x0AA;
```

to return the actual failing bits.

This code is better, but not exactly what I would want. The problem with just putting in this correction is that the IF_Test function returns after the first failure. Ideally, it should include all the failing bits. To do this, both 0x0AA and 0x055 are tested and the return error bits should be returned, rather than a pass/fail value. To do this, I would OR the failing bits of each test together as in the following revision to the function:

```
int IF_Test()                    //  Test the Example Interface
{                                //   - Enhanced Error Return

int retvalue;                    //  Return Code is Built from Actual Data
                                 //   Values

  IFOut( 0x0AA );                //  Write the First Pattern
  IFLatch();                     //    Latch it into the "Output"
  IFOut( 0x055 );                //  Put out a different Pattern to clear
                                 //    the Interface
   retvalue = IFIn() ^ 0x0AA;    //  Record the Failing bits

  IFOut( 0x055 );                //  Test the Complement
  IFLatch();
  IFOut( 0x0AA );                //  Put out a different Pattern to clear
                                 //    the Interface
   return retvalue | ( IFIn() ^ 0x055 );
                                 //  Return the Failing Bits

 } //  End IF_Test
```

In this function, the failing bits are identified by XORing the returned (actual) value with the expected value. The advantage of this is that any individual failing bits are identified for easier debug and if all the bits are set (IF_Test returns 0x0FF), it can be assumed that the PC's interface is not working or the device is not connected to the PC. This level of debugging is all that is required for an end user and will give the field or manufacturing technician a better idea of the problem.

For debugging an interface/device, this code is a start. To make the technician's life easier, the device must be designed with feedback for all internal registers and the status of the hardware execution must be available in read-only registers that can be read back by the PC through the device interface. Unfortunately, this was not designed into the PC itself, which can make motherboard and adapter debug very difficult.

When the defect information is returned for debugging, it should be displayed with expected values. If your application provides this level of information for the technician when running a debugging diagnostic and the technician had access to register maps referenced to the device's schematics, then they would most likely be able to debug the device quite easily.

Part of the debugging process is to place a logic or oscilloscope probe on individual pins to discover if a problem is within a chip or is another chip's output. To help facilitate this effort, a set of "scope loops" should be written that will send data to a specific register address repeatedly so that a technician can look at the "nets" on the card and at the chip pins to find the problem.

This technique will work on individual hardware registers, but it is not sufficient for testing memory arrays. I use the term *arrays* to describe memory because that is what it basically is, an array of bits the size of which is the number of addressing bits to the power of two by the size of the memory word. I could probably write volumes about testing memory, but I just want to give you a few tips to help you find problems.

For my own applications that have built-in memory, I typically run three tests to identify stuck bits or address lines in a *static RAM (SRAM)* memory array. I make the distinction between static RAM and *dynamic RAM (DRAM)* because SRAM problems tend to remain constant (i.e., the same bits), whereas DRAM problems can "jump" to different locations in the chip (or collection of chips). Except for video graphics adapters, very few adapters have DRAM designed in. For this reason (and if I were to describe DRAM test strategies, it would require *several* volumes), I just concentrate on the three tests that I use for SRAM.

The first two tests are known as *flood* or *fill* tests in which the memory is loaded with all 1s or all 0s. These tests find problems in the data lines that lead to the memory chips or to individual cells within the chips. A typical fill routine looks like:

```
int Fill_0s()              //  Fill the Memory with 0s and check to
{                          //   to see it was stored there.

int i;                     //  Index into the Memory
int retvalue = 0;

  for ( i = MemStart; i MemEnd; i++ )
    Memory[ i ] = 0;       //  Fill the Memory with 0s

  for ( i = MemStart; i< MemEnd; i++ )
    if ( Memory[ i ] != 0 ) {   //  Check to see that the Memory is
                           //  filled with 0s
```

```
        printf( "Error at address %i of Fill_0s, %x Read Back\n",
          i, Memory[ i ]);
        retvalue = -1;
      }

  return retvalue;

} // End Fill_0s
```

In this function, I print out the address and value of every location that is not equal to zero. From this information, if every memory location has the same bit error, then I can look at the data bits into the chips. Individual errors should point you to a defective cell in one of the memory chips.

The other type of memory test that I always run is the "data equals address" test. This test is exactly what the name implies; it writes the address of the memory word into itself. The purpose of this test is to test the address lines and find any that are open or shorted. The code for this test is:

```
int Data_Addr()              // Fill the Memory with its Address
{                            // to see it the Address Lines are
                             // OK.

int i;                       // Index into the Memory
int retvalue = 0;

  for ( i = MemStart; i < MemEnd; i++ )
    Memory[ i ] = i;         // Fill the Memory with its Address

  for ( i = MemStart; i < MemEnd; i++ )
    if ( Memory[ i ] != i ) {    // Check to see that the Memory is
                             //   filled with the Address
      printf( "Error at address %i of Data_Addr, %x Read Back\n",
        i, Memory[ i ]);
      retvalue = -1;
    }

  return retvalue;

} // End Data_Addr
```

Determining the specific error bit is a bit trickier than in the fill tests. To determine the error, you have to note that if a bit is defective, then one half of the memory will have the problem. For example, if address bit 2 of a 16-byte memory was stuck low and this test was run, you would get the error messages:

```
Error at address 4 of Data_Addr, 0 Read Back
Error at address 5 of Data_Addr, 1 Read Back
Error at address 6 of Data_Addr, 2 Read Back
Error at address 7 of Data_Addr, 3 Read Back
Error at address 12 of Data_Addr, 8 Read Back
Error at address 13 of Data_Addr, 9 Read Back
Error at address 14 of Data_Addr, 10 Read Back
Error at address 15 of Data_Addr, 11 Read Back
```

If address bit 2 of the memory array was stuck high, you would get the error messages:

```
Error at address 0 of Data_addr, 4 Read Back
Error at address 1 of Data_addr, 5 Read Back
Error at address 2 of Data_addr, 6 Read Back
Error at address 3 of Data_addr, 7 Read Back
Error at address 8 of Data_addr, 12 Read Back
Error at address 9 of Data_addr, 13 Read Back
Error at address 10 of Data_addr, 14 Read Back
Error at address 11 of Data_addr, 15 Read Back
```

Finding the defective bit is actually quite easy. From these two outputs, you can identify a bit that is stuck low if the error address is not zero. The stuck low error bit is the base-two logarithm of the address of the error. For a bit that is stuck high, address zero will have the first bad data and the base-two logarithm of the actual data will be the data bit that is in error.

User Feedback

The last point I want to make about errors and hardware interface programming is that the user must be aware of what is going on. In the previous section, I noted that many applications do not notify the user that the interface is unavailable or has errors. I also find that many applications don't properly notify the user as to how the application is running and the current status of data transfers.

The user must be notified as to the "health" of the link to the interface device. Next, the user has to be kept up to date as to the status of hardware operations. Last, the user must have control over the interface's operation in terms of both starting and stopping—even if the current operation is not complete. These requirements probably seem very basic and easy to do (which they are), but a surprising number of applications do not provide them.

The previous section presented the need to be able to "ping" a device on an interface. This ping should be asynchronous to the operation of the device and will be serviced—even when other operations are occurring. For most applications, I ping the device once every second and update the user interface as to the status of the ping. The user-interface indicator should be easily visible and the state easily discernible. I put a flag in the upper right corner of the display with it brightly lit for "on" and dark for "off." In doing this, I am not trying to overwhelm the user, but make them aware of the current status.

I find that Web browsers are one of the biggest culprits for not telling users whether or not the Internet link is actually working and if the page they are requesting will ever be displayed.

During a data transfer that takes a noticeable amount of time, the user should be kept apprised of the progress of any on-going transfers. This is really a visual indicator to the user that everything is well with the system and whether or not they have time to go get a coffee before the operation completes. This indicator is often missing in such applications as terminal emulator download functions, which lead the user to wonder whether or not it is

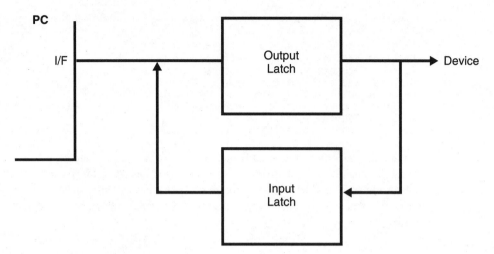

FIGURE 18-2 **Hardware interface with feedback.**

actually working or if the interface has a problem. The actual status is probably shown with a bar-graph display that will give the user an idea of how quickly the transfer is occurring and estimate how long it will take to complete.

Again, Web browsers stand out as culprits in this area, but this is mostly caused by their ability to load multiple files simultaneously. Ideally, I would like to see a series of bar graphs showing the progress of all the files being loaded for the page rather than a single bar graph or a message indicating how many files to download are remaining.

The last feature that I feel should be included in a hardware-device user interface is the ability to stop the action if it is going to take a significant amount of time. This option is usually missing in such applications as programmers and controllers because the software developer does not see the need to stop a transfer. Often, because of system errors, applications will continue to attempt transfers—even when the link is down and the system is seriously corrupted. Adding a Stop button to the application will allow the user to halt the progress of the application, rather than end the application forcefully (usually using *Ctrl-Alt-Delete*).

To demonstrate how I think these interfaces should look, I created the fictitious Programmer Dialog Box shown in Fig. 18-3. This dialog box contains the ping indicator (the circle in the top right corner), the progress indicator bar graph and the ability for the user to stop the transfer for whatever reason. These simple controls are very self-explanatory. They would allow the user to feel confident that the programming operation is occurring as expected and problems would become obvious very quickly.

There is also one other type of user feedback that you should be aware of and that is actual "user feedback". Before an application is considered "released", you should "Beta" it to a number of the actual users to see if they are happy with the application's operation and if they can find any problems with it. In the tester application I discussed earlier in the chapter, this was not done and resulted in major customer dissatisfaction until the interface and operational problems were fixed.

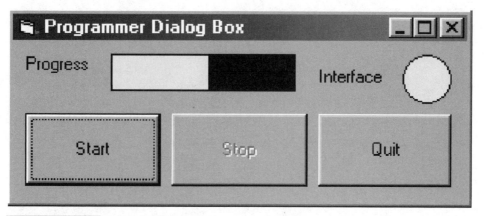

FIGURE 18-3   Hardware interface with user status.

I am reminded of the great luggage TV commercial of twenty years ago in which a suit-case was put into a gorrilla's cage and then thrown about to demonstrate its high quality. With all my software, I do the same thing; I give my product to a bunch of hairy, unkept knuckle draggers to find out which seams will burst.

HARDWARE

INTERFACING

A PC

TO USE

FOR EXPERIMENTS

CONTENTS AT A GLANCE

Hardware Requirements	**Reset Control**
Software Requirements	**Test Equipment Adapter**

When I was writing this book, I called the file used to store this chapter *ExPC*, which is actually quite ironic when you consider the use of this PC. I recommend that you find an old PC that you can design ISA cards or just play around with adding your own interfaces. The reason for suggesting that you use an old PC for this function is because damaging it and having to replace a 386 motherboard is a lot less painful than a 450-MHz Pentium III motherboard.

When I first created the circuits in this book, I tried them out on an old 80386 PC (Fig. 19-1) that I found in a used computer shop for $30.00 (with a $35 color monitor, a $15 ISA VGA card, a $10 keyboard, and a $10 diskette drive). To really impress you, note that these prices are in Canadian dollars.

Surprisingly enough, I did not damage the PC during the writing of this book, but using this system gave me piece of mind when I was plugging in my prototype board and not knowing whether it was wired correctly.

FIGURE 19-1   My experimental PC.

I bought my PC from a used computer store, the monitor from an appliance consignment store, and bits and pieces from an electronics surplus store. I'm lucky that I live in a large city and I was able to look around for the best bargains. If you aren't able to do this, I recommend that you look for used PCs in your local newspaper, put up a request at your supermarket, or try to "borrow" your Uncle Elmer's PC that he bought 10 years ago when he retired and decided it was just too hard to use. It isn't that hard to find a usable one and you can easily find a suitable PC over a weekend.

Hardware Requirements

The hardware requirements for this PC will probably seem quite lengthy and specific, but I have made them in order for you to work with the basic hardware and software that is presented in this book. They include:

- 386 SX processor running at 16 MHz
- PC/AT-style motherboard (Fig. 19-2)
- 1 MB of DRAM
- 20-MB hard drive
- 1.44-MB 3.5" diskette drive
- 256-KB VGA Driver Card
- At least one free ISA port
- RS-232 port
- Parallel port

- PC/AT enhanced keyboard (12 function keys)
- Color VGA display

You might be surprised that I specified a VGA adapter and color monitor. You should be able to pick up a used VGA color monitor for $50 (or less) without much looking around. I specify the VGA adapter because if you look for an MDA, CGA, or EGA adapter, you will have a monitor that is about 15 years old and is probably barely serviceable. Using a VGA adapter means that if you have any problems with the monitor, you can quickly and easily replace it (which I had to do a week before I sent in the book because I dropped a screw when the PC was powered on).

Just one bit of caution. When looking at used color VGA monitors, you will probably see a lot of IBM 8513 monitors available. These should be avoided because they had a design problem and a number of production lots could catch fire. IBM did have a replacement program for the affected lots, but there really is no way for you to know whether or not the monitor you are looking at was one of the problem ones and whether or not it was fixed.

Also note that I specify that a PC/AT-style motherboard. This is the most common format for older PCs; if you manage to damage it, a replacement can usually be picked up from a bin in a surplus store for $10 or less. When you buy a motherboard (or the whole PC to go with it), be sure that it will "beep" before you pay for it and take it out of the store. Most surplus stores will have power supplies or even used cases and keyboards that you can use to try the motherboard before buying it (and consider it "As is" as soon as you leave the store).

FIGURE 19-2   PC replacement motherboard installed in PC.

If you buy a "name brand" PC, notice that the motherboard might not be in the PC/AT format and if you have problems, you might not be able to replace it. The motherboard in Fig. 19-2 is my "spare" motherboard. If I were to damage the motherboard in the PC that I am using, I would simply swap it out for the one in the photograph.

On your motherboard, check to see how many ISA slots are available and be sure that any EISA slots do not take up all the available slots. In the PC I used for experiments, after the diskette controller, VGA, and serial/parallel cards were put in, I found that I only had one ISA slot left for experimentation. This wasn't a major problem in my case, but it could have been if I wanted to add more than one ISA card to the system.

I specified the 3.5" diskette drive for passing applications between the primary PC and the one used for experiments. Later, the book shows how the serial ports on two PCs can be used to transfer data quickly between them, but for this system, I recommend being sure you have a common diskette drive between your systems. The experimental PC that I bought only had a 1.2-MB 5.25" diskette drive, to which I added $10 refurbished 3.5" drive.

Chances are that you will assemble some of the different components to get a working PC. Although the information contained in this book could be considered enough for you to create your own PC from "scratch," I have not provided enough information to put together a PC from miscellaneous parts. There are some excellent books on this subject that are available in used book stores for 80386 PCs.

Software Requirements

The software required to test your hardware creations on the experimental PC is actually quite modest. I developed the software applications presented in this book on another PC and passing the compiled code over to the experimental PC using diskette or a serial cable.

The most basic software requirement is MS-DOS. I have the operating system loaded on a hard disk for faster booting and utility execution. You should install MS-DOS 5.0 (or later), although MS-DOS 3.3 will probably work acceptably. MS-DOS 3.3 really seems to be the first version of MS-DOS that implements the full Int 21h API functions required for modern PCs and applications.

Along with the hard file being formatted with MS-DOS, I set up a DOS subdirectory for utilities. This subdirectory should be entered into the Path statement of the PC's AUTOEXEC.BAT.

Other software that you should have loaded onto the hard disk includes an editor and debugger. These utilities are required to find the problems with your applications, both from a hardware and software perspective.

The editor should be an MS-DOS full-screen editor, ideally with the capability of handling individual bits in a file, rather than just full ASCII words. I have not been able to find an editor that I like that can handle the data in ASCII and the hex values. I typically have two editors; one well suited to editing ASCII data and one that can be used to change the individual bits and bytes of a file.

Being able to change bits and bytes might seem unnecessary when I have gone to great pains in the book to point out the advantages of only using straight ASCII files. You'll find problems that require the application code to be changed. In some cases, the easiest way of doing this is looking for a repeating bit pattern and changing it directly.

If you have loaded MS-DOS onto your hard file and loaded the utilities into a DOS sub-directory, you'll already have DEBUG.COM available for use. DEBUG.COM is accept-able for many types of debugging. Ideally you should have CodeView or a similar source-level debugger to make stepping through your application and finding the problem easier.

Over the years, I have collected a number of utilities that I use for MS-DOS application development. These include PKZIP, unerase utilities, file-attribute editors, etc. I normally put these applications with the editors in a DOSUTIL subdirectory. Like DOS, I add DO-SUTIL subdirectory to the AUTOEXEC.BAT file "PATH" statement as well.

You might have noticed that, for this PC, I have recommended neither using a Windows operating system or a mouse. The reason for avoiding Windows is that chances are your experimental PC will only have enough hard drive and memory space to be able to run Windows 3.1, which uses the 16-bit kernel. A PC running with the 16-bit kernel cannot be used for the applications presented in this book and all modern systems use the 32-bit Windows kernel.

Attempting to run Windows 95/98/NT on a simple system like this is probably not pos-sible. Even if it successfully loaded, it would run very slowly.

I also do not recommend using a mouse with the PC for many of the same reasons, fo-cusing on the resources (the serial port and memory) required to add a mouse to the PC. Ideally, most of the code development should be done on another PC, which allows you to easily keep the resources required on this PC to a minimum.

If you are just starting out with writing applications (especially ones that write to the MS-DOS file system), chances are that you're going to "trash" the hard drive. Keeping the amount of code that you have to load to a minimum (and keeping diskettes nearby) will re-ally be helpful when the inevitable happens. If this is the case, I find it best to reformat the hard file and just reload everything again.

For hardware development, you might end up writing two sets of software for the appli-cation. The first set will be used on the experimental PC and written just in MS-DOS. The second set will be the required Windows device drivers and applications. Although re-quiring a bit more work, creating the hardware interface for MS-DOS can be an advantage because of the ease in which interface code can be debugged (which is a lot easier than with a straight Windows application).

Reset Control

When selecting an experimental PC, I suggest looking for one with a reset switch on the front panel. The reset switch is usually connected to the PC's power supply and resets the "PwrGood" signal on the PC. This feature was very common in 80386 clones, so this fea-ture should not be hard to find.

If the PC does not have a built-in reset, you might want to look at building your own. To do this, you will have to cut the PwrGood line in the cable running from the PC's power

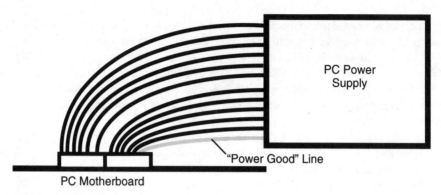

"Power Good" Line

PC Motherboard

FIGURE 19-3   **PC power connections.**

supply to the motherboard. The PwrGood line is normally on pin 1 of the connector (Fig. 19-3).

Once this line is cut, an SPDT switch can be wired into the line (Fig. 19-4) to hold the line inactive (low) and then allow it to be driven high by the PC's power supply. This will allow you to reset the PC's motherboard on command, which will (hopefully) get you out of trouble when your application locks up the PC without going through the hassle of powering down and powering back up again.

I realize that powering a PC down and then back up doesn't seem like a lot of effort or require a lot of time, but trust me when I say that having this type of switch will help out a lot.

In some PC motherboards, this switch will not work properly because of the bouncing of the PwrGood signal to the motherboard's reset circuitry. In this case, you will have to design a debounced PwrGood control. Ideally, the PwrGood should be inactive for at least one second.

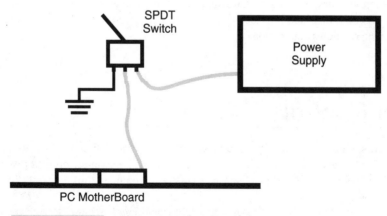

FIGURE 19-4   **"Power Good" reset circuit.**

Using PwrGood to reset the PC is superior to *Ctrl-Alt-Delete* ("the three-fingered salute") because the PC's reset hardware is cycled and the signal is passed along to the adapter cards in the system. This should reset all the hardware in the PC if it has been put into an invalid state.

If it doesn't, then you are going to have to lean over and cycle the *BRS (Big Red Switch)*, power down, and start all over.

Test Equipment Adapter

One day, a coworker complimented me for a couple of wires soldered onto a connector that I was using to power a logic probe while debugging an ISA adapter card that I had designed. I was really surprised by how much he liked the little tool. I first made one more than 10 years ago and have always used it (or one of the later versions) when I had to put a logic or oscilloscope probe into a PC (Fig. 19-5).

This tool simply consists of the mating male connector to a diskette drive power connector soldered to a red (V_{cc}) and black (ground) wires. The genesis for this adapter was when I had to 'scope a failing adapter card within a PC and had nowhere to put the probe's ground connector. In virtually all PCs, one or two spare disk-drive power-supply connectors can be used for this purpose.

When I wire the tool, I put on a relatively short, red, V_{cc} wire and a longer, black, ground wire. I use a pretty heavy-gauge wire (such as #14 stranded), not because I'm worried about handling a heavy current draw, but because they're fairly rigid and will survive multiple alligator-clip attachments.

When you don't have anything clipped to the wires and are leaving it inside of the PC, I suggest that you put on some insulated clips or home wiring "wire nuts" to eliminate the possibility of shorts within the PC. This is particularly important because most PC power supplies are capable of a 50- or 60-A output on the +5-V (V_{cc}) line. A V_{cc} wire swinging around inside the grounded cabinet is like an arc welder's electrode running around loose.

When I'm 'scoping, I've found the ground provided by this tool to be more than adequate for seeing the signals on ISA and PCI adapters. I would not think that this is true for high-speed motherboard signals (i.e., 100-MHz processor local bus signals), but this is really not required in a modern PC, unless you are debugging the motherboard. In this case, specialized oscilloscope and logic analyzer probes would be used.

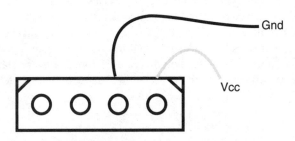

FIGURE 19-5   Test equipment adapter for the PC.

PRECISE

TIMING

IN THE PC

The holy grail of PC interfacing is understanding how to precisely time signals and control hardware down to the submillisecond level of granularity. Like "grasshopper's" attempts to snatch the pebble out of the blind master's hand, before you can really say that you understand how to interface hardware to the PC, you must be able to precisely time signals on the I/O ports and busses.

This chapter goes quite deep into the PC's operation and shows you why relying on instruction timing is unacceptable. Although you can rely on some hardware devices and software functions to provide constant timings across different PCs, this method might not be reliable across all of the different PCs with which your application will have to work. The information provided here is somewhat ironic because for highly precise timing for applications, I believe that you should create custom hardware (ideally, using crystal-driven counters), instead of using the tricks I will show in this chapter.

Real-Time Clock Timing

The *RTC* chip is the battery-backed-up 32.768-kHz driven chip that has been built into the PC's motherboard since the PC/AT. Time within one PC uses the Intel 8253/8254 timer chip that is run by the 1.193-MHz system clock. In different documentation, both devices are referred to as "real-time clocks".

A later section, presents the 8253/8254 timer chips as a tool for reasonably precise timing events for delays in the magnitude of seconds. This section concerns the RTC chip and its poor suitability for use as a subsecond timing device for PC-interface applications (it is totally incapable of providing submillisecond timing).

There are really two problems with using the RTC chip to provide a stable clock for interfacing applications. The first is that although some RTC chips will allow you to access the subsecond counter values, the Motorola MC146818 will not. In the MC146818, the 32.768-MHz clock is divided by 32,768, which gives an internal clock "tick" of once per second.

As well, the RTC BIOS APIs will read to the second, but do not provide any subsecond information.

The other problem is that the time registers are usually indirectly addressed (requiring writes to index registers in the device before read/write accesses can occur). This will add a certain amount of uncertainty to the length of time needed to set up and pass data quickly between the device and the PC.

Even when I want to time applications to the second (or longer), I use the 8253/8254 interrupt and timer information. This information can be read easily from the PC's system variable area (at segment 0x040) or be retrieved by using standard BIOS or MS-DOS APIs.

Bus Timing Strategies

Although monitoring the 8253/8254 is an acceptable way to provide a gross level of timing (at a granularity of 55 ms), it is not useful for providing an accurate method of submillisecond timing on the PC. To get finer resolution and more-accurate timing, reads and writes to the ISA (or another) bus are often timed and used as a method to provide more accuracy. This is possible, but it is a very inconsistent method to actually define an operation of a known period of time.

To show how this could be done, I created the PortTime application, which waits for an RTC clock interrupt (which causes the word at 0x040:0x06C to be incremented) and then counts how many times the data port of a printer port could be read from and written to in the 54.925 ms to the next clock interrupt.

```
/*  PortTime - Time the Reads/Writes to LPT

    This is a Quick and Dirty Program to check how fast an I/O Port can
    be accessed.

    Myke Predko
    Started: 98.11.11
```

```
            Updated: xx.xx.xx

                                                                    */

    //   Include Files
    #include (stdio.h)
    #include (dos.h)


    //   Defines - Located in "global.var"
    #define LPT1 0x0378            //  LPT1's Port Address
    #define LPT2 0x0278

    //   Subroutines


    //   Global Variables


    //   Mainline Code
    main(argc, argv, envp)
       int argc;
       char *argv[];
       char *envp[];
    {

    int       BaseAddr;
    long      Ctr = 0;            //   Counter Of the Number of I/Os
    unsigned CurCtr;             //   Current Clock Value
    unsigned far * ClkCtr;       //   Clock Counter

      if ( argc == 2 )           //   Port Specified?
        if ( strncmp( &argv[ 1 ], "1", 2 ) == 0 )
          BaseAddr = LPT1;       //   Set the Port Address
        else
          BaseAddr = LPT2;
      else
        BaseAddr = LPT1;         //   Default to LPT1

      (long) ClkCtr = 0x00040006C;  //  Get the Pointer to the Clock

      CurCtr = *ClkCtr;          //   Wait for an RTC Interrupt
      while ( CurCtr == *ClkCtr );

      CurCtr++;                  //   Increment

      while ( CurCtr == *ClkCtr ) {
        Ctr++;                   //   Count Number of I/Os in 55 msec
        outp( BaseAddr, inp( BaseAddr ));
      }  // End while

      printf( "%lu Loops in 55 msec\n", Ctr );

    }  // End PortTime
```

After compiling this application, I ran it on a number of different PCs in a different number of configurations eight times to see what kind of results I would get. To try and understand what happened most efficiently, I found the mean, as well as the standard deviation, both as an absolute value (*S/D*), as well as a percentage (*%S/D*) of the mean. The program was run from the MS-DOS Prompt dialog box in Windows (if available) and from the MS-DOS command line.

Some PCs have no hardware for LPT2, but I checked the address anyway. If the port wasn't present, I marked it as *LPT2(No H/W)*. For Windows 95 and Windows 98 PCs, I

3

did not mark the MS-DOS version because it is largely indeterminate when *Shutdown - MS-DOS* is selected. *D/T* is an abbreviation for *desktop*, just as *L/T* is for *Laptop*.

```
PC                O/S            LPT Port         Mean        S/D      %S/D
16 MHz '386 D/T   MS-DOS 5.00    LPT1             2910        0.35     0.012%
                                 LPT2(No H/W)     2910        0.35     0.012%
90 MHz '486 L/T   Windows 3.11   LPT1            14755        4526     30.6%
                                 LPT2(No H/W)    10711        2904     27.1%
                  MS-DOS 5.00    LPT1             8596        1202     14.0%
                                 LPT2(No H/W)     8094        1235     15.3%
150 MHz Pen. D/T  Windows/95     LPT1            17309         326      1.9%
                                 LPT2(No H/W)     7903        3929     49.7%
                  MS-DOS LPT1                    18863          25      0.1%
                                 LPT2(No H/W)    18672        0.46      0.0%
166 MHz Pen. L/T  Windows/95     LPT1            45525         946      2.1%
                                 LPT2(No H/W)    47250         514      1.1%
                  MS-DOS LPT1                    49582        0.35      0.0%
                                 LPT2(No H/W)    49583        1.77      0.0%
300 MHz PII D/T   Windows/98     LPT1            13899         515      3.7%
                                 LPT2           14085         233      1.7%
                  MS-DOS         LPT1            14562        0.35      0.0%
                                 LPT2           14562           0      0.0%
```

Notice a few interesting things from this listing. For the most part, executing from generic DOS allowed more reads/writes than executing from Windows. This is expected because Windows adds a level of complexity over MS-DOS and could have some task switching (although I really didn't see any evidence of that in running this application). I was expecting accesses to LPT2 to be slower if there wasn't any hardware in the PC to support it. This was largely confirmed by this experiment.

It is important to see that the '386 PC has very consistent results for both present and missing hardware. That is because everything is timed to the ISA port data rates and will provide a constant speed for all accesses on the bus (I/O addresses 0x0100 to 0x03FF).

The number of unexpected results in many ways validated what I want to say in this section: the I/O Port reads and writes should not be used to provide a time base for an application. You might be surprised to see that the faster printer I/O is not the fastest processor (not by a long shot). To a certain extent, this was an expected result. I knew that as PCs have gotten more complex, with ASICs taking up more of the I/O functions of the PC, that I/O timings would be sporadic at best. The ASICs within laptops are connected to the processor bus, rather than the PCI/ISA busses, which means that accesses execute much more quickly and, in their BIOS routines, delays are built in to match expected timings.

This is confirmed by comparing the results of the two laptops with the two desktop PCs. It is interesting (for me) to see that the laptops both performed in the same neighborhood and much faster than the Pentium desktops.

The biggest problem with this method of timing events in the PC (confirmed by this experiment) was the variability in the I/O reads and writes. Although, for the most part, most results have very little variability, some results have incredibly large variability (as noted by the standard deviation of the samples). The most surprising for me was the standard deviation of almost 50 percent of the mean for the 150-MHz Pentium desktop accessing a non-existent LPT2.

This result was completely unexpected. In fact, I was expecting the largest variability to be present in the laptops, because of the I/O ASIC being connected to the processor's bus and not through the standard PCI/ISA interfaces. The 300-MHz Pentium II desktop shows very minimal deviation over the samples and the 90-MHz '486 laptop's large variability seems to bear out this theory.

The conclusion that I get when I see these results are; it is impossible to create a general rule for using an I/O port for doing precise timing in the PC. If you were going to run the application on a single PC that you could characterize, using something like PortTime and confirm that the variability of I/O accesses was minimal (less than 5% for the standard deviation as a percentage of the mean), then I would say that you could accomplish it successfully.

But I would never recommend it. More than 10 years ago, I replaced a 30-year old computer on a piece of test equipment using an 80286 PC. Rather than create a "proper" ISA interface, I decided to be clever and use the parallel port. The advantage was that I didn't have to create an ISA card for the interface. As you have probably guessed, a couple of years ago, the PC died and when a new Pentium one was slated to replace it, the interface software would no longer work. I spent almost a month recreating 10-year-old code (and the compiler and linker to process the source), getting it working again.

The lesson for this was to not depend on I/O port timings to get constant timings out of the PC.

As I was writing this book, I created the "El Cheapo" PICMicro Programmer. Programming the PICMicro devices requires a minimum time delay for loading data and waiting for the programming operation to complete. For this device, which is connected to the PC's parallel port, I added an RC network that could be charged/discharged by the parallel port's control. By doing this, I was able to time the I/O quite effectively, easily and cheaply. For the "El Cheapo" design, look at my web page.

Using the Timer for Microsecond Precision

The most precise way I've found to time signals on a PC is to use the built-in timer to monitor how long the application has been running. This timer is driven by a 1.19-MHz clock and is constant within all versions of the PC. Neither the 1.19-MHz timer frequency (which is 14.31818 MHz divided by 12) nor the timer's operation changes with continual improvement in processors and other hardware put into PCs. However, using the timer can have some limitations.

As I've noted earlier in the book, in the PC, three 16-bit timers are built into the motherboard's 8253/8254 timer chip. Timer 0 is a system timer used to track the current time since the PC was first booted. Timer 1 is used for DRAM refresh and must never be accessed in case the refresh operation of the memory is inadvertently affected. The last timer, Timer 2, is normally used for the simple speaker on the motherboard and is my primary choice for an application timer.

I use Timer 2 for two reasons. First, it is not crucial to the operation of any operating system code or applications within the PC. The second is, that I can start and restart it at my discretion. These reasons make it quite easy to implement a reasonably precise timer in the PC.

If you look in the Delay subdirectory of the CD-ROM, you will find the DELAY.ASM file, which carries out a delay by executing:

```
Temp = inp( 061h );                 //  Save the Timer Gate Value

outp( 0x043, 0x0B6 );               //  Set up Timer 2 as a 16 Bit Binary
                                    //   Timer
outp( 0x042, 0 );                   //  Reset the timer
outp( 0x042, 0 );

outp( 0x061, Temp | 1 );            //  Enable the Timer

while ((( inp( 0x042 ) * 256 ) + inp( 0x042 )) < Dlay );
                                    //  Wait for the Specified "Dlay"
outp( 0x061, Temp );                //  Turn Off the Timer Clock
```

This code sets up Timer 2 as a 16-bit counter driven by the 1.19-MHz clock. The timer is then reset and allowed to run until it reaches the delay value. The delay value is calculated using the formula:

$$Dlay = Required\ delay/0.838\ ns$$

In Delay_C.C, you'll see how I output my attempt to get a 10-μs active clock signal:

```
while ( GetKeyStat() != 0  ) {

  CLI();                            //  Disable Interrupts

  StrobeActive();                   //  Output the Active Request

  Dlay();                           //  Call the 10 usec Delay Routine

  StrobeInActive();

  STI();                            //  Turn Interrupts On Again

  }
GetKey();
```

This code disables interrupts while the clock is active to provide the most accurate output clock possible. When I looked at it on an oscilloscope, I saw the output waveform shown in Fig. 20-1.

You can see that the actual pulse output is about twice the expected delay (it's about 20 μs when a *Delay* value of 10 or 8.4 μs was specified). The extra delay is caused by two factors. The first is the delay of the instructions built in the PC that I was using.

The second aspect of the delay is the operation of Windows that is operating on the PC. When I ran this utility for Fig. 20-1, I ran it on my Windows 98 machine from the MS-DOS prompt and the disabling of the interrupts is not pervasive throughout the PC. This program runs with a 10- to 12-μs pulse in a "true" MS-DOS environment. To get an absolutely accurate delay, you will have to experiment with different values for a particular PC. For a 10-μs delay, as I've shown here, this actual value could be as much as 200-percent longer than the calculated and expected value. For larger delays, the actual difference will approach zero. This is why I usually consider this method of delaying to be submillisecond accurate.

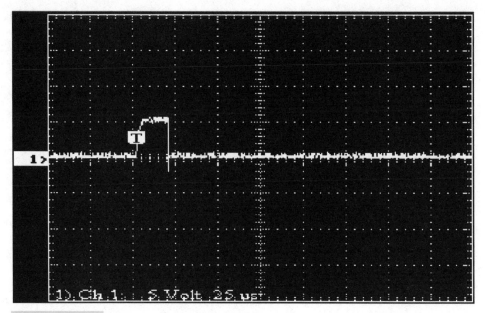

FIGURE 20-1 10 μsec timing delay.

Also, when this program runs in a Windows PC, the pulse also stays active for up to 250 μs periodically. This occurs when the Dlay subroutine is interrupted by the 55-ms timer within the PC. The *cli* instructions do not disable system interrupts when the MS-DOS prompt is active. For applications that run within a Windows PC from the MS-DOS prompt, you should design your application to work with variable length pulses because it will be almost impossible to precisely time them for every cycle.

When interfacing to hardware, I recommend using this code as a minimum pulse to load or initiate adapter hardware. Doing multiple signals with this method can cause problems again because of excess delay with interrupts disabled.

I have also included the misnamed file, DELAY_2, which shows how the Dlay subroutine can be implemented using Timer 0. In C code, it could be blocked out as:

```
Dlay = ( inp( 0x040 ) * 256 ) + inp( 0x040 ) + Dlay;
if ( Dlay > 0x0FFFA )
Dlay = 1;
while ((( inp( 0x040 ) * 256 ) + inp( 0x040 )) < Dlay );
```

Which is simpler, requires fewer overhead I/O accesses (i.e., to set up Timer 2), but has one major potential problem. The problem occurs if the timer plus the delay value is very close to the overflow value of the timer. From 0x0FFFF, the overflow is zero, which cannot have an integer compared to be less than it. This means that the delay can never be precisely timed—even in an MS-DOS system.

With the results presented here, I have to conclude that microsecond-precise delays are impossible for the "standard" PC hardware. If absolutely precise timings are required, then you will have to design your hardware application to generate the delays on board. Hopefully, you will read this conclusion here, rather than have to come up with it on your own, trying to get a hardware interface to work.

THE KEYBOARD

AND

MOUSE PORTS

The PC's keyboard and mouse ports operate with a synchronous serial data protocol that was first introduced with the original IBM PC. This protocol allows data to be sent from the keyboard in such a way that multiple-pressed keys can be recognized within the PC without any key presses being lost. The standard was enhanced with the PC/AT as a bidirectional communication method. Three years later, when the PS/2 was introduced, the mouse interface also used the keyboard's protocol, freeing up a serial port or ISA slot, which was used for the mouse interface. The keyboard protocol used in the PC was so successful that virtually all system manufacturers used it for all its PC, terminal, workstation and server product lines that have been developed since 1981.

A good measure of this protocol is the industry that has sprung up for creating compatible keyboards, mice (or other pointing devices), and peripherals that enhance the operation of the PC. These peripherals are usually barcode scanners or magnetic-strip readers, and the data is passed to the PC as if it were coming from the keyboard.

The operation of these peripherals brings up an important point; the keyboard and mouse interface ports have a specific function in the PC to provide keyboard and mouse data into the PC. Nothing more. They should not be used for any other functions. I have seen some projects in the past that use the keyboard as a way to interface with outside devices. Using the keyboard port in this manner should be discouraged.

It is possible to piggy back hardware onto the keyboard port and send instructions between the PC and keyboard, but it is quite impossible to get this same function in Windows, unless you would be willing to rewrite the keyboard interface.

This chapter does not describe how to design your own keyboard or mouse. There are a few reasons. The first is, the design is very device and hardware specific. Creating new functions for the keyboard and mouse ports will require a large software effort to change the BIOS and operating system access to these ports. Also, I feel that looking at keyboard and mouse design is really outside the realm of this book. As well, I can't help but think that with all of the different device interfaces available, something must meet your requirements so that you don't have to design something.

I do think it's appropriate to discuss the interface so that if you are designing a device for the handicapped or an auxiliary data reader (such as a bar-code scanner), you will have the information required to implement the keyboard port adapter successfully.

Keyboard Synchronous Protocol

The bidirectional keyboard protocol should not present any surprises if you've worked with I2C, Microwire, or other synchronous data protocols. The PC's keyboard communication protocol is set up to pass data between the PC and keyboard with auxiliary devices in parallel, which, in turn, can monitor and pass data with the other devices.

The keyboard connector (facing out) is shown in Fig. 21-1 with data passed via the clock and data lines. The port can usually supply up to 100 mA over and above the keyboard requirements. The power (+5 Vdc) might not be fused, so any hardware put on the port must not draw excessive current to prevent damage to the PC's motherboard and power supply.

Data from the keyboard looks that shown in Fig. 21-2. The parity bit is an odd number (eight data bits plus the parity). The data line should not change for at least 5 usecs from the change of the clock line. The clock line should be high or low for at least 30 usecs (with 40 usecs being typical).

Data sent from the system unit is similar, but with the clock inverted. The data changes while the clock is low and is latched in when the clock goes high (Fig. 21-3).

When data is sent from the keyboard, the clock is pulled low and then data is sent with the keyboard accepting data when the clock is pulsed high. The bit timings are the same as data from the keyboard.

These two protocols are used to allow a device wired in parallel to monitor the communication to and from the PC.

Appendix D lists the "scan" codes from the keyboard to the PC. The PC itself has a number of commands that it can send to the keyboard:

CODE	FUNCTION
0x0ED	Set indicator LEDs. The next character out is the LED status
0x0EE	Echo - Keyboard returns 0x0EE
0x0EF-0x0F2	Ignored by the keyboard
0x0F3	Set Typematic rate, next character is the rate
0x0F4	Enable key scanning
0x0F5	Set to default (no LEDs on, default Typematic rate) and disable key scanning
0x0F6	Set to default (no LEDs on, default Typematic rate) and enable key scanning
0x0F7-0x0FD	Ignored by the keyboard
0x0FE	Request keyboard to resend the last character
0x0FF	Reset the keyboard's microcontroller

3

HARDWARE INTERFACING

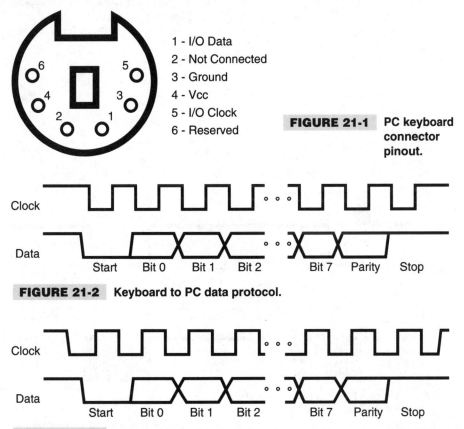

1 - I/O Data
2 - Not Connected
3 - Ground
4 - Vcc
5 - I/O Clock
6 - Reserved

FIGURE 21-1   PC keyboard connector pinout.

Clock

Data

Start   Bit 0   Bit 1   Bit 2   Bit 7   Parity   Stop

FIGURE 21-2   Keyboard to PC data protocol.

Clock

Data

Start   Bit 0   Bit 1   Bit 2   Bit 7   Parity   Stop

FIGURE 21-3   PC to keyboard data protocol.

In all of these cases (except for the Ignore and Echo commands), the keyboard sends back the Acknowledge character, 0x0FA.

The actual signals used to send a keystroke from the keyboard into the PC looks like Fig. 21-4. To get these pictures, I used a keyboard extender and spliced into the middle of it. Using a DMM, I found the Ground, Data, and Clock lines of the port. When doing this, notice that the diagram presented in Chapter 2 is from the PC motherboard; the actual pins will have to be transposed when beeping out the cable. I only mention this because I forgot to do this and I spent five minutes scratching my head until I figured out what I did wrong.

If you create a cable like this, please be careful stripping off the cable insulation, as well as the insulation on each wire. Care must be taken in how you allow the cable to rest. The +5-V line on this port might be fused, which will prevent you from having to buy a new power supply or motherboard for your PC, but it is still a pain to replace if you do blow it. If you probe the lines, I highly suggest that you only do it on an experimental PC that will not cause major problems if you short something.

For each byte sent, a 0x0F0 character is sent first to notify the PC that the character is coming, followed by the actual keyboard scan code. Figure 21-5 shows an expanded oscilloscope picture of the actual character.

The key that I pressed (I can't say that I sent a character) is labeled with *E* and sends a scan code of 0x012. If you look at the set bits in Fig. 21-5, you will see that if you check the bits starting after a 0 start bit, 0x012 is indeed sent to the PC. The last bit sent is a parity bit.

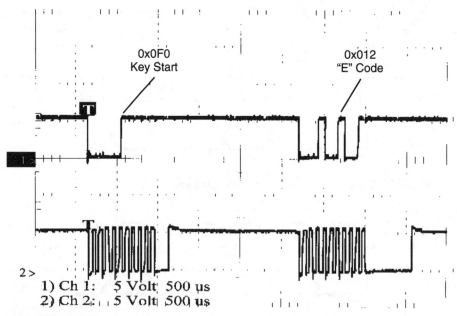

FIGURE 21-4 Keyboard sending "E" to the PC.

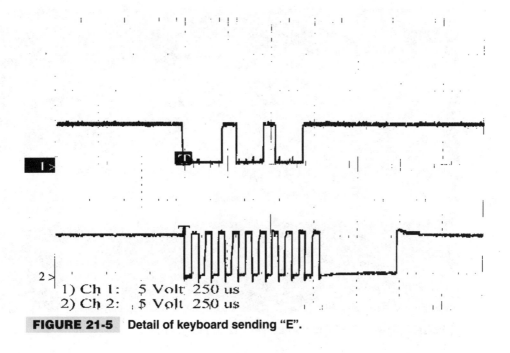

FIGURE 21-5   **Detail of keyboard sending "E".**

Looking at the actual oscilloscope pictures in Figs. 21-4 and 21-5, you'll see the actual timing. For the keyboard that I have scoped, which is a "Cirque Wave Keyboard 2," the clock high and low are each roughly 30 usecs in duration.

The long clock "low " period at the end of the packet is used to give the PC time to process the incoming data byte before another keyboard device is allowed to transmit on the bus.

Keyboard Port Software Interfaces

Appendix D lists the scan codes that are returned from the keyboard. Appendix H lists the keyboard BIOS-interrupt APIs; the previous chapters introduce how to use the keyboard port to get characters and process them in the application. This chapter regards the practical aspects of using the keyboard interfaces, complete with a few tips.

When the PC/AT first came out, it used a copy of the original IBM 84 keyboard. This keyboard was quite compact, with 10 function keys along the left side of the QWERTY keys and a single numeric keypad/cursor control to its right. This keyboard was superseded in 1985 with the more-familiar layout of the cursor keys between the QWERTY keys and a separate numeric keypad on the right side along, with 12 (not the original 10) function keys across the top. To maintain compatibility with this original keyboard, IBM did not change the basic top (Fig. 21-6). BIOS APIs; instead, they added APIs (AH function values) for the newer keyboards.

FIGURE 21-6 PC/AT keyboard with 12 function keys.

The most important thing to remember about using the keyboard BIOS APIs is to use the "extended" APIs instead of the basic APIs. The extended APIs will give you full access to the PC's keyboard, including *F11* and *F12* and the numeric keypad and cursor-control keys of the advanced PC/AT keyboard.

I do not recommend accessing any APIs other than the Read Keyboard Buffer, Check Keyboard Buffer Status, and Read Keyboard Shift Status. Setting the Typematic rate or sending characters to the keyboard (especially in Windows) could adversely affect how the PC operates when the application has finished. Changes to the keyboard's functionality should only be made through the operating system interfaces so the operating system does not receive keyboard data unexpectedly and run erratically.

When keystrokes are received, two bytes are returned. The most-significant byte is the scan code (as can be found in Appendix D) with the least-significant byte being the ASCII code of the key pressed. For most applications, just the least-significant byte can be used and the scan code can be discarded.

In the PC, non-ASCII keys are represented by either a 0x000 or 0x0E0 character in the ASCII portion of the two-byte scan and ASCII code return. If you receive one of these characters after issuing a keyboard read, then the actual key read can be decoded by looking at the table in Appendix D. This feature makes it very easy to process keystrokes in an application.

For example, to simply process a keystroke in C, the following switch code could be used:

```
switch(( KeySave = KEYREAD()) & 0xOFF ) { // Process the Key
  case 0x000:                              // Special Function Keys
  case 0x0E0:
    KeySave = ( KeySave > > 8 ) & 0xOFF;   // process the Scan Code
   :
  break;
  case 0x00D:                              // Handle "Enter"
   :
  break;
   :                                       // Handle Other Special Keys
  default:                                 // Other, Unneeded Keys
   :
} // endswitch
```

The PC keyboard is a marvelous invention that is useful for much more than just operating as a keyboard. Each key press sends at least two different packets of information. The first is the "Make" code, which is repeated at the Typematic rate while the key is pressed. The second is the "Break" code, which is sent when the key is released.

In the "true" IBM design, when two keys are pressed and one is released, the keyboard will continue to send Make codes from the last pressed key until one is released. This can be of particular advantage in games or applications where the keyboard is used for device control. But, to take advantage of it, your application will have to take over the keyboard BIOS functions and redirect the BIOS Interrupt handler vector. This is not very difficult to do, but you will have to save the original vector to the keyboard interrupt handler and restore it when you are returning to MS-DOS.

If your application is going to take over the handling of keyboard functions, then it will have to be able to accept the scan codes from the keyboard. These scan codes are identical to what comes from the keyboard BIOS functions as the high byte of the returned two-byte value. Your routines could either convert these scan codes to ASCII codes or use them "raw" in the application.

A user-defined keyboard interrupt handler would simply be:

```
Int KeyInt()
{

  Buffer = KeyControl();       // Read the Character Coming in
                               //   and Save it
  Int_Cntl( EOI );             // Reset the Interrupt Controller

} // End KeyInt - Return from the Interrupt Handler
```

With *Buffer* being either a variable (or array) for saving keystrokes or a function that processes the incoming Make and Break codes. An example of the function could be an array of bits that is set when specific Make codes are received and reset when a Break code is received. The mainline code could then poll these bits to see which keys are currently being pressed.

Taking over the keyboard interrupt vector is not something that I would recommend for an application that runs under Windows (or even MS-DOS). Instead, link into the keyboard interrupt and process the incoming data after the system has processed it.

Keyboard Controller

The interface to the keyboard/mouse in the PC/AT (and later PCs) is an 8042 microcontroller that provides the I/O interface to the keyboard (and just receives) data from the mouse. Along with the keyboard interface, the 8042 provides a keyboard lock up (with password) interface and control over address bit 20 of the PC's processor to prevent differences between the 8088 and 80286 in some addressing situations.

The 8042 can be accessed at I/O address 0x060 and 0x064. Port 0x060 is the data port. When a byte has been received from either the keyboard or mouse (auxiliary) port requests an interrupt of the PC's processor. When this byte is read, the most-recent byte received is output and, if set, the keyboard interrupt line is reset.

Data written to address 0x060 is sent to the keyboard unless the 8042 has a previous command sent to it, which requires a follow-up data byte.

Port 0x064 is the command/status port which when read will return the current status of the 8042 and the keyboard/mouse hardware. The bits are defined as:

BIT	FUNCTION
7	Parity - Set if received character parity is invalid
6	Timeout - If not all the bits of a packet were received
5	Auxiliary Device Buffer Full - Set to indicate a byte had been received from the mouse/pointing device port
4	Password - Bit is set if the Password function of the 8042 is enabled
3	Set if port 0x060 is expecting another command byte
2	Set when Bit 2 of the system flag byte is written. Reset on power up
1	Input Buffer Full - Waiting for the PC to read back the keyboard/mouse data ports
0	Output Buffer Full - Waiting for the keyboard to accept data from the PC

To change the operation of the 8042, a byte is written to it via I/O address 0x064:

```
Command              Function
0x020-0x02F          Read Controller RAM. Next read at 0x060 will return
                     Byte at the specified internal buffer address (0x000
                     to 0x00F)
0x060-0x06F          Write to Control RAM. Next Byte written to 0x060
                     will be written at the specified internal buffer
                     address (0x000 to 0x00F)
```

```
0x0A4                    Test Password Installed. If installed, Read of 0x064
                         will return 0x0FA. Read of 0x064 will return 0x0F1
                         if not installed
0x0A6                    Enable Password
0x0A8                    Enable Mouse Port
0x0A9                    Test Auxiliary Device (Mouse) interface. Checks to
                         see if any of the mouse lines are "stuck". 0x000 is
                         returned on a Read of 0x060 if no lines are stuck
                         high or low
0x0AA                    Run 8042 Self-Test. 0x055 is read from 0x060 if 8042
                         is okay
0x0AB                    Keyboard Interface Test. Checks to see if any of the
                         keyboard lines are "stuck". 0x000 is returned on a
                         Read of 0x060 if no lines are stuck high or low
0x0AD                    Disable Keyboard Interface
0x0AE                    Enable Keyboard Interface
0x0C0                    Read input port - 0x060 will have the value read.
                         Only to be used when the buffer doesn't have any
                         waiting keys
0x0D2                    Write output port - Next byte written to 0x060 will
                         be available for read back from 0x060
```

When the keyboard interface is enabled, then interrupt requests (int 009h) are automatically enabled when data is received from the keyboard. The keyboard interrupt handler is part of BIOS and should never be relocated. Only very rarely should it be shared with other handlers. The only time sharing the interrupt should be used is in applications that cannot poll the keyboard status.

If you look at your PC's motherboard, you probably won't see a chip labeled *8042*. In most modern PCs, the chip's functions are located within the super I/O chip as a macro that emulates the 8042 hardware with the keyboard firmware installed.

Sharing the Keyboard Port

The best way to add a device to the PC's keyboard port is by connecting it in parallel to the keyboard. Providing the parallel interface will allow you to pass data to the PC without having to buffer keystrokes off the PC instructions (Fig. 21-7).

When connecting a device to the keyboard port, it is important to remember that the keyboard port's bus is open collector, which means that your device can only pull down the clock and data lines. A "high" voltage cannot be driven onto the keyboard connector.

To send data to the PC, the device must simply send keyboard scan codes in the same format as the keyboard. While the device is operating, it must monitor the traffic between the PC and keyboard and wait to send data to the PC until the currently transmitting "packet" has completed.

This is relatively easy. Problems can occur when your device begins to transmit a scan code and either the keyboard or PC transmitting a byte at the same time. Without some kind of "arbitration", the data will become garbled and both of the packets lost. The chances of this happening are quite remote, but if data got garbled, the PC might stop working correctly or wrong data could be processed.

This "garbling" occurs when two devices are driving the bus low at different times within the "packets." To avoid this problem, your device should stop transmitting when

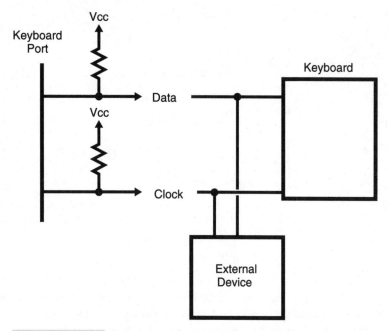

FIGURE 21-7   Sharing a keyboard with another device.

unexpected data shows up on the line. In Fig. 21-8, Device 1 should have stopped after the second bit because, while it is attempting to transmit a *1*, a *0* is actually being driven onto the line. After stopping transmitting because of another device forcing unwanted *0*s on the line, the device should wait a few milliseconds before attempting to transmit again.

Another way to detect when another device is transmitting at the same time as the current device is to check to see if the clock is being held low at unexpected times.

To send scan codes and monitor the keyboard signals, I would recommend the circuit shown in Fig. 21-9.

FIGURE 21-8   Waveform for shared keyboard devices.

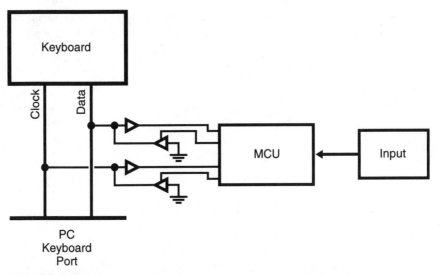

FIGURE 21-9 Actual circuit for shared keyboard devices.

In this circuit, a microcontroller is used to control the input device and send data by pulling down the clock and data lines. These lines are also monitored to give you an opportunity to stop the scan-code transmission if a miscompare, as described, occurs between what's going out from the microcontroller and what's actually on the bus.

This method of collision detection is widely used in simple microcontroller networks (such as I2C or CAN). In these protocols, often the devices try to synchronize their clocks to avoid problems with the data passing. I don't consider this necessary for the keyboard port, and not synchronizing clocks gives you another opportunity to discover that another device is transmitting at the same time.

The Mouse Port Interface

The mouse port itself uses an identical data protocol as that of the keyboard. The big difference between the two is that the PC does not drive data back to the mouse. The mouse information can be passed to the PC one of two ways. When the mouse was first provided to the PC, it used a serial port and typically transmitted three data bytes at 9600 bps. The mouse interface (also known as the *pointing device interface*) is unidirectional; only sends data to the PC, but it cannot receive data as the keyboard does.

The PS/2-style mouse uses the same connectors and protocol as the keyboard port. When power is applied to the mouse's microcontroller, an ASCII *M* is sent to the PC to indicate that the device on this port is a mouse. The PS/2-style mouse was first introduced by IBM with the PS/2 computer in 1987. Most modern PCs use the PS/2-style mouse, which is the focus of this section.

The PS/2-style mouse uses the keyboard port with a single-bit asynchronous data protocol, which consists of three types sending serially to the PC every 50 ms or so:

```
Byte Number        Function/Value
1                  Start of Data
                   Bit 7 - 0
                   Bit 6 - 1
                   Bit 5 - Set if the "left button" is pressed
                   Bit 4 - Set if the "right button" is pressed
                   Bit 3 - Bit 6 of the "Delta Y"
                   Bit 2 - Bit 7 of the "Delta Y"
                   Bit 1 - Bit 6 of the "Delta X"
                   Bit 0 - Bit 7 of the "Delta X"
2                  "Delta X" Position
                   Bit 7 - 0
                   Bit 6 - 0
                   Bit 5 - 0 - Bits 5 - 0 of "Delta X"
3                  "Delta Y" Position
                   Bit 7 - 0
                   Bit 6 - 0
                   Bit 5 - 0 - Bits 5 - 0 of "Delta Y"
```

The three bytes can be seen in Fig. 21-10. Notice that a delay of roughly 200 usecs occurs between each byte transmission; at the end of each byte, the clock "dead zone" is active to allow the PC to process the incoming byte.

Figure 21-11 shows what the three bytes would look like if the left button is pressed and the position is not changed. Figure 21-12 shows how the waveform changes for a position change with the Y delta position change being passed to the PC.

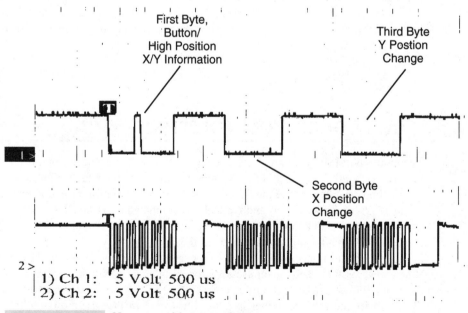

FIGURE 21-10 Mouse position waveforms.

3
HARDWARE INTERFACING

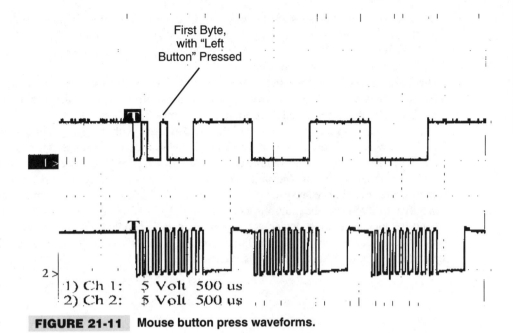

First Byte,
with "Left
Button" Pressed

1) Ch 1:   5 Volt 500 us
2) Ch 2:   5 Volt 500 us

FIGURE 21-11   Mouse button press waveforms.

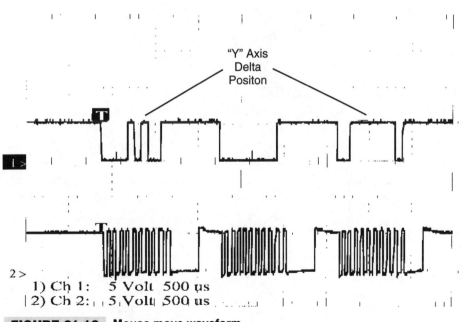

"Y" Axis
Delta
Positon

1) Ch 1:   5 Volt 500 us
2) Ch 2:   5 Volt 500 us

FIGURE 21-12   Mouse move waveform.

Delta X and Delta Y values are the position differences of the mouse/pointing device since the last time the three bytes were sent (just less than 50 ms before). These deltas are used by the mouse BIOS software to calculate the current position of the mouse on the screen, based on the previous position.

The 20 times-per-second position update (from the 50-ms interval between bytes) is a reasonable update rate, which allows the user to move the mouse on the display very smoothly without any perceived discontinuities or jumps in motion.

While writing this section, I discovered that the keyboard with integral pointing device (the Cirque Wave Keyboard 2), from which I took the oscilloscope pictures, does not send these three bytes every 50 ms as I noted previously. Instead, the three bytes are only sent when there is something to transmit. This is a more-efficient way to implement the pointer-device function because the PC is not continually interrupted with information that basically tells it to leave the mouse where it is.

How the mouse/pointing device actually sends data is handled within the operating-system/mouse device drivers. The Int 33h mouse BIOS and OS APIs do not make any differentiation as far as the application is concerned.

PRACTICAL
KEYBOARD
INTERFACING

As indicated in the previous chapter, the keyboard and mouse ports should only be used to replicate the functions provided by standard keyboards and mice. These ports should not be used to provide any other arbitrary functions or interfaces to the PC. This limits any designs on the keyboard and mouse ports, but this limitation is good because it will allow you to develop new and innovative ways to receive user control to the PC.

When you design your application, always use the +5-V power supply, which is available on the ports. This will simplify your design and make wiring interfaces much easier and convenient.

Keyboard Monitor

I feel like I've described a lot about understanding how the keyboard port works in this book and how external devices are connected to it. For a better idea how the interface works, I created a simple monitor for the keyboard port, in which I have monitored the performance of both the keyboard, as well as the mouse. The actual results are interesting and I gained some new insights about how the PC's keyboard works.

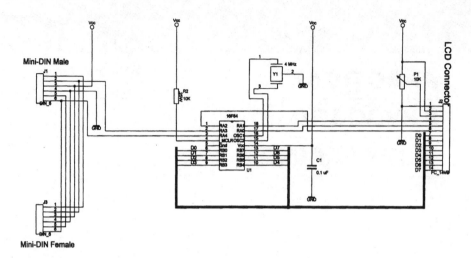

FIGURE 22-1   Keyboard minor schematic.

The circuit (Fig. 22-1) is based on the joystick communications adapter (i.e., I used the circuit after I was finished with it). If you already have one available, it can be made in less than an hour. I used the keyboard extender cord that I modified in the previous chapter to look at the keyboard signals as the interface. Despite this, I found that it took all of my concentration to wire the circuit because of the complexity of the point-to-point wiring that I used for the joystick adapter.

When you are doing this wiring, be careful. First, be sure that none of the wiring shorts together. When I created the joystick communicator, I designed it to work on a Radio Shack dual general-purpose PC board (#276-148A) and left some space on one side to accommodate both the 15-pin D-shell joystick connector and pushing in the exposed connections of the keyboard extender cable. This actually worked out quite well (although it has some pretty fiddly soldering) to keep the bare conductors from touching each other. I left the Case Ground line of the extender available to clip oscilloscope probes to, but as it turned out, this function wasn't necessary. After soldering the connectors, I tied the insulated keyboard-extender cables to the card with wire-wrap wire to provide some measure of strain relief.

Secondly, notice which conductor is which in the cable when you wire up the circuit. In keeping with the convention that I established in the previous chapter (where I labeled everything from male keyboard connector), I wired the various connections to the mirror-image values in the circuit.

I do not recommend building this circuit on a "solderless" prototype board or with wire wrapping, simply because of the danger of lines becoming shorted or pulling loose. Soldering will take a few extra minutes, but it is worth it in terms of circuit reliability (and avoiding the opportunity of blowing up your PC's motherboard or power supply).

This application is a PICMicro-based interface and I followed a multitiered development effort to first ensure that I could display information on the LCD, followed by tracking information from the keyboard, and then data from both the keyboard and the PC itself.

To read data from the keyboard, I used the following algorithm:

```
KeyboardRead()                        //  Read the outgoing Keyboard Byte
{

int  Count;                           //  Delay 9 Bits
char ReadByte;                        //  Data Byte Read

  while ( Data == 1 );                //  Wait for the Clock to Go High

  for ( Count = 0; Count < 9; Count++ ) { //  Read through the Next
                                      //   Nine Characters
    while ( Clock == 1 );             //  Wait for the Clock to Strobe

    ReadByte = ( ReadByte >> 1 ) + ( Data << 7 );
                                      //  Store in the Byte
    while ( Clock == 0 );             //  Wait for Strobe to Go Low

  }

  while ( Clock == 1 );               //  Skip Over Parity
  while ( Clock == 0 );

  while ( Clock == 1 );               //  Wait for the Stop Bit

  Output( "k" );                      //  Indicate the Keyboard
  OutputHex( ReadByte );              //  Output the Data Byte in Hex

} // KeyboardRead
```

The read serial data byte code is used quite a bit in microcontrollers. Although this application is a bit unique, sample code should be easy for you to find for other microcontrollers.

The actual data is sent to the LCD screen as first the source ("k"eyboard or "P"C), followed by a two-character ASCII value. In the code, I used worst-case timing delays for the data to be accepted within the LCD, which was probably a mistake. Instead, I should have polled the Busy bit of the LCD and used it to determine when data could be sent. This wasn't a problem with the keyboard, but it was when connecting the keyboard monitor to the mouse port.

The actual application software development was very straightforward and I didn't experience any problems. Surprises did occur in the boot sequence of the keyboard. I was always under the impression that the sequence was very straightforward, with the PC passing a Reset request to the keyboard and the keyboard ready to transmit data virtually autonomously, without prompting from the PC. When I watched the keyboard's boot, I got the data:

```
Keyboard:  0x0E8  0x0FA
PC:        0x0FE
Keyboard:  0x0FA  0x0AA
```

before the end of the 16-character LCD line that I was using was filled with I/O communications.

In this sequence, the keyboard boots on its own. Then the PC requests the keyboard to resend the last character (which it does), followed by a hex 0x0AA character. Unfortunately (and this is one of my first observations), I should have used a larger LCD or passed the data serially to another device.

Sometime later during the boot, the keyboard is reset with many (not one) 0x0FF characters from the PC. Although I expected one, I did not expect the literally hundreds that showed up. Once the initial Windows screen came up, this operation stopped (and then I was able to log into the PC), and the keyboard and PC behaved as I would expect.

I tried out the *Caps Lock* key and got the sequence:

```
Keyboard:  0x058
PC:        0x0ED
Keyboard:  0x0FD
```

This sequence is somewhat surprising because I would have expected the *0x0FD* to come from the PC, not the keyboard. I suspect that this is a problem with the delay that I put into the LCD because as long as the LCD write is occurring, the keyboard data lines are not being polled. In this case, there is a chance that I have picked up the PC's transmission and identified it incorrectly in my PICMicro code.

This conclusion is also based on how the second keyboard value changes sometimes to 0x0FE during multiple iterations of this operation.

I also placed this circuit in line with the "mouse" (actually a touchpad) port on my PC to observe what was being sent there as well. In this case, I found that the data being sent was what I expected, but was at such a volume that the LCD could not keep up and display all the data. Like the keyboard port, to get meaningful information, I would have to provide a larger LCD and poll the Busy bit or use another, higher-speed method to store the incoming data and display it.

RS-232—THE
NON-STANDARD

The RS-232 port is most commonly used in the PC. But, when you look through Web pages and catalogs at different devices designed to be connected to the PC, you'll see that they often use the other interfaces available. If you are a new engineer or technician, fresh out of school (and have had serial ports explained to you), you probably wonder why this is the case.

The basic reason is pretty logical and obvious once you start working with RS-232. RS-232 can be used in an awful lot of different ways to interconnect devices with many different options and quirks that you have to understand before you can successfully use the PC's serial ports to interface with other devices.

You can wire two RS-232 devices together 16 different basic ways (and when all of the small variances are taken into account, there is probably twice that number of different ways again). This is a real impediment to this method of communications if you think you can just wire two devices together in five minutes and keep going. If you've ever attempted to wire two devices together, even if you have a good understanding of what's required, it can become a real headache.

I remember an article in *Byte* a number of years ago by Jerry Pournelle in which he described his efforts trying to connect an ASCII terminal to a computer using RS-232. It took him a month to get it working—even after he called in some very technical friends! Even in my own case (and I consider myself to be pretty knowledgeable about RS-232), I feel like I have spent decades debugging RS-232 connections between different computers and devices.

So, after reading this, you're probably thinking that you should skip on and read about the parallel port.

First, the serial port is not that difficult to understand and implement. RS-232 does have a few quirks and will probably cause you to reach for a bottle of aspirin before you've done your first connection, but it is a much simpler (and, in many cases, cheaper) method of interfacing devices to the PC than the parallel port or the ISA bus. Understanding how it works will give you an option on how to connect external devices and help you handle the inevitable problems when you're first handed an application that needs to be connected to RS-232 and be told to "make it work."

This chapter contains a lot of information, including rules and suggestions for creating an RS-232 interface on the PC. Most of this information concerns the "standards" and how you can create an interface that will work well with them. You're probably wondering if you follow all these rules, will you be able to get an RS-232 interface application between the PC and an external device working on the first time?

The short answer is "no", but if you followed my recommendations, you will be able to create and debug an RS-232 interface with a lot less problems and much more quickly than if you attempt it without them.

Introduction to Asynchronous Serial Communications and RS-232

Man's long-distance electronic communications has always been based on asynchronous serial communications technology. This is true whether talking about telegraphy, teletypes, or computer communications; data is sent one character at a time, with each character broken up into smaller individual symbols (whether they are called *dits/dahs*, *Baudot characters*, or *ASCII bytes*). Computer RS-232 (also known as *EIA-232*) communications are a direct evolution from the telegraphy. It represents continuous improvements while retaining the best features of its ancestors.

Telegraphy was the first form of modern long-distance electronic asynchronous serial communications. When I say "asynchronous," I mean that data communication can start at any time and the receiver must be ready for it at any time. *Synchronous* communications means that the receiver is synchronized to the transmitter and only polls the incoming data bits when the transmitter is expected to be sending them.

The transmitter and receiver for the telegraph systems were simply humans operating a circuit that looked something like that shown in Fig. 23-1.

In this circuit, a 20-mA current would continuously flow through the speakers' magnets. When this current was removed (i.e., shorting out the source by pressing the telegraph key) the speakers would "relax" and make a clicking sound. Releasing the key would cause current to start flowing through the speakers again, causing it to deform (and click again), waiting for the next "dit" or "dah" to be transmitted.

The primary disadvantage of this system was the need for skilled telegraphers. If you don't think that learning Morse code is a skill, try to learn reading incoming Morse at 25 words per minute (the minimum required for getting your ham license). It is actually quite difficult to learn how to decode the incoming signals.

One clever feature of this system is still being used today: the error-detection features that are built into the circuit shown in Fig. 23-1. Now, you're probably wondering what kind of error-detection hardware can you put into a circuit that only has five components and wire?

The error detection is in how the Rest (nothing being sent) state is implemented. In this telegraphy circuit diagram, what happens if the wire linking the two stations is broken or shorted to ground?

If the wire breaks, the current source station will detect the problem because of no response from the other station or the speaker will be much louder because twice the amount of current is passing through the speaker.

If the line is shorted, no current is available to Station A and its speaker will not respond to keys pressed by either operator. The cause of this problem could be either the wire has made a circuit to ground short or bandits have shot the other station's operator and he is slumped over his key. In either case, the problem can easily be detected and appropriate action be taken.

This is known as *Non-Return to Zero (NRZ)* and it is a basic part of all asynchronous serial communications. During idle (Rest) periods, a *1* or Mark signal is sent. A 0 is known as a *space* because if you were to look at the voltage on the telegraph lines, you would see long periods of high voltages, punctuated by spaces pulling the voltage to ground.

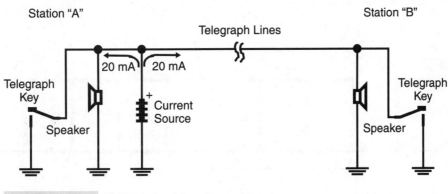

FIGURE 23-1   Telegraph wiring.

The next major innovation in asynchronous long-distance communications was the Baudot Teletype. This device mechanically (and, later, electronically) sent a string of electrical signals (called *bits*) to a receiving printer.

This data packet format is still used today for asynchronous transmission (including RS-232). With the invention of the Teletype, data could be sent and retrieved automatically without having an operator sitting by the equipment all night, unless an urgent message was expected. Normally, the nightly messages could be read in the morning.

Some people get unreasonably angry about the definition and usage of the terms *data rate* and *baud rate*. The *baud rate* is the maximum number of possible data-bit transitions per second. This includes the Start, Parity, and Stop bits at the ends of the data "packet" shown in Fig. 23-2, as well as the five data bits in the middle. I use the term *packet* because more than just data is included (some additional information is in there, too), so *character* or *byte* (if there were eight bits of data) are not appropriate terms.

Thus, for every five data bits transmitted, eight bits in total are transmitted (which means that nearly 40% of the data-transmission bandwidth is lost in Teletype asynchronous serial communications).

The *data rate* is the number of data bits transmitted per second. For this example, if you were transmitting at 110 baud (a common Teletype data speed), the actual data rate is 68.75 bits per second (or, assuming five bits per character, 13.75 characters per second).

I tend to use the term *data rate* to describe the *baud rate*. So, when I say *data rate*, I am specifying the number of bits of all types that can be transmitted in a given period of time (usually one second). I realize that this is not absolutely correct, but it makes sense to me to use it in this form and I will be consistent throughout the book (and not use the term *baud rate*).

With only five data bits, the Baudot code could only transmit as many as 32 distinct characters. To handle a complete character set, a specific five-digit code was used to notify the receiving Teletype that the next five-bit character would be an extended character. With the alphabet and most common punctuation characters in the "primary" 32, this second data packet wasn't required very often.

The data packet diagram shows three control bits. The Start bit is used to synchronize the receiver to the incoming data. All asynchronous serial receivers have an overspeed clock (usually running at 16 times the incoming bit speed) that samples the incoming data and verifies whether or not the data is valid (Fig. 23-3).

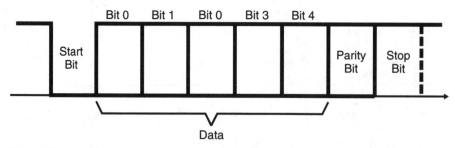

FIGURE 23-2   **Baudot asynchronous serial data.**

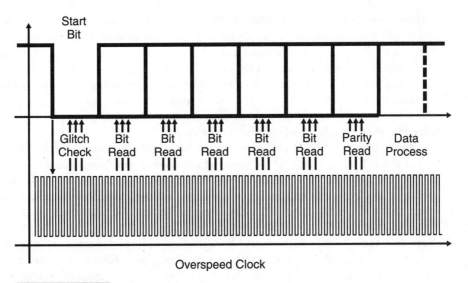

FIGURE 23-3   Reading an asynch data packet.

When waiting for a character, the receiver hardware polls the line repeatedly at 1/16-bit period intervals until a *0* (Space) is detected. The receiver then waits half a cycle before polling
the line again to see if a glitch was detected and not a Start bit. Notice that polling will occur
in the middle of each bit to avoid problems with bit transitions (or if the transmitter's clock
is slightly different from the receivers, the chance of misreading a bit will be minimized).

Once the Start bit is validated, the receiver hardware polls the incoming data once every
bit period multiple times (again to ensure that glitches are not read as incorrect data).

The Stop bit (at "Data Process" in Fig. 23-3) was originally provided to give both the receiver and the transmitter some time before the next packet is transferred (in early computers, the serial data stream was created and processed by the computers and not custom
hardware, as in modern computers).

The Parity bit is a crude method of error detection that was first brought in with Teletypes. The purpose of the parity bit is to indicate whether the data was received correctly.
An odd parity meant that if all the data bits and parity bits set to a Mark were counted, then
the result would be an odd number. Even parity is checking all the data and parity bits and
seeing if the number of Mark bits is an even number.

Along with even and odd parity are Mark, Space, and No parity. *Mark parity* means that
the parity bit is always set to a *1*, *Space parity* is always having a *0* for the parity bit, and
No parity is eliminating the parity bit altogether.

The most common form of asynchronous serial data packet is *8-N-1*, which means eight
data bits, no parity, and one stop bit. This reflects the capabilities of modern computers to
handle the maximum amount of data with the minimum amount of overhead and with a
very high degree of confidence that the data will be correct.

I stated that parity bits are a "crude" form of error detection and because they can only
detect one bit error (i.e., if two bits are in error, the parity check will not detect the problem). If you are working in a high induced-noise environment, you might want to use a
data protocol that can detect (and, ideally, correct) multiple bit errors.

The five-bit Baudot code was okay for Teletypes, but it was not sufficient for computers and higher-speed communications. Computers typically worked with eight-bit numbers and a bit-to-character system (which you know as *ASCII*) was developed for computers to communicate with one another in a standard format.

At this point, we're up to the early days of computing (the 1950s). Although data could be transmitted at high speed, it couldn't be processed and read new incoming data back continuously. So, a set of handshaking lines and protocols were developed for what became known as *RS-232 serial communications*.

With RS-232, the typical packet contained seven bits (the number of bits that each ASCII character contained). This simplified the transmission of man-readable text, but made sending object code and data (which were arranged as bytes) more complex because each byte would have to be split up into two *nybbles* (which are four bits long). Further complicating this is that the first 32 characters of the ASCII character set are defined as "special" characters (e.g., *Carriage Return, Back Space*, etc.). So, the representative data characters would have to be converted or (shifted up) into valid characters (this is why, if you ever see binary data transmitted from a modem or embedded in an e-mail message, data is either sent as hex codes or the letters *A* to *Q*). With this protocol, to send a single byte of data, two bytes (with the overhead bits resulting in 20 bits in total) would have to be sent (and, surprisingly enough, sending data would take twice as long as sending a text file of the same length).

As I pointed out, modern asynchronous serial data transmission is normally eight bits at a time, which will avoid this problem and allow transmission of full bytes without breaking them up or converting them.

With this background, you should probably be comfortable with the idea that there is a standard for allowing computers to communicate and have some ideas of what to look for when you are going to connect computers together.

The actual RS-232 communications model is shown in Fig. 23-4.

In RS-232, different equipment is wired according to the functions they perform.

DTE (Data Terminal Equipment) is meant to be the connector used for computers (the PC uses this type of connection). *DCE (Data Communications Equipment)* was meant for "modems" that transfer the data.

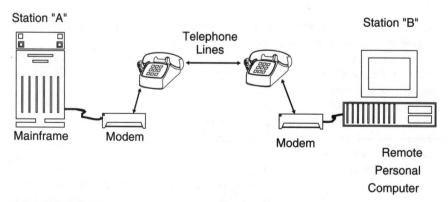

FIGURE 23-4   **2 computer communication via modem.**

Understanding what RS-232 model different equipment fits under is crucial to successfully connecting two devices by RS-232. With a pretty good understanding of the serial data, we can now look at the actual voltage signals.

As mentioned, when RS-232 was first developed into a standard, the computers and the electronics that drive them were still very primitive and unreliable. Because of that, we've got a couple of legacies to deal with.

The first is the voltage levels of the data. A Mark (*1*) is actually -12 V and a Space (*0*) is +12 V.

From Fig. 23-5, you should see that the hardware interface is not simply a TTL or CMOS level buffer. Later, this chapter introduces some methods of generating and detecting these interface voltages. Voltages in the "switching region" ($+/-3$ V) could be read as a 0 or 1, depending on the device. You should always ensure that the voltages going into a PC are in the "valid" regions.

Of more concern are the handshaking signals. These six additional lines (which are at the same logic levels as the transmit/receive lines (Fig. 23-5)) are used to interface between devices and control the flow of information between computers.

The *Request To Send (RTS)* and *Clear To Send (CTS)* lines are used to control data flow between the computer (DCE) and the modem (DTE device). When the PC is ready to send data, it asserts (outputs a Mark) on RTS. If the DTE device is capable of receiving data, it will assert the CTS line. If the PC is unable to receive data (i.e., the buffer is full or it is processing what it already has), it will de-assert the RTS line to notify the DTE device that it cannot receive any additional information.

The *Data Transmitter Ready (DTR)* and *Data Set Ready (DSR)* lines are used to establish communications. When the PC is ready to communicate with the DTE device, it asserts DTR. If the DTE device is available and ready to accept data, it will assert DSR to notify the computer that the link is up and ready for data transmission. If a hardware error is in the link, then the DTE device will de-assert the DSR line to notify the computer of the problem. Modems, if the carrier between the receiver is lost, will de-assert the DSR line.

You should be aware of two more handshaking lines in the RS-232 standard, even though, chances are that you will never connect anything to them. The first is the *Data Carrier Detect (DCD)*, which is asserted when the modem has connected with another de-

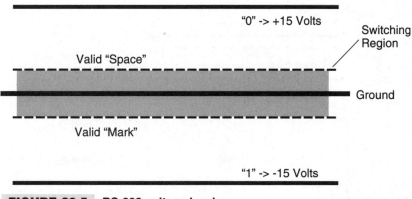

FIGURE 23-5   RS-232 voltage levels.

vice (i.e., the other device has "picked up the phone"). The *Ring Indicator (RI)* informs the PC whether or not the phone on the other end of the line is ringing or if it is busy.

A common ground connection is made between the DCE and DTE devices. This connection is crucial for the RS-232 level converters to determine the actual incoming voltages. The ground pin should never be connected to a chassis or shield ground (to avoid large current flows or be shifted and prevent accurate reading of incoming voltage signals). Incorrect grounding of an application can result in the computer or the device that it is interfacing to reset or have the power supplies blow a fuse or burn out. The latter consequences are unlikely, but I have seen it happen in a few cases. To avoid these problems, be sure that chassis and signal grounds are separate.

The handshaking lines are almost never used in RS-232 communications. The handshaking protocols were added to the RS-232 standard when computers were very slow and unreliable. In this environment, data transmission had to be stopped periodically to allow the receiving equipment to catch up.

Today, this is much less of a concern and normally three-wire RS-232 connections are implemented. This is done by shorting the DTR/DSR and RTS/CTS lines together at the PC. The DCD and RI lines are left unconnected.

With the handshaking lines shorted together, data can be sent and received without having to develop software to handle the different handshaking protocols. The next section explains why you would want to do this.

Now, a few points on three-wire RS-232. First, it cannot be implemented blindly; in about 20% of the RS-232 applications that I have done over the years, I have had to implement some subset of the total seven-wire (transmit, receive, ground and four handshaking lines) protocol lines. Interestingly enough, I have never had to implement the full hardware protocol. This still means that four out of five times, if you wire the connection as shown in Fig. 23-6, the application will work.

Three wire RS-232 is always a good starting place.

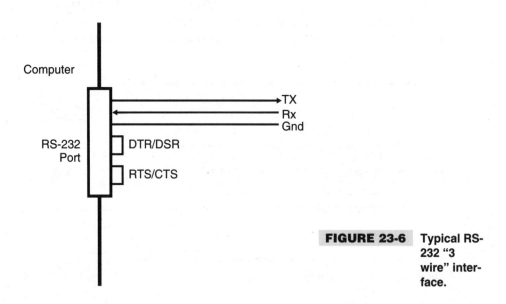

FIGURE 23-6   Typical RS-232 "3 wire" interface.

With the three-wire RS-232 protocol, you might not want to implement the hardware handshaking in some applications (the DTR, DSR, RTS, and CTS lines), you might want to implement software handshaking. Two primary standards are in place. The first is the XON/XOFF protocol, in which the receiver sends an XOFF (DC3, character 0x013) when it can't accept any more data. When it is able to receive data, it sends an XON (DC1, character 0x011) to notify the transmitter that it can receive more data.

The final aspect of the RS-232 covered here is the speed in which data is transferred. When you first see the speeds (such as 300, 2400, and 9600 bits per second), they seem rather arbitrary. The original serial data speeds were chosen for Teletypes because they gave the mechanical device enough time to print the current character and reset before the next one came in. Over time, these speeds have become standards and, as faster devices have become available, they've just been doubled (e.g., 9600 bps is 300 bps doubled five times).

To produce these data rates, the PC uses a 1.8432-MHz oscillator input into its serial controller. This frequency is divided by integers to get the nominal RS-232 speeds.

The problem occurs when you want to use another device (such as a microcontroller) and a 1.8432-MHz oscillator (or other frequency that is evenly divisible by 300) is not available or appropriate for the application. The answer lies in what I call RS-232's strange relationship with the number 13.

If you invert (to get the period of a bit) the data speeds and convert the units to microseconds, you will discover that the periods are almost exactly divisible by 13. This means that you can use an even-MHz oscillator in the hardware to communicate with the PC.

For example, if you had an external microcontroller running with a 20-MHz instruction clock and you wanted to communicate with a PC at 9600 bps, you would determine the number of cycles to delay:

1 Find the bit period in microseconds. For 9600 bps, this is 104 usecs.
2 Divide this bit period by 13 to get a multiple number. For 104 usecs, this is 8.

Now, if the external device is running at 20 MHz (which means a 50-ns cycle time), you can figure out the number of cycles as multiples of 8×13 in the number of cycles in 1 usecs. For 20 MHz, 20 cycles execute per microsecond. To get the total number of cycles for the 104-usecs bit period, simply evaluate:

$$20 \text{ cycles/usecs} \times 13 \times 8 \text{ usecs/bit} = 2080 \text{ cycles/bit}$$

So, in the external microcontroller, running at 20 MHz, 2080 instruction clock cycles must execute to delay one bit.

The PC's RS-232 Ports

The PC's serial ports consist of basically the same hardware and BIOS interfaces that was first introduced with the first PC in 1981. Since that time, a 9-pin connector has been specified for the port (in the PC/AT) and one significant hardware upgrade was introduced when the PS/2 was announced. For the most part, the serial port has changed the least of any component in the PC for the past 17+ years.

DB-25 (Male)   D-9 (Male)

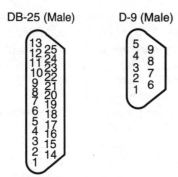

FIGURE 23-7   IBM PC DB-25 and D-9 pin RS-
232 connectors.

Either a male 25-pin or male 9-pin connector is available on the back of the PC for each serial port (Fig. 23-7).

These connectors are wired as:

PIN NAME	25 PIN	9 PIN	I/O DIRECTION
TxD	2	3	Output (O)
RxD	3	2	Input (I)
Gnd	7	5	
RTS	4	7	O
CTS	5	8	I
DTR	20	4	O
DSR	6	6	I
RI	22	9	I
DCD	8	1	I

The 9-pin standard was originally developed for the PC/AT because the serial port was put on the same adapter card as the printer port and there wasn't enough room for the serial port and parallel port to both use 25-pin D-Shell connectors. Actually, I prefer the smaller form factor connector.

Up to four serial ports can be addressed by the PC and of these probably only two will be usable for connecting external devices to the PC.

The serial port base addresses are:

PORT	BASE ADDRESS	INTERRUPT NUMBER
COM1	0x03F8	0x00C
COM2	0x02F8	0x00B
COM3	0x03E8	0x00C
COM4	0x02E8	0x00B

Later, this section shows that each base address is used as an initial offset to eight registers that are used by the serial port controller (the 8250). The *interrupt number* is the interrupt vector requested when an interrupt condition is encountered.

When IBM was specifying port addresses for the PS/2 and developed the 8514/A graphics adapter (which has become known as *Super VGA*), the designers found they didn't have enough available I/O port addresses left to support the registers they wanted to put in. So, they used the addresses reserved for COM4 assuming that very few people connect four serial ports to their PC. This means that virtually all modern PCs cannot work with COM4 and a Super VGA display at the same time.

When I was interfacing a device to a PC with four serial ports (it was a bad assumption), I found that writing to the COM4 port addresses caused my PC's screen to go black. The application was changed to only work with three serial ports and an ISA adapter.

To be on the safe side, don't attempt to put a serial port at COM4.

Chances are that you'll have a modem in your PC. As I've noted in the PC's architecture, although the PC has four sets of I/O addresses set aside for serial devices, for practical purposes, there are only two serial ports available when a modem is used. This is reduced to one if a serial mouse is used.

For serial (COM) ports 1 and 3, interrupt level 4 (which is actually interrupt 12 (or 0x00C) in the PC's interrupt table) is used. COM Ports 2 and 4 use "level" 3, interrupt 11 (or 0x00B). By setting your modem to COM2, you are leaving COM1 and COM3 free for interfacing to external devices without worrying about sharing interrupts with the software used by COM2. Although interrupts can be shared between applications and many try to work together, you should avoid sharing them whenever possible.

The block diagram of the 8250 *Universal Asynchronous Receiver/Transmitter (UART)* is quite simple and if you were to design your own device, its block diagram would probably look like the 8250's.

Figure 23-8 shows the data paths for the serial communications. You might want to refer back to this diagram, as I explain how the various registers work.

To avoid any confusion later, the 8250 is not an Intel part. Quite a few engineers notice that the PC's interrupt controller is the Intel 8259A, the original switch configuration and keyboard interface was an Intel 8255 and the DMA controller is an Intel 8237. Although it seems logical that the 8250 is from Intel, it is not. Looking at the Intel Web site for data sheets on the part will not yield you anything.

What is not shown in Fig. 23-8 are the interrupt registers and data paths. Interrupts are generated by changes in the status of the different hardware functions. I will go through interrupts in greater detail in this and the next subchapter.

The 8250 serial interface chip is the primary chip used for serial communications. Along with the 8250, the 16450 and the 16550 were introduced with the PS/2 as 8250 replacements. These chips can execute the same basic instructions as the 8250, but with additional circuits put into the chips to allow buffering of data (using *First In/First Out, FIFO, memories*) coming in and out.

I focus in on the 8250's operation and bypass the FIFO-equipped chips for two reasons. First, the FIFO is really not needed, except for very high data speeds (57,600 bps and faster). Most software programs written for the RS-232 Ports don't attempt to use the buffering FIFO hardware.

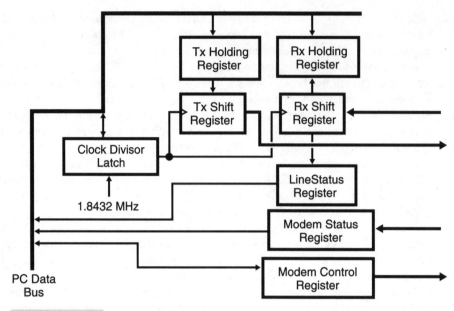

FIGURE 23-8 **8250 block diagram.**

This might be surprising, but most programs ignore the FIFOs for the same reason why I do: many of the FIFO-equipped chips simply don't work properly or as the specifications indicate. It is much safer to use the standard 8250 functions as they are guaranteed to work.

There are methods for detecting whether or not you have a working FIFO-equipped chip, but for most practical serial communication applications, the FIFO is not required.

The 8250 consists of eight registers offset from the "base address:"

BASE ADDRESS OFFSET	REGISTER NAME
0	Transmitter holding register/receiver character buffer/LSB divisor latch
1	Interrupt enable register/MSB divisor latch
2	Interrupt identification register
3	Line-control register
4	Modem-Control register
5	Line-status register
6	Modem-status register
7	Scratchpad register

Each of these registers controls or monitors hardware actions is in the 8250. Before explaining the operations of each register, here are a few points.

The data speed is set by inputting a 16-bit divisor value into the Rx/Tx holding register and interrupt enable register addresses. To change the function of these two registers, bit 7 of the line-control register is set. The value loaded into the register is multiplied by 16 and divided into 1.8432 MHz to get the actual data rate.

As a formula, this is:

$$Data\ rate = 1.8432\ \text{MHz}/(16 \times Divisor)$$

The divisors for different standard data rates are:

DATA RATE	DIVISOR
110 bps	0x0417
300 bps	0x0180
600 bps	0x00C0
1200 bps	0x0060
2400 bps	0x0030
9600 bps	0x000C
19200 bps	0x0006
115200 bps	0x0001

The divisors can either be loaded into the divisor registers by using the BIOS serial port initialize API.

When you have finished loading in the data rate, resetting bit 7 of the line-control register returns operation to its Normal mode.

After a character is received, it will set a number of conditions (including error conditions) that can only be reset by reading the character in the receive-holding register. If you are waiting for a character (but don't care what it is), and if you haven't read the previous one, "overrun" errors will occur as "live" data comes in because a new interrupt won't be generated for it.

For this reason it's always a good idea to read the serial port at the start of an application. By reading the port, you are clearing out any status and left-over characters.

By reading a character from the serial port at the start of the application, you are also "claiming" the serial port resource for the application in Win32 operating systems if you are executing from the MS-DOS prompt. By reading the port, you are in no way affecting the serial port hardware, except to clear the character received flags.

When you write to the base address (with no offset added), you are loading a character into the "transmit holding register", which the byte will pass to the shift out register when it has completed sending the previous character. Often, when starting transmission, nothing will be in the shift register, so the character is loaded immediately into the shift register, freeing the holding register for the next character.

Thus, if the holding register is kept full at all times (reloading when the value is moved into the shift register), you can send a continuous stream of data, the start bit of one packet immediately following the stop bit of the packet before it.

By reading the base address, you are reading the contents of the serial receiver holding register. If you're going to read the register, be sure that there is a new character to read by checking the "line-status register" for "data ready".

Interrupts can be generated upon the completion of the current packet transmission and the contents of the holding register stored into the shift register can be shifted out, if the modem status bits change state or if data has been received and is either in error or ready to be processed. If any of these events occur with the appropriate interrupt enable register bit set, which is located at the base address plus one, then an interrupt request will be generated by the 8250.

When any interrupts are enabled in the 8250, they will output an interrupt request. This might not be desirable, so, in the PC, some hardware was added to globally mask the interrupt (Fig. 23-9). _Out2 is controlled within the modem-control register.

The *interrupt-enable register* (at the base address plus one) is used to enable the interrupt requests out of the 8250, based on different events:

BIT	DESCRIPTION
7-4	Unused, normally set to zero
3	When set an interrupt request on change of state for modem-interface lines
2	Request interrupt for change in receiver holding register status
1	Request interrupt if the holding register is empty
0	Request interrupt for received character

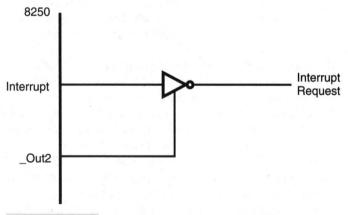

FIGURE 23-9   IBM PC serial interrupt enable hardware.

3

The modem input lines are DSR, CTS, RI, and DCD. They can cause an interrupt request in the PC when they change state. The event that caused the interrupt request is stored in the modem-status register.

Just as a note, in the 8250, the modem bits are what I've called *handshaking lines* earlier in this chapter.

The receiver line-status bits will request an interrupt when something unusual is happening on the receiver line. These conditions include a data overrun, incorrect parity in the data packet received, framing errors in the received data packet, or a break in the line is detected.

This interrupt request is given the highest priority so that errors can be responded to first.

The transmit-holding register-empty interrupt indicates that the holding register is able to accept another character and is shifting out the one that used to be in the holding register.

It might seem surprising to use a holding register, rather than the actual shift register when transmitting data. Using the transmitter-holding register is actually an advantage in applications where data has to be transmitted as quickly as possible with a minimum of overhead or "dead air" (nothing is being sent).

When sending data at full speed, the start bit of the next packet has to follow the stop bit of the previous packet. One option is to continuously poll the serial port to wait for the stop bit to be sent and load the shift register with the next character to send when it is empty. You could also let the transmit-holding register load the shift register when the shift register has finished sending the previous packet and then reload the holding register when it's convenient to the application (i.e., when an interrupt request is received).

The last event that can generate an interrupt request is when a character is received. This interrupt request is at the second highest priority (after the receive line-status interrupt request) to ensure that the received characters and status are serviced as quickly as possible (and avoid framing errors).

When the serial port interrupt request is being serviced, the *interrupt identification register* (base address plus two) is used to determine the cause of the interrupt.

BITS	DESCRIPTION			
7-3	Unused, normally set to zero			
2-1	Interrupt ID bits			
	B2	B1	Priority	Request Type
	0	0	Lowest	Change in modem-status lines
	0	1	Third	Transmitter holding register empty
	1	0	Second	Data received
	1	1	Highest	Receive line-status change

These bits correspond to the interrupt mask bits used in the interrupt-enable register and should be checked before responding to what you think is the interrupt. I put this caution in because after reading from the received data register (at the base address); the contents of the interrupt identification register are lost.

The *line-control register* (at base address plus three) is used to set the operating conditions of the data transmitter/receiver.

BIT	DESCRIPTION
7	When set, the transmitter holding and interrupt-enable registers are used to load the data-speed divisor
6	When set, the 8250 outputs a break condition (sending a space) until this bit is reset
5-3	Parity Type Specification
	B5 B4 B3
	0 0 0 - No parity
	0 0 1 - Odd parity
	0 1 0 - No parity
	0 1 1 - Even parity
	1 0 0 - No parity
	1 0 1 - Mark parity
	1 1 0 - No parity
	1 1 1 - Space parity
2	When set, two stop bits are sent in the packet, otherwise one
1-0	Number of data bits sent in a packet
	B1 B1
	0 0 - 5 bits
	0 1 - 6 bits
	1 0 - 7 bits
	1 1 - 8 bits

Most modern serial communications use 8-N-1 (eight data bits, no parity, one stop bit) for data transmission. Because this is the simplest and most flexible (fewest overhead bits and can transfer a full byte) method to transfer data. To set the line-control register to 8-N-1, load it with 0b000000011 (or 0x003).

The *modem-control register* (at the base address plus four) is used to control the modem-control pins, as well as two other functions.

3

BIT	PIN	DESCRIPTION
7-5		Unused, normally set to zero
4	Loop	When set, data from the transmitter is looped internally to the receiver
3	Out2	When set, interrupt requests from the 8250 are unmasked
2	Out1	This bit/pin is not controlling any hardware features in the serial port
1	_RTS	When this bit is reset, the RTS line is at Mark state
0	_DTR	When this bit is reset, the DTR line is at Mark state

The Loop bit (feature) is useful when debugging an application or seeing how the serial port works. By simply setting this bit, transmitted data is passed directly to the receiver without going outside the chip. When debugging an application that is using the serial port, I'll often set this bit in a debugger and then manually output a byte to the transmitter-holding register to see how the program responds.

I have found a few computers, usually laptops (although I've seen some newer mother-board's SuperIO chips with integrated 8250s), where the Loop function isn't implemented in the serial port. In these cases, you might be frustrated that the character is not received. To debug the applications on these PCs, you will have to make a small connector with pins 2 and 3 shorted together to provide the loop-back feature.

As described later in this chapter, I try to stay away from controlling external devices with the modem-control pins wherever possible.

The *line-status register* (base address plus five) is a read-only register with the current status of the 8250.

BIT	DESCRIPTION
7	Unused, normally set to zero
6	Set when the transmitter shift register is empty
5	Set when the transmitter holding register is empty
4	Set when the receive line is held at a space value for longer than the current packet size
3	This bit is set when the last character had a framing error (i.e., stop bit set to Space)
2	Set when the last character had a parity error
1	Set when the latest character has overrun the receiver-holding register
0	Set when a character has been received, but not read

When you are debugging a serial port application, always remember that the contents of the line-status register should normally be 0x060 (no character being sent and no character in the transmitter-holding register waiting to be sent) or 0x061 (no character being sent, no character in the transmitter holding register waiting to be sent, and a character has been received but not read in). If you see any other value in this register, then an error has occurred with transmitting or receiving the data.

The *modem-status register* (at the base address plus six) is a read-only register dedicated to returning the current status of the modem (DCE) device connected to the PC's serial port.

BIT	PIN	DESCRIPTION
7	DCD	When set, an asserted DCD signal is being received
6	RI	When set, the modem is detecting a ring on the device to which it is connected
5	DSR	When set, a DSR Mark is being received
4	CTS	When set, a CTS Mark is being received
3	DCD	When this bit is set, the DCD line has changed state since the last check
2	RI	When set, this bit indicates that the ring-indicator line has changed from a Mark to a Space
1	DSR	When this bit is set, the DSR line has changed state since the last check
0	CTS	When this bit is set, the CTS line has changed state since the last check

When this register is read, the least-significant four (known as the *delta bits*) are reset. Therefore, two reads of this register, one immediately after the other, could result in different values being returned.

The delta bits are used for the modem-status change interrupt request. If interrupts are not used in your application, these bits can be polled for changes in the modem-control lines.

At base address plus seven, in some serial hardware, you can read from and write to a *scratchpad register* without affecting any other hardware. This register should not be counted upon being present in all serial interfaces.

Like the scratchpad register, the FIFO transmitter and receiver buffers might not be present in the serial interface (or worse, they might not work correctly). As well, very few applications really require this hardware because it really isn't very hard for the PC's processor to keep up with most incoming data speeds.

In the register definitions, I have only presented the lowest-common denominator, the 8250.

The only application where I could see the FIFO being required is if the PC was communicating with more than one other device continuously at high speed (above 9600 bps for multiple devices). If this were the case, instead of using the standard serial ports, I would recommend using some of the available multiple serial-port adapters with built-in buffers to reduce the processor's workload.

Making the Connection

RS-232 and PC serial communications have a reputation for being difficult to use and I have to disagree. Implementing RS-232 with a PC isn't very hard when a few rules are followed and you have a good idea of what's possible. The rest of this chapter covers the PC hardware and software RS-232 interfaces, followed by what types of interfaces are required for the devices on the other side of the RS-232 cable and a few hints on getting the connection to work properly.

Like the other hardware devices in the PC, the serial ports have a BIOS interrupt (Int 0x014) for generic operations. These BIOS functions allow you to set up the interface, as well as send and receive characters. When I am creating RS-232 applications, I very rarely use the BIOS functions (or when I do, I just use the port setup) because the BIOS values are quite limited in their capabilities and force you into working in a specific manner.

The most useful serial BIOS requests are "Port Initialize" (AH = 0) and "Extended Port Initialize" (AH = 4). The Extended Port Initialize is available in PS/2 (and later) PCs (which really means all PCs built after 1987). These functions will set up the serial port with regard to speed. The following data speeds are supported:

110 bps
150 bps
300 bps
600 bps
1200 bps
2400 bps
4800 bps
9600 bps
19,200 bps

As well as parity type (None, Odd, Even, Mark, and Space), number of stop bits (1 or 2), and the number of data bits (7 or 8). The extended port initialize will also allow you to transmit a "Break" (a "Space" longer than a data packet). Typically, data communications works at 8-N-1 (eight data bits, no parity, and one stop bit), which can be written into the line-control register directly. But, you might want to use the BIOS port-initialize functions to set up the speed of the port without having to set the divisor manually.

Actually, the only reason why I ever use the port-initialize function is to set the data speed (although if I'm creating an application that runs faster than 19,200 bps or at a non-standard speed, then I will have to do it manually anyway).

The character-send BIOS function works as:

```
DTR = 1;                    // Indicate that the Port is active
RTS = 1;
```

```
for ( TimeOut = SetValue; ( TimeOut != 0 ) && ( DSR == 0 ) &&
  ( CTS == 0 ); TimeOut- ); // Wait for Receiver to become ready

if (( DSR == 0 ) || ( CTS == 0 ))
  return TimeOutError;  // Return the Timeout Error
else {                  // Else, Send the Character
  TxHoldingRegister = Character;
  return 0;
} // endif
```

To receive a character, a similar process is followed:

```
DTR = 1;                    //  Indicate Port is Active and Ready to
                            //  Receive

for ( TimeOut = SetValue; ( TimeOut != 0 ) && ( DSR == 0 );
  TimeOut- );               //  Wait for Transmitter to become ready

if ( DSR == 0 )            //  Did the DSR Line NOT Get Set?
  return TimeOutError;      //  Yes, Return Error
else {                      //  No, Get the Character

  for ( TimeOut = SetValue; ( TimeOut != 0 ) && ( RxChar == 0 );
    TimeOut- -);            //  Wait for a Character to be Received and Set
                            //  "RxChar"

  if ( RxChar == 0 )       //  No Character Received
    return NoRxChar;
  else {                    //  Character was Received
    Character = RxHoldingRegister;  //  Return the Character Read
    return 0;
  } // endif
} // endif
```

Along with these functions, there is a fourth function that returns the contents of the line-status register and the modem status register contents (which can be read and processed directly).

There are a number of problems with these functions. Because the handshaking lines are used, you cannot hook up a simple three-wire RS-232 connection, except as shown in Fig. 23-6. Before transmitting data, the transmitter-holding register is not checked (which means that before you call the character-transmit BIOS function, you must check the port status to be sure that the transmitter-holding register is empty. As well, an interrupt request on any state cannot be implemented.

This is why I typically read and write directly to the port registers and check the status (either before sending a character or after receiving one) in the application.

Causing an interrupt on the transmitter-holding register empty or on a character received is quite easy. Now, you can also have an interrupt on the changing modem-status lines or on a change of state in the received line (such as an overrun or Break condition), but for three-wire operations with interrupts being used, I really haven't found a need for this.

To enable interrupts for COM1/COM3 (at interrupt 0x00C), the following code could be used:

```
SetInt( 0x0C, SerIntHndlr );        //  Point the Interrupt Handler to
                                    //  the Correct Handler
Dummy = inp( RxHoldingRegister );   //  Turn Off any Pending
                                    //  Interrupts
```

```
outp( IntMaskRegister, inp( IntMaskRegister ) & 0x0FB );
                                // Enable COM1/COM3
                                // Interrupts in Controller
outp( InterruptEnableRegister, 0x003 );
// Request Interrupts on TxHolding
                                // Register Empty and Rx
                                // Holding
                                // Register Full
outp( ModemControlRegister, inp( ModemControlRegister ) | Out2) ;
                                // Unmask Interrupt Requests from
                                // 8250
```

Notice that before I enable any interrupts, I read from the serial port to clear out anything that is pending. This is very important to do because it both "claims" the serial port in the operating system as well as clears out any inadvertent problems that you can't expect (such as an earlier executing program leaving the serial port in an unknown state).

Once an interrupt request is made by the hardware control is passed to the service routine:

```
SerIntHndlr:                // Serial Interrupt Handler

//  #### - Assume that the Interrupting COM port is identified

   switch ( InterruptIDRegister ) { // Handle the Interrupt Request
     case 4:                  // Received Character
       InString[ i++ ] = RxHoldingRegister;
       break;
     case 2:                  // TxHolding Register Empty
       TxHoldingRegister = OutString[ j++ ];  // Send the Next Character
       break;
     default:                 // Some other kind of Interrupt
       Dummy = RxHoldingRegister;  // Clear the Receiving Data
   } // endswitch

   InterruptControlRegister = EOI;  // Reset the Interrupt Controller

   returnFromInterrupt;       // Return from the Interrupt.
```

This code passes data to and from the strings, incrementing their pointers each time. In a real application, the interrupt handler would ensure that it was executing on the correct port (with this code, it is assumed that only one port can cause an interrupt request). The application would be notified when data was available (or, if a table was being saved, if an end character, such as a carriage return, was encountered, then the handler would then notify the mainline).

When implementing an RS-232 interface, you can make your life easier by doing a few simple things.

The first is the connection. Whenever I do an application, I standardize using a 9-pin D-shell with the DTE interface (the one that comes out of the PC with Pin 3 as the serial data output) and use "straight through" cables wherever possible. In doing this, I always know what my pinout is at the end of the cable when I'm about to hook up another device to a PC.

By making the external device DCE always and using a standard pinout, I don't have to fool around with "null modems" or making my own cables.

When I am creating the external device, I also loop back the DTR/DSR and CTS/RTS data pairs inside the external device, rather than at the PC or in the cable. This allows me to use a standard PC and straight through cable without having to do any wiring on my own or any modifications. It looks a lot more professional, as well.

Tying DTR/DSR and CTS/RTS also means that I can take advantage of built-in terminal emulators. Virtually all operating systems have a built-in dumb terminal emulator that can be used to debug the external device without requiring the PC code to run. Getting the external device working before debugging the PC application code should simplify your work.

The last point is, although I can develop applications that run up to 115,200 bps (by writing a *1* into the two data-divisor registers), I typically run at 9600 or 19,200 bps. By keeping the data rates reasonable, then I can run the applications to reasonable lengths (up to about a 1000 feet with shielded cabling) without requiring special protocols because of bit errors.

Longer cable lengths can be accommodated by using a modem and the local phone lines, instead of cabling between the PC and device yourself and will probably be cheaper and easier for you. I have not described connecting a modem to your PC, but this information is typically found in a modem's documentation. If you are running with a Hayes-compatible or "AT command set" modem, you can send the "AT commands" directly to the modem as character strings.

Converting RS-232 Logic Levels to TTL/CMOS

As I went through the RS-232 electrical standard earlier in the chapter, you were probably concerned about interfacing standard, modern technology (i.e., TTL and CMOS) devices to other RS-232 devices. This is actually a legitimate concern because, without proper voltage-level conversion, you will not be able to read from or write to external TTL or CMOS devices. Fortunately, certain methods can make this conversion quite easy.

If you look at the original IBM PC RS-232 port specification, you'll see that 1488/1489 RS-232 level-converter circuits were used for the RS-232 serial port interfaces.

To transmit data with the 1488/1489 components, each transceiver (except for *1*) is actually a NAND gate (with the inputs being #A and #B outputting on #Y). When I wire in a 1488, I ensure that the second input to a driver is always pulled high (as I've done with 2B in Fig. 23-10).

In the 1489 receiver, the #C input is a flow control for the gates (normally, RS-232 comes in the #A pin and is driven as TTL out of #Y). This pin is normally left floating.

These chips are still available and work very well (up to 1,156,200 bps max PC RS-232 data rate), but I'd never use them in my own projects because the 1488 (transmitter) requires $+/-12$-V Sources in order to produce valid RS-232 signal voltages. Actually, the PC motherboard, $+/-12$ V is only used for RS-232 level conversion, although $+12$ V may be required from the power supply for disk and diskette drives.

I wanted to present three methods that you could choose from for converting RS-232 signal levels to TTL/CMOS (and back again) when you are creating projects that interface with the PC's serial ports. These three methods do not require $+/-12$ V; in fact, they just require the $+5$-V supply that is used for logic power.

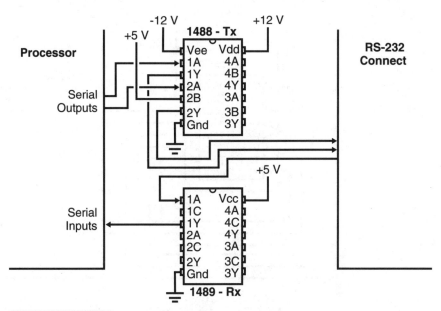

FIGURE 23-10   1488/1489 RS-232 connections.

The first method is using an RS-232 converter that has a built-in charge-pump to create the $+/-12$ V required for the RS-232 signal levels. Probably the most well-known chip used for this function is the MAXIM MAX232 (Fig. 23-11).

This chip is ideal for implementing three-wire RS-232 interfaces (or add a simple DTR/DSR or RTS/CTS handshaking interface). The ground for the incoming signal is connected to the processor ground (which is not the case's ground).

Along with the MAX232, MAXIM and some other chip vendors have a number of other RS-232 charge-pump-equipped devices that will allow you to handle more RS-232 lines (to include the handshaking lines). Some charge-pump devices that are also available do not require the external capacitors that the MAX232 chip does, which will simplify the layout of your circuit (although these chips do cost quite a bit more).

The next method of translating RS-232 and TTL/CMOS voltage levels is to use the transmitter's negative voltage (Fig. 23-12).

This circuit relies off the RS-232 communications only running in Half-Duplex mode (i.e., only one device can transmit at a given time). When the external device "wants" to transmit to the PC, it sends the data either as a Mark (leaving the voltage being returned to the PC as a negative value) or as a Space by turning on the transistor and enabling the positive voltage output to the PC's receivers. If you go back to the RS-232-voltage specification drawing, you'll see that +5 V is within the valid voltage range for RS-232 Spaces.

This method works very well (consuming just about no power) and is obviously a very cheap way to implement a three-wire RS-232 bidirectional interface.

There are a few comments I want to make about the circuit in Fig. 23-12. This diagram shows a NMOS device simply because it does not require a base-current-limiting transistor the same way that a bipolar transistor would.

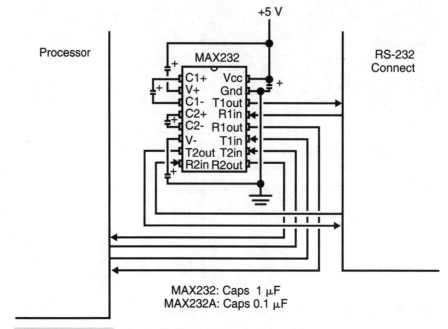

FIGURE 23-11   Maxim MAX232 RS-232 connections.

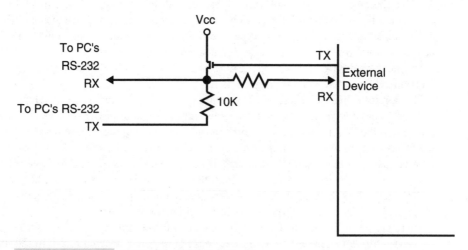

FIGURE 23-12   RS-232 to external device.

When the PC transmits a byte to the external device through this circuit, it will receive the packet it's sent because this circuit connects the PC's receiver (more or less) directly to its transmitter. The software running in the PC (as well as the external device) will have to handle this.

You also have to be absolutely that sure you are only transmitting in Half-Duplex mode. If both the PC and the external device attempt to transmit at the same time, then both messages will be garbled. Instead, the transmission protocol that you use should wait for requested responses, rather than sending them asynchronously. Or, you could have one device (either the PC or external devices) wait for a request for data from the other.

Another issue is that data out of the external device will have to be inverted to get the correct transmission voltage levels (i.e., a *0* will output a *1*) to ensure the transistor turns on at the right time (i.e., a positive voltage for a Space).

Unfortunately, this means that the built-in serial port for many microcontrollers cannot be used because they cannot invert the data output, as is required by the circuit (although an inverter could be inserted between the serial port and the RS-232 conversion circuit).

One chip, the Dallas Semiconductor DS1275, basically incorporates the circuit above (with a built-in inverter) into a single package (Fig. 23-13).

The DS1275 has two part numbers with the same pinout, the DS1275 and the DS275. Both work exactly the same way, but the 1275 is a later version of the part.

Before going on to the last interface circuit, I should point out a big advantage of the circuit above. The advantage results in the fact that the PC's RS-232 transmitter is connected to the PC's RS-232 receiver if the external device (with this circuit) is connected to the PC. This means that the PC can "ping" (send a command that is ignored by the external device) via the RS-232 port and see if the external device is connected.

But, there is one hitch. Even though the circuit is connected, how do you know that the external device is working?

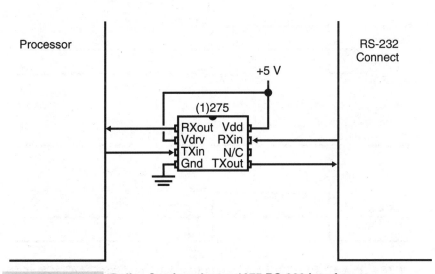

FIGURE 23-13   Dallas Semiconductor 1275 RS-232 interface.

Actually, this isn't that difficult. Simply specify the ping character as something that the external device can recognize and have it modify it so that the PC's software can recognize that the interface is working.

The method that I have used in the past is to use a microcontroller with "bit-banging" software (described in the next section) to change some Mark bits when it recognizes that a ping character is being received.

Figure 23-14 shows a ping character of 0x0F0 that is modified by the external device (by turning on the transistor) to change some bits into Spaces.

If the PC receives nothing or 0x0F0, then the external device is not working.

The last interface circuit is simply a resistor (Fig. 23-15).

This method of receiving data from an RS-232 device to a logic input probably seems absurdly simple and could not work. But it does and very well.

This interface relies on clamping diodes in the receiving device to hold the voltage at the maximum allowable for the receiver. The 10-K resistor limits any possible current flows (Fig. 23-16). The actual circuit looks like Fig. 23-17.

Some devices that do not have clamping diodes internal to the I/O pin (e.g., in some microcontrollers). In that case, they can be added in the configuration shown in Fig. 23-17.

This implementation has a few rules. Some people like to use this configuration with a 100-K resistor instead of the 10 K shown in the figure. Personally, I don't like to use anything higher than 10 K because of the possibilities of induced noise with a CMOS input (this is less likely with TTL) causing an incorrect value to be read.

You will probably have to have the PC running before the external device if this circuit is to be used. With this circuit, your ground will have to match the signal ground of the PC's serial port, if you power up before this ground is matched, then the device might not receive properly or be reset when the PC powers up.

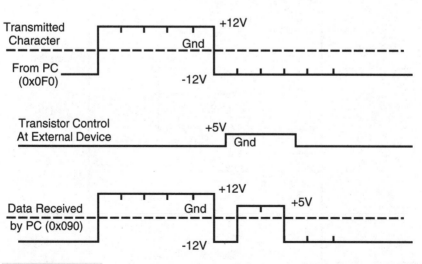

FIGURE 23-14   RS-232 "Ping" using transistor/resistor TTL/CMOS voltage conversion circuit.

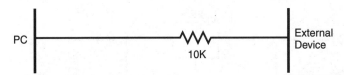

FIGURE 23-15 Simple RS-232 to TTL/CMOS voltage conversion.

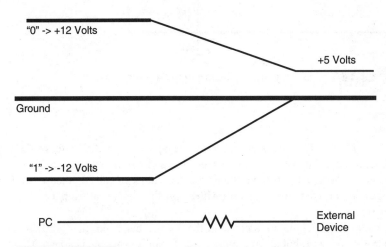

FIGURE 23-16 RS-232/resistor voltage conversion.

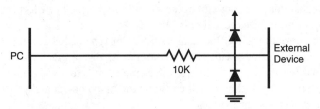

FIGURE 23-17 Simple RS-232 to TTL/CMOS voltage conversion with clamping diodes.

Obviously, this circuit is only usable for devices being written to by a "true" RS-232 device. When using this circuit (and the transistor/resistor transceiver circuit) the data read (and write) is inverted to what the data (the bits consist of Marks and Spaces) actually is.

As a final warning. Many people will use simple resistor/diode circuits for parsing TTL/CMOS logic levels for RS-232 and they will work most of the time. I always seem to be interfacing to devices which need proper RS-232 voltage levels. For this reason, I only drive "true" RS-232 voltages with a negative voltage greater than −5V.

POWERING YOUR CREATION FROM THE PC'S RS-232 PORT

With the availability of many CMOS devices requiring very minimal amounts of current to operate, you might be wondering about different options for powering your circuit. One of the most innovative that I have come across is using the PC's RS-232 ports itself as powering devices that are attached to it using the circuit (Fig. 23-18):

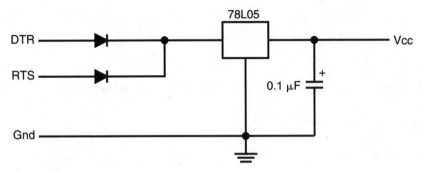

FIGURE 23-18   "Stealing" power from the PC's serial port.

When the DTR and RTS lines are outputting a Space, a positive voltage (relative to ground) is available. This voltage can be regulated and the output used to power the devices attached to the serial port (up to about 5 mA). For extra current, the transmitter line can also be added into the circuit, as well with a "break" being sent from the PC to output a positive voltage.

Some people prefer regulators other than the 78L05, but I like the 78L05's ability to source up to 100 mA and shut down if more current than is available is drawn. Many of the other low-power +5-V regulators can be burned out quite easily with too much current. I use a 0.1-μF filtering capacitor on this circuit because it minimizes the in-rush current and there should be no opportunity for large switching transients.

The 5 mA is enough current to power the transistor/resistor type of RS-232 transmitter and a CMOS microcontroller, along with some additional hardware (such as an LCD). You will not be able to drive an LED with this circuit. Some circuits that you normally use for such things as pull-ups and pull-downs will consume too much power and you'll have to specify different (higher) resistance values.

Now, with this method of powering the external device, you do have use of the hand-shaking lines, but the savings of not having to provide an external power supply (or battery) will outweigh the disadvantages of having to create a software pinging and handshaking protocol. Externally powering a device attached to the RS-232 port is ideal for input devices, such as serial mice, which do not require a lot of power.

Choosing RS-232 for Applications

One of the biggest root causes difficulties using RS-232 is how RS-232 is used. In these situations, the PC's RS-232 port is modified to work in a manner in which it was not originally designed or some feature is exploited to provide a specific function. Often, these types of applications do not work well, or, if they work on one type of PC, they won't work on others. I tend to feel that these types of applications are not appropriate for the serial port and others should be considered first.

An application that is appropriate for PC-serial communications has the following characteristics:

1 A standard PC serial port is to be used on at least one end.
2 Only two computing devices are connected together.
3 These two devices might be an arbitrary distance apart (from inches to miles to astronomical distances).
4 Relatively small amounts of data need to be transferred in real time (on the order of hundreds of kilobytes per hour).
5 Man-readable commands are transmitted between the devices and data is transmitted using standard protocols.

If an application does not fit all of these criteria, then you should probably look for another method to communicate between the PC and another device.

The PC's serial port and the built-in BIOS are designed to provide RS-232 communications. The BIOS interface is a significant advantage for developing applications. It is available on all PCs and will ensure that the serial port works the same way, regardless of the hardware on which it's running.

Having BIOS APIs suitable for communications is not available for any other "standard" interface for the PC.

The second criteria, that only two computing devices are to be connected together is important, even though RS-232 can become a "multidrop" network if the transistor-resistor or DS1275 RS-232 drivers are used to transmit data to the PC. This would make the PC's RS-232 receiver behave like a dotted AND bus.

A typical dotted AND bus consists of a pulled-up bus line with multiple open-collector (or open drivers, as shown) drivers being able to pull the line down. When each of the drivers are sending a Mark, then the bus remains at the Mark state. If any one of the devices pulls down the line (sends a Space), then no other devices can transmit a Mark because the line is already being pulled down (Fig. 23-19).

In RS-232 terms, this could be set up with the V_{cc} connection being connected to -12 V, and the Ground connections attached to +5- or +12-V, as shown.

The problem with implementing a shared bus on a PC's RS-232 line is developing a data "collision" detection and resolution protocol. In a synchronous multidrop network (such as I2C), there are rules for transmitting.

This makes detecting problems much simpler. For example, if two devices begin to transmit at the same time on a dotted AND bus, their signals become confused.

In this example, TxB can alter the message that TxA has put on the bus by pulling the line low when TxA is letting the line stay high. And, TxA also changes the data output of TxB, resulting in a garbled combination of the two.

In synchronous protocols, this is not a problem because often the transmitters are monitoring the line to see what's actually being transmitted. In the example shown in (Fig. 23-20), TxA, if it were monitoring the Bus, would detect that when it was trying to transmit a Mark (at bit 0), a Space was being transmitted instead. At this point, it would stop transmitting (and will start again, according to the rules of the protocol) and let TxB transmit without garbling TxB's message.

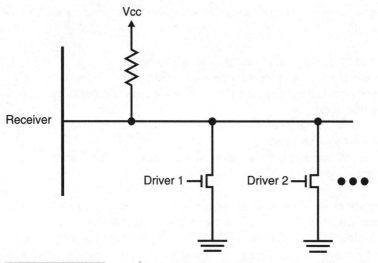

FIGURE 23-19 "ANDing" multiple drivers on a "Dotted AND" bus.

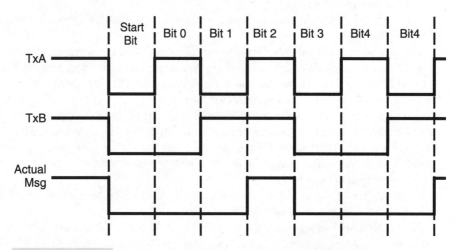

FIGURE 23-20 "AND" bus collisions and message changes.

This isn't possible in RS-232 because data is sent a byte at a time with no monitoring of the data as it's sent. In this example, the final message would be garbled and the PC would have to detect the garbled message and the devices driving TxA and TxB would have to detect the errors and wait to attempt retransmitting.

This method of resolving collisions is much more complex than what a synchronous serial protocol would have to implement.

As well, an additional problem with collisions might not be readily apparent from this example. What happens with data being sent from independent devices? In this example, it was shown what happens when the collision occurs when the bits are perfectly aligned, but what happens if halfway through one byte, another starts transmitting?

3

In this case, a much more complex collision detection and resolution protocol is required. This is not only for the transmitting devices, but the PC RS-232 receiver. The receiver might be able to receive two overlapping data packets as two separate packets or a byte with an invalid stop bit or as an overrun if the first byte isn't read from the receiver's buffer fast enough. Another source of error is if the application has not finished parsing previous bytes of the message.

This discussion really boils down to the fact that RS-232 is not meant for implementing networks. RS-232 is really designed to pass data between two systems.

The next rule, that these devices can be an arbitrary distance apart, is used to define how the data transmitting works. Unless the device is going to always be connected directly to another device sitting on a bench, you should plan for the worst case.

What is the worst case? Here's a very possible situation.

You have developed an application that is controlling a piece of manufacturing process equipment. Using RS-232, you could do your development on the floor, right by the equipment. As you gain confidence in it and don't have to be physically near it, you could run the RS-232 line to the PC at your desk, requiring a few hundred feet of cable.

At this point, you might want to be able to check the machine's operation from home. If you get called with a problem, you might want to be able to use the modem in your PC at home, rather than have to come in to work to tweak a parameter.

With the equipment connected to a modem, your boss now feels that this would be a good time to transfer it to your plant in Asia, where you will be able to monitor it via intercontinental phone lines using geosynchronous satellites. In this case, the data transmissions will encounter significant delays (up to a quarter of a second) and significantly more opportunities for missed bits.

This is actually an excellent opportunity to use RS-232 with standard transmission/ reception protocols because the range of the communications can be expanded significantly. It is also a good match because standard RS-232 equipment (i.e., modems) and data-transmission/reception protocols will meet all of the requirements of this application with minimal software changes or upgrades with the relocation of the equipment.

When I say "relatively" small amounts of data are to be transferred, I am really talking in the order of hundreds of kilobytes per hour. For larger amounts of data, networks and Internet communication protocols are much more appropriate.

The fifth point, sending and receiving man-readable commands, might seem like a waste of some good cycles, but it is really an extension of the previous points. Rather than using the RS-232 port for serial communications, it might seem possible to use the output pins (RTS, DTR, and the "break" feature, TX) for simple applications. Doing this eliminates one of the big advantages of sending serial data. It is timed at standard data speeds, which eliminates much of the work of timing the application to work on different PCs.

This section has hinted that communications should only be between two intelligent devices. When I was working on my first book (*Programming and Customizing the PIC Microcontroller*), I created a PICMicro programmer and, following the direction that had set before by others, I used a PC's parallel port to provide the timing signals for writing data into the device being programmed. The PC software was written for the MS-DOS command line.

After I got the programmer running on my PC at home, I tried it on a number of other PCs, owned by different people. I found that it was hit or (more often) miss whether the software would work. I had to do a lot of tweaking and modifications to the PC software to get the programmer to run properly.

I found that if I put in a PICMicro for programming and created a RS-232 interface, I could control the programming operations using a standard terminal emulator, rather than create a custom interface on the PC. This is actually quite liberating because for this application, the PC software was very complex (requiring several thousand lines of C and assembler code), it didn't use a Windows interface, and it also didn't work that well.

By using the PICMicro to take commands from the PC serially and execute them, not only was I freed from the task of writing my own PC interface, but I had a device that would work on a number of different systems. Not only would the programmer work on a PC running DOS, but it would work on a PC running Windows (including Windows NT), a Macintosh, or a UNIX workstation without modification, using whatever terminal emulator software was available.

To further simplify how the program worked, I used the Text Download function to send the program to be loaded into the device to be programmed. This again eliminated work for me because the file read functions were taken care of within the terminal emulator and the programmer microcontroller used the incoming serial data stream to program the device.

This story is really used for the last criteria for deciding whether or not an interface is appropriate for RS-232. Even if you are going to create your own interface, you should make the commands man-readable and producible. This will allow you to debug the external device by simply sending and receiving data from the terminal emulator without having to develop debug software that is of no use to anybody when the application is finished.

When I've talked about this, I usually receive the reply this is terribly wasteful. A command to the external device, or coming back to the PC, which might take one byte in binary form could require up to 10 bytes in man-readable form (one byte for each bit of the command and a carriage return and line-feed characters added to the end of the command). This requires 1000% more data to be sent than if binary data was just used.

When this concern is raised, I usually tend to respond with "What's the problem?" By definition, commands are telling a device to start doing something. The commands should not be that complex or frequent (this raises a pretty obvious concern, which is addressed in a couple of paragraphs). If 10 bytes are required instead of one in a command that is sent once per second, why is this a bad thing?

If 10 bytes are sent per command at 9600 bps, this will require 0.0104 seconds, as opposed to 0.00104 seconds for a single-byte command. As humans, we cannot perceive the difference between something happening at 1/100 second, versus 1/1000 second. If this command is sent to initiate an action, I don't believe that you will see the difference in the operation of the external device.

In external equipment (such as a graphics plotter), the commands are sent multiple times per second and such a difference would be noticeable. I don't consider these strings to be commands, I consider them to be data. In the programmer example, the program to be burned into the device was a series of instruction words (in an Intel IH8XS9A-formatted file). In this case, I downloaded the program (as a text file using an editor) and then parsed the lines and burned them into the device.

In a graphics plotter, the pen commands would really be considered data as well. In this case, *commands* would be nongraphing commands, such as Start, Stop, and Eject.

Transferring data between a PC and an external device should be done with as standard a protocol as possible. Some of the most popular protocols include "Kermit" (developed by Columbia University) and "ZMODEM" (the result of evolving PC asynchronous data protocols). For both of these cases, you can get the specifications or use prewritten programs without licensing fees. Personally, I prefer ZModem for no other reason than for most terminal programs; you can send files without having to prepare the receiver by selecting the Receive function. Normally, when they see the ZMODEM preamble, they know that a file is coming and starts receiving it without preparing the receiver.

Or, you can use a straight text transfer to send data. Text transfers send data as is, without any changes or checking. A few years ago, I worked with an engineer that was trying to send a data file to a vendor. They agreed that the data would be sent as a text file and the vendor set up a PC with a modem to receive it. Every time the engineer sent the data, the receive would fail because his modem hung up the phone.

Halfway through his file was the string *ATH* followed by a Carriage Return character. This is the Hayes modem command for hanging up a modem.

The lesson of this was (at least to me), never transfer data through a modem using a text transfer. Ideally data should be send in a ".hex" format with no opportunities for AT command set strings to be sent.

"Bit-Banging" Serial Interface Software for Microcontrollers

In this chapter, I've probably screwed up your plans to create a new product that will sell in the millions; you wanted to create a simple device that could be attached to the serial port using a nonstandard protocol. To make matters worse, you've probably designed it using a cheap microcontroller (to maximize your profits) that does not have a standard serial port.

Maybe your microcontroller has a serial port, but, to minimize costs, you want to use the single-resistor interface and the microcontroller can't receive inverted (TTL/CMOS Mark and Space states).

What are you going to do?

Before you try out your nonstandard interface, here are two suggestions for creating your own serial interface on a cheap and simple microcontroller.

For the microcontroller C programs presented in this section, I really only use C to demonstrate how the data receives and transmits work. I would be amazed if a microcontroller C language could take this code without modification and be able to send and receive serial data. I would expect the actual code used for serial communications to be written in assembler.

The first method to send and receive serial data is commonly referred to as *bit banging*. You manually shift in and out the serial packet. This isn't very sophisticated, but it works well for applications where you don't have to do anything while the data is being sent or received (for this case, I'll describe a different method).

Simply shifting data out can be accomplished by:

```
SerOut( data )                              //  Subroutine to Shift Data
{                                           //    out

int i;

  outp( inp( SerPort ) & !( 1 << bit );     //  Output the "Start Bit"
  BitDlay();                                //    and delay one bit period

  for ( i = 0; i < 8; i++ ) {               //  Shift Out all 8 Bits

    outp(( inp( SerPort ) & !( 1 << bit ) | (( data & 1 ) << bit ));
    BitDlay();                              //  Delay one bit period
                                            //    after Outputting the
                                            //    Current Bit
    data = data >> 1;                       //  Make the Next Highest Bit
                                            //    the Lowest to Check

  }  //  endfor

  outp( inp( SerPort ) & ( 1 << bit ));     //   Output "Stop Bit"
  BitDlay();

}  //  End SerOut
```

In this example routine I've really simplified how it would work and assumed that each instruction (except for BitDlay) takes no time at all to execute. If you were to implement this routine, you would have to carefully time it and provide accurate delays to be sure that each bit was output after the correct (and same) number of cycles from the previous bit.

Receiving data would be fairly similar, with the operation starting at the detection of the start bit (Fig. 23-21).

In this case, when the start bit was detected (either through polling or an interrupt on state change), the software waits a half-bit period, polls the start bit again to be sure that it's still low (and not a glitch) and then, after waiting a full bit period, polls each of the incoming bits.

A C-code interrupt handler could be used to receive the data coming in.

```
interrupt SerIn()                           //  Interrupt Handler to
{                                           //    Receive an incoming
                                            //    Serial Byte
int i;

char data;

  pushContext();                            //  Save the Context
  HalfBitDlay();                            //    Registers

  if (( inp( SerPort ) & ( 1 << bit )) == 0 ) {    //  Have the Start Bit

    for ( i = 0; i < 8; i++ ) {             //  Shift Out all 8 Bits

      data = ( data << 1 ) + (( inp( SerPort ) >> 1 ) & 1 );
                                            //  Shift the Bit In
      BitDlay();                            //  Delay one bit period
```

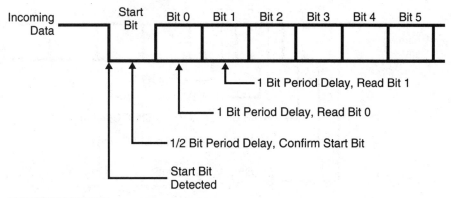

FIGURE 23-21   "Bit Banging" RS-232 data receive.

```
        } // endfor

      SaveRx( data );                          // Save the Received Data

    } // endif

    EnableInt();                               // Re-Enable Interrupt

    popContext();                              // Restore Context Registers

  } // End SerIn - Return from Interupt
```

If an interrupt is not available, then the line in can be polled continuously.

One important aspect of the code might make it a bit confusing. I have taken the most general case for accessing the transmit/receive bit. This means that I have put in ANDs, ORs, and shifts based on the bit value, which might not be required in some applications where the position of the I/O bits are specified in such a way to make writing the code easier.

An important point about this method is that, by placing the location of the poll right in the middle of the expected bits, it maximizes the chance that what it reads is correct because it's as far away as possible from a bit transition.

Although this method does work, consider the large downsides. The first, and most obvious, is that while data is being sent or received, the microcontroller isn't capable of doing anything else. Thus, if a character comes in while one is being sent, it will be ignored or read incorrectly if a space is in the incoming data.

The second downside is the amount of overhead of this method. If you are receiving a large amount of data (i.e., data packets coming in one after another), you will have very little time in the mainline to actually process information).

A much better way, all around is to set up a timer to interrupt every third of a bit period and from here, the data can be sent or received (Fig. 23-22).

In this method, when the interrupt is received, the incoming data is polled to see if a space (start bit) is being received. If it is, a receiving flag is set and, after waiting an extra (1/3-bit period) cycle, the line is polled every three cycles until all eight bits are received.

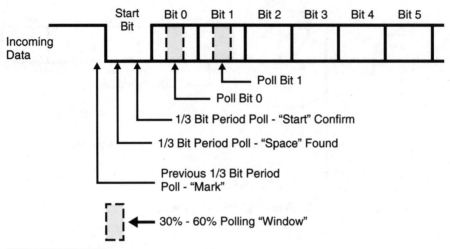

FIGURE 23-22   1/3rd bit polling RS-232 data receive.

By using a 1/3-bit period timer and then waiting 4/3-bit periods, the incoming data is polled between (approximately) 30% and 60% of a bit period from the start of the bit. Thus, we are always within 20% of the middle of the bit (which isn't as good as the previous method, but still more than sufficient for receiving data from the PC).

```
interrupt SerIn()                       //  Receive Serial Data
{

  pushContext();                        //  Save the Context
                                        //   Registers
  ThirdBitDlay();                       //  Set the Timer to a 1/3rd
  EnableInts();                         //   Bit Delay and Enable
                                        //   Ints
  if ( RxData )                         //  Are we Rxing Something?
    if ( !ReadData )                    //  Is this the Confirm?
      if (( inp( SerPort ) & ( 1 << bit )) == 0 ) {
        ReadData = 1;                   //  Yes, Mark the Flag
        ReadCount = 3;                  //  Wait three Cycles for
        ReadBit = 8;                    //   Bit Poll
      } else                            //  No - Keep Polling
        RxData = 0;
    else                                //  Else, Have a Bit to Read?
      if (( --ReadCount ) == 0 ) {      //   Is the Count == 0?
        data = ( data << 1 ) + (( inp( SerPort ) >> 1 ) & 1 );
                                        //  Shift the Bit In
        ReadCount = 3;                  //  Poll another 3 bits
        if (( --ReadBit ) == 0 ) {      //  Read All Bits in?
          RxData = 0;                   //  Yes, Turn Off Reading
          ReadData = 0;                 //   Bits
          SaveRx( data );               //  Save the Data Bit
        } // endif
      } // endif
  else                                  //  Do we have the Start Bit?
```

```
    if (( inp( SerPort ) & ( 1 « bit )) == 0 )
        ReadBit = 1;                            //   Yes, Mark that it is to
                                                //   be checked on the next
                                                //   cycle.

    popContext();                               //  Restore Context Registers

}   //  End SerIn - Return from Interupt
```

This code is simply an interrupt handler in the mainline of the application. The following flags must be declared globally:

```
RxData            - This is set when the Start Bit has been received
ReadData          - This is set when the Start Bit has been Confirmed
```

along with two counters for the current bit (one to count down from three for each full-bit
period and one to count the bits).

A big advantage to this method of handling serial reception is that transmission can be
integrated along with it. In this case, in every three interrupt-handler invocations, a bit is
output. To add sending of the byte TData, TxData, and TxOut flags are added along with
two counters (one for delaying three cycles and the other to count the bits) and, before the
if (RxData) statement in the code, I would add:

```
    if ( TxData )                       //   Is Data Being
                                        //     Transmitted?
        if ( !TxOut ) {                 //   Has the Start Bit been
                                        //     Sent Yet?
            outp( inp( SerPort ) & !( 1 « bit ));        //   No - Send Start
                                        //   Bit
            TxCount = 3;                //   Setup the Tx Bit
            TxBit = 8;
        } else
            if (( —TxCount ) == 0 ) {   //   Send a new Bit?
                outp(( inp( SerPort ) & !( 1 « bit )) | (( TData & 1 )«bit));
                TData = TData » 1;      //   Shift down to the Next
                                        //   Bit
                TxCount = 3;            //   Reset the Cycle Count
                if (( − −TxBit ) == 0 ) //   Have Sent all the Bits?
                    TxData = TxOut = 0; //   Yes, Reset the Flags
            } else
                TxDlay();               //   Make Sure the Cycles
                                        //     match
    else                                //   No Transmission
        TxDlay();                       //     Make sure Cycles match
```

Just remember to be sure that the same number of cycles is executed for each path of the
data-transmission code to ensure that the receive code always ends up on the same cycle.

This method has some very significant advantages over the first one. Actually, all of the
downsides of the previous method are eliminated with this technique.

And, notwithstanding the effort to time the transmitting code, this is probably simpler to
code than the first methods. It probably seems hard to believe when you look at it, but not
having to time up each bit (along with the effort in figuring out how many cycles is required for the delays) is actually a major help.

It has a few other advantages. The first is in code; you can treat the serial receive and
transmit like a hardware device; you give it data to send or poll a data-received bit and

that's it. As well, you can have your interrupt handler load from and store to a buffer, which means that the main line doesn't have to bother with sending or receiving data until a complete command has been transferred. To further simplify your mainline, an intelligent buffer can be set up, where the mainline is only notified if a complete command (including a CR character) has been received.

One of the biggest advantages of this method is its ability to use any pin of the microcontroller to receive data. In the first method, if interrupts are to be used, then only specific pins can be used to receive the data. These pins might be better used for other parts of the application.

What happens if you want to use the second method, but your microcontroller doesn't have a timer interrupt available? In this case, you will have to time your application so that the SerIn routine is called after a set number of instruction cycles. This way, your mainlines execution will become the timer.

When you do this, you're going to find that sometimes you just can't get the 1/3 cycles without using up a lot of instructions. In these cases, you should just ignore using only 1/3 cycles and use one or two cycles extra, but be sure that they are placed in such a way that this can only happen once per byte being received.

Microcontroller timers are really beyond the scope of this book, I want to leave with you with one last trick to implement the second method of transmitting/receiving asynchronous data.

Most microcontrollers have an eight-bit counter that either counts up or counts down and causes an interrupt when it has to carry or borrow. The time required to jump to the interrupt handler might be nondeterministic or writing to the timer might change other hardware (such as a prescaler with undesirable effects).

With this in mind, consider the speeds required to implement the 1/3-bit polling routine. If the timer overflows once every 256 clock cycles, you can take advantage of something.

The speed needed to drive the internal clock and poll data coming in on the line every 1/3 bit at 9600 bps could be calculated as:

$$9600 \text{ bits/second} \times 3 \text{ polls/bit} \times 256 \text{ cycles/poll}$$

$$= 7{,}372{,}800 \text{ cycles/second}$$

Which is a standard frequency for crystals (along with 14.7456 MHz) and would allow you to implement this method of a software transmit/receive without ever having to update the clock (once the clock overflows, it is allowed to run to the next overflow without being updated). This will ensure that you will poll the data precisely every cycle.

PRACTICAL

RS-232 INTERFACING

In the previous chapter, I have really outlined what I consider to be the "right" way to provide an RS-232 interface. The receiver should be intelligent and able to work from a standard terminal screen without any special software. This will allow the interface hardware to be debugged separately from the PC application. Creating the interface in such a way that it can be used separately allows you to reduce variables when you develop interfaces. Reducing variables is a good thing that will allow you to more easily debug your application.

When I originally started this book, I was going to describe how my YAP (a microchip PICMicro programmer that I described in "Programming and Customizing the PIC Microcontroller") is a good example of this. But as I was writing this book, I bought a new PC with Windows 98 installed. I discovered that the download function wouldn't work and the application execute had a problem when the *Ctrl-C* key sequence was pressed to stop the PICMicro from executing.

As I debugged the problems, I discovered a few things. First, don't count on "canned" (operating system) utilities being the same between versions. This probably sounds like a "no-brainer," but many of the MS-DOS utilities have not changed since MS-DOS Version 1.0. I took for granted this would be also true for Windows; it's not, at least where "HyperTerminal" is concerned.

In the new version of HyperTerminal, I found that when a text file is downloaded, every line is terminated with only a carriage return (0x00D) and not a carriage-return/line-feed (0x00A) combination—even if the source file includes them. If you attempt to change the application's properties, you'll find it crashes.

This lead me to realize that a much more general case is required for handling line ends. Not surprisingly, I had already written such an algorithm for use in printing data to the VRAM (similar to *printf*):

```
Int CharHandle( char In_Char )      //  Display Character on the Screen
{

int  Retvalue = 0;

  switch( In_Char ) {               //  Handle the Different Characters
    case CR:                        //  Handle the Carriage Return
      if ( Last_Char == LF )        //  If Last Character was LF
        Last_Char = Retvalue = 0;   //  Don't Return Anything
      else  {                       //  Else, Process the CR
        NewLine();                  //  Scroll the Display Up?
        Last_Char = CR;
        Retvalue = 1;               //  Indicate there's a New Line
      }
      break;
    case LF:                        //  Handle the Line Feed
      if ( Last_Char == CR )        //  If Last Character was a CR
        Last_Char = Retvalue = 0;   //  Don't Return Anything
      else  {                       //  Else, Process the LF
        NewLine();                  //  Scroll the Display Up?
        Last_Char = LF;
        Retvalue = 1;               //  Indicate there's a New Line
      }
      break;

      :                             //  Handle Other Characters

    default:                        //  Handle Display Characters
      Output( In_Char );            //  Put Character on the Display
      Last_Char = Retvalue = 0;     //  Note, No New Line
  }

  return Retvalue;                  //  Return New Line to Caller

}  //  End CharHandle
```

This code will return a *1* the first time a CR/LF is encountered and when the following is the other, it will ignore it. *Last_Char* is a global variable that saves the last character that indicated the end of the line.

A Break consists of the serial line being held at *0* for more than one full serial byte. This aspect of the NRZ standard, while not unusual in PC and workstation serial ports, is not often implemented in many microcontroller's built-in serial ports. To avoid potential problems, you should use *Ctrl-C*, which is simply ASCII 0x003 and an accepted way of passing Break information to an external device.

In many ways, it should go without saying, but three-wire RS-232 with no handshaking is the best way to design your applications. Going along with this, I always use standard cables with RTS-CTS and DSR-DTR shorted together at the device's RS-232 interface.

This will allow the terminal emulator to execute—even if the handshaking option is still enabled in the emulator.

Serial Data Transfer Between Two PCs

One of the biggest problem areas I find people run into is hooking up two PCs together for transferring files. The problems seem to stem in a "bipolar" distribution: people either think they don't understand the RS-232 specification or think that they do. In either case, the engineer or technician that tries to create something on their own, invariably runs into problems and spends a lot of time spinning wheels trying to figure out what is wrong. In this sub-chapter, I wanted to show how I could use two PCs' serial ports and default software to provide a quick and dirty interface between them for transferring files (Fig. 24-1).

I've found that deciding upon a convention and sticking to it makes serial interfacing a lot easier. The convention that I use is to keep the PC's serial port as a 9-pin male DTE connection. This standard was set with the PC/AT. I prefer it to the PC/XT 25-pin standard simply because it is physically smaller.

In some cases, this means converting a 25-pin connector to 9 pins and this can be done either using commercial cables or a molded plastic 25-pin to 9-pin interface. Normally, I run a six or 10-foot extension cable that is a "straight through," which means that the PC's serial output format is available wherever I need it.

This also brings up another important aspect of my convention: I don't make any cables or connectors if I can help it. This is true for connecting to another PC and it is true when I am connecting to an external device. Life is too short to be making cables of any type and good-quality straight-through 9-pin cable can be purchased for as little as $5. Buying two D-shell connectors, plastic shields, and appropriate cables will set you back at least that much and are a real pain to wire up.

Now, I can easily interconnect two PCs, each with the same output, using a null modem. The name *null modem* comes from the idea that to connect two computers together serially, they are normally connected to a modem and then through telephone lines to the other PC. A null modem is used to simulate this connection and allow two computers to communicate without the use of a modem, simply by passing the appropriate signals to each computer.

9-Pin Female
to Female
"Gender Changer"

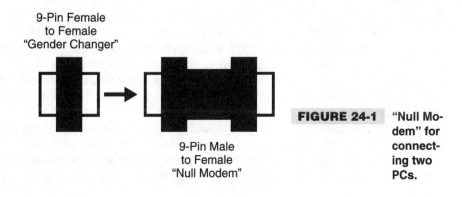

9-Pin Male
to Female
"Null Modem"

FIGURE 24-1 "Null Modem" for connecting two PCs.

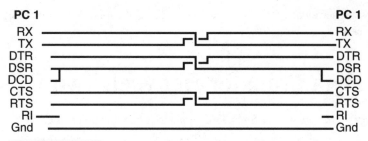

FIGURE 24-2   PC to PC serial connection ("Null Modem").

A typical PC null modem can be a cable or a small box (as is shown in Fig. 24-1). The wiring of a PC null modem is shown in Fig. 24-2. This wiring will allow a PC to communicate with another PC—even with hardware handshaking enabled. For this application, the null modem should have female connectors on both ends.

As indicated, it is quite simple to buy a null modem cable or small box to convert it for just a few dollars. Most of them have a male and a female connector attached. For the null modem to work properly with the DTE 9-pin male D-shell connector that I use, I add a female-to-female gender changer to the end of the box. After doing this, I end up with a null modem with two female connectors that can be connected directly to the serial extension cables without any modification.

The minimum parts that you will require for this is a straight-through male-to-female 9-pin cable, the null modem box, and the gender changer. These parts can often be found when you are on a business trip, at a local "Business Depot." I have been able to impress and help out co-workers and managers on several occasions when they have forgotten their laptop's diskette or CD-ROM drives when on a business trip and need to transfer data between two PCs.

With the serial connection created, you can use HyperTerminal (in Windows 95 and Windows 98), Terminal (in Windows 3.x) or any freeware terminal emulator with file-transfer capability to connect the two PCs. Once the two PC's are wired together, then you can test the link by sending a message, such as shown in Fig. 24-3.

To set up the link, create a new "direct connect" session in the terminal emulator. If the message isn't passed to the other PC or is garbled, check the data rate and format to ensure they are common between the two PCs. If no message comes up, chances are that you haven't selected the correct serial port in one or the other PCs. If this is the case, be sure to keep track of which serial ports have been tried and go through every combination.

For a fully configured PC with three possible serial ports (assuming that COM4 has the same I/O addresses as the SVGA control registers), nine connection combinations are possible for each of the PC's three serial ports. Realistically, for a laptop PC, you will only have COM1 and COM2, which means that you only have four test connection combinations to test before finding the correct interfaces. With a bit of practice, you will be able to complete the connections in less than 30 seconds—even if you have never worked with the two PCs before.

When making the connection, you can theoretically go up to 115,200 bps, but I typically stick to 38,400 bps. The reason for not going at the maximum theoretical speed is not that the simple terminal emulators provided with Windows or available free of charge over the Internet cannot keep up with this maximum speed but at higher speeds, the probability of an in-

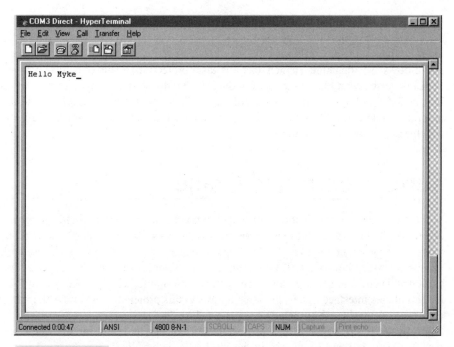

FIGURE 24-3   PC serial connection using "Hyperterminal".

correctly read bit is higher. This means that to have a completely reliable connection, you should go with a somewhat slower speed. I typically only work with the 8-N-1 protocol and any errors that would have to be caught by parity are not handled well by the terminal emulators.

At 38,400 bps, a 1-MB file can be transferred in about four and a half minutes.

When transferring the file, I always use one of the binary file transfer protocols, such as Kermit, X-Modem, Y-Modem, or Z-Modem that are built into the terminal emulator. These protocols do provide a modicum of error checking and will provide you with feedback as to the status of the transfer in some emulators. As well, these protocols allow you to set up the receiver before the transmitter without a short timeout occurring.

When transferring multiple files, I find it useful to first "PKZIP" them together into one file. This allows one single transfer instead of having to monitor the progress of each transfer and re-initiate sending multiple files.

When you look at serial cables in computer stores, you will probably see something that is labeled *PC-to-PC Serial Interconnect Cable*, which will have two female 9-pin D-shells (and optionally two 25-pin D-shells) and seems exactly what you are looking for. It will seem that by just buying this cable, you will dispense with the hassle of buying and connecting the null modem and gender changer. Before you buy this cable check to see if it provides internal null-modem capabilities, chances are it won't: instead, it will be wired to provide "LapLink" support, which is not a true null modem. Buying this type of cable will mean that you will have to buy the "LapLink" software as well.

"LapLink" is an excellent product and has been continually updated to allow PCs to pass files between each other as if they were on local hard drives. LapLink was first introduced in the mid-1980s when laptops first became available with 3.5" floppy drives and a serial (or parallel) cable and software was a much cheaper solution than adding a 3.5" floppy drive to a desktop machine. The LapLink process is very fast, avoids the need to "PKZIP" multiple files and is probably the only way in which you will be able to transfer files with a Windows NT machine (which has file/disk protection). The only disadvantage to LapLink versus what I have shown previously is that my solution can be carried out for as little as $10, but LapLink and cables will set you back roughly $200. LapLink and the appropriate cable can also be somewhat of an unusual commodity in some retail outlets, which can also be a disadvantage.

Serial Controlled Crane

Most of the interface applications presented in this book are what I would call *forced examples* of PC interfaces and their presence is really to show how interfaces work, rather than providing something of real value. This project shows how the PC can be used to control the electric motors of a toy crane using an RS-232 interface (Fig. 24-4). The actual operation and hardware/software interface itself is very simple, which allows you to focus on the actual user interface. Later, the book returns to this project to show how an interesting dialog-box control can be created very simply (Fig. 24-5).

For the serial motor controller, I decided to use a design and raw card that I first created for "Programming and Customizing the 8051 Microcontroller" (Fig. 24-6). This circuit uses an Atmel AT89C2051 8051-compatible microcontroller to provide the interface to the PC. The RS-232 conversion uses the Dallas Semiconductor 275 RS-232 interface and the motors are driven by the Unitrode 293D motor driver.

This circuit uses two 9-V batteries to independently power the AT89C2051 and the motors. For the microcontroller power (which requires 5 V), a 78L05 regulator is used. When the circuit is connected to the PC, a 9-pin D-shell connector, wired in a DCE configuration with the DSR/DTR and CTS/RTS pairs are shorted together to allow a straight-through RS-232 cable to interface with the circuit with hardware handshaking enabled. The motor interface uses screw terminals to allow easy connection/removal. For "Programming and Customizing the 8051 Microcontroller," I designed a small circuit board and I used this for the simplicity of not having to wire my own application.

When you look at the circuit and how the 275 is wired, you will see that the V_{drv} pin is connected to +5 V (V_{cc}), rather than +9 V, which would give a wider RS-232 voltage swing. I did not put in this wiring because, when I designed the card, I didn't think to do it. The card itself has provisions for a switch on both of the +9-V battery connectors, which are shorted in this application (the battery and connector themselves are used as the switch). The 9-V power trace "downstream" from the switch could have been used for the V_{drv} voltage and would give a +9 V to PC RS-232 negative voltage (which is normally -12 V).

I wanted to make the interface as simple as possible (to avoid creating complex 8051) source code and allow it to run from Windows HyperTerminal by a user very easily. I came up with the single instruction format:

```
#C<CR>
```

FIGURE 24-4   Toy crane.

FIGURE 24-5   8051 based serial motor interface.

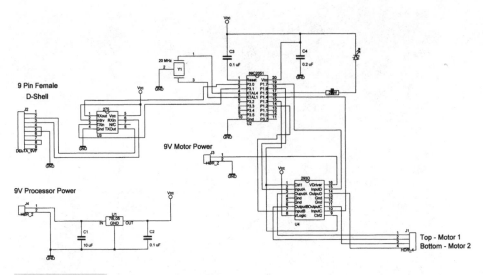

FIGURE 24-6 Serial motor controller circuit.

Where # is the number of the motor to control (the circuit can control two motors, *1* and *2*). *C* is the command. For this application, the only commands are *F* (Forward), *B* (Backward), and *S* (Stop). This is shown in (Fig. 24-7).

A 2400-bps 8-N-1 interface is used and, within the microcontroller application, the characters that are sent are echoed back by the microcontroller to show that the link is up. This feature is important later in the book when checking to see if the interface is up and enabled.

If the user can see that they are entering the wrong value, then they can backspace over the data that was sent. In the microcontroller, only two parameters are loaded; anything other than a carriage return (*Enter* on the PC's keyboard) or *Backspace* will be ignored. If the values sent are invalid, the microcontroller places a "-" at the end of the line and ignores the command. This is also shown in Fig. 24-7.

The toy crane I used for the application was part of a "construction playground" I bought from "Toys'R Us" for $20. The crane uses two C-cell batteries that provide a nominal 3 V to the motor. To simplify how I wanted the application to be wired, I used a 9-V battery with a 50% duty cycle PWM. This gives an average effective voltage of 4.5 V to the 293D that has a 1.5-V drop across the drivers. This results in an effective 3-V average drive to the motors in the toy crane.

The code itself is very simple and was originally written in 8051 assembler for the UMPS development system. A built-in timer interrupt is used for the PWM and polling is used for the RS-232 serial interface, as well as turning on and off the motors.

Rather than reproduce it here, I will show how it works in C pseudo-code:

```
//  Motor - Controlling two Motors using an 8051 and Serial Port
//
//  Serial Commands:
//   #F - Run Motor # Forward.
//   #B - Run Motor # Backwards.
```

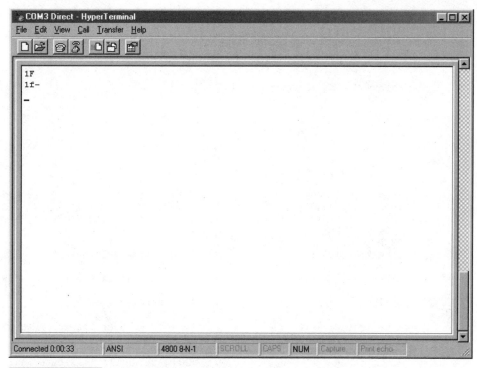

FIGURE 24-7   Serial motor controller "HyperTerminal" I/F.

```
//    #S - Stop Motor #.
//
//  Timer 1 Interrupt Rate: 75.76 KHz (for a 18.94 KHz PWM Frequency)
//
//  Serial Interface Speed: 2400 bps (Actually)
//
//  Myke Predko
//  98.10.19
//
//  Hardware Notes:
//  AT89C2051 is used as the Microcontroller
//   - Oscillator Speed is 20 MHz
//  Serial Output is on P3.1
//  Serial Input is on P3.0
//  LED Control is at P1.5
//  Motor PWM is p1.3
//  Motor 1 + Control is P1.6
//  Motor 1 - Control is P1.2
//  Motor 2 + Control is P1.7
//  Motor 2 - Control is P1.4

//  Constant Declarations
TimerReload EQU OEAh            //  Value to Reload the Timer With

//  Variable Declarations
int Counter = 020h;             //  Real Time Counter
int Motor = 0;                  //  Motor Specified
int Direction = 0;              //  Direction for Wheels to Turn
```

```
// Subroutines
org 01Bh                        // Timer 1 - PWM Handler

int Timer1()                    // Run the Motor at Quarter Data Check
{                               //   Speed

  MotorPWM = ( ++Counter > > 1 ) & 1;

}  // End Timer1


// Mainline

  P1 = %00100011;               // Turn off Motors

  SCON = %01010000;             // Serial Port in Asynch 8 Bit Mode
  TMOD = %00100001;             // Timer1 in 8 Bit Reload
  TH1 = TL1 = TimerReload;      // Set up Timer with 2400 bps Reload
  TCON != 040h;                 // Enable Timer1
  SMOD &= 07Fh;                 // Reset SMOD Bit
  IE = %10001000;               // Enable Timer1 Interrupt

  SBUF = BS;                    // Start Application off with a BS

  while ( 1 == 1 ) {            // Loop Forever

    while ( RI == 0 );          // Wait for a User Character to be
                                //   Received
    switch( SBUF ) {            // Handle the Character
      case CR:                  // Carriage Return - Execute Ins?
        switch( Motor ) {       // Handle for Each Motor
          case "1":             //   Motor1?
            switch( Direction ) {
              case 'F':         // Move Forward
                Motor1 = Forward;
                break;
              case 'B':         // Move Backwards
                Motor1 = Backwards;
                break;
              case 'S':         // Stop Motor
                Motor1 = Stop;
                break;
              default:          // Invalid Command
                SBUF = '-';
            }
            break;
          case "2":             //   Motor2?
            switch( Direction ) {
              case 'F':         // Move Forward
                Motor2 = Forward;
                break;
              case 'B':         // Move Backwards
                Motor2 = Backwards;
                break;
              case 'S':         // Stop Motor
                Motor2 = Stop;
                break;
              default:          // Invalid Command
                SBUF = '-';
            }
            break;
```

```
      default:                      //  Invalid Motor Specification
        SBUF = '-';                 //   Output Invalid Message Char
    }
    SBUF = CR;                      //  Echo Back the Character
    Motor = Direction = 0;          //  Clear the Variables
    break;
  case LF:                          //  Line Feed Character - Echo Back
    SBUF = LF;
    break;
  case BS:                          //  BackSpace Character - Go Back
    if ( Direction != 0 ) {
      Direction = 0;                //  Clear the Value
      SBUF = BS;                    //  BackSpace on "HyperTerminal"
    } else if ( Motor != 0 ) {
      Motor = 0;                    //  Clear the Value
      SBUF = BS;                    //  BackSpace on "HyperTerminal"
    } else;                         //  If at Start, No Backspace
    break;
  default:                          //  Else, Add the Character
    if ( Motor == 0 ) {             //   Add the Motor Character
      Motor = SBUF;
      SBUF = Motor;                 //  Echo Back to the Display
    } else if ( Direction == 0 ) {
      Direction = SBUF;             //  Load up the Direction and
      SBUF = Direction;             //   Echo it Back
    } else;                         //  Else, Can't add, ignore character
    }
  }
} // End Motor
```

The assembly-language source code doesn't take up too many more lines than this pseudo-code.

Now, in your own applications, simple "help" or "welcome" information can be included. For the purposes of this application, which was to demonstrate how a simple serial PC interface application, which doesn't require any PC software, no user information is really needed. This application is designed to be controlled by the Visual Basic front end that is presented later in the book.

25

THE

CENTRONICS

PARALLEL

PORT

Several years before the IBM PC first became available, "Centronics" built and sold printers using a simple parallel bus interface. This bus was used to pass data from a computer to a printer and poll the printer status, waiting until additional characters could be sent. As part of the format, a special connector was also used.

This connector format became very popular and was adopted by a number of printer manufacturers and quickly became an industry standard. The Centronics printer port's advantages were that its hardware could be replicated by using a few simple components, it was relatively fast (compared to RS-232 ports), and software could be easily written for it.

Today, the parallel port is the first device most people look to when simple I/O expansion must be implemented in the PC. I consider this unfortunate because this port is actually poorly designed for the purpose. If you are looking for efficient digital input/digital output in the PC, ISA or USB busses should be considered first.

Hardware Configuration

The parallel port itself is very simple; the design in the PC/AT consists of just seven TTL chips. When I originally wrote this chapter, I felt bad that I didn't provide an essay going back over 100 years, as I did with the serial port, but the parallel (printer) port is really a hardware design solution to interface with a specific device. Actually, before the Centronics interface design was available, printers were typically attached to computers via an RS-232 interface.

Over the last 20 years, as PCs have gotten more complex, so have the printers. When the PC was first introduced, the standard printer was a relabeled (to "IBM") Epson dot-matrix Centronics-compatible graphics printer, which used the parallel port's data and handshaking lines to control the data transfer (a byte at a time) from the PC. The early printers, after receiving a byte, would hold the Host PC from sending the next byte by indicating that it was Busy.

This method of printing works well, but is inefficient for large volumes of data. To counteract this, MS-DOS could run a print application as a TSR, sending the data each time the handshaking lines indicated that the data had been transmitted and the printer was ready for the next byte. This method was somewhat inefficient (especially with the relatively slow early PCs) and a common solution was to add a hardware printer buffer, which would store the print data and pass it to the printer without involving the PC. These solutions were adequate for simple text data, but, as applications became more complex and graphics orientated, this became less than adequate.

Modern "ink bubble" and "Laser" printers typically buffer an entire page or more of data before they start printing. This allows the PC to send data at the full speed of the parallel port that is limited to the I/O bus where it is connected. This data rate is usually on the order of 300,000 bytes per second and avoids the problems of early printers (although, in terms of speeds, things haven't changed much). A graphics-filled Web page might have several megabytes of data that will take several seconds to send to the printer; this complexity brings the effective print speed down to 20 (or more) seconds per page. This is similar to that of the early dot-matrix and daisy-wheel printers.

As the capabilities of printers have improved, the need for bidirectional data transfer came about as Laser and other full-sheet printers became available. This requirement has actually spawned a new class of device, including portable diskette drivers, scanners, etc., which use this bidirectional data-transfer protocol to pass data back to the PC via the parallel port. Most modern devices connected to the parallel port use a bidirectional data protocol and really avoid using the handshaking lines.

To model the parallel port, I usually go to the base circuit (Fig. 25-1).

This diagram shows the parallel-port connector pin out, along with the registers involved with passing data and the appropriate bits for the different functions. The control register is used to enable the data-output latch drivers and enable-interrupt requests from the parallel-port hardware.

In Fig. 25-1, it is assumed that the parallel port is a 25-pin DB-25 male connector. The true Centronics printer connector is a 36-pin shell, but this shell is connected to the PC's

Data Bus

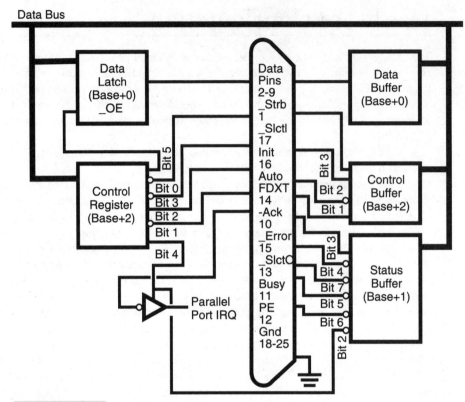

FIGURE 25-1   Parallel port block diagram.

DB-25F parallel-port connector via a male connector and several feet of cable. When developing hardware that interfaces to the PC, I normally use Straight-through DB-25M to DB-25F (female) cable. This cable is normally used as straight through serial cables and extensions to the Centronics connector cables. The advantage of using this type of cable is that the output can be brought from your PC to your bench and not be translated in any way. This is an advantage in applications where the hardware interface will be connected directly to the parallel port on the PC.

   If you look at the PC/AT technical reference manual, you will see that the parallel port is designed with 74LS TTL logic, which is capable of driving 20 mA (or greater) loads. It is a very dangerous assumption to make that all PCs have this kind of parallel-port drive capability. Most modern PCs have the parallel-port function embedded in the "Super I/O" chip. This chip is an ASIC that has most of the user I/O functions, as well as timers and the interrupt controllers for the PC. In this case, the parallel port (at best) will only be able to source a couple of mA or so. To be on the safe side, I recommend that no more than 1 mA ever be sourced by a parallel-port pin.

The registers that provide the functions are:

REGISTER	ADDRESS	FUNCTION
Data	Base + 0	Pass 8 bits of data to and from the PC
Control	Base + 2	Pass control signals to the external device
Status	Base + 1	Return the printer status

Where the Base addresses are 0x0378 and 0x0278 for LPT1 and LPT2, respectively. Hardware interrupt requests can be initiated from the hardware, interrupt 0x00F for LPT1 and 0x00D from LPT2. Although some standards provide for an LPT3 and LPT4, these are somewhat "loose" and might not be possible to implement in some PCs and adapter types and configurations.

When the parallel port passes data to a printer, the I/O pins create the basic waveform shown in Fig. 25-2.

It is important to note that the Printer BIOS routines will not send a new character to the printer until it is no longer busy. When *Busy* is no longer active, the *Ack* line is pulsed active, which can be used to request an interrupt to indicate to data output code that the printer is ready to accept another character.

The timing of the circuit for printer applications is quite simple with 0.5-μsecs minimum delays needed between edges on the waveforms in Fig. 25-2.

When interfacing to the parallel port, because the different port pins are seemingly inverted at random, I use a set of functions that I created a number of years ago to eliminate the confusion. These routines change all the input and output lines to being positively active (to simplify trying to figure out what is happening).

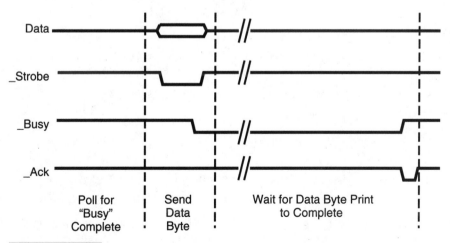

FIGURE 25-2   **Parallel port printer byte write waveform.**

```
PPortOut( int BaseAddr )        // Enable Data Bit Drivers
{

  outp( BaseAddr + 2, inp( BaseAddr + 2 ) & 0x0DF );

} // End PPortOut

PPortIn( int BaseAddr )         // Disable Data Bit Drivers
{

  outp( BaseAddr + 2, inp( BaseAddr + 2 ) | 0x020 );

} // End PPortIn

PPortIRQEn( int BaseAddr )      // Enable the Parallel Ports Interrupt
{                               //   Requesting Hardware

  outp( BaseAddr + 2, inp( BaseAddr + 2 ) | 0x010 );

} // End PPortIRQEn

PPortIRQDis( int BaseAddr )     // Disable the Parallel Ports Interrupt
{                               //   Requesting Hardware

  outp( BaseAddr + 2, inp( BaseAddr + 2 ) & 0x0EF );

} // End PPortIRQDis

PPortHiSLCT( Int BaseAddr )     // Set "SLCT In" (Pin 17) to an
{                               //   Electrical "High"

  outp( BaseAddr + 2, inp( BaseAddr + 2 ) | 0x008 );

} // End PPortHiSLCT

PPortLoSLCT( Int BaseAddr )     // Set "SLCT In" (Pin 17) to an
{                               //   Electrical "low"

  outp( BaseAddr + 2, inp( BaseAddr + 2 ) & 0x0F7 );

} // End PPortLoSLCT

PPortHiInit( Int BaseAddr )     // Set "Init" (Pin 16) to an
{                               //   Electrical "High"

  outp( BaseAddr + 2, inp( BaseAddr + 2 ) & 0x0FB );

} // End PPortHiInit

PPortLoInit( Int BaseAddr )     // Set "Init" (Pin 16) to an
{                               //   Electrical "low"

  outp( BaseAddr + 2, inp( BaseAddr + 2 ) | 0x004 );

} // End PPortLoInit

PPortHiAuto( Int BaseAddr )     // Set "Auto FDXT" (Pin 14) to an
{                               //   Electrical "High"

  outp( BaseAddr + 2, inp( BaseAddr + 2 ) & 0x0FD );
```

```
}  //  End PPortHiAuto

PPortLoAuto( Int BaseAddr )      //  Set "Auto FDXT" (Pin 14) to an
{                                //    Electrical "low"

   outp( BaseAddr + 2, inp( BaseAddr + 2 ) | 0x002 );

}  //  End PPortLoAuto

PPortHiStrobe( Int BaseAddr )    //  Set "Strobe" (Pin 1) to an
{                                //    Electrical "High"

   outp( BaseAddr + 2, inp( BaseAddr + 2 ) & 0x0FE );

}  //  End PPortHiStrobe

PPortLoStrobe( Int BaseAddr )    //  Set "Strobe" (Pin 1) to an
{                                //    Electrical "low"

   outp( BaseAddr + 2, inp( BaseAddr + 2 ) | 0x001 );

}  //  End PPortLoStrobe
```

In the Status bit read routines, note that I have not included reads for bits that are driven in from the control port. I assume that the control register latches are good and that the devices connected to the port are not holding it high or low. Also, for the Status bit read routines, the result returned is either zero or one and inverted, if appropriate.

```
PPortRdBusy( Int BaseAddr )      //  Read the "Busy" (Pin 11) handshaking
{                                //    line

   return 1 ^ (( inp( BaseAddr + 1 ) & 0x080 ) >> 7 );

}  //  End PPortRdBusy

PPortRdError( Int BaseAddr )     //  Read the "Printer Error" (Pin 12)
{                                //    handshaking line

   return 1 ^ (( inp( BaseAddr + 1 ) & 0x020 ) >> 5 );

}  //  End PPortRdBusy

PPortRdSLCTO( Int BaseAddr )     //  Read the "SLCT Out" (Pin 13)
{                                //    handshaking line

   return 1 ^ (( inp( BaseAddr + 1 ) & 0x010 ) >> 4 );

}  //  End PPortRdSLCTO

PPortRdAck( Int BaseAddr )       //  Read the "Ack" (Pin 10) handshaking
{                                //    line

   return ( inp( BaseAddr + 1 ) & 0x008 ) >> 3;

}  //  End PportRdAck
```

With these routines, external digital hardware can be controlled by the four output bits driven to the parallel port and data is either read from or written to and an additional four input pins are available.

Types of Interfaces

In a surprising number of ways, the parallel port can be used to interface with external hardware. This section shows how the parallel port can be used to provide a simple hardware interface between bus I/O devices, I2C devices, and LEDs. I'll leave it as an "exercise for the reader" to come up with your own interfaces to straight logic.

Interfacing to a bus I/O device, such as an 8250 UART, is quite easy with the parallel port (Fig. 25-3).

In this case, the eight data bits are used to emulate a microprocessor's data bus and also to provide simple register addressing information to the chip. These addresses are stored in a latch using _STROBE_ to load it in. The chip Read and Write lines are provided by the remaining two outputs and I used the parallel port's _Ack_ interrupt as the interrupt for the serial port. For this application, the chip-select line on the 8250 should always be active.

To send data to the chip, the following code could be used:

```
PPortOut( LPT1 );        // Enable the Parallel Port for output
Dlay();                  // 0.5 usec Delay

outp( LPT1, 0 );         // Set Address 0
Dlay();
```

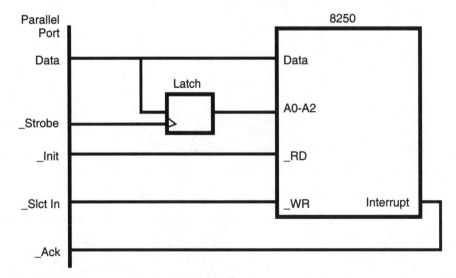

FIGURE 25-3   Connecting an 8250 to a parallel port.

3

```
PPortHIStrobe( LPT1 );      //  Strobe in the Address
PPortloStrobe( LPT1 );
Dlay();

outp( LPT1, DataByte );     //  Strobe out the Data Byte
Dlay();

PPortHIStrobe( LPT1 );      //  Strobe out the Data
PPortloStrobe( LPT1 );
```

This would result in the output waveform shown in Fig. 25-4. Reading a byte from the 8250 would use similar code:

```
PPortOut( LPT1 );           //  Enable the Parallel Port for output
Dlay();                     //  0.5 usec Delay

outp( LPT1, 0 );            //  Set Address 0
Dlay();

PPortHIStrobe( LPT1 );      //  Strobe in the Address
PPortloStrobe( LPT1 );
Dlay();

PPortIn( LPT1 );            //  Disable the Parallel Port's Data Drivers
Dlay();

PPortHIStrobe( LPT1 );      //  Read in the Data on the Strobe
DataByte = inp( LPT1 );
PPortloStrobe( LPT1 );
```

Notice that I have included explicit timing delays for the data to be set up within the 8250. As I've described, these delays are not extremely precise and you cannot depend on the parallel port to provide reliable timings for you.

I2C is a bus protocol that was first developed by Philips in the 1970s as a way of providing a simple I/O bus for microprocessors. Today, it is most widely used with microcontrollers although most modern PC motherboards do have an I2C bus for system monitoring (usually to sense the temperature of the processor). The motherboard I2C bus is usually not available for interfacing to the PC, but you can use the parallel port to provide a simulated I2C bus master (Fig. 25-5).

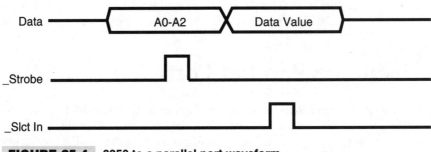

FIGURE 25-4   8250 to a parallel port waveform.

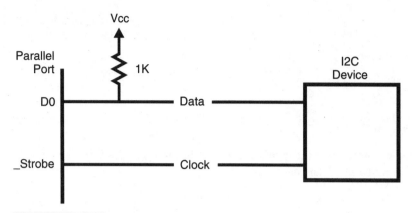

FIGURE 25-5   Connecting an I2C bus to a parallel port.

The beginning of sending an I2C byte would look something like Fig. 25-6. Using the parallel-port functions presented in the previous section and earlier in this one, the writes can be implemented using the basic parallel-port I/O functions. Reading and acknowledge bits will require the data driver to be turned off with the clock still driving the circuit. The pull up on the data line allows data to be driven by I2C devices pulling the line low.

You can find out more about I2C by looking at Philips Semiconductor's Web page.

Single and multisegment LEDs can be wired to the parallel port (Fig. 25-7). The three output bits are used with an eight-bit decoder (the 74S138) as the data is output for each display digit. When this happens reasonably fast (on the order of 500 times per segment per second), the human eye cannot distinguish between when the LED displays are on or off, and it appears that all eight displays are on simultaneously, each one showing different characters.

I use TTL buffers to drive the LED segments and do not use the built-in drivers or the parallel port. If you look at the *PC/AT Technical Reference*, you will see that 74LS TTL parts are used for drivers and should have the capability of driving LEDs on these lines. The problem is with modern PCs that might use CMOS ASIC drivers in a central ASIC for the parallel port.

Very rarely can these CMOS ASIC drivers provide enough current to run LEDs safely for an extended period of time; they could burn out (along with the ASIC). If you wanted to control an LCD display from a parallel port, I would have no concerns about using the parallel port to provide the signals and the power for the device. But for high-current devices, such as LEDs, the parallel port must be buffered against high-current loads.

Using the Parallel Port

I have used the parallel port for a number of applications and I think I'm being honest and accurate when I say *don't use it to interface with hardware unless you absolutely have to and have thought about it a lot.* The problems with using the parallel port include inconsistent timing and limited and confusing I/O capabilities.

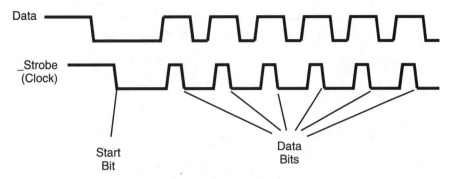

FIGURE 25-6   8250 to a parallel port waveform.

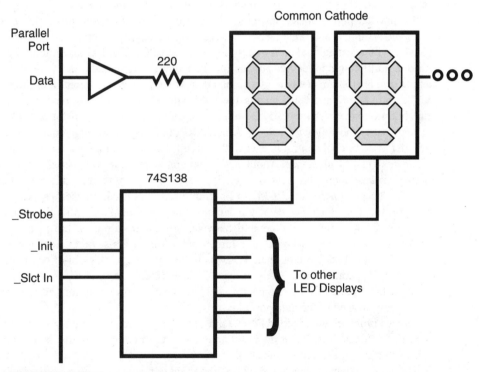

FIGURE 25-7   Connecting a LEDs to a parallel port.

Timing might seem like a surprising complaint—especially when you look at how homogeneous modern PCs have become. It is actually the biggest problem with using the parallel port across a variety of PCs. With modern PCs, the ASICs and adapters used to provide the parallel-port function can vary in how they work and how they are connected to the processor. These connections can range from ISA, PCI, and the processors Local Bus (which is often the case for laptops). This means that the code:

```
Mov DX, Base+2          ; Load DX with the Control Register
Mov AL, Strobe          ; Load a Strobe Active Value
Out DX, AL              ; Make the "_STROBE" Line Active
Mov AL, NotStrobe
Out DX, AL              ; Make the "_STROBE" Line Inactive
```

can range from 1 instruction cycle (as fast as 2 ns on current PCs) to more than 1.5 μsecs with a PC that uses an ISA parallel-port adapter.

This represents a variability of three orders of magnitude.

These timing problems can be worked out in software, as shown in Chapter 20, but this can make the parallel-port application much more complex and difficult to work with when other applications are involved. If the software route is not desired, a single-shot circuit can be used to provide constant signals widths, which makes the application hardware (and software because the single shot has to be monitored) more complex.

The parallel port, at best, has eight bidirectional *DI/DO (digital input/digital output)* pins, and six inputs and three outputs. I have used these pins for different applications, but usually with a struggle when moving them between PCs. The lack of digital outputs can make a multiple-output device application difficult or require additional pins. A good example of this problem is when I developed that Atmel 20-pin microcontroller programmer for "Programming and Customizing the 8051 Microcontroller." The device cannot only run, but program, an Atmel 8051 20-pin device using the parallel port for control. I could have provided the ability to "run" an Atmel AVR, but this would have required an address decoder or additional control latches in the circuit. Neither solution was acceptable for the "footprint" that I had chosen. Another problem you have is the wide variability in parallel ports your customers may have on their PCs. As I was proof reading this book, I created the "El Cheapo" microchip PICMicro Programmer. The PICMicro uses a serial programming protocol in which the "data" pin can be input or output. To simplify the design, I initially used a data pin and alternated between input and output on the parallel port as required. I was amazed when I got many e-mails from users saying that the programers they build would not work on their PCs which did not have working bi-direction data pins on their PC's parallel ports. Many of these PC's were '286s & '386s.

To fix the problem I used two hand shake lines (with a current limiting resistor to avoid contention) instead of the data port pins.

The last problem, the inverted DI/DO pins, probably seem pretty minor and in the grand scheme of things, it is. But it does add an extra layer of complexity that is not present in other interfaces presented in this book.

After cutting down the port, I think it's important to point out some conditions where the parallel port is useful. One of these is with the dongle application I presented in the next chapter. For limited I/O that is time insensitive (or can be easily timed up using the system timer resource), it is a good fit. It is also an appropriate interface when you can guarantee that a single PC will be used with just a few I/O and the timing can be "tuned" to the PC and device. This latter condition can be very hard to guarantee and should not be taken lightly; applications have a way of lasting "forever" if they are found to be useful.

PRACTICAL

PARALLEL-PORT

INTERFACING

As I have indicated, the parallel port is not a trivial piece of hardware for interfacing. The biggest issues revolve around timing and how to provide constant timings for multiple applications.

To ensure constant timings is to use a hardware timer (such as the 55-ms RTC clock period) one way exclusively for timing the parallel-port signals. This delay is easy to monitor and is constant in all PC systems. This RTC interrupt can be monitored by polling on the clock BIOS system variables (the double word at 0x040:0x06C, specifically) or by hooking into the RTC interrupt (level 0 or interrupt 8). The former method is preferred because it is simpler and has less opportunity to "crash" your PC.

For example, to time a strobe output, you would use the code:

```
outp( BaseAddr + Ctrl, inp( BaseAddr + Ctrl ) & !Strobe );
                            // Make the Strobe Active

 i = Word PTR @ 0x040:0x06C;      // Get the Current RTC Clock Tick
Count

while ( Word PTR @ 0x040:0x06C != ( I + 2 ));
                            // Wait for two Cycles

outp( BaseAddr + Ctrl, inp( BaseAddr + Ctrl ) ! Strobe );
                            // Make the Strobe Inactive
```

The problem with this method is that the strobe will be active anywhere between 55 and 110 ms. Despite this long period, the timing is not going to be so short that the interface hardware cannot respond. Another method of providing the timing is to output a clock signal or delay from the board you are interfacing to.

Another issue to watch for is that the parallel port cannot be used to drive any significant loads. The ISA parallel-port adapter card on my PC is capable of driving LEDs (with appropriate current-limiting resistors). The other parallel port in the system is part of a super I/O ASIC on the motherboard. These ASICs are incredibly complex and problems with the hardware that the parallel port is connected to could result in this chip being blown. This means an expensive repair to the PC or a new motherboard. When I have designed a new parallel-port interface and am testing it, I usually use a cheap plug in ISA parallel-port card that is much cheaper and easier to replace if something goes wrong, or if I've wired the adapter incorrectly.

A Software-Protection Dongle

If you've been around PC's long enough in a technical capacity, you're probably very familiar with (and hate) the "dongle". The *dongle* is a small hardware device that plugs into a parallel port between your PC and printer and provides a "go/no go" indicator to an application. Dongle-protected software is usually used with high-cost, low-volume software (usually used by engineers) because the temptation to illegally copy the software is great. Like just about everybody else, I hate dongles because it means crawling on all fours to attach it to any PC. As well, they generally don't work in multiples or with some printers. For the manufacturer of the application that is "protected" by the dongle, the actual protection provided is quite modest.

The dongle project presented here does have all of these drawbacks, but it is an easy-to-wire application and does show off many of the good and bad points of interfacing to a parallel port (Figs. 26-1 and 26-2).

When I created this project, I did not do any kind of patent or prior art search about dongles. The design presented here was developed over a weekend in December 1998. The way this device works might be in violation of other company's patents and although the design and code have certainly not been taken from any applications. I suspect that this design is probably very simplistic, compared to other dongle designs available, and does not provide more than a minimal amount of protection for application code.

Having said this, if you do search for this design and find that it is unique and want to use it in your design, just remember two things. First, people will probably hate you for even considering adding a dongle to your application; secondly, contact me to find out my rates for licensing this apparently wonderful design.

As indicated, the circuit is very simple with two connectors, a board to wire the design on and four electronic components (Fig. 26-3). The main component is a Microchip 12C509 microcontroller that you should acquaint yourself with (along with its 12C508 sibling with smaller memory)—even if you aren't planning on using microcontrollers; they're handy little devices that are useful in a wide variety of applications.

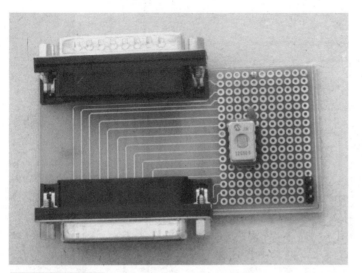

FIGURE 26-1   Dongle top.

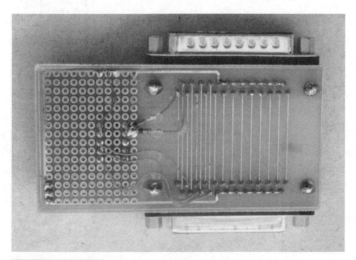

FIGURE 26-2   Dongle bottom showing wiring.

The circuit is wired so that the parallel port itself powers the 12C509. When I originally wired this circuit, I used _STROBE for V_{dd} (V_{cc}) and _Auto FDXT for ground. For my PC, I found that the parallel port was only able to source about 1.5 mA per pin. According to the 12C509 data sheet (and tested empirically), the 12C509 requires at least 2 mA to operate, which meant that I had to source two pins in parallel to provide the needed current. This was done with diodes to make sure the signals output on _STROBE and _Auto FDXT pins would not interfere with each other. I wanted to ensure that the dongle would co-exist with a printer.

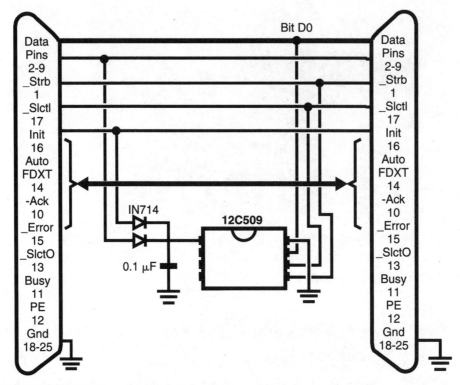

FIGURE 26-3   Parallel port "Dongle" circuit.

A Select and Clock line were taken from the _Slct In and Init lines of the parallel port. To allow the PC to work with the printer, both lines have to be reset for the 123C509 to recognize that the dongle is being accessed. This is an invalid condition with the printer and it will ignore this output (just as the 12C509's code will ignore anything it considers invalid).

The 12C509 code was designed using the pseudo-code:

```
main()                   //  Dongle Response Code
{

eight DataOut;           //  Eight Bytes for the data out

  while ( 1 == 1 ) {     //  Loop Forever

    DataOut = 0x078563412FF0055AA;  //  Least Significant 4 Bytes is
                         //    "Check"
                         //  Most Significant 4 Bytes is the
                         //    "Decrypt"

    while (( Strobe == 0 ) & ( Select == 0 )) {

      Output = Enabled;    //  Can Drive D0

      Output = DataOut & 1;//  Output the Least Significant Bit
```

```
        DataOut = Dataout > > 1;      // Move the Next Bit for Output

        while (( Strobe == 0 ) & ( Select == 0 ));

        if (( Strobe == 1 ) && ( Select == 0 ))  // Next Bit Request

            while (( Strobe == 1 ) || ( Select == 0 ));

      }  // endwhile

    Output = Disabled;         // Can't Output Anything

  }  // end Mainline
```

This code starts when the 12C509 powers up, loads a default value into the DataOut shift variable and then waits for the valid Strobe and Select conditions to appear on its I/O pins. When they do, the first bit is output onto the data bus at D0. Because "Strobe" and "Select" being inactive are invalid conditions for a printer, it's safe to assume that the dongle is being communicated with.

After both bits go low and the least-significant bit is output, the value in *DataOut* is shifted down by one bit and then the parallel port is polled for a Strobe, after which, it outputs the next bit if the next value is the expected Strobe and Select low. If the sequence is lost, the output bit is disabled and the *DataOut* variable is re-initialized.

The total 12C509 code is only 53 instructions long and I was able to get it working on my first attempt.

Three PC programs are needed to successfully use the dongle: the application itself; DONGLE2.COM, which is inserted into the application to read the dongle; and dongmkr, which inserts DONGLE2.COM into the application. Dongmkr was taken from the "Operating Systemless" code written in C and uses many of the same functions. For the actual application, I used .COM MS-DOS applications because of the ease to work with them.

From this application, I learned not to name everything so similarly. Entering *dongle2*, *dongapp*, and *dongmkr* really allowed for typos when going through the debug of the application.

Dongle2 actually consists of two parts. The first part reads lpt2 to see if the dongle is present. This code starts at address 0x0100 (the starting address of .COM applications). If the dongle is present, then the code will be overwritten by the actual application (which has been loaded after this part). This is done by reading the 64 bits of the application and checking the first 32 for 0x0FF0055AA. If this value is not present or invalid, then an error message is output and control is returned to the MS-DOS command line.

This code can be blocked out as having the following functions:

1 0x0E4 is written to LPT2's control register, which sets the _STROBE and _Auto FDXT lines and resets the _Slct In and Init lines.
2 The 64 bits of data is read into a shift variable.
3 To strobe in the data, LPT2's control register is written with 0x0E0.
4 0x0E8 is written to LPT's control register to return it to its original state.
5 The first 32 bits are checked for the 0x0FF0055AA sequence.

Between each bit, I delay one system clock tick (55 ms). This draws out this sequence to about eight seconds long, but I have tried it on a number of different PCs without any problems with the code not being read in. I could have used the timer code shown in Chapter 20, but I wanted to keep the code as simple as possible.

If you do decide to go with a faster clock (which would be appropriate in a commercial system), I suggest that you keep the initial 300-ms delay to allow the 12C509 to power up and then use no less than a 30-usecs clock to strobe out the data. In the 12C509, the I/O pins are polled (interrupts are not available in the 12C509) and the response is limited to about 5 usecs per polling loop.

Another, better solution that I came up with as I was proofreading the book was to use the 12C508 to toggle a data line after a set period of time to indicate to the PC the next operation could take place.

If the value is present and valid, then the second part uses the second 32 bits to decode the encrypted application and move it into memory starting at address 0x0100 and jump to this address to execute the application. This code "XORs" the application code with the 32 decrypt value returned from the dongle as the most significant 32 bits of the 64-bit number. As mentioned, this code also moves the application from above the first part to starting at 0x0100, so it can execute as an unmodified .COM application.

The code used is:

```
DecodeExecute:

    mov    AX, DI              ;  Do we Have an Odd/Even Word?
    and    AX, 2               ;  If Not Zero, Have Odd Word
    jnz    DecodeExecuteOdd

DecodeExecuteEven:             ;  Even Word - Use the First 16 Bits

    mov    AX, BX

    jmp    SHORT DecodeExecuteDo

DecodeExecuteOdd:              ;  Odd Word - use the Second 16 Bits

    mov    AX, BP

DecodeExecuteDo:              ;  Now Convert the Value and Save It

    xor    AX, WORD PTR DS:[SI] ;  Get the Decoded Byte
    add    SI, 2               ;  Simulate the "LODSW"
;   lodsw                      ;  Get the Straight Byte
    stosw                      ;  Store the Word

    loop   DecodeExecute

    xor    AX, AX              ;  Zero Out the Registers
    xor    BX, BX
    xor    DX, DX              ;  CX is Zero By "Loop" Instruction
    xor    DI, DI
    xor    SI, SI
    xor    BP, BP

    jmp    DongEnd             ;  Jump to the Variable Address
```

I handle the data as 16-bit words instead of bytes. This speeds up the conversion/copy process and takes advantage of the 8086's ability to move and manipulate the data consistently. Because I transfer "words", I increment the count to ensure that I don't miss anything. In doing this, I might transfer the first byte of the DecodeExecute code and incorrectly translate and move it at the end of the application code. This should not be a problem because if the code is properly written, it will never be executed. The last thing to notice is the *jmp DongEnd* instruction at the end of the program. *DongEnd* is actually a variable and not a label. The 8086 does not have an absolute direct address jump instruction, so I had to use a jump to contents of a variable (which is initialized to 0x0100).

To combine the DONGLE2.COM and the application code, I use a C utility called *dongmkr*. This application takes DONGLE2.COM writes the first part into a buffer, reads the application code into the buffer and encrypts it. With the application ready, the second part of DONGLE2.COM is loaded into the buffer, then the buffer is written back out as the application's name.

The 32-bit encryption value that I decided to use is:

```
0x078563412
```

which is really an arbitrary value. This might not look that effective, but for my sample application DONGAPP.COM (Fig. 26-4). This application simply displays the message: "Dongle Decoded Me Correctly" and then returns control to MS-DOS. One nice feature of this application is that it uses compiled and linked applications, instead of encrypting the code as part of the operation. This allows you to debug your application before "releasing" it with the dongle. The encrypted application looks like Fig. 26-5, which bears absolutely no relationship with the original code. In DEBUG.COM, I set a break point at the *jmp DongEnd* of the code to see what the decoded value was and I was very happy to see Fig. 26-6. When it was allowed to execute, the code worked without any problems.

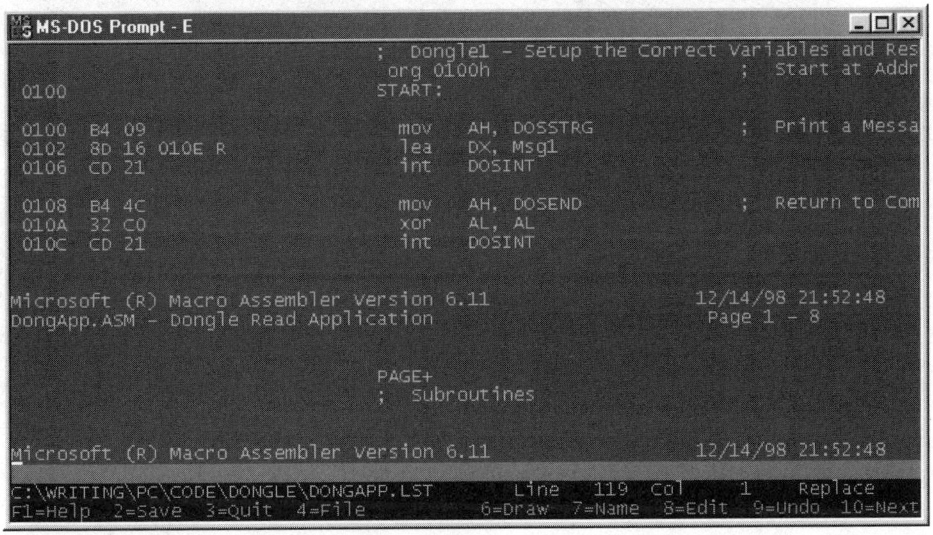

FIGURE 26-4 "DongApp" code.

```
MS-DOS Prompt - DEBUG                                              _ □ ×
C:\writing\pc\code\dongle>debug dongapp.com
-u 1e7
19E0:01E7 A6            CMPSB
19E0:01E8 3DDB6E        CMP      AX,6EDB
19E0:01EB 1C35          SBB      AL,35
19E0:01ED 9B            WAIT
19E0:01EE 59            POP      CX
19E0:01EF A6            CMPSB
19E0:01F0 7864          JS       0256
19E0:01F2 B8DF15        MOV      AX,15DF
19E0:01F5 1217          ADC      DL,[BX]
19E0:01F7 7C53          JL       024C
19E0:01F9 3A1D          CMP      BL,[DI]
19E0:01FB 327033        XOR      DH,[BX+SI+33]
19E0:01FE 1B7D50        SBB      DI,[DI+50]
19E0:0201 331C          XOR      BX,[SI]
19E0:0203 327933        XOR      BH,[BX+DI+33]
19E0:0206 58            POP      AX
-
```

FIGURE 26-5   "Dongle" encrypted code.

```
MS-DOS Prompt - DEBUG                                              _ □ ×
AX=0000  BX=0000  CX=0000  DX=0000  SP=FFFE  BP=0000  SI=0000  DI=0000
DS=19E0  ES=19E0  SS=19E0  CS=19E0  IP=0234    NV UP EI PL ZR NA PE NC
19E0:0234 CC            INT      3
-u 100
19E0:0100 B409          MOV      AH,09
19E0:0102 8D160E01      LEA      DX,[010E]
19E0:0106 CD21          INT      21
19E0:0108 B44C          MOV      AH,4C
19E0:010A 32C0          XOR      AL,AL
19E0:010C CD21          INT      21
19E0:010E 44            INC      SP
19E0:010F 6F            DB       6F
19E0:0110 6E            DB       6E
19E0:0111 67            DB       67
19E0:0112 6C            DB       6C
19E0:0113 65            DB       65
19E0:0114 204465        AND      [SI+65],AL
19E0:0117 63            DB       63
19E0:0118 6F            DB       6F
19E0:0119 64            DB       64
19E0:011A 65            DB       65
19E0:011B 64            DB       64
19E0:011C 204D65        AND      [DI+65],CL
19E0:011F 20436F        AND      [BP+DI+6F],AL
-
```

FIGURE 26-6   "Dongle" de-crypted code.

The advantages of this dongle type is its encryption of the code before it is received in the user's hands and the decryption information is not available within the code. To successfully decode the application, the dongle must be present. Although the .COM format is limiting in terms of space, this technique could be used to encrypt and decrypt code and data segments in an .EXE program randomly, providing a much greater level of security.

Also, the dongle must be present at least once. To someone that is familiar with 8086 code and can use a debugger, this program would take about 10 minutes to break. Actually, with the information contained in this book up to this point, I would be surprised if it took you any longer than 20 minutes to initialize the *DataRd* variables to the correct *Check* and *Encrypt* values. With this done, it is fairly simple to save the hacked application under debug, eliminating the need for the dongle at all.

This is one of the biggest problems with dongles and other application-security measures. They will succeed in keeping people with little systems programming skills from stealing the application. But, for somebody with even a modest amount of knowledge about PC programming, a cracked version of the code could be up on the Internet before you have a chance to get a cup of coffee after releasing a new version of the protected code. There are more-complex algorithms for dongle code/data encryption and other hardware protection (including storing sections of code in the dongle) methods, but to a knowledgeable hacker, they are really of little protection (so don't use them and make me crawl under my desk to get to the back of my PC).

3

HARDWARE INTERFACING

27

THE

ISA

BUS

CONTENTS AT A GLANCE

Bus Signals
I/O REGISTER ADDRESSING
MEMORY ADDRESSING
8-/16-BIT DATA TRANSFERS

BUILT-IN HARDWARE DIFFERENCES
INTERRUPTS
DMA

The ISA bus has been included on virtually every PC built since the first one in 1981 and has really only been excluded on laptops. Although the PC/99 specification indicates that new PCs should not have an ISA bus, I expect PCs will have it built in for a number of years to come. Simply too many adapters are on the market are designed for the bus and the bus is a very good tool for creating complex interfaces to the PC.

The ISA bus was originally designed as a method to convert the 8088's multiplexed bus into a 20-bit address, 8-bit data bus for devices on the motherboard and peripherals. Along with the address, data and control busses, ISA also provides an interrupt and DMA interface to adapters. I believe that this complete, easy-to-interface-to bus is the primary reason why the PC became so popular after it was first introduced.

ISA is ideally suited for simple, low-cost, and relatively slow hardware interfaces. In a modern PC, this usually consists of serial and parallel devices, as well as simple hardware interfaces. The next chapter presents an ISA prototyping card that will interface to the ISA bus. The purpose of this will be to show you how I/O is accomplished in the ISA bus and how software is written to interface with it.

Bus Signals

The title of this section was originally "Understanding Bus Timing," but I realized that there really isn't a lot to understand. If you look at the Intel 8088 datasheet, you'll see that the multiplex address/data bus with DMA and interrupts is actually quite complex. When the PC was designed, IBM designed the motherboard and specified the ISA "slots" in such a way that the complexity of the bus was hidden from the user.

A PC with ISA busses can be thought of as a processor with its data, address, and control/interrupt/DMA lines being passed directly to a number of ISA "slots" (Fig. 27-1).

Looking at the PC's motherboard and ISA slots from this perspective, it should be no surprise that the read/write cycle on the ISA bus looks like Fig. 27-2.

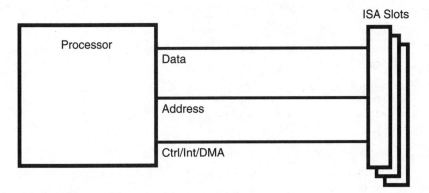

FIGURE 27-1   **Processor/ISA block diagram.**

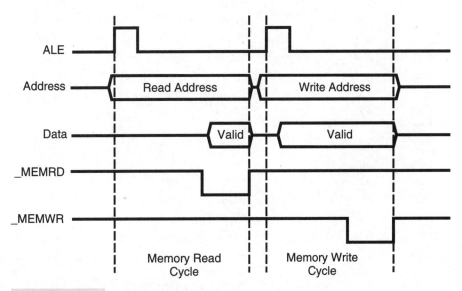

FIGURE 27-2   **ISA bus timing.**

The "ALE" bit is a little surprise. This bit becomes active when the address is valid. The original purpose of this bit was to initiate the RAS/CAS address multiplexing for reading and writing to memory on the ISA bus. Today, with memory never attached to the ISA bus, this bit is actually of little use. This waveform is identical for the I/O reads and writes.

To transfer data, the time between ALE active and the data available is normally 760 ns for eight-bit transfers and 125 ns for 16-bit transfers. The faster access for 16-bit transfers was a function of the PC/AT and the need for moving memory data faster in the 80286 system.

The eight-bit ISA bus consists of a two-sided 31-pin card edge connector with the pins defined as:

PIN	"A" (CONNECTOR)	"B" (SOLDER)
1	I/O CH CHK	Ground
2	D7	Reset
3	D6	+5 V
4	D5	IRQ2
5	D4	+5 V
6	D3	DRQ2
7	D2	-12 V
8	D1	-CARD SLCTD
9	D0	+12 V
10	+IO CH RDY	Ground
11	AEN	-MEMW
12	A19	-MEMR
13	A18	-IOW
14	A17	-IOR
15	A16	-DACK3
16	A15	DRQ3
17	A14	-DACK1
18	A13	DRQ1
19	A12	-DACK0 (-REFRESH)
20	A11	OSC
21	A10	IRQ7
22	A9	IRQ6
23	A8	IRQ5
24	A7	IRQ4
25	A6	IRQ3
26	A5	-DACK2
27	A4	T/C
28	A3	BALE
29	A2	+5 V
30	A1	CLOCK - 14.31818 MHz
31	A0	Gnd

The 16-bit extension connector is a separate two-sided 18-pin connector:

PIN	"C" (CONNECTOR)	"D" (SOLDER)
1	SBHE	-MEM CS16
2	LA23	-I/O CS16
3	LA22	IRQ10
4	LA21	IRQ11
5	LA20	IRQ12
6	LA19	IRQ15
7	LA18	IRQ14
8	LA17	-DACK0
9	-MEMR	DRQ0
10	-MEMW	-DACK5
11	SD8	DRQ5
12	SD9	-DACK6
13	SD10	DRQ6
14	SD11	-DACK7
15	SD12	DRQ7
16	SD13	+5 V
17	SD14	-MASTER
18	SD15	Ground

The data and address busses are buffered to the processor, this should be of no surprise, but it is important to recognize.

Notice that if A20 is to be output onto the bus, hardware in the keyboard controller must be enabled. When I first saw this function, I puzzled over it for quite a bit because I didn't understand why anybody would want address bit 20 to be disabled. I finally understood why this was done as I was writing this book. When the PC/AT was introduced with the 80286, if the address went above the 1-MB boundary (for example, accessing data at 0x0FFFF:0x0FFFF), the physical address output would be above the 1-MB boundary and not "wrapped" around to the first 64-KB segment, as in the 8088. By disabling the A20 bit, the 80286 (and faster processors) would work identically to the 8088 for this condition.

BALE (Buffered ALE) was the term used in the original PC because the ALE line was produced by the 8088's instruction-sequence clock. This pin was buffered to avoid having the ISA bus directly processor driven. Today, this bit is more commonly known as *ALE* and it provides essentially the same operation and timing as BALE.

-I/O CH CHK was designed for use with parity checked memory. If a byte was read that did not match the saved parity, an NMI interrupt request was made of the processor.

I/O CH RDY is a line driven low by an adapter if it needs more time to complete an operation. This is yet another pin that was really specific to the times when DRAM was put on the ISA bus. During each processor cycle (of 760 ns in the 8088), while the pin was high, the ISA read/write cycle would wait full processor cycles until the line was dropped low. In the PC/AT (and faster) PCs, this delay has a granularity of 210 ns.

-IOR and -IOW are used to read and write data from the ISA bus into the processor's I/O space. As noted elsewhere, only I/O addresses 0x0100 to 0x03FF are used for the ISA bus I/O registers.

-SMEMR and -SMEMW are only active for eight-bit reads and writes in the first 1-MB addresses. For reads and writes in higher memory, the -MEMR and -MEMW pins should be used; they are active throughout the entire ISA 16-MB range.

The faster 16-bit transfers are initiated by the adapter card making the -MEM CS16 or -IO CS16 bits active when BALE is high. If these pins are not active, then the PC transfers eight bits of data at 760-ns cycle times.

The -*SBHE* signal is input/output and is used by either the motherboard or adapter to indicate that a 16-bit read/write operation is active. Adapters using 16-bit busses will enable this line for every transfer. The motherboard activates this line when eight bits are being transferred over the upper eight bits of the ISA adapter (SD8 to SD15).

Pins IRQ3 through IRQ7, IRQ9 through IRQ12, IRQ14, and IRQ15 request hardware interrupts. When these lines are driven high, the 8259As on the motherboard will process the request in a descending order of priority. These lines must be kept high until the processor resets the requesting hardware. I suggest that before designing an adapter that uses these functions, you go back and read the chapter on interrupts and look at the example code.

The CLOCK line is a four times colorburst clock that runs at 14.31818 MHz and was the system clock in the original PC. This clock was divided by three for use in the 4.77-MHz 8088 clock in the original PC. This clock is not running at the 200+ MHz of your Pentium processor. The 14.31818-MHz clock was distributed to the system to provide clocking for the MDA and CGA video display cards. This clock can be useful for providing a simple clock for microcontroller and other clocked devices on adapter cards.

The OSC pin is driven at up to 8 MHz. The pin was originally added to the 16-bit ISA specification as the actual clock speed for memory adapters connected to the bus. As PC clock speeds have gone up, this pin's speed hasn't. The pin is capped at 8 MHz to provide a clock for hardware operations and not provide significant radiated noise problems.

DMA, which is addressed (no pun intended) later in the chapter, uses four types of pins. The DRQ# pins request a DMA transfer to occur. When the corresponding DACK# pin is driven high, the DMA controller is reading or writing an I/O address of an adapter card. When the DMA controllers have control of the bus over the processor, the AEN pin is active to indicate to other adapters that a DMA operation is in process. When all the DMA data has been transferred, the T/C bit is pulsed high to indicate the operation has completed. When the T/C bit becomes active, the adapter should request a hardware interrupt to indicate to software that the operation is complete.

DRQ1 to DRQ4 are used to request eight-bit DMA transfers (DMA channel 0 is used for the DRAM refresh circuitry) and DRQ4 through DRQ7 are used to request 16-bit DMA transfers.

The -REFRESH or -DACK0 pin is active when the DMA controller's channel 0 is active and doing a RAS-only refresh of the system memory. The purpose of this pin is to be distributed to ISA DRAM memory cards and use the address on the lower eight to 10 bits of the bus for refreshing the memory card's DRAM. In modern PCs, this line might be active, depending on how DRAM memory is implemented.

The last pin is the -MASTER, which is driven by an adapter when it "wants" to take over the bus and drive its own signals. This is a way of providing DMA to the system without using the 8237s or allowing another processor to access the system resources. There are a few potential problems with this pin and its usage. One of the most important things to watch for is that holding the line active for longer than 15 usecs might result in a missed refresh interval. The -MASTER pin is also not all that useful because it cannot be used to drive data to the motherboard's hardware. It is best suited to passing data between adapters.

Despite the plethora of pins in this interface, you can create ISA adapters quite easily. For example, to provide an ISA Hitachi 44780-controlled LCD interface, the circuit shown in Fig. 27-3 is all that is required for passing data to the LCD and reading status and data back from the device.

Notice that I do not use ALE and just use the address data and I/O read and write pins. Eight-bit transfers have the -IOR and -IOW pins active for more than the 450 ns required

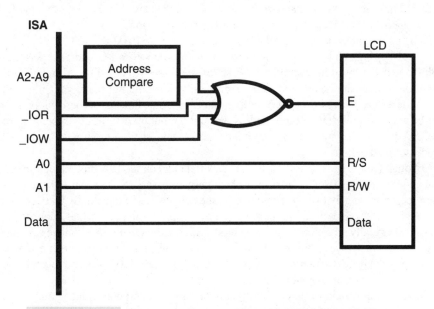

FIGURE 27-3   SA connection to a Hitatchi 44780 based LCD.

for the LCD interface to work. The next chapter presents a prototyping card with user-selectable addressing to provide a simple interface for user-designed projects to the ISA bus.

I/O REGISTER ADDRESSING

Interfacing to (reading from and writing to) I/O registers on the ISA bus is quite simple, as shown in the previous section. A few points will help you become successful in developing your ISA interface cards. Keep these comments in the back of your mind when developing your adapter cards to keep from encountering problems that will require you to re-read this book and/or another with the ISA specification.

The first issue to understand with the ISA bus is that the original PC and PC/AT only decodes the least-significant 10 bits of the 16-bit I/O address bus. Modern PCs often have registers above this limit or might not decode any of the bits above this limit. The PC was originally released with 1024 device addresses that only decode the ISA address pins zero to nine. If register address was accessed above this address, the most-significant address bits are ignored when the device selections are made.

You might have an idea for a device that you want to put at I/O space address 0x0420, but, in the PC, the motherboard will interpret this as address 0x020, which is the primary interrupt controller.

The current Pentium II & III Northbridge and Southbridge chips have registers at addresses above 0x03FF (the 10-bit limit). These addresses have been chosen to work with the standard I/O addresses within the PC and not cause any conflicts with them. As well, in these chips, many of the standard functions are decoded within the chips and the full 16 bits are used for the decoding, which simplifies the operation.

To be on the safe side, just use the I/O addresses from 0x0100 to 0x0300.

This also brings up the second point. If you look at the PC's I/O address specification, you'll see that a lot of holes are in the first 256 addresses (to 0x0100). Although you can count on devices not being at specific addresses, you should not place your interfaces at these addresses. The reason is very simple: in the ISA bus, devices at these addresses may not be read back. Writes to these addresses can be monitored from devices connected to the ISA bus, but in some PCs they cannot drive data at these addresses and have the processor read them.

Although the PC can support 16-bit I/O data transfers on the ISA bus, I recommend that you avoid using this feature unless it's absolutely necessary. Sixteen-bit I/O accesses can be processed strangely (as explained later in the chapter) and can actually take longer than two eight-bit accesses in some hardware. Few chips are available that supports 16-bit transfers (virtually all support eight data bits), which means that you will have to create the interface yourself. Developing a 16-bit interface might not be unreasonable if you are working with an ASIC design, but if you are using discrete devices, save yourself a lot of grief and stick with an eight-bit interface.

The last point shouldn't be that surprising: be sure that you don't place your devices at the same addresses as other adapters in the system. I have talked about Plug'n'Play and the possibility that devices can be placed at unexpected addresses. If you are not designing a Plug'n'Play adapter in a system that does have them, be sure that you change the I/O ad-

3

dresses (along with the RAM/ROM/interrupt/DMA addresses) so that your device does not conflict with anything else in the system.

MEMORY ADDRESSING

The comments for providing memory on an ISA bus will largely echo the comments that I made about I/O register addressing in the previous section. When the PC was originally designed, the ISA bus was the primary method of adding to the systems memory, and it provided standard I/O functions. Today, the ISA bus is primarily to interface relatively slow-speed peripherals that provide some level of nonstandard function to an individual PC. These peripherals include network adapters and interfaces to backup storage devices, such as streaming tape.

Like the I/O addresses, ROM and RAM built into an adapter must be movable to avoid conflict problems with Plug'n'Play devices. To find possible conflicts, you can use the memory program described earlier in the book or use your PC's set-up utility to understand the addresses used by the Plug'n'Play cards in the system.

If you are adding an ISA hardware device to a PC equipped with Plug'n'Play devices, it is a good idea to only have one non-Plug'n'Play device in the PC. This will make it much easier to avoid resource conflicts.

RAM and ROM must be located within 0x0C8000 and 0x0DFFFF. Any other addresses can conflict with other addresses used within the PC.

I suggest that only modest amounts of memory be used on an adapter card (this also goes for PCI). Only 96 KB is available in the memory space from 0x0C8000 to 0x0DFFFF; adding a device with large RAMs and ROMs will make it more difficult for your hardware to co-exist with other adapters installed in the system. I personally like to keep an adapter's total RAM and ROM to 16 KB (or less) to allow easy installation with other devices.

Keeping the ROM to a minimum might mean that code you had hoped to put on the device will have to be installed from a diskette or CD-ROM. This might seem like an unreasonable compromise, but it will be much easier for you when a user calls and asks for your help in installing your card in their PC.

8-/16-BIT DATA TRANSFERS

Earlier in this chapter, I noted that one 16-bit data transfer could actually take longer in a modern PC than two eight-bit transfers. This probably seems pretty hard to believe, but when you look at how hardware in the PC operates, it is not that unlikely. In the first 80286 and 80386 PCs, 16 bit ISA transfers did have advantages over eight bit ones.

All PCs have a central eight-bit I/O control bus that is used to access motherboard device registers. These devices include the timer, interrupt controllers, DMA controllers, and page registers, along with other hardware miscellaneous control devices. In modern PCs, this bus is the primary low-speed interface to the system.

When 16-bit data transfers are requested by the processor, the motherboard logic breaks the request into two eight-bit requests. The hardware can be blocked out as in Fig. 27-4.

In this block diagram, the low eight bits are passed through the central bus first and latched. When both sets of eight bits are ready, the hardware controlling the operation of

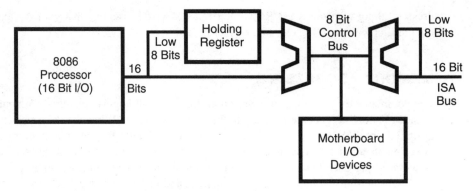

FIGURE 27-4   16 Bit to 8 bit I/O circuitry.

the ISA bus performs the write. In comparison, two eight-bit writes could flow through this hardware chain reasonably unimpeded and unbuffered.

If it seems like I'm steering you away from creating 16-bit ISA adapter interfaces, you are right. For the low-speed bus and the devices that are appropriate for it, it just isn't the cost or effort effective to put 16-bit devices on the bus, it's the speed and complexity issues.

BUILT-IN HARDWARE DIFFERENCES

Depending on your PC's motherboard, a number of differences can occur in the hardware addresses that are driven out onto the ISA bus. I realize that earlier I stated that I/O addresses 0x0100 to 0x03FF and memory addresses 0x0C8000 to 0x0DFFFF can be accessed on the ISA bus, but in some cases, this isn't true. The reasons for this can cause problems with creating ISA adapters.

The problems with these data accesses center around what is built into the motherboard and what is already on the PCI bus. Many motherboards now have the disk controllers, video graphics adapter, networking hardware, sound card hardware, etc. built in. The addresses traditionally reserved for these devices and available on the ISA bus are no longer passed out.

Thus, in your application design, you have to be absolutely sure of where your adapter is going to reside in the PC. My original intention, when I was creating the concept for this book, was to present a list of addresses that you could use without fear of conflict with other devices. When I looked at PC technical references, I found that many addresses were specified for specific devices, so this goal seemed very possible.

In actuality, this is just not possible. Over time, different adapters have used virtually all addresses, which makes trying to define addresses more of a "bob and weave" operation specific to an individual PC than carrying it out by rote. You will have to design your adapters with the capability of being able to relocate addresses, either by switches or Plug'n'Play.

INTERRUPTS

Interrupts in the ISA bus are positive-active, edge-triggered, TTL/CMOS inputs that are passed to two 8259As on the PC's motherboard. The interrupts work reasonably well, although you should be aware of a few issues. This section introduces the ISA bus operation; more information can be found in Chapter 7.

The biggest issue for me is the inability of the pins to safely work with multiple sources under all conditions. This might seem surprising, based on the text in Chapter 7, which showed how vectors could be shared in software and how the interrupt request pin could be driven by multiple devices.

This means that when planning which interrupt to use, understanding the current usage in the PC is important before a new adapter is configured to a specific request line. Using the serial or parallel port interrupts (IRQ3, IRQ4, or IRQ7) is usually a safe bet because most modern PC motherboards have this hardware built in and there is no danger of a problem from having multiple sources drive the line and "loose" an edge.

In terms of which interrupts to select, I have suggested IRQs 3, 4, and 7. If they are not available for whatever reason, then you should consider IRQs 10, 11, 12, 14, or 15.

If an interrupt appears to be used, check to see if there is anything driving the line on the motherboard's ISA slots. This can be done with a common logic probe, which can indicate High, Low, or Open conditions. If nothing normally drives the line, then you can use the circuit shown in Fig. 27-5 for enabling a tri-state driver output as a high logic level only when the interrupt is being requested. This should drastically cut down on the opportunity for bus contention or missed interrupt requests.

Once you have specified the interrupt, you can set the interrupt vector to the handler using the following steps:

1 Save the original vector using MS-DOS interrupt 021h AH = 035h API.
2 Set the new vector using MS-DOS interrupt 021h AH = 025h API.
3 Enable the interrupt request mask bit in the 8259.

To enable the interrupt request mask bit in the 8259, the appropriate interrupt mask register bit has to be reset. This register is at the 8259's base address plus one.

This can be done with the following statement:

```
outp( IntBase + 1, inp( IntBase + 1 ) & (( 0x0FF ^ ( 1 < Bit )));
```

In this statement, the interrupt mask register is read in, the appropriate bit cleared and then written back. Nothing more needs to be done with the 8259.

To "release" the interrupt vector and the interrupt source at the end of the application, do the following steps:

1 Disable the interrupt request mask bit in the 8259.
2 Restore the original vector using MS-DOS Interrupt 021h AH = 025h API.

I restore the interrupt vector to the original value because it is normally pointing to the D11 routine, which causes the requesting interrupt to be masked off and never responded to again.

Interrupts themselves should be active until they are serviced by the interrupt handler code. Although interrupt requests can be blips or pulses from the adapter hardware, this is

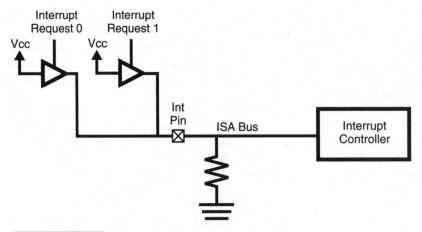

FIGURE 27-5   Multiple interrupt request circuit.

not recommended because the interrupts might be missed at the end of a shared interrupt handler when any pending interrupts are polled.

Unless you are designing a Plug 'n 'Play adapter card or an adapter for only one application, you will have to set up a switch block with multiple interrupt request numbers. I do not recommend hard wiring the interrupt request number because this might make your application unworkable in some situations. I realize that this solution is less than optimal because most users lose their documentation on how to set the application's software for different device addresses. The only suggestion to this problem is to be sure that you have a Web page with the documentation available for downloading.

This section reiterates much of the information in Chapter 7. I have tried to move away from the other chapter's general terms and get into practical specifics with the ISA bus interrupt-request lines. It is unfortunate that positive edge-triggered interrupts were chosen by IBM when specifying the original PC's interrupt because this can cause problems in your applications. Ideally, you should be designing ISA hardware adapters and software that can use any of the IRQ lines on the ISA bus. They should also be designed to be active for a short period of time to minimize the opportunity for "missed" interrupts in an application.

DMA

If you look through IBM's documentation on the PC, you'll see a lot of confusing, complex documentation on how DMA is implemented in the PC and how it works. This section shows how the DMA controllers are programmed to pass data between the PC's memory and an ISA DMA device and how an ISA DMA card could be designed. A few comments are also included relating to how I think DMA should be used.

As I noted elsewhere, the Intel 8237 DMA controller accomplishes DMA in the PC. The 8237 is used in a "fly-by" mode, where it sets up an ISA transfer consisting of an I/O and memory read/write. Data is never stored within the DMA controller; it is passed between the PC's memory and the I/O device as is shown in Fig. 27-7.

During the transfer, the processor is disabled and the DMA controller is responsible for the data transfer, along with driving the address and control lines. Throughout this section, I have been careful to be sure that I referenced DMA transfers as ISA only. The ISA bus is the only bus in the PC that makes use of DMA using the 8237s built into the motherboard.

For example, if eight bits were to be transferred from the diskette drive into memory, the following operations would occur:

1 The diskette controller would make -DRQ2 active.

2 The DMA controller would request a hold of the PC's processor.

3 When the processor was ready to allow the DMA controller to take control of the bus, it will tri-state its ISA bus data, address, and control drivers and make the DMA HoldA (Hold Active) line active.

4 When the active Hold Ack is recognized by the DMA controller, it will make the _MEMW, _IOR, and DACK2 lines active and drive the memory address where the byte is to be stored.

5 The DMA channel 2 page register drives ISA address lines A16 to A23.

6 The requesting device will drive the byte of data onto the ISA bus.

7 The DMA controller will enable DACK2 for the requesting device to end the DMA request and prepare for the next transfer.

8 The _MEMW line will latch the byte into the PC's memory.

9 The DMA controller will disable its address bus, _MEMW, and _IOR lines to terminate the DMA transfer.

10 The Hold line to the PC's processor will be made inactive.

11 The PC's processor will resume its execution and driving the ISA bus.

If you have read descriptions of DMA transfers, this process should seem quite normal, except that I don't say that the processor finishes the current instruction and then gives up control of the bus. This is how DMA is typically described, but with advanced Pentium processors, the processor might give up ownership of the bus, but continue executing out of cache. In some PCs, the processor might continue operating without pausing because of its local bus and instruction/data caches. The only time it would stop (or even have to suffer a few wait states) is if the ISA transfer is active when the processor attempts to do an I/O read/write. The operation of the ISA DMA transfer can be seen in Fig. 27-7.

In the PC's ISA bus, DMA transfers are typically only between I/O and memory. Memory-to-memory transfers are possible, but take longer to execute than using the processor to transfer the data in software. This is because of the need of buffering the byte to be transferred in the DMA controller.

The memory address output from the 8237 is only 16 bits wide and is placed on A0 to A15 of the ISA bus (Fig. 27-6). In the original PC, a four-bit by four-bit "page" memory was added to the hardware to give a full 20-bit address transfer range. When the PC/AT was designed, the size was increased to eight bits, to give the capability of using DMA anywhere in the 80286's 16-MB data range.

Since moving from the 80286, the page registers have not changed. This has left the PC's data only able to access the lowest 16 MB of memory. The appropriate register is addressed by the active DACK# bit. The page registers themselves drive from ISA address line A16 to A23 (Fig. 27-8), which means that data is transferred, not in segments, but in

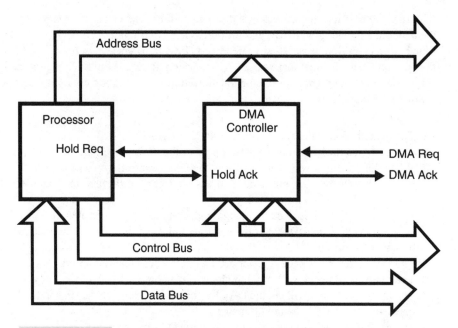

FIGURE 27-6   Direct memory access with processor.

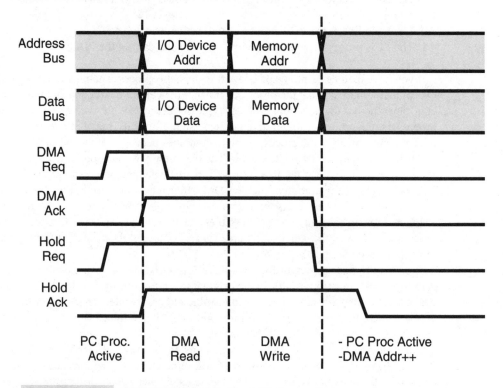

FIGURE 27-7   DMA I/O to memory operating waveform.

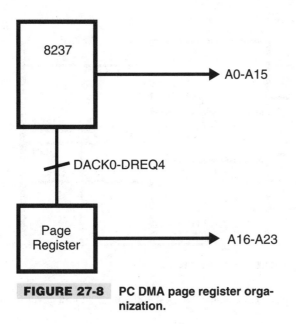

FIGURE 27-8   PC DMA page register organization.

64 KB "pages" (64-KB "blocks"). This can cause some problems if the transfer is going across the page boundary and you do not compensate for it correctly.

For example, if you have a buffer set address 0x05678:0x01234 and require a DMA transfer of 48 KB of data, you will find that the page register will be set to 0x05 (as you would expect) and the start of the transfer is at A0 to A15 of 0x079B4. Moving 48 KB of data will increment this offset to 0x0139B4, which is in page 0x06 (again, as you would expect). As the DMA operation executes, you will end up "wrapping around" back to offset zero within page 0x05 after 34,380 bytes have been transferred. The subsequent writes will start at address 0x05678:0x00000, which is not where the buffer is located and will probably overwrite data or code in the application or cause a memory allocation error.

To avoid this, you have to be sure that your buffer is correctly set up to receive the data within the same page and not the same segment. This error can be exceedingly hard to find the first time that it occurs when the wrong address is set up and unexpected memory is trashed. The first time that I attempted a DMA transfer, I ran into this problem and not only was my application overwritten, but also the debugger that I was using. I had absolutely no idea what was happening, other than that the PC had stopped responding to the keyboard.

The adapter hardware to make a DMA request can be quite simple. For the example shown (a DMA transfer from I/O space to memory) could use the adapter shown in Fig. 27-9.

In this circuit, when the data is ready to DMA out, it is latched into the register and the DMA request line is made active. When the DMA request is acknowledged and the _IOR lines are both low (active), the latch's drivers are enabled and the byte to transfer is driven onto the bus.

Look at this circuit and Fig. 27-7. You might have already noticed one aspect of memory and I/O space transfers. The DMA controller does not drive an I/O address onto the ISA bus. Instead the _IOR and DACK# lines are used to determine that the device's DMA

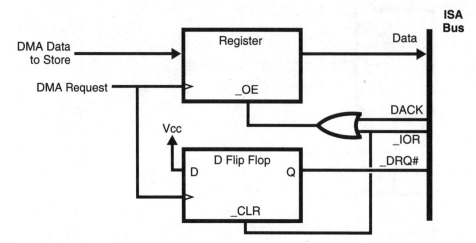

FIGURE 27-9   **PC DMA request sample circuit.**

I/O registers have to be accessed. This means that DMA channels should never be shared between devices.

When all the bytes for the DMA transfer have been passed, the T/C line on the ISA bus becomes active along with the appropriate DACK# line. This is normally used within an adapter to make a hardware interrupt request, which is used to notify the software application that the DMA has completed and it can disable the DMA requesting hardware. A possible DMA completion interrupt request circuit could be like that shown in Fig. 27-10. When the DACK# line goes low and the T/C line is high, the D flip-flop's output is set. This active line can be used to drive the interrupt request line.

Two 8237s (or equivalent circuits) are used in modern PCs, each able to handle four DMA sources. The primary DMA controller (starting at base I/O address 0) handles eight-bit DMA requests 0 through 3. The secondary DMA controller (starting at base I/O address 0x0D0) handles the 16-bit DMA transfers 4-7. This difference is important to remember as the data-transfer sizes cannot be changed.

In most modern PCs, the diskette controller uses DMA channel 2 and the SoundBlaster card uses DMA channel 1. For most user-created adapters, DMA Channel 0 is used.

The software for using the DMA controller is actually quite simple. In fact, as you work with the device, you only have to be concerned with six registers. The first register (at address 0x00C or 0x00D8) is the DMA-clear selected channel. Writing to this register will stop any in progress transfers on the last selection channel.

The *mask register* (at address 0x00A and 0x00D4) is used to select which register is to be written to:

BIT	FUNCTION
7-3	Not used
2	Set mask bit
1-0	Select channel

3

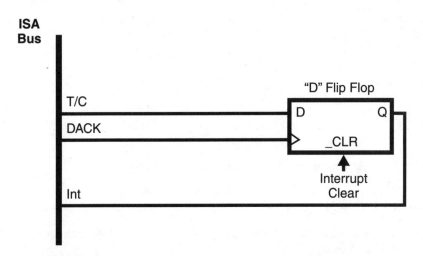

FIGURE 27-10 PC DMA interrupt request sample circuit.

When the register is "masked," the register will pause, which means that no DMA requests will be serviced until it is unmasked. The purpose of masking a channel is to allow changes to the DMA channel registers without inadvertent requests causing problems or changing values before the application is ready to accept DMA transfers.

The *mode register* (at address 0x0B or 0x0D6) is used to set the operating mode of the DMA channel.

BIT	FUNCTION
7-6	Operating mode
5	Address increment select
3	Initialization mode
3-2	Data movement
	00 - Verify - verify
	01 - Write (I/O to memory)
	10 - Read (memory to I/O)
1-0	Channel select

The most common modes are 0b00100,01cc or 0b00100,10cc (where "cc" is the channel), which is writing and reading data.

With the mask and mode setup, the offset register for the channel, the page register for the channel, and the count registers are written to. The *offset* and *count registers* are 16 bits long and have the low byte followed by the high byte when reading and writing to them. The addresses of the registers are:

CHANNEL	OFFSET REG	COUNT REG	PAGE REG
0	0x000	0x001	0x087
1	0x002	0x003	0x083
2	0x004	0x005	0x081
3	0x006	0x007	0x082
4	0x0C0	0x0C2	0x08F
5	0x0C4	0x0C6	0x08B
6	0x0C8	0x0CA	0x089
7	0x0CC	0x0CE	0x08A

Later in this book, there is a demonstration showing how a DMA transfer is set up with the SoundBlaster card.

Understanding and using DMA in the PC really isn't that complex. Like interrupts, you do not have to initialize a device; you only have to enable it for the channel you want to use. Despite this, I want to recommend that DMA not be used and other methods of data transfer between a PC and ISA adapter are used. The reason for making this recommendation is the way that the page registers work and the difficulty interfacing a reasonable page, I/O address, and interrupt handler in Windows. Ideally, the entire driver code should be located in Ring 0 or Real mode of the PC's processor.

Dual-port memory Because DMA is difficult to work with (and this gets worse if you are working with a Protect-mode 32-bit operating system, such as Windows), you might want to avoid using it altogether and instead opt for dual-ported memory instead.

This type of memory has two methods of access, the first uses double-speed clocked memory interface in which each interface (the adapter and PC) is given a time slice to interface with the memory (Fig. 27-11).

This type of memory interface is often used with VRAM, where the accesses can be easily predicted and proper timing is crucial. This method is, however, quite complex and difficult to implement. The problems lie in the buffering needed to save data going to and coming from the memory, which allows it to be synched with the ISA bus and the adapter reads and writes.

A more traditional way to provide access to both the ISA bus and adapter card is by using an asynchronous arbitration scheme (the first method used a synchronous access scheme), with accesses between the two devices prioritized. In this scheme (Fig. 27-12), the priority encoder determines which source should get access to the RAM. For example, the adapter interface could have priority in accessing the memory, unless the PC is writing to it. The truth table for the priority encoder could look like:

	ADAPTER INACTIVE	ADAPTER READ	ADAPTER WRITE
PC inactive	No access	Adapter access	Adapter access
PC read	PC access	Adapter access	Adapter access
PC write	PC access	PC access	Adapter access

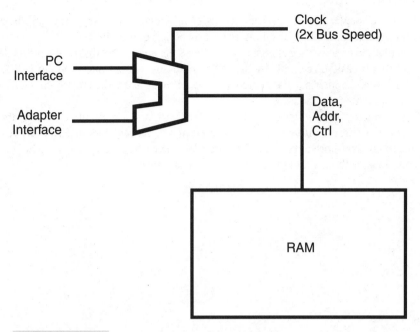

FIGURE 27-11 Double speed clock interface.

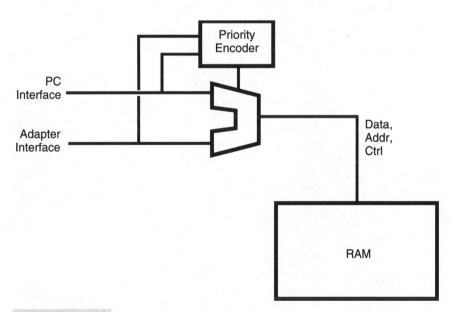

FIGURE 27-12 Dual port memory interface.

3
HARDWARE INTERFACING

When the adapter is given priority, the ISA bus is held with wait states until the adapter has finished; then, the ISA bus transfer is allowed to go through.

This method of providing shared access allows the adapter hardware to save its data in a format that is easily accessible by the PC's processor without interrupting the PC. Using this interface, the interface hardware can execute reads and writes totally in a DMA manner, without affecting the PC.

This method is used in the IDE disk interface with one important difference: the interface requires address information to be stored in adapter registers, followed by reads and writes to the dual-ported memory. This method is even stingier in terms of hardware than the previous method, although it is a bit slower to access data.

28

ISA I/O PORT AND
RAM/ROM
PROTOTYPING CARD

CONTENTS AT A GLANCE

If you've ever been in the market for an ISA prototyping card, you've probably been pretty disappointed by what is available. Virtually all prototyping cards just consist of a blank card, fully drilled for wire wrapping and with pads and traces routed in a pattern suitable for installation in a PC's ISA eight- or 16-bit ISA slot. These cards are generally very expensive ($70 or more) for what you get and you will have to provide all of the logic and wiring.

When both the PC and PC/AT were first announced, IBM sold a prototyping adapter that could be used to develop simple example circuits. This adapter had traces and chip prototypes on the card to decode the I/O bus and set a line active when the I/O address was I/O addresses 0x0300 to 0x031F. This adapter is actually one of the better prototyping systems that has been on the market, but the limited address range made it difficult to users to develop general applications.

I've always wanted to create a board that would provide more than the IBM prototyping card and still give a lot of flexibility in development of the actual circuit. This chapter presents my idea for an ISA prototyping card and an ISA NTSC composite video frame-grabber application that shows how the ISA interface works and some of the issues that surround it.

The prototyping card that I have come up with for this book consists of an I/O and memory address decode circuit that can be selected by a user. To simplify working with the card, I have designed it to use a simple menuing system that uses a couple of buttons and an LCD (Figs. 28-1 through 28-3).

The LCD and address decode ranges are controlled by a Microchip 16C64 microcontroller. This chip outputs select values, monitors the MFG_PORT address, and controls access to an eight-KB RAM that can be used for RAM or simulating boot ROM (Fig. 28-4).

The LCD used in this application is a Wirz Electronics SLI-OEM which is a simple card that takes serial data and displays it on a standard Hitachi 44780-controlled liquid crystal display. When the card first boots up, the 16C64 can default to the MFG_PORT address (0x0080) and the value written to this port will be displayed on the LCD, allowing you to monitor the boot of the PC.

A switch on the card selects whether or not the card I/O selects address range 0x0080 to 0x87 (the MFG_PORT/DMA page registers) or 0x0300 to 0x0307 (which is in the prototyping space) for the I/O address space. Depending on how the card is configured, booting with address 0x0300 might be required to avoid conflicts with the DMA page register.

Two buttons connected to the PC are used to select the prototyping card's operating mode and addresses. One button is used to select the menu (MFG_PORT value and I/O address select, RAM address select, and RAM write enable).

The actual circuit will seem very complex, but it is actually quite simple. I was surprised to discover this was a first-off design and prototype built for me. My design worked first time and the microcontroller's software, despite being very simple, works exactly as I wanted it to (Fig. 28-5).

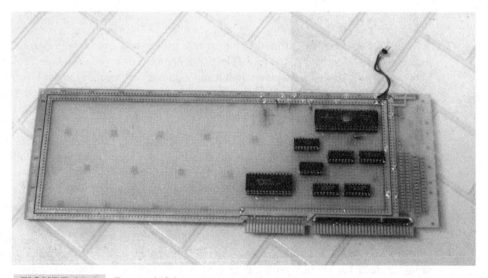

FIGURE 28-1   Front of ISA prototype card.

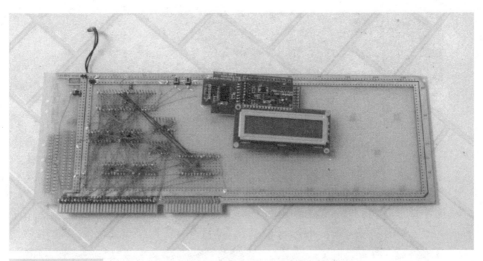

FIGURE 28-2   Back of ISA prototype card with LCD installed.

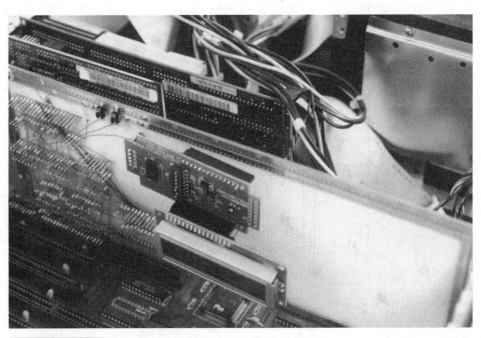

FIGURE 28-3   ISA prototype card installed in system.

FIGURE 28-4   "MFG-Port" display of ISA prototype card.

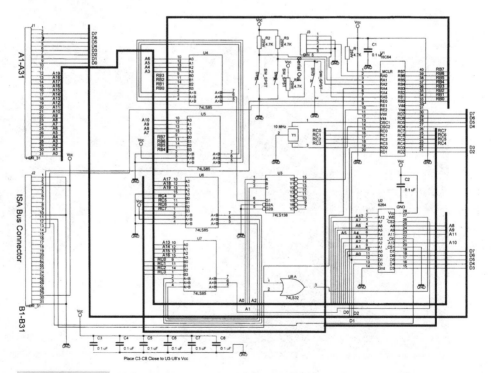

FIGURE 28-5   ISA prototype card schematic.

I/O Port Reads and Writes

The register input/output section of this design can be blocked out (as in Fig. 28-6), which uses the parallel slave port function of the 16C64 to monitor the base I/O address and display whatever is written to it. This feature is nominally used for monitoring the MFG_PORT during the PC's boot-up operation.

The I/O addresses that can be selected are eight bytes apart because of the 74LS138 that I use to decode the least-significant bits of the I/O address. The reason for using the 73LS138 for the actual address decoding is to piggy back up to seven other hardware I/O addresses from the '138.

Normally, upon boot up, the 16C64 microcontroller will output an I/O comparator value of 0x080, which is the MFG_PORT address. It is quite fascinating to watch the PC boot with the changing MFG_PORT values. When I actually started using the prototype with hardware connected to it, I found that the default address of 0x080 caused problems with hardware contention with the DMA page registers. To allow hardware to be placed in the circuit, I added the switch that would select between I/O address 0x080 and 0x0300 before booting up. With the address set to 0x0300 (the prototype adapter address), hardware added to the circuit will not cause problems with the DMA page registers.

This address can be changed. I wrote the 16C64 firmware to accept the address 0x080 and the range 0x0100 to 0x03F8. I avoided the range from 0x000 0x078 and 0x088 to 0x0F8 to prevent adapter hardware from being inadvertently being set to a hardware address that is also used for motherboard hardware. The I/O addresses 0x0100 to 0x03F8 are for hardware nominally on the ISA bus.

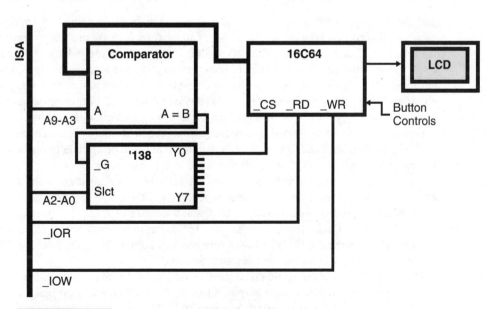

FIGURE 28-6   **ISA prototyping card I/O circuit.**

In the decode circuitry, I tied the two high-order bits to ground and in the comparator. This gives the circuit seven bits with which to decode the I/O address with the three bits used with the 74LS138. These are the 10 I/O address bits of the PC/AT. As pointed out, using only 10 bits means that if one of the upper six bits are set, the prototype adapter will respond as if only the lower 10 bits were active.

This means that the following I/O addresses are all the same to the ISA prototype adapter:

```
0x00300
0x00700
0x00B00
0x00F00
0x01300
   :
0x0FF00
```

The output of the 74LS138 should be ORed with the ISA bus' _IOR or _IOW lines to provide a valid Select negatively active signal to the peripheral that you've added to the I/O card.

Without this gate, any time that the lower 10 bits of the address bus have the I/O decode address, the select will become active. This means that you could have problems with the adapter driving the bus during memory reads and writes, as well as invalid I/O operations. To simplify things, you can also use the negative active chip enables in the 74LS138 for this function, as I do in the NTSC-compatible frame grabber shown later in this chapter.

Memory Reads and Writes

The ISA prototype card, even though it is designed to make prototyping ISA applications easier, is also an ISA application itself. As an application, you are probably surprised by the amount of LS (Low-Power, Schottkey) TTL logic on the board, which operates relatively slowly, compared to other technologies. In designing this hardware, I wanted to take advantage of the 760-ns access times and not develop a card that will require fast (expensive) parts or require a significant amount of silicon to design it. I didn't want to get a flood of e-mail from people that couldn't get their prototype adapter circuits working.

This fairly slow access speed is especially important with the memory access. In the card, I created an interface to an eight-KB memory that could be optionally read and written and used as a boot ROM (which is described in the next section).

On power up, the most-significant bit from the 16C64 to the comparator is set, while the corresponding bit within the comparator is reset (Fig. 28-6). This ensures that there can never be an ISA address/16C64 address comparator match and have data driven on or read from the ISA bus. The high-order bit from the 16C64 has to be reset for any addresses ever to be matched. When the 16C64's high-order memory-address bit is set, I describe this as "disabled" on the LCD for the memory address menu.

The comparator is wired so that the upper seven bits of the ISA's address bus (address bits 13 to 19) are compared to the output of the 16C64. With an 8K RAM that requires 13 bits, these seven bits allow access to the entire 20-bit ISA memory address space.

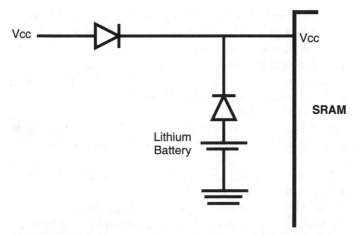

FIGURE 28-7   Battery backup for SRAM loaded with ROM.

Once these seven bits are set with a valid address (from 0x0C8000 to 0x0DE000), the RAM will be addressable from the ISA bus and, if the optional write-enable bit from the 16C64 is reset, it can also be written to. The purpose of the write-enable bit was to disable writes from the PC's processor to the SRAM and allow it to behave as ROM from the processor's point of view.

To allow the SRAM to work like ROM and retain its contents on power up, a lithium back-up battery, wired in the configuration shown in Fig. 28-7 can be used. In this circuit, when power is turned off within the PC, the Lithium cell powers the SRAM.

Although the RAM-selection hardware in the ISA prototype card works very well, I would like to see this portion of the board modified. Ideally, I would like the eight KB expanded to allow at least 32 KB of memory to be added to the card to provide a reasonable amount of ROM/RAM memory for the prototype circuit. As well, I would like to see the 16C64 provide a RAM/ROM window, in which the function of portions of the SRAM could be selected as either type of memory and give more flexible access for applications.

Expansion ROM and ROM Boot

The RAM in the prototyping card can be used as a boot ROM when you are developing new applications that will use a ROM. The program in the ROM subdirectory will save a .COM program in the specified RAM address and can be executed as ROM the next time the PC is booted.

The Romload program is written totally in C and is executed from the MS-DOS command line as:

```
romload segment file.com
```

Where *segment* is the 8-KB address starting at 0x0C8000 and going up to 0x0DE000. The segment itself can only be 8 KB in size on an 8-KB boundary.

The .COM file can be no more than 7936 bytes in size because 256 bytes of the 8192 bytes available in the SRAM are used for application header information.

To load the code, the address of the SRAM in the ISA prototyping card must be set to a valid address (i.e., not disabled) and writes to memory must be enabled.

After the SRAM has been loaded, writes to it should be disabled. The Power Good line is then cycled or the *Ctrl-Alt-Delete* key sequence is entered. In both cases, the ROM area is scanned and any ROM code encountered is executed.

You could also add an external power source to the SRAM (i.e., a battery) to ensure the contents are not lost on power down. I use lithium PC battery in the configuration shown in Fig. 28-7.

At the end of your .COM file's execution, a far return instruction (0x0CB) has to be executed to allow the PC to continue booting.

The .COM file is loaded into the RAM directly by romload. When creating the .COM file, you should use the same rules as doing an OSLess boot. No MS-DOS APIs or functions should be executed because they're simply not there. As well, in this application, I set registers to .COM default (AX, BX, CX, DX, SI, and DI to zero, SP to 0x0FFFE, and all four segment registers to the same value).

If you look at this application and the "OSLess" disk boot, you will probably feel like I use the .COM/binary format a lot. I don't really, but they are very useful to provide a quick-and-dirty way to test applications that execute within the PC with an operating system being loaded. I have found that using .COM to be a very effective way to test applications or simple code because issues with the segment registers can be ignored.

ISA NTSC Composite
Video Frame Grabber

With the ISA prototype card designed and tested, I wanted to see how useful it would be in designing an actual application for the PC. The application I came up with was an NTSC composite video frame grabber. This circuit was designed to be used with the prototype card and actually helped me to add an improvement to the card itself.

A *frame grabber* is a circuit that treats video data as a stream of analog serial data (which is exactly what it is) and converts it into a series of bytes, which represent the data on the video display. It can be displayed on a computer monitor exactly like graphical data. The circuit presented here converts a single frame of monochrome video into a 64- by 64-pixel array of bytes that can be processed by the PC.

This circuit was a good demonstration of my project-management skills because I planned to take seven evenings to design it and get it working. This is exactly what was required. The circuit was built onto the ISA prototype card after the prototype circuitry was built and tested. I used MS-DOS C code to debug the circuit and display the output. After I finished debugging it, I was amazed to discover that the final circuit was actually quite a bit simpler than what I started out with.

3

WINDOWS PROGRAMMING

Despite saying this, this not a trivial circuit to build and debug. I had always wanted to design and build a frame grabber, so I had some ideas about how I wanted it to work. When you work through the circuit, I suggest that you follow the steps that I have laid out here and try to understand how I expect it to work. This is a circuit (along with the software) where you will have to be 100-percent satisfied with what's happening before you move on. I made this mistake and had to go back and work through a problem with the design.

A very important part of using the circuit is a source of monochrome composite video. I used a *Tyco* toy video camera that I bought from Toys'R Us a few years ago (my wife is always amazed at how many electronic projects I've used it for) as the video source. The video output is straight NTSC luminance video information without a colorburst signal (used by a TV to lock into the line's color phase information) or color information (Fig. 28-8). If you are going to use a video source with color information embedded in it, then colorburst and 3.579-MHz color signal will have to be filtered out (which can be done easily).

To decode the frame information, I used a National LM1881 synch separator and used the vertical synch output (VertOut from the chip) to start the frame-grab operation and the horizontal synch output (Burst from the chip) to start the sampling of each line. The vertical synch output was used as a clock input to a D flip-flop (a 74HCT74), which was used to control the sampling circuit (Fig. 28-9).

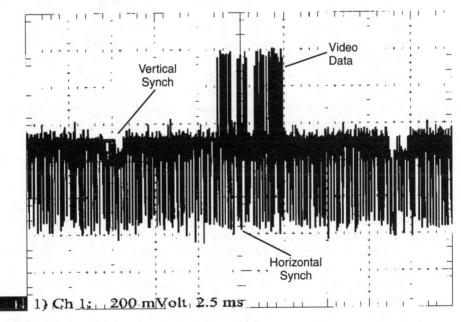

1) Ch 1:   200 mVolt 2.5 ms

FIGURE 28-8   NTSC composite video field.

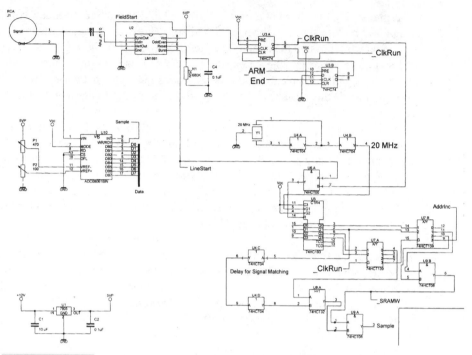

FIGURE 28-9   **Frame grabber-analog and pixel timing.**

The 74HCT74 is put in a cleared or reset state when the address counters have reached the end of the frame. To start the frame grab, the reset control is disabled; when the vertical synch pulse is detected by the LM1881, the process of sampling the data begins.

The circuit is clocked by a 20-MHz ceramic resonator timer (giving a 50-ns system clock), which is divided by 16 to get an 800-ns pixel sample clock. A 74HCT193 divides this clock down and the output of the counter is run through some combinatorial circuits to get the waveform shown for the ADC08061 "_W" bit in Fig. 28-10. The ADC08061 is a 1.5-MHz flash analog-to-digital converter with sample and hold, which runs at a maximum speed of 1.5 megasamples per second. For the 800-ns pixel timing, the device actually runs at 1.25 megasamples per second.

The ADC08061 runs in "_WR-_RD (Mode Pin High)" Reduced Interface System Connection mode, which allowed the ADC to run with a fairly simple control signals. At sample load in Fig. 28-10, the analog value to be sampled is loaded into the device. At Data Write, the analog voltage is output and written into the frame grabber's RAM.

The input to the ADC08061 is the straight 75-Ohm terminated output from the video camera. For the LM1881 to operate properly, it must be filtered by a 0.1-µF polyester capacitor. When I wired my circuit, the video input was simply a #30 wire wrap wire that traveled over the length of the ISA prototype address-line decode circuitry. I did not find a problem with induced noise on this line.

Where I did find a problem with noise was with the +5-V supply, available from the PC onto the prototype card. Measuring it on an oscilloscope, I found it to be upwards of 500 mV of noise at the ADC08061 and LM1881. To reduce this, I created a separate +5-V

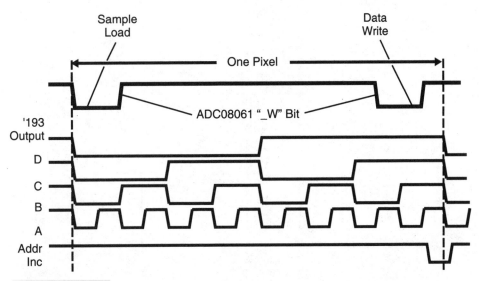

FIGURE 28-10   Frame grabber pixel timing.

power supply using a 7805 to regulate the ISA's +12-V supply to +5 V. After doing this, I found the voltage ripple to be below 10 mV at the ADC and LM1881.

In the original circuit, I used 5VP and Gnd for $+V_{ref}$ and $-V_{ref}$, respectively. I found that this caused problems with the dynamic range of the input, so the voltage references were changed to the dual potentiometers that you can see in Fig. 28-9. This allowed me to "tune" the circuit to the actual voltage output from the video camera.

The pixel timing circuit is only active when the frame grab is occurring and a horizontal scan line is active. When the scan line is inactive, the pixel clock does not run and the column counter is reset.

As mentioned, with the video data being sampled, the pixel clock not only controls the ADC08061, but also strobes the data into the 6264 SRAM. When deciding how to sample the frame, I decided upon using a 64- by 64-pixel size that uses 4 KB of the 8 KB SRAM. When sampling, I sample 64 times for each line taking 51.2 of the 53.6 μsecs available on the line. This means that I miss the rightmost 2.4 μsecs of the frame, but this really isn't a problem.

Only one out of every four lines is actually saved before the row counter is incremented. In normal NTSC video, each frame consists of two fields of 262.5 lines. I actually sample 256 lines of one field and save 64 lines of the field. Obviously, I am not doing a complete sample to the maximum available data, but I do get a good representation of the video frame.

The circuit is controlled by the unused pins of the '138 I/O address selector of the ISA prototyping card. When you look at Fig. 28-11, you'll notice that I use the output signals from the '138 (CS1 through CS5) without ORing them with the ISA bus' _IOR line. To avoid having to add a number of OR gates and the wiring associated with them, I rewired one of the '138s chip-enable lines to the ISA bus' _IOR. This actually results in slightly faster signals (no additional gates) and about 15 less wires to wrap.

Having all the signals as "Read" was not an issue as I used the chip selects to initiate the functions and the only data transfer was from the card to the PC (Read).

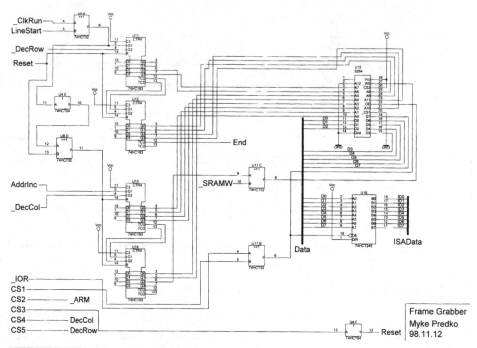

FIGURE 28-11   **Frame grabber-memory addressing.**

This gave the signals the addresses:

LINE	ADDRESS	FUNCTION
CS1	Base+1	Read data from the SRAM
CS2	Base+2	Arm the circuit (start frame grab after next vertical synch)
CS3	Base+3	Reset the address counters
CS4	Base+4	Decrement the column counter
CS5	Base+5	Decrement the row counter

After I first used the circuit, I discovered that the PC would fail POST because of a DMA page register failure. Looking at the circuit and my PC references, I noticed that the ISA prototype card booted up at address 0x080 (which would be *Base*). At address 0x081, *Base+1*, data was driven onto the bus by the frame grabber and caused bus contention problems with the DMA page registers.

To fix the problem, I added the Base-Address Select switch on the ISA prototype card, which would allow me to select between 0x080 and 0x0300 (the prototype card base address).

With the card in place, I first worked through the data-sampling functions. These were fairly easy to debug. The only problem was that I could not get an acceptable spacing between the data sample and data write (I was getting 470 ns, instead of the minimum

550 ns). By adding the two inverters in the clocking circuit, I was able to get the specified timing.

Next, I worked through the row timing. I felt this was more important because it is used to stop the frame-grab operation. To only save the samples on the fourth line, I ignored the least-significant two bits of the counter and used the carry output to stop the sampling.

As described, the column counters are incremented when the horizontal line data is valid. To avoid problems with overwriting data in the RAM, when the counter is greater than 64, I mask off writes to the SRAM.

To initiate a sample, the counters are reset and the circuit is armed:

```
inp( Reset );              // Reset the Counter

inp( Arm );                // Arm Circuit to Wait for Field
```

To ensure that the operation is completed, I waited two RTC "ticks" before reading the data out of the SRAM.

```
i = *ClkVar + 2;           // Wait a Minimum of 55 msecs for
while ( i != *ClkVar );    //   a full field to be sampled.
```

Reading data uses the counters in a decrement mode (which again saved wiring that I would have had to use if I worked through the increment lines). This meant I had to read into the destination array backwards. The code to do this is actually quite simple:

```
inp( Reset );              // Reset the Counter Again

for ( i = 0; I < 64; i++ ) {  // Read through the Data

  inp( DecRow );              // Go to the Previous Row

  for ( j = 0; j < 192; j ++ )
    inp( DecCol );            // Go to the Start of the Line

  for ( j = 0; j < 64; j++ ) {  // Read the Data

    inp( DecCol );             // Point to the Column

    VarBuffer[ 63 - i ][ 63 - j ] = inp( ByteRead );

  } // endfor

  inp( DecRow );               // Go to the End of the Row
  inp( DecRow );
  inp( DecRow );

} // endfor
```

After *VarBuffer* is loaded, I displayed the information on the PC one of two ways. The first was as an array of numbers. This was supposed to be a quick-and-dirty method to see if the program worked. The second was to use *Mode 13h* and display the information graphically.

When I first ran the number-array program, I was able to see a difference between light and dark. I tried putting a black piece of cardboard across half of the camera's lens, but I couldn't see a line showing a difference in light levels. After playing around with it a bit and seeing some results, I decided that the reduced data displayed (only the top leftmost 32- by 32-pixel values are displayed) was not getting the edge of the cardboard.

I forged on ahead with the graphics program. When I tried to look at a picture, all I got was garbage. After pulling my hair for a while, I went back to the original grabber program and worked through the data reads. As I did that, I found an error in how I designed the column counter circuit and I was able to fix it (and simplify the circuit in the process). With the fix in place, I was able to observe the differences between light and black in grabber and then I went on to the graphics programs.

When I first ran them, I found that the image was reversed. This was actually because I tried to guess what was the correct values and saturating the ADC08061. After playing around with values, I decided to put in the potentiometers that are in Fig. 28-9 and then "tuned" the circuit to the voltage-level output from the video camera.

Even with the potentiometer reference-level tuning, I found that the toy video camera and frame-grabber combination does not give a great range of analog voltages. I confirmed this by connecting the camera into a VCR, as well as then looking at the output on an oscilloscope. To get better dynamic range, a better video source would have to be used.

Later in this book, in a Visual Basic application for this application, a few example frame grabs are shown from the circuit. I could not get a good screen print or photograph from a PC screen to include in this section.

If I were to review the circuit, I would give it pretty high marks. Even though the schematics seem complex, the circuit is actually quite simple. I would like to see it run at a higher resolution. To do that, I would have to add a larger SRAM and faster ADC. I could have done it in the original circuit, but I did not feel like doing the extra wiring.

The use of the address decodes to initiate functions greatly simplifies the interface and provides all the necessary functions for the circuit. When you are designing your own ISA circuits, you might want to use this method instead of registers that have to have data written to them to initiate hardware functions. The only gating factor in this method is that it does take up I/O addresses (of which there aren't many in the PC).

Other things I might consider looking at in the future would be to have an interrupt requested when the frame grab is completed. If the circuit has no valid NTSC input, it will remain armed indefinitely without any way to check this from the application code. This is really the only deficiency I see with the circuit.

You might be tempted to use DMA with this circuit instead of the SRAM. Although this would seem to use less circuitry and would be simpler, you have to recognize that it wouldn't work. DMA is dependent on when the processor stops using the bus and will allow the DMA controllers to take it over. In this circuit, data is timed quite precisely; if the processor does not give up the bus in time for the DMA controller, pixels (which come at 800 ns intervals) will be lost.

DMA is best used for requests that are 10 μsecs (or more) apart with data latched. This gives the processor time to finish the current instruction and carry out the DMA transfer before the next byte of data is available. In the diskette drive, data can come in as slowly as 20 μsecs per byte, which gives the processor lots of time to finish its current operation before having another request to process.

Even going to a 16-bit DMA, which will double the data period to 1.6 μsecs per transfer, will still be too fast for the processor to reliably load using DMA.

29

THE
PCI
BUS

CONTENTS AT A GLANCE

Bus I/O	**Interrupts**
Configuration and PnP	**DMA**

There seems to be a winner in the competition to provide a high-speed adapter card interface to the PC. This competition was started by IBM with the introduction of the *Micro-Channel Architecture (MCA)* as a successor to the ISA bus. It was then challenged by *Enhanced ISA (EISA)* followed by Local Bus and "won" by "PCI" ("Peripheral Channel Interface"). The advantage of PCI is that it is not only available on PCs, but also Macintoshes and work stations (Silicon Graphics, specifically), which simplifies the work of the developer to only having to design one adapter card to all these systems.

PCI is primarily a high-speed (33/66 MHz) bus that is really only suited to devices that can benefit from this speed. Currently, the typical cards that require PCI are video adapters, very fast networking cards, and high-speed disk controllers. To provide fast access for these devices, the PCI Bus specification is actually quite complex and really not suitable for casual applications, such as shown in this book.

One problem with PCI is the lack of good documentation and learning aids available. To truly understand how to develop adapter cards (and their constituent ASICs), you will have to enter into a *Non-Disclosure Agreement (NDA)* with Intel on the operation of PCI and the PC's bridge chips. This makes casual applications unlikely and the applications for the bus only suitable for adapters that are planned to have at least 10,000 built and sold.

Making PCI even less desirable to learn is the PC/9x specification that has been released by Intel and Microsoft as a guide to PC designers and manufacturers for their future products. This specification only provides for USB and Firewire (IEEE 1394) interfaces to the PC and ideally no internal busses (which makes both ISA and PCI obsolete). The goal of the PC/9x specification is to create a PC that the user will never have to open up to add adapters and not have any switches to set

This chapter is an introduction to the PCI bus, but without applications or interfaces.

Bus I/O

If you download the PCI 2.1 document from the PCI *Special Interest Group (SIG)*, you'll see that the bus can be designed for a variety of different bus interconnect formats. Along with the familiar PC card adapter, the PCI bus has been adapted to embedded applications (CompactPCI), VME card format, among other form factors. These differing mechanical designs, although physically different, are electronically the same. In this chapter, I will focus on the PC's PCI adapter's electrical connections, although the I/O information can be applied to a PCI card in any form factor.

The PC's PCI card can use +5-V or +3.3-V logic with the card "keys" in the 32-bit card edge connector used to prevent cards being connected into systems that cannot provide the appropriate power. The following table shows the connections for the 32-bit connector:

PIN NUMBER	COMPONENT SIDE	SOLDER SIDE	KEY LOCATION
1	-12 V	-TRST	
2	TCK	+12V	
3	Gnd	TMS	
4	TDO	TDI	
5	+5 V	+5 V	
6	+5 V	-INTA	
7	-INTB	-INTC	
8	-INTD	+5 V	
9	-PRSNT1	Reserved	
10	Reserved	+I/O voltage	
11	-PRSNT2	Reserved	
12	Gnd	Gnd	3.3 V Key Position
13	Gnd	Gnd	3.3 V Key Position
14	Reserved	Reserved	
15	Gnd	-RST	
16	Clk	+I/O voltage	

17	Gnd	-GRNT
18	REQ	Gnd
19	+I/O voltage	Reserved
20	AD31	AD30
21	AD29	+3.3 V
22	Gnd	AD28
23	AD27	AD26
24	AD25	Gnd
25	+3.3 V	AD24
26	C/BE3	IDSEL
27	AD23	+3.3 V
28	Gnd	AD22
29	AD21	AD20
30	AD19	Gnd
31	+3.3 V	AD18
32	AD17	AD16
33	C/BE2	+3.3 V
34	Gnd	-FRAME
35	-IRDY	Gnd
36	+3.3 V	-TRDY
37	-DEVSEL	Gnd
38	Gnd	-STOP
39	-LOCK	+3.3 V
40	-PERR	SDONE
41	+3.3 V	-SBO
42	-SERR	Gnd
43	+3.3 V	PAR
44	C/BE1	AD15
45	AD14	+3.3 V
46	Gnd	AD13
47	AD12	AD11
48	AD10	AD9
49	Gnd	Gnd
50	Gnd	Gnd	5 V Key Position

51	Gnd	Gnd	5 V Key Position
52	AD8	C/BE0	
53	AD7	+3.3 V	
54	+3.3 V	AD6	
55	AD5	AD4	
56	AD3	Gnd	
57	Gnd	AD2	
58	AD1	AD0	
59	+I/O voltage	+I/O voltage	
60	-ACK64	-REQ64	
61	+5 V	+5 V	
62	+5 V	+5 V	

Both keys can be cut out of the card if it can run on both +5- and +3.3-V power.

PCI is also capable of supporting 32- or 64-bit data transfers. During the data-transfer attempt, the -REQ64 pin is made active and if the card responds with -ACK64, then a full 64-bit transfer is executed.

To carry out a 64-bit transfer, a second connector is added to the card:

PCI PIN	CONNECTOR PIN	COMPONENT SIDE	SOLDER SIDE
63	1	Reserved	Gnd
64	2	Gnd	C/BE7
65	3	C/BE6	C/BE5
66	4	C/BE4	+I/O voltage
67	5	Gnd	PAR64
68	6	AD63	AD62
69	7	AD61	Gnd
70	8	+I/O voltage	AD60
71	9	AD59	AD58
72	10	AD57	Gnd
73	11	Gnd	AD56
74	12	AD55	AD54
75	13	AD53	+I/O voltage
76	14	Gnd	AD52
77	15	AD51	AD50

78	16	AD49	Gnd
79	17	+I/O voltage	AD48
80	18	AD47	AD46
81	19	AD45	Gnd
82	20	Gnd	AD44
83	21	AD43	AD42
84	22	AD41	+I/O voltage
85	23	Gnd	AD40
86	24	AD39	AD38
87	25	AD37	Gnd
88	26	+I/O voltage	AD36
89	27	AD35	AD34
90	28	AD33	Gnd
91	29	+I/O voltage	AD32
92	30	Reserved	Reserved
93	31	Reserved	Gnd
94	32	Gnd	Reserved

As is implied by the pin names, the data and address lines are multiplexed. The transfer is initiated by special-function pins, which handshake with the PCI controller. The handshake lines include -FRAME, which is used to notify all the devices on the bus that a transfer is going to happen. The C/BE# bits are output from the bus controller, which is used to indicate what operation is going to occur. The four pins can select the following operations:

C/BE	FUNCTION
0b00000	Interrupt acknowledge
0b00001	Special cycle
0b00010	I/O read
0b00011	I/O write
0b00100	Reserved
0b00101	Reserved
0b00110	Memory read
0b00111	Memory write
0b01000	Reserved

0b01001	Reserved
0b01010	Configuration word read
0b01011	Configuration word write
0b01100	Multiple memory read
0b01101	Dual address cycle
0b01110	Memory read line
0b01111	Memory write invalidate

This chapter focuses on using the PCI adapter as an I/O space adapter, but there are a few PCI transfers I should comment on. The first is that each slot can be individually addressed by the PCI controller from the PC's processor. This is used at boot up to read the configuration information and is described in more detail in the next section.

The interrupt-acknowledge operation works similarly to how an 8086 acknowledges an interrupt from the 8259 with the processor putting the interrupt vector on the bus. This really leaves the I/O and memory data-transfer operations. These operations execute in a similar manner, keyed off the 33-MHz PCI bus clock. A single-word transfer looks like Fig. 29-1.

In the address phase, the address is selected or broadcast over the bus. When the master is ready to transfer data, it makes the -IRDY line active. If an adapter has I/O or memory matching the address, the adapter will pull the -TRDY line low. The PCI controller will acknowledge the -TRDY signal by asserting the -DEVSEL line to indicate that the data will be following.

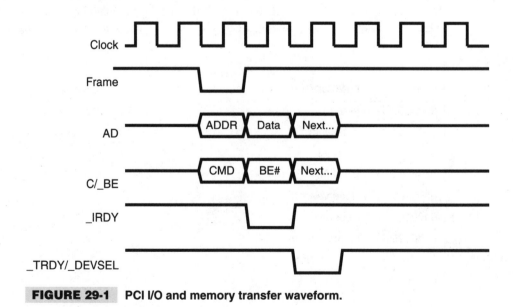

FIGURE 29-1 PCI I/O and memory transfer waveform.

3
WINDOWS PROGRAMMING

If the address phase yields no response, the PC's PCI controller will automatically pass the I/O operation to the PC's ISA bus. Thus, if an adapter is available in the PCI bus at a given I/O or memory address, the I/O or memory read/write operation will not be driven on the ISA bus.

The start of the next cycle is the start of when data has to read or written. This is actually very fast for most I/O and memory devices, so the provision for inserting wait cycles by the PCI adapter into the transfer process (Fig. 29-2) is possible by delaying the assertion of -TRDY for a cycle or two.

An extreme example of wait states is if an adapter does not decode an address quickly enough. In most modern PC chipsets, if the time required for an ISA transfer passes the PCI transfer ends and the ISA transfer is assumed to be the default case. In this way, the PC can determine whether an address is a PCI (quick response) or an ISA transfer. The Plug'n'Play configuration information can also be used by the PC to determine where ISA and PCI devices are located, but this could be overridden if the PCI card takes an unexpectedly long time to respond.

A nice feature of PCI is that multiple sequential word I/O operations can occur after the address phase is passed. This allows the PCI bus to take full advantage of the 33-MHz clock to provide fast block transfers (Fig. 29-3).

Notice that the -FRAME line stays active until the next-to-last word transfer. This indicates to the adapter that the PCI controller is waiting for additional data to be passed. This feature allows large amounts of data to be passed to sequential devices (such as SCSI ports and video adapters).

These multiple-word transfers can continue indefinitely, but a timer will temporarily stop them and respond to pending bus requests (such as for interrupts, new masters, and memory refreshes).

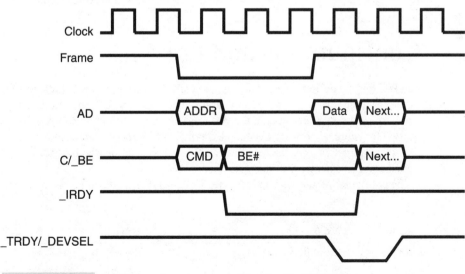

FIGURE 29-2   PCI I/O and memory waveform with "Waits".

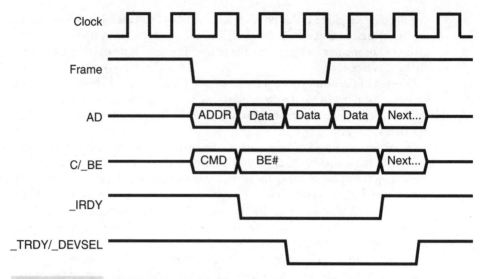

FIGURE 29-3   Multiple word PCI I/O and memory waveform.

It is actually quite easy to implement a simple I/O card using PCI. The information up to this point will be sufficient for you to create your own non-PnP adapter, although I should caution you on the potential problems of running hardwired device addresses with change-able PnP selectable device addresses.

Memory transfers are somewhat more complex and have to be fully integrated into the system. To successfully do this, you will have to get a copy of the PCI specification (Version 2.1 is the latest, as of this writing) and understand how memory is located on the PCI bus and passed to the system. This is a function of the configuration/PnP information stored in the adapter card. It is presented in greater detail in the next section.

Configuration and PnP

The PCI bus, by definition, contains dynamically allocated resources (adapters or targets). These resources are designed with the ability that memory, I/O port and interrupt-request numbers can be relocated within the system. The previous section showed that PCI could be used for simple, hardware-decoded I/O ports, but for more-complex operations, the PCI uses its *configuration memory* as Plug 'n 'Play data to allow the host to poll what is installed and then specify the addresses used.

The configuration memory is 256 bytes in size and is accessed 32 bits at a time:

ADDR	BYTE 0	BYTE 1	BYTE 2	BYTE 3
0000h	Vendor ID	<-	Device ID	<-
0004h	PCI CMD	<-	PCI Status	<-

0008h	Revision	Class Code	<-	<-
000Ch	Cache size	Latency Tmr	Header Type	BIST
0010h	BAR0	<-	<-	<-
0014h	BAR1	<-	<-	<-
0018h	BAR2	<-	<-	<-
001Ch	BAR3	<-	<-	<-
0020h	BAR4	<-	<-	<-
0024h	BAR5	<-	<-	<-
0028h	RESERVED	<-	<-	<-
002Ch	RESERVED	<-	<-	<-
0030h	Expansion ROM base	<-	<-	<-
0034h	RESERVED	<-	<-	<-
0038h	RESERVED	<-	<-	<-
003Ch	Int Reg	Int Pin	Min Grant	Max Latency

In this table <- indicates that the byte is a carry-over from the previous byte. *Vendor ID* and *Device ID* perform the same service as their counterparts in ISA PnP. *Vendor ID* specifies the card model and *Device ID* specifies the serial number of the device with every device of a card model given a unique serial number. This allows multiple cards of the same type to be placed in a system, recognized, and uniquely addressed.

The *BAR#* values are base address registers. Upon power up, they contain the resource type (I/O or memory) and the number of bytes required for the resource. During PnP setup, the resource addresses are written to. The expansion ROM addresses and interrupt resources work similarly.

The PCI PnP resources are identified at boot time, along with the ISA resources. The PCI PnP operation works like:

```
 1. Set Slot Index to Zero.
 2. Read Vendor ID. If Invalid, Jump to Step 4.
 3. Read and Save Resources.
 4. Increment the Slot Index.
 5. If Slot Index is not Past the Last Slot goto 2.
 6. Construct a Resource Map.
 7. Set Slot Index to Zero.
 8. If Invalid Device (from 2.) goto 10.
 9. Write Device Resource Map Settings.
10. Increment the Slot Index.
11. If Slot Index is not Past the Last Slot goto 8.
12. Continue Boot Operation.
```

When Windows 95/98/NT boots, it loads a "device registry" file from disk. This file contains all the configuration information of the previously installed adapters. The contents of this file are checked against the Resource Map, the system created upon boot up and appropriate drivers are loaded into memory. If the drivers are not loaded on the system's hard disk, then the user will be prompted to load them. In many cases, when new hardware is added to the system, Windows can use the configuration registers Vendor ID and Device ID to load the correct drivers automatically. At the end of the operating system boot, the registry file is updated with the correct system information.

Using configuration registers with Plug'n'Play moves PCI beyond the scope of what a hobbyist or casual one-off design is appropriate for with PCI. Both Altera and XILINX have PLD prototypes for PCI interfaces, but to create your own PnP cards, they will have to be registered and an appropriate set of drivers written. This is also especially true for implementing PCI cards with interrupts and DMA, as is shown in the next two sections.

Interrupts

Interrupt requests from PCI adapters must also be set up as part of the configuration/PnP process. Four interrupt lines on the PnP bus might have to be shared among multiple devices. Like the configuration/PnP set up, interrupt set up is not trivial.

When an interrupt request is acknowledged by the PCI bus controller, the PCI bus controller outputs the interrupt acknowledge CMD on the bus with the AD lines having the interrupt handler vector address driven onto the bus (Fig. 29-4).

The interrupt acknowledge can be sagely ignored on the bus and the request should be turned off when the PC has recognized the source and resets the interrupt-requesting hardware via register writes. As part of the interrupt-handler device driver, code must be put in to check-status registers built into the adapter card, which is a mirror of the request bit. If the bit is active, then the device driver can service the interrupt. The purpose of this method of handling interrupts is to allow the four interrupt lines to share multiple interrupt sources and provide a mechanism to determine which interrupt request is active.

The PCI interrupt-request hardware avoids the problems identified with the ISA interrupt-request hardware. The lines are negatively level triggered and allow multiple de-

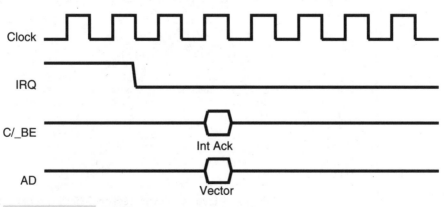

FIGURE 29-4 **PCI interrupt request waveforms.**

vices on the bus to pull down the line, with no opportunity for interrupt requests to be missed.

DMA

When I presented the PCI bus signals at the start of this chapter, you might have been surprised to see that no DRQ, DACK, or TC bits are in the bus. These lines are used by the ISA to carry out DMA requests; it is only natural to assume that the PCI bus would have the same capabilities. The reason why the DMA lines are not present is simple; DMA, as it exists on the ISA bus, doesn't exist in the PCI bus. Instead, the PCI's "bus-mastering" capabilities are used to allow an adapter to interface directly with other devices on the PCI bus to transfer data.

This might seem surprising, but, in reality, that is exactly how traditional DMA works. The processor is isolated form the data, address, and control busses and another device drives the transfer. In the PCI bus case, the PC itself is presented to the controller as a device that requests the bus.

When an adapter wants to do a transfer from memory to I/O, it must carry out the following steps:

1 Assert the _REQ line to request control of the bus.
2 Wait for the _GRNT line from the controller to become active to indicate that the adapter has control of the bus.
3 Do the data transfer.
4 Release the _REQ line to free up the bus before the last transfer.

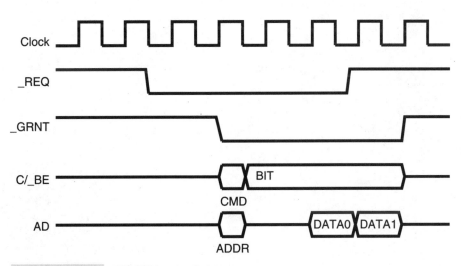

FIGURE 29-5 **PCI DMA waveforms.**

The bus waveforms look like Fig. 29-5. To carry out the bus master request, the equivalent circuit of a DMA controller (or microprocessor) must be present on each DMA-equipped PCI adapter card. This feature is actually responsible for much of the complexity of the primary PCI bus interface ASICs on adapter cards.

THE JOYSTICK
INTERFACE

One very common device on the PC that has always felt like it was an afterthought was the joystick interface. The IBM-designed interface was not even present in the original PC. It was made available by IBM both as a hardware adapter card and BIOS API interface when the PC/XT was announced.

The joystick port itself is not a marvel of engineering; the BIOS code that is provided with most PCs can be quite "clunky," slow, and difficult to integrate with games. As well, the way the port works can result in a fair amount of jitter caused by the analog-to-digital conversion not being very repeatable.

This has lead games manufacturers to use the joystick port as almost a digital left/ right/up/down device without using the proportional features of the joystick. Some other game manufacturers use large-granularity zones to simplify their programming, as well as cut down on the jitter that is inherent in the design.

Figure 30-1 shows the Microsoft Precision Pro joystick, which can avoid the joystick port of my PC altogether and use the USB port. This allows good precision in the operation of the joystick and avoids the jitter that is inherent in the analog-to-digital conversion process.

This chapter is an introduction to the analog joystick port and how it works, along with a method of using it as a bidirectional communications port for your PC.

FIGURE 30-1 Microsoft "Sidewinder Precision Pro" joystick.

How the PC Reads Analog Input

I, along with many other people, felt that IBM regarded that "business machines" in the name did not include equipment for playing games. Thus, the PC was not released with a joystick. Although the keyboard was very well designed for playing games, many applications that required an analog input for control (including games) did not have a very efficient interface available. The lack of a joystick made the PC a second runner compared to the "home" computers, which all had joystick ports, as well as graphics and sound hardware dedicated to making writing game applications easier.

When the PC/XT was announced, IBM also announced BIOS APIs for the joystick, as well as a simple joystick interface that was based at I/O address 0x0201. The block diagram of this port is shown in Fig. 30-2. To connect to a joystick, a 15-pin female D-Shell connector was placed on the end of the joystick port adapter. The _IOR and _IOW signals are the _IOR and _IOW lines of the ISA bus ORed with the address bus decoded to 0x0201.

The four buttons provided with the joystick (port 0x0201 bits 4 through 7) are simple pull-ups that are shorted to ground when a button is pressed. To read the buttons, the current state is simply read through the four-bit tri-state buffer. The button presses are not debounced or latched in any way by the joystick port hardware.

The analog-to-digital functions built in to the joystick are actually quite simple and often used for digital applications when the hardware supports timing better than a bus for an

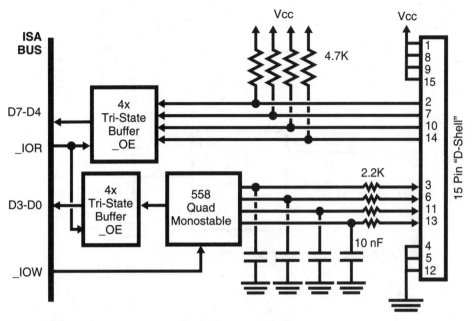

FIGURE 30-2 Typical PC joystick port implementation.

ADC. The characteristic rise/fall time of an RC network is used to determine the current location of the pot within the joystick.

The actual circuit for carrying out this analog to digital conversion (Fig. 30-5) consists of a monostable multivibrator, which triggers the analog-to-digital conversion. In steady state, the control (attached to the capacitor and resistor network) is at a low voltage and the State output is high.

When the trigger is pulsed, the State output is latched low and the output capacitor is allowed to charge. When the capacitor voltage reaches the threshold voltage, a 1 is latched in to the State output and the capacitor voltage is returned to a low state. This operation can be seen in the oscilloscope picture (Fig. 30-4), in which a 10-K resistor, along with a potentiometer set to 90K shows the waveforms produced by the joystick circuit.

To read a joystick's position, code writes to the port at 0x0201 with any value (the act of writing to the port is what activates the monostable multivibrator's trigger) and then polls port 0x0201 until the appropriate bit becomes set. This code is quite simple, although the timing issues are described elsewhere. Later, this section and the next one show some examples of how the code works.

To create this test of the joystick port, I built the circuit shown in Fig. 30-3. Because the trigger is common to all four joystick outputs, I wanted to see how two different resistor values performed. This circuit (along with the following code) allowed me to produce the waveforms shown in Fig. 30-4.

This circuit is very simple. When I built it, I didn't bother with a prototype card, I simply wired the potentiometer, resistor, and switch onto the back of a 15-pin male D-shell connector. As the circuit is wired, the button is read from bit 4 of port 0x0201, the 10-K

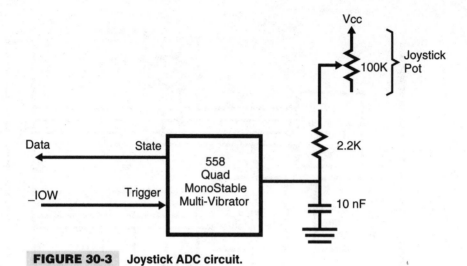

FIGURE 30-3   Joystick ADC circuit.

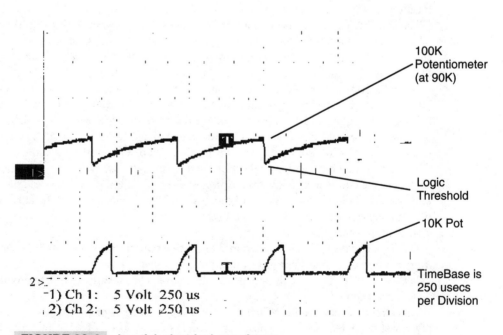

FIGURE 30-4   Joystick electrical waveforms.

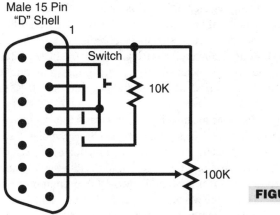

Male 15 Pin
"D" Shell

Switch

10K

100K

FIGURE 30-5   PC joystick test circuit.

3

HARDWARE INTERFACING

resistor is read from bit 0 of port 0x0201 and the 100-K potentiometer is read from bit 1 of port 0x0201.

To produce the differing waveforms, I executed DEBUG.COM from the MS-DOS prompt in Windows and entered the following program:

```
C:\WINDOWS>debug
-a 100
299B:0100 mov al, ff
299B:0102 mov dx, 201
299B:0105 mov bx, ffff
299B:0108 mov cx, ffff
299B:010B out dx, al
299B:010C in al, dx
299B:010D and al, 2
299B:010F jnz 10C
299B:0111 in al, dx
299B:0112 and al, 10
299B:0114 jz 11b
299B:0116 loop 10b
299B:0118 dec bx
299B:0119 jnz 10b
299B:011B int 3
-
```

This code is quite simple and could be pseudo-coded as:

```
unsigned long i = 0x0FFFFFFFF;

  while (( i != 0 ) && (( inp( 0x0201 ) & 0x010 ) != 0 ) {
                        //  Repeat for Count and Button Not
                        //   Pressed
    i--;                //  Decrement the Counter

    outp( 0x0201, 0xOFF );    //  Trigger Start of Pot Position Read
    while (( inp( 0x0201 ) & 0x002 ) == 0 );

  }  //  end while
```

In this code, a 32-bit counter (using registers BX:CX) is loaded with 0x0FFFFFFFF and provides a hard stop for the application, if you have to walk away from the application for any reason. Otherwise, a button press is used to stop the application.

Within the loop, the analog-to-digital conversion is triggered and the PC polls on this address until a *1* is returned for the potentiometer bit. By changing the value on the potentiometer, you can change the total period of the operation, but the 10-K resistor's waveform never changes.

I put the source code in DEBUG.COM to show how simply assembly-language test applications can be written to test hardware. The source code can be saved one of two ways. The most obvious way is to print it out using the Print Screen function of the PC. If you are working with a Windows MS-DOS prompt, you will have to disable the Windows Clipboard save of the Print Screen function from within the MS-DOS prompt properties. Another way of saving the code is to use the Mark function of Windows and save the code (which can be displayed using the Unassemble command) into an editor.

When working on this application, I discovered how truly awful the PC's joystick port is. On my development PC in which the joystick port is a part of the SoundBlaster-compatible sound card, I found that it was a lot of work trying to get the joystick port operational. I ended up giving up (with either the analog-to-digital converter or the button read working, but not both) and going with my experimental PC instead.

Once I had a fully working port, I found that the real-time clock interrupts significantly affected the timing and polling of the bits with a lot of potential "jitter" induced in the process. As well, I found a lot of variances between ports when I tried the 100-K potentiometer applied to different ports (up to 20 percent across the four ADC bits).

To see this, I bought a Microsoft Sidewinder Precision Pro joystick and a copy of Microsoft Combat Flight Simulator, which was done purely in the quest for knowledge and understanding how the joystick port worked in a practical application. The Sidewinder Precision Pro joystick can be connected to the PC—either through the joystick port or the USB bus. I found that when the joystick was connected to the joystick port, the control was quite poor and difficult to work through. When I attached the joystick to the USB port, I found the tracking to be much more precise and the aircraft in the Combat Flight Simulator much easier to control and "fly."

Another issue with the joystick port on the PC is the potential for problems with a MIDI port connected to the device. The following table presents the purpose of the original port, along with the typical modern port that is part of a SoundBlaster-compatible card. If you are going to develop a joystick application, you should use the SoundBlaster-compatible port to ensure that no problems occur with different PCs.

PIN	ORIGINAL PC PORT	SOUNDBLASTER PORT	JOYSTICK FUNCTION
1	V_{CC}	V_{CC}	Joystick 1 Pot Common
2	Button 1 (Bit 4)	Button 1 (Bit 4)	Joystick 1 Button 1
3	Pot 1 (Bit 0)	Pot 1 (Bit 0)	Joystick 1 X Axis
4	Ground	Ground	Joystick 1 Button Common
5	Ground	Ground	Joystick 2 Button Common

6	Pot 2 (Bit 1)	Pot 2 (Bit 1)	Joystick 1 Y Axis
7	Button 2 (Bit 5)	Button 2 (Bit 5)	Joystick 1 Button 2
8	V_{CC}	Not Used	
9	V_{CC}	V_{CC}	Joystick 2 Pot Common
10	Button 3 (Bit 6)	Button 3 (Bit 6)	Joystick 2 Button 1
11	Pot 3 (Bit 2)	Pot 3 (Bit 2)	Joystick 2 X Axis
12	Ground	MIDI Output	
13	Pot 4 (Bit 3)	Pot 4 (Bit 3)	Joystick 2 Y Axis
14	Button 4 (Bit 7)	Button 4 (Bit 7)	Joystick 2 Button 2
15	V_{CC}	MIDI Input	

To avoid potential problems with the MIDI circuitry in a SoundBlaster-based joystick card, the potentiometers and buttons should be wired with the pins indicated for the "SoundBlaster".

Digital Control Using the Joystick

If you play "flight simulator" computer games, you are probably aware of the "high tech" joysticks (like the Microsoft Precision Pro joystick shown at the beginning of this chapter) that have a multitude of buttons and features. When you look at the information I've provided above, you are probably wondering how the PC can "communicate" with the joystick and provide these extra functions. Not only must the joystick pass the data to the PC, but also the PC must pass data to the joystick to indicate how it is configured and is expected to work.

The previous section showed how different resistance values behave when the resistance measuring operation is initiated. Using this knowledge of how the RC circuits operate, I felt I could come up with a simple method of passing data back and forth between the PC and a microcontroller connected to the joystick port (Fig. 30-6).

To send data from the PC to the joystick device, I decided to use the characteristic RC rise curves and send pulses at varying rates for different bit values. In my application, I send two pulses with a very small delay between them to send a *1* and place a noticeable delay (greater than 50 μsecs) between the two pulses (Fig. 30-7).

To produce these differing pulses, I used the code:

```
BitPulse( int Value )
{

int  i;

  outp( 0x0201, 0 );              // Send out the Pulse
  while (( inp( 0x0201 ) & 1 ) != 0 );
```

FIGURE 30-6   LCD interface using the joystick port.

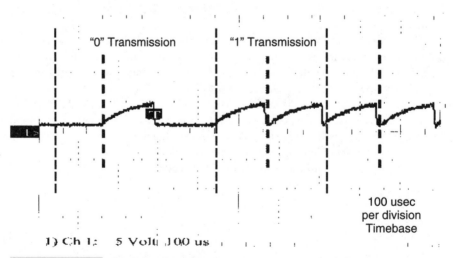

FIGURE 30-7   Joystick "communicator" data transmissions.

```
for ( i = 2 + (( Value ^ 1 ) * 98 ); i > 0; i-- )
  inp( 0x0300 );                    // Put in ISA "Read" Delays

outp( 0x0201, 0 );                  // Send the Second Pulse
while (( inp( 0x0201 ) & 1 ) != 0 );

for ( i = 0; i < 5; i++ )
  inp( 0x0300 );                    // Let the MCU "Settle"

}  //  End BitPulse
```

This code sends a pulse, waits for it to end and then places a delay of variable length (depending on the bit value passed to the routine) before sending the next delay. I use dummy reads to the first ISA prototype card I/O address to provide the delay. Notice that when I am sending a *1*, I still put in two *inp(0x0300);* operations to be sure the line has a noticeable settling time before the second pulse is sent.

Using the ISA bus and *inp(0x0300)* is a quick and dirty way of providing a fairly precise delay for applications. I hesitate to recommend it because it is not really applicable for all PCs. With an ISA bus, I could pretty much guarantee that the operation would take between 760 ns to 1.5μsecs. PCs following the Intel/Microsoft PC9x specification do not have ISA busses and the timing of the *inp(0x0300)* operation is indeterminate or could cause an access violation. Neither of these situations is desirable. While timing using ISA ports might appear easy to use, I don't recommend it.

To send a full byte, I used the following subroutine:

```
int ByteSend( char DataOut )     // Send the Byte Out
{

int  i;
int  Parity = 0;

  for ( i = 0; i < 8; i++ ) {      // Send the Data a Bit at a Time
    if (( DataOut & 0x080 ) == 0 )
      Parity++;                    // Keep Track of the Parity
    BitPulse(( DataOut >> 7 ) & 1 );
    DataOut = ( DataOut << 1 ) & 0x0FF;
  } /* endfor */

  BitPulse(( Parity & 1 ) ^ 1 );  // Send the Parity

  outp( 0x0201, 0 );  i = 0;      // Now, Look for the Ack
  while (( inp( 0x0201 ) & 1 ) != 0 )
    if (( inp( 0x0201 ) & 0x010 ) == 0 )
      i = 1;

  return i ^ 1;                    // Return "0" For Good

}  // End ByteSend
```

This routine sends data a bit at a time (using BitPulse) with the most-significant bit first and ending with an even parity bit and looks for an acknowledgement from the joystick device. When I first coded this, I didn't know how reliable the data transmission would be (especially using a number of different PCs), so I placed this level of control.

The joystick device that I used was a Microchip PICMicro 16F84 connected to the joystick port and a Hitachi 44780-based LCD (Fig. 30-8). The Pot1 pin was put in a typical

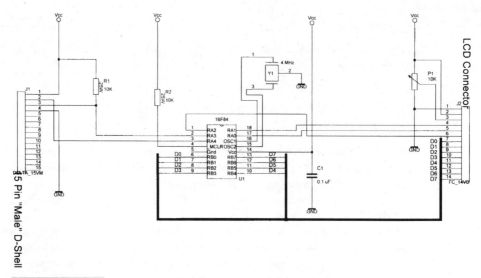

FIGURE 30-8 Joystick "communicator" circuit.

potentiometer application with a 10-K resistor pulled up to V_{cc} (which is provided by the joystick port). This gave me a characteristic R/C rise/fall time of about 100 μsecs, which the PICMicro could easily detect and decode the time between incoming pulse pairs.

This circuit is not trivial to wire, as can be seen in Fig. 30-9. If I would create another device like this again, I would probably use the LCD's 4-bit mode instead of the 8-bit mode to simplify the wiring.

To read a bit, I first waited for the first pulse to be read and then the time to the next pulse measured using the built-in timer. The bit read operation could be written in C as:

```
BitRead()                    //  Read the Incoming Bit
{

  while ( Pulse_In == 0 );    //  Wait for the First Pulse

  while ( Pulse_In != 0 );    //  Wait for the First Pulse to End

  TMR0 = 0;                   //  Reset the Timer

  while ( Pulse_In == 0 )     //  Wait for the Next Pulse
    if ( TMR0 == 0x0FF )      //  Have Timed Out the Wait
      break;

  if ( TMR0 == 0x0FF )        //  If Time Out
    return -1;                //    Indicate Bit Not Read
  else {

    while( Pulse_In != 0 );   //  Wait for the Pulse to End

    if ( TMR0 > 50usec )      //  If Time > 50 usec, then "0" Sent
      return 0;
    else
      return 1;

  }

}  // End BitRead
```

FIGURE 30-9 Backside of LCD joystick interface.

In this code, I look for the timer to almost reset (at 0x0FF). If it does reach this value, I assume that a problem has occurred at the PC and the second pulse is not coming. Actually, in the assembler code, I also have a timeout for the first bit pulse as well. In this way, if the PC's software ends or cannot send data in the correct protocol, the PICMicro ignores any potentially invalid instructions.

At the end of the byte being sent, the PC sends a single pulse for the joystick device to acknowledge successful reception of the data. If the parity received by the microcontroller matches the bit count kept by the microcontroller matches, then the PICMicro pulls the Button 1 line down for the PC to acknowledge that the byte was received correctly.

The code for the PC and PICMicro can be found in the Joystick subdirectory of the CD-ROM as JOYSTC.C and JOYSTC.ASM, respectively. The PC's JOYSTCK.EXE code waits for the user to enter keyboard data. If it isn't a carriage return (Enter), which ends the application, it sends the character to the PICMicro and the PICMicro displays the character on the LCD. The application is surprisingly robust. In my testing, I found that it would work on a number of different PCs with no observed data transmission errors. In each case, I used a six-foot joystick extender cable to connect the joystick to the PC (to avoid getting on hands and knees to look at what the LCD is displaying).

The PC software would return with a "No Acknowledgement" error message if the joystick device was disconnected from the PC's joystick port.

Passing data back to the PC was not investigated other than simply sending the Acknowledgment bit, but with a user-designed protocol, the button pull-down circuitry used

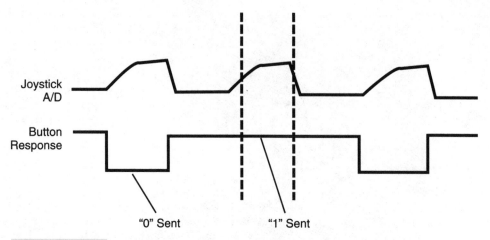

Joystick
A/D

Button
Response

"0" Sent   "1" Sent

FIGURE 30-10 Joystick "communicator" data transmissions.

with the microcontroller could be used to pass data back very easily and very quickly. Figure 30-9 shows how the joystick A/D pulses can be polled by an external device and bit values sent back when the pulses are read as high voltage values.

The protocol for sending and receiving data could be as simple as sending a byte with bit 7 set to send a command byte and sending a byte with bit 7 reset to indicate that the following eight pulses would be used to receive a byte from the joystick. The return protocol could include a parity bit, as does the transmit operation, but with the reliability that I saw I might be easily persuaded to stop using the parity bit and acknowledge bit to make the code simpler.

Like for the dongle presented for the parallel port, the method presented here for sending data between the PC and the joystick is my own invention. I have no idea how commercial units perform this operation, although I suspect that they carry it out in a manner that is similar to this. Although I did test this interface on a number of different PCs, they were really quite homogeneous; all were desktops running Windows 95 or Windows 98 on 100+ MHz Pentiums and Pentium IIs with ISA busses. If you want to use this type of protocol, you should test it out on a wide variety of PCs using a wide variety of operating systems.

THE
SOUNDBLASTER
CARD

Creative Technology, founded in Singapore, is an interesting company as one of the first to see the potential of multimedia in personal computers. From the beginning, Creative Technology has worked with the goal of providing advanced audio (and now video) to the PC.

The first SoundBlaster card was introduced in 1989 as an 11 "voice" FM synthesizer with a MIDI/joystick interface. The package was bundled with software that gave Sound-Blaster the capability of speech synthesis and the ability to generate user-defined sounds. The card very quickly became the "standard" for PC audio. Almost all PCs shipped today have a SoundBlaster 32, 64, or 128 equivalent audio card shipped with them.

Along with giving "life" to PC games, the SoundBlaster is an excellent tool for learning more about interfacing the PC and can be used for experiments without the need of creating unique hardware.

This book primarily describes the original SoundBlaster. All SoundBlaster-compatible hardware shipped since 1989 contains a "superset" of these capabilities. What is present here should be applicable for all these cards, but you might find some differences in operation for different chip sets and devices.

Register Interface

Every six months or so, I rediscover how much fun it is to write to SoundBlaster's registers to add some simple sounds to an application. The big advantage of the SoundBlaster is the ease in which simple tones and chords can be added to an application, along with special effects that catch the user's attention. These tones are much clearer and less "clipped" than what you would get out of the PC's speaker with the timer. Using the SoundBlaster means that you do not have to access the timer for tones and you can use it as a precise time delay. Creating simple music and special effects is actually quite easy and one of these days I'm going to write a front-end music synthesizer for working through specialized sounds with the device.

This section presents the register interface to the original SoundBlaster. All enhanced SoundBlaster devices support this interface and the software presented for this section (in the "SB_REGS" subdirectory of the CD-ROM) can be run in any device that is identified as being SoundBlaster compatible.

The SoundBlaster is actually quite an impressive specification, with up to nine voices capable of being output at a time. Each voice can output an independent tone with a user-defined envelope to allow you to very easily program chirps, steady tones, or ringing sounds into your applications. Along with the sound outputs, two timers are built into the card, which will allow you to independently time events without having to use the system timer.

The normal set up for a SoundBlaster card in the PC is to have port addresses 0x0220 and 0x0221 used to address the card and interrupt Level 5 and DMA channel 1 set up for DMA operations. This section presents the register operations, along with a few simple applications that I have written to demonstrate how the SoundBlaster works. The next section works through a DMA example with the SoundBlaster.

The SoundBlaster is really a write-only device with a number of different addresses used to control the different channels of the card. These addresses are:

ADDRESS	FUNCTION
001h	Execute SoundBlaster self-test/waveform control
002h	Timer1 count register
003h	Timer2 count register
004h	Timer control register
008h	Speech synthesis control
020h–035h	Amplitude modulation/vibrator/envelope generator/frequency-modulation control
040h–055h	Key scaling/output-level control
060h–075h	Attack/decay rate control
080h–095h	Sustain-level/release-rate control
0A0h–0A8h	Channel frequency control low 8 bits

0B0h–0B8h	Channel key-on/octave/frequency-high 8 bits control
0BDh	AM depth/vibrato depth/rhythm control
0C0h–0C0h	Feedback-strength control
0E0h–0F5h	Wave-select control

I will concentrate on simply outputting a tone and leave it up to you to play with the other controls to see what kind of sounds you can create.

Writing to the SoundBlaster's registers is accomplished by writing to an address/status register at I/O address 0x0220. After writing the register address, you can then write the contents of the register via I/O address 0x0221. For proper operation, a 3.3 µsecs must be made after writing to 0x0220 and before writing to 0x0221 and 23 µsecs after writing the register value to 0x0221 and writing a new address to 0x0220.

For most of my applications, I would simply create a specific delay, but when I was writing this book, I discovered that the nominal SoundBlaster write cycle time is 760 ns. Thus, the 3.3-µsecs delay can be created by executing six dummy reads to the SoundBlaster and the 23-µsecs delay can be created with 35 dummy reads.

To do this, I use the function:

```
SBWrite( int Addr, int Value )  //  Write the Value to the SB Card
{

int  i;

    outp( 0x0220, Addr );        //  Write the Address to the SB Port
    for ( i = 0; i < 6; i++ )     //    Delay 3.3 µsecs for Operation
      inp( 0x0220 );              //    to complete

    outp( 0x0221, Value );        //  Output the Value and Wait 23 µsecs
    for ( i = 0; i < 35; i++ )    //    for the Operation to Complete
      inp( 0x0220 );

}  //  End SBWrite
```

The SoundBlaster has nine channels that can be used for independently outputting a sound. Each channel has two "operators" that can be set with different parameters and combined to create sound effects. The addressing for these channels is a bit strange and will help answer any questions you had in the table of SoundBlaster addresses.

With nine channels and two operators per channel, 22 possible addresses are needed for each register type. As can be seen in the previous table, a 32-byte (0x020) register area is devoted to the register type. I call the first address the *base register address*.

Each channel operator is given an offset to the start of the register type address and is separated from the other operator by three; for channel 1, operator 1 is at address 0 and operator 2 is at address 3.

This leads to the unusual operator offset table shown:

CHANNEL	1	2	3	4	5	6	7	8	9
Operator 1	000h	001h	002h	008h	009h	00Ah	010h	011h	012h
Operator 2	003h	004h	005h	00Bh	00Ch	00Dh	013h	014h	015h

As I go through the following sample sound applications, this addressing scheme will become clearer.

Register 0x001 is used to test the SoundBlaster hardware and should normally be set to zero. If the FM chips are to control the waveforms of the different operators, bit 5 (known as *WS*) should be set.

The SoundBlaster's timer is quite straightforward with register 0x004 being used to control the operation of the device. The timeout status is returned when address 0x0220 is read with the bits defined as:

BITS	FUNCTION
7	Set if either timer has timed out
6	Set if Timer 1 has timed out
5	Set if Timer 2 has timed out
4–0	Unused

When a timer is started, every 80 μsecs it is incremented by the SoundBlaster's internal clock. When the timer overflows ("times out"), the interrupt request bits in the timer control register (0x004) is set along with the appropriate bits in the address 0x0220 status register.

The *control register* is defined as:

BITS	FUNCTION
7	Time out and enable reset bit. When reset, both timers are disabled
6	Timer 1 Interrupt mask bit. If set, Timer 1 cannot request a hardware interrupt
5	Timer 2 Interrupt mask bit. If set, Timer 2 cannot request a hardware interrupt
4–2	Unused
1	Timer 2 control bit. When set, register at address 0x003 is incremented every 80 μsecs
0	Timer 1 control bit. When set, register at address 0x002 is incremented every 80 μsecs

To delay a specific amount of time, you must take the desired delay and divide by 80 μsecs. This is the number of ticks that the timer must count up to overflow at the end of the delay. The actual value loaded into the timer is 256 minus the number of ticks calculated.

For example, for a 10-ms delay, the timer would be loaded with:

$$Timer\ initial\ value = 256 - (10\ ms/80\ \mu secs)$$
$$= 256 - 125$$
$$= 131$$

With an 80-μsecs timer tick, the full delay is no more than 20.480 ms. To get longer delays, the timer will have to overflow a certain number of times. The overflow can be monitored within software.

To create a sound to be output, first the address 0x020 register *(amplitude modulation/vibrato/envelope generator type/frequency-modulation control)* must be set up. The bit definition for these registers is:

BITS	FUNCTION
7	Amplitude modulation. Apply when set
6	Vibrato. Apply when set
5	Envelope generator. When Set, the Volume of the note is maintained until it is released. When reset, decay starts after "sustain" has completed
4	Keyboard Scaling Rate. When Bit is set, if the frequency output is increased, the volume output is decreased
3–0	Frequency Modulation. These bits are used to specify the key the output is in
	0000 One Octave Below
	0001 At the Specified Frequency
	0010 One Octave
	0011 One Octave and a Fifth Above
	0100 Two Octaves Above
	0101 Two Octaves and a Major Third Above
	0110 Two Octaves and a Fifth Above
	0111 Two Octaves and a Minor Seventh Above
	1000 Three Octaves Above
	1001 Three Octaves and a Major Second Above
	1010 Three Octaves and a Major Third Above
	1011 Three Octaves and a Major Third Above
	1100 Three Octaves and a Fifth Above
	1101 Three Octaves and a Fifth Above
	1110 Three Octaves and a Minor Seventh Above
	1111 Three Octaves and a Minor Seventh Above

This is a rather large and complex function. For most applications, I set this register for the channel's two operators to simply 0x001, which doesn't do anything funky, but outputs a note at the specified frequency.

The *channel registers* with base address 0x040 are used to set the channel level, as well as diminish the sound as the frequency rises:

BITS	FUNCTION
7–6	Diminish output as frequency rises 00 – No Change 01 – 1.5 dB/Octave 10 – 3.0 dB/Octave 11 – 6.0 dB/Octave
5–0	Output level. 0 is the highest, 0x03F is the lowest

For most applications, a value of *0x020* is used for a moderate volume.

The next two registers are used to control the envelope of the sound produced. *Envelope* is the technical term for the volume profile the sound makes. As shown in Fig. 31-1, the profile consists of three parts. *Attack* is how quickly the sound reaches full volume. *Sustain* is the volume level after the attack has completed and it might not be the full volume of the sound. If it is less that the full value, then the volume drops off immediately. *Decay* or *release* is the volume slope when either the sound's volume is allowed to drop "naturally" (decay) or if the channel is turned off explicitly (release). Base registers 0x060 and 0x080 control these parameters.

Base register 0x060 bits are defined as:

BITS	FUNCTION
7–4	"Attack" Rate of the Envelope. 0 is the slowest, 0x0F is the fastest
3–0	"Decay" Rate of the Envelope. 0 is the slowest, 0x0F is the fastest

Base register 0x080 bits are defined as:

BITS	FUNCTION
7–4	"Sustain" Level. 0 is highest, 0x0F is the softest
3–0	"Release" Rate of the Envelope. 0 is the slowest, 0x0F is the fastest

Base address registers 0x0A0 and 0x0B0 are used to specify the frequency (and octave) the channel's output. Each channel can only work with one frequency, so the described offset method doesn't apply, instead channel 1 is at offset 0 in the base Address, channel 2 is at offset 1, etc.

Base *address 0x0B0* contains the upper two bits of the frequency, along with the operating octave and channel output enable. The bits are defined as:

BITS	FUNCTION
7–6	Unused
5	Enable. When set, the Channel Output is Enabled
4–2	Octave Channel operates in
1–0	Most Significant two bits of the sound frequency

Base address 0x0A0 is defined as:

BIT	FUNCTION
7–0	Least Significant eight bits of the sound frequency

The sound frequency is a 10-bit value written to the two registers (usually base address 0x0A0 first). This value is generated to be relative to the internal SoundBlaster clock. For standard notes at the octave below middle C, you can use:

NOTE	FREQUENCY	VALUE
C	263 Hz	0x0157
C#	277 Hz	0x016B
D	294 Hz	0x0181
D#	311 Hz	0x0198
E	330 Hz	0x01B0
F	350 Hz	0x01CA
F#	370 Hz	0x01E5
G	392 Hz	0x0202
G#	415 Hz	0x0220
A	440 Hz	0x0241
A#	466 Hz	0x0263
B	494 Hz	0x0287

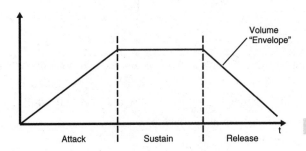

FIGURE 31-1 Sound effect "envelope".

Normally, the 0x0A0 base address register is written first and the 0x0B0 base address register is written with Bit 5 set to enable the channel sound output. To release the channel, the 0x0B0 base address register is written with bit 5 reset.

The *feedback base register* at address 0x0C0 is used to add feedback to the channel. This can give your applications an interesting Jimi Hendrix Experience sound. After saying this, you're probably not surprised that I rarely use it.

BITS	FUNCTION
7–4	Unused
3–1	Level of Feedback provided. 1 is the minimum, 7 would be appropriate for Woodstock
0	Modulation Control. If reset, operator 1 modulates operator 2. If set, both operators generate sound.

The *waveform-select base register* at address 0x0E0 is used to select the operator's output waveform. Although a sine wave is continually output, "rectifiers" and clipping can be applied for sound effects.

BITS	FUNCTION
7–2	Unused
1–0	Waveform select 00 Sine Wave output 01 Half Wave Rectified Sine Wave Output 10 Full Wave Rectified Sine Wave Output 11 Half Wave Rectified Sine Wave with Clipping

The last register is the *amplitude-modulation depth/vibrato/rhythm-control* register at address 0x0BD in the SoundBlaster. This register is a central control to the current operation of the SoundBlaster and provides a central On/Off switch to many special sound effects.

BITS	FUNCTION
7	Amplitude Modulation Depth Control. When set, AM depth is 4.8 dB, 1.0 dB when reset
6	Vibrato Depth Control. When set, Vibrato is 14% and 7% when reset
5	Rhythm Control. When set, Rhythm enabled

4	Bass Drum Synthesis control. When set, enabled
3	Snare Drum Synthesis control. When set, enabled
2	Tom-tom Synthesis Control. When set, enabled
1	Cymbal Synthesis Control. When set, enabled
0	Hi-hat Synthesis Control. When set, enabled

The best way to see what you can do with these controls is to play with them. To give you a head start, the SB_REGS subdirectory of the CD-ROM includes three small MS-DOS C applications to show what can be done with the SoundBlaster via the register interface.

SBTEST simply outputs a C note that is one octave below middle C for two seconds. SBTEST2 plays around with the envelope shaping registers to give you an interesting sound suitable for Star Trek sound effects. SBTEST3 outputs a C major chord using three channels. These applications will give you an idea of what is possible for very little programming effort.

The last application in the SB_REGS subdirectory is a little practical joke you can play called SBSCREEN. As the SBTEST2 sound is output, the MS-DOS prompt screen is cleared line by line. This is done by direct writes to the VRAM (after saving the screen contents). After the screen is cleared, the sound stops and will be restored when any key is pressed. It is a gentle practical joke, although if I were 10 years younger," I would probably move it into a TSR that would it execute every time the user entered something like "dir" on the command line. This joke could be disabled just before a repairman arrives to look at the PC, then turned back on the minute they leave.

DSP/MIXER REGISTER INTERFACE

Along with the voice outputs, which are designed to create sounds manually, the Sound-Blaster card also has two sets of registers that are designed to control the *Digital Signal Processor (DSP)* and the on-board mixer functions. For basic register "beeps" and "boops," these functions are not accessed, but they are very useful for producing complex sounds. Along with the DSP and mixer, stereo output control registers, FM music, CD-ROM, AdLib sound card, and MPU-401 MIDI driver registers are available in most systems. These functions are sure to be enhanced as sound cards beyond the current (PCI 128) standard are created. This section concentrates on the DSP and Mixer functions because these are most accessible to the casual user.

The DSP interface consists of kind of a peculiar arrangement of three registers. These registers are used to send commands and data to the SoundBlaster's DSP, poll the completion of operations, and poll to see whether or not data is available. Although the functions are quite straightforward, their operations are not.

Writing data or commands to the DSP first requires I/O register address 0x022C's bit 7 to be polled until it goes reset. After the bit goes low, data can be written to this I/O register address as a command (or data that follows a command). A typical WriteDSP C function looks like:

```
WriteDSP( int Value )              //  Wait for the Port to be free and
{                                  //    then Write a Command

  while (( inp( 0x022C ) & 0x080 ) != 0 );

  outp( 0x022C, Value );

}  // WriteDSP
```

To read data from the DSP, I/O register address 0x022E is polled until bit 7 is set. When the bit is set, then the data can be read from I/O register address 0x022A. A typical ReadDSP C function looks like:

```
int ReadDSP()                      //  Wait for the ADC Operation to
{                                  //    Complete

  while (( inp( 0x022E ) & 0x080 ) == 0 );

  return inp( 0x022A );            //  Return the DSP Data When Ready

}  //  End ReadDSP
```

These functions are used with the following commands to control the operation of the DSP in the SoundBlaster card:

COMMAND	FUNCTION
010h	Direct DAC output. The byte sent to 022Ch following the 010h command is an 8 bit value to be output on the DSP's DAC.
014h	Initiate DAC DMA. The two bytes sent to 022Ch following the 014h command is the low byte followed by the high byte of the number of bytes to transfer via DMA. The length should be the number of samples minus one. Length = Samples − 1
016h	Initiate 8-bit ADPCM DAC DMA. The two bytes sent to 0x022C following the 016h command is the low byte followed by the high byte of the number of samples to transmit. To get the correct length, use the formula: Length = ((Samples − 1) + 3) / 4
017h	Initiate 8-bit ADPCM DAC DMA with a new reference byte. The two bytes sent to 0x022C following the 017h command is the low byte followed by the high byte of the number of samples to transmit. To get the correct length, use the formula: Length = (((Samples − 1) + 3) / 4) + 1
01Ch	Auto-Initialize 8-Bit DAC DMA. Set up the DMA for PCM output. No length specification required. To get the correct length, use the formula: Length = ((Samples + 1) / 4) − 1

01Fh	Auto-Initialize 8-Bit DAC DMA with a new reference byte. Set up the DMA for PCM output. Set up the DMA for PCM for output. To get the correct number, use the formulas: SampleBytes = ((Samples + 3) / 4) + 1 Length = ((Samplebytes + 1) / 2) − 1
020h	Do Direct 8-Bit ADC Read. Read the Current ADC Voltage Level.
024h	Initiate 8-Bit DMA Transfer. Operation the same as function 014h.
028h	Burst Direct 8-Bit ADC Read. After function set, each valid read to 022Ah will return the next line in analog voltage level.
02Ch	Auto-Initialize 8-Bit DAC DMA. Same as function 01Ch.
030h	Read the MIDI Code when available. After sending this command, the first MIDI byte received will be returned at address 022Ah.
031h	MIDI Read Interrupt. Generates an Interrupt Request when the MIDI Code is Available.
032h	MIDI Read Timestamp. Returns 24 bit time (in msecs) since the last MIDI command was received. followed by the MIDI command.
033h	MIDI Read Timestamp Interrupt. Generates an Interrupt Request when the MIDI command is received. Returns 24 bit time (in msecs) since the last MIDI command was received.
034h	MIDI Read Poll and Write Poll. Enables the MIDI's "UART mode" in which all DSP reads and writes are interpreted as MIDI I/O.
035h	MIDI Read Interrupt and Write Poll. Outputs all DSP writes are sent as MIDI Commands and Requests an Interrupt when a Read Command is Received.
037h	MIDI Read Timestamp Interrupt and Write Poll. Outputs all DSP writes are sent as MIDI Commands and Requests an Interrupt when a Read Command is Received. When the Read is made, the 24 bit time (in msecs) since the last MIDI command receive is returned.
038h	MIDI Write Poll. The next byte is written as a MIDI Command out.
040h	Set Time Constant. Set the sample rate through the internal I/O transfer timer. The time constant is sent after the command and is found using the formula: TimeConstant = 256 − (1000000/(SampleChannels*SampleRate))
041h	Set Sample Rate. Set the sample rate independent of the number of Sample Channels. The two bytes (low first) that are sent following 041h is the sampling rate in Hz.
045h	Continue Auto-initialize 8-Bit DMA. This command continues a halted auto-initialized 8-Bit DMA transfer.
047h	Continue Auto-initialize 16-Bit DMA. This command continues a halted auto-initialized 16-Bit DMA transfer.
048h	Set DMA Block Size. Set the DMA Block Size to transfer. The next byte is the low byte of the block size and is followed by the high byte.

074h	Initiate 4-bit ADPCM DMA transfer. This command starts a four bit PCM DMA transfer. The number of bytes follow as and are sent low byte followed by high byte. The length is calculated as:
	Length = Samples / 2
075h	Initiate 4-bit ADPCM DMA transfer with reference byte. This command starts a four bit PCM DMA transfer. The number of bytes follow as and are sent low byte followed by high byte. The length is calculated as:
	Length = (Samples / 2) + 1
076h	Initiate 4.6-bit ADPCM DMA transfer. This command starts a 2.6 bit PCM DMA transfer with accumulated reference byte. The number of bytes follow as and are sent low byte followed by high byte. The length is calculated as:
	Length = (Samples + 2) / 3
077h	Initiate 4.6-bit ADPCM DMA transfer with Reference Byte. This command starts a 2.6 bit PCM DMA transfer with accumulated reference byte. The number of bytes follow as and are sent low byte followed by high byte. The length is calculated as:
	Length = ((Samples + 2) / 3) + 1
07Dh	Auto-Initialize 4-bit ADPCM DMA transfer. This command starts a four bit PCM DMA transfer. The length is calculated as:
	Length = ((Samples + 1) / 3) + 1
07Fh	Auto-Initialize 4-bit ADPCM DMA transfer with reference byte. This command starts a four bit PCM DMA transfer. The length is calculated as:
	SampleBytes = ((Samples + 1) / 2) + 1
	Length = ((SampleBytes + 1) / 2) − 1
080h	Silence DAC for Specified Number of Samples. The number is defined by the following byte (low value) and the high value.
090h	Auto-Initialize 8-Bit DAC DMA for high-speed (> 23 KHz) signals. Set up the DMA for PCM output. No length specification required.
098h	Auto-Initialize 8-Bit DAC DMA for high-speed (> 23 KHz) signals. Same as 090h.
0A0h	Disable Stereo Input.
0A8h	Enable Stereo Input.
0Bxh/0Cxh	Generic DAC/ADC DMA for 8 and 16 Bit Transfers. Force a DMA transfer in software. Similar to operation of 080h.
0D0h	Halt 8-Bit DMA Transfer.
0D1h	Enable Speaker.
0D3h	Disable Speaker.
0D4h	Continue Halted 8-Bit DMA Transfer.
0D5h	Halt 16-Bit DMA Transfer.
0D6h	Continue Halted 16-Bit DMA Transfer.
0D8h	Read the Speaker Status. If 000h is returned, the Speaker is disabled.

0D9h	Exit Auto-Initialize 16-Bit DMA Operation. Stop operation at the end of the current block.
0DAh	Exit Auto-Initialize 8-Bit DMA Operation. Stop operation at the end of the current block.
0E0h	DSP "Ping Function". After command, send check byte. Complement of check byte read back (from I/O Register Address 022Ah) if SoundBlaster is present.
0E1h	Read DSP Version. After Sending this command the DSP responds with the Version Number as the Major Version Code (first Byte) and Minor Version Code (second Byte).
0E3h	DSP Copyright. After sending this command, the DSP copyright information is returned for each read of I/O Register Address 022Ah. The operation is terminated when 000h is read.
0E4h	Write the Test Register. The byte following the command is saved in the DSP's internal "Test Register".
0E8h	Read the Test Register. After this command, the Test Register can be read back at I/O Register Address 022Ah.
0F0h	Output a Diagnostic Sine Wave. After this command, a 2 KHz Sine Wave is output. This function is turned off by a DSP Reset.
0F2h	Make an 8-Bit Interrupt Request.
0F3h	Make a 16-Bit Interrupt Request.

0FBh	DSP Status Register Read. Return the Information about Pending DSP operations in I/O Register Address 022Ah.

Bit	Function
7	Set if the Time Constant has been Modified
6–5	Reserved
4	Set if the "Virtual Speaker" is Active
3	Set if DMA ADC for 16-Bit is Active
2	Set if DMA DAC for 16-Bit is Active
1	Set if DMA ADC for 8-Bit is Active
0	Set if DMA DAC for 8-Bit is Active

0FCh	DSP Auxiliary Status Register Read. Return the Status for DMA Operations in I/O Register Address 022A.

Bit	Function
7–5	Reserved
4	Set if Auto-Init 16-Bit DMA is Active
3	Reserved
2	Set if Auto-Init 8-Bit DMA is Active
1	Set if DAC/ADC Simultaneous DMA is Taking Place
0	Reserved

0FDh	DSP Command Status. Return the last successful DSP Command Sent to the DSP in I/O Register Address 022Ah.

To reset the DSP, register 0226h is written to with 001h and left for at least 3.3 μsecs. Once the 3.3 μsecs has passed, then it is written with 000h to enable DSP execution. When the initialization is complete, the DSP will return 0x0AA at 0x022A. The code that I usually use for this is:

```
int ResetDSP()                 //  Reset the SoundBlaster DSP
{

int i;
int retvalue = -1;             //  Assume a Failure

  outp( 0x0226, 0x001 );       //  Rest the DSP
  for ( i = 0; i < 5; i++ )    //  Delay Based on 760 ns ISA
    inp( 0x0226 );             //    bus
  outp( 0x0226, 0x000 );

  for ( i = 0; ( i < 256 ) && ( retvalue == -1 ); i++ )
    if ( inp( 0x022A ) == 0x0AA )
      retvalue = 0;

  return retvalue;             //  Indicate whether or not SB Reset

}  //  End ResetDSP
```

Notice that I assume that an 8-bit ISA card is used for the SoundBlaster function that provides the 3.3-μsecs delay. For my PC, this is a valid assumption. This may not be valid for all PCs which have integrated SoundBlasters on their motherboards. The issue is further confused for enhanced versions of the SoundBlaster which do not need the full 3.3-μsecs delay. Chances are that this code will work properly, although it is not something you can count on for all PCs.

The mixer is used to combine different signals together. For the PCI 128 SoundBlaster, this function is actually quite complex, as is shown in Fig. 31-2. In the original Sound-Blaster, the mixer function is used to combine the audio signals from the DSP (known as *DAC*), the FM output circuits, the microphone, the line in, and the CD-ROM. For most application programming, I recommend setting the DSP (DAC) output to maximum and ignore the other sources.

I/O register address 0224h is used as the address register to send commands to the mixer. The mixer address register cannot be read. I/O register address 0225h is the mixer's data port; it can be read from or written to.

At least a 100-μsecs delay should occur between writing to the mixer address register and accessing the register itself.

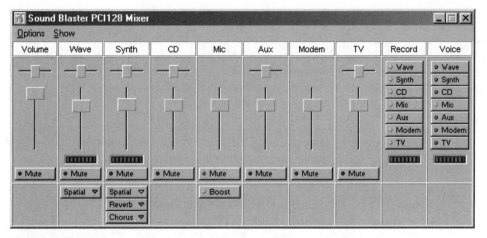

FIGURE 31-2   PCI 128 SoundBlaster mixer utility.

REGISTER	FUNCTION
000h	Reset. Write 000h to Register to Reset the Mixer.
001h	Re-read Status. Return the previous value Read from 0x0225.
002h	Master Volume. Bits 7–5 for Left Volume, Bits 3–1 for Right Volume. 000 is low volume, 111 is high. 099h is the default value.
004h	DAC Volume. Bits 7–5 for Left DAC Volume, Bits 3–1 for Right Volume. 000 is low volume, 111 is high. 099h is the default value.
006h	FM Output Control. Used to add FM Output to the SoundBlaster output.

Bits	Function
7	Reserved
6	Set to Enable Right Channel
5	Set to Enable Left Channel
4	Reserved
3–1	FM Volume Level (000 is low, 111 is high)
0	Reserved

00Ah	Microphone Input Level Control. Used to specify the Input Pre-Amp Volume Level.

Bits	Function
7–3	Reserved
2–1	SoundBlaster Pro Input Level Bits 2–1
0	Input Level Bit 0

00Ch	Input/Filter select. Set the Filtering information for the SoundBlaster Pro.

Bits	Function
7–6	Reserved
5	Set if Filter Input is On
4	Reserved
3	Set for Lowpass Filter Enabled
2–1	Input Select:
	00–Microphone
	01– CD Audio
	11–Line Input
0	Reserved

00Eh	Output/Stereo Select. Specify the output operating mode.

Bits	Function
7–6	Reserved
5	Set if Output is Filtered
4–2	Reserved
1	Set if Stereo Output
0	Reserved

022h	Master Volume. Same as 002h.

026h	FM Level. Set the volume level of the FM input.

Bits	Function
7–5	SoundBlaster Pro Left Channel Volume bits 3–1
4	Left Channel Volume Bit 0
3–1	SoundBlaster Pro Right Channel Volume Bits 3–1
0	Right Channel Volume Bit 0

028h	CD Audio Level. Set the volume level of the CD input.

Bits	Function
7–5	SoundBlaster Pro Left Channel Volume Bits 3–1
4	Left Channel Volume Bit 0
3–1	SoundBlaster Pro Right Channel Volume Bits 3–1
0	Right Channel Volume Bit 0

02Eh	Line In Level. Set the volume level of the Line In Input.

Bits	Function
7–5	SoundBlaster Pro Left Channel Volume Bits 3–1
4	Left Channel Volume Bit 0
3–1	SoundBlaster Pro Right Channel Volume Bits 3–1
0	Right Channel Volume Bit 0

030h	Master Volume Left. Bits 7–4 in common with Register 022h.

Bit	Function
7–3	Volume Control
2–0	Reserved

031h   Master Volume Right. Bits 7–4 in common with bits 3–0 of register 022h.

            Bit   Function
            7–3   Volume Control
            2–0   Reserved

032h   DAC Volume Left. Bits 7–4 in common with Register 004h.

            Bit   Function
            7–3   Volume Control
            2–0   Reserved

033h   DAC Volume Right. Bits 7–4 in common with bits 3–0 of register 004h.

            Bit   Function
            7–3   Volume Control
            2–0   Reserved

034h   FM Volume Left. Bits 7–4 in common with Register 026h.

            Bit   Function
            7–3   Volume Control
            2–0   Reserved

035h   FM Volume Right. Bits 7–4 in common with bits 3–0 of Register 026h.

            Bit   Function
            7–3   Volume Control
            2–0   Reserved

036h   CD Volume Left. Bits 7–4 in common with Register 028h.

            Bit   Function
            7–3   Volume Control
            2–0   Reserved

037h   CD Volume Right. Bits 7–4 in common with bits 3–0 of Register 028h.

            Bit   Function
            7–3   Volume Control
            2–0   Reserved

038h   Line In Volume Left. Bits 7–4 in common with Register 02Eh.

            Bit   Function
            7–3   Volume Control
            2–0   Reserved

039h   Line In Volume Right. Bits 7–4 in common with bits 3–0 of Register 02Eh.

            Bit   Function
            7–3   Volume Control
            2–0   Reserved

03Ah   Microphone Level.

            Bit   Function
            7–3   Volume Control
            2–0   Reserved

3

HARDWARE INTERFACING

03Bh	PC Speaker Volume Level.

	Bit	Function
	7–6	Volume Control
	5–0	Reserved

03Ch	Output Control. Specify Mixer Sources for Mono output.

	Bit	Function
	7–5	Reserved
	4	Set for Left Line In
	3	Set for Right Line In
	2	Set for Left CD
	1	Set for Right CD
	0	Set for Microphone

03Dh	Input Control Left. Select the Sources for the Left Output.

	Bit	Function
	7	Reserved
	6	Set for Left FM
	5	Set for Right FM
	4	Set for Left Line In
	3	Set for Right Line In
	2	Set for Left CD
	1	Set for Right CD
	0	Set for Microphone

03Eh	Input Control Right. Select the Sources for the Right Output.

	Bit	Function
	7	Reserved
	6	Set for Left FM
	5	Set for Right FM
	4	Set for Left Line In
	3	Set for Right Line In
	2	Set for Left CD
	1	Set for Right CD
	0	Set for Microphone

03Fh	Input Gain Control Left. Specify the Gain on the Input Sources.

	Bit	Function
	7–6	Left Input Gain Control
	5–0	Reserved

040h	Input Gain Control Right. Specify the Gain on the Input Sources.

	Bit	Function
	7–6	Right Input Gain Control
	5–0	Reserved

041h	Output Gain Control Left. Specify the Gain on the Output Sources.

	Bit	Function
	7–6	Left Output Gain Control
	5–0	Reserved

042h   Output Gain Control Right. Specify the Gain on the Output Sources.

Bit   Function
7–6   Right Output Gain Control
5–0   Reserved

043h   Automatic Gain Control. When Bit 0 is set, Automatically Gain Control
                    is active to maximize input signal strength.

044h   Left Treble Control. Set the High-Frequency Characteristic Output of
                    the Left Channel.

Bit   Function
7–4   Treble Control
3–0   Reserved

045h   Right Treble Control. Set the High-Frequency Characteristic Output of
                    the Right Channel.

Bit   Function
7–4   Treble Control
3–0   Reserved

046h   Left Bass Control. Set the Low-Frequency Characteristic Output of the
                    Left Channel.

Bit   Function
7–4   Bass Control
3–0   Reserved

047h   Right Bass Control. Set the Low-Frequency Characteristic Output of the
                    Right Channel.

Bit   Function
7–4   Bass Control
3–0   Reserved

080h   IRQ Select. Select the Interrupt Number used by the SoundBlaster.
                    Normally IRQ 5 used. This value is not affected by Mixer Reset or *Ctrl-
                    Alt-Delete* Reboot.

Bit   Function
7–4   Reserved
3   Set to Enable IRQ10
2   Set to Enable IRQ7
1   Set to Enable IRQ5
0   Set to Enable IRQ2

081h   DMA Select. Select the DMA Channel used by the SoundBlaster. DMA
                    Channel 1 normally used. This value is not affected by the Mixer Reset
                    of the *Ctrl-Alt-Delete* Reboot.

Bit   Function
7   Set for DMA7 (16-Bit)
6   Set for DMA6 (16-Bit)
5   Set for DMA5 (16-Bit)
4   Reserved

3

HARDWARE INTERFACING

	3	Set for DMA3 (8-Bit)
	2	Reserved
	1	Set for DMA1 (8-Bit)
	0	Set for DMA0 (8-Bit)
082h		IRQ Status. This Read-Only Register Returns the Interrupt Pending Status.
	Bit	Function
	7–3	Reserved
	2	Set if MPU–401 Interrupt Requested
	1	Set if 16-Bit Interrupt Requested
	0	Set if 8-Bit Interrupt Requested

The command registers are defined as:

To demonstrate how these functions work, I have created two functions. The first is *RegSampl,* which is an MS-DOS command-line program that records input from the microphone and then plays it back. This is a "poor man's" version of Window's multimedia Sound Recorder (Fig. 31-3). This application provides the microphone sampling by polling the ADC as quickly as possible to get the information.

The source code for the application is actually quite simple. You should be able to cross reference the register reads and writes with the previous code. When this application is invoked, the 32-KB buffer is filled with sample information from the microphone. After the sample has been taken, the data is output.

```
RegSampl - Do a Register Sample/Output for the SoundBlaster
//
//   This program is a "C" rewrite of sample assembly code found on
//   the web. This application does a Sample Read of the Input ADC
//   line and then saves it in an array. When the Load is Complete,
//   the array is output through the speaker ports.
//
//   Myke Predko
//   99.02.22
//

//   Defines
#include <stdio.h>
```

FIGURE 31-3   Windows "Sound Recorder".

```c
#include <asmprocs.h>

// Global Variables
char far * Buffer;                  // buffer of the Read in Data


// Subroutines
WriteDSP( int Value )               // Wait for the Port to be free and
{                                   //   then Write a Command

  while (( inp( 0x022C ) & 0x080 ) != 0 );

  outp( 0x022C, Value );

} // WriteDSP

int ReadDSP()                       // Wait for the ADC Operation to
{                                   //   Complete

  while (( inp( 0x022E ) & 0x080 ) == 0 );

  return inp( 0x022A );             // Return the DSP Data When Ready

} // End ReadDSP


// Mainline
main(argc, argv, envp)
  int argc;
  char *argv[];
  char *envp;
{

int i, j;

  Buffer = GETMEM( 0x08000L );

  printf( "RegSampl - Myke Predko\n" );
  printf( "          99.02.22\n\n" );

  printf( "Speak into the Microphone, Press Any Key when Done\n\n\n" );

  while ( GETKEYSTAT() != 0 )
    GETKEY();                       // Clear the Keyboard Buffer

  printf( "Recording" );

  for ( i = 0; ( i < 0x08000 ) && ( GETKEYSTAT() == 0 ); i++ ) {

    if (( i & 0x01FF ) == 0 )
      printf( "." );                // Printing 64 Dots

    WriteDSP( 0x020 );              // Do a Direct Read
    Buffer[ i ] = ReadDSP();        // Wait for the DMA to Complete

  } // endfor

  printf( "\n" );                   // Start the Next Line
```

```
if ( GETKEYSTAT() == 0 ) {      // Only Output if No Key Pressed

  printf( "\nPlayback" );

  WriteDSP( 0x0D1 );            // Enable the Speaker for Output

  for ( i = 0; ( i < 0x08000 ) && ( GETKEYSTAT() == 0 ); i++ ) {

    if (( i & 0x01FF ) == 0 )
      printf( "." );           // Printing 64 Dots

    WriteDSP( 0x010 );         // Output DAC Data Byte
    WriteDSP( Buffer[ i ]);
    ReadDSP();

  } // endfor

  WriteDSP( 0x0D3 );           // Turn Off the Speaker

} // endif

while ( GETKEYSTAT() != 0 )    // Clear the Keyboard Buffer
  GETKEY();                    // If Keys Used to End Operation

FREEMEM( Buffer );

} // End RegSampl
```

The sound quality of this application is admittedly very poor (and barely understandable). The reason for the poor quality of the output is because of the untimed execution of the sample and playback. Because DMA is not used for this application, the time between samplings is variable because of how the PC is operating and what other applications are running concurrently under Windows. For best results, this application should be run from MS-DOS (no Windows invoked) to minimize this variability.

The next section presents an application that eliminates this variability by using the DMA capability of the SoundBlaster to output a .WAV file.

For some PCs (especially with newer SoundBlaster variants), you might find that the audio input or output does not work. If this is the case, you will have to get the developer's kit for your sound card and understand the differences in the registers and their operation. Ideally, in your applications, to avoid these problems, you should do direct reads and writes. Instead, system device drivers should be used to avoid any direct register compatibility issues with different hardware.

WAV File Output Program with DMA

When you run the *RegSampl* application, I'm sure that you will be pretty disappointed with the device's performance. What is missing is a set time base for sampling and outputting the data. The SoundBlaster does provide this capability using the DMA channels built into the PC. The *Wavdma* application outputs a .WAV file, up to 32 KB in size.

If you are not familiar with .WAV files, they are used throughout the PC for outputting audio information because they are designed for the SoundBlaster's DMA capability. Once the files are loaded in and identified, the data area can be run through the Sound-Blaster directly without modification to play the audio file.

The file format is:

OFFSET	DATA TYPE	DESCRIPTION
0x0000	4 Bytes	"RIFF" String
0x0004	Double Word	Length of the .WAV file
0x0008	4 Bytes	"WAVE" String
0x000C	4 Bytes	"fmt" String
0x0010	Double Word	Header Size (Normally 0x010)
0x0014	Word	File Type (1 for PCM Data File)
0x0016	Word	Number of Channels Used for the File
0x0018	Word	Left or Single Channel Samples Per Second
0x001A	Word	Left or Single Channel Byte Per Second Rate (usually 0)
0x001C	Word	Right Number of Samples Per Second (Normally the same as Left)
0x001E	Word	Right Number of Bytes Per Second Rate (Normally the same as Left)
0x0020	Word	Repeat of the Number of Channels
0x0022	Word	Channel Data Size in Bits (Normally 8)
0x0024	4 Bytes	"data" string
0x0028	Double Word	Number of Bytes of the Wave Data to Play
0x002C	Unknown	Wave Data to Play
Last	Byte	0x000 to Indicate Data End

Wavedma only supports .WAV files of up to 32 KB in size. The reason for this is to ensure that the DMA controller does not move over the page. In the code, I allocate 64 KB and look at the actual address to see whether or not a full 32-KB buffer is present at offset zero of the page or offset 0x08000. This allows the DMA controller to access 32 KB without any opportunity to go over a page boundary.

The DMA controller is set up as you would have expected from earlier in the book. The process that I went through was:

1 Mask the DMA channel
2 Clear out any pending requests
3 Set the mode as memory to I/O
4 Load the starting address in the page (either offset 0x00000 or 0x08000)

5 Load the size of the data to transfer

6 Unmask the DMA channel

Next, the SoundBlaster is set up for DMA transfers using DSP function 0x014, with the data length passed after the command byte. When the DMA transfer is executing, I simply poll on bit 1 of the DMA channel 1 status register to find out when all the bytes are transferred.

One area that I really haven't explained about the SoundBlaster is the mixer. For later versions of the SoundBlaster, before you can actually hear anything, the mixer must be set up to pass data from the DSP DAC. I spent a frustrating three days trying to find this problem until I discovered the SBSetup code on the Internet.

The Wavedma source file is a good source of snippets and reference information. Besides the SoundBlaster reading and writing, the areas that I would suggest you look at in particular are:

1 The file read and processing. This code checks for an extension. If none is present, it adds .WAV.

2 The buffer and ActBuffer set up. This code will provide 32 KB of memory on a 32-KB boundary for easy accessing.

3 The file format test. Rather than check every byte, I check some known features in the file and work from there.

The actual source code for Wavedma is:

```
//   WAVEDMA - Application to Play "Wave file" data on a PC using DMA
//
//   This program loads the specified ".WAV" file and plays it through
//    the PC's SoundBlaster card using the DMA controller to pass the
//    data at a specific sampling rate (specified within the .WAV
//    file).
//
//   Myke Predko
//   99.02.23
//

//   Defines
#include <stdio.h>
#include <dos.h>
#include <asmprocs.h>
#include <fcntl.h>
#include <sys\types.h>
#include <sys\stat.h>
#include <io.h>
#include <string.h>

#define DMA0Addr  0x000          // DMA Address Register
#define DMA0Word  0x001          // DMA Word count Register
#define DMA1Addr  0x002
#define DMA1Word  0x003
#define DMA2Addr  0x004
#define DMA2Word  0x005
#define DMA3Addr  0x006
#define DMA3Word  0x007
#define DMA1Stat  0x008          // DMA Status/Command Register
```

```
#define DMA1Write 0x009        //   DMA Write Request Register
#define DMA1Mask  0x00A        //   DMA Mask Register
#define DMA1Chnl  0x00B        //   DMA Channel Mode Register
#define DMA1Clr   0x00C        //   DMA Clear Byte Pointer
#define DMA1Mstr  0x00D        //   DMA MasterRegister
#define DMA1CMsk  0x00E        //   DMA Clear Mask Register
#define DMA1WMsk  0x00F        //   DMA Write Mask Register
#define DMA2Page  0x081        //   DMA Channel 2 Page Address
#define DMA3Page  0x082        //   DMA Channel 3 Page Address
#define DMA1Page  0x083        //   DMA Channel 1 Page Address


//  Global Variables
char far * Buffer;             //   For Loading the File Into
char FileName[ 256 ];          //   Plan for the Worst Possible Case


//  Subroutines
WriteDSP( int Value )          //   Wait for the Port to be free and
{                              //     then Write a Command

  while (( inp( 0x022C ) & 0x080 ) != 0 );

  outp( 0x022C, Value );

}  // WriteDSP

int ReadDSP()                  //   Wait for the ADC Operation to
{                              //     Complete

  while (( inp( 0x022E ) & 0x080 ) == 0 );

  return inp( 0x022A );        //   Return the DSP Data When Ready

}  // End ReadDSP

int ResetDSP()                 //   Initialize the SoundBlaster
{

int  i;
int  retvalue = -1;

  outp( 0x0226, 0x001 );       //   Start Reset Operation
  for ( i = 0; i < 5; i++ )
    inp( 0x0226 );
  outp( 0x0226, 0x000 );       //   Complete the Reset

  for ( i = 0; ( i < 256 ) && ( retvalue == - 1 ); i++ )
    if ( inp( 0x022A ) == 0x0AA )
      retvalue = 0;            //   Reset Successful

  return retvalue;

}  // End ResetDSP

SBSetup()                      //   Look for Sound Blaster Version
{                              //     3.x or Later for Mixer
```

```c
int VerMajor, VerMinor;


  WriteDSP( 0x0E1 );                  //  Get Version Information
  VerMajor = ReadDSP();
  VerMinor = ReadDSP();

  if ( VerMajor == 3 ) {              //  Setup Mixer if Version 3.x

    outp( 0x0224, 0x000 );  outp( 0x0225, 0x0FF );
    outp( 0x0224, 0x004 );  outp( 0x0225, 0x0FF );
    outp( 0x0224, 0x00A );  outp( 0x0225, 0x000 );
    outp( 0x0224, 0x00C );  outp( 0x0225, 0x026 );
    outp( 0x0224, 0x00E );  outp( 0x0225, 0x020 );
    outp( 0x0224, 0x022 );  outp( 0x0225, 0x099 );
    outp( 0x0224, 0x026 );  outp( 0x0225, 0x000 );
    outp( 0x0224, 0x028 );  outp( 0x0225, 0x000 );
    outp( 0x0224, 0x02E );  outp( 0x0225, 0x000 );

  } /* endif */
} // End SBSetup


//  Mainline
main(argc, argv, envp)
  int argc;
  char *argv[];
  char *envp;
{

int  i;
int  handle;
long size;
int  temp;
long addrtemp;

char far * ActBuffer;          //  Actual Location in Buffer
int  Samples;                  //  Samples per Second
int  DataSize;                 //  Number of Bytes to Send


  printf( "\"WAVEDMA\" - Play a .WAV File on the PC\n" );
  printf( "Myke Predko\n\n" );

  if ( argc != 2 )             //  File Specified?
    printf( "No .WAV File Specified\n" );
  else {                       //  Load the File/Read it

    strcpy( FileName, argv[ 1 ]); //  Get Proper FileName
    for ( i = strlen( FileName ) - 1; ( i > 0 ) &&
        ( FileName[ i ] != '.' ) && ( FileName[ i ] != '\\' ); i-- );
    if ( FileName[ i ] != '.' )
      strcat( FileName, ".wav" );

    if (( handle = open( FileName, O_RDONLY | O_BINARY )) == - 1 )
      printf( "\"%s\" could not be found\n", FileName );
    else {                     //  Go Ahead and Process the File

      if (( size = lseek( handle, 0L, SEEK_END )) > 0x08000L )
        printf( "\"%s\" is Too Large for the Application\n", FileName );
```

```
else                      //  Can Handle the Application
  if (( Buffer = GETMEM( 0x010000L )) == 0L )
    printf( "Unable to Allocate Required Memory for wavedma\n" );
  else {                  //  Can Execute the Application
    lseek( handle, 0L, SEEK_SET );

    addrtemp = ( GETSEG( Buffer ) << 4 ) & 0x0FFFFL;
    if ( addrtemp > 0x08000 )
      (long) ActBuffer =
      (((long) GETSEG( Buffer ) & 0x0F000L ) + 0x01000L ) << 16;
    else                  //  Calculate Actual Buffer Address
      (long) ActBuffer =
      (((long) GETSEG( Buffer ) & 0x0F000L ) + 0x00800L ) << 16;

    read( handle, ActBuffer, size );  //  Read in the File

    if (( strncmp( &ActBuffer[ 0 ], "RIFF", 4 ) != 0 ) ||
          ( strncmp( &ActBuffer[ 8 ], "WAVE", 4 ) != 0 ) ||
          ( strncmp( &ActBuffer[ 12 ], "fmt ", 4 ) != 0 ) ||
          ( strncmp( &ActBuffer[ 36 ], "data", 4 ) != 0 ))
      printf( "\"%s\" is not a Valid .WAV File\n", FileName );
    else                  //  Process the .WAV File
      if ( ResetDSP() != 0 )
        printf( "No SoundBlaster in PC\n" );
      else {              //  Go ahead and Process the File

        SBSetup();        //  Setup the SoundBlaster Output

        temp = ActBuffer[ 24 ] + ( ActBuffer[ 25 ] * 256 );
        Samples = 256 - ( 1000000L / temp );
        WriteDSP( 0x040 );  //  Setup the Sample Rate
        WriteDSP( Samples );

        WriteDSP( 0x0D1 );  //  Turn the Speaker On

        DataSize = ActBuffer[ 40 ] + ( ActBuffer[ 41 ] * 256 );
        DataSize--;       //  Have the Data to Send

        outp( DMA1Mask, 0x005 );  //  Mask Channel 1
        outp( DMA1Clr, 0x000 );   //  Clear
        outp( DMA1Chnl, 0x049 );  //  Set Mode
        outp( DMA1Addr, 0x000 );  //  Load Start Address
        if ( addrtemp > 0x08000 )
          outp( DMA1Addr, 0x000 );
        else
          outp( DMA1Addr, 0x080 );
        outp( DMA1Page, (unsigned long) ActBuffer >> 28.);
        outp( DMA1Word, DataSize & 0x0FF );
        outp( DMA1Word, ( DataSize >> 8 ) & 0x0FF );
        outp( DMA1Mask, 1 );      //  Unmask DMA

        WriteDSP( 0x014 );  //  Enable DSP DMA
        WriteDSP( DataSize & 0x0FF );
        WriteDSP(( DataSize >> 8 ) & 0x0FF );

        while (( inp( DMA1Stat ) & 2 ) == 0 );
                          //  Wait for DMA Output to End

        WriteDSP( 0x0D3 );  //  Turn off the Speaker

      }
```

```
        FREEMEM( Buffer );

      }  /*  endif  */
    close( handle );

  }
 }

} // End WAVEDMA
```

To find source files on which to run Wavedma, execute:

```
dir *.wav /s | more
```

from the root subdirectory in your PC. You should find lots of interesting sounds to try out with this program. I found some excellent example sounds in the Visual C++ sample subdirectories that show you the capabilities of the program and SoundBlaster. As you would expect, the Internet is another good source for WAV files.

WINDOWS

PROGRAMMING

32

WINDOWS
ARCHITECTURE

CONTENTS AT A GLANCE

Arenas and Rings   V86 MODE

Virtual Machines   **COM/OLE/ActiveX**
VIRTUAL MACHINE MANAGER

Most Windows application code can be written directly from the Windows development tools (such as Visual Basic) without ever having to know anything about how Protect mode in the processor works or how Windows actually operates. But, to interface with hardware, a good understanding of how Windows operates and how device drivers interface to it is imperative.

The next few chapters contain many terms that you are familiar with, have heard in passing, and some that you will never have heard before. Although I will try to define all of them, I must confess that you might need more information before you can continue to develop your own application.

Like so many aspects of the PC, if I were to try to explain everything concerning the Windows operating system to the lowest possible level of detail, I would end up writing a book that is many times as thick as it is now. For more information, I have to recommend that you read through the books recommended in Appendix B to round out your knowledge of how Windows is architected and works.

Arenas and Rings

As described elsewhere in the book, Windows applications execute as "processes" with each process given a virtual Protect-mode 32-bit (4.3 GB) memory space from which it can execute from within. This makes the actual application structure very simple and allows the application designer to completely forget about the segment selector registers in the application. These registers provide the same function as the segment registers in the 8086.

Each process is created by the *Virtual Memory Manager (VMM)* and consists of four different arenas, as shown in Fig. 32-1. A process uses the full 32-addressing bits available and segregates each arena into set addresses, which can be available to the kernel or to other processes.

The operating system (OS) arena contains the VxD device drivers for the file system. This arena is common to all of the Windows processes and cannot be read from or written to; just the APIs are located in this 1-GB arena. The top four MB of the OS arena is not available and a protection error or "Access Violation" will be flagged if an application attempts to access it.

The shared arena is a one GB area that is shared by all the Windows Processes. It can be read from and written to by the application and contains memory-mapped files and *Dynamically Linked Device Drivers (DLLs)*. The system video RAM can be accessed from this arena.

The private arena is where the application code is loaded. This 2-GB arena can be read from or written to by the application (but no others) and contains both code and data. Ear-

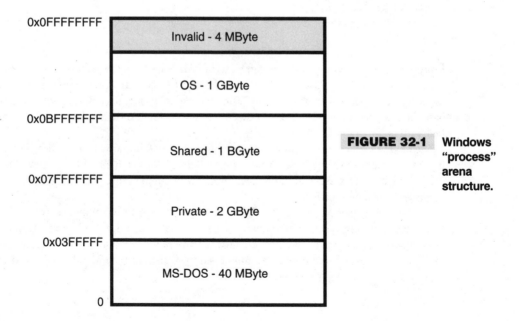

FIGURE 32-1   **Windows "process" arena structure.**

lier in this section, I noted that the 32-bit Protect-mode made application execution very simple. This is especially true with the private arena, which can be arbitrarily read from and written to. But, be careful not to overwrite code in this arena.

The private arena can be up to 2 GB in size. Two GB are not automatically allocated to the application (this would mean applications would be a uniform 2 GB in size and would be incredibly wasteful of hard disk space). Memory can be dynamically "reserved" (allocated) or "released" (freed) with a granularity of 64 KB. As part of this process, physical memory can be committed to the application's private arena as well.

When the application runs, the entire application might not be loaded into memory at all times. When the user requests other applications to run, pages of the applications might be loaded or stored on the PC's hard file in paging files. When the processor attempts to access code or data that is part of the application, it goes through the process shown in Fig. 32-2.

If the data to be accessed is not in RAM, the processor's paging hardware takes over and invokes the operating system. The operating system first confirms whether or not the memory to be accessed actually "exists" in the application; if it doesn't, it flags an access violation.

If the memory is in the paging file, the operating system looks for available memory to load it into. If no memory is available, the least recently used page is located and stored in its paging file.

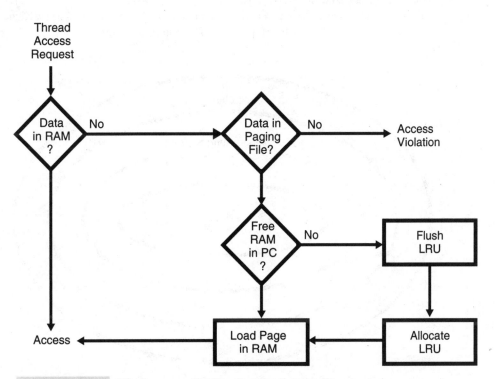

FIGURE 32-2   Windows application "paging" operation.

Once there is memory for the page, it is loaded into the page and then the access is allowed to continue. If many applications are loaded and executing in a PC with very little main memory, this paging operation will happen very often and slow down the execution of the applications significantly more than just loading additional applications. This is caused by the excessive paging that is necessary; this happens when the system is said to be in the throes of "thrashing."

To fix this problem, fewer applications should be run or more memory added to the PC.

This total operation is actually very similar to caching in the Pentium processors. The difference between caching and paging is that caching retrieves missing data from the pages, whereas paging retrieves data from the hard disk. Because of this similarity of the two operations, you might find that in some systems, main memory is referred to the Level-3 cache, where Level 1 is the processor's onboard cache and Level 2 is the high-speed cache, external to the processor chip. A good example of this is the IBM 308x mainframe processors; the main memory is only identified as *L3 cache* (buffered disk data is referred to as the *L4 cache*).

The Windows executable (.EXE) file is normally loaded directly into the process. In some operating systems, a paging file can be built from the executable directly before the application starts to execute to speed up the initial paging operations.

The MS-DOS arena is inaccessible by the application and is used by the MS-DOS prompt (virtual 8086) and 16-bit Windows applications. This arena should not be accessed because it contains the system variables and interrupt vectors. Incorrect changes to these values could cause the system to crash.

Protect mode used in Windows takes advantage of the four execution privilege rings available in the PC's processor (Fig. 32-3). The outermost rings have less privileges and

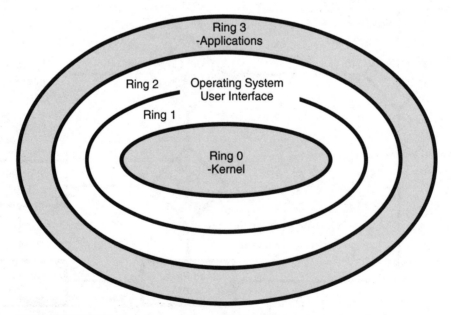

FIGURE 32-3   Windows "rings" organization.

resource access than the inner rings. Windows applications are run in the outside ring (Ring 3), which minimizes the application's opportunity to overwrite crucial system data.

The innermost ring, is known as *ring 0*, and can access any physical address or I/O address in the processor. Device drivers and the Win32 kernel code normally inhabit this ring. As device drivers are presented in this book, I will present Ring 0 operation and how communication with Ring 3 is implemented for the various types of device drivers.

Between Ring 0 and Ring 3, the middle two rings are devoted to the Windows operating system and user interface. These rings are primarily used to manage specific resources, such as main memory and video RAM, but do not access actual hardware. For the purposes of this book, these rings and the APIs associated within them are not normally accessed by Windows applications.

High-level languages normally provide API interfacing to these rings. If you were to write an assembly-language Windows application, you would have to be familiar with them as well.

Virtual Machines

The concept of virtual machines is one that I find most people are able to understand very easily, but have a hard time understanding the implications of running a PC this way. Before looking at the Virtual Memory Manager and how processes (applications) execute under Windows, I wanted to spend a bit of time explaining how virtual machines work and some of the issues involved. The previous section showed how the memory is allocated and how the application runs, but this section describes how applications interface to the hardware and the operating system (Fig. 32-4).

As I was writing this section in Microsoft Word, I had my Web browser enabled and I was listening to a CD (Genesis "Lamb Lies Down on Broadway"). I then started up the two games presented in this book, Tic-Tac-Toe and the game of Life to give you an idea of what is possible for concurrent application execution under Windows. Each of these applications display information on the screen and use the keyboard (as well as the mouse) for user input. Some applications, such as the CD player and Web browser also interface with other hardware devices. This should seem very natural to you, but you have to realize that the hardware interfaces have all been *virtualized* to allow the different processes to interact with them.

A *process* is defined as an application that is running in a virtual machine of the PC's processor. From the process's perspective, it is running all by itself in a PC's processor without anything else available, except for the standard hardware interfaces and the operating-system APIs. To access hardware, part of the application is used to pass API requests from the application to the actual hardware. This is done using a *virtualized* driver (Fig. 32-5). Currently, the most common type of virtual device driver is the VxD (Virtual x Device Driver). This type of device driver "intercepts" requests to hardware and BIOS, MS-DOS, and Windows operating-system APIs and ensures that the requests between the different processes don't interfere with one another.

For many types of devices, this is done by tracking which process (and which dialog box) has the focus of the Windows Desktop. In Fig. 32-4, Tic-Tac-Toe has focus on

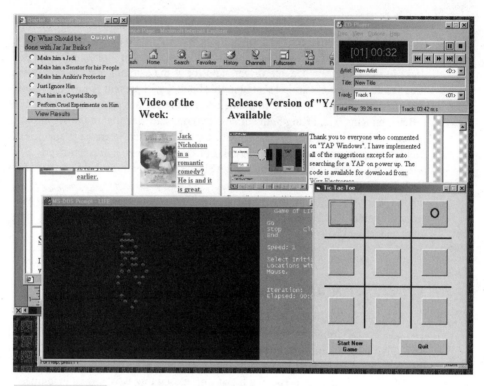

FIGURE 32-4   Windows "virtual" process operation.

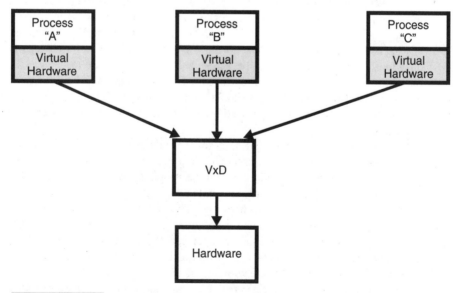

FIGURE 32-5   VxD operation.

the desktop. For this application, any keystrokes that are entered by the user are passed to Tic-Tac-Toe until it loses the focus of the desktop. The keystrokes are not passed to the other applications until they are given the focus of the desktop. When this happens, they will receive keystrokes from the operator, as if they were the only application running in the PC.

As an aside, the Windows task that has focus is normally brought forward to the top of the desktop and the top line of the application is highlighted (colored blue instead of gray). In other operating systems, focus is achieved differently. For example, in Sun's Solaris operating system, the dialog box that has focus is the one that the mouse is currently moved over. In Solaris, the dialog box does not have to be clicked or brought to the top of the desktop to have focus that is in direct contrast with Windows. When a Solaris dialog box has the focus, much of it can be obscured, which is also not possible in Windows.

The keyboard is a simple example of virtualization, but it becomes much more complex for other devices. In Fig. 32-4, all the applications shown on the desktop, with the exception of Tic-Tac-Toe, can update the display automatically without the user intervening or requesting the application to execute. Each of the different applications continue to run in time slices given to them by the virtual memory manager, as if they were the only applications in the PC and they will continue to pass display (or dialog box) update requests, even though they do not have focus.

Thus, the display-virtualized device driver is actually quite a bit more complex than the keyboard device driver; not only must it display the current focus application's dialog box up to date, but also the other applications as well. In this case, the virtualized device driver must track how each dialog box appears on the Desktop (and whether or not it is partially obscured by others) and display the data appropriately.

Going further, the disk subsystem device drivers must monitor disk I/O requests from the different applications and keep them straight. If you have worked with other multitasking operating systems, you are aware of the term *Serialization*. For the disk (and other hardware interfaces) to be serialized, individual processes must be given complete control over the resource.

VIRTUAL MACHINE MANAGER

Virtualization is the magic of Windows and most other multitasking GUI operating systems. Virtual machines is a very common method to provide this level of ease in application operation for the user. In this book, I will discuss creating Virtual Device Drivers that will work with one or more applications accessing hardware resources. To understand exactly what is required to create a virtualizing device driver and understand what is happening when there is a problem, you must have a good idea of how the processor and operating system are operating.

Loading and controlling the execution of the virtual machine processes is the job of the *Virtual Machine Manager (VMM)*. This operating system function is responsible for making space available for an application, as a process, with all of the appropriate resources and APIs available. As shown at the start of the chapter, each application is executed within Windows as its own virtual machine within the PC's processor. Along with loading the application into Windows, the virtual memory manager also has to ensure that the application can interface to the operating-system APIs and drivers, as well as any hardware VxDs.

The actual application is loaded into what I call the *Windows execution pyramid* with the application on top and the hardware on the bottom Fig. 32-6.

I feel like this is an appropriate way to visualize how applications work under Windows. The application itself runs in a virtual machine with no direct interfaces to hardware or the operating system. These interfaces are provided as the KERNEL, USER, and GDI DLLs and are passed down to the device drivers responsible for interfacing with the hardware.

The application at the top of the pyramid has the fewest privileges in terms of accessing system resources on its own. As it passes requests down the pyramid, each level has a greater amount of access to the system hardware, with the bottom level, the Virtual Machine Manager and VxDs having the ability to read from or write to any resource in the PC.

The Virtual Machine Manager can load three types of applications:

1 16-bit MS-DOS applications
2 16-bit Windows 3.x applications
3 32-bit Windows 95/98/NT/2000 applications

Some versions of Windows NT can also load and execute "OS/2" applications.

When Windows loads and executes the application as a process, it allocates space for the application both in the physical system memory and any overflow into a paging file. For each of the different types of applications, creating the process virtual machine is slightly different. This is why, when I described arenas at the start of the chapter, some of the information probably seemed strange (such as the MS-DOS arena that can't be accessed). The arena structure is designed to provide virtual machines for each of the three different types of executable files. When I described the arena structure, I only showed how it was

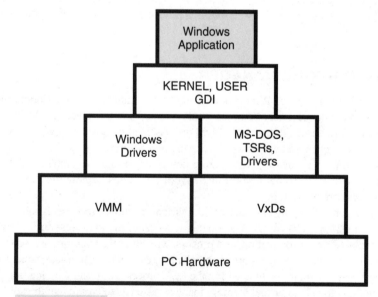

FIGURE 32-6   Windows application execution model.

used for Win32 kernel applications. The inaccessible arenas are used for the other types of executables.

The application is also linked with the KERNEL, USER, and GDI DLLs. Once this has been accomplished, the application can execute in virtual memory and access operating-system functions, as well as memory.

With all of the applications loaded and executing as processes, the Virtual Machine Manager still has two important tasks to perform. The first is providing the "time slices" for each application to give the appearance that they are all running concurrently. This is actually quite a simple requirement, with the Virtual Machine Manager saving the context information of the current application and passing control to another.

The last function that the Virtual Machine Manager provides is communications between executing threads in the system.

I hope I have not given the impression that each process is capable of running a single execution instance because that is not true. Each process (or application) consists of one or more threads. Each thread is a small program unto itself and is often known by the name of *task*.

With multiple threads possible for each process, the Virtual Machine Manager provides a communication function for them to pass messages to one another. This message passing extends beyond a single process and can include multiple processes or the operating-system APIs. Messages and multitasking application design is really beyond the scope of this book, but I wanted to be sure that you had the right terms before you began to research Windows to create your own applications. Using the multithreaded capability of Windows can make creating some applications much easier and more efficient.

Windows is normally referred to as a *multithreaded* operating system and not a *multiprocess* or *multitasking* operating system. I realize that this is a subtle, semantic difference, but it is very important if you are going to communicate with other people about your Windows applications.

V86 MODE

I would love to find out who is responsible for the *Virtual 8086 (V86)* capabilities of Windows and thank them. When you use Windows, the V86 is best known as the MS-DOS prompt dialog box that you can use to run MS-DOS applications under Windows. This amazing tool allows me to debug my MS-DOS applications without fear of trashing the operating system or system variables, along with quickly bringing up a new dialog box in case my application crashes or gets into a loop from which it can't escape.

The V86 mode also shows off the virtualization capabilities of Windows. For example, I can run two separate instances of The Game of Life under two V86 dialog boxes. Even though they are both running the same application, because each runs in its own virtual machine, they can run independently without affecting each other (Fig. 32-7).

Each of the two instances of The Game of Life are running with only the one that has the Desktop's "focus" is being passed keystrokes and mouse information. Despite this, the display drivers are able to keep track of where the data is to be displayed, even with one dialog box "behind" the other.

In the applications themselves, they are writing to local VRAM as if they were the only application running in a PC. These writes are passed to virtual VRAM that is recognized

FIGURE 32-7   Windows "virtual 8086" operation.

within the Virtual Machine Manager and the display VxD. The writes to the virtual VRAM cause the VMM to stop the application thread and pass the data to the display VxD. The display VxD then places the display byte at the appropriate location on the Desktop.

For the MS-DOS and BIOS API requests, a somewhat different process is used. These APIs are interrupt based for a table located starting at address 0x00000:0x00000 in the virtual 8086. As shown in Fig. 32-8, the virtual 8086's interrupt table actually points to VxD APIs.

When the *int ##* instruction is executed, the interrupt table redirects the virtual 8086 operation to a VxD API interface. This interface then passes the BIOS/MS-DOS request to the appropriate device driver within the Windows operating system. This method of providing the software-interrupt APIs is quite clever because it allows applications to overwrite (redirect) the API addresses without having to change the VxD. It also allows MS-DOS applications to run in either pure MS-DOS or Windows MS-DOS prompt dialog boxes without any regard to where the application is running.

However, three aspects of the virtual 8086 in Windows can cause problems. First, do not use graphics modes from the MS-DOS prompt. If you do, the MS-DOS prompt application will be given the entire display as if it were the only application running. This can cause some serious problems if multiple programs are outputting graphics.

The second issue is with TSR programs. If you are familiar with MS-DOS, you'll know that TSRs are normally loaded in at boot time from within AUTOEXEC.BAT. This is also true for Windows, but when a TSR is loaded at boot time, it is stored into the Protect-mode MS-DOS arena. In some ways, this is good because it means that TSRs do not take up any of the 640 KB used for applications.

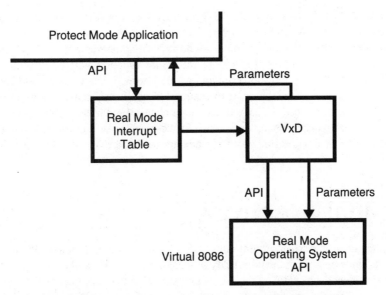

FIGURE 32-8   Windows application to BIOS/MS-DOS path.

It can be a bad thing if you want to use a TSR for some MS-DOS applications and not others. In this case, the TSR will have to be loaded from within the appropriate MS-DOS prompt dialog box before the application that needs it is run. This is not a major inconvenience, but I guarantee you that as you debug an application that needs a separate TSR, you'll forget to load it and then spend hours trying to find why the application has stopped running.

For this reason, I have sworn off TSRs for all applications wherever possible. The only exception to this rule is that I load a keystroke-retriever TSR that I've used for a long time with all my MS-DOS command-line applications.

Interestingly enough, OS/2 can be thought of being somewhat better than Windows in this regard. In OS/2, virtual 8086 MS-DOS prompt dialog boxes can be defined with their own AUTOEXEC.BAT files. These AUTOEXEC.BAT files can be specific to applications and are useful to set up with paths and initial operating conditions for using/debugging an application.

The last issue with the virtual 8086 is in the area of physical memory and I/O addresses. Under MS-DOS, an application can access any address within the system. Under Windows, efforts have been made to provide the ability of interfacing to I/O ports, but not memory addresses. Actual physical memory addresses cannot be accessed at all, which means that if you are debugging hardware-interface applications under Windows' MS-DOS prompt, you are limited to only being able to use the I/O ports.

Under Windows, standard interface device I/O ports are usually allocated to VxDs and are not available to MS-DOS prompt applications. Unfortunately, if an application attempts to access an I/O port that has already been assigned to another virtual 8086 or VxD, you will not be alerted to the problem by an access violation error. To avoid this problem, when you are debugging an MS-DOS application in Windows, check to see that you can access and use the I/O ports from the debugger that you are using. If you can't, then you will have to work from MS-DOS directly.

In terms of I/O port allocation, I have found that, in some versions of Windows, you must access specific registers first before the entire function will be allocated to the MS-DOS prompt process. For the serial and parallel ports, it is always a good idea to do an initial dummy read of the data port to ensure that you have been allocated the device. For arbitrary I/O addresses, you have to take your chances and hope that Windows will allow you to access the port. To maximize the chances of this, use I/O addresses that are not allocated to specific devices (the prototype adapter card addresses, 0x0300 to 0x031F, are always a good choice).

COM/OLE/ActiveX

Probably the most important assumptions you must make about a modern PC is that it is not a stand-alone unit. With the popularity of local-area networks and the Internet, PCs are very rarely connected to networks that contain external data or applications. To make this easier, Microsoft came up with the *Component Object Model (COM)* to allow the code and data to be shared as if it were local to the PC.

COM "hides" the network protocols and device drivers from the application developer. In the straight COM, all data and resources are presented as "objects" to the application. In *Distributed COM (DCOM)* systems, data is transferred between the network and the PC as if the data were located locally on the PC. As I write this, COM is only available on Windows NT machines (but will run under Windows 2000). The high-level COM operation looks like the illustration in Fig. 32-9.

Like many of the new interfaces built into the current and future Windows operating systems, COM is an object-orientated binary standard for API calling. Methods for each object allow the application to ID the object quickly and allow data to be passed directly to the requesting application. Along with data, device drivers can also be COM objects, which allows hardware interfaces on remote PCs to be interfaced as if they were on the local machine.

ActiveX is an enhancement to DCOM, which allows objects located on long latency networks (the Internet being a good example of this) to be interfaced as COM objects to applications.

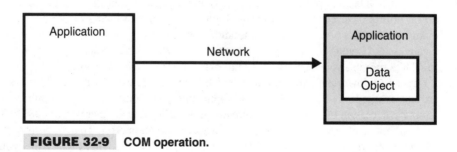

FIGURE 32-9   COM operation.

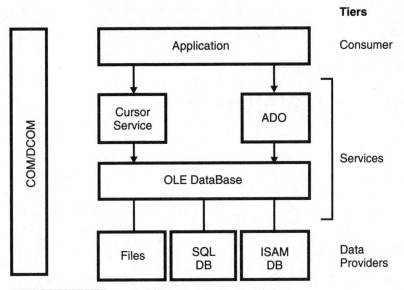

FIGURE 32-10 COM/OLE block diagram.

COM grew out of the *Object Linking and Embedding (OLE)* database technology. OLE (pronounced "olé") is used for network data-base operations in which records are composed of compound documents. A *compound document* consists of text files, data-base records, graphics, animations, audio files, and any other digital data that can be stored in a PC system. When you look up information on OLE, you will probably see a diagram like that in Fig. 32-10.

COM technology should not be confused with TCP/IP and other Internet-connection technologies. COM is a Microsoft method to provide data interfaces for Windows NT applications. Although TCP/IP is often used as the low-level network interface to pass the data, it is not accessed from application code, instead COM is used.

33

WINDOWS

PROGRAMMING

Two types of programming are used for Microsoft Windows. The first is application programming, including Visual Basic and Visual C++. Application programming is generally data-processing applications, although recently it has come to mean network and database programming as well. These languages can only use built-in APIs that access standard hardware in the PC, such as the file system and the Windows Desktop. Many excellent books have been written on how to develop applications in Windows.

To access custom hardware device drivers, which are created using systems programming techniques, this chapter introduces you to the different types of Windows device drivers and the issues of operating in Ring 0 of the operating system (normally, Windows applications execute in Ring 3). Unfortunately, much fewer resources are available to developing systems-level code for Windows.

Learning how to develop Windows applications is really not that daunting a task. You will find that you can be proficient in less than a month. This is accomplished by focussing on the high level, documenting what you want your application to do, and walking through the low-level information to get exactly what you need. I feel that this is the most efficient way to starting to be a genius in developing Windows hardware and software applications.

To be honest, I did not go through this route and I feel like it has really cost me in terms of my efficiency in developing applications. I think I have a good grasp on how to create Windows applications and device drivers, but I sure feel like I could have gained this knowledge easier and been more efficient in developing my applications.

Program Development

Even when different tools are used to develop Windows applications, I recommend that the same process is used to develop the dialog boxes used and the application code and logic behind them. Despite the apparent complexity of many Windows applications; the actual structure of the application can be developed very quickly with prototype code available to show users at very early stages of development. This section goes through my philosophies for developing Windows applications, including some ideas on how the application-development plan can be presented to your customers and superiors.

I must confess that the central concept presented here was not developed by me. I am an avid reader of *Aviation Week* and my philosophies for developing Windows applications really came about from a series of articles presented in one issue on developing graphical displays for pilots. Traditionally, in aerospace applications, computer displays and their underlying code was developed using highly structured processes designed to produce a very high-quality end product.

The problem with using rigorous design processes is that final products tend to take a very long time to develop and require a lot of *NRE (Non-Recurring Expenses)* that have to be amortized over the life of the product. As well, the products tended to be a follow-on to what was already available; the process really stifled innovation.

In the series of articles, the development of a tool that could be used to mock-up the cockpit display was used to create a quick-and-dirty display to show to pilots and experts. This was in contrast to the original process, in which surveys were taken of perceived needs and a product definition derived from the results of the surveys.

By using mock-ups of the displays and presenting them, the users were able to suggest changes and help in overall design of the product. Once the display formats were agreed upon, the underlying code was developed and the products released.

Virtually all Windows development tools support this type of development. To begin, I design my dialog boxes with just enough code to allow the movement between child and parent dialog boxes to be seen and understood. In Visual Basic and Visual C++, Dialog boxes can be developed and executed without the need of any underlying code. Normally, just the X in the top right corner of the dialog box is all that is required to stop the execution of the dialog boxes.

Once I am happy with the dialog boxes, I then work through any data file formats and the file system Open/Read/Write/Close code. As described for MS-DOS programming, I only work with code that is in a man-readable format. This allows me to see errors in the code quickly and allows me to create test cases without having to develop applications to convert what I understand to what the application understands.

With the file operations working, I am then able to move on and work through the program and dialog-box logic. To help me visually keep track of what needs to be done, I'll often disable dialog box controls so that their labels (and captions) show up as gray, rather than black, characters. As I work through the application and add functionality to the different controls, I enable the controls so that their labels and captions show up as black.

Once I am happy with the functionality of the application, I put in the actual hardware interfaces. Chances are that as I work through the application, I will discover better ways to interface to the hardware, so if I were to start off with specific interfaces, I would probably find that I have to rewrite them.

Hardware interfaces should be as generic as possible and also very well documented. As you look at my Visual Basic and Visual C++ code in this book, you'll see that they are very minimally commented. This is really a function of me creating the underlying code very quickly and having a good understanding of how I want things to work. For the most part, this is a reasonable strategy, but it can be a problem where complex hardware interfaces are involved or complex processing is required.

When developing hardware interfaces, I often create simple Windows applications to test them out. Often in an application, the user must accomplish a large number of operations before hardware can actually be accessed. As I work through my applications, I find this to be tiresome. To avoid this boring work, I create simple applications to test out the hardware and then place the interface code in the application itself.

I have talked to some people who feel that this method of code development is too "seat of the pants" for them to be comfortable. As well, many people prefer a "bottoms up" approach to application development, where this is just about the ultimate in "top down" coding. To be honest, I prefer doing my MS-DOS coding using a "bottoms up" philosophy because I prefer having the hardware interface before the user's.

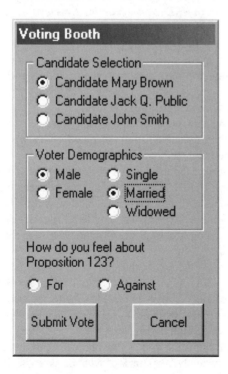

FIGURE 33-1 Sample dialog box.

Resource Files

Resource files (which normally end in *.RC*) specify dialog boxes. These files consist of the type of dialog controls, their properties and labels, as well as other information needed to create the application. When I first started programming for a GUI environment (it was OS/2), a text editor created the resource file. This wasn't that hard, although it was tedious. Visual C++ has an integrated graphic dialog editor that makes creating the resource file quite easy. Visual Basic does not produce a resource file the same way that Visual C++ does, so the information in this section really doesn't apply to it.

For this section, I created the following dialog box in Visual C++ (Fig. 33-1), which has the associated resource file:

```
//Microsoft Developer Studio generated resource script.
//
#include "resource.h"

#define APSTUDIO_READONLY_SYMBOLS
/////////////////////////////////////////////////////////////////////////////
//////
//
// Generated from the TEXTINCLUDE 2 resource.
//
#include "afxres.h"


/////////////////////////////////////////////////////////////////////////////
///
#undef APSTUDIO_READONLY_SYMBOLS

/////////////////////////////////////////////////////////////////////////////
//////
// English (U.S.) resources

#if !defined(AFX_RESOURCE_DLL) || defined(AFX_TARG_ENU)
#ifdef _WIN32
LANGUAGE LANG_ENGLISH, SUBLANG_ENGLISH_US
#pragma code_page(1252)
#endif //_WIN32

#ifdef APSTUDIO_INVOKED
/////////////////////////////////////////////////////////////////////////////
//////
//
// TEXTINCLUDE
//

1 TEXTINCLUDE DISCARDABLE
BEGIN
    "resource.h\0"
END

2 TEXTINCLUDE DISCARDABLE
BEGIN
    "#include ""afxres.h""\r\n"
    "\0"
END

3 TEXTINCLUDE DISCARDABLE
```

```
        BEGIN
            "#define _AFX_NO_SPLITTER_RESOURCES\r\n"
            "#define _AFX_NO_OLE_RESOURCES\r\n"
            "#define _AFX_NO_TRACKER_RESOURCES\r\n"
            "#define _AFX_NO_PROPERTY_RESOURCES\r\n"
            "\r\n"
            "#if !defined(AFX_RESOURCE_DLL) || defined(AFX_TARG_ENU)\r\n"
            "#ifdef _WIN32\r\n"
            "LANGUAGE 9, 1\r\n"
            "#pragma code_page(1252)\r\n"
            "#endif //_WIN32\r\n"
            "#include ""res\\temp.rc2""  // non-Microsoft Visual C++ edited
        resources\r\n"
            "#include ""afxres.rc""           // Standard components\r\n"
            "#endif\r\n"
            "\0"
        END

        #endif    // APSTUDIO_INVOKED


        //////////////////////////////////////////////////////////////////////
        //////
        //
        // Icon
        //

        // Icon with lowest ID value placed first to ensure application icon
        // remains consistent on all systems.
        IDR_MAINFRAME           ICON    DISCARDABLE     "res\\temp.ico"

        //////////////////////////////////////////////////////////////////////
        //////
        //
        // Dialog
        //


        IDD_TEMP_DIALOG DIALOGEX 0, 0, 156, 164
        STYLE DS_MODALFRAME | WS_POPUP | WS_VISIBLE | WS_CAPTION | WS_SYSMENU
        EXSTYLE WS_EX_APPWINDOW
        CAPTION "temp"
        FONT 8, "MS Sans Serif"
        BEGIN
            DEFPUSHBUTTON   "OK",IDOK,7,143,50,14
            PUSHBUTTON      "Cancel",IDCANCEL,99,143,50,14
            LTEXT           "How do you feel about Proposition
        123?",IDC_STATIC,16,
                            110,122,16
            CONTROL
            "For",IDC_RADIO1,"Button", BS_AUTORADIOBUTTON,16,129,26,9
            CONTROL
            "Against",IDC_RADIO2,"Button", BS_AUTORADIOBUTTON,43,129,
                            44,9
            LTEXT           "Voting Booth",IDC_STATIC,57,7,45,8
            CONTROL         "Candidate John Smith",IDC_RADIO3,"Button",
                            BS_AUTORADIOBUTTON,13,24,88,11
            CONTROL         "Candidate Jack Q Public",IDC_RADIO4,"Button",
                            BS_AUTORADIOBUTTON,13,34,96,15
            CONTROL         "Candidate Mary Brown",IDC_RADIO5,"Button",
                            BS_AUTORADIOBUTTON,13,50,96,9
            LTEXT           "Demographics",IDC_STATIC,50,66,49,8
```

```
        CONTROL
        "Male",IDC_RADIO6,"Button", BS_AUTORADIOBUTTON,16,73,37,9
        CONTROL
        "Female",IDC_RADIO7,"Button", BS_AUTORADIOBUTTON,16,84,42,8
        CONTROL
        "Single",IDC_RADIO10,"Button", BS_AUTORADIOBUTTON,73,74,63,9
        CONTROL
        "Married",IDC_RADIO11,"Button", BS_AUTORADIOBUTTON,73,83,62,9
        CONTROL
        "Widowed",IDC_RADIO12,"Button",BS_AUTORADIOBUTTON,73,92,63,10
END


#ifndef _MAC
/////////////////////////////////////////////////////////////////////////
//////
//
// Version
//

VS_VERSION_INFO VERSIONINFO
 FILEVERSION 1,0,0,1
 PRODUCTVERSION 1,0,0,1
 FILEFLAGSMASK 0x3fL
#ifdef _DEBUG
 FILEFLAGS 0x1L
#else
 FILEFLAGS 0x0L
#endif
 FILEOS 0x4L
 FILETYPE 0x1L
 FILESUBTYPE 0x0L
BEGIN
    BLOCK "StringFileInfo"
    BEGIN
        BLOCK "040904B0"
        BEGIN
            VALUE "CompanyName", "\0"
            VALUE "FileDescription", "temp MFC Application\0"
            VALUE "FileVersion", "1, 0, 0, 1\0"
            VALUE "InternalName", "temp\0"
            VALUE "LegalCopyright", "Copyright (C) 1999\0"
            VALUE "LegalTrademarks", "\0"
            VALUE "OriginalFilename", "temp.EXE\0"
            VALUE "ProductName", "temp Application\0"
            VALUE "ProductVersion", "1, 0, 0, 1\0"
        END
    END
    BLOCK "VarFileInfo"
    BEGIN
        VALUE "Translation", 0x409, 1200
    END
END

#endif    // !_MAC


/////////////////////////////////////////////////////////////////////////
//////
//
// DESIGNINFO
```

```
//

#ifdef APSTUDIO_INVOKED
GUIDELINES DESIGNINFO DISCARDABLE
BEGIN
    IDD_TEMP_DIALOG, DIALOG
    BEGIN
        LEFTMARGIN, 7
        RIGHTMARGIN, 149
        TOPMARGIN, 7
        BOTTOMMARGIN, 157
    END
END
#endif    // APSTUDIO_INVOKED

#endif    // English (U.S.) resources
///////////////////////////////////////////////////////////////////////
//////

#ifndef APSTUDIO_INVOKED
///////////////////////////////////////////////////////////////////////
//////
//
// Generated from the TEXTINCLUDE 3 resource.
//
#define _AFX_NO_SPLITTER_RESOURCES
#define _AFX_NO_OLE_RESOURCES
#define _AFX_NO_TRACKER_RESOURCES
#define _AFX_NO_PROPERTY_RESOURCES

#if !defined(AFX_RESOURCE_DLL) || defined(AFX_TARG_ENU)
#ifdef _WIN32
LANGUAGE 9, 1
#pragma code_page(1252)
#endif //_WIN32
#include "res\temp.rc2"   // non-Microsoft Visual C++ edited resources
#include "afxres.rc"        // Standard components
#endif


///////////////////////////////////////////////////////////////////////
//////
#endif    // not APSTUDIO_INVOKED
```

Creating the resource file by a text editor is possible, but to do it, you will have to understand how the resource file actually works. As you can see in this listing, the resource file is not a straight text file, but it's actually a C++ source file that is assembled and linked into the rest of the application.

In several applications, I have created my own dialog boxes using an editor. The advantage of working with the text instead of the Visual C++ graphic tool is the columns can be precisely lined up when I first created the dialog box shown in Fig. 33-1, the button resources were not precisely lined up). When manually editing the resource file, I have two rules.

First, put on all of the required controls into the dialog boxes before manually editing the files. This will give you all the controls to be used, meaning that they just have to be repositioned from the editor.

Second, I only modify the actual dialog-box control information in the resource file. In the example file, this is:

```
/////////////////////////////////////////////////////////////////////////////
//////
//
// Dialog
//

IDD_TEMP_DIALOG DIALOGEX 0, 0, 156, 164
STYLE DS_MODALFRAME | WS_POPUP | WS_VISIBLE | WS_CAPTION | WS_SYSMENU
EXSTYLE WS_EX_APPWINDOW
CAPTION "temp"
FONT 8, "MS Sans Serif"
BEGIN
    DEFPUSHBUTTON   "OK",IDOK,7,143,50,14
    PUSHBUTTON      "Cancel",IDCANCEL,99,143,50,14
    LTEXT           "How do you feel about Proposition
                    110,122,16
    CONTROL
    "For",IDC_RADIO1,"Button",BS_AUTORADIOBUTTON,16,129,26,9
    CONTROL
    "Against",IDC_RADIO2,"Button",BS_AUTORADIOBUTTON,43,129,
                    44,9
    LTEXT           "Voting Booth",IDC_STATIC,57,7,45,8
    CONTROL         "Candidate John Smith",IDC_RADIO3,"Button",
                    BS_AUTORADIOBUTTON,13,24,88,11
    CONTROL         "Candidate Jack Q Public",IDC_RADIO4,"Button",
                    BS_AUTORADIOBUTTON,13,34,96,15
    CONTROL         "Candidate Mary Brown",IDC_RADIO5,"Button",
                    BS_AUTORADIOBUTTON,13,50,96,9
    LTEXT           "Demographics",IDC_STATIC,50,66,49,8
    CONTROL
"Male",IDC_RADIO6,"Button",BS_AUTORADIOBUTTON,16,73,37,9
    CONTROL
"Female",IDC_RADIO7,"Button",BS_AUTORADIOBUTTON,16,84,42,
                    8
    CONTROL
"Single",IDC_RADIO10,"Button",BS_AUTORADIOBUTTON,73,74,
                    63,9
    CONTROL
"Married",IDC_RADIO11,"Button",BS_AUTORADIOBUTTON,73,83,
                    62,9
    CONTROL
"Widowed",IDC_RADIO12,"Button",BS_AUTORADIOBUTTON,73,92,
                    63,10
END
```

When I modify these controls, I primarily just change the starting coordinates (the first two numbers of each control is the *X* and *Y* position with 0, 0 at the top left corner) and then the size of the control (which is the second two numbers in the control). For button properties, other than the caption, I use the graphical dialog editor in Visual C++. This seems to be the most efficient way to combine the Visual C++ tools with the manual process.

Practical Windows Interfaces

A plethora of books and courses are dedicated to developing effective Microsoft Windows interfaces. The purpose of this and the following sections is not to repeat what these references say, but try to give some pointers on how to provide a reasonably intuitive interface to your hardware. This is important, not only for the users, but well-designed user interfaces can be an advantage for debugging application hardware, as well. The rest of this chapter describes the aspects of designing Windows hardware interfaces for both your customers and yourself. Some of this information is repeated in Chapter 18, but the focus in this chapter is on creating efficient interfaces for your users.

As you work through Visual Basic (and, to a lessor extent, Visual C++), you'll discover that creating dialog boxes for playing with application hardware to be much less painful than creating debugging code using C, Q-BASIC, or other MS-DOS development tools. The code that you write for debugging hardware should not be confused with the final user interfaces. This code should be designed to test specific functions quickly and, as shown later in the chapter, it should be designed to allow you to debug the functions as well.

DESIGNING HUMAN USER INTERFACES

If you are a "thirty-something" like me, you'll probably remember such TV shows as *Star Trek* or *Voyage to the Bottom of the Sea*, in which computer interfaces were large arrays of flashing lights and unlabeled buttons. Often, the technicians would stare at intently and remark upon an impending emergency from the subtleties of what was being displayed. Usually, the reply from the commanding officer would be a caustic comment about the years spent training the technician and he should have noticed a problem earlier.

As a kid, I felt that was unfair because if it were me in that situation, 90 percent of the training would have been learning what the different lights displayed and what the switch functions controlled. It seemed a waste to me that the important function of the board, plotting an efficient course through interstellar space or keeping a nuclear reactor from melting down, took a backseat to learning how the controls and displays worked.

I realize now that the people who built the sets, didn't have a clue as to how a modern or futuristic computer would work. When I look at some hardware-interface applications, I have to wonder if they were created by the same people who built the props for the TV shows 30 years ago.

My biggest complaint is that, for the most part, hardware displays do not show what's happening in the mechanical, electrical, or whatever system being controlled. There are some notable exceptions to this; in my HP DeskJet printer, the status of the paper going through the printer is displayed on the PC's screen and, on my IBM ThinkPad 755, the modem-status dialog boxes are a series of virtual LEDs, which show the modem's current status. These examples are rare and few and far between.

If you want to see good examples of how graphic displays can be used to help the user, the next time you are taking a flight, ask to go into the cockpit and have one of the pilots show you the electrical bus or hydraulic subsystem displays (Fig. 33-2). These displays graphically show what the status is of each element in the system. If there is a problem, it

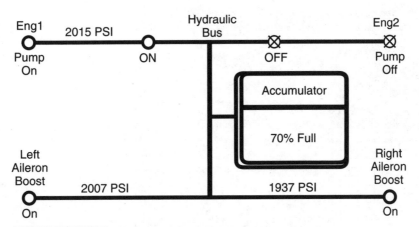

FIGURE 33-2   Aircraft engine hydraulic system display.

is immediately apparent (either by changing colors or flashing lights). By following the flow paths, the extent of the problem can be easily determined and the appropriate corrective action is obvious.

Figure 33-2 shows the status of one engine's hydraulic pump being off line and the valve leading to it shut off. By using different text for "OFF" and marking the closed valve and shut down pump, the current situation is very easy to understand after looking at the display.

Not having this information can really change a routine error into a life-or-death emergency. In the last 20 years, the inclusion of electronic displays in the cockpit with this sort of display is one of the biggest factors responsible for eliminating the need for the flight engineer. Previously, the flight engineer's job was to monitor "steam gauges" and determine whether everything was working properly. This has done a lot to make air travel much more efficient and safer.

Along with graphical displays showing a system's status, I feel that it is important to provide bar graphs, gauges, etc., to show what is going on in the most appropriate manner. For example, if the PC is controlling a battery charger, you might want to put in a bar graph of the current charge on the battery (Fig. 33-3).

This display, in a tool like Visual Basic, is remarkably easy to create and use. Later chapters show how these types of displays can be quickly and easily created using Visual Basic.

I've found that humans look first at a graphic display to get a rough idea of the current status and then look for detail on what's actually happening if what they see is unexpected. In the battery-charger example, the battery could explode if its charge goes above 90 percent (the dotted line on the battery graphic). By placing the dotted line on the bar-graph display, the user can check to see if the charge is near the danger point and if the charging operation is close enough to stop without losing a significant amount of capacity. The numeric value displayed helps give the user a good idea of exactly what is happening in the situation.

Feedback to a program working is also important. This is really because of the bad applications that lock up either themselves or the PC. We've been conditioned to expect this condition over the years.

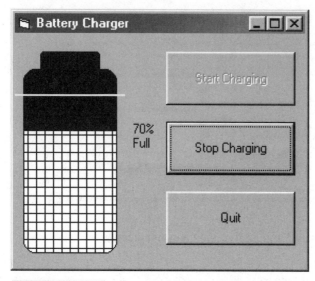

FIGURE 33-3 Sample Windows dialog box.

In Microsoft Windows, program active indicators can be animations (such as a ball bouncing up and down in the dialog box) or messages ("Loading......."). Personally, I prefer animation, but it should be keyed to the application execution and not a separate timer. If the application stops, then the animation/message should also stop.

HARDWARE DEBUGGING INTERFACES

Earlier in this chapter, I indicated that you could create debugging applications in Windows easier than what could be done in MS-DOS. This probably seems surprising, but it's actually true. Debugging applications can be created in Windows quite quickly and can work through specific sequences with very little development effort. As you learn Visual Basic and Visual C++, you'll see how easy it is to develop custom dialog boxes and supporting code. This section provides some strategies to create dialog boxes to simplify your hardware card software debugging.

When debugging a register-based interface, I like to first create a simple program with button controls for reading and writing data.

Like the dialog box in Fig. 33-4, multiple sets of registers can be "peeked" and "poked" from the dialog box while you look at what is being loaded or read onto the card. This allows you to probe the hardware easily to see what happens. Writing your applications this way allows you to create and debug the routines that will be used later in the application interface with the hardware.

When first reading and writing registers, I recommend putting in a message to yourself to explain what is happening. Figure 33-5 shows how this could be done.

I always find that when I am debugging, I get lost with what I expect to see what is happening. Having information presented in a format like this makes debug of a card much easier.

In these examples, I have used constant values for the reading and writing. This could be enhanced by placing a text-input box into your dialog box and passing the value to the

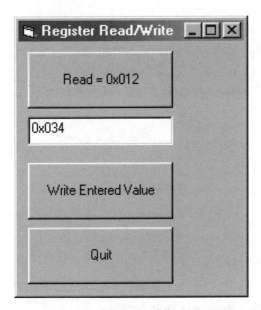

FIGURE 33-4 Register read/write test dialog box.

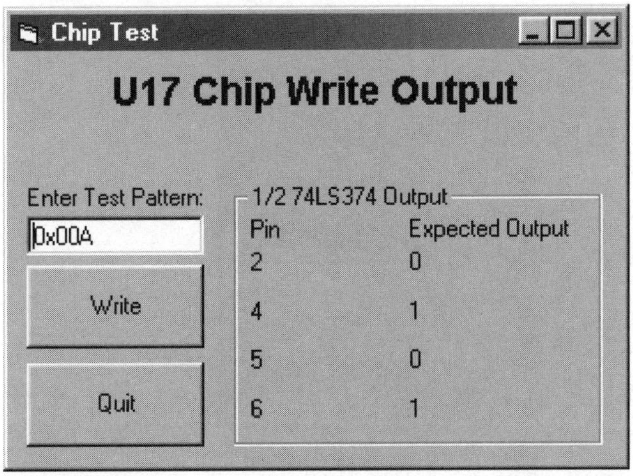

FIGURE 33-5 Register write test with chip text display.

hardware. The problem with doing this is you will have to write code that parses/processes the data. I find it easier to just write constant values and go from there. If I have specific cases, I just add more controls.

Custom controls can be used to good advantage in different situations. For example, if you're reading an analog value, how about using a bar graph, as demonstrated in the Chapter 35? Different types of analog values are shown in Fig. 33-6.

If you have an *analog-to-digital converter (ADC)* attached to the PC, the bar graph could show information more meaningfully than a numeric value.

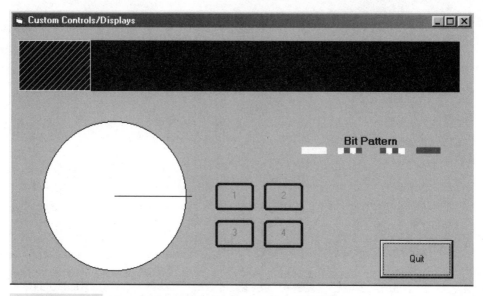

FIGURE 33-6   Bar graph analog display/custom controls.

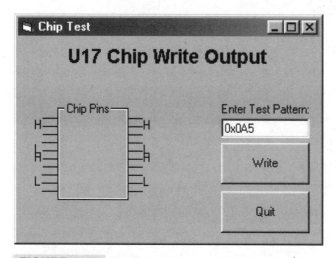

FIGURE 33-7   Register write test with chip pin display.

Custom displays could also be used to display bit values or even how to check a chip (Fig. 33-7)

None of these custom controls require a lot of effort to create over just a standard display. For this section, I was able to create the dialog boxes shown in the diagrams in Visual Basic in less than half an hour.

When developing debugging dialogs, I have a few rules that should be followed. The first is, the dialogs can be placed in the application, but when you release the application, be sure that the debugging dialogs are disabled, password protected or taken out alto-gether. Chances are that your hardware has to be accessed in a specific order or manner. By accessing registers incorrectly, the hardware will not function properly later. Many users like to "prowl;" seeing something called *debug* will probably peak their interest.

When creating dialog boxes to debug hardware, I recommend starting with just reading and writing registers and memory, then moving your way up to sequences of instructions, interrupt handlers, and the application sequence.

4

WINDOWS PROGRAMMING

VISUAL

BASIC

PROGRAMMING

Microsoft's Visual Basic is the fastest way to get into Microsoft Windows application programming. I was amazed that after an hour of going through the *Learning Visual Basic* CD-ROM, I was able to create the reasonably complex Tic-Tac-Toe game that is described later in this chapter. This ease of using the language and development system also makes it great as a "what if" tool and allows you to write an application quickly to try out new ideas.

Without taking too much thunder from later in the chapter, the Visual Basic IDE really works the way I would want a Windows development system to. To create an application, the Primary dialog box (known as a "form") is created first, with different features (I/O boxes, buttons, etc.). These features are known as *controls* within Visual Basic (Fig. 34-1). With the Window defined, by simply double clicking on the different controls, subroutine prototypes to handle events (such as mouse clicks over these features) are automatically created. Additional features in Visual Basic's source code editor allow you to specify the control parameters (known as *properties*).

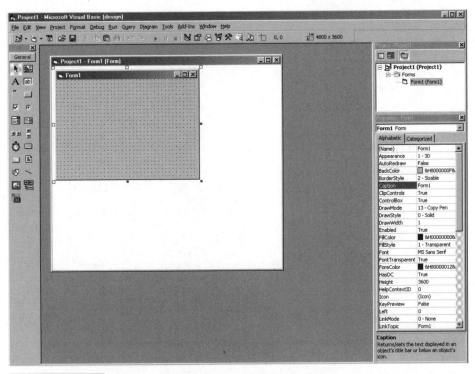

FIGURE 34-1   "Visual Basic" Development System.

Buy the "learning editions" of Microsoft Visual Toolkit development products first. The learning editions cost considerably less than the Professional or Enterprise editions and include multimedia CD-ROMs that will walk you through the languages and help you to create your own applications and provide an additional reference for you.

If you work with the Learning Edition products, notice that the executable files (.EXE) cannot be commercially distributed. If you are going to create code for sale, you will have to recompile them using the Professional or Enterprise editions. The good news is that Microsoft offers a rebate for users that start with the Learning Editions and then upgrade or graduate to the commercial versions.

Visual Basic Features

To characterize Visual Basic, I tend to think of it primarily as a development tool, rather than as a language. Visual C++ and other Windows application-development tools can perform the same functions as Visual Basic, but are much more difficult to learn. Visual Basic is the Windows development tool that I would use as I was designing a Microsoft Windows development environment.

Visual Basic applications are built around The Dialog Box Editor desktop. When application development is started, Visual Basic prompts you with the initial dialog box of your application (Fig. 34-1).

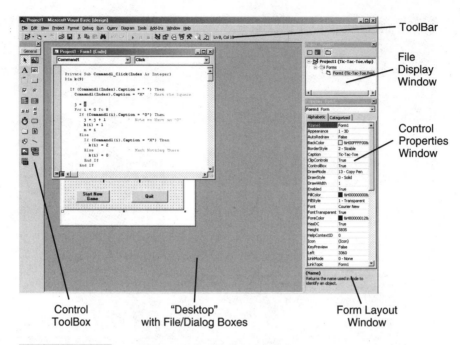

ToolBar

File
Display
Window

Control
Properties
Window

Control
ToolBox

"Desktop"
with File/Dialog Boxes

Form Layout
Window

FIGURE 34-2   Visual basic desktop.

From here, dialog resources are selected from the ToolBox and placed upon the dialog. The standard dialog controls that can be placed on a dialog box include:

CONTROL	DESCRIPTION
Pull Downs	Selected from the Menu Editor icon on the ToolBar
PictureBox	Display Bitmaps and other graphic files on the Dialog Box
Label	Put Text in the Dialog Box
TextBox	Input/Output Text Box
Frame	Put a Frame around Resources
CommandButton	Button for Code Operation
CheckBox	For Checking Multiple Selections
OptionButton	Also known as the *Radio Button*. For Checking one selection for a list of Multiple options
ComboBox	Select or Enter Text in a Box/List
ListBox	List Data (with User Controlled Scrolling)
HScrollBar	Provide Horizontal Scrolling in a Text or Graphic Output Control
VscrollBar	Provide Vertical Scrolling in a Text or Graphic Output Control
Timer	Cause a periodic interrupt

DriveListBox	Select a Drive for File I/O
DirListBox	Select a Subdirectory for File I/O on a Specific Drive
FileListBox	Display Files for a Specific Subdirectory on a Specific Drive
Shape	Put a Graphics Shape on the Dialog Box
Line	Draw a Line on the Dialog Box
Image	Display an Image File on the Dialog Box
OLE	Insert OLE Objects to the Dialog

Along with these controls, a number of optional controls (such as *serial I/O*) can be added to the toolbox, as well. These controls are used for advanced applications and provide additional capabilities to Visual Basic.

Once the dialog box is designed and looks the way you want it, you can start writing the code. The easiest way to create the application code is by double clicking on the control in the Dialog Box Editor and a subroutine prototype will appear to allow you to add code to respond to when the control is "clicked" by the user.

In Fig. 34-3, I double clicked on Help and Quit to bring up the event handler prototypes (the code to respond to when the control is clicked by the user). For Quit, you can see that the End statement is used to end the application and clear it from memory. In Help's case, I will spawn a new dialog box to explain how the application works and who the author is.

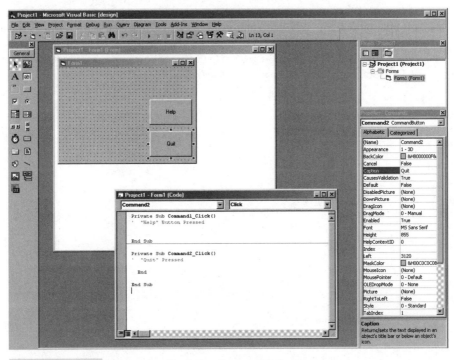

FIGURE 34-3   Visual basic dialog box control set up.

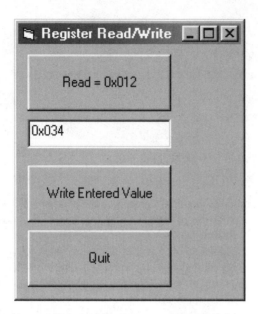

FIGURE 34-4 Visual Basic register read/write form.

To set the control attributes (also known as *properties*), they can be changed within the Control Properties window of the Desktop or from the code itself. To demonstrate this, I created the simple program called *Traffic*, which is on the CD-ROM. The dialog box itself is very simple with the individual buttons set to the appropriate colors (i.e., Red, Yellow, and Green). When one of these buttons is pressed, the appropriate action is displayed on a Text box to the right of the light buttons. Figure 34-4 shows a form in which the top control can be changed depending on the register value read.

The Event handler code that responds to the user clicking on these buttons and changing the Text-box caption property is:

```
Private Sub Command1_Click()
'   "Red" Button

    Label1.Caption = "Stop"

End Sub

Private Sub Command3_Click()
'   "Green" Light

    Label1.Caption = "Go"

End Sub

Private Sub Command4_Click()
'   "Yellow" Light

    Label1.Caption = "Slow"

End Sub

Private Sub Command2_Click()
'   "Quit" CommandButton

    End

End Sub
```

As can be seen from the code, when one of the buttons (such as *Command1 - Red*) is clicked with the mouse's left button, the string *Stop* is copied into the *Label1* caption property. This code is repeated for the other two buttons.

A number of controls cannot be activated with a left button click; the one that is most used is the Timer. This control causes an event after a set period of microseconds. This control can be set within the dialog editor or modified within the application itself. The Timer can provide many different advanced functions without requiring any interrupt interfaces.

The Event Handler's code is written in pretty standard Microsoft BASIC. Once the handler prototypes are created by Visual Basic, it is up to the application developer (you) to add the response code for the application. Visual Basic provides a large number of built-in functions, including trigonometric, logarithms, and the ability to interface with the file system and dialog controls.

Variables in Visual Basic are typically "real," which is to say that they are floating-point values in the ranges provided by the floating-point coprocessor built into the PC's processor. Integer variables can be specified by putting a $ character at the start of the variable name. One important thing to note about variables is that they are local to the event routine where they are used, unless they are declared globally in the general module, which executes at the beginning of the application and is not specific to any controls.

The only real deficit I can see in Visual Basic is its inability to handle binary data. All files must be in ASCII text format with only carriage return and line feed as the only control characters. This actually fits in nicely with what I wrote earlier in the book with only using man-readable files.

Visual Basic is a gigantic programming language and code specification. As well, it also encompasses OLE devices and other Windows application-development tools. Despite the vast abilities available, the BASIC language used in the application is the Microsoft standard established with GW-BASIC and continued in QBASIC.

Learning Visual Basic

Learning Visual Basic is actually quite an easy proposition with the Learning Edition of the tool because included with it is a CD-ROM that contains an audio-visual course and sample applications showing how Visual Basic applications are created. I found that I needed about a week of mornings to go through the CD-ROM and work through the example applications. At the end of the week, I felt I was comfortable with Visual Basic and ready to start doing my own applications.

At the end of the CD-ROM course, you will be able to create what I would call *intermediate applications*, which do not interface with any external hardware or operating-system APIs, but do work through the language very completely. After working through the course and developing some sample applications for yourself, you are ready for the next step to start controlling hardware from your applications. The next chapter shows some built-in controls. Later, the book presents Windows device drivers and how to interface Visual Basic to the hardware.

For Visual Basic and Visual C++, the Learning Edition of the tools, even though they are the least expensive, provide the best information for getting you off the ground. The multimedia CD-ROMs are quite good and references you can go back to when you've upgraded to Professional and Enterprise editions.

An even better reason for starting with the Learning Edition of the development tools, Microsoft offers a substantial rebate on the cost of the Learning Edition if you upgrade to the Professional and Enterprise editions of the development tools. This will save you quite a bit of money over buying low-level books to learn how to develop Visual Basic and Visual C++ applications.

To learn the operations of the BASIC language statements, I suggest that you find a used copy of the QBASIC specification. This will provide you with the syntax of the instructions, as well as a list of what is available.

TIC-TAC-TOE SHOWING OFF VISUAL BASIC

This chapter shows how quickly you can begin working with Visual Basic, but I wanted to give you an actual example. As I went through the Learning Edition's training CD-ROM, after I completed a chapter (the Visual Basic CD-ROM has 11 chapters), I created my own application. After the first chapter, I created the Tic-Tac-Toe game presented here. I realize that a few features used are presented in later chapters, but once you get the basic ideas, you can really run with it.

The application presented here is quite simple, with an array of nine tiles that you or the computer can mark. The object of the game is to mark three tiles in a row, up and down, side to side, or diagonally before the computer can.

The preceding paragraph will probably make you feel like you have a chance to win. If you feel like you can win, you are wrong. The best you can hope for against this game is a tie (nobody wins). The computer starts first and places its first move in one of the four corner tiles. This follows with the strategy of getting to the point where it can win by marking one of two tiles, leaving you with the impossible task of trying to mark the two. This strategy is shown in Fig. 34-5. It is possible to block the computer from winning, but you'll have to figure out how.

Each tile in the dialog box is part of a three-by-three array of control buttons. This means that when one of the tile buttons is clicked, a central event handler, which is common to the nine tiles, is invoked. When the event handler is invoked, the array number of the last tile to be selected is returned.

The strategy used by the event handler is pretty simple. First, it checks to see if the tile is free; if it is not, then the event is ignored. If the tile is free, the user move is marked. A simple algorithm checks the current captions in the nine tiles and responds with a move in the following priority sequence.

1 If the move results in a win
2 If the user can win on their next move, the user is blocked
3 If a corner is open, follow the strategy in Fig. 34-5
4 Mark the first available free tile

When the computer wins, you'll notice that the empty tiles are marked with a period (.) to prevent the user from marking any more additional moves. The reason for doing this is

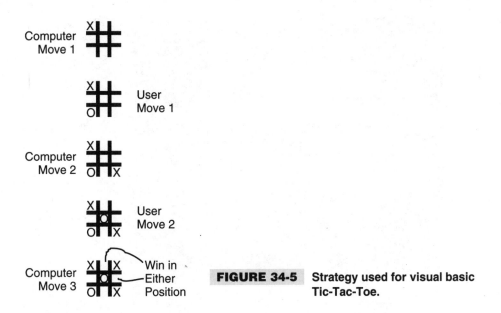

Computer Move 1

User Move 1

Computer Move 2

User Move 2

Computer Move 3 — Win in Either Position

FIGURE 34-5   Strategy used for visual basic Tic-Tac-Toe.

to avoid the need for having any global variables. The code itself just checks the tile captions, rather than use a global array variable. To reset the game, the tiles' captions are cleared when the computer makes the first move.

Notice that the computer can start in any corner, based on the 0.01 second of the current time when the New Game button is clicked. This is a simple way to add randomness to an application.

Creating the game you see here took me about two hours and was started after I had only an hour's introduction to Visual Basic and the Learning Edition's multimedia CD-ROM.

Developing and Debugging Visual Basic Applications

I use the Visual Basic development system IDE and the method of Visual Basic or Windows application-development process I outlined earlier in the book. The application is developed by starting with the dialog box first (which, by the way, can be run and ended by clicking on the *X* at the upper right corner box). Next, the simple control interfaces are coded and tested. Finally, the complete application code is added to the application and tested. By going through this process, there really won't be a lot of opportunities for difficult-to-debug errors to creep in.

Another good idea to simplify debugging of the application is to save the current project and all its files between each step in this process (or after every major feature of the application has been installed). That way, if you discover that you've taken a wrong turn somewhere in your development, you can go back and take a look at the problem from its inception, rather than repair the damage.

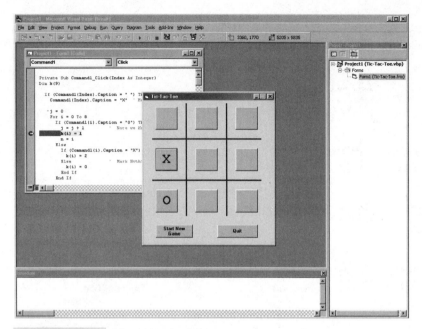

FIGURE 34-6 Visual basic debug screen.

With this type of code development, there is one potential problem that you can run into and that is not properly commenting and documenting the source code. If you look at the Tic-Tac-Toe example in the previous section, you'll see virtually no comments and as you start working with Visual Basic as a "what if" tool, you'll often discover that you've completed the application without any comments at all! Force yourself, as much as possible, to add appropriate comments while you are developing the application code.

When the code executes it is possible to set breakpoints and monitor variables within the Debug menu that becomes active at breakpoints or if errors occur during the application (Fig. 34-6).

To set a breakpoint, the cursor is set to the line of code you want to stop at and the breakpoint is set either by pressing *F9* or right mouse button is clicked and the breakpoint option is selected from the Debug pull down. Variables and control properties can be watched or queried from the Window at the bottom of the Debug screen. The debug keystrokes follow the CodeView convention.

This level of debugging is not as complete as what you would get from full debuggers, such as the Visual C++ debugger or "CodeView" tools. However, it is more than sufficient for monitoring the execution of your applications and finding where the execution of your Visual Basic is executing incorrectly and fix it.

35

VISUAL

BASIC

CONTROLS

CONTENTS AT A GLANCE

Standard Controls

Custom Controls

MSComm Serial Control
VISUAL BASIC CRANE CONTROL

As described in the previous chapter code is written to support the different features or controls of the dialog boxes. These controls can be visible, invisible, and can be affected by different program operations or all interfaces with hardware in the PC. You will find that working with them within Visual Basic is really quite simple.

Controls are buttons, text boxes, graphics, and whatever else is to be displayed within the dialog box of a Visual Basic application. These controls can either be taken from the toolbox (Fig. 35-1) or created in software as a custom control.

Visual Basic controls are governed by Properties (Fig. 35-2), which are unique to each type of control and each instance of the control. Properties can be set at application development time or during run time to change the look, value, or operation of the control. This chapter covers the different Visual Basic controls in more detail, as well as introduce you to the MSCOMM control that allows Visual Basic applications to interface directly with the PC's serial port.

Although I have focussed on Visual Basic, these controls are also appropriate for Visual C++ and other Windows application-development tools.

Visual
Basic
"ToolBox"
of
Controls

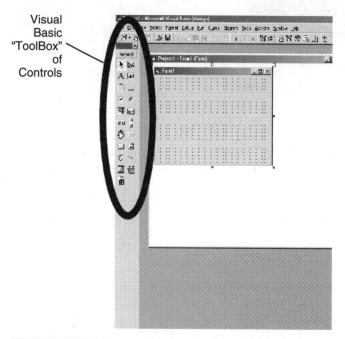

FIGURE 35-1 Visual basic control "toolbox".

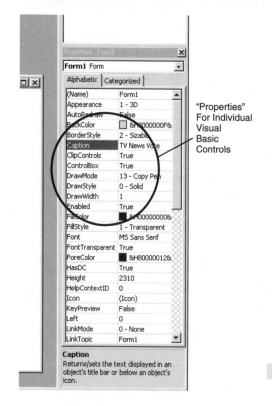

"Properties"
For Individual
Visual
Basic
Controls

FIGURE 35-2 Visual basic control
"properties".

Standard Controls

When creating Visual Basic applications, I usually break the available controls into a few categories that simplify what is to be done. This section covers the categories that are best suited for hardware interfaces and how to use them. These categories are actually quite simple and range from simple I/O to controls that you can create yourself (shown in the next section).

The most basic controls in Windows dialog boxes are buttons. These buttons respond to mouse clicks as the only input. The basic button control is the CommandButton (Command1 on Fig. 35-3). The CommandButton responds when the mouse is pointing to it and the left button is clicked.

Data can be selected either by manually entering it into a buttons text box or by putting up OptionButtons or CheckBoxes. These buttons are used to select different options from a list. To have them work correctly in this fashion, they should be loaded as groups or arrays.

OptionButtons will only allow one button of the array to be selected at any one time while multiple CheckBoxes can be selected at the same time. Normally, for these types of buttons, an action is not taken for selecting one of them, but is instead used to tabulate information and when a CommandButton is clicked, the information is processed.

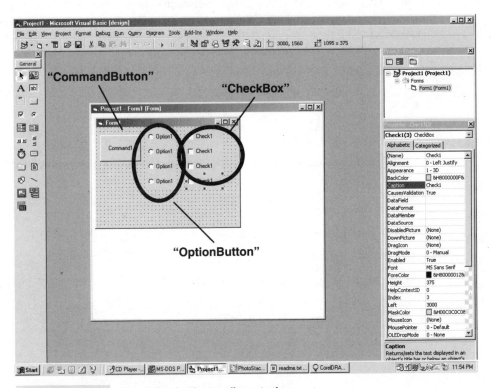

FIGURE 35-3 Visual basic "button" controls.

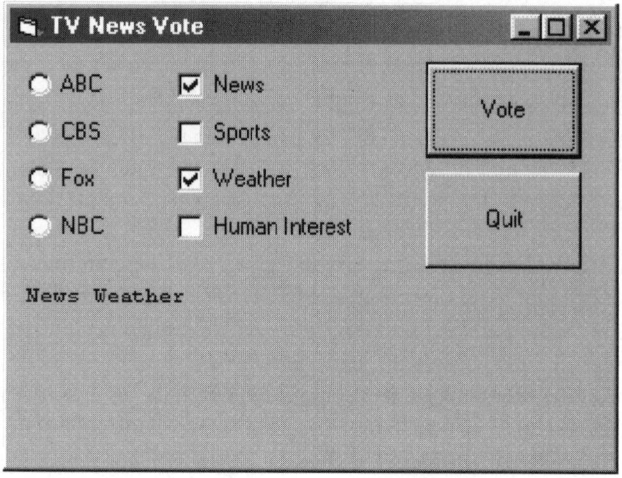

FIGURE 35-4   "News Ballot" dialog box.

Rearranging Fig. 35-3, I created the Voting Application (shown in Fig. 35-4) for allowing a viewer select which TV network they get their news from and what segments they watch most closely.

Notice that I have added the Quit CommandButton, which is used to end the application. Its code is very simple and double clicking on the control in the Object dialog box creates the procedure prototype for it. Next, the processing code is entered into the prototype.

Quit in most Visual Basic applications is usually very simple:

```
Private Sub Command2_Click()

  End  '  Quite the Program

End Sub
```

And the "Vote" code shows how the network and New item selection is processed:

```
Private Sub Command1_Click()
'  Tabulate Results

  Label1.Caption = ""

  If Option1(0).Value = True Then
    Label1.Caption = "ABC "
  ElseIf Option1(1).Value = True Then
    Label1.Caption = "CBS "
  ElseIf Option1(2).Value = True Then
    Label1.Caption = "Fox "
  ElseIf Option1(3).Value = True Then
    Label1.Caption = "NBC "
  End If

  If Check1(0) = 1 Then
    Label1.Caption = Label1.Caption & "News "
```

```
   End If
.  If Check1(1) = 1 Then
      Label1.Caption = Label1.Caption & "Sports "
   End If
   If Check1(2) = 1 Then
      Label1.Caption = Label1.Caption & "Weather "
   End If
   If Check1(3) = 1 Then
      Label1.Caption = Label1.Caption & "Human Interest "
   End If

End Sub
```

Text data can be displayed and entered with a dialog box in three different formats as well (Fig. 35-5).

In each of these cases, the application code can write to the text boxes Caption property to print information back to the user. When the user inputs text data, it overwrites the previous caption value. Normally, text boxes are designed so that the text caption data doesn't shift beyond the control limits (although this can be changed by the Properties).

In the News Ballot example, I use the text block Caption property to temporarily store data that is displayed to the user. As I tabulate more data to display, I use the Concatenate function (the "&" for strings) of Visual Basic to add selected values to the output string.

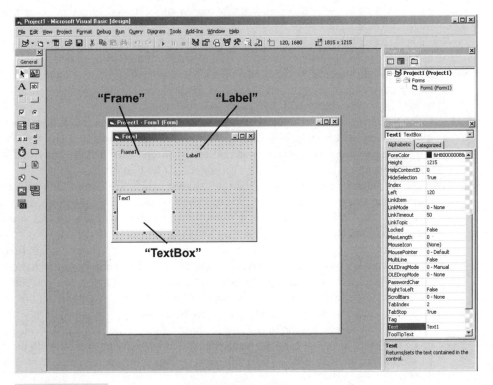

FIGURE 35-5   Different types of "text controls".

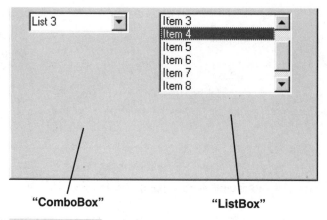

"ComboBox"   "ListBox"

FIGURE 35-6   Different types of "list controls".

The two list controls: ComboBox and ListBox are an interesting combination of the button controls and text controls presented previously (Fig. 35-6).

The ComboBox can display a text message and take user input, or a pull-down menu can be displayed with a list of different selections that can be used to save the user the effort of keying in a selection. This can be a useful control when hardware is used because it allows the casual user to use predefined controls, but for application debugging, or the advanced user, a specific value can be displayed.

The ListBox presents a list of different items for the user to choose from in a scrolling box. This control is really analogous to the OptionButton described previously. The ListBox has the difference that it can take up a lot less space than a list of options and, by selecting the control and keying in a letter (or number), the control will automatically scroll to the first list element, which starts with that character.

The list controls should be used with an Execute button, as does the Button Controls to initiate action by the application. Double clicking on the controls will bring up a control procedure prototype as for the CommandButton, but the user will probably find it awkward and nonintuitive to have to click on or press *Enter* to initiate an action.

The OLE and File Specification controls (known as one "Common Controls") are well documented in the Learning Visual Basic CD-ROM, as well as numerous introductory texts to Visual Basic. Although I won't go into them here, I will suggest that you should use these controls to give your application a "standard" feel.

Graphics can add quite a bit to your application—even if they are quite small. In the Tic-Tac-Toe game presented in the previous section, I added some lines to the dialog box to delineate the different squares on the playing surface. I found that it really added a lot to the game and made the operation much more intuitive. The bomb graphic for this application was created using "Paint" that comes with Windows.

To create the graphic, I first set Paint to show a bitmap the size that I wanted for the bomb (64 by 128) and then set the background to a light gray to blend in with the default background of the dialog box. The bomb itself is black with a white stripe to give the illu-

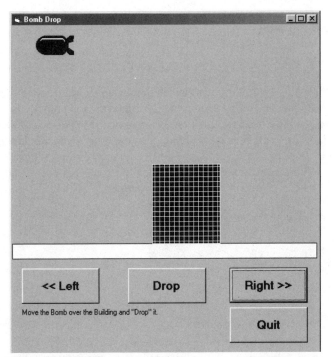

FIGURE 35-7   "Bomb drop" visual basic application.

sion that it is round. Using Paint, I was able to create the bomb bitmap is just a few minutes. More-complex graphics programs can be used, but for most bitmap icon and graphic creation, I find Paint to be more than adequate.

With graphics, animation can be simply implemented and add a lot to the application. To show what I mean, I created the simple game Bomb Drop (Fig. 35-7).

In this game, the user moves the bomb left and right. When they feel it is over the building, it can be dropped. When the bomb is dropped, its position is changed by 130 pixels every second until it impacts on the building or the terrain below.

Changing the bomb's position vertically was accomplished by using a timer and moving the bomb graphic control's position every time the time interval passed. The code that does this is very simple:

```
Private Sub Timer1_Timer()
'  Time the Falling of the Bomb

  If Image1.Top < 3360 Then
    Image1.Top = Image1.Top + 130
  Else  '  Bomb has landed
    Timer1.Enabled = False
    If ((Image1.Left >= 3000) And (Image1.Left <= 5640)) Then
      Label1.Caption = "*** Hit *** - Press 'Reset' to Start Again"
    Else
      Label1.Caption = "Miss - Press 'Reset' to Start Again"
```

```
    End If
    Command3.Caption = "Reset"
  End If

End Sub
```

In this code, each time the timer overflows (which is four times per second), the bomb image is moved down by incrementing its top property. When the top property is equal to the top of the building, then its horizontal position is compared to the position of the building and if the bomb is at least half over the building, then the drop is classified as a "hit."

Before the Bomb is dropped, the bomb is moved using the < *Left* and *Right* > CommandButtons. These buttons each move the bomb when the control is clicked on. In the following code, here is the < *Left* control response subroutine:

```
Private Sub Command1_Click()
' Move Left

  If Command3.Caption = "Drop" Then
    If Image1.Left > 240 Then
      Image1.Left = Image1.Left - 20
    End If
  End If

End Sub
```

Notice that I only check to see that the bomb is not beyond the left edge of the dialog box. When moving to the right, I only check for the bomb going past the right boundary. I also ensure the bomb isn't falling when the button is pressed. If it is, then the move is not allowed. These simple rules allow the movement on the screen to be very simple.

After trying out Bomb Drop, you'll probably feel like I wasn't very successful with it; the game is really not a significant challenge and moving the bomb left and right is tedious. The purpose of this application is not to amuse you and replace "Solitaire" in your Windows Games folder, but to show what was possible with very little effort.

For both graphics and animation, I find that less is more. One or two graphics "smarten up" an application's dialog box and give it a very professional appearance. Animation is an excellent tool to show that something is happening when, normally, the screen would just sit doing nothing, waiting for the hardware operation to complete and ignoring the user's input.

If multiple graphics and animation are used, then the application will take on the appearance of an arcade game and be hard for the user to follow what's going on. As well, graphics or icons that you create and think are completely intuitive might be indecipherable to different users (especially if they are from different cultures).

Just as a follow up to the "arcade game" comment, I think it's interesting to note that using the controls presented in this section, along with animation, you now have all the information to recreate many early arcade games. With what I've shown here, Pong is an obvious one (although you'll have to come up with a good two-player interface), but many others could be replicated with surprising ease.

This really shows the power of Visual Basic. Many of these games can be recreated in Visual Basic with very little effort and will run as well (or better) on a modern PC. If you do come up with anything interesting, please let me know.

Along with these standard controls, Visual Basic also has a number of controls that can be added to the application, including serial and ActiveX controls. Later this chapter shows how these controls can be added to the toolbox running down the left-hand side of the Visual Basic IDE. In advanced Visual Basic texts, you can also learn how to develop your own controls and link them into the Toolbox for use in applications, as if they were provided with Visual Basic.

Custom Controls

One of the aspects that I like the most about Visual Basic is its ability to create custom controls for different situations. After looking at the Visual Basic's IDE, you might feel like you are limited to just text boxes or bringing up graphics on cue. With a bit of ingenuity, you can come up with some interesting displays that will really enhance your application and make it easier to work with the user.

For this section, I came up with the Visual Basic application in the Custom subdirectory. In this application, I show how an analog bar graph can be implemented, some simple animation, using lights for displaying bits and some buttons that I have "rolled" on my own. These are not full controls, but they can be created and used easily and add a lot to the application.

When you run CUSTOM.EXE (Fig. 35-8), you'll see the bar graph at the top "grow" to the end, then move to the far left and start growing again. In the circle, a line will turn around, looking like an old-style radar display. As the bar graph grows, the bit pattern shows the width of the diagonal yellow bar and if you click the mouse over the four buttons, you'll see the background turn yellow for a quarter of a second. It is an interesting display (although it might flash a bit because a lot of pixels are being updated on the display).

The code needed to create this dialog box is actually quite simple and you should be able to develop a similar display with only an introduction to Visual Basic programming. To provide the motion and action, I use three timers to interrupt and cause motion. Instead of using the timers, the displays can be used for showing information from sensors or used with the mouse to select a new position for the hardware.

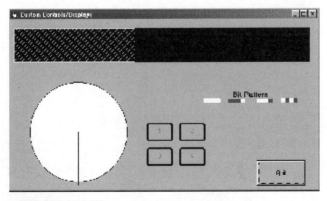

FIGURE 35-8   Custom control dialog box.

Using two rectangular shapes with the size of the top one arbitrarily varied produced the bar graph at the top of the dialog box. The diagonal yellow box is overlaid over the black-filled box and its width is varied according to the value to be displayed. For the custom application, I used a timer to delay 100 ms before incrementing the display. To display an actual value, as a fraction of the total size, the timer event routine could be replaced with:

```
Shape2.Width = Size * Shape1.Width
```

As the yellow diagonal box grows, it also displays the numeric value as a set of bits (bit pattern). This was produced by a series of boxes, which I change the DrawMode property from whiteness (value 16) to draw pen (value 9). This changes each bit from white, to the fill color, which I've set to red.

The "radar scope" at the bottom left of the display consists of a circle with eight radial lines. Normally, each line is set with the Visible property set to False. To imitate motion, every 50 ms, one of the line's Visible property is set to True, while the previous one is set to False. This gives the illusion of movement without having to move or load/create lines. Another way to do this (and is demonstrated at the end of this chapter) is to use Visual Basic's trigonometric functions (i.e., sine and cosine) to place one end of the line on the correct location on the circle for the current angle.

Each of these three types of displays uses tricks that would be familiar to early PC games programmers. If you ever worked with the graphics on the Atari 400/800 or Commodore 64, the changing of properties should seem familiar to you as a fast way to provide graphic motion. Using the technique of simply changing the properties of controls on a dialog box can give you some quite impressive capabilities without investing a significant amount of programming effort.

The new input controls (the 1, 2, 3, and 4 boxes in the lower center of the dialog box) turn yellow for 250 ms when you click on them. These controls were built using a rounded rectangle with a text box in the middle of them. For the text boxes, I set the Enabled property to False so that being clicked on the text box would not prevent the mouse press from being sampled. I found that if the Enabled property was True, then mouse clicks over the numbers would not be picked up.

The code that monitors the mouse clicks checks the position of the mouse when the left button is down and if it is within one of the button's boundaries, sets the appropriate button as Active.

```
Private Sub Form_MouseDown(Button As Integer, Shift As Integer,
                           X As Single, Y As Single)

If (Y >= 3000) And (Y <= 3495) Then
   If (X >= 4080) And (X <= 4815) Then
      Shape5(0).FillStyle = 0
      Timer3.Enabled = True
   ElseIf (X >= 5040) And (X <= 5775) Then
      Shape5(1).FillStyle = 0
      Timer3.Enabled = True
   End If
ElseIf (Y >= 3720) And (Y <= 4215) Then
   If (X >= 4080) And (X <= 4815) Then
      Shape5(2).FillStyle = 0
      Timer3.Enabled = True
   ElseIf (X >= 5040) And (X <= 5775) Then
```

```
        Shape5(3).FillStyle = 0
        Timer3.Enabled = True
      End If
   End If

End Sub
```

When the routine is entered, the current position of the mouse is given as X and Y. This value is then checked for the start of the box, as well as the furthest edge. If the mouse is within these borders, the FillStyle is set to Solid (value 0) from Transparent (value 1).

Once the button is pressed, then Timer3 is enabled to time out after 250 ms to turn itself off, as well as turn all the buttons back to Transparent FillStyle.

This method of providing a separate event monitor for the mouse can also be used to specify exact positions. For example, using MouseMove, a dragged mouse could be used to specify the position of a control (such as the bar graph in the custom example).

The use of custom controls really shows off the capabilities of Visual Basic and should give you an idea of how Visual Basic can be used as an excellent "what if" tool. The "custom" application, although I probably spent a couple of hours getting in the format for this section, could probably be created in 10 minutes or less by experienced Visual Basic programmers that have an idea of exactly what they want to see in their application.

Using these techniques and ideas, you can come up with controls that are well suited to your hardware to give special meaning to how the circuitry works. Later in this chapter, I'll show what I mean.

What I have shown here is only halfway to creating "full" custom controls. I define a *full custom control* as being compilable into a control that can be selected from the toolbox on the left of the Visual Basic integrated development environment. The custom controls shown here are really just custom graphics that can be added to an application. I haven't gone the full way and linked them into the toolbox simply because it is not required in this application. It might be required and desired to be separately compiled and stored in the toolbox if the controls are going to be used in multiple applications.

I should also point out that there are a plethora of controls available both at a price as well as free of charge from the internet. These controls range from giving your application the appearances of having a LCD alpha-numeric display to giving your application "analog" controls.

MSComm Serial Control

In Visual Basic, if you are willing to "prowl" around and look through what kind of "extra" controls are available, you will find that there is the MSComm serial communications control. This control allows you direct access to the serial ports within the PC and allows you to interface directly with the serial port hardware without having to load in device drivers. The MSComm control itself is very easy to use; the biggest problem that you will have is trying to figure out how to enable it.

When you first load up Visual Basic, you are given a basic number of controls in the toolbox down the left side of the development screen. These controls, as pointed out earlier in the chapter, are a basic number needed to execute most initial (beginner's) Visual Basic applications. The basic controls can be expanded with not only the MSComm Serial Port Con-

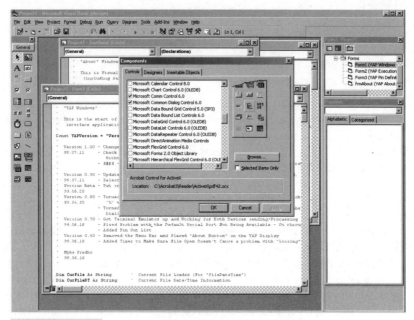

FIGURE 35-9   Setting up the "MSComm" control.

trols, but also Microsoft ActiveX and OLE controls, but "Kodak Image" and "Macrovision" "Shockwave" controls, along with a lot of other controls and objects that you can use.

For adding the MSComm serial port control to the available selection, you can click on Project, followed by Component and then Apply Microsoft Comm Control, as shown in Fig. 35-9.

With the control added to the toolbox, you can now use MSComm with your applications.

To demonstrate how simple MSComm is to work with, I created the tag crane control that is discussed later in the chapter. I have also used MSComm to provide an initial Visual Basic front end to my "YAP" Microchip PICMicro programmer. The "YAP" programmer is a fairly complex programmer that was designed to interface only with PC and workstation serial ports to program PICMicros. This programmer follows that the philosophy I introduced earlier in the book for serial devices, which is that they have to be usable from a simple terminal emulator without requiring special software.

With the programmer working, I wanted to provide a simple Windows front end to demonstrate and simplify how the programmer works. The initial dialog box, I came up with is shown in Fig. 35-10.

To work with the MSComm control, after loading the control onto the toolbox, I placed MSComm's Telephone icon on the dialog box, similarly as I would with the timer. When the application is executing, the telephone is invisible to the user.

To initialize the MSComm control, I used the recommended sequence that consists of:

1 Specify the hardware serial port to be used.
2 Set the speed and data format to be used.
3 Define the buffer size.
4 Open the port and begin to use it.

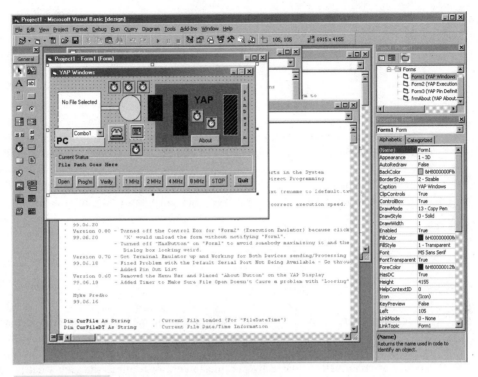

FIGURE 35-10 "YAP" "MSComm" control.

The code used to perform these functions are placed in the Form_Load subroutine, which means that the port is enabled before the primary dialog box is executing. Although the control values should be self-explanatory, they are covered in greater detail later in the chapter.

```
Private Sub Form_Load()
'  On Form Load, Setup Serial Port 3 for YAP Programmer

  MSComm3.CommPort = 3

  MSComm3.Settings = "1200,N,8,1"

  MSComm3.InputLen = 0

  MSComm3.PortOpen = True

  Text1.Text = "Turn on YAP Programmer"

End Sub
```

With the port initialized and executing, I use a 50-ms timer to continually poll the serial port and display data in the Text box when it is received.

```
Private Sub Timer1_Timer()
'  Interrupt every 50 msecs and Read in the Buffer
Dim InputString

  InputString = MSComm3.Input
```

```
    If (InputString <> "") Then
       If (Text1.Text = "Turn on YAP Programmer") Then
         Text1.Text = ""  ' Clear the Display Buffer
       End If
       Text1.Text = Text1.Text + InputString
    End If

End Sub
```

This application code first prompts the user to turn on the programmer. If it is when data is received, the Text display is cleared and data is placed in sequence on the display.

For specialized operations (such as starting device programming), I used CommandButton controls, which send data to the YAP via the serial port using the code:

```
Private Sub Command1_Click()
'  Open File for Processing

    handle = open L)

End Sub
```

With these controls, the YAP can be controlled using the buttons and the mouse with the dialog much more quickly and efficiently (i.e., little chance for error) than if the commands were entered manually by the user. One nice feature of this application is the text box that is continually updated by the timer interrupt routine, showing what is actually happening with the YAP and allow the user to debug problems very quickly.

Once the MSComm control is placed on the display, the following properties are used to control it:

PROPERTY	SETTING	DESCRIPTION
Break	True/False	When set to True, Break Sends a *0* break signal until the property is changed to False.
CDHolding	True/False	Read-only property that indicates if the Carrier Detect line is active. This is an important line to poll in applications which use modems.
CommEvent	Integer	Read-only property that is only available while the application is running. If the application is running without any problems, this property returns zero. This property is read by the OnComm event handler code to process the reason why the event was caused.
CommID	Object	Read-only property that returns an identifier for the serial port assigned to the MSComm control.
CommPort	Integer	Specify the "COMx" (1-3) serial port that is used by the MSComm control.

CTSHolding	True/False	Read-only property that returns the current state of the serial port's Clear To Send line.
DSRHolding	True/False	Read-only property that returns the current state of the serial port's Data Set Ready line.
DTREnable	True/False	Property used to specify the state of the Data Terminal Ready line.
EOFEnable	True/False	Specify whether or not an OnComm event will be generated if an End-Of-File character (0x01A) is encountered.
Handshaking	0, 1, 2 or 3	Sets the current handshaking protocol for the serial port: 0 - No handshaking (default) 1 - XON/XOFF Handshaking 2 - RTS/CTS (Hardware) Handshaking 3 - Both XON/XOFF and RTS/CTS Handshaking
InBufferCount	Integer	Read-only property indicating how many characters have been received by the serial port.
InBufferSize	Integer	Property used to specify the number of bytes available for the Input Data Buffer. The default size is 1024 bytes.
Input	String	Return a String of Characters from the Input Buffer.
InputMode	Integer	Specify how data is to be retrieved using the Input property. Zero specifies data will be received as Text (Default). One will specify that data will be passed without editing (Binary format).
InputLen	Integer	Sets the maximum number of characters that will be returned when the Input property is accessed. Setting this value to zero will return the entire buffer.
NullDiscard	True/False	Specify whether or not Null Characters are transferred from the port to the receiver buffer.
OutBufferCount	Integer	Read-only property that returns the Number of Characters waiting in the Output Buffer.
OutBufferSize	Integer	Specify the size of the Output Buffer. The default is 512 Bytes.
Output	Integer	Output a string of characters through the serial port.
ParityReplace	Integer	Specify the character that will replace characters which have a Parity Error. The default character is *?* and the ASCII code for the replacement character must be specified.
PortOpen	True/False	Specify whether or not the data port is to be transmitting and receiving data. Normally, a port is closed (False).

4

WINDOWS PROGRAMMING

Rthreshold	Integer	Specify the number of characters before there is an OnComm event. The default value of zero disables event generation. Setting the *Rthreshold* to *one* will cause an OnComm event each time a character is received.
RTSEnable	True/False	Specify the value output on the Request To Send line.
Settings	String	Send a String to the Serial Port to specify its operating characteristics. The String is in the format *Speed, Parity, Length, Stop*, with the following valid parameter values:

Speed: Data Rate of the Communication
    110
    300
    600
    1200
    2400
    9600 (Default)
    14400
    19200
    28800
    38400
    56000
    128000
    256000

Parity: The type of error checking sent with the byte
E - Even Parity
M - Mark Parity
N - No Parity (Default)
O - Odd Parity
S - Space Parity

Length: The number of bits transmitted at a time
4 - 4 Bits
5 - 5 Bits
6 - 6 Bits
7 - 7 Bits
8 - 8 Bits (Default)

Stop: The number of stop bits transmitted with the byte
1 - 1 Stop Bit (Default)
1.5 - 1.5 Stop Bits
2 - 2 Stop Bits

Sthreshold	Integer	Specify the number of bytes to be transmitted before an OnComm event is generated. The default is zero (which means no OnComm event is generated for transmission). Setting this value to one will cause an OnComm event after each character is transmitted.

These properties are quite simple to use and will allow you to quickly develop and debug serial Visual Basic applications.

Further enhancing the usefulness of the MSComm control is the OnComm event. This routine is similar to an interrupt because it is requested after specified events in the serial port. The CommEvent property contains the reason code for the event. These codes include:

COMMEVENT IDENTIFIER	COMMEVENT CODE	DESCRIPTION
comEvSend	1	Specified Number of Characters Sent
comEvReceive	2	Specified Number of Characters Received
comEvCTS	3	Change in the Clear To Send line
comEvDSR	4	Change in the Data Set Ready line
comEvCD	5	Change in the Carrier Detect line
comEvRing	6	Ring Detect is Active
comEvEOF	7	End-of-File Character Detected
comEventBreak	1001	Break Signal Received
comEventFrame	1004	Framing Error in incoming data
comEventOverrun	1006	Receive Port Overrun
comEventRxOver	1008	Receive Buffer Overflow
comEventRxParity	1009	Parity Error in Received Data
comEventTxFull	1010	Transmit Buffer Full
comEventDCB	1011	Unexpected Device Control Block Error

These values can be processed in the OnComm event handler, as in:

```
Private Sub Object_OnComm()
' Handle Serial Port Events

  Select Case Object.CommEvent
    Case comEventBreak  ' Handle a "Break" Received
      Beep
      :                      '  Handle other events
  End Select
End Sub
```

To identify the serial port object, I have italicized the word "Object" in the OnComm event handler to make the label used for the serial port more noticeable in the code above.

For basic OnComm events, to allow the OnComm handler to respond to the problems, the OnComm handler code simply has to be written. If the handler is not present and the error or event occurs, then it will be simply ignored by Visual Basic.

FIGURE 35-11 Toy crane.

VISUAL BASIC CRANE CONTROL

Usually when programming languages and development systems are described by their owners, such adjectives as "efficient," "fast," and "simple" are used. This is unfortunate because the adjective I would use for Visual Basic is "fun." I really enjoy coming up with new ways to work with the language and development tools and, with a little work, you can come up with something that is pretty spectacular, such as the Visual Basic Crane Control, which I created one afternoon in less than three hours (Fig. 35-12).

This application is an extension of the serial motor controller presented earlier in the book and encompasses many of the concepts in terms of user interfacing, error handling, and developing unique controls for applications. When I developed the application, I wanted to simulate the crane (shown in Fig. 35-11) on a dialog box. By using the Lines and Shapes tool of Visual Basic, I created a crane shape (with a moving hook) along with an Angle circle to show where the crane is located (Fig. 35-12).

The Button controls to the left of the hook and at the bottom of the circle are used to initiate movement of the two degrees of freedom of the crane (hook up/down and turning), as well as stop them. The operation of the Visual Basic application shows the current position of these values, as well as continually poll the serial link to see if the crane control is active (this is displayed by a small dot in the upper right corner of the dialog box). The development of the dialog box (and with it, the application) is shown in Fig. 35-13.

Communication with the serial motor controller is accomplished by the MSComm control that is added to the application, as described. For the movement, I timed the operation of the crane and do not provide any feedback to the actual position to the user. The display

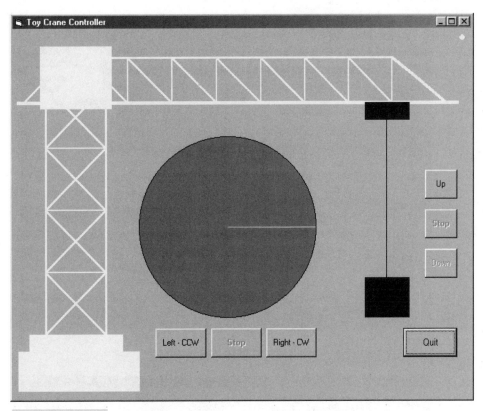

FIGURE 35-12 Serial crane control using motor controller.

shown is a rough guess (based on an assumed initial position. When the hook reaches the "top" or "bottom" of its travel (which takes 20 seconds), I stop the motors and disable the button control that would push it further. Ideally, the crane would have some way to report its position back to the controller to allow the user to know exactly the location of the various items.

Every second, a timer event (Timer1) is used to "ping" the serial control and see if the connection is still valid. The ping consists of sending an x ASCII character, followed by a carriage return. If this value is not returned by the serial controller, the application turns off the "Up light" (the circle in the upper right hand corner of the form) and disables the controls to the two motors (Fig. 35-14). When the link goes back up, the Up light is turned back on and the appropriate movement controls are enabled. This works quite well and gives the user some immediate feedback concerning the state of the link and what is happening (and prevents them from thinking that something is happening that is not).

The last point on serial interfacing has to do with the semaphore variable in the application. When you read through the code, you will see that I have set up a variable that is used to indicate whether an event handler is already working with the serial port when the current one is executing. This is important because although most of the movement commands are initiated by the user, the ping is accomplished by the timer event handlers and the semaphore is used to ensure that two different commands are not passed to the serial controller.

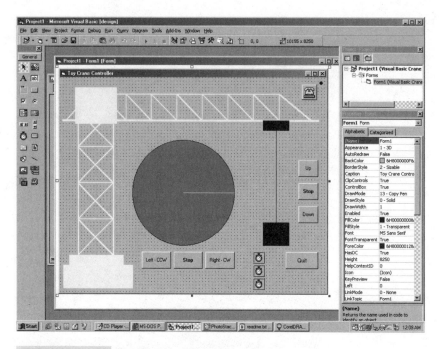

FIGURE 35-13 Serial crane dialog box design.

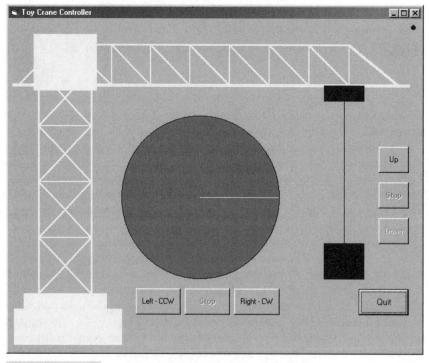

FIGURE 35-14 Serial crane with RS-232 link down.

When the Timer1 event handler is active, it sends x and CR to the serial motor controller. Rather than wait for the reply, it initiates Timer3 and ends. When Timer3 times out (in 0.100 seconds), it checks the received data for anything (actually x-, CR should be received) and, if the value is correct, it allows communications from the control buttons. If the link is down, then the buttons are disabled.

The operation of the semaphore is quite simple. In an event handler, if it is sending data to the serial port, it sets the semaphore and resets it when it is complete. The Timer1/Timer2 event handlers use a value of 2 to indicate that they have control of the serial port and are waiting for the reply to see if the link is available.

The actual application is quite complex, although it was very easy to develop. When you go through the source code for the application, you should look at the individual event handlers, each of which contains no more than 21 lines:

```
'  Crane Controller Declarations

Public Height2 As Integer
Public Direction As Integer
Public Semaphore As Integer
Public MoveState As Integer
Public TurnState As Integer
Public SerOn As Integer
Public StringIn As String
Public Text As String


Private Sub Command1_Click()
'  Application Finished

 End

End Sub

Private Sub Command2_Click()
'  Move the Crane Up
  If (SerOn = 0) And (Semaphore = 0) Then GoTo Command2End
  Semaphore = 1

  MoveState = 1
  If Timer2.Enabled = False Then Timer2.Enabled = True
  Command6.Enabled = True

'  Moving Motor 1 Up
  MSComm1.Output = "1B" + Chr$(13)
  Semaphore = 0
Command2End:

End Sub


Private Sub Command3_Click()
'  Move the Crane Down
  If (SerOn = 0) And (Semaphore = 0) Then GoTo Command3End
  Semaphore = 1

  MoveState = -1
  If Timer2.Enabled = False Then Timer2.Enabled = True
  Command6.Enabled = True
```

```
'   Moving Motor 1 Down
  MSComm1.Output = "1F" + Chr$(13)
  Semaphore = 0
Command3End:

End Sub

Private Sub Command4_Click()
'   Move the Crane Left/Counter ClockWise
  If (SerOn = 0) And (Semaphore = 0) Then GoTo Command4End
  Semaphore = 1

  TurnState = -1
  If Timer2.Enabled = False Then Timer2.Enabled = True
  Command7.Enabled = True

' Move the Crane Left/Counter Clockwise
  MSComm1.Output = "2F" + Chr$(13)
  Semaphore = 0
Command4End:

End Sub

Private Sub Command5_Click()
'   Move the Crane Left/Counter ClockWise
  If (SerOn = 0) And (Semaphore = 0) Then GoTo Command5End
  Semaphore = 1

  TurnState = 1
  If Timer2.Enabled = False Then Timer2.Enabled = True
  Command7.Enabled = True

' Move the Crane Right/Clockwise
  MSComm1.Output = "2B" + Chr$(13)
  Semaphore = 0
Command5End:

End Sub

Private Sub Command6_Click()
' Stop the Crane From Moving Up
  If (SerOn = 0) And (Semaphore = 0) Then GoTo Command6End
  Semaphore = 1

  MoveState = 0
  Command6.Enabled = False

'   "Stop" Motor 1
  MSComm1.Output = "1S" + Chr$(13)
  Semaphore = 0
Command6End:

End Sub

Private Sub Command7_Click()
'   Stop the Crane from Turning
  If (SerOn = 0) And (Semaphore = 0) Then GoTo Command7End
  Semaphore = 1

  TurnState = 0
  Command7.Enabled = False
```

```
'  "Stop" Motor 2
  MSComm1.Output = "2B" + Chr$(13)
  Semaphore = 0
Command7End:

End Sub

Private Sub Form_Load()

  Height2 = 0        '  Starting at the Bottom
  Direction = 0      '  Starting at Angle == 0
  Semaphore = 0      '  Nobody using the Serial Port
  MoveState = 0      '  Assume the Crane is not Moving
  TurnState = 0
  SerOn = 0          '  Assume that the Link is Down

  MSComm1.CommPort = 3  '  Turn on the Serial Port
  MSComm1.Settings = "2400,N,8,1"
  MSComm1.InputLen = 0
  MSComm1.PortOpen = True

End Sub

Private Sub Timer1_Timer()
' One second "Ping" Timer
If Semaphore = 1 Then GoTo Timer1End

  StringIn = MSComm1.Input  '  Clear the Input Buffer

  Semaphore = 2             '  Mark What is Happening

  MSComm1.Output = "x" + Chr$(13)   '  Do a Ping on Serial Card

  Timer3.Enabled = True     '  Wait for Character to Come in

Timer1End:
End Sub

Private Sub Timer2_Timer()
' Half Second Movement Update Timer
  If SerOn = 1 Then GoTo Timer2Do
                            '  Link Failed:
  MoveState = 0             '  Stop Moving
  TurnState = 0

  Command2.Enabled = False
  Command3.Enabled = False
  Command4.Enabled = False
  Command5.Enabled = False
  Command6.Enabled = False
  Command7.Enabled = False

  GoTo Timer2Done

Timer2Do:

  If MoveState = 0 Then GoTo NoMove

    If MoveState = 1 Then Shape5.Top = Shape5.Top - 81 Else Shape5.Top =
Shape5.Top + 81
```

```
      If MoveState = 1 Then Line32.Y2 = Line32.Y2 - 81 Else Line32.Y2 =
Line32.Y2 + 81

      If Shape5.Top < 2041 Then MoveState = 0: Command2.Enabled = False:
Command6.Enabled = False Else Command2.Enabled = True

      If Shape5.Top > 5279 Then MoveState = 0: Command3.Enabled = False:
Command6.Enabled = False Else Command3.Enabled = True

      If MoveState <> 0 Then GoTo NoMove

' Turn off the "Move" Motor
   Semaphore = 1
   MSComm1.Output = "1S" + Chr$(13)
   Semaphore = 0

NoMove:                        ' Look for Updating the Turning Value

   If TurnState = 0 Then GoTo Timer2Done

   If TurnState = -1 Then Direction = Direction - 3 Else Direction =
Direction + 3
      If Direction > 359 Then Direction = Direction - 360
      If Direction < 0 Then Direction = Direction + 360

      Line34.X2 = (Cos((Direction * 3.141593) / 180) * 1920) + 4680
      Line34.Y2 = (Sin((Direction * 3.141593) / 180) * 1920) + 4200

Timer2Done:                    ' Finished with Timer2

End Sub

Private Sub Timer3_Timer()
'  Check to See if "Ping" Came Back

   Text = MSComm1.Input

   If Left(Text, 1) = "x" Then Shape7.FillColor = &H80FFFF: SerOn = 1
Else Shape7.FillColor = &H0&: SerOn = 0

   Timer3.Enabled = False     ' Turn Off Timer when Done

   Semaphore = 2              ' Clear the Semaphore

   If SerOn = 0 Then GoTo Timer3End

   If Shape5.Top > 2040 Then Command2.Enabled = True
   If Shape5.Top < 5280 Then Command3.Enabled = True

   Command4.Enabled = True
   Command5.Enabled = True

Timer3End:
End Sub
```

When I created the application, I first started with the dialog box. Next, I worked through the dialog-box animation controls. The code to move the crane position and hook was accomplished very quickly and surprisingly easily. With this done, I added the ping code and then ensured that the dialog box enables behaved appropriately if the application lost communication with the serial motor controller.

In many ways, this was a "text book" Visual Basic application development. This is really indicative of what I think is possible with Visual Basic. For just a few hours work, I was able to create an application very quickly and with a very high level of quality (few errors). The errors that I did have were easy to find and resolve during the development process.

36

VISUAL

C++

CONTENTS AT A GLANCE

Looking From 30,000 Feet

The Visual C++ Language
CLASSES

Microsoft Development Studio
APPSWIZARD
CLASSWIZARD

Microsoft Function Classes (MFC)

Debugging Visual C++ Programs

Tic-Tac-Toe—A First Visual C++ Program

If you are going through the entire book, the hardest thing to learn is Microsoft's Visual C++. Conceptually, Visual C++ is similar to Visual Basic. I found my biggest problem to be keeping track of the different "standard" classes and having appropriate reference information at my beck and call. When you go through introductory books and the training CD-ROM that comes with the Learning Edition, it won't seem that hard. The problems arise when you have completed the basic training and you feel like you are ready to create your own application. The most depressing sight in the world is the first time you see the Classview window (Fig. 36-1) after you have run through the AppsWizard.

As you go through this chapter, I hope you won't be disappointed to find out that I am not as comfortable with Visual C++ as I am with Visual Basic or even straight C. Visual C++ is not a programming environment where you can buy a beginner-level book and be

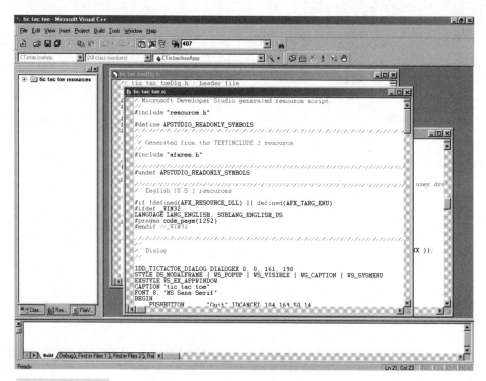

FIGURE 36-1   Visual C++ start up screen.

proficient within a week. I have talked to people who have been programming in Visual C++ for literally years and still feel like they are beginners.

Looking From 30,000 Feet

Throughout my professional career, when giving presentations, I've been told to give the "30,000-foot view." The purpose of a very high-level overview is to give the people being presented to an idea of what you are going to be doing and the major features that can be observed without getting lost in the weeds at "ground level." I've also found that this analogy is a potentially dangerous (at least from the viewpoint of the presenter) because an explanation of what is actually happening is lost when compared to lines of code (Fig. 36-2).

This is especially true when working with Visual C++. From 30,000 feet (or whatever overview height you want to use), the language and development environment appears identical to Visual Basic. Like Visual Basic, I develop applications by first developing dialog boxes and prototyping the application. Once the dialog boxes are up and working, the Windows development path that I presented earlier in the book (and use for Visual Basic) can also be used for Visual C++.

What is lost in a high-level overview is the complexity of working with Visual C++. When I work with Visual Basic, I find that I am able to work through it quite intuitively (relying on my half-remembered GW-BASIC skills) and quickly. This is not true with Vi-

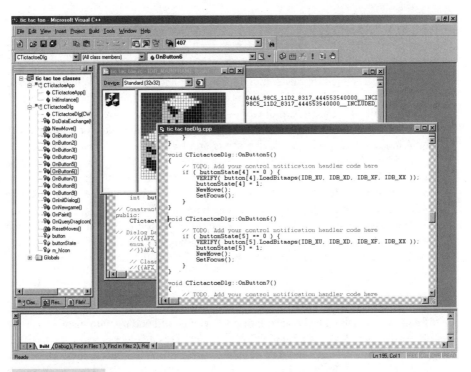

FIGURE 36-2

sual C++, where I have to continually go back and look at previous and demonstration applications to find code that shows what I want to do. As well, back referencing to Class and function information is required (and this seems to be a requirement that doesn't go away).

I'm sure that once I get a few years under my belt of exclusively working with Visual C++, this comment will have less relevance as I am able to work with the various classes and have a large library of code from which to draw. Having a large resource of code that I have developed on my own and can reuse is the secret to being able to efficiently develop Visual C++ applications.

Visual C++ might appear to be very similar to Visual Basic for Windows application development. The difficulty in initially getting the information you require will make initial application development effort quite difficult and a lot longer than you are probably used to. Visual C++ really shines in its ability to create code for a wide range of applications (including Windows command line and device drivers), which Visual Basic cannot match. As well, Visual C++, because it is object orientated, allows the reuse of classes and code much easier than Visual Basic and other languages.

My ideal development environment is to use Visual Basic for application code and C++ for developing hardware drivers. I find C++ to be a natural language for device-driver development because of its object-orientated bias. Device drivers tend to be very much "event driven," with much low-level programming, which is, to me at least, natural for C/C++. Visual C++ does have the built-in ability to naturally create *Dynamic Link Libraries (DLLs)*, along with extensions for the Microsoft *Software Development Kit (SDK)*, Microsoft *Device Driver Kit (DDK)*, and driver-development tools, such as Vireo's VtoolsD. Visual C++ also has the capability of creating straight "C" command line applications as well.

The Visual C++ Language

Visual C++ is much more than just Microsoft's implementation of the C++ language. Visual C++ is designed for developing highly complex and flexible Windows System applications. Because Visual C++'s focus is on Systems programming, becoming effective and efficient will take a great deal of work—much more than Visual Basic.

Visual C++ is a super-set of C, with extensions built in to make application development for Windows dialog box and device-driver applications. Visual C++ can be characterized as working similarly to Visual Basic, with the idea that dialog boxes can be created and controls clicked and prototype code generated for the programmer to enter in the appropriate responses. But the added complexity of Classes, both unique to the application and MFC makes creating simple programs much more difficult.

I have tried to structure this chapter as an introduction to Visual C++ and help explain the concepts that are used to develop Windows applications. Later, this book approaches creating Windows device drivers using Visual C++ as the base.

CLASSES

If you were to take the classes out of C++, you would end up with just C. Classes and the object-orientated programming philosophy that they engender is really the basis of C++ as a language and Visual C++ as a Windows programming environment. The concepts behind classes and objects are really quite simple; I find that the problems that I have with the language come from my unfamiliarity in programming with them and understanding exactly what is already available.

Visual C++ has all of the same characteristics of C and I highly recommend that before even attempting to learn C++, you are thoroughly versed and very comfortable with a MS-DOS command-line C implementation.

A class can be thought of as an advanced structure. Although a typical structure in C is used to describe a data type; the class is used to describe everything about an object.

An object in Visual C++ can be anything you want it to be; it can be a file, data records, Windows dialog boxes, etc. Objects can also be used to represent physical objects, such as a car, with four wheels, and an engine. Classes are instantiated in memory as data and functions, which represent the objects that are to be used in the application.

To manipulate the objects, instead of modifying the data used to represent the objects, the "methods" (usually functions) of the object are accessed instead. This provides a common interface to the object's properties and allows for type and value checking, which can help eliminate many of the common errors in applications and makes developing interfaces and APIs much easier.

Structures are available within C++, but I tend to avoid using them simply because I find them confusing when they are used with classes. This is also recommended in many introductory Visual C++ texts for exactly the same reason. Object-orientated programming really eschews the concept of data structures. If you are processing data in a specific format (such as recorded in a file), I could see the usefulness of using structures in this case. Otherwise, I would have to recommend that structures be avoided at all costs to minimize the confusion in the application code.

An object is declared much the same way as you would with a C variable. The class is analogous to C's type definition and is used exactly the same way to instantiate an object as a variable is declared:

```
ClassName ObjectName;
```

The term *instantiation* is really a $10 way of saying *declare and initialize* the object. When an object is instantiated, the data variables within the object are initialized using a Constructor function that prepares the data for the operation of the application.

Instantiating an object in the source, as shown previously, is known as *static instantiation* because the object is defined at application compile time. Objects can be instantiated "dynamically" during program execution using the *New* prefix to define an object to a pointer.

```
NewBall * Ball;

NewBall = new Ball();
```

In this example, *NewBall*, which is a pointer to data type *Ball*, has an object dynamically instantiated and given its pointer.

To delete a dynamically instantiated object, the "delete" operation is used. To delete the object created for *NewBall* in the previous example, the following code should be used:

```
delete NewBall;
```

Dynamic instantiation uses memory from the C++ heap space. The *heap space* in a high-level language is a block of memory used to temporarily store data, as well as provide a cache of memory for temporary data structures. In Visual C++, the heap provides the same function and care must be used with dynamically instantiating objects to ensure that they are all kept track of and before a pointer is changed, the object it is pointed to is either passed to another pointer or deleted.

Object classes consist of the blueprint for the object and contain the data variables (known as *data members*) and subroutines (known as *function members*), which process the object's data and provide an interface to the object's data, as well as application function. If a function member is used to access data members, it is known as a *method*.

It is considered bad object-orientated programming form to provide access outside of an object to the data members, instead, the function members should be the only interface to the data.

A class declaration can look like:

```
class Desk {                            //   Doing an Office Application -
                                        //     Need a Desk object type
private:                                //   Variable information
  int xPos, yPos;                       //   Position of the Desk
  color Color;                          //   Color of the Desk
  int Drawers;                          //   Number of Drawers

public:                                 //   Interface to the class/object
```

```
void SetPosition( int X, int Y );   //   Set the Position of the Desk
int  GetXPosition();                //   Return the "X" axis Position
int  GetYPosition();                //   Return the "Y" axis Position
int  Open_Drawer( int Num );        //   Open One of the Drawers

}  //  End "Desk" Class Definition
```

The member data and member functions, can be described as "public," "protected," or "private" (the default), which allows specific access to the different functions. These access specifiers are defined as operating as:

SPECIFIER	DATA MEMBERS	METHODS	CLASS DESCRIPTOR
Public	Can be Accessed throughout the application	Can be Accessed anywhere the Class can be accessed	Derived Class Inherits Base Class Public and Private Members
Protected	Can only be Accessed within the class and Derived classes	Can only be Accessed within the class and Derived classes	Derived Class Inherits Base Class Members and Makes them "protected"
Private	Can only be Accessed by Class Function Members	Can only be Accessed within the Class	Derived Class Inherits Base Class Members as "private" members of its Class

The data members should always be classed as *private* and the methods should always be classed as *Public*. Any intermediate class functions should be classed as *Private* to prevent inadvertent access by other classes.

As can be seen from this table, classes can be derived from previously defined classes. The Base class is the originating class that the derived one is built from. Data members and function members from one class can be enhanced, changed ("overloaded"), or deleted in a Derived class. Derived classes are a method of modifying available code into exactly what you need without having to copy all the code and variables that aren't changed.

In a derived class, the members that are not changed are known as the "inherited" members of the derived class.

This class declaration is exactly the same as the function prototype of a C function. The function prototypes in the class description are the function prototypes of the actual member functions of the class. Normally, the class descriptor and member functions are kept in separate files to help keep the object-orientated concept of class/code separation.

A member function takes the form:

```
ReturnValue ClassName::FunctionName( parameters... )
{

// Function Code

}  //  End ClassName::FunctionName
```

The C++ function member is very straightforward and, other than the *ClassName* identifier, is identical to C functions. The two colons (::) are used to delimit the class and function name, and identify to the compiler that the function belongs to a class.

Member functions can be repeated within the class in a process known as *overloading*. Overloaded functions each have multiple parameter types (which is used to differentiate them). For example, if you had a class of type *Box* and moving it, you might want to use Cartesian or radial coordinate systems. The Methods could be defined using the Move member function name as:

```
void Box::Move( int X, int Y );

void Box::Move( float Radius, int Angle );
```

Earlier in this section, I noted that *instantiation* meant that when the variable was defined and memory allocated for it, the data members were also initialized. This is carried out using the *Constructor* member function. This function, which has the same name as the class, is used to initialize the member data items.

For the Desk class described, the constructor could be:

```
Desk::Desk()          //  Initialize the "Desk" Variables
{

  xPos = yPos = 0;    //  Put it in the center of the room

  Color = Black;

  Drawers = 3;

}  //  End "Desk" Constructor
```

Once an object of class Desk is declared, during the instantiation process *Desk::Desk* would be called and the variables initialized. The constructor can also have parameters that are passed at instantiation and used to initialize the data members to a specific set of values. The constructor cannot return a parameter (it cannot be called by the application code and the system code is not designed to handle a returned parameter).

One very nice feature of Visual C++ is that if you forget to create a constructor for your object (one is required for each class), then, at compile time, Visual C++ will create a null one for you.

Along with the constructor is a *destructor*, which executes at the end of the application (if the object was statically instantiated) or when an object is deleted. The destructor function name is the class name, like the constructor, but has a tilde (~) in front of it to indicate that this is a destructor. Like constructors, if no destructor is specified by the programmer, Visual C++ will create a null one at compile time.

Destructors are really only appropriate in cases where the object's data must be saved and cannot be lost. If memory or objects unique to the object being destroyed have been allocated, then the memory used should be freed up within the destructor.

When accessing object member functions (Methods), the object followed by the method is used, separated by a dot (.). Going back to the Desk class, to open a door, the following code could be used:

```
DeskObject.Open_Drawer( 1 );
```

In regular C, this function might be provided by the statement:

```
Drawer[ 1 ] = Open;
```

The C example presumes that the programmer understands exactly how the data is formatted and what is the correct value to use. In the object-orientated C++ example, the programmer is saved from having to understand how the function works at the low level.

Microsoft Development Studio

The Microsoft Development Studio is designed for the Visual C++ development environment. The Window that comes up provides source code editors, dialog box editors and easy access to help information (which you'll access a lot). As well, development studio provides access to the Visual C++ compilers, linkers, and debuggers.

The default Desktop (Fig. 36-3) is the most comfortable way that I've found to work with Visual C++. The data type to be displayed or edited is selected by the Tabs highlighted in Fig. 36-3. These tabs allow you to select between the Class (source) file view, the Resource (dialog box and bitmap) view and the complete file source view. Like Visual Basic, by clicking on dialog box controls, the methods for handling control events are prototypes and brought up.

Visual C++'s Development Studio does work like Visual Basic's IDE, but it has many extensions needed to help you interface with and create the classes necessary for a func-

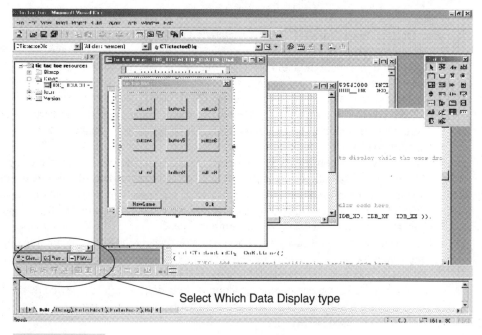

Select Which Data Display type

FIGURE 36-3   Visual C++ display selection "Tabs".

tional Visual C++ application. The next two sections expand upon this and show how the two Wizards provide the tools necessary to create a Visual C++ application.

APPSWIZARD

The Applications Wizard (AppsWizard) is invoked upon starting a new Visual C++ application. The AppsWizard is a series of dialog boxes that are used to let you select the "gross" operating characteristics of your application. Upon selecting "New" from the File pull down, you are greeted with the AppsWizard and given the opportunity to select individual files or projects. These projects are typically MFC applications but also include the ability to create custom Wizards, device drivers, and other types of executable files (Fig. 36-4).

The AppsWizard creates a framework of classes and objects for your application and helps to set up the basic mode of operation for your menus and dialog boxes.

Once the operating characteristics of the application have been selected, the AppsWizard displays a simple dialog box for you to review what was selected (Fig. 36-5).

If you are not happy with the selections made, you can click on Cancel and restart the AppsWizard operation.

The AppsWizard is really a wonderful tool, although I don't like one minor thing. When you first start working with Visual C++, AppsWizard will seem overwhelming. A lot of choices need to be made and when you first start working with Visual C++, you won't understand the ramifications of the different selections. This can be a frustrating experi-

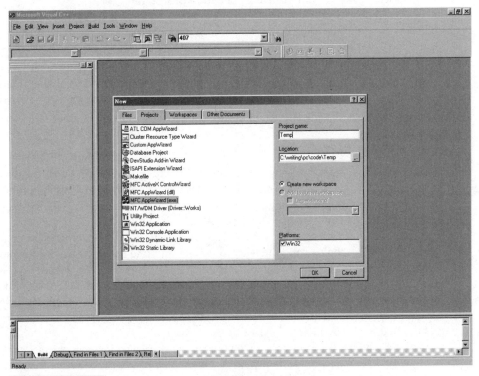

FIGURE 36-4   "AppWizard" application selection.

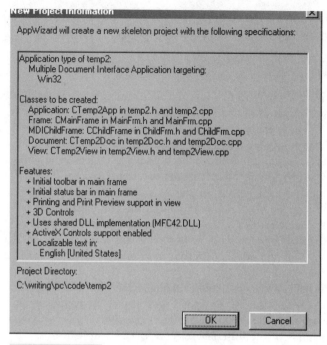

FIGURE 36-5   "AppWizard" application prototype review.

ence—especially if the wrong selections are made and your application won't respond in any kind of manner that you are expecting. When you first start working with Visual C++, leave the "default" selections in AppsWizard alone unless you are explicitly instructed to change them in the instructions for learning Visual C++.

CLASSWIZARD

Once you have started the application and are ready to start writing your code, you will have to create member functions and variables using ClassWizard. This feature of Visual C++ could be thought of being loosely analogous to the Visual Basic IDE to specify controls and the functions invoked by the controls.

One of the primary interfaces to the Class information is the WizardBar function of Visual C++. This allows you to quickly maneuver and find specific member functions and variables within a class specific to the application. In Fig. 36-6, the Wizard Bar is shown with the different member functions of the CTictactoeDlg class of the Tic-Tac-Toe application described at the end of the chapter. From here and a with few mouse clicks, you can move very quickly to different functions. Other methods can be used to find these routines, but I find the Wizard Bar to be the fastest.

Along with the Wizard Bar, a dialog box can be displayed for each object and class and is the primary interface to Class Wizard. Figure 36-7 shows the Message Maps, in which the member functions used and available in a class are displayed, specified, and linked

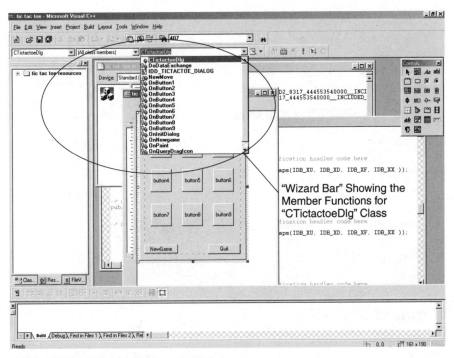

FIGURE 36-6   Visual C++'s "Wizard Bar".

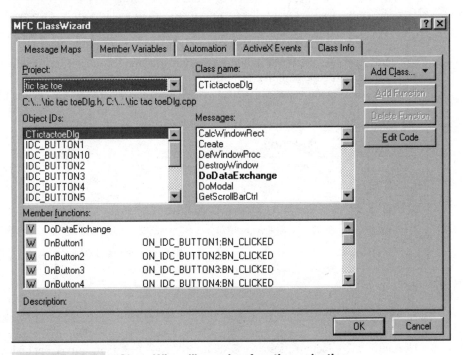

FIGURE 36-7   "Class Wizard" member function selection.

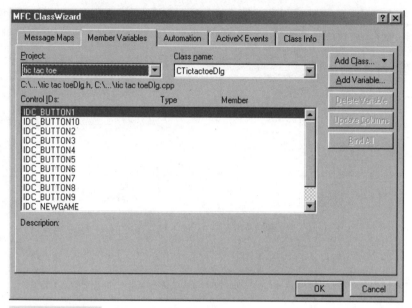

FIGURE 36-8   Visual C++ "Class Wizard".

with events. In Fig. 36-8, the Member Variables tag has been selected and the different variables created in the class for each of the controls of the CTictactoeDlg box are displayed. From the Class Wizard, the various members of a class can be displayed, prototypes created and destroyed.

Although classes, along with their member functions and variables, can be created manually, using the Class Wizard will link them in with the application and ensure that the format is correct before the compiler is used.

In every C++ Windows application, there are five primary MicroSoft Foundation Classes:

CLASS	FUNCTION
CMainFrame	The Application's MDI Interface
CaboutDlg	The Application's About Dialog Box
CChildFrame	The MDI Interface Child Dialog Boxes
CnoHandsApp	The Application Behavior Control
CnoHandsView	Class which controls how documents are displayed

These are the base classes needed to run a *Multiple Document Interface (MDI)* Visual C++ application. These applications provide a large area that can be written to with text or graphics by the application or user. Figure 36-9 shows a sample of an MDI application.

Normally, MDI documents are the default for Visual C++ applications, but dialog boxes can also be created, as shown in the Tic-Tac-Toe application at the end of the chapter.

FIGURE 36-9   Basic Visual C++ menu base application.

The six classes (and their associated objects) shown, are created by Application Wizard when the application is first started. Once AppsWizard has completed, the Class Wizard is used to display the class member function code for editing and creating the application.

Most of the controls that are available in Visual Basic dialog boxes are also available in Visual C++ dialog boxes. The big difference is in the controls that interface to hardware, which includes timing and serial-port functions.

When controls are put onto a dialog box, the dialog box's class information is also updated by subroutine functions of Class Wizard. The Properties of the controls in Visual Basic are analogous to the member data and member functions of the dialog box's class. These properties can be updated via the class's methods or by using the property boxes in the dialog box editor.

Using Application Wizard and Class Wizard works very well with my method of creating Windows applications. Class Wizard is not as easy to use as the Visual Basic IDE, but, as shown in the rest of this chapter, once you understand how classes work in Visual C++ you can develop Object Oriented Programming applications.

Microsoft Function Classes (MFC)

As I was working through the applications in this book, I discovered a big difference in the applications in which Visual Basic and Visual C++ are best suited. Visual Basic is best suited for applications that use a dialog box and button controls to execute applications, whereas Visual C++ is best for applications that are data intensive and require more data displaying and optional user editing. Now, this classification of the two development systems and best applications might not be shared by other people, but it is a difference that works for me and one that I can apply when deciding which tool to use for a specific application.

The data-handling and displaying capabilities are really a function of the *Microsoft Foundation Classes (MFC)* built into Visual C++. These classes, when used with AppsWizard and ClassWizard, give you a tool that allows you to create Windows Menu dialog applications with large areas for data editing or presenting (Fig. 36-9).

With this perspective, I find it quite easy to understand how Visual C++ can be best used to create Windows applications using the basic classes, without having to work through creating your own classes, modifying controls, or adding methods before you are comfortable with the language.

You should be aware of the seven basic MFC classes used for running applications and displaying dialog boxes on a PC:

CLASS	FUNCTION
CObject	Base Class used for the Visual C++ Classes responsible for displaying data on the Windows Display. All the other MFC classes are derived from this Class.
CWinApp	The class that defines the basic operation of the application. This is created by AppsWizard and should never be modified in an application.
CWnd	This is the base class for Windows in Visual C++. The purpose of this class is to give you access to drawing and moving Dialog Boxes within your application.
CDialog	Built from CWnd, this class is used to create Dialog Boxes. Most Dialog Box types that are built into MFC are derived from this class.
CMDIFrameWnd	This class, derived from CWnd, is used to display multiple Windows in the Application's Dialog Box at the same time. *MDI* is the *Multiple Document Interface* that is part of MFC.
CToolBar	The class used to create and display Toolbars on the Dialog Box. This Class is derived from CWnd and not from CDialog. The derived class CDialogBar allows both buttons and text information (CToolBar) just allows buttons. The derived class CStatusBar is used to display status information on the Dialog Box and is also derived from CToolBar.
CDC	Derived from CObject (but for some reason not shown on the hierarchy chart, CDC is used to display text and graphics. All Graphics Commands are Member Functions of this class.

Appendix K includes the Microsoft Foundation Class hierarchy chart. This is a useful reference to have available at all times. I have printed out a copy of it from the *Microsoft Developer's Network Library* CD-ROM that comes with Visual C++. One copy is on my wall in my office at work and another is in my workshop at home. When you look at this chart, you should notice that all these classes are derived from the base class of CObject.

Along with these basic classes are the simple value types which include:

VALUE	FUNCTION
CPoint	Pointer to Objects.
CRect	Rectangle Object.
CSize	Derived from Windows SIZE Structure. This is used to define the size of a Graphic Object.
CString	ASCIIZ String Implementation.
CTime	Represents Time and Date.
CTimeSpan	Representation of a Time Span.

These values are used with and within the MFC to provide data parameters to the class member functions. Standard C++ data types, such as *int*, *long*, etc., cannot be used with these functions. Along with these data types, Visual C++ also uses standard data types for interfacing with the kernel, user and GDI DLLs.

This section is really no more than an introduction to the MFC. I have not listed the methods available and how to work with them. Once you have a good understanding of what the MFC classes do, you will then have to learn how to work with them. To do this, I suggest working through the Visual C++ Help scripts and going through examples in the books listed in Appendix B.

Debugging Visual C++ Programs

When you see a completed Visual C++ program, you will probably be amazed by the simplicity of the user code that is required to carry out the application's functions. Often in class functions, the actual statements will only consist of one or two lines with the actual operation of the code being quite easy to understand. In this way, Visual C++ is very similar to Visual Basic; with the resources available in the built-in debugger, on the Internet, and available in books, finding samples showing how to create application code can be found reasonably easily.

The big difference between Visual C++ and Visual Basic is the ease in which the initial application can be created when you are first starting out with the language. Whereas Visual Basic is very straightforward and really follows established programming techniques, Visual C++ requires a complete understanding of class implementation, along with a good understanding of C programming and the theory behind object-orientated programming. Without this background, you'll spend a lot of time staring at the Visual C++ development windows, trying to figure out how the application is supposed to be implemented.

Debugging Visual C++ applications requires familiarity with the built-in Visual C++ debugger, which has many of the same features and key sequences as CodeView. The Visual C++ debugger is not the first and most important thing you will have to learn. Instead, you should familiarize yourself with the *MSDN Library* Help function with dialog box built into Visual C++. When you install Visual C++, you have the option of installing these programs on your PC's hard drive or leaving them on the CD-ROMs that they come on. When you first start your applications, be sure that you install them on your hard drive; you will be looking at them for virtually every line you write at the beginning.

When I use the tool, I normally only work with the Search option and Visual C++ documentation (Fig. 36-10). The *MSDN Library* CD-ROMs contain help information for all of the Visual Studio development tools, including Visual FoxPro and .DLL development information. If you select All for the Active Subset, you'll find that you have to do a lot of filtering between the different tools when you are looking for specific information.

When working through the Help dialog box, I find that it's useful to print out the information for classes and other information. I can't display as much information on my PC's screen as what I could see on a page of paper. Chances are that I'll have to look back at the information to fix problems later in the application.

When I write an application, I find that Visual C++, like Visual Basic, is well designed for creating small functions and debugging them before writing the entire application. Despite this, I still make a number of syntax errors.

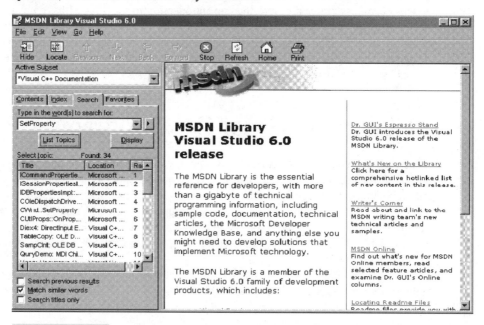

FIGURE 36-10 Visual C++ MSDN help dialog.

In order, I find that they are:

1 Using the incorrect method with derived classes. This is especially a problem with such controls as *CButton* and *CBitmapButton*.

2 Not using the correct overloaded member function. Visual C++'s editor will prompt you with all the available function parameter lists.

3 Forgetting to make member functions that don't return anything of at least type void. The only functions that do not have any returned values are the constructors and destructors.

4 Using a . for a new object when –> should be used.

5 Putting ; at the end of a *#define*.

6 Forgetting to initialize a variable.

This list is probably unique to me. However, other people that program in Visual C++ agree as to the importance of checking this list when syntax errors are flagged by the compiler.

As in any programming environment, when trying to find defective code, try to break it down into pieces to find the problem. This is actually much easier in Visual C++ than it probably sounds because of the nature of objects. Despite what I said about it being difficult to create a Visual C++ program, it is surprisingly easy to debug it.

Tic-Tac-Toe: A First Visual C++ Program

I thought it would be interesting to show how the Visual Basic Tic-Tac-Toe program could be implemented in C++ (Fig. 36-11). As you will no doubt expect, this exercise turned into a large amount of work with me learning a lot about C++, as well as how to find sample code and help for developing my own Visual C++ programs. Contrasting how I was able to develop the Visual Basic Tic-Tac-Toe program after only working with Visual Basic for about an hour and working through the first "chapter" of the *Learning Visual Basic* CD-ROM. I found that developing the same level of knowledge took me about five days, full time. Talking to some people who are well versed in Visual Basic and Visual C++, this seems to be in the right order of magnitude for the difference when developing your first applications.

When I started this application, I wanted to use the same interface—a dialog box with standard controls. Normally, Visual C++ applications use a Menu, which is a graphic area, which can be written to with text, simple figures (lines and polygons) or keyboard characters. The data entered onto the menu can be read back and mouse clicks on it can also be observed. The AppsWizard specifying this looks like Fig. 36-12.

Using the Menu interface, which is known as *MDI (Multiple Document Interface)*, is the default and is relatively easy to use because it is quite simple. Dialog box functions have to be created by the user.

4

WINDOWS PROGRAMMING

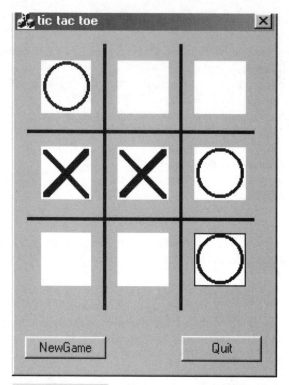

FIGURE 36-11   Visual C++ Tic-Tac-Toe dialog box.

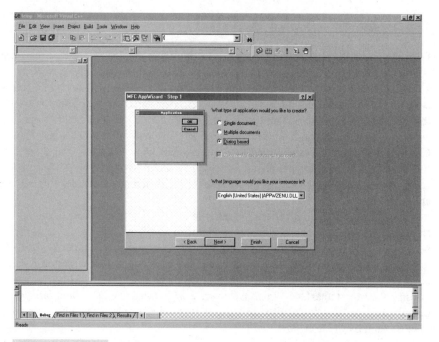

FIGURE 36-12   Visual C++ Tic-Tac-Toe dialog specification.

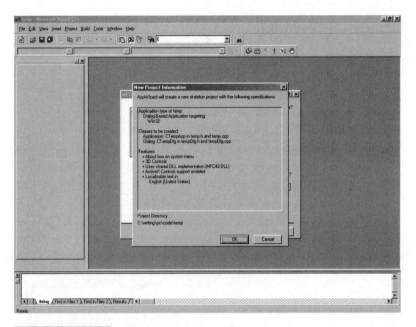

FIGURE 36-13   Visual C++ Tic-Tac-Toe project.

Because the Tic-Tac-Toe application is control based and does not really display any data when I used AppsWizard to create the base information, I selected a dialog-based application during set up. This actually makes the application harder to create scan if it were menu based.

Selecting a dialog-based application when you are creating it is simply done by clicking on the appropriate radio button during AppsWizard project setup. After selecting a dialog-based application, I allowed AppsWizard to select the defaults for the application, except for the About dialog box. For this application, I felt I did not need the dialog box showing the release information, so this option was disabled.

When I finished with AppsWizard, I was given the following information on the set up (Fig. 36-13).

Following my Windows development procedures, I first created the dialog box to be used in the application and its controls. For the Tic-Tac-Toe boxes, I decided to use standard buttons (of the CButton class) and I would then use bitmaps for the different characters. Figure 36-14 shows how the dialog boxes are defined with the Properties dialog box.

For this application, it is important that the OwnerDraw box is selected. This allows me to specify bitmaps for each of the nine character boxes. You should also notice that I have set the button's Caption to be similar to the button's ID. This is very important and I spent quite a few days trying to figure out why I couldn't load bitmaps into the buttons (which is covered in greater detail).

Once I had a rough outline of the dialog box, I then closed Visual C++ and opened up the dialog box in the WordPad editor. From here, I played around with the order of the controls on the dialog box and their positions to get them properly aligned. It is possible to do this from within the Visual C++ dialog-box editing functions, but I find it much faster to do it manually.

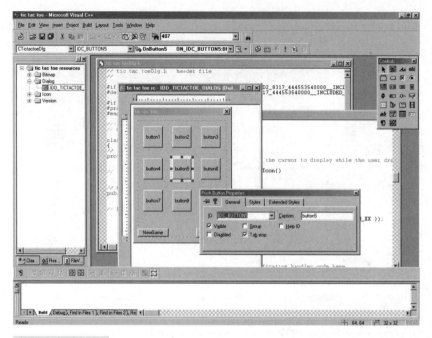

FIGURE 36-14 Visual C++ **Tic-Tac-Toe button specification.**

When I go through the Resource file (which ends in *.RC*), I look for the // *Dialog* line, after which, the controls are listed. For this application, this section of the resource file looks like:

```
//////////////////////////////////////////////////////////////////////
//////
//
// Dialog
//

IDD_TICTACTOE_DIALOG DIALOGEX 0, 0, 161, 190
STYLE DS_MODALFRAME | WS_POPUP | WS_VISIBLE | WS_CAPTION | WS_SYSMENU
EXSTYLE WS_EX_APPWINDOW
CAPTION "tic tac toe"
FONT 8, "MS Sans Serif"
BEGIN
    PUSHBUTTON      "Quit",IDCANCEL,104,169,50,14
    CONTROL         "button1",IDC_BUTTON1,"Button",BS_OWNERDRAW |
                    WS_TABSTOP,16,16,32,32
    CONTROL         "button2",IDC_BUTTON2,"Button",BS_OWNERDRAW |
                    WS_TABSTOP,64,16,32,32
    CONTROL         "button3",IDC_BUTTON3,"Button",BS_OWNERDRAW |
                    WS_TABSTOP,112,16,32,32
    CONTROL         "button4",IDC_BUTTON4,"Button",BS_OWNERDRAW |
                    WS_TABSTOP,16,64,32,32
    CONTROL         "button5",IDC_BUTTON5,"Button",BS_OWNERDRAW |
                    WS_TABSTOP,64,64,32,32
    CONTROL         "button6",IDC_BUTTON6,"Button",BS_OWNERDRAW |
                    WS_TABSTOP,112,64,32,32
```

```
        CONTROL         "button7",IDC_BUTTON7,"Button",BS_OWNERDRAW |
                        WS_TABSTOP,16,112,32,32
        CONTROL         "button8",IDC_BUTTON8,"Button",BS_OWNERDRAW |
                        WS_TABSTOP,64,112,32,32
        CONTROL         "button9",IDC_BUTTON9,"Button",BS_OWNERDRAW |
                        WS_TABSTOP,112,112,32,32
        PUSHBUTTON      "NewGame",IDC_NEWGAME,6,170,51,12
END
```

From the button controls, you should be able to see the properties quite easily. As well as checking that the positions are correct, you can change these parameters manually, as well (which is faster than using the GUI interface).

Coming up with the idea of changing the control properties manually is really a function of my experience with creating dialog boxes for OS/2 (which has no dialog-box editors). To be honest, I get a few raised eyebrows at work when people see me do it. Normally, this is not required. For this application, where I wanted to ensure that all buttons are aligned and the same size and as I was trying to figure out how to get the bitmaps displayed, manual editing of the resource file made my life a lot easier and avoids a lot of eyestrain.

With the dialog box set up, I then went ahead and created the bitmaps I wanted to have displayed on the Tic-Tac-Toe dialog box. Fortunately, "X"s and "O"s are quite easy to create using the Bitmap editor built into Visual C++.

For each symbol displayed on the Tic-Tac-Toe board, I created four actual bitmaps. These bitmaps are used in the different cases of button execution. The normal or "Up" bitmap (which ends in "U") displays the bitmap normally. Tabbing over to the bitmap button causes it to be "focussed," which uses the "F" ending. As can be seen in Fig. 36-15, I put a simple black line around the focussed bitmap to make it visually obvious that the user

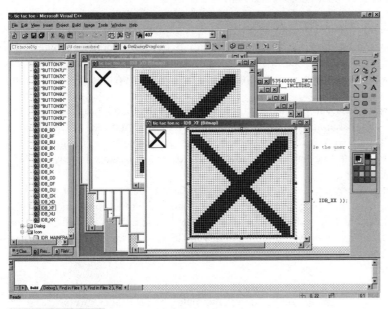

FIGURE 36-15 "Tic Tac Toe" bitmap.

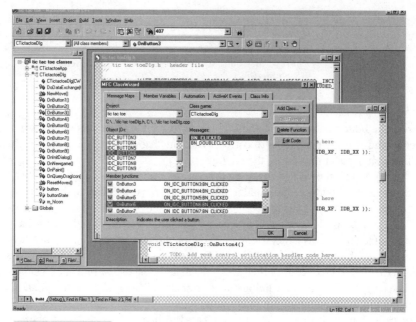

FIGURE 36-16 Tic-Tac-Toe button member function.

has tabbed over on it. Normally in Windows applications, the focus is shown as either a three-dimensional bitmap or as a broken line. The solid line that I used was the easiest to create for the application and it does work well.

The remaining two bitmaps, the Down (when the user clicks the left mouse button while over the control) and Disabled (ending in X) are simply copies of the "U" bitmap.

Actually putting the graphics on the control turned into a major undertaking that is not very well documented, either in the Microsoft MSDN or in the book documentation that I have found. As well, changing bitmaps on the fly, as this application does, does not seem well supported within MFC.

A few things are necessary to get the bitmaps to work properly. First be sure that the control's ID and Caption match, as shown in Fig. 36-16. If the Caption doesn't match the ID value after the Visual C++ provided *IDC_*, you will never be able to get the graphics to work (this took me about two days to figure out). Ditto for not having the OwnerDraw property selected.

Once the buttons are created, default (blank) bitmaps have to be created in the same format. For Visual C++ to reference them correctly, they should be the same as the Caption, except in upper case and within double quotes ("). The default bitmap identifiers can be seen in the Resource View box on the left hand of Fig. 36-16. For the other bitmaps (i.e., X, O, and disabled), I left the Visual C++ specified *IDB_* label and just added a letter to make identification for me easier.

To load the button controls with the bitmaps, first the buttons have to be defined as being in the CBitmapButton class. This is done in the dialog boxes header (prototype) definition. For this application, I defined them as a protected array:

```
//  Put in the Button Definition
protected:
        CBitmapButton button[9];
```

I made the button classes protected to prevent any other objects from accessing the buttons and I used an array because it is easier to access the data instead of having to come up with nine unique identifiers.

To load the default bitmaps, I used the "AutoLoad" method of the CBitmapButton class in the dialog's OnInitDialog function:

```
VERIFY( button[0].AutoLoad(IDC_BUTTON1, this));
VERIFY( button[1].AutoLoad(IDC_BUTTON2, this));
VERIFY( button[2].AutoLoad(IDC_BUTTON3, this));
VERIFY( button[3].AutoLoad(IDC_BUTTON4, this));
VERIFY( button[4].AutoLoad(IDC_BUTTON5, this));
VERIFY( button[5].AutoLoad(IDC_BUTTON6, this));
VERIFY( button[6].AutoLoad(IDC_BUTTON7, this));
VERIFY( button[7].AutoLoad(IDC_BUTTON8, this));
VERIFY( button[8].AutoLoad(IDC_BUTTON9, this));
```

The VERIFY function causes an Abort/Retry/Ignore error in the execution if a problem occurs with the function. The AutoLoad function returns a Boolean value to indicate whether or not there were any problems with the bitmap load. With this code, when the dialog box is loaded, the Tic-Tac-Toe button controls are also loaded with their default bitmaps.

The procedure I've shown here is very simple, but getting to this point just about gave me a nervous breakdown. Before working on this application, my Visual C++ experience had to do with .DLLs and simple Menu applications. The upside of all this frustration was that I learned a lot about finding snippets and getting questions answered in Visual C++.

Before going any further, I then wanted to put in the vertical and horizontal bars that separate the values in the Tic-Tac-Toe controls. This is actually very straightforward and is accomplished by using the basic graphic functions in Visual C++. To draw the bars, I used the following code within the "OnDraw" function.

```
CRect rect;
GetClientRect(&rect);
CClientDC dc(this);
CPen mypen;
mypen.CreatePen(PS_SOLID, 3, RGB(0, 0, 0));
CPen* oldpen = dc.SelectObject(&mypen);

dc.MoveTo( 84, 12 );
dc.LineTo( 84, 250 );

dc.MoveTo( 155, 12 );
dc.LineTo( 155, 250 );

dc.MoveTo( 12, 90 );
dc.LineTo( 222, 90 );
dc.MoveTo( 12, 169 );
dc.LineTo( 222, 169 );

// end of added code

dc.SelectObject(oldpen);
```

This code defines the rectangle of the dialog box, followed by a pointer to it (dc). Next, a pen is defined with a specific color and pixel width. The color definition, *RGB(#, #, #)*, probably seems straightforward, but for a color to be fully on, its value is zero and not 255.

The code to write the bars can be used either with a dialog box (as in this case) or on a menu without change. With the *rect* variable loaded with the position and size of the dialog box, I could have arithmetically defined the position of the bars as fractions of the window width, but I found it easier to explicitly specify the values.

With the initial bitmaps loaded and the graphic bars displayed, I then turned my attention to changing the bitmaps when the control is clicked on. To do this, I first created the dialog class OnButton member functions. This is done by selecting the dialog class (CTictactoeDlg, in this example) in the Class View window of the Visual C++ development screen, right button clicking on the dialog class, and then selecting Add Member Function. I did this for each of the nine Tic-Tac-Toe buttons and the New Game button.

Once the member functions are created, their operation can be checked in ClassWizard.

When the user is playing the game, positions are selected by clicking on the buttons. To keep track of the state of the buttons, I created the *buttonState* variable, which is loaded with zero, for the square being available, one for the user (X) selecting it, two for the computer move (O), and three for game over. The button cannot be accessed. A typical On-Button function looks like:

```
void CTictactoeDlg::OnButton6()
{
    // TODO: Add your control notification handler code here
    if ( buttonState[5] == 0 ) {
        VERIFY( button[5].LoadBitmaps(IDB_XU, IDB_XD, IDB_XF,
                IDB_XX ));
        buttonState[5] = 1;
        NewMove();
        SetFocus();
    }
}
```

In these functions, I check to see if the *buttonState* is zero and if it's not, I ignore it. From here, the control's bitmap is loaded with the *X* bitmaps, the *buttonState* variable is updated and the *NewMove* function, which allows the computer to respond, is called. At the end of the *OnButton* function, I call the *CWnd* class (from which both the *CBitmapButton* and dialog box classes are derived) function SetFocus to ensure that the dialog box and control are updated.

Having the buttons update automatically is a problem for this application and is a function, as pointed out. The MFC CBitmapButton class does not "expect" to be updated, which makes the bitmap updates only become visible when the button has the focus of the dialog box. This can be forced using the *SetFocus* function.

With the button bitmaps displayed and updateable, I then spent 20 minutes creating the logic for the application (the *NewMove* function). This aspect of the application is really nontypical because I had the advantage of already creating the application in Visual Basic and knowing exactly how the application should behave.

Looking over what I have written, I feel like I have really minimized the effort I put in trying to figure out how to display bitmaps on buttons. It was really hard work and should not be regarded as trivial. At the same time, I feel like I also got a good handle on how applications are created within Visual C++ and the importance of having:

1 A copy of the *MSDN Library* CD-ROM.
2 A number of Visual C++ reference books. I had four that I continually pour over when I work with Visual C++.
3 An Internet connection.

Along with documentation for Visual C++ and MFC, the *MSDN Library* CD-ROM also contains more than 20 example applications that will help show you what to do. I have four Visual C++ reference books that are falling apart from all of the time that I have spent pouring over them. Even with these references, I have to recommend an Internet connection and bookmarking the Web sites listed in Appendix B, as well as subscribing to the Microsoft MSDN Developer's Network. With these resources, you will be able to puzzle out how to create your own applications.

As simple as this Tic-Tac-Toe application is, if you look through beginner's Visual C++ books, you'll discover that the bitmap application is really an "advanced" application. I used this project because I wanted this application to help me understand how dialog boxes are implemented within Visual C++. Before this application, I did try to use the CBitmap-Button class to link bitmaps with buttons twice before and gave up each time because I couldn't get them to work. For this application, I really went through all the resources that I had and toughed it out until I got the bitmap controls working with the application.

WINDOWS

DEVICE

DRIVERS

37

DEVICE
DRIVER
TYPES

CONTENTS AT A GLANCE

Dynamic Link Libraries (.DLLs)　　　　Win32 Device Models (.WDMs)

Virtual Device Drivers (.VxDs)

As mentioned earlier in the book, device drivers are used to provide a common access method to I/O devices, as well as providing system functions for applications. Personally, I don't use device drivers in MS-DOS because typically only one application is active at any time and the lack of protect mode operation does not make device drivers mandatory. In Windows applications where hardware is being accessed, the operation of device drivers is the only way for accessing hardware and working with interrupts.

Device drivers for Windows are notoriously hard to write and debug. As well, device drivers are considered "dangerous" because they have access to all the system resources without any type of protection. These points are certainly true to an extent. I agree that they are hard to develop if the developer does not understand how Windows works or is unsure about how device drivers work. I find they're quite straightforward with a good basic grounding on Windows and the PC hardware.

The rest of the book focuses on PC hardware access from Windows. Device drivers are the most common for Windows 95/NT and Windows 2000 operation and will be useful for a very long period of time. If you have a modern version of Windows loaded into your PC and look in your SYSTEM subdirectory, you will find a number of different types of device drivers available to the system. Along with .VxD and .WDM filename extensions, you will also see .DLLs and .386. These device drivers are designed for Legacy applications and are given a low level of support. For all new applications, I recommend that you only look at developing device drivers in the .WDM format. One point about Windows device drivers that I have never liked; hopefully, I can take this opportunity to change this when they are initially created. I generally find that Windows device drivers (especially their early incarnations) are very poorly written. I often find them to have a number of problems and can cause the PC to lock up or lose data—and I'm not alone in this observation. I beseech you when you develop your device drivers to keep them simple and don't consider them ready for "release" unless you are absolutely sure that they work perfectly. Currently, too many devices on the market today have substandard drivers, which hurts both the product's chance in the market and consumer's confidence in the quality of the products they buy. This leads the consumer to the conclusion that the PC is getting too complex. This is unfortunate because I believe that these feelings will impede the speed in which such innovations as WDMS, USB and Firewire will be accepted in the marketplace.

Dynamic Link Libraries (.DLLs)

My first foray into Windows device drivers was in the *Dynamic Link Libraries (.DLL)* because of my initial experiences with them for OS/2. .DLLs are device drivers that are loaded in with the application and execute Ring 0 operations. When the application is unloaded from Windows, the .DLL is unloaded as well. .DLLs have started out as the simplest form of device drivers that you can have for a Windows application, with the most basic three providing system access and allows interprocess communication.

.DLLs work differently for different execution model applications. I was originally going to write operating system instead execution model because that is how the issue is normally presented. In Win16 systems, .DLLs are available to all the applications running in the PC. In Win32 systems, .DLLs are available to the applications that loaded them as subroutines and functions as if they were local to the application.

Win16 .DLLs behave in Windows 95/98/2000 as they would in a Windows 3.x system even though the operating system is based on the Win32 kernel. This book focuses on the Win32 kernel .DLL format, largely because I do not believe there are any currently supported Win16 application tools available. The secondary reason why I do not include the Win16 kernel .DLL format is because support for the Win16 kernel is waning in Microsoft operaing-system products and I would not be surprised to see that it has been eliminated all together in the operating system after Windows 2000.

Virtual Device Drivers (.VxDs)

As has been covered at length earlier in the book, Windows 95/98/2000 are true 32-bit operating systems running applications in a virtual machine. The Virtual Machine Manager provides access to the console and I/O functions for the application as if it were the only application that the processor was running. When adding new hardware functions in Windows, typically a device driver is used to allow access to the new hardware to all applications within the PC. The most typical Windows device driver is known as the *VxD*.

With my experience with multitasking operating systems before Windows (usually as shells over MS-DOS), when providing device drivers for common functions, the device driver and operating system functions must be serialized. As I've covered elsewhere in this book, this is normally accomplished in MS-DOS by intercepting API calls (usually by redirecting the API interrupt) from processes and not allowing the calls to pass to the operating system and hardware unless the hardware was idle (all the previous requests had completed). I've always known this action as *serialization*. The operating system function, in this case, serializes the requests to occur one after each other. This is much of what virtualization is all about, with one important difference. Windows VxDs not only serialize the requests passed to the device drivers from the processes, but also to provide an interface to each requesting process that gives the appearance that it is the only application requesting the device driver in the system. The difference probably seems trivial, but it is actually quite important. An example of this could be shown with the keyboard API. A serializing device driver would hold off on any process requests until the previous ones were completed, whereas a virtualizing device driver would hold off a processes requests until it had the console's focus (i.e., its dialog box was highlighted) and then respond to its requests. In the serialization example, keystrokes could be passed to a process that did not have focus (and the keystrokes would be inappropriate for the specific virtual machine), whereas in the virtualized device driver only the appropriate keystrokes are passed to the process.

VxDs run in Ring 0 of the process without any memory protection. This means that the opportunity for a VxD to cause mischief in the system is very high and care must be taken in developing the device driver. Later, the book goes through a VxD to give you an idea of how they are created and how to keep them from "running amok."

1 Provide communications links between the "substrate" MS-DO S/BIOS and Windows processes.
2 Arbitrate contention between requesting processes (Virtual Machines).
3 Create virtual (simulated) hardware to help develop application software before the hardware is available.
4 Redirect I/O and provide standard interfaces to nonstandard hardware.
5 Monitor the system's behavior.

Win32 Device Models (.WDMs)

In the early 1990s, there was a divergence in PC products. With the wide-spread acceptance of LANs and the emergence of the Internet, PCs split into two different types. Desktop and laptop PCs were designed to provide a cost-effective tool for users to access and develop applications, and servers provided interconnectivity between PCs and other computers. Servers also provided central storage of crucial data and centralized application execution (such as database searches). This schism resulted in vastly different PC philosophies, with desk and laptop PCs being simpler and somewhat cheaper than the server products. This difference was also apparent in the operating systems provided between the two types of PCs.

In the desk and laptop PC world, the operating systems followed the MS-DOS path with Windows 3.x and Windows 95 being essentially "overlays" to MS-DOS. These operating environments (looking at them critically, I'm reluctant to call them "operating systems") reflected this philosophy as well, taking on an evolutionary development approach, adding sophisticated features slowly, and not taking advantage of the hardware features built into the processor and support chips. This has resulted in Windows receiving some hard knocks from critics for not providing the system maintenance functions expected of a mature operating system. In Windows 3.x, application failures regularly "crashed" the entire PC. In Windows 95, legacy applications and drivers could cause problems with crashing themselves and possibly the PC, but these problems have been reduced as time has passed. The Windows 3.x and Windows 9x operating systems use a device driver structure that can be traced back to MS-DOS. This structure is based on the 16-bit operating model and causes unnecessary complexity and lost robustness over a properly designed 32-bit device driver.

In the server product line, Windows NT has emerged as the premier operating system with the ability to provide full multitasking for multiprocessor systems, enhanced network connectivity features, and reliability. Windows NT used a unique device driver model that was found to be quite difficult to program and debug. As laptop and desktop hardware has become more complex and tasks have required more networking and larger applications, the software requirements have literally brought the PCs up to the same level as the servers, with many of the same operating integrity and networking features from the operating system.

Microsoft, rather than continuing to enhance the MS-DOS-based operating systems, has decided to merge the two operating systems lines into one. This is now known as "Windows 2000" (originally Windows NT 5.0). A key initiative of this effort was to provide a new device-driver structure that is native to the 32-bit operating system and is much easier to program than previous device drivers. This new device driver structure is known as the *Win32 Device Model (W DM)*. Personally, I find that it is the best of the three formats presented here, it is definitely the most efficient to code for and, to me, it makes the most sense. WDM is an event-based programming model that is well suited to object-orientated programming languages, such as C++. This structure brings device-driver creation in line with Visual Tools code development and eliminates the need for conceptually understanding multiple PC programming philosophies to develop a software/hardware interface application. WDM has actually been around for a number of years. It was first made available for Windows 95 OSR 2.0 (OEM System Release 2.0) for use with the initial USB ports provided with motherboards built in the 1996 and later timeframe. Since this time, the device-driver handlers have become much more stable with more device drivers being written for the execution mode 1. Before writing this book, I already had some experience with USB devices and I have been impressed with the ease in which they can be installed and applications added. I am excited about how easily new and powerful peripherals can be created and interfaced in future PCs using USB with WDM drivers.

5

WINDOWS DEVICE DRIVERS

CREATING

DLLS

I'm always surprised to discover that DLLs are normally placed in the back of Windows System Programming texts, as if they are actually harder to write than VxDs. DLLs are fairly simple to create in Visual C++, as well as update.

DLLs are loaded into Ring 0 of a process when the application is loaded. The purpose of DLLs is to provide interfaces to hardware, as well as standard software functions to applications. DLLs consist of a set of function interfaces that can be called from an application.

Throughout this book, when describing Windows, the focus has been on the Win32 kernel and not the Win16 kernel. For VxDs, this is really not an issue (other than the need for a separate 16-bit and 32-bit compiler), but for DLLs it is because they operate differently in the different kernels if multiple iterations of the same DLL are loaded with an application. In the Win16 environment, if a DLL is required by multiple processes, then a single iteration is shared. In the Win32 environment, a separate DLL data area is loaded for each invocation. This has implications on how the DLLs are written for the different kernels.

Creating .DLLs

DLLs can be created in Visual C++ using the APP Wizard available for new applications. After specifying how MFC is going to work with the DLL, you will get a New Project In-

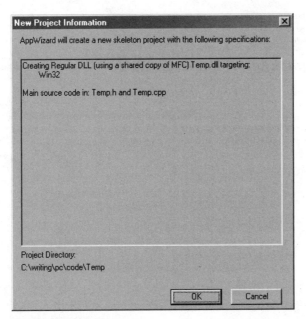

FIGURE 38-1   Visual C++ DLL wizard operation.

formation dialog box (Figure 38-1). With this complete, you can then add member functions to the DLL Application class (DLLNameDLLApp, shown in Figure 38-2) using the Class Wizard as you would any other Visual C++ application. Adding member functions is shown in Figure 38-3.

This is really all there is to creating a basic DLL in Visual C++. One paragraph and three screen shots obviously don't give you the entire story, including how to share variables between DLLs, as well as executables and DLLs, but this will give you a start to how DLLs work.

From Visual C++, you could also create a DLL using just C source, but I don't recommend that because the features and advantages of Visual C++ will not be available to you.

Visual C++ developed DLLs are designed to be used only with Visual C++ applications. This has resulted in the DLLs interface names to be different than what you specify (usually the @8 characters are put at the end of the DLL name). To allow Visual C++ DLLs to be used with other Windows development tools, you should add the line:

```
#pragma (comment(linker,"/expert:ActFunc=VC++Func")
```

where *ActFunc* is the Actual Function name that you want applications to access and *VC++Func* is the label that Visual C++ gives to the function. As indicated, the difference is usually the characters @8 added to the end of the Visual C++ function name.

DLL Operation

DLLs can be loaded with an application one of two ways. The first is *implicit loading*— that which is from within a library when the application loads. The second is *explicit load-*

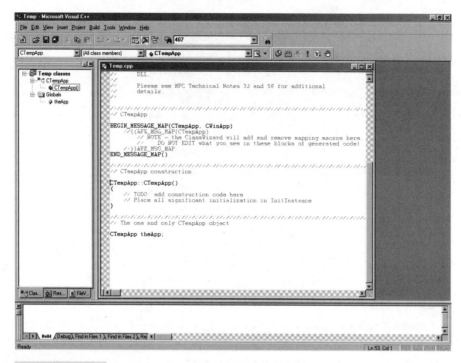

FIGURE 38-2 Visual C++ DLL main class source code.

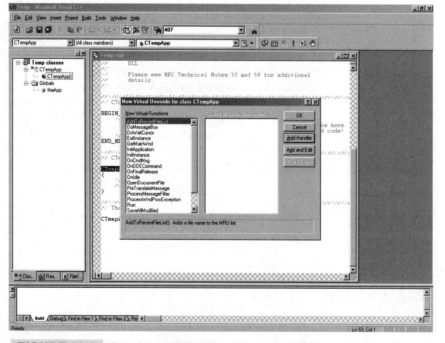

FIGURE 38-3 DLL Class Wizard function delaration.

ing—with the application specifying the DLLs that are required. Normally implicit loading is used unless the DLL is being debugged or a new version is being tried out in an application.

An implicit load follows a search path trying to find the file that is specified in the library. This search checks the following locations:

1 Directory where .EXE was loaded from
2 Current directory
3 C:\WINDOWS\SYSTEM directory
4 D:\WINDOWS directory
5 PATH-specified directories

If the DLL cannot be found in any of these directories, an error message is displayed when the application loads.

Explicit loads uses the LoadLibrary or LoadLibraryEx APIs, which return the address of the image of the DLL that was loaded.

When the DLL is loaded, it shows up in the system Registry information. Under Windows 95, it is under the heading *Known DLLS*; in Windows 98, it can be found under *16-bit Modules Loaded* or *32-Bit Modules Loaded* (Figure 38-4).

When the application is through with the DLL, it can invoke a FreeLibrary API, which will remove the DLL from the process. If multiple copies of the DLL are loaded, then only the appropriate data is freed from the system. When all previous iterations are removed, the code is removed as well.

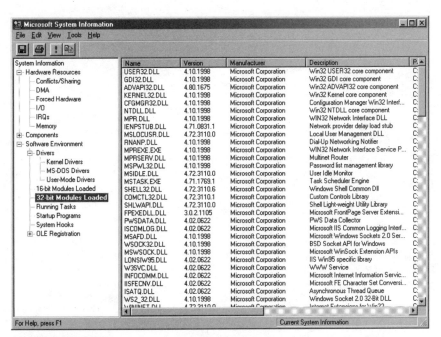

FIGURE 38-4   DLL system registry information.

WINDOWS DEVICE DRIVERS

5

Normal MyLib DLL load code is:

```
int MylibLoad = 0;
HINSTANCE hinstDLL;

  HinstDLL = GetModule( "MyLib" );  //  Look for DLL installed
  If ( HinstDLL == NULL ) {
    HinstDLL = LoadLibrary( "MyLib" );  // If not installed, load
    MylibLoad = 1;                      //   Explicitly
  }
```

The best unload code is:

```
  If ( GetModuleUsage( HinstDLL ) == 1 )
    FreeLibrary( HinstDLL );
```

This code checks for the situation where the loading process ends before the current one and the DLL's code could be unloaded before all instances of it being required have been eliminated. This is a bit of a failing of different versions of Windows to properly keep track of the number of active iterations of a DLL and where it is located.

Although the DLL keeps track explicitly of the different processes that are running and using it, it cannot keep track and implicitly virtualize the requests multiple threads in a process are placing on it. To avoid this problem, I recommend that you only access a DLL from one thread per process.

SURVIVING

THE

VxD EXPERIENCE

CONTENTS AT A GLANCE

As described earlier in the book, VxDs seem like wonderful programming tools and are able to do much more than just provide a virtualized device driver. They can be used like MS-DOS device drivers to enhance the operation of the PC by intercepting I/O operations or by providing advanced processing and filtering functions to hardware.

VxDs also allow Microsoft to enhance the Windows Operating System without having to destroy all of the previous device drivers written. For example, in Windows 98, among the different VxDs used in the system are a number of VxDs that were used in Windows 95. They include:

DEVICE	VXD
Display	VDD.VxD
Keyboard	VKD.VxD
Mouse	VMD.VxD

VxDs provide a virtual interface to hardware and software functions. This virtual interface is used by the different Windows application processes to provide the interface functions. From Fig. 39-1, you can see how the virtual hardware actually "appears" as part of the process virtual machine and interfaces to the VxD code.

VxDs can be nested or used to interface with hardware or enhance software functions. For example, in Fig. 39-2, the hardware provides an interrupt request, which is handled by the interrupt controller (the 8259A) VxD and passed onto the device VxD.

This capability gives VxDs a great deal of flexibility and allows them to be used for simulating hardware or enhancing previously available features.

This chapter is an introduction to the tools used to develop VxDs, how they are formatted for creating them in Visual C++, as well as some advanced functions, including linking to BIOS/MS-DOS APIs and handling interrupts.

VxD Operations

Of the three types of device drivers presented in this book, I find that VxDs are the hardest to understand and visualize. This is really because of how VxDs operate within the PC and the operating system and permeate all aspects of Windows' operation. This previous sentence is important because it implies that VxDs are actually part of the operating system, which they are. VxDs are application specified enhancements to the operating system and this design philosophy affects how they are loaded into a PC's memory and operate.

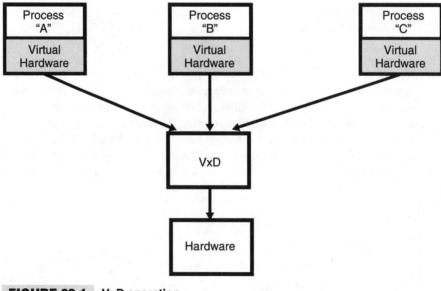

FIGURE 39-1 VxD operation.

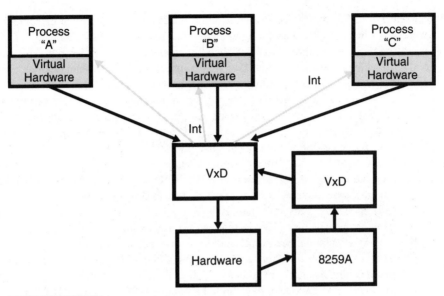

FIGURE 39-2   VxD operation with interrupts.

VxDs are loaded into the same memory/data selector that the virtual machine manager executes in and can access the entire 4.3 GB of the PC's physical memory space. When a VxD is executing, all the selectors (CS, DS, ES, SS, and GS) are loaded with 0 and the size limit is set to the full 4.3 GB addressable by the processor. When a VxD is operating with a V86 virtual machine, it can only access the first 1 MB of the virtual machine (which is where the application is executing).

A VxD is hard to visualize and graphically show in the system because it exists simultaneously in the OS-devoted memory, each of the processes that are loaded and executing and allocates data specifically for the different processes.

VxDs are primarily "flow-control device drivers". That is to say that they intercept the file system and return "handles" and interpret or output streams (or flows) of data. VxDs are capable of not only accessing other VxDs, but are also able to send messages to the virtual machine manager. This flexibility in operation allows the VxD to be used in a variety of applications that you wouldn't expect. Two examples of this would be monitoring and logging system calls to another VxD to aid in debugging (VxDs are notoriously hard to debug) or creating a hardware emulator VxD to allow application development while the actual hardware interface device driver is being created.

VxDs can be represented as an event-driven programming model, with the different messages passed to the VxD represented in software as events and programmed to respond to the events. These events can come from external sources or the VxD can run threads that are unique to it. These threads run at a higher priority than applications and should be interrupt/timer event driven to avoid "starving" the application and operating system threads of CPU cycles.

Control transfer from processes to the VxDs occur through the virtual machine manager, which provides device I/O capturing and virtualization, VxD API interfacing, hooking into other VxD APIs and interrupt and fault-handling conversion to VxD events. This makes the VxD/virtual machine manager interface very complex, although from a programmer's point of view (i.e., ours), this complexity gives us a somewhat easier interface with which to work.

Device virtualization is carried out by the virtual machine manager that controls the data path between the application and the device VxD. The data path from the application through the virtual machine manager to the VxD is accomplished by the VxDs (when they are loaded) requesting application events using virtual machine manager APIs. Along with device driver requests, the virtual machine manager can pass I/O operations from the application to an appropriate VxD using the Install_IO_Handler API from within the VxD. Hardware interrupts can be passed as events to the VxD by using the VPICD_Set_Int_Request API. The Hook_V86_Int_Chain API will cause the virtual machine manager to pass software interrupts (i.e., int 21h API requests) to the VxD for processing.

When VxD APIs (which are event handlers) are created, normally two are provided—one for V86 requests and one for Protect-mode requests. The APIs used to provide this API from the virtual machine manager are Allocate_V86_Call_Back or Allocate_PM_Call_Back.

Control messages to VxDs in the Win32 kernel use W32_DEVICEIOCONTROL event handler. In the Win16 kernel, the Virtual Device Service Table is used to provide a similar function with software interrupt 20h.

Hooking another VxD's API will pass the input and output parameters to the VxD. To hook into the APIs provided by other VxDs, the following APIs are used: Hook_Device_Service, Hook_Device_PM_API, and Hook_Device_V86_API. Once a VxD's API is "hooked," it can be invoked by the VxD using the Hook_Device_Service_Ex API. The last API is useful for debugging APIs by sending a specific message to a VxD without requiring application code.

This section is an introduction to some of the most important APIs available to VxDs. You probably won't be surprised to find that almost 1000 different APIs are available to VxDs. The main categories of these APIs are:

1 Breakpoints
2 Debugging
3 Error conditions/events
4 Events
5 Faults
6 Information
7 Initialization
8 Interrupts
9 I/O traps
10 Linked lists
11 Nested execution
12 Protect-mode execution
13 Scheduling
14 Thread execution
15 Timers

These APIs can be found in the Microsoft Device Driver Development (DDK) or VtoolsD documentation.

VXD STRUCTURE

In MS-DOS and Windows, how a file is loaded and executed is often based on the extension given to the file name. For 32-bit VxDs running under the Win32 kernel, the extension .VxD is used, while for 32-bit VxDs running under the Win16 kernel, the extension .386 is used. The format is known as *LE'* (which is pronounced "elle ee prime") and was originally developed for IBM's OS/2 Version 2.0 as a means to provide a file format for 16- and 32-bit programs.

Every VxD has a Data Descriptor Block (DDB), which is used by the virtual machine manager to determine how to load the file into Ring 0, the files initialization sequence, control message handler address, and establish links to applications and other VxDs.

The format of the DBB is:

FIELD	DESCRIPTOR
Next	Used by the VMM to Link VxDs as a singly linked list
SDK_Version	DDK Version used to build the VxD
Req_Device_Number	Device ID used by other VxDs, V86 and Protect-Mode Applications
Dev_Major_Version	VxD Version Number
Dev_Minor_Version	VxD Version Number
Flags	Bits indicating Initialization Calls are complete
Name	Eight-byte Device Name (with Blanks in Unused Positions)
Init_Order	Initialization Order, can request VMM to load other VxDs before current can initialize
Control_Proc	Offset of the Control Procedure
V86_API_Proc	Offset to the V86 APIs
PM_API_Proc	Offset to the Protect-Mode APIs
V86_API_CSIP	CS:IP stored by VMM, which is used by V86 applications "reflected" to V86_API_Proc
PM_API_CSIP	CS:IP stored by VMM, which is used by Protect-Mode applications "reflected" to V86_API_Proc
Reference_Data	Reference Data from Real Mode
VxD_Service_Table_Pointer	Pointer to VxD service Table, which identifies Services called from other VxDs
VxD_Service_Table_Size	Number of Services in Table

5

WINDOWS DEVICE DRIVERS

A number of memory options are available for the code/data in a VxD when the device driver is linked. These include:

FORMAT	DESCRIPTION
Locked Code	Code must always be in physical memory
Locked Data	Read/Write Data must always be in physical memory
PageableCode	Code can be swapped out into a "page" file
Pageable Data	Read/Write data can be swapped out into a "page" file
Static Code	Code will be left in memory after VxD is unloaded
Static Data	Read/Write Data will be left in memory after VxD is unloaded
Debug_Only Code	Code only loaded if a debugger is present
Debug_Only Data	Read/Write data only loaded if a debugger is present
Init Code	Code is executed for VxD initialization and unloaded afterward
Init Data	Read/Write Data used for VxD initialization and unloaded afterward
Init Message	Message to be displayed when VxD is loaded

CONTROL MESSAGES

Control messages are notifications of event occurrences from the virtual machine manager to the VxD. They can be sent for application device interface requests, interrupts, or Private Control Messages, which is a method for VxDs to communicate with one another. I tend to think of control messages as events to be processed—even though the actual mechanism is not quite what you would expect for event-driven programming.

The device interface request control messages include:

1 System Preparation (thread/process creation or destruction)
2 Thread switching
3 I/O operations
4 Application VxD API calls
5 Hooked VxD API calls
6 Interrupts

Event Processing

A properly written VxD maintains an "event list" for each thread currently executing in the system, along with a global event list. Each list is created upon the loading of the VxD or when new threads begin executing in the PC.

Before passing thread VxD requests on, the virtual machine manager first passes on any pending Global or virtual machine events. These events indicate changes in the operation of the system or in the processes loaded into the PC.

VxDs can be static (loaded at system initialization) or dynamic (loaded/unloaded based on demand). Dynamic VxDs have two specific events that must be handled during loading and unloading, SYS_DYNAMIC_DEVICE_INT and SYS_DYNAMIC_DEVICE_EXT, respectively.

The VxD global-event APIs are (in the order of priority):

```
Call_Global_Event
Call_Priority_VM_Event
Call_Restricted_Event
Call_VM_Event
Cancel_Priority_VM_Event
Cancel_VM_Event
Schedule_Global_Event
Schedule_Thread_Event
Schedule_VM_Event
Shell_CallAtAppyTime
```

VxDs can also monitor the virtual machine manager for faults in Ring 0 and in the applications. The APIs to request VxD events for faults are:

```
Hook_VMM_Fault
Hook_PM_Fault
Hook_V86_Fault
```

Call backs are part of the event process and are used to request the virtual machine manager to "call back" a VxD on the following specific events. These call backs include:

API EVENT	DESCRIPTION
Call_When_Idle	Execute when the system is idle
Call_When_Not_Critical_Execute	Execute when the critical code section of the Virtual Machine Manager is not executing
Call_When_Task_Switched	Executed when a Task Switch is taking place by the Virtual Machine Manager
Call_When_Thread_Switched	Executed when a Thread Switch is taking place by the Virtual Machine Manager
Call_When_VM_Ints_Enabled	Execute when the Virtual Machine's Interrupts are enabled
Call_When_VM_Returns	Execute when Virtual Machine Interrupt Handler executes the *iret* instruction

5

WINDOWS DEVICE DRIVERS

HARDWARE INTERRUPTS

As you've read through this chapter, you probably realize that the 8259A aspects of hardware interrupt requests are handled by the virtual machine manager and that a VxD-specified interrupt handler is responsible for processing the interrupt request. This division of tasks actually makes VxD interrupt handling quite easy to understand and work with.

During the VxD initialization, hardware interrupt levels are claimed from the virtual machine manager using the VPICD_Virtualize_IRQ API request. The parameters to this API are stored in a structure that consists of the addresses of the interrupt event handler and the IRQ that will be processed by the VxD.

Once the interrupt request is acknowledged by the virtual machine manager, the VxD's interrupt event handler is called. The VxD's interrupt handler can interface with the requesting hardware, but should not attempt to interface with the PC's 8259A interrupt controllers (generally referred to as the *PIC*). Once the interrupt has been processed and the requesting hardware reset, the interrupt event handler simply returns to its caller.

Multiple VxDs can claim the same interrupt, although each VxD should be checking the hardware that is specific to a shared interrupt source. Like Real-mode interrupt handlers, the VxD interrupt handlers should reset the interrupt-request mechanism as quickly as possible and then process the interrupt. Resetting the request source will allow subsequent interrupt requests to be acknowledged and minimize the potential for them to be missed.

Interrupts can be globally "masked" from within a VxD (using the *cli* instruction), but I don't recommend it. Even though the intention is to minimize the time that the processor executes without hardware interrupts, actual virtual machine manager and VxD API calls while interrupts are masked can take a surprisingly long time (especially with interrupts masked). Missed clock ticks, disk operations or other hardware events that request interrupts can cause problems in the operating system or other applications that are very hard to debug.

For code that has crucial execution requirements, you should use the synchronization features that follow.

Request Synchronization

For any kind of device driver in a multitasking/multithreading operating system, synchronizing requests from applications and other device drivers is crucial. Elsewhere in the book, I have introduced the concept of virtualization, in which a device driver appears to be dedicated to a virtual machine process. As part of this requirement, a device driver has to be able to handle multiple thread requests appropriately and not take requests out of order or lose the thread serialization. Windows has four primary tools for providing this serialization: semaphores, mutexes, Global Critical Section, and synchronization IDs.

The need for serialization is shown in Fig. 39-3, in which three threads are sending requests to a device driver. Thread A is only sending one request, thread B has sent two, and thread C has sent three. In the device driver, a strategy must be developed to determine which request is to be handled next. This strategy must be created with the threads' in-

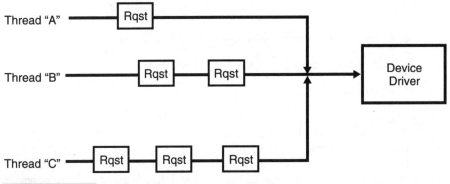

FIGURE 39-3 **Messaging without synchronization.**

volvement. If the threads are not involved, then the device driver will have to arbitrarily pick out which requests it has to handle in the appropriate order.

This is crucial for device drivers that handle devices (such as a disk drive) in which multiple requests from different tasks can be expected. Correctly serializing the requests is needed for the operation of the disk for the different tasks. The serializing methods presented here are also available for standard Windows applications.

The first type of serialization tool is the semaphore. A *semaphore* is a token that is claimed by a specific thread and other threads will wait for this token to become free and then claim it for its own use before sending requests to the device drivers. The four semaphore requests are Create, Destroy, Wait, and Signal. Normally, the semaphore is created by the device driver and then claimed (by Wait) by an application or device driver thread. Signal will poll the semaphore to see if it is free. To find the semaphore's ID, a separate request, designed to be accessed by multiple threads (i.e., is reentrant), is used to request the ID from the device driver.

Mutex is a combination of the two words *mutually exclusive* and is a tool used to indicate code that can only be executed for one thread at a time. In the device driver, this code is identified using *CreateMutex*. When the device driver shuts down, it is freed using *DestroyMutex*. Application code will enter the mutex code and then leave it when the execution is complete. This is similar to the semaphore, but it is used in inline code and cannot "Signal" or poll the code to determine whether it is available (if it isn't, then the thread waits for the mutex code to become available).

The virtual machine manager has Global Critical Section code, which is similar to the mutex, but is part of the operating system. A thread first claims the Critical Section and then begins to execute the code within it and returns. When the Critical Section is no longer needed (only one is available in the system), it is ended and returned for use by other device drivers. The Critical Section code is used when code must have priority over the entire system and no other threads or operation can execute.

The last synchronization tool is the synchronization ID, which is a simple form of messaging between threads in Windows. The Synchronization ID tool is used by a thread when it is waiting for another thread to complete. An example (Fig. 39-4) shows how

Thread "A"   **Thread "B"**

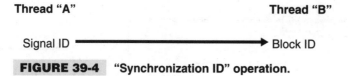

Signal ID ──────────────────────► Block ID

FIGURE 39-4   "Synchronization ID" operation.

Thread B will wait for Thread A to send a synchronization ID to it. Like any form of messaging, understanding exactly how the program is expected to flow is crucial.

In Fig. 39-4, if Thread A is, in any way, dependent on Thread B's downstream (from the Block ID statement) code, then Thread B's Block ID statement will never complete. In this case, the two threads will wait for information or a message that will not come.

These synchronization tools are not limited to VxD's. They can be used with any code that executes within the Windows Operating System.

VxD Debugging

When you research more about VxDs, you will discover they are perceived by most people (including experienced programmers) as being very hard to debug. Unfortunately, this perception is correct; VxDs are very hard to debug because, as indicated, loaded VxDs are an extension to the PC's operating system. Being operating system extensions, modern debugging techniques cannot be used with them; instead, you will have to resort to methods and procedures that were used 20 years ago to debug applications.

If you are a relatively old programmer like me, you'll remember that programming classes used to specify that status messages had to be put in source code to allow you to track how the code was executing. For example, to follow a branch path in C, you would put in the statements:

```
if ( condition == TRUE ) {

  printf( "condition == TRUE\n" ); //  ####

  :                        // Put in Code to Execute Condition TRUE

} else {

  printf( "condition == FALSE\n" ); //  ####

  :                        // Put in Code to Execute Condition
                           //    FALSE
}
```

This code, although easy to understand, is an absolute pain to maintain and when your application was ready. It was difficult to find all the occurrences of the *printf* debug statements. This is where I started to put in the #### indications in the source code to allow me to search on them and find the occurrences to delete them.

If you are working with VtoolsD, stream I/O can be used for these statements:

```
x out << "message or Variable = " < Value < <endl;   //   #####
```

The x*out* can be *dout* for serial output (*vdbostream*), *dmono* for monochrome display output (*vmonostream*) or *din* for serial input (*vdbistream*). To take advantage of any of these stream I/O paths, additional hardware will have to be added to the PC and the streams will have to be initialized when the VxD executes its Load or Create code.

Two interactive VxD debuggers are available that can be loaded with the VxD and use an external PC (via a serial cable) to debug the VxD.

WDEB386 is an assembly-language debugger (similar to MS-DOS' DEBUG.COM) that comes with the Microsoft DDK. A small kernel runs in the PC with the VxD, which communicates over a serial link to another PC running the actual debugger interface. I have used WDEB386 on two occasions and I would consider it to be a tool of last resort. It is very difficult to exactly find your location in an application (especially if you are running C++ code) and does not provide trace functions (which at least can show you how the code is executing).

Compuware's *Soft-ICE* is somewhat better because it provides a source-level debugger on the serially connected PC. Unfortunately, C++ classes are hard to work with in Soft-ICE, which makes the tool only useful for VxDs written in C.

My general rule when writing VxDs is to keep them very simple. Complex operations can be virtually impossible to debug (especially in your initial attempts). Second, you should use the layering capabilities of VxDs as much as possible to develop complex applications without complicating the code. Last, the VxD code should be tested in MS-DOS applications before trying it in a VxD, to ensure that the data-processing functions work as required.

These rules won't help you when it is 2:00 AM and you've been staring at a problem that needed to be fixed two days before, but they will help minimize the chances of being in that situation.

VtoolsD

Reading through the previous 10 pages, I have probably made you very nervous about VxD writing and having the appropriate information at your fingertips to efficiently create the code. If you have worked through learning Visual C++ and creating your own application, you will have learned how much effort it is to find all the class information and example code to work from. With this background, creating VxDs probably seems very scary.

This is not a unique impression on VxD writing and Vireo tools (now Compuware Nu-Mega) has come up with a product known as *VtoolsD*, which makes writing VxDs much easier and makes it very similar to creating a Visual C++ application. As pointed out elsewhere, VtoolsD does not require a Microsoft DDK to create VxDs, but does require Visual

C++ (Version 5.0 or later) or a Borland C compiler for application development. This book focuses on the Visual C++ source creation because that is my primary VxD development tool.

To create a VxD, the QuickVxD program is launched and from the dialog box that comes up (Fig. 39-5), you will enter in the device driver name, its ID and other parameters, and then execute it. When QuickVxD has completed, you will have a skeleton framework for the VxD, into which you just enter code. This is very similar to the Visual C++ Apps Wizard. For this reason, I consider QuickVxD to be a wizard in its own right.

Under the Device Parameters tab, along with specifying the device name and ID, the architecture framework is specified, along with the device initialization order, the version code, debug flagging, whether the VxD is static or dynamically loaded, and if it supports the *Network Device Interface Specification (NDIS)*. The VxD ID parameter is only entered if the VxD is going to supply services to other VxDs.

The device initialization order specifies the point in the Windows initialization where the VxD's create code executes. Normally, if a VxD has specific initialization order requirements, it is because it must have another VxD active before it can be loaded in.

The Debug/Retail flag is used to specify whether or not debug hooks for the I/O streaming or one of the serial debug interfaces is going to be used. For the VxDs that I have written, I have left the Debug flag active. I have not had to ship any of my VxDs (they have all been used in a manufacturing environment), but this flag should only be set to Retail before shipping the VxD and product to customers.

The Control Message tabs are used to create classes and skeleton member functions for C++. In C, it creates skeleton code for the ControlDispatcher that will be used in the VxD.

As can be seen in Fig. 39-5, the API tab is used to specify the event-handler entry points the VxD will support (either V86 or Protect mode). Checking the boxes will create C++ skeleton member functions or C skeleton interface code. The vendor-specific entry point

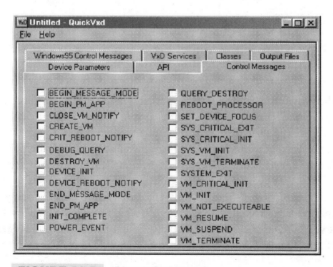

FIGURE 39-5   "VtoolsD" Wizard.

is used to create code skeletons or member functions that are appropriate entry points, based on the VxD's name.

VxD services allow you to specify APIs for other VxDs to access the current VxD and member function skeletons or skeleton interface code will be created as required.

If you are going to allow other VxDs to interface with the current one, then you should always be sure that a *Get_Version* API is available, which, by convention, is used to determine whether or not a specific VxD is loaded in the system. If the Get_Version fails, then the calling VxD can output an error message to the user.

The Classes tab is only active for C++ output framework and is used to specify the class names used in the application.

Once the previous five tab's parameters have been entered, you can then click on Output and generate the VxDs:

1 Include files
2 Code module
3 Make file

The actual parameters entered can be saved using the File pull down on the QuickVxD dialog box. This file is saved with a .QVX extension.

One thing that usually screws new users up is the need for the environment variable *VTOOLSD* to be embedded in the PC's Environment Block. This is done by adding the line in your PC's autoexec.bat file where "D:PATH" is the path information where the VtoolsD utilities have been loaded.

```
SET VTOOLSD=D:PATH
```

Normally, this is taken care of by the VtoolsD installation program, although sometimes it doesn't work or the AUTOEXEC.BAT gets modified and the line is deleted.

VTOOLSD CLASS LIBRARY

The biggest advantage of the VtoolsD Class library is how clearly it displays how VxDs are structured and work. QuickVxD takes excellent advantage of object-orientated programming techniques and Wizards for application development. The class library focuses on the VxD operation, rather than on the format and avoids the low-level virtual machine manager interface issues. This is a good thing because it allows you to focus on what is important in the VxD: the actual operation and whether you have created the VxD source exactly as the compiler and linker require.

Three primary classes are provided by VtoolsD. The VtoolsD base class is the "VDevice" class, which is analogous to CObject in Visual C++. The device classes are derived from this base class. The VVirtualMachine class is used to provide data structures for each virtual machine (Process) instance in the PC's Windows virtual machine manager. The last primary class is VThread, which is the same as VVirtualMachine, but is devoted to individual threads, rather than processes.

QuickVxD-specified application entry points can be overridden by user-written code with different parameters passed from the caller to the VxD. These entry points are defined in VVirtualMachine and VDevice classes. By overriding them, you are creating a handler for that message.

OnCreateVM and OnDestroyVM are often used user VxD code to allocate and free memory that is needed to keep track of the information required by the Process to access the VxD. These entry points are usually overridden by the VxD programmer to allocate resources needed for each process.

When an API is added to a VxD, QuickVxD carries out a number of tasks to ensure that the API is integrated throughout the VxD's source code. These operations are similar to what happens in Visual C++ when a new member function is added to an application.

For example, if the GetVersion API (used by other VxDs to determine whether or not a VxD is installed and active) was added to a VxD from within QuickVxD in MyVxD, first a prototype of the API would be created:

```
class MyVxDDevice: public Vdevice
{
public:
 static DWORD MyVxD_GetVersion();

}
```

Next, the API is added to the driver's service table, which resides in the *MyVxD.h* function prototype file using the macros:

```
Begin_VxD_Service_Table( MyVxD )
 VxD_Service( MyVxD_Get_Version )
End_VxD_Service_Table
```

Pipe classes are often used to provide a data path between applications and VxDs or just between VxDs. Figure 39-6 shows that a pipe is a serialization mechanism that presents only one request at a time to the VxD. All requests are queued inside the pipe, according to the order in which they are received.

The class VPipe is specific to VtoolsD and provides a byte stream data-transfer mechanism and can be for a unique VxD/process pair. When a specific pipe is used, then all the

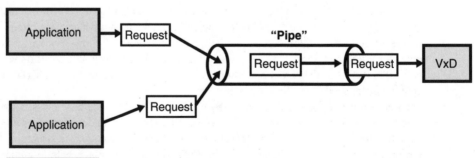

FIGURE 39-6   VxD "Pipe" serialization operation.

requests for a specific process can be handled and when the requests are finished, the VxD can poll pipes connected to other applications and execute any requests waiting for the VxD to process.

Events in a VxD can either be requests from applications or other VxDs or hardware interrupt requests. The event handlers are created in the VxD by carrying out the following steps:

1 Determine the appropriate base class
2 Derive a class with a constructor and override the member function holder
3 Create the Constructor, optional Destructor, and Event Handler
4 Generate a new Object for the class
5 Call the member function hook to link the event handler into the operating system

The class declaration for a function to handle the *Ctrl-C* keystroke (which executes when the PC's user presses a *Ctrl* key followed by the *C* key) would be:

```
class CtrlCEvent: public VHotkey
{                               //  Define the "CtrlEvent" Class with a
                                //   Constructor
public:
 CtrlCEvent();                  //  Constructor
 Virtual VOID handler( BYTE, keyaction_t, DWORD, DWORD, DWORD );
}

CtrlCEvent::CtrlCEvent():VHotKey( SCAN_Code_C, SCAN_NORMAL, HKSS_Ctrl,
CallOnPress )
{                               //  Constructor Code

//  #### - Put in the Constructor Code for the "VHotKey" VxD Class

}

CtrlCEvent::handler( BYTE scan, keyaction_t ka, DWORD shift, DWORD ref-
Data, DWORD elapsed )
{

//  #### - Put in the Handler Code for the "Ctrl-C" event

}
```

To create the object and "hook" it into the operating system, the following code is used:

```
CtrlCEvent * pCC = new CtrlCEvent();    //  Create the New CtrlCEvent
                                //   Object  and Execute the
                                //   "Constructor"
 if ( pCC -> hook())            //  Not Zero - Successful

//  #### - Handle the successful object creation and "hook"

 else                           //  Zero - Not Successful

//  #### - Report the error in "hooking" the "CtrlCEvent" object
```

The event types supported in VtoolsD are

EVENT TYPE	DESCRIPTION/COMMENTS
VPreChainV86Int	V86-Mode Interrupt Handler
VInChainV86Int	V86-Mode Interrupt Handler
VInChainPMInt	Protect-Mode Interrupt Handler
VHardwareInt	Hardware Interrupt Handler
VHotkey	Keystroke Hotkey Event Handler
VprotModeFault	Protect-Mode Fault Event Handler
VV86ModeFault	V86-Mode Fault Event Handler
VVMMFault	Virtual Machine Manager Fault Handler
VInvalidPageFault	Page-Access Fault Handler
VDeviceAPI	VxD Device API Handler
VglobalEvent	Global System Event Handler
VVMEvent	Virtual Machine Manager Event Handler
VThreadEvent	Thread Event Handler
VPriorityVMEvent	Priority Process Event Handler
VV86Callback	Callback in V86-Mode Event Handler
VProtModeCallback	Callback in Protect-Mode Event Handler
VIOPort	Specific I/O Port Access Event Handler
VMTimeOut	Notification of Elapsed Time Interval

WIN32

DEVICE

MODELS

CONTENTS AT A GLANCE

As described earlier in the book, the *Win32 Device Model (WDM)* was originally de-signed for Windows NT 5.0 (now known as *Windows 2000*) and was based off the Win-dows NT device-driver structure. When Microsoft decided to integrate the operating-system product lines, they saw it as an opportunity to create a device-driver structure that was sim-pler than the existing structures and also had the ability to natively support Plug'n'Play. I think that the developers deserve a pat on the back for design of WDMs because they re-ally are simpler to code and more effective to use than previous device drivers used in MS-DOS and Windows.

WDM consists of a set of class drivers, which provide generic support for certain types of drivers (such as streaming devices, including CD-ROMs, and human interface devices, including keyboards) and allow the user to create their own unique driver classes, derived from the primary classes. Once you are comfortable with C++ and creating your own objects, you won't have any problems understanding how WDM drivers are created.

The WDM driver (Fig. 40-1) interfaces to the application through the system services/I/O manager interface. The system services provides a traditional interface for applications and allows WDMs to appear to the applications identical to any other device driver written for a PC. The I/O manager converts the device driver request into an *I/O Request Packet (IRP)* and passes it to the WDM driver. This architecture makes implementation of layered drivers (such as the OSI communications model) quite easy and logical to implement, as well as allows you to create dummy drivers to debug application code before the actual hardware drivers are ready.

There are two primary types of WDMs, both of which can link to other drivers. The first is the class driver, which provides a common interface to a type of device. An example of a class driver could be the diskette interface; PCs can use disk drives that use a traditional diskette controller, a parallel-port interface (which is often used with laptops), or a diskette that interfaces through the USB port. When an application needs to access diskette data, the programmers don't want to worry about how the diskette is actually implemented; instead, just having a common API is all that is desired. The class driver provides this.

The mini driver is the second type of driver and is used primarily for handling specific services. Whereas the class driver provides a common interface for applications, the mini driver provides the "bits and bytes" movement. Going back to the diskette example, the mini driver would be the interface to the ISA diskette controller, the parallel port, or the USB port and be accessed by the class driver, instead of the application directly.

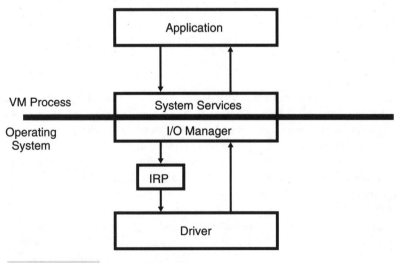

FIGURE 40-1   Basic WDM operation.

Device Objects

In the Windows system services module, device driver and object information is stored in a directory of symbolic links. These symbolic links are objects that contain a pointer to another object. As you go down the chain, you might discover that multiple symbolic links lead to the same device object, which is known as a *WDM*. These links are used by system services to allow accessing of specific WDM objects.

Device objects controls the hardware devices that it represents and passes control requests to the actual hardware via a *Hardware Abstraction Layer (HAL)*. The HAL allows WDMs to access specific hardware devices without having access to the actual device address (which might be at an unexpected address because of Plug'n'Play. The HAL overlay is shown in Fig. 40-2.

The device object may simply pass on I/O request objects to other WDMs or VxDs without accessing a HAL. In this case, layers of WDMs are used to pass the requests to the actual hardware (Fig. 40-3). This is described in more detail in the next section.

The operating system maintains a set of *Physical Device Objects (PDO)* representations for the devices that are listed in the system registry. The PDO contains the device parameters and passes this information into a driver-created object known as the *Function Device Object (FDO)*. Multiple function device objects can be attached to a single PDO to represent multiple instances of similar devices (such as multiple diskette drives in a system).

As well as providing an interface into the Windows registry, the HAL also provides physical access information. An example of this is the digital thermometer used in modern PCs to monitor the current temperature of the processor in the system. The output of this device is used to determine whether or not a processor specific fan should be run to cool it

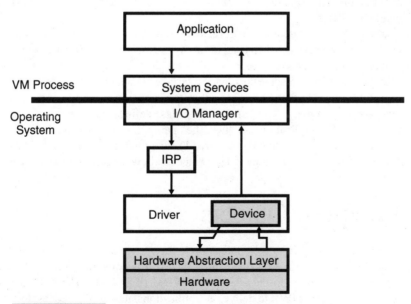

FIGURE 40-2   WDM device driver data path/operation.

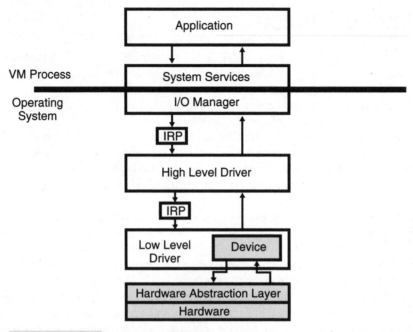

FIGURE 40-3   **Multi-layer WDM device driver.**

down. In most modern PCs, a small I2C bus is provided on the motherboard and is connected to the digital thermometer. In future systems, the I2C bus might be forsaken for the USB bus. In either case, the device would have the same interface to the WDM, but the HAL would be different.

Memory objects are located in virtual memory to pass data to and from a direct I/O device. The memory objects are often used to supply the memory required by the I/O request objects to carry out the data transfer.

The last type of WDM object is the device interface, which provides a defined set of I/O request object services to the HAL. These objects are instantiated by the presence of specific device objects in the system. An Interface class defines functionality for the device interface objects. The application can query the operating system for symbolic links to all devices that are registered within the required Device Interface class. Each Device Interface class is identified with a unique *GUID* value to allow the search to take place.

I/O Request Objects

When a request is passed from the application to the system services module of the operating system, if the request is destined for a WDM, it is converted into an *I/O Request Packet (IRP)* and is passed to the appropriate WDM (Fig. 40-1). The I/O manager and WDMs themselves create IRPs to deliver an application data-transfer request to the driver object and back to the caller.

The device driver itself can have a queue of requests or process the request immediately. This chapter includes information concerning the queuing and synchronization options available to WDMs.

WDMs and the I/O request packets can be architected one of two ways in the Windows 98 or Windows 2000 PC operating system. The first method (shown in Fig. 40-2) is an expansion of the basic application/WDM operation (shown in Fig. 40-1). Figure 40-2 shows the actual operation of the WDM as a driver interface to the application along with a built-in device driver for the hardware.

Notice that the hardware itself is not accessed directly by the device-driver portion of the WDM. Instead, a HAL is used. This kind of "mini" device driver is managed by the Windows system registry and provides interface information for standard devices to the WDMs.

As pointed out at the beginning of this chapter, WDMs can be nested with other WDMs to provide functionality layers for interfacing. An example of this could be creating a page scanner interface for PC applications. The top-level WDM is a standard interface to the application and provides the application with an interface to request to pass specific parameters to the scanner or receive scan information. The middle layer could be a manufacturer-specific interface, in which the scanner commands are converted into manufacturer-specific command strings. The bottom layer would be a communications layer and would pass the requests to the scanner on whatever communications medium is used. Using this WDM architecture, an application could work with scanners available from a variety of different manufacturers that interface over such diverse busses as ISA, SCSI, or USB.

In this layering capacity, WDMs are actually filtering and processing requests in the same manner as VxDs.

A two-WDM layer example is shown in Fig. 40-3.

The most common IRP operations used by WDMs are Create, Close (destroy), Read, Write, and DeviceControl. These operations are used to create and send an IRP to another device and when one is received, read its contents, and reply to it or destroy it. It is important (for application performance) for these operations to be executed as quickly as possible.

Containers

The data-storage and manipulation capabilities of WDMs and system services is actually better than that of other device drivers (and even that of standard application modes) with a number of basic data types built in to both standards. These different methods allow the WDM to easily manipulate data and pass IRPs between system services, WDMs, and HAL drivers.

The primary data structures is the Doubly Linked List (Fig. 40-4) and the First-In/First-Out List (Fig. 40-5). These two list types are available in standard C and C++ as well as *Driver::Works*. Both data structures use pointers to address a previous or following list data record element and keep track of which element is to be accessed next.

The two types of lists are best for message passing without any access of any of the "inside" elements ("Element 2" in both Figs. 40-4 and 40-5).

List "Head"   List "Tail"

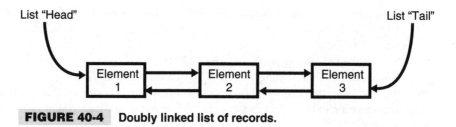

FIGURE 40-4   **Doubly linked list of records.**

Transmitter   Receiver

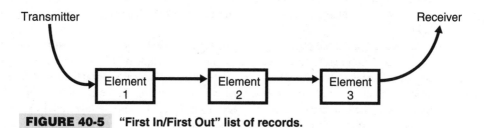

FIGURE 40-5   **"First In/First Out" list of records.**

File data can be accessed from within a WDM with the (very standard) operations: Create, Open, Close, Read, Write, Seek, Query, and Set Properties. Because of the relatively long time needed for these operations to complete, the code used for the file operations should only execute at the lowest IRQL (explained in the following paragraphs) priority level possible.

To carry out the file operations, WDMs typically create system threads to handle the file operations without impacting the responsiveness of the WDM itself.

One thing that has bugged me for 10 years (and probably more) is error messages in Windows and Windows device drivers. In versions of Windows previous to Windows 98, you either got the "blue screen of death" or a dialog box indicating that there was a problem with your application or device driver. In either case, when the display changes, you usually get a list of register contents, data information, or a code listing, none of which does you or a help desk person any good.

These error indicators were probably set up by the application or device-driver programmer to help them debug their code. Unfortunately, this code is meaningless to anybody else and should have been replaced by a simple message, such as "Adapter Bust, Replace, and Reboot." Which, despite its flippancy, is a lot more useful to a user than the processor register contents at the time of the failure.

WDMs allow you to create an event log of everything that has lead up to the error event. An *event log* is a record of all events of a WDM with software-generated messages added in as well. This file consists of a number of fixed-length entries, which can contain text, binary data, or whatever is appropriate, and can be read out using System Administration Tools.

The Event Logs allows the software developer to have the information needed to initially debug the application and still put in simple, meaningful messages for the user, in the form of a dialog box with simple instructions on how to respond to the problem.

Strings in WDMs are normally in UNICODE format. This format is not really a string, but a data structure, with a set buffer for saving text data along with the current size of data stored and the maximum buffer size for the text data. Although not as flexible as an ASCIIZ string, the UNICODE buffer is well suited to working with WDMs with fixed-data sizes.

The last data structure to be aware of when working with WDMs is the *heap*. The *Heap* gets its name from the idea that data is "piled" up with each element ordered specifically in relation to the element above it and when the actual structure is displayed, it looks like a real mess. If you look at the heap in Fig. 40-6, you'll see exactly what I mean.

The heap represented in Fig. 40-6 is a binary heap with each element able to point to up to two elements below it. This characteristic allows the heap to carry out some programming tasks very quickly with a minimal amount of code. If each element in Fig. 40-6 pointed to the lesser element to the left and the greater element to the right, you should be able to see how random data could be stored into the heap structure very easily. When it was time to read back the data, by retrieving the heap elements from left to right, you would be able to read out the data in a sorted format.

Another classic use of a heap is to parse an arithmetic statement. Figure 40-7 shows a reasonably complex statement that is then broken down into its constituent parts in "order of operations" priority (i.e., multiplication and division must execute before addition or subtraction).

To place the statement's data and operations into the heap, I have gone through the full statement and placed the lowest priority operation at the top of each "sub-heap." The first operation to execute is either the addition or division. Because division is of a higher priority than addition, I placed addition at the top of the heap. This then results in the two statements $((A * B) - C)$ and D / E, which are then broken down the same way.

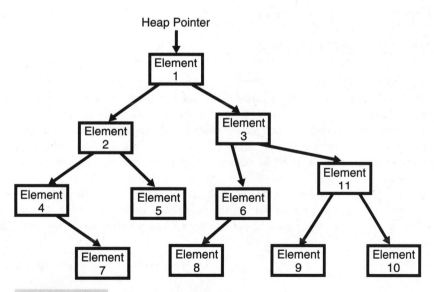

FIGURE 40-6 "Heap" record structure.

Statement = ((A * B) – C) + D / E

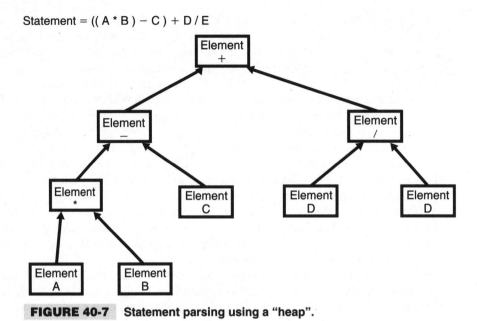

FIGURE 40-7   **Statement parsing using a "heap".**

To evaluate the statement, the values are either retrieved or calculated from the bottom up. In this example, the *A * B* will be executed first, followed by the subtraction and division operations, and finally the addition. Like the sorting operation, using a heap to process an arithmetic statement, which seems quite hard, can be carried out quite easily.

Request Control and Synchronization Objects

Like VxDs, WDMs have to provide their own request synchronization and control to ensure that requests from multiple applications and threads are "synchronized" and "virtualized." A few specific WDM types and built-in features can help you carry out these tasks.

The first control object is the *Queue*, which serializes requests from multiple applications. A *queue object* is shown as part of a device object in Fig. 40-8. Multiple Queue Objects can be created in a WDM device object to service the requests from multiple processes.

In Fig. 40-8, you can see that the queue object consists of a singly linked list of IRPs. To read an IRP and take it out of the list, the pointer to the last IRP must be found and its pointer to the queue object must be put into the second last IRP. To do this, the following code could be used:

```
IRP * GetLastIRP()              //  Function to Retrieve the Last
{                               //   IRP in a Queue Object

IRP * CurIRP, PrevIRP;          //  Pointers into the IRP List
```

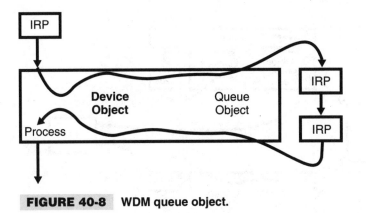

FIGURE 40-8   WDM queue object.

```
if ( QueueStart == QueueEnd )       //  Are there any Queue Elements?
   return NULL;                      //   - No
 else {                             //  Read through the Queue

   CurIRP = QueueStart;             //  Get First Element in the Queue

   if ( CurIRP -> NextIRP == QueueEnd ) {
     QueueStart = QueueEnd;         //  Only One Queue Element
     return CurIRP;                 //   Return It and Empty Queue
   } else {                         //  Else, Read through the Queue

     while ( CurIRP -> NextIRP != QueueEnd ) {
       PrevIRP = CurIRP;             //  Go through List to Last Element
       CurIRP = CurIRP -> NextIRP;
     }

     PrevIRP -> NextIRP = QueueEnd;//  CurIRP is the Last Element
     Return CurIRP;                 //  Make Previous Point to Queue
//   End
   }
 }
} // End GetLastIRP
```

Multiple-device objects can access a single HAL using a control object to arbitrate which device object should have access. Figure 40-9 is the block diagram of a situation, where multiple WDMs are accessing a common hardware device.

Requests to the control object are prioritized within the control object and passed back to indicate to the device object that it can access the HAL.

Along with the queue and control objects, a number of different functions are built into WDMs to allow for access synchronization and execution control. These functions include "spin locks" and "dispatcher" objects. Each of these functions is used in a variety of different cases to provide control over access to the hardware device.

Spin locks are used in multiprocessor systems to halt one processor while it is waiting for a message from one of the other processors in the system. Like the other multiprocessor features described in this chapter, spin locks are not something that will be routinely accessed in most people's PCs.

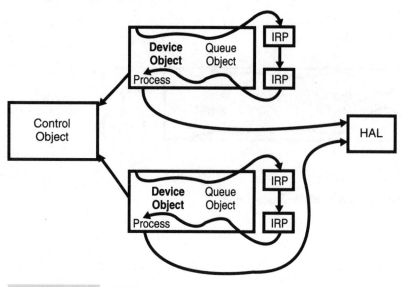

FIGURE 40-9   WDM control object.

Dispatcher objects is a term used for objects that are used to provide synchronization and scheduling of the WDM's execution. The actual objects are very similar to what is available in VxDs.

The *event object* is simply an event handler that waits for an event to occur in the system. Along with waiting on user input, timers, and interrupts, hardware states can be used as events to key off of the WDM.

Semaphores are token counters that can be incremented and waited on for a specific event. For example, in a WDM, a semaphore can be used to keep track of the number of IRPs in a queue. When the semaphore value becomes zero, the WDM should block on the semaphore because there are no more requests to process.

For multithreaded applications, mutexes ("mutually exclusive" sections of code) can be declared to prevent multiple threads from accessing the same code at the same time. This feature is identical to the corresponding VxD feature.

System timer functions can be used to either generate events or provide timed callbacks to the WDM thread. This capability is useful when long delays between hardware events are needed.

The last synchronization/request control function available to a WDM is the system thread. The system thread is an independent thread created by the WDM to carry out tasks to either access hardware or help synchronize the operation of the WDM. System threads are often created to do background operations like register polling at the lowest operating ("IRQL") level of the processor. Other uses include background event logging and file operations.

Interrupts

To prioritize the use of the processor, in Windows systems with WDM capability, execution is set at specific *Interrupt Request Levels (IRQL)*, with 31 being the highest and 0 being the lowest. This scheme is important to understand when interrupt requests are waiting to be processed by WDMs, as well as understanding how the system is working and why it is ignoring some requests.

When Windows is executing, the processor can only be interrupted by a request at a higher level than what the processor is currently running. For example, if the processor is running at level 2, it cannot be interrupted by a level 2, 1, or 0 request. It can be interrupted by any request from level 3 to 31. Ideally, the processor should always be running at the lowest possible interrupt request level to ensure that all interrupt requests can be serviced.

If an interrupt request cannot be serviced because the processor is running at a higher level, then it is said to be *starved*. To prevent starvation of interrupt requests, WDM interrupt handlers (which are given the IRQL execution level by the windows hardware registry) should be as short as possible and return to the level 0, 1, or 2 (the normal execution levels) as quickly as possible.

The IRQLs built into the system are:

PRIORITY	IRQL	DESCRIPTION
Highest	31	Bus Error
	30	Power Failure
	29	Interprocessor Communications
	28	System Timers
	27–3	I/O Device Interrupts
	2	Dispatch Level
	1	APC Level
Lowest	0	Passive Level

All of the IRQLs should be self explanatory, except for interprocessor communications. This IRQL is reserved for systems with multiple processors.

The system associates a specific IRQL to each interrupt registry key (Object). To give an idea of how the interrupts are set up in a system, I have printed out my registry IRQ information in Fig. 40-10. From this information, you can see how the interrupts are set according to the hardware IRQ levels.

The IRQ information is converted into IRQLs by Windows system services. Hardware interrupt IRQLs are known as *Direct IRQLs (DIRQLs)* and are mapped into IRQLs 3 through 27. Along with this mapping, the IRQL registry entries also contain the attributes of the IRQ. These attributes are the bus type, the vector number (the IRQ in Fig. 40-10) and its mode.

5

WINDOWS DEVICE DRIVERS

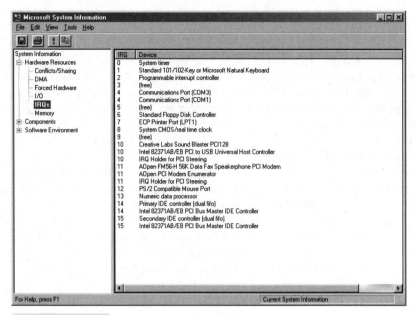

FIGURE 40-10 Interrupt register display.

Notice that multiple interrupt sources can be shared. In this case, all of the interrupt handler routines (known as *Interrupt Service Routines, ISRs*) are called when a specific hardware interrupt is requested. If the hardware associated with a specific interrupt handler did not request an interrupt, then the ISR ignores the interrupt and simply returns.

These ISRs are "connected" when the WDM is loaded into the system.

Ideally, for fast interrupt response and minimized "starving" of other interrupt requests or threads, the ISR should be short and execute as quickly as possible to avoid having the processor spending so much time in the higher-priority IRQL level that lower-level IRQL requests are starved. One way to ensure that this will occur is to have the data-handling routines execute at IRQL level 2 or lower. For this operation to be successful, the data-handling routines must be built before the ISR is connected to the system.

WDM Initialization and Unloading

When a WDM is loaded, system services creates driver objects for the WDM that requires a constructor (which executes immediately) and a Destructor (which executes when the WDM is unloaded or the PC is shut down). The entry points for these functions are built into the WDM structure itself.

The WDM constructor is known as *DriverEntry* and can be as simple as just a variable initialization. Typically, DriverEntry is used to query the Windows registry for devices needed for the WDM to operate. The registry is queried to load the device's control (i.e., Plug'n'Play) addresses and HAL interfaces and not the actual physical address of the device. The memory required for the DriverEntry code is usually discarded after it has successfully executed.

Re-initialization functions are normally built into the WDM and run the DriverEntry constructor repeatedly during the system boot and WDM load operation. The reason for the requirement to run the DriverEntry multiple times is to ensure that if required WDMs (and VxDs) are loaded after the current WDM, then the linkages with them can be repeatedly pinged until all the device drivers are loaded into the system. Only after all the other device drivers have been loaded can a WDM flag an error, indicating that a required device driver is not present.

When the WDM is no longer needed (such as when the system shuts down), Unload is used as a destructor. It determines which resources have been allocated to the WDM and then frees them up for other device drivers. It is important that WDMs do not allocate devices; they simply get the device access information stored in the Windows registry.

Some crucial system drivers, such as console, disk and user input, do not have the Unload destructor because they are always required in the system. I was going to write that these types of device drivers are primarily only needed for operating-system and user-interface functions, but I realized that this was wrong because I could come up with a number of devices that would be required as long as the system was active. These devices could be a network interface for "thin clients," system-status recorders, alternative audio output, external system controllers, etc.

Driver::Works

Earlier, the book described how I liked to develop Windows applications; Visual Basic was used for the user interface and the application code and Visual C++ was used for the device drivers and hardware interface. When creating WDMs for Windows 98 and Windows 2000, this works perfectly with Vireo's (now Compuware's) Driver::Works tool.

Driver::Works is a Visual C++ enhancement, which integrates a new wizard for developing WDM skeleton code for the actual device driver. During Driver::Works installation, the Wizard code is loaded into Visual C++'s Template and BIN subdirectories. Like Visual C++, Driver::Works has its own Help HTML code for guiding the user.

The Wizard carries out the following functions needed for WDMs:

1 Allocates hardware resources
2 Creates registry entries
3 Creates registry variables
4 Defines I/O controls

Driver::Works also includes Driver::Monitor, which is a simple debug tool that allows monitoring of the WDM state from the Windows Desktop. Using Driver::Monitor, you can display the output from WDMs, dynamically configure the start and stop driver for testing WDMs without application code and use it to load and link VxDs.

To use Driver::Works, Visual C++ Version 5.0 or later must be installed on the development PC.

DRIVER::WORKS CLASSES

Driver Works has provided a number of base classes for you to use with your applications. Like any other C++ classes, the prototype information and skeleton methods can be viewed from the Visual C++ IDE.

USB:
THE INTERFACE
OF THE
FUTURE

41

WHAT

IS

USB?

CONTENTS AT A GLANCE

CONNECTIONS TO THE PC

DATA PACKET FORMATS

DATA TRANSFER TYPES

DEVICE ENUMERATION

PC HOST CONFIGURATION

The *Universal Serial Bus (USB)* is an interface protocol developed by Intel and Microsoft to provide a "hot pluggable," relatively low-speed PC connection scheme that could be used by all PC users to attach peripherals. USB is a cornerstone of the Intel/Microsoft PC/98 specification, which is noted for its elimination of the need to open up the PC to add and configure peripheral devices because of its use of only USB and Firewire connectors for attaching peripherals.

USB was designed with three attributes that distinguish it from other methods of attaching hardware to the PC. The first is ease of use. This was achieved by making devices *hot pluggable/unpluggable* (meaning that they can be connected or disconnected while the PC is operating) and dynamically configurable. *Dynamically configurable* means that the device address on the USB network is determined by software when the device is *enumerated* (recognized with its software set up by the PC). These two features eliminate many of the issues associated with adding hardware to PCs and the problems users can have.

The second attribute of USB is its ability to transfer voice-quality audio data over the bus. This gave a certain performance requirement (about 40 KBps) which was used as USB's lower limit. It is important to note that *voice quality* is not *CD quality* or even *data quality*, both of which have much more stringent error-rate requirements. *Voice quality* simply means that USB will have to pass data at the same quality as you would expect on the telephone and does not require special cabling or high-speed electronic devices for passing data.

The last quality required for USB is expandability. As I have been writing this book, I have been racking my brain as to how many PCs I've had on my desk at work or at home over the past two decades. I think the number is somewhere around 15. Of all those PCs, I would have to guess that at least 90 percent of them have had all their I/O slots used up. For the early PCs, the video and disk controllers did take up a good fraction of the available slots, but the 127 devices possible in USB would have been welcome for many of these PCs.

This section introduces USB and how to create PC peripherals using the Cypress CY7C6xx microcontroller. I am excited about USB because I see it as a viable, useful method to add peripherals to the PC.

CONNECTIONS TO THE PC

USB is most often described as a "tiered star network" and then is described with a diagram looking something like that in Fig. 41-1 that really doesn't make any sense (or look like a "star"). I find USB is most easy to understand from its description.

USB consists of a token-passing ring in which the host (the PC) initiates contact with the various devices on the network. This network is best described as a "ring" because all devices are serially connected to one another through a "single" connection with data flowing in one direction (Fig. 41-2). Each device on the ring monitors the data passing by and only responds to the messages directed toward it.

Each USB connection consists of two connectors (A and B) and four wires. The A connector is the connection to the USB host or "upstream" hub, and the B connector is the

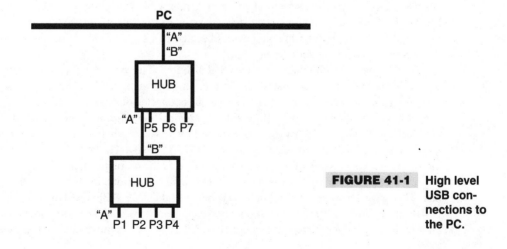

FIGURE 41-1   High level USB connections to the PC.

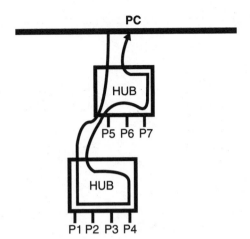

PC

HUB

P5 P6 P7

HUB

P1 P2 P3 P4

FIGURE 41-2   Actual USB connections to the PC.

connection to the peripheral or "downstream" device. A USB cable consists of an A and a B connector at each end of the wire.

Electrically, the cable consists of four connections. Two connections are used for the bidirectional signal between the host/hub/peripheral. The PC drives the signals on these two lines (which are differential voltages to enhance electrical noise immunity). The peripheral hardware drives data, at appropriate times, on these lines.

The other two lines in the USB cable are power (+5 volts and ground). Normally, a USB PC or hub can supply up to 100 mA to each peripheral device connected to it. The PC and some hubs can supply up to 500 mA to a device, but this shouldn't be counted upon in your applications. If more than 100 mA is required in an application, an external power source should be provided.

The maximum 12-MBps data rate means that the cable does not have to be shielded or treated specially in any way. Along with the maximum 12-MBps data rate, USB also can be used with a 1.5-MBps "slow" data rate, which is designed for keyboards and other low-speed, low-data rate devices.

I have not included much more detail in how packets are decoded; the following sections explain how this is accomplished. The actual network decode operations are quite complex and will require specially designed parts (such as ASICs or microcontrollers) to decode the signals. This is best performed by hardware designed especially for the task.

DATA PACKET FORMATS

Information passed between the USB device and the host consists of groups of packets sent at 12 MBps. Five different types of packets are available for use. These packets consist of a synch field, which is used to synchronize the USB device to the host. The next field, the PID, is used to specify the type of packet that is being passed. Following the PID is the packet information and an optional CRC.

The PID field is an eight-bit field with four bits of data repeated twice (for error detection). The four bits are specified as:

PACKET TYPE	PID NAME	PID3-PID0
Token	Out	0001
Token	In	1001
SOF		0101
Token	Setup	1101
Data	Data0	0011
Data	Data1	1011
Handshake	Ack	0010
Handshake	Nak	1010
Handshake	Stall	1110
Special	Pre	1100

The start-of-frame packet is broadcast by the host to each device every millisecond. The purpose of the packet is to notify the USB device that a set of packets is coming. The format of the packet is shown in Fig. 41-3.

Data packets are prompted by In or Out start-of-frame packets, with the buffer specified as either *Data0* or *Data1* (Fig. 41-4).

In all types of requests, except for isochronous data requests, a data packet is followed by a handshake packet that is simply like that in Fig. 41-5. The special preamble packet is sent by the host to notify a low-speed device (1.5 MBps) that it will communicate with it (Fig. 41-6).

These basic packet types are built into the USB data-transfer specification that is explained in the next section.

DATA TRANSFER TYPES

In USB, data is transmitted in packets, with each packet consisting of a number of fields. Different packets are used to create different message types, which are initiated by the PC host. It is important to note that the PC host only initiates all requests; this operation affects how "interrupts" and other USB device originated data transfers work.

Synch	PID = SOF	FRAME #	CRC

FIGURE 41-3   USB start of frame packet.

Synch	PID = Data	Data0 I Data 1	CRC

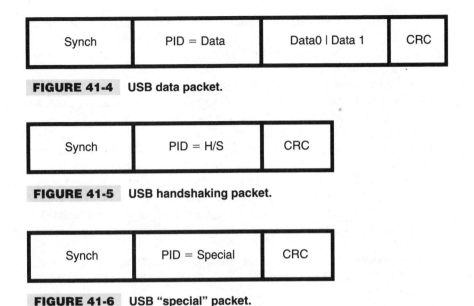

FIGURE 41-4 **USB data packet.**

Synch	PID = H/S	CRC

FIGURE 41-5 **USB handshaking packet.**

Synch	PID = Special	CRC

FIGURE 41-6 **USB "special" packet.**

The four USB data transfer types are: control, isochronous, bulk, and interrupt. Each type consists of two or three stages of a startup, optional data, and status. Startup passes the request type to the USB device and the data, if required, is returned in the next stage.

At the end of any data transfer, an Ack, Nak, or Stall is returned from the DMA transfers. *Ack* indicates that the operation completed successfully, *Nak* indicates that the operation cannot complete, and *Stall* indicates that PC host help is required. The best way I can visualize Stall is having the host prompt the user to put in a diskette so that a read can occur.

A control transfer is used to asynchronously pass data between the host and USB device. This type of transfer is used for general device reads and writes.

An isochronous transfer is completed within the USB communications frame (a 1-ms window for data transfer to occur). When an In token is received by the USB device, it will send data; when an Out token is received, it will wait to receive data. There is no handshake phase after data is transferred, which makes this type of transfer appropriate for telephony applications where erroneous data can be tolerated.

The bulk transfer is similar to that of the isochronous transfer, except that a handshake is passed after each frame.

The final type of USB data transfer is the interrupt data transfer. For this type of transfer, the host checks the USB device once per millisecond to see if something has changed. This check is responded to by a data packet (with the interrupt information) and a Nak or Stall. The PC host responds with an Ack, Nak, or Stall. This type of transfer is designed for such devices as keyboards or mice that only interrupt at a reasonably slow (for a computer) rate.

DEVICE ENUMERATION

Enumeration is the process that the PC goes through when it first powers up to recognize and link in the USB devices onto the system resources tables. This process can occur at any time and gives USB true "hot" Plug'n'Play capability. *Hot Plug'n'Play* means that devices can be plugged in and unplugged at any time when the PC is operating. The actual process consists of five steps with the USB device being accessed by applications using a .WDM file.

There are five steps to the enumeration process (Fig. 41-7).

The USB hub has two 15-K resistors pulling down the USB channel. When the USB device is attached, a pull up on the D+ or D- pins will change this state, causing the hub to recognize that the device is connected (Fig. 41-8).

The host PC then issues a Port Enable and Reset command to the hub address, where the new device is attached. At this point, 100 mA is supplied to the USB device.

The device will be put into its Default condition and wait for the host to poll it using a *GetDescriptor(Device)* set up packet and the device will respond with the device information. After the information has been received, the PC will issue a SetAddress to the device. This will set an address for the device to monitor requests to and respond when it is being addressed.

Once the address has been specified, a *GetDescriptor(Device)* command is re-issued, followed by a *GetDescriptor(Configuration)* command to have the device send its configuration information.

With the device's configuration set, the host sends a *SetDescriptor(Configuration)* command to indicate to the device that it is set up and can receive requests from the host at any time.

PC HOST CONFIGURATION

To use USB, you will need a PC loaded with at least one USB port (which can be built into the motherboard or on an adapter card) and a USB-enabled operating system. A hub is optional (but recommended).

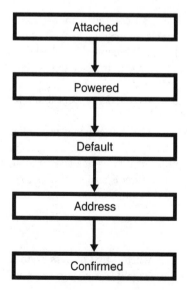

FIGURE 41-7   USB enumeration process.

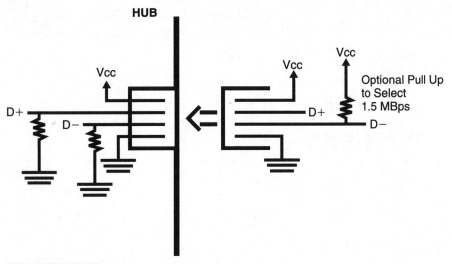

FIGURE 41-8 USB connector operation.

Fortunately, the hardware requirement has been a part of the PC de facto "standard" since 1996. USB-enabled operating systems (Windows 95 OSR 2.1 and Windows 98) have been available since late 1997. As time goes on, USB devices designed as PC peripherals will become more and more prevalent—especially with the availability of such hardware as the Cypress CY7C6xx microcontroller.

6

USB: THE INTERFACE OF THE FUTURE

42

THE
CYPRESS
CY7C6XX

If you're familiar with my previous books, you probably feel like I'm on familiar ground. The Cypress CY7C6xx family of microcontrollers (Fig. 42-1) do largely conform to the modern microcontroller model. They use a RISC processor architecture, have built-in RAM and ROM, internal clocking and control, and user-defined I/O. What makes them different is their ability to interface directly with a USB bus running at 1.5 MBps (the minimum speed specification).

This chapter introduces you to the Cypress microcontroller and goes through the hardware needed to interface with the Universal Serial Bus from the microcontroller's perspective. The next chapter covers the PC's software to interface with USB devices, such as the Cypress CY7C6xx.

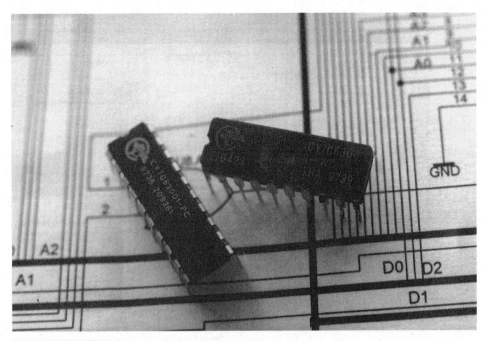

FIGURE 42-1   **Cypress CY7C6xx microcontrollers.**

Processor Architecture

A number of parts are in the CY7C6xx family, with differences in EPROM (control store) and RAM sizes, along with the number of port pins and their functions. What is common is the processor core, which Cypress describes as an eight-bit RISC processor with 35 instructions and 128 to 256 bytes of on chip RAM. The core is actually two different pieces of hardware. For the low-end devices (CY7C630xx/CY7C61xx/CY7C62xx), the core is known as *CPU A*. For the high-end devices (CY7C64xx/CY7C65xx) the core is known as CPU B. Minor differences exist between the two cores, centered primarily around how much control store is available to the processor.

Like I did with the 8086, I always want to be able to visualize how the processor is architected and be able to visualize in my mind how instructions execute. The CY7C6xx is actually a Harvard architected processor with three separate, addressable memory and I/O spaces (Fig. 42-2).

The control store memory is *nonvolatile* (which means that its contents aren't lost upon power down) and stores the application code for the processor. Each instruction in control store is eight or 16 bytes long, which generally includes the instruction and parameter. The parameter is an address, explicit value, or an offset to an index.

RAM consists of 128 bytes or more of RAM that can be used for application variables. This doesn't seem like an awful lot (especially in comparison to modern PCs), but it will be more than adequate to fulfill the requirements. The RAM can be accessed directly or using an index register.

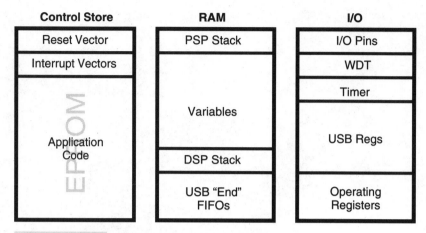

FIGURE 42-2   **CY7C6xx memory architecture.**

The final memory space isn't one at all, it is a set of addressable hardware registers that are used to read and write to the I/O ports, the USB control ports, timers, and miscellaneous control hardware. To access this hardware, specialized *iord* and *iowr* instructions are used.

These memory and I/O spaces fit together with various registers to become the computer architecture shown in Fig. 42-3. The different elements interact to execute the processor's instruction set.

For example, to execute a *mov A, Variable* instruction (load the accumulator with the contents of *Variable*), the instruction would be loaded from Control Store EPROM into the instruction register. The instruction register is part of an instruction decode/execution unit, which decodes it and places the address of variable on the address bus. The instruction decode/execution unit then reads the data from *Variable* and latches it into the accumulator (Fig. 42-4).

The Status Register bits (CY/ZR flags in Fig. 42-4) record the results of an arithmetic or bit instruction. This register only consists of a carry (CY) flag and a zero (ZR) flag. The zero flag is set after an arithmetic (or bit) instruction if the result placed in the accumulator is zero (000h).

The carry flag is set if the result of an addition is greater than 0x0FF or the result of a subtraction is less than -256. In either case, the carry flag is set when the result of an addition or subtraction should affect the next higher byte in a multibyte operation.

The shift and rotate instructions can also be used to pass data between the accumulator and carry flag. As well as using *jc/jnc* [jump on (no) carry] conditional branches. The rotate instructions can be used to load the carry flag into the accumulator.

The zero and carry flags cannot be directly accessed, instead instruction sequences designed to set or reset them must be used.

To set the zero flag:

```
    and    A, 0         ; ( Accumulator & 0 ) Always == 0
```

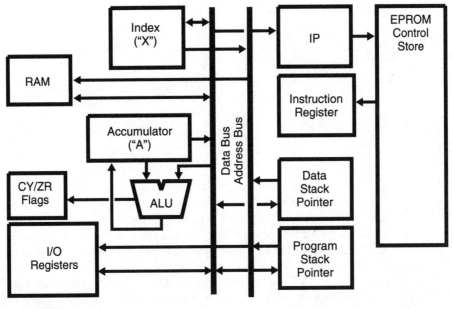

FIGURE 42-3   CY7C6xx processor architecture.

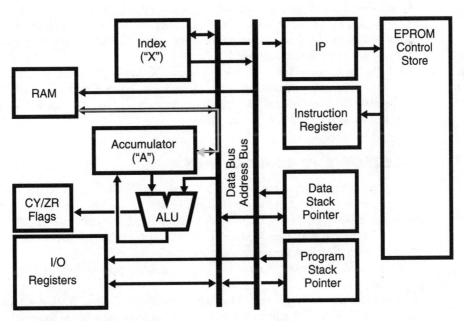

FIGURE 42-4   "Mov A, variable" instruction data flow.

To reset the zero flag:

```
or    A, 0AAh      ; ( Accumulator | !0 ) Always != 0
```

To set the carry flag:

```
mov   A, 0FFh      ; Load up the Accumulator and Shift
rlc                ;   a Set Bit into the Carry Flag
```

To reset the carry flag:

```
mov   A, 0         ; Clear the Accumulator and Shift
rlc                ;   a reset Bit into the Carry Flag
```

The CY7C6xx's instruction pointer is 14 bits long, which means that up to 16 KB of control store can be addressed. The instruction pointer is broken up into two registers, a six-bit PCH or high instruction pointer register and an eight-bit PCL, which is the lower eight bits of the instruction pointer. There is an issue with this because jumps and calls only have 12-bit address values. These instructions can only use the 12 bits to specify addresses in the least-significant 4096 bytes of the CY7C6xx's memory space.

To access the full 16 KB of control store, the long-call instruction is used to call subroutines and functions in any control store more than 4 KB. This instruction is only available in the high-end (CPU B) processors.

The code *page size* is determined by the PCL register, which is eight bits wide and only 256 bytes long. When an instruction reaches address 0FFh, it does not increment to 0100h, as you would expect; instead, it jumps back to address 000h. To allow code to flow into the next page, the assembler automatically inserts an XPAGE instruction into the code. The XPAGE instruction increments the PCH register.

If the XPAGE instruction falls on an address two bytes away from the page boundary (i.e., 0FEh) and the next instruction is two bytes long, the assembler will insert a NOP instruction before the XPAGE instruction. This will ensure that both bytes of the following instruction is located in the same page.

This is the basic architecture to the CY7C6xx microcontroller's processor. From this description, you should have a reasonable understanding of how software executes in the device. The next two sections expand on the instructions available within the CY7C6xx and the hardware that is available within the chips.

THE STACK AND SUBROUTINES

The memory and stack organization are a bit unusual in the Cypress CY7C8xx. Instead of having one stack for both the program counter and data, two stacks, one for the instruction pointer (which uses the PSP stack pointer) and one for data (which uses the DSP stack pointer). Sorting out how they are to be used is a bit confusing, although quite logical, when you understand how the processor works.

In the low-end CY7C6xx, which has 128 bytes of RAM, upon power-up is arranged as in Fig. 42-5.

Both the PSP and DSP registers are initialized to zero upon powerup. This is not a problem for the PSP because the IP is pushed onto the stack during a call or interrupt request and the operation is a post increment of the PSP stack pointer.

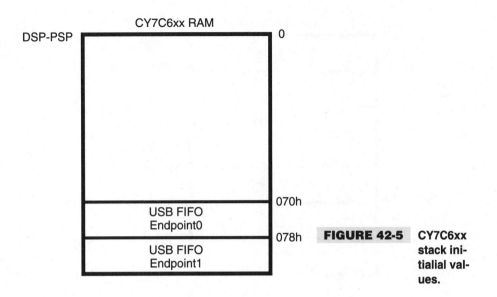

FIGURE 42-5   CY7C6xx stack initialial values.

The DSP stack pointer, which is used for pushing and popping from the data stack works with a *Pre Decrment*, which means that if the DSP is not changed before a push, the data will be stored at address 0x0FF or 0x07F, either of which is invalid. At the end of the RAM is the two USB endpoint memory blocks, which should not be accessed or overwritten by stack operations.

To avoid this potential problem, the DSP should be set to a different address at the top of the available RAM, which, in the 128-byte RAM CY7C6xx's case, is 0x068. This is accomplished by using the *swap A, DSP* instruction and would be set up as:

```
Mov   A, 068h
Swap  A, DSP
```

These two instructions should be executed at the start of the application (right after reset).

With the PSP and DSP set up, you should now decide how much memory is going to be used by the instruction pointer stack and the data stack. If you are not planning to have nested interrupts or subroutines and you are expecting to use the stack very little, you could probably get away with only allocating eight bytes for both the instruction pointer stack and data stack (Fig. 42-6).

This would leave you with 96 bytes of RAM for variables and arrays. You might wish to change these values according to the needs of your application.

When subroutines are called, the 16-bit instruction pointer is pushed onto the stack before the actual address is stored in there. As noted previously, each byte of the current instruction pointer will be saved onto the stack, followed by an increment of the PSP stack pointer.

To return from a subroutine, a *ret* instruction is executed, which pops the return address off the PSP stack and into the IP.

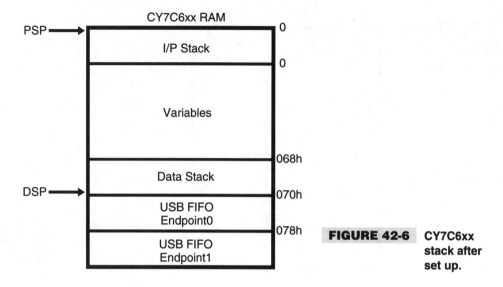

FIGURE 42-6 CY7C6xx stack after set up.

Subroutine parameters can be passed to a subroutine one of three ways. The first is to pass the data in the accumulator and index registers. This will allow up to 16 bits to be passed to and from the subroutine.

Another method is to use a block of variables in the RAM area. The problem with this method is that the CY7C6xx does not have a log of RAM available and, if nested subroutines are used (or if you call subroutines from an interrupt handler), your application will become quite complex, trying to figure out which block of variables to use.

The most elegant way that I've found to pass parameters is to take a chapter from the PC and use the CY7C6xx's Index (X) register as a base pointer. Parameter data can be loaded in reverse order (like C) onto the data stack and, in the subroutine, the data can be accessed as an offset to the current DSP.

```
;  Routine( Parm1, Parm2, Parm3 ) - Simulate "C" Subroutine Call

   mov  A, Parm3              ;  Save the Parameters on the DSP
   push A
   mov  A, Parm2
   push A
   mov  A, Parm1
   push A

   call Routine              ; Call the Subroutine

   swap A, DSP               ;  Restore the Stack Pointer to the
   add  A, 3                 ;   Correct Address
   swap A, DSP

    :

;  Routine( int Parm1, int Parm2, int Parm3 ) - Simulate the "C"
Routine:                     ;   Subroutine Operation
```

```
    push X                       ;  Save the Index Register

    swap A, DSP                  ;  X = DSP for Accessing Parameters
    mov  Rtn_DSP, A
    swap A, DSP
    mov  X, Rtn_DSP

      :

;  if ( Parm2 == 7 ) - Show how Parameters are Accessed

    mov  A, [X + 3]              ;  Use the Parameter in the Operation
    cmp  A, 7
    jnz  Skip

      :

;  Return from "Routine" subroutine

    pop  X                       ;  Restore the Index Register

    ret                          ;  Return to Caller
```

This method of passing parameters allows you to track the input parameters very easily as just the parameter number plus one. Local variables can be implemented by simply pushing their initial values onto the DSP stack and accessing them along with the passed parameters. In this case, the passed parameter offset would be the index shown in the example plus the size of the local variable area.

INTERRUPTS

The previous section shows how the CY7C6xx's data stack and index register can be used to provide a subroutine parameter pointer that is remarkably similar to the Base Pointer (BP) register in the 8086. Another similar function in the CY7C6xx to the 8086 is the way that interrupts are handled and processed.

The first 16 bytes in the CY7C6xx's control store is dedicated to providing a vector space to the reset and interrupt vectors:

ADDRESS	INTERRUPT VECTOR	TYPE
0000h	N/A	Reset Vector
0002h	0	GIER Register Vector 0
0004h	1	GIER Register Vector 1
0006h	2	GIER Register Vector 2
0008h	3	GIER Register Vector 3
000Ah	4	GIER Register Vector 4
000Bh	5	GIER Register Vector 5
000Ch	6	GIER Register Vector 6
000Eh	7	GIER Register Vector 7

6

USB: THE INTERFACE OF THE FUTURE

The *GIER (Global Interrupt Enable Register)* is used to provide masks to the CY7C6xx's interrupt controller. When a bit is set and an interrupt request corresponding to that vector is received, the current instruction pointer and CY and Zero flags are pushed onto the stack (which requires three bytes). All the bits in the GIER are masked off (reset) and execution jumps to the appropriate vector address.

Normally, at each vector address, a *jmp IntVectorAddr* instruction is used. The Reset vector is treated exactly this way and should be a *jmp ResetAddr*.

This is very similar to how interrupt requests are processed in the 8086 with one big exception: the interrupt vector table cannot be overwritten by software (because it is in EPROM control store). The reset vector (Address 0) corresponds to the 8086's reset vector at address 0x0FFFF0.

The interrupt handlers themselves are quite simple and similar to the 8086's as well.

Upon entry into the interrupt handler, the context registers (Acc and X) should be saved on the stack, the hardware interrupt should be addressed, the hardware controller reset, the context registers restored (popped off the stack), and an interrupt return instruction executed.

Different interrupt return instructions are used in different devices. The IPRET instruction, available in the low-end or CPU A devices, not only returns from the interrupt, pops the Carry and Zero flags off the stack as well. It also stores the contents of the accumulator into the specified register and then pops the accumulator off the stack.

Using IPRET, the interrupt handler takes the form:

```
IntHandler:

    push A                    ;  Save Context Registers
    push X

;   Handle Requested Interrupt

    mov   A, [mask]           ;  Restore the Interrupt Mask

    pop   X                   ;  Restore the Index Register

    ipret GIE                 ;  Return from Interrupt with GIE Reset
```

For the high-end devices (CPU B), the *reti* instruction just pops the carry and zero information off the stack followed by the return instruction pointer address. The high-end CY7C6xx device's interrupt handlers should be in the form:

```
IntHandler:

    push A                    ;  Save Context Registers
    push X

;   Handle Requested Interrupt

    mov   A, [mask]           ;  Restore the Interrupt Mask
    iowr GIE

    pop   X                   ;  Restore Context Registers
    pop   A

    reti
```

Interrupt handlers should be short. This is an issue because while an interrupt handler is executing, other interrupts are being masked. By keeping the interrupt short, you won't keep the requests waiting for an unacceptably long time.

The interrupt handlers (and reset address) vectors must always be within the first 2048-byte page of control store. This will allow the *jmp* instruction to always be valid.

The last point has to do with invalid interrupts. In Cypress's example code, if an invalid interrupt is executed, the vector is set to the routine:

```
SysUnused:

  push A
  mov  A,[mask]

  ipret GIE
```

I am not 100-percent happy with this because if the code jumps to an unused interrupt, I feel that it is not operating properly and should be reset by the watchdog timer. To do this, my SysUnused handler goes into a hard loop with interrupts disabled (which they would be, by default, by the interrupt operation) until the watchdog timer overflows:

```
SysUnused:

  jmp   SysUnused
```

I realize that this would cause the CY7C6xx to drop out of the USB network, but it is much safer than simply resetting the interrupt mask and continuing.

Instruction Set

The Cypress CY7C6xx's instruction set is very straightforward and a lot less complicated than the 8086's. If you are familiar with Intel 8051, Zilog Z80, or Motorola 6800 assembly-language programming, you won't have any trouble understanding how the Cypress CY7C6xx works. Having said this, I'll have to be honest; there are a few quirks with subroutines and interrupts, as well as some differences between the CPU A (what I call the *low end*) and CPU B (high end) processors.

Moving data within the CY7C6xx is accomplished by using the *mov* instruction (Figs. 42-7 and 42-8), which use the Intel format:

```
Mov   Dest, Source
```

This format is used for all data movement instructions (including addition, subtraction, and bitwise operations, which have source and destinations).

Constants, variables, and array elements can be moved into the accumulator (A) and index (X) registers very simply. These instructions load the registers with the specified values.

Storing data from the accumulator into a variable or array can be accomplished by the *mov [Dest], A* instructions (see Fig. 42-9). If the contents of other registers are to be stored into a variable, then they will have to be moved to the accumulator first.

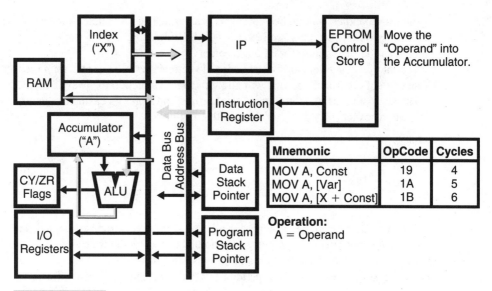

FIGURE 42-7   CY7C6xx "Mov A, operand" instruction.

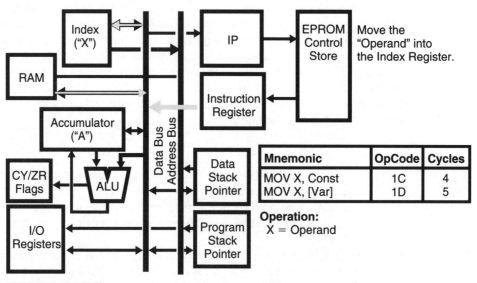

FIGURE 42-8   CY76xx "Mov X, operand" instruction.

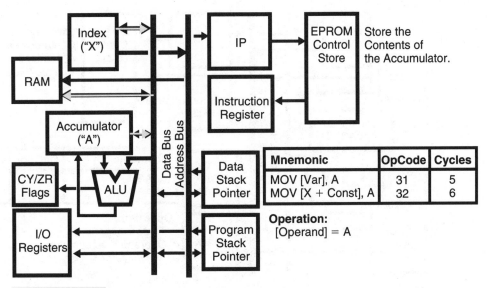

FIGURE 42-9   CY7C6xx "Mov operand, A" instruction.

Passing data between the index (X) and DSP registers in CPU A is accomplished by using the swap instruction (Fig. 42-10). This instruction exchanges the contents of the two registers. When using this instruction to load the accumulator with the contents of the other registers, you have to be sure that you are moving in a valid (for the application) value.

This is especially important for the DSP, which can be used in an interrupt handler. If this register is set to an invalid value, the stack or variables could be overwritten.

In CPU B (the high-end processor) architecture, additional instructions have been included to help with moving data between the accumulator X and DSP (Figs. 42-11 and 42-12).

Notice that the PSP can only be read from and not written to. The execution stack in the CY7C6xx cannot be changed and must always return to a value of zero when the mainline is executing. I realize that this is pretty standard advice, but I have seen a number of applications where the author, instead of returning to all the called routines and returning from there, just resets the stack. This is not possible in the CY7C6xx.

Another method of loading and storing the accumulator and index registers is to use the DSP stack and the *Push* and *Pop* instructions (Figs. 42-13 and 42-14). *Push* is very straightforward and traditional and works just as you would expect with the stack pointer being decremented before the data is saved. Popping data is accomplished by retrieving the data pushed onto the stack, storing it into the specified register, and then incrementing the DSP register. As indicated earlier in this chapter, with the index register, this can be an effective method of passing parameters to a subroutine.

Data can be passed between the I/O ports and the accumulator using the *IORD*, *IOWR*, and *IOWX* instructions (Figs. 42-15, 42-16, and 42-17). The first two instructions are analogous to the 8086's in and out instructions and *IOWX* does a write using the Index register as a base pointer. The *IOWX* instruction allows single subroutines to be used for accessing the different endpoint control registers.

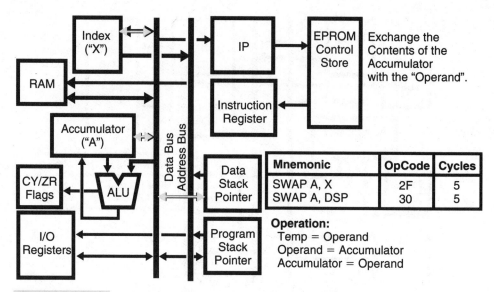

FIGURE 42-10   CY7C6xx "Swap A, operand" instruction.

Exchange the Contents of the Accumulator with the "Operand".

Mnemonic	OpCode	Cycles
SWAP A, X	2F	5
SWAP A, DSP	30	5

Operation:
Temp = Operand
Operand = Accumulator
Accumulator = Operand

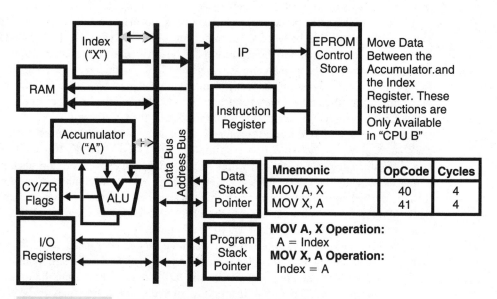

FIGURE 42-11   CY7C6xx "Mov A, X/X,A" instruction.

Move Data Between the Accumulator and the Index Register. These Instructions are Only Available in "CPU B"

Mnemonic	OpCode	Cycles
MOV A, X	40	4
MOV X, A	41	4

MOV A, X Operation:
A = Index
MOV X, A Operation:
Index = A

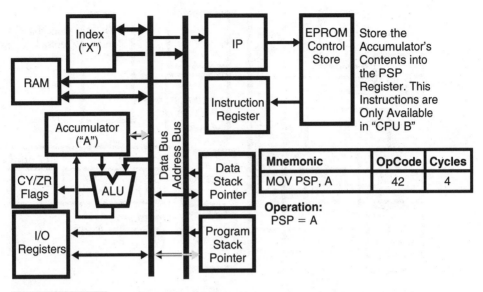

Store the Accumulator's Contents into the PSP Register. This Instructions are Only Available in "CPU B"

Mnemonic	OpCode	Cycles
MOV PSP, A	42	4

Operation:
PSP = A

FIGURE 42-12 CY7C6xx "Mov PSP,A" instruction.

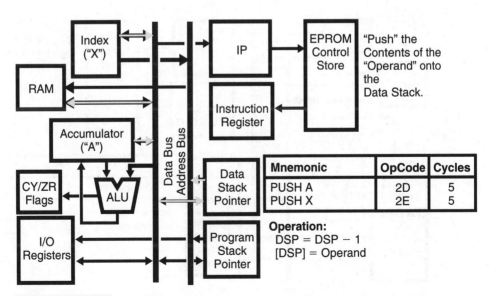

"Push" the Contents of the "Operand" onto the Data Stack.

Mnemonic	OpCode	Cycles
PUSH A	2D	5
PUSH X	2E	5

Operation:
DSP = DSP − 1
[DSP] = Operand

FIGURE 42-13 CY7C6xx "Push operand" instruction.

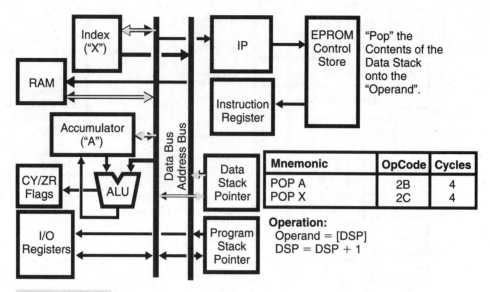

"Pop" the Contents of the Data Stack onto the "Operand".

Mnemonic	OpCode	Cycles
POP A	2B	4
POP X	2C	4

Operation:
Operand = [DSP]
DSP = DSP + 1

FIGURE 42-14 CY7C6xx "Pop operand" instruction.

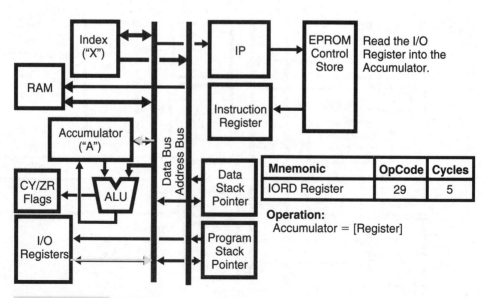

Read the I/O Register into the Accumulator.

Mnemonic	OpCode	Cycles
IORD Register	29	5

Operation:
Accumulator = [Register]

FIGURE 42-15 CY7C6xx "lord operand" instruction.

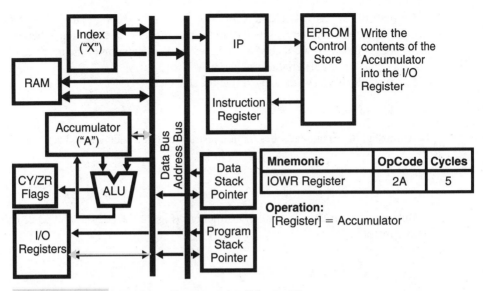

Mnemonic	OpCode	Cycles
IOWR Register	2A	5

Operation:
  [Register] = Accumulator

FIGURE 42-16 CY7C6xx "Iowr operand" instruction.

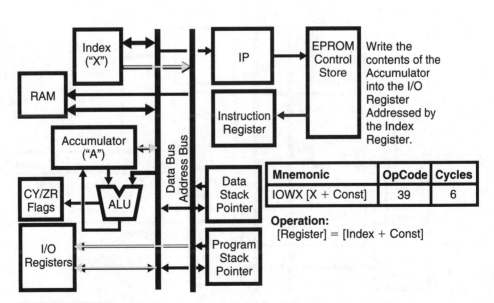

Mnemonic	OpCode	Cycles
IOWX [X + Const]	39	6

Operation:
  [Register] = [Index + Const]

FIGURE 42-17 CY7C6xx "Iowx operand" instruction.

6

Bit operations (AND, OR, and XOR, see Figs. 42-18, 42-19, and 42-20) perform bit-wise logical operations on the contents of the accumulator. The zero flag is set with the result. These operations are nicely set up because the destination of the result can either be the accumulator or the variable brought in.

For example, if you wanted to execute the statement:

```
VarA = VarA & 0x055
```

Just using the accumulator destination instructions, the code would be:

```
mov  A, [VarA]
and  A, 055h
mov  [VarA], A
```

But, with the variable destination instructions (Figs. 42-21, 42-22, and 42-23), the code is simplified to:

```
mov  A, 055h
and  [VarA], A
```

The addition and subtraction instructions (Figs. 42-24 and 42-25) are very easy to use with the result stored in the accumulator (there aren't any variable destination addition and subtraction instructions) with the carry and zero results stored in the Flags register. Carry is set on an addition result greater than 0x0FF or a subtraction result less than zero (borrow).

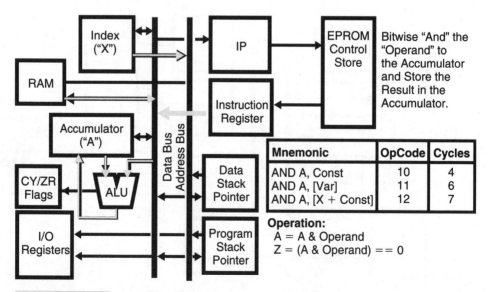

Mnemonic	OpCode	Cycles
AND A, Const	10	4
AND A, [Var]	11	6
AND A, [X + Const]	12	7

Operation:
A = A & Operand
Z = (A & Operand) == 0

Bitwise "And" the "Operand" to the Accumulator and Store the Result in the Accumulator.

FIGURE 42-18 CY7C6xx "And A, operand" instruction.

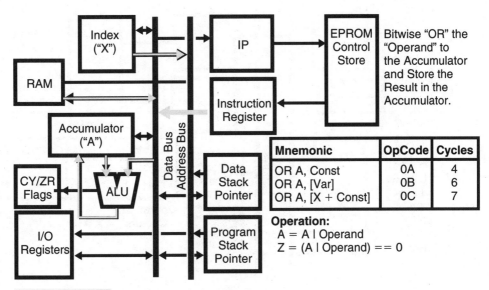

Bitwise "OR" the "Operand" to the Accumulator and Store the Result in the Accumulator.

Mnemonic	OpCode	Cycles
OR A, Const	0A	4
OR A, [Var]	0B	6
OR A, [X + Const]	0C	7

Operation:
A = A | Operand
Z = (A | Operand) == 0

FIGURE 42-19 CY7C6xx "Or A, operand" instruction.

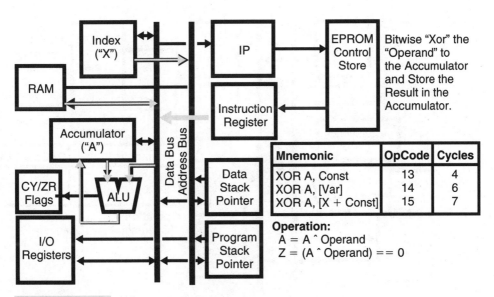

Bitwise "Xor" the "Operand" to the Accumulator and Store the Result in the Accumulator.

Mnemonic	OpCode	Cycles
XOR A, Const	13	4
XOR A, [Var]	14	6
XOR A, [X + Const]	15	7

Operation:
A = A ^ Operand
Z = (A ^ Operand) == 0

FIGURE 42-20 CY7C6xx "Xor A, operand" instruction.

6

USB: THE INTERFACE OF THE FUTURE

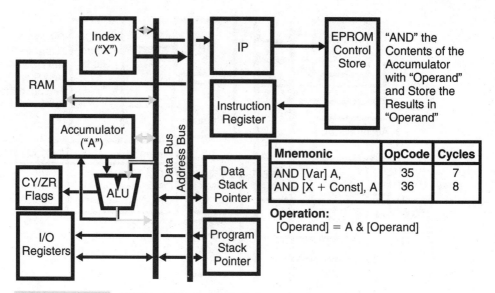

Mnemonic	OpCode	Cycles
AND [Var] A,	35	7
AND [X + Const], A	36	8

Operation:
[Operand] = A & [Operand]

FIGURE 42-21   CY7C6xx "And operand, A" instruction.

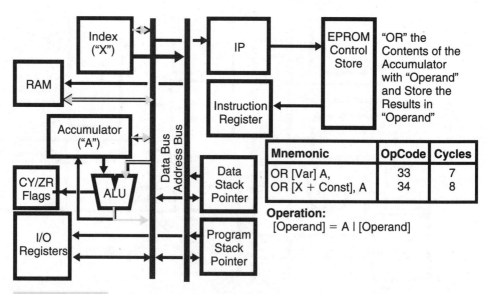

Mnemonic	OpCode	Cycles
OR [Var] A,	33	7
OR [X + Const], A	34	8

Operation:
[Operand] = A | [Operand]

FIGURE 42-22   CY7C6xx "Or operand, A" instruction.

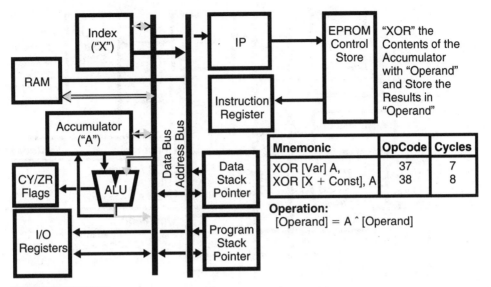

Mnemonic	OpCode	Cycles
XOR [Var] A,	37	7
XOR [X + Const], A	38	8

"XOR" the Contents of the Accumulator with "Operand" and Store the Results in "Operand"

Operation:
[Operand] = A ^ [Operand]

FIGURE 42-23 CY7C6xx "Xor operand, A" instruction.

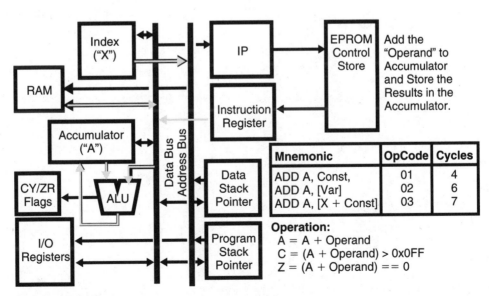

Add the "Operand" to Accumulator and Store the Results in the Accumulator.

Mnemonic	OpCode	Cycles
ADD A, Const,	01	4
ADD A, [Var]	02	6
ADD A, [X + Const]	03	7

Operation:
A = A + Operand
C = (A + Operand) > 0x0FF
Z = (A + Operand) == 0

FIGURE 42-24 CY7C6xx "Add A, operand" instruction.

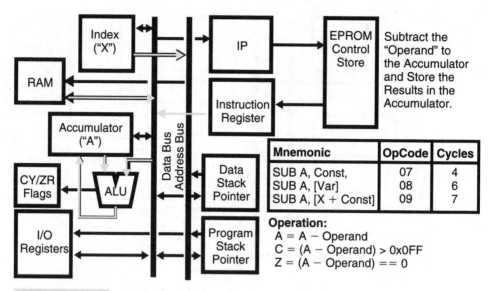

FIGURE 42-25 CY7C6xx "Sub A, operand" instruction.

Sixteen bit (or more) addition and subtraction operations can be easily carried out by using the add with carry and subtract with carry instructions (Figs. 42-26 and 42-27). These instructions add or subtract the stat of the carry flag to the operands to get the correct high-order byte result.

For example, 16-bit addition for:

```
VarA = VarB + VarC
```

would be coded as:

```
mov   A, [VarB]          ;  Do Low Byte Add
add   A, [VarC]
mov   [VarA], A

mov   A, [VarB + 1]      ;  Do Upper Byte Add
adc   A, [VarC + 1]
mov   [VarA + 1], A
```

and subtraction for:

```
VarA = VarB - VarC
```

is coded as:

```
mov   A, [VarB]          ;  Low Byte Subtract
sub   A, [VarC]
mov   [VarA], A

mov   A, [VarB + 1]      ;  Upper Byte Subtract
sbb   A, [VarC + 1]
mov   [VarA + 1], A
```

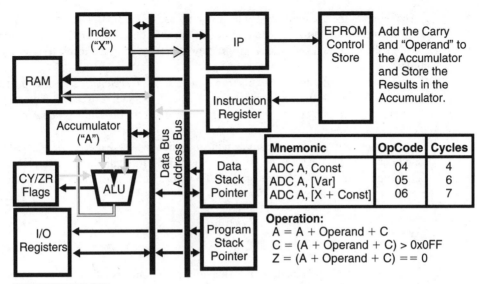

Add the Carry and "Operand" to the Accumulator and Store the Results in the Accumulator.

Mnemonic	OpCode	Cycles
ADC A, Const	04	4
ADC A, [Var]	05	6
ADC A, [X + Const]	06	7

Operation:
A = A + Operand + C
C = (A + Operand + C) > 0x0FF
Z = (A + Operand + C) == 0

FIGURE 42-26 CY7C6xx "Adc A, operand" instruction.

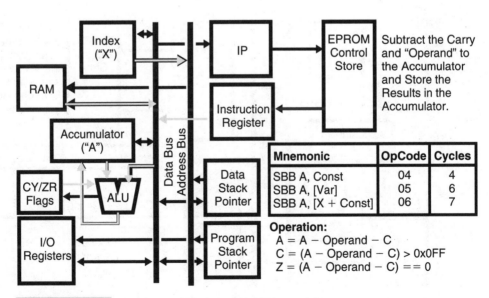

Subtract the Carry and "Operand" to the Accumulator and Store the Results in the Accumulator.

Mnemonic	OpCode	Cycles
SBB A, Const	04	4
SBB A, [Var]	05	6
SBB A, [X + Const]	06	7

Operation:
A = A − Operand − C
C = (A − Operand − C) > 0x0FF
Z = (A − Operand − C) == 0

FIGURE 42-27 CY7C6xx "Sbb A, operand" instruction.

The value in the accumulator can be tested by use of the CMP instruction (Fig. 42-28). This instruction performs a subtract (without borrow) on the contents of the accumulator and sets the carry and zero flag appropriately without storing the result back in the accumulator.

A simple form of addition/subtraction is to use the *increment/decrement* instructions (Figs. 42-29 and 42-30). These instructions change the contents of the accumulator, index registers, or a variable byte by one value. If the result of the operation is equal to zero, then the zero flag is set.

Data in accumulator can be complemented (which means that each bit is inverted (Fig. 42-31) or shifted and rotated up or down (Figs. 42-32 through 42-36). Complementing is not doing a two's complement negation of a value. To do that, a value must be complemented and then incremented:

```
cpl                    ;   A = A ^ 0x0FF
inc   A                ;   A = ( A & 0x0FF ) + 1
                       ;     = -A
```

It can be a little hard to understand when to use Shift and Rotate. I like to always visualize them *shift table* and *rotate wheel* (Fig. 42-31).

When data is shifted, the bits that are shifted out of the accumulator (into the carry flag in the CY7C6xx) are lost forever; they have fallen off into space, never to be recovered. Rotates, on the other hand, keeps rotating the bits around and around. No matter how many positions the rotate wheel is turned, the data can always be recovered.

Jumping to addresses in the CY7C6xx takes three different forms. The first is the traditional nonconditional jump (Fig. 42-37), which jumps to a specified address. The next type is the conditional jump (Figs. 42-38 and 42-39). These jumps allow the execution to change to a new address within the current 4-KB code segment.

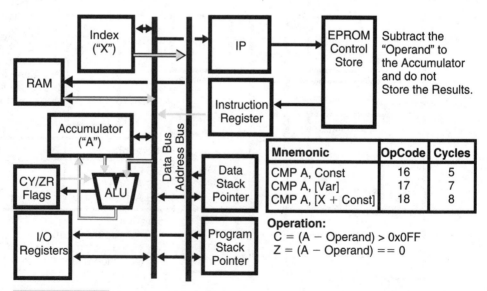

Mnemonic	OpCode	Cycles
CMP A, Const	16	5
CMP A, [Var]	17	7
CMP A, [X + Const]	18	8

Operation:
C = (A − Operand) > 0x0FF
Z = (A − Operand) == 0

FIGURE 42-28 CY7C6xx "Cmp A, operand" instruction.

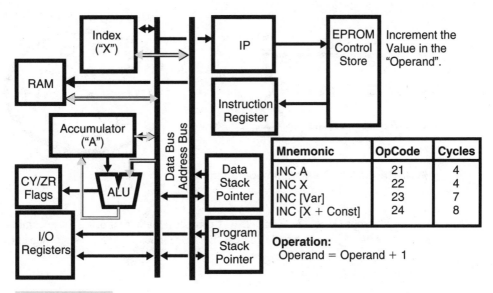

Mnemonic	OpCode	Cycles
INC A	21	4
INC X	22	4
INC [Var]	23	7
INC [X + Const]	24	8

Operation:
  Operand = Operand + 1

FIGURE 42-29 CY7C6xx "Inc operand" instruction.

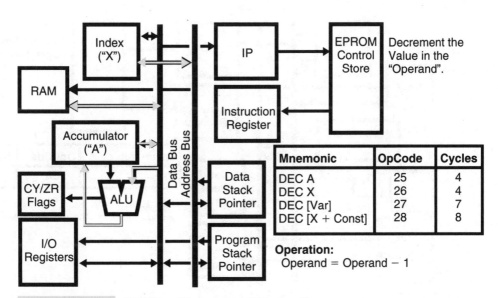

Mnemonic	OpCode	Cycles
DEC A	25	4
DEC X	26	4
DEC [Var]	27	7
DEC [X + Const]	28	8

Operation:
  Operand = Operand − 1

FIGURE 42-30 CY7C6xx "Dec operand" instruction.

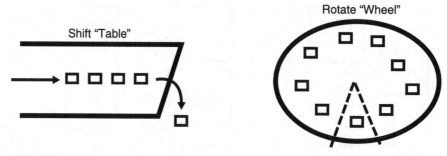

FIGURE 42-31 Rotate/shift operation.

Indexed jumps (Figs. 42-40 and 42-41), provide a method of using the accumulator and index registers to jump to a table address. For these indexed jumps, I suggest using a jump to a list of jmp statements, such as:

```
Asl
Swap  A, X
Index Table      ;  Do the Indexed Jump

Table:
  Jmp   X_0       ;  Jump to Code for Accumulator = 0
  Jmp   X_1
   :
```

In this example, the contents of the accumulator are doubled before moving into the Index register. Then, when the jump is executed, a unique address with a separate routine starts executing.

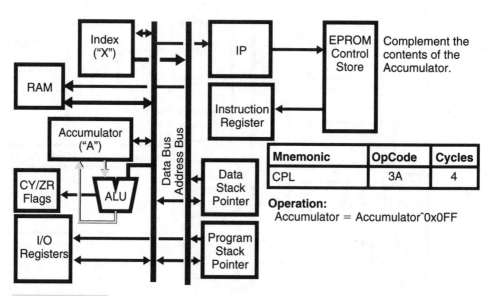

Mnemonic	OpCode	Cycles
CPL	3A	4

Operation:
Accumulator = Accumulator^0x0FF

FIGURE 42-32 CY7C6xx "Cpl" instruction.

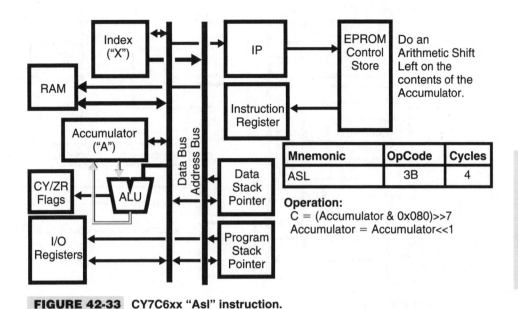

Do an Arithmetic Shift Left on the contents of the Accumulator.

Mnemonic	OpCode	Cycles
ASL	3B	4

Operation:
C = (Accumulator & 0x080)>>7
Accumulator = Accumulator<<1

FIGURE 42-33 CY7C6xx "Asl" instruction.

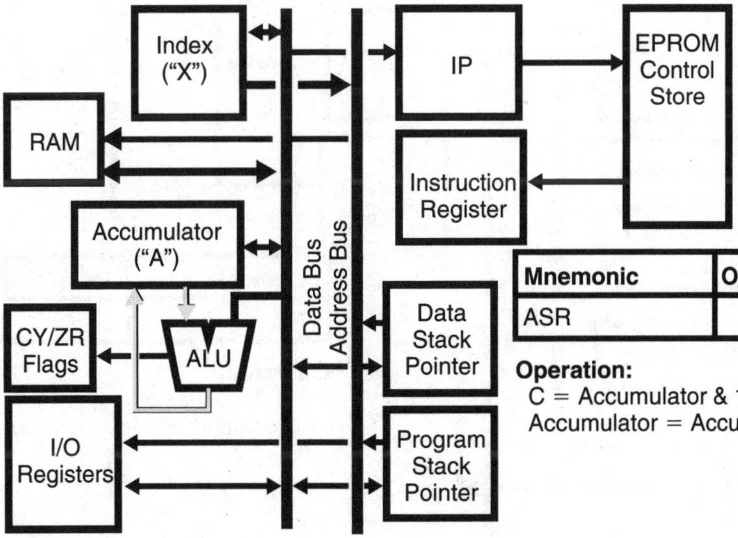

Do an Arithmetic Shift Right on the contents of the Accumulator.

Mnemonic	OpCode	Cycles
ASR	3C	4

Operation:
C = Accumulator & 1
Accumulator = Accumulator>>1

FIGURE 42-34 CY7C6xx "Asr" instruction.

6

USB: THE INTERFACE OF THE FUTURE

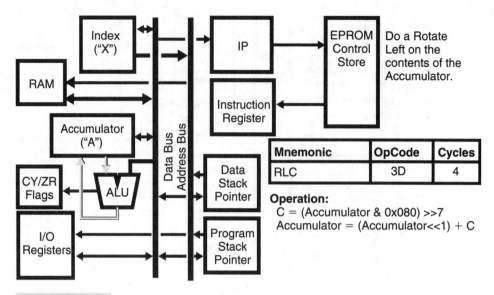

Do a Rotate Left on the contents of the Accumulator.

Mnemonic	OpCode	Cycles
RLC	3D	4

Operation:
C = (Accumulator & 0x080) >>7
Accumulator = (Accumulator<<1) + C

FIGURE 42-35   CY7C6xx "Rlc" instruction.

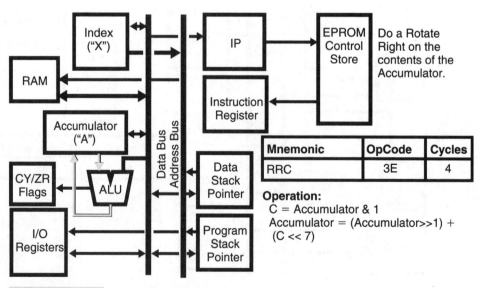

Do a Rotate Right on the contents of the Accumulator.

Mnemonic	OpCode	Cycles
RRC	3E	4

Operation:
C = Accumulator & 1
Accumulator = (Accumulator>>1) + (C << 7)

FIGURE 42-36   CY7C6xx "Rrc" instruction.

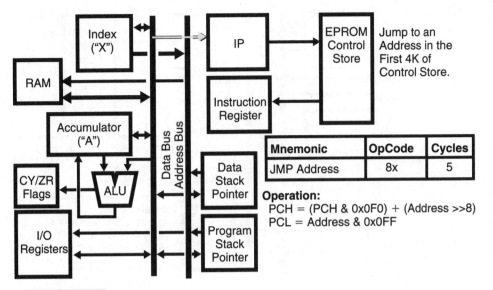

FIGURE 42-37 CY7C6xx "Jmp address" instruction.

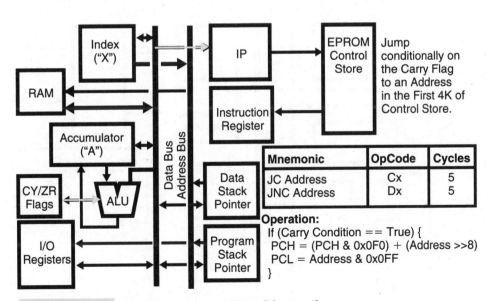

FIGURE 42-38 CY7C6xx "Jc/Jnc address" instruction.

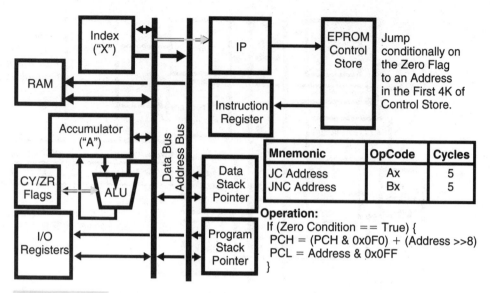

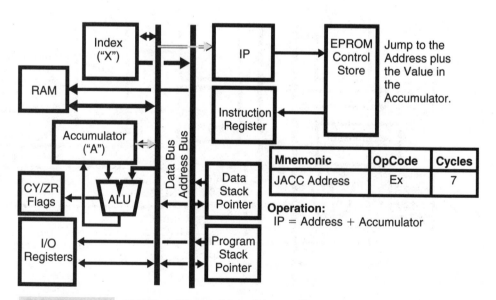

FIGURE 42-39 CY7C6xx "Jz/Jnz address" instruction.

Mnemonic	OpCode	Cycles
JC Address	Ax	5
JNC Address	Bx	5

Operation:
If (Zero Condition == True) {
  PCH = (PCH & 0x0F0) + (Address >>8)
  PCL = Address & 0x0FF
}

Jump conditionally on the Zero Flag to an Address in the First 4K of Control Store.

Mnemonic	OpCode	Cycles
JACC Address	Ex	7

Operation:
IP = Address + Accumulator

Jump to the Address plus the Value in the Accumulator.

FIGURE 42-40 CY7C6xx "Jacc address" instruction.

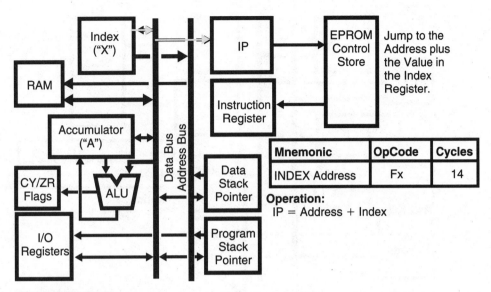

Mnemonic	OpCode	Cycles
INDEX Address	Fx	14

Operation:
IP = Address + Index

FIGURE 42-41 CY7C6xx "Index Address" instruction.

I touched on the *XPAGE* instruction (Fig. 42-42) earlier in the chapter when I presented the CY7C6xx's processor architecture. This instruction should really be ignored and just have the assembler insert them automatically for you. Putting *XPAGE* instructions manually into the code runs the risk of incrementing the high byte of the instruction pointer at the wrong times. As well, when patching code, be sure that you don't overwrite any *XPAGE* instructions in the code or change their absolute addresses.

In the previous two sections, I have explained interrupts and subroutines instructions (Figs. 42-43 through 42-48) in pretty good detail, which I won't repeat here. Subroutines and interrupts are quite easy to work with in the CY7C6xx architecture.

The two processor control instructions *Halt* and *Nop* (Figs. 42-49 and 42-50) are very common in most processor architectures (even the 8086 has them). The *Nop* is used to insert empty instruction cycles while crucially timed applications are executing.

Halt stops the processor, to save power, until a reset or enabled interrupt request is encountered.

The CY7C6xx's instruction set is very complete, but I consider two instructions to be missing: an I/O port bit set and reset. These two instructions are very important in all microcontrollers and their functions can be simulated using a macro in the format:

```
BitSet MACRO Reg, Bit
  IORD Reg
  OR   A, 1 << Bit
  IOWR Reg
ENDM
```

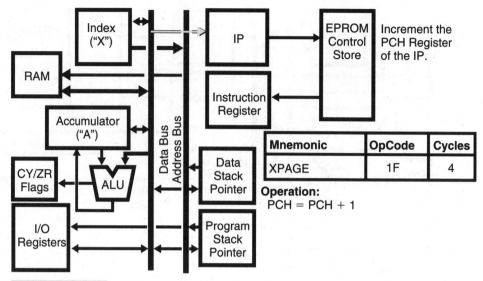

Mnemonic	OpCode	Cycles
XPAGE	1F	4

Operation:
PCH = PCH + 1

Increment the
PCH Register
of the IP.

FIGURE 42-42   **CY7C6xx "Xpage" instruction.**

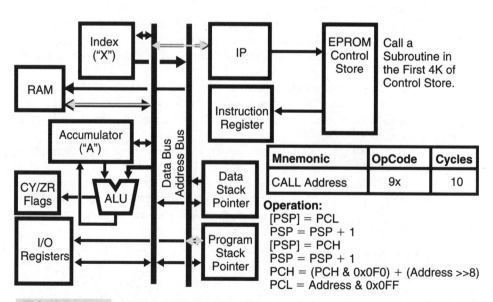

Mnemonic	OpCode	Cycles
CALL Address	9x	10

Call a
Subroutine in
the First 4K of
Control Store.

Operation:
[PSP] = PCL
PSP = PSP + 1
[PSP] = PCH
PSP = PSP + 1
PCH = (PCH & 0x0F0) + (Address >>8)
PCL = Address & 0x0FF

FIGURE 42-43   **CY7C6xx "Call address" instruction.**

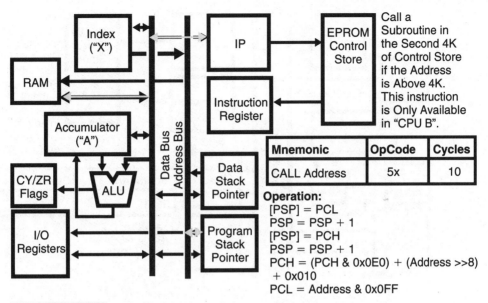

Call a Subroutine in the Second 4K of Control Store if the Address is Above 4K. This instruction is Only Available in "CPU B".

Mnemonic	OpCode	Cycles
CALL Address	5x	10

Operation:
[PSP] = PCL
PSP = PSP + 1
[PSP] = PCH
PSP = PSP + 1
PCH = (PCH & 0x0E0) + (Address >>8) + 0x010
PCL = Address & 0x0FF

FIGURE 42-44 CY7C6xx CPU B "Call Address" instruction.

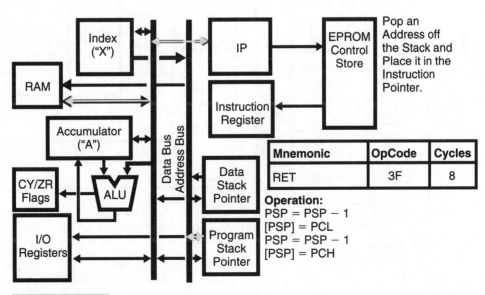

Pop an Address off the Stack and Place it in the Instruction Pointer.

Mnemonic	OpCode	Cycles
RET	3F	8

Operation:
PSP = PSP − 1
[PSP] = PCL
PSP = PSP − 1
[PSP] = PCH

FIGURE 42-45 CY7C6xx "Ret" instruction.

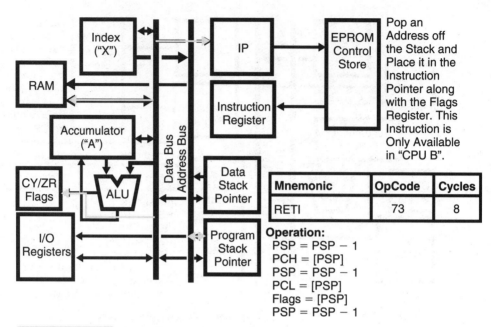

Pop an Address off the Stack and Place it in the Instruction Pointer along with the Flags Register. This Instruction is Only Available in "CPU B".

Mnemonic	OpCode	Cycles
RETI	73	8

Operation:
PSP = PSP − 1
PCH = [PSP]
PSP = PSP − 1
PCL = [PSP]
Flags = [PSP]
PSP = PSP − 1

FIGURE 42-46 CY7C6xx "Reti" instruction.

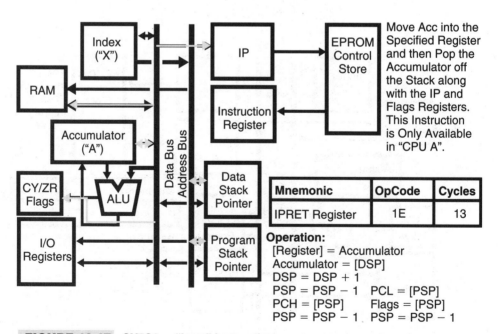

Move Acc into the Specified Register and then Pop the Accumulator off the Stack along with the IP and Flags Registers. This Instruction is Only Available in "CPU A".

Mnemonic	OpCode	Cycles
IPRET Register	1E	13

Operation:
[Register] = Accumulator
Accumulator = [DSP]
DSP = DSP + 1
PSP = PSP − 1   PCL = [PSP]
PCH = [PSP]   Flags = [PSP]
PSP = PSP − 1   PSP = PSP − 1

FIGURE 42-47 CY7C6xx "Ipret" instruction.

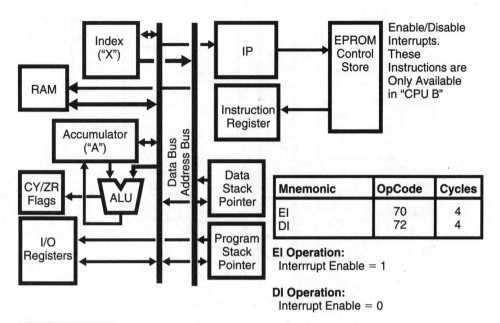

Enable/Disable
Interrupts.
These
Instructions are
Only Available
in "CPU B"

Mnemonic	OpCode	Cycles
EI	70	4
DI	72	4

EI Operation:
Interrrupt Enable = 1

DI Operation:
Interrupt Enable = 0

FIGURE 42-48   CY7C6xx "Ei/Di" instructions.

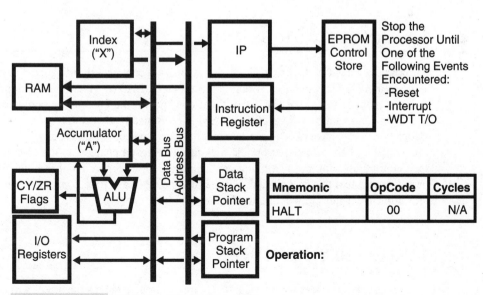

Stop the
Processor Until
One of the
Following Events
Encountered:
-Reset
-Interrupt
-WDT T/O

Mnemonic	OpCode	Cycles
HALT	00	N/A

Operation:

FIGURE 42-49   CY7C6xx "Halt" instruction.

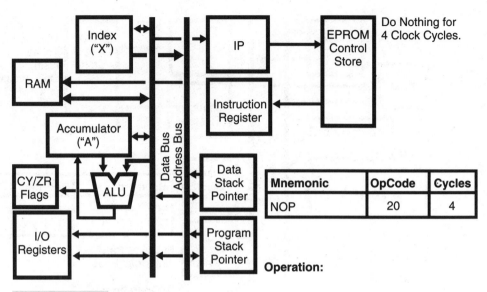

FIGURE 42-50 CY7C6xx "Nop" instruction.

Mnemonic	OpCode	Cycles
NOP	20	4

Or

```
BitReset MACRO Reg, Bit
  IORD Reg
  And   A, 0x0FF ^ ( 1 << Bit )
  IOWR Reg
ENDM
```

Development Tools

Unfortunately, the CY7C6xx development kit does not contain a significant amount of development tools for you to use. Along with sample DS1620 (the thermometer application source was burned into the CY7C6300 that comes with the kit), the kit comes with the MS-DOS command-line assembler CYASM. Unfortunately, this is it.

Ideally, I would have liked to see a simulator to test code out on and because of it not being available, I have focussed on just making incremental changes to the source, rather than coming up with my own unique applications. As I become more familiar with the part, I'm sure that this will change. For the time being I have only done applications that are simple extensions to what is already there.

Hardware Features

Before describing how to wire the CY7C6xx into a circuit and how the timers and USB interface hardware works, here are a few comments about how the chip is built. These comments are quite cursory, but I felt it was important for you to get a better idea of the different devices and the technologies used with them.

The CY7C6xx is built from CMOS technology with (*Erasable Programmable Read Only Memory) EPROM* control store (program memory). CMOS is a push-pull logic technology with very low power requirements. EPROM, as its name implies, is a user-programmable memory that can be erased by exposure to *ultraviolet (UV) light*. Combined, they make the CY7C6xx a fairly user-friendly device that can be reprogrammed repeatedly using the cypress programming equipment that comes with the USB development kit.

The chips themselves are packaged in solid plastic or a windowed ceramic. The plastic parts are known as *One-Time Programmable (OTP)* because the parts can only be loaded with a program once because the UV light cannot penetrate the plastic to erase the EPROM. A windowed ceramic package is a ceramic package that has a quartz window, allowing UV light to be applied to the chip to erase the EPROM (Fig. 42-51).

The chips themselves come in two pin types. *Pin Through Hole (PTH)* consists of packages with long vertical pins that are pushed through holes of vias in a card and soldered to make electrical contact (Fig. 42-52).

The advantage of pin through hole is that it is very easy to solder in circuits or can use inexpensive sockets and wire wrapping, which allows for easy removal and replacement. For virtually all the projects presented in this book, I used wire wrapping as the method of assembly because it is well suited to one-off projects.

Surface-Mount Technology (SMT) uses chips with horizontal leads that are soldered to the surface of the card (Fig. 42-53).

The CY7C6xx can be purchased as gull-wing *Surface-Mounted Devices (SMD)*. Gull wing is easier for hobbyists to solder and inspect than the J-leaded parts (which can be packed more densely on a card). The SMT parts have leads on 0.050 (50 mil) centers, whereas the PTH parts have 0.100 (100 mil) centers. This smaller pin pitch allows a much higher number of chips to be put in a given space than PTH (as well as having parts on the backside).

The disadvantage of SMT is that it generally requires the resources of a manufacturing plant to place and rework components, whereas PTH does not. SMT is best used in high-volume applications, where lower parts costs (smaller and cheaper boards and cheaper parts) and high-volume chip shooting equipment availability make it attractive.

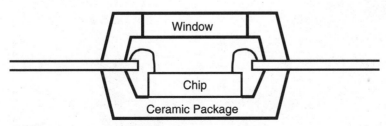

FIGURE 42-51 Windowed ceramic package.

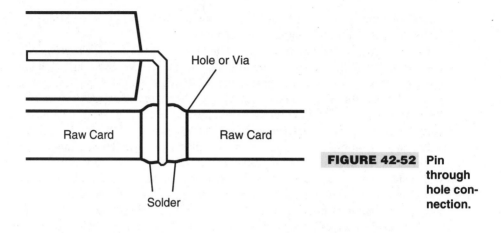

FIGURE 42-52 Pin through hole connection.

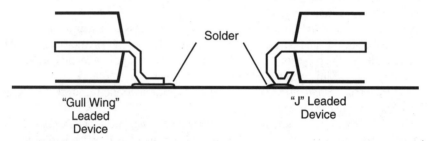

FIGURE 42-53 Surface mount technology packages.

A number of different CY7C6xx parts are available:

PART NUMBER	EPROM SIZE	# OF I/O PINS	PACKAGE TYPES
CY7C63200	2 KB	10	PTH
CY7C63201	4 KB	10	PTH, Windowed
CY7C63000	2 KB	12	PTH, SMT
CY7C63001	4 KB	12	PTH, SMT, Windowed
CY7C63100	2 KB	16	SMT
CY7C63101	4 KB	16	SMT, Windowed
CY7C63411	4 KB	32	PTH, SMT
CY7C63511	4 KB	32	SMT
CY7C63412	6 KB	32	PTH, SMT
CY7C63512	6 KB	32	SMT
CY7C63413	8 KB	32	PTH, SMT, Windowed
CY7C63513	8 KB	32	SMT

The packages come in a variety of types and sizes. The CY7C63/4/5 parts are 40- and 48-pin packages and have all of the features of CY7C64x- (the high end) parts, along with extra I/O pins and analog-to-digital converters. Actual features, pin outs, and part dimensions are listed in the Cypress datasheets.

POWER AND CLOCKING

One very nice feature of the CY7C6xx microcontrollers is the ease in which it can be wired into a circuit. USB is designed to provide up to 100 mA of current at +5 V to the network devices and this power is usually all that is required by the CY7C6xx (Fig. 42-54).

Going with this simple philosophy is the use of a 6-MHz crystal or ceramic oscillator just connected to the XTALIN and XTALOUT pins. The oscillator does not require any external components, such as capacitors or resistors. Inside the chip, the 6 MHz is doubled to 12 MHz.

The 6-MHz clock speed is crucial for proper operation of the 1.5-MBps USB link. The 7.5-K resistor between D- and V_{cc} is used to indicate to the host that the CY7C6xx USB device runs at 1.5 MBps and not 12 MBps.

The CY7C6xx also has one other important feature: the suspend in which the clock is stopped and the device is held in its lowest power state. It can be brought out of this state by power cycling, a watchdog timer reset, or an enabled interrupt.

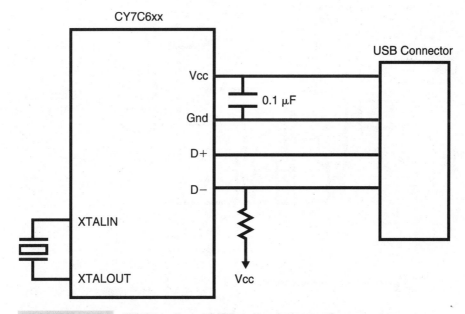

FIGURE 42-54 CY7C6xx Power/USB network connections.

6

USB: THE INTERFACE OF THE FUTURE

TIMERS

The CY7C6xx has one basic 11-bit timer that runs at 1 MHz. This clock is free running and is read only. It is used to provide interrupts to the processor, as well as provide a driver to the watchdog timer. Some CY7C6xx's also have an external RC network circuit for providing user-defined displays. The clock functions probably seem quite complex, but they are actually quite simple to work with. The complete timer circuit is shown in Fig. 42-55.

The clock itself runs at 1 MHz, derived from the 6-MHz instruction clock, and cannot be stopped or written to. The least-significant eight bits can be read and used for simple timing functions. As the timer increments, bit 6 and bit 9 of the timer can be used to provide interrupts to the mainline at 128- and 1024-microsecond intervals, respectively.

The 1024-microsecond overflow is used to increment the three-bit watchdog timer. The watchdog timer counter cannot be disabled and has to be continually reset to prevent the microcontroller from resetting itself. The reset operation is usually the first operation carried out by the 1024-microsecond interrupt handler. To reset the watchdog timer, a write to the WatchDog register will reset the counter.

The other method of timing within the CY7C6xx is to use the optional CExt pin with a simple RC network (Fig. 42-56). When the CExt bit is reset in the CExt register, the capacitor is allowed to discharge through the microcontroller. Setting the CExt bit places this pin in a high-impedance state, which allows the capacitor to change through the resistor. When the capacitor reaches the logic threshold of the pin (nominally 1.4 volts), a CExt interrupt request is generated.

The values for C and R do not follow any rules and you'll have to experiment with different values until the correct result is achieved. I suggest starting with R = 10 K and C = 0.1 μF and changing the resistor value in 1-K increments to a minimum of 1 K before changing the capacitor value.

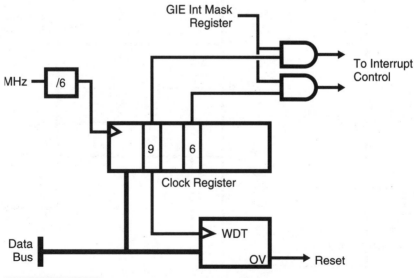

FIGURE 42-55   CY7C6xx timer block diagram.

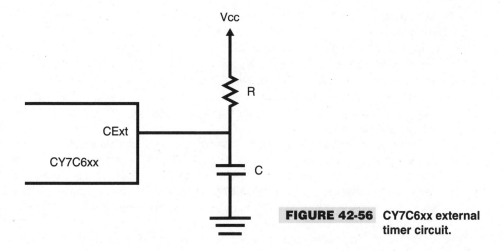

FIGURE 42-56 CY7C6xx external timer circuit.

I/O PORTS

One thing I don't like about the CY7C6xx's documentation is the apparently complex operation of the I/O pins. The I/O pins are in actuality not very complex. If you've worked with an 8051 you won't have any problems understanding how they work (Figure 42-57).

The CY7C6xx's GPIO pins work very similarly to the 8051's. A 0 or 1 can be written out and, if the port pull up bit is set, the weak pull up (16 KB) on the pin will be enabled. If a 0 is written to the pin, then the N-MOS transistor will be turned on and the pin will be pulled to ground through the user-definable constant-current source. Because of the weak

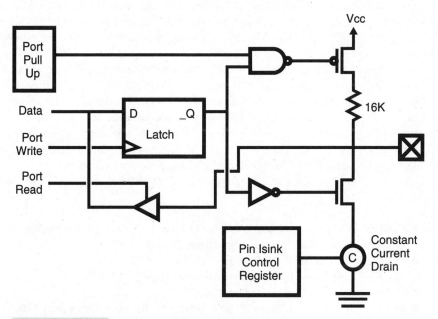

FIGURE 42-57 CY7C6xx I/O pin block diagram.

pull up, the pin can be easily overpowered by external devices during a bus-contention situation, or the pin is used for input with the pull up enabled.

Reading a GPIO pin is accomplished by writing a 1 to the pin's output bit and then reading back the logic level. Normally, the built-in pull up will be disabled, although (as hinted previously), most logic families will be able to overpower the 16-K resistor.

Each pin has an I_{sink} register associated with it to control the constant-current drain built into the pull down transistor. The constant-current drain is used to select how much current the pin can sink.

For most applications, this feature is superfluous and I would recommend setting the I_{sink} register for every output bit at the highest value and forgetting about it. At the highest current value, some GPIO pins will be able to drive LEDs without requiring external drivers. The reason why the controllable drain is placed on the pins is to ensure that the total pins do not sink so much current that the 100 mA maximum for the USB application is exceeded.

The pin state transistors can be used to generate interrupt requests as well. Each port has an interrupt-enable register with each pin in the register assigned to a pin in the GPIO registers. To enable interrupt requests for a specific pin, the appropriate *Port n Interrupt Enable Register* bit is set. If the pull-up bit is set, then an interrupt will be generated on a low-to-high transition on the pin. If the pull up bit is reset, then an interrupt request will be generated for a high-to-low transition.

USB SIE INTERFACE

The *SIE (Serial Interface Engine)* provides the USB interface between the CY7C6xx microcontroller and the host PC. The SIE is designed to minimize the software overhead required by the processor, as well as in hardware. For software, two end points are supported within the SIE, which are loaded and written from automatically by the SIE. When connecting the CY7C6xx to the USB connector, simply straight-through connections are required without any buffering (Fig. 42-54).

EP0 and EP1 are the labels given to the two end points that are supported within the SIE. Enumeration/Control data is passed through the EP0 FIFO while data from the microcontroller is passed when the host PC reads the EP1 FIFO. This use of FIFOs allows the microcontroller to execute while the USB communication is occurring, without having to dedicate the microcontroller to the USB communications operations. This is similar to the operation of DMA or shared memory in a PC's hardware adapter card that allows the adapter operation in the background of the PC's application execution.

To enumerate a CY7C6xx microcontroller USB application to a host PC, the following steps are used:

1 The Host sends a Setup packet, followed by a Data Packet to USB Device Address 0. This request is for the Device's Descriptor Block.

2 The CY7C6xx Decodes the Request from 1.

3 The CY7C6xx Loads its Device Descriptor into the EP1 FIFO.

4 The Host Requests the Device Descriptor.

5 The Host Sends the CY7C6xx its USB Device Address in a Setup/Data Packet combination.

6 The CY7C6xx Stores the Device Address.
7 The CY7C6xx Loads EP1 FIFO with the Device Descriptor again.
8 The Host Requests the Device Descriptor.
9 The CY7C6xx Loads EP1 FIFO with the Configuration and Reporting Descriptors.
10 The Host Requests the information loaded in EP1 FIFO.

The enumeration process is complete when the host has retrieved the information loaded into EP1's FIFO in step 10.

For USB communications, only a few registers are required to manage the USB communication. They consist of the EP0 receive status register (at address 014h), the EP0 transmit configuration register (at address 010h), the EP1 transmit configuration register (at address 011h), and the USB status and control register (at address 013h). These registers allow EP0 to be used as a bidirectional communications path for the CY7C6xx while EP1 can only transmit information. As noted, the actual data is passed through the FIFOs, rather than by individual bytes loaded by the microcontroller.

The *EP0 transmit configuration register* (address 0x010) is written to after the EP0 FIFO has been used loaded, to allow the PC host to request its data.

BITS	FUNCTION
7	Enable Response to Data Packets. Send Data in FIFO.
6	Set Data State (1 or 0).
5	STALL. Set STALL instead of Ack for Packet Requests.
4	RX Data Error. Bit Set if Error in Received Data Packet.
3–0	Count. Number of FIFO Data Bytes to be Transmitted.

The *EP1 transmit configuration register* (address 0x011) performs similarly to the EP0 transmit configuration, with the only difference being that EP1 cannot receive data.

BITS	FUNCTION
7	Enable Response to Data Packets. Send Data in FIFO.
6	Set Data State (1 or 0).
5	STALL. Set STALL instead of Ack for Packet Requests.
4	RX Data Error. Bit Set if Error in Received Data Packet.
3–0	Count. Number of FIFO Data Bytes to be Transmitted.

6

USB: THE INTERFACE OF THE FUTURE

The *EP0 receive status register* (address 0x014) is used to indicate what is the status of incoming packets and how the SIE has responded to them.

BITS	FUNCTION
7–4	Count. Number of Bytes Received in Data Packet.
3	Data Toggle. Flipped when a Data Packet Received.
2	In. Set when a Valid In Token is Received. Reset for other Tokens.
1	Out. Set when a Valid Out Token is Received. Reset for other Tokens.
0	Setup. Set when a Valid Setup Token is received.

The last register, the *USB status and control register* (address 0x013) allows the CY7C6xx application to initiate the operation of the USB port, as well as enable the microcontroller to poll the status of the USB communications.

BITS	FUNCTION
7–5	Reserved = 0.
4	Write Enable. When Set, Data from an Out endpoint responds with an *Ack*.
3	Status Output. When Reset, Automatically Responds to a Status Stage out of Control Read Transfer on EP0 (Data1 Packet, 0 Bytes of Data). When the bit is set, SIE responds to valid Status Out with *Ack* and all others with a *Stall*.
2	Reserved = 0.
1	Set to Force a Resume Signal to the Host.
0	Set if anything but Idle on the line.

43

USB

INTERFACE

PROJECTS

CONTENTS AT A GLANCE

Cypress USB Example
Thermometer Application

To finish off the book, I wanted to show how the USB interface, which is built into virtually every modern PC, works. I decided to stay with the Cypress USB Starter Kit and the CY7C6xx microcontrollers. Other manufacturer's USB introduction kits can be used, but I do recommend the Cypress kit because of the reasonable cost and ease in which applications can be developed. The CY7C6xx with its 12-MHz clock speed is not a speedy device, but can be used for a variety of applications, including keyboards, mice, serial communications, and games interfaces.

The recommendation is somewhat reserved because I would like to see some better tools for the part, either from Cypress or from third parties.

Cypress USB Example
Thermometer Application

It might seem like I'm copping out by introducing the application that comes with the Cypress USB Starter Kit, but I found that it was a useful exercise to get it running before attempting my own application (Fig. 43-1). Actually, it was more than that. I had to expend quite a bit of effort to get the thermometer running and loading the software properly.

The initial connection to the PC was through a Belkin ExpressBus Hub. This four-channel USB hub is powered externally from the PC. You can use the built-in USB hubs in your PC, but I choose the separate hub to avoid any potential problems with the USB port on my PC being damaged. I realize that the opportunities of this happening with the starter kit are quite remote, but I'd rather be safe than have to replace my motherboard.

When the Starter Kit board is first plugged into the hub and the PC powered up, the powered LED on the Starter Kit board comes on, but not the ENUM (Enumerated) LED. After Windows has loaded, you are prompted to insert the drivers (which come on a CD with the kit). After doing this and rebooting, the ENUM LED would come up (indicating that the .WDM drivers were loaded for the device and allowed it to be enumerated).

The problem came when I tried to run the application. The application itself would not recognize the Starter Kit board. After working through the Control Panel settings in Windows 98, I decided to attempt a reload and the thermometer started working (Fig. 43-2).

After getting the USB thermometer working, I tried clicking on the X in the upper right corner and got a GPF problem. This is a known problem with the software.

Along with buying the hub, I also got a Cypress CY7C6xx USB device introductory folder with a CD-ROM. The CD-ROM included with this folder complements the information in the CD-ROM that comes with the Starter Kit and includes datasheets on both the USB products, but Cypress's full range of products as well.

FIGURE 43-1   Cypress USB Thermometer/CY7C6xx Development kit.

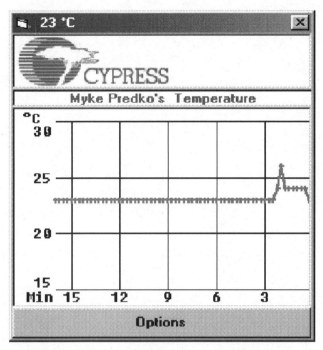

FIGURE 43-2   Dialog box from the CY7C6xx thermometer.

CONCLUSION

44

IN

CLOSING

Along with the Pentium, a fair number of high-end processors are available for PCs and servers. Just off the top of my head, I can think of the Motorola 68000 and PowerPC, MIPS, SPARC, and ALPHA. These processors all enjoy a fair amount of success in the marketplace with the workstations and applications they are used in. I wanted to end this book by saying that even though there are a number of processors out there that many people will argue are better than the 8086 derivatives (which includes the Pentium processor), I see the PC being the primary device used for most business and engineering applications in the foreseeable future. This means that the investment you put into learning the architecture of the processor and the hardware, as well as in the operating system software of the 8086 family of microprocessors and the PC will be useful for you for a very long time.

In the almost 20 years of the PC, the basic core hardware has remained essentially unchanged, undoubtedly with improvements, but with few changes. The PC is really defined by the cliché:

Plus ca change, plus ces le mem chose.

Which translated literally means "The more things change, the more they stay the same."

I first wanted to write this book in the mid-1980s, but didn't because of the PC/AT and what I saw as a brave new world with capabilities and opportunities. Again, around 1990, I returned to this subject, only to be scared off again because of Windows 3.1 and the 80486 and Pentium processors. Finally, as I started this book, Microsoft and Intel released the PC 99 specification that would firmly entrenche Windows 2000 and suggests the elimination of the ISA and PCI busses in favor of USB and Firewire.

Despite these changes, the core of the PC has remained unchanged with the processor, I/O devices with DMA and interrupts, memory, and video all located in the first 1 MB of system memory and the first 1024 I/O space addresses. Having a clear understanding of how this core works and how to interface to it is crucial to creating hardware interfaces no matter what the interface and the code needed to control it.

The purpose of this book was to give you an insight into the PC and the knowledge required to develop some very advanced applications for the different PC operating systems available today along with the capability of interfacing to external hardware. I think this book (as thick as it is) meets this goal.

In the various explanations, sample code and applications presented here, I hope I have given you the confidence to go out and create your own applications. At the very least, when nothing is working and smoke is curling up from your application, you will not give up hope totally. Maybe you will find a few answers here to discover what might have gone wrong and some hints in how to fix it.

I always look forward to hearing what the readers of my books have to say and this one is no exception. As well, I also suggest that you check my Web page periodically for updates and errata to the mistakes I'm sure that I've made.

Good luck and I'm looking forward to hearing about your successes,

Myke

Toronto, Canada

January 1999

APPENDICES

GLOSSARY

Even if you've worked around PCs for a while, I'm sure I've thrown in a number of terms and acronyms that you will not be familiar with. I've tried to give a complete list of all the acronyms, terms, and expressions that may be unfamiliar to you. Acronyms are explained before they are described.

8086 First Intel 16-bit microprocessor. Processor basis for the 8088 used in the first PC.

8087 Numeric coprocessor chip. A parallel processor used with the 8086/8088 to provide "number crunching" capability to the PC.

8088 Processor used in the first PC. Twenty-bit data bus and eight-bit external bus. Sixteen-bit internal 8086 core.

80186/80188 Microcontrollers designed by Intel to be used in the place of the 8086/8087 with support chips.

80286/80287 Enhanced 8086 (a Protect mode capable of accessing 16 MB of memory added) that was provided with the PC/AT.

80386/80387 Thirty-two bit enhancement to the 8086. Capable of running "emulated" 8086s in up to 4.3 GB of memory.

80386SX/80387SX Cost-reduced version of the 80386. Sixteen-bit external data bus and up to 16 MB of external memory.

8042 Bus-interface 8051-compatible microcontroller used for controlling the keyboard in the PC/AT system unit.

80486 Cache and clock-enhanced performance 80386.

80486SX/80486SX A cost-reduced 80486 with 16-bit external data bus and up to 16 MB of memory access. Contrary to popular myth, these are not defective 80486s.

8237 A DMA controller used in the PC. Sixteen-bit addresses output—"page" registers used for full 24-bit addressing.

8253/8254 Timer chips used in the PC. 1.19 MHz used for the clock input, which can be reduced to 18.2-ms ticks.

8259 Interrupt controller used in the PC, which has eight input sources including slave 8259 devices, providing additional interrupts. Also known as the "PIC".

8514/A Introduced by IBM with the PS/2 and VGA. The 8514/A standard is the basis for SVGA.

AC Abbreviation for *Alternating Current*. Normal North American household (and office) power is 100 Vac.

Accumulator Register used as a temporary storage register for an operation's data source and destination.

ACPI Abbreviation for *Advanced Configuration and Power Interface*. Updated version of APM that can be used in both laptops and desktop PCs.

Active Components Generally integrated circuits and transistors. Devices that require external power to operate.

ActiveX An enhanced version of COM that allows code and data used by a PC to be spread over large networks.

ADC *Analog-to-Digital Converter*. Hardware devoted to converting the value of a dc voltage into a digital representation. See *DAC*.

Address The location a register, RAM byte, or instruction word is located at within its specific memory space.

ADO Abbreviation for *ActiveX Data Object*.

AGP Abbreviation for *Advanced Graphic Processor*. AGP was developed by Intel as a fast graphics adapter interface to the Pentium processor and display-update protocol.

Amps A measure of current. One amp is the movement of one coulomb of electrons in one second.

Analog A quantity at a fractional value, rather than a binary, one or zero. Analog voltages are the quantity most often measured.

AND A logic gate that outputs a *1* when all inputs are a *1*.

ANSI Abbreviation for the *American National Standards Institute*. Best known for the ANSI console interface, which is used to control the PCs (and other terminals) and workstation's display.

API Abbreviation for *Application Program Interface*. The interface to standard resources within the PC.

APM Abbreviation for *Advanced Power Management*. This set of Interfaces is used to control the processor speed and motherboard operation of a PC.

Array Data that has been stored in a series of addressable indices within a variable. Arrays can have multiple "dimensions."

ASCII *American Standard Character Interchange Interface*. Bit-to-character representation standard most used in computer systems.

ASCIIZ A contiguous string of ASCII characters terminated by a null (0x000) character. This data format is often used for passing strings in the PC.

ASIC Abbreviation for *Application Specific Integrated Circuit*. A chip designed to be configured for a specific application before packaging. Many standard functions in the PC are provided by ASICs.

Assembler A computer program that converts assembly-language source to object code.

Assembly Language A set of word symbols used to represent the instructions of a processor. Along with a primary instruction, parameters are used to specify values, registers, or addresses.

Asynchronous Serial Data sent serially to a receiver without clocking information. Instead, data synching information for the receiver is available inside the data packet or as part of each bit.

Autoexec.bat A batch file that is run when a PC first boots up and is used to configure the MS-DOS command-line operating environment. It is also used to set directory paths for libraries and often-used files.

Bare Board See *Raw Card*.

BASIC Acronym for *Beginners All-purpose Symbolic Interface Code*. A beginner's computer language that has been available in different forms for the PC since it was first available.

Baud A term to describe serial data rate. Normally, this value is used to describe data in "bits per second," although this is not the exact definition.

Baudot A five-bit serial code developed for use with Teletype machines. One of the fore runners to modern asynchronous serial communication.

BCD Abbreviation for *Binary Code Decimal*. Using four bits to represent a decimal number (zero to nine).

Binary Numbers Numbers represented as powers of two. Each digit is two raised to a specific power. For example, 37 Decimal is $32 + 4 + 1 = 2**4 + 2**2 + 2**0 = 00010101$ binary. Binary can be represented in the forms: *0b0nnnn*, *B'nnnn'*, or *%nnnn*, where *nnnn* is a multidigit binary number comprising of 1s and 0s.

BIOS Acronym for *Basic Input/Output System*. The BIOS APIs provide a consistent interface to hardware within the PC.

Bipolar Logic Logic circuits made from bipolar transistors (either discrete devices or those integrated onto a chip).

Bit The smallest unit of data available in digital logic. A bit can have one of two states: On or Off.

Bitmap Saving graphic data directly from VRAM is called *bitmap data*. This format is quite inefficient in terms of space used and resolution.

Bit Mask A bit pattern that is ANDed with a value to turn off specific bits.

Blue Screen of Death When a Windows program fails or causes Windows itself to fail, the video output is changed to a blue text display which is known as the "Blue Screen of Death."

Boolean Logic Invented by the theologian George Boole in the nineteenth century, it is the mathematical basis for digital logic.

Borland The company responsible for many tools for the PC, including "Turbo Pascal," which was the first popular inexpensive Integrated Development Environment ("IDE") for the PC.

BPS Abbreviation for "Bits Per Second." The measure of data transfer in serial applications is normally in "Bits Per Second." BPS is similar to, but not exactly the same as the "Baud" rate.

BRS Abbreviation for "Big Red Switch." When all else fails in a program, you will have to cycle the "BRS" to turn it on and off.

8 APPENDICES

Burning See "Programming."

Bus An electrical connection between multiple devices, each using the connection for passing data.

Bus Contention The situation that arises when more than one circuit is driving a value onto a bus. If the output values are different, then the actual electrical value is indeterminate.

Bus Mastering A technique to provide bus control to multiple devices (or "masters").

Byte Eight bits which are combined to form a data character or a control statement. This is the normal smallest unit of data used in PC applications.

C Structured programming language that is often described as a "structured assembly." C is widely used across many computer systems and is often used for systems programming.

C++ An object-oriented programming version of C. C++ (pronounced "See-Plus-Plus") is often used for Windows application development.

Cache Relatively small, high-speed memory directly connected to a PC's processor to bypass the relatively slow reads from DRAM.

Capacitor A device used to store an electrical charge. Often used in microcontroller circuits for filtering signals and input power by reducing transient voltages.

CAS Acronym for *Column Address Strobe*. The CAS line on a DRAM is used to specify that the column address data is being driven on the multiplexed address bus.

CD Abbreviation for a serial port's *Carrier Detect* line. This line is active when a modem connected to the serial port is receiving a carrier signal from another device.

CD-ROM A 5.25" disc that contains information stored in an optical format instead of using the traditional magnetic methods. The CD-ROM is a derivation of the audio compact disc.

Celeron A cost- and performance-reduced Pentium processor introduced by Intel.

Ceramic Resonator A clocking device that is less accurate than a crystal, but cheaper and more robust.

CGA Abbreviation for *Color Graphics Adapter*. Introduced with the first PC as a method of displaying graphical data, as well as (low resolution) text.

Character A series of bits used to represent an alphabetic, numeric, control, or other symbol or representation. See *ASCII*.

CISC Abbreviation for *Complex Instruction Set Computer*. A type of computer architecture that uses a large number of very complete instructions, rather than a few short instructions. See *RISC*.

Clock A repeating signal used to run a processor's instruction sequence.

Clock Cycle The operation of a microcontroller's primary oscillator going from a low voltage to a high voltage and back again. This is normally referenced as the speed the device runs at. Multiple clock cycles can be used to make up one instruction cycle.

CMOS Logic Logic circuits made from N-channel and P-channel MOSFET *(Metal-Oxide Silicon Field-Effect Transistors)* devices (either discrete devices or integrated onto a chip).

COM Acronym for *Component Object Model*. The use of objects for code and data within a Windows PC.

Comparator A device that compares two voltages and returns a logic *1* or a *0*, based on the relative values.

Compiler A program that converts a high-level Language source file to either assembly-language code or object code for a microcontroller.

CONFIG.SYS A text file that specifies the operating environment and default device drivers for a PC.

Constant A numeric value used as a parameter for an operation or instruction. This differs from a variable value, which is stored in a RAM or register memory location.

Constructors Functions defined in object-orientated programming to initialize variables and memory areas.

Control Characters, ASCII Hex codes 0x000 to 0x01F have been given special meanings in ASCII for controlling communication with other devices. In the PC, these codes are used to display custom characters on the video monitor.

Controls The name given to buttons, sliders, and other features in Windows dialog boxes, which are used to control the behavior of an application.

CPU Abbreviation for *Central Processing Unit*; what I refer to as the microcontroller's "processor."

CR Abbreviation for the ASCII *Carriage Return (0x00D) character*. This character is nominally used to indicate the end of the line to a printer (and have it return its carriage to the left side of the page). In the PC, the CR character is normally used to indicate the user has pressed *Enter*.

CRC Abbreviation for *Cyclical Redundancy Check*. A CRC is a hardware device used to produce a checksum, based on a serial stream of data that has been received.

CS Abbreviation for a device's *Chip Select line*. This line is used to indicate that the data to be transferred will be coming from/going to the selected chip. In TTL, this line may also use the G reference.

CRT Abbreviation for *Cathode-Ray Tube*. The CRT is the basis for the video display used in PCs (and your TV set).

Crystal Device used for providing precise clock signals.

CTS Abbreviation for serial port *Clear-To-Send line*. This line is received from an external device to indicate that it is able to receive characters.

CUI Abbreviation for *Console User Interface*. This term used for a standard MS-DOS interface in which the user enters data from the keyboard from a prompt on the display. Event-driven programming techniques are not used for this type of interface.

Current The measurement of the number of electrons that pass by a point in a second each second. The units are *amps*, which are coulombs per second. One Coulomb of charge requires $1.6 \times 10 ** 19$ electrons.

DAC Abbreviation for *digital-to-analog converter*. Hardware designed to convert a digital representation of an analog dc voltage into an analog voltage. See *ADC*.

DC Abbreviation for *direct current*. An unchanging voltage applied to a circuit.

DCD Abbreviation for the *data carrier detect line* in a serial port. This line is active when two modems are synched and capable of communication.

DCE The abbreviation for *data communications equipment,* the RS-232 standard by which modems are usually wired. See *DTE*.

DCOM Abbreviation for *Distributed COM*. DCOM is the mechanism used to provide code and data to PCs over a network.

DDB Abbreviation for *Data Descriptor Block*. This data area, at the start of a VxD is used by the Virtual Machine Manager to load parameters about the VxD.

Debugger   A program used by an application programmer to find the problems in the application. This program is normally run on the target system on the application to run on.

Decimal Numbers   Base-10 numbers used for constants. These values are normally converted into hex or binary numbers for the microcontroller.

Desktop   The term used for a PC, which can only use 110 Vac power and uses a CRT for video display. In Windows, a Desktop is the base display for loading and displaying application dialog boxes.

Destructors   An object-oriented programming function, which is called when an object is no longer needed to free up any resources allocated by the object.

Device Drivers   Software used to provide a common, low-level interface to hardware devices.

Dialog Box   What most new users would call a *window*. A dialog box displays the current status of a Windows application, as well as the controls needed to take user input.

Digital   A term used to describe a variety of logic families, where values are either high (1) or low (0). For most logic families, the voltage levels are either approximately 0 volts or approximately 5 volts with a switching level somewhere between 1.4 and 2.5 volts.

DIP   Acronym for *Dual In-line Package*. This type of chip package has two rows of legs that are pushed into a PTH board or socket.

Directory   Also known as a *subdirectory* or a *folder*. A file directory is used as a high-level descriptor for a set of files falling under one category. The terms *directory* and *subdirectory* are typically MS-DOS terms.

.DLLs   Abbreviation and file type for *Dynamically Linked Libraries*. DLLs are Windows device drivers that are loaded with the application and not specified by CONFIG.SYS, as MS-DOS device drivers are.

DMA   Abbreviation for *Direct Memory Access*. DMA is used to pass data between I/O devices and memory without requiring the PC's processor to intervene.

DMM   Abbreviation for *Digital Multi-Meter*. A voltmeter/ammeter/ohmmeter (and other instruments) built into one package. The most common type of test equipment.

Docking Station   A device used with laptops to provide an easy way to connect/disconnect interface to keyboards, CRT displays, and networks in a desktop environment.

DOS   Acronym for *Disk Operating System*. This is a generic term for operating systems that are centered on the disk or diskette subsystem.

Double Word   In the PC, when 32 bits of data are required, the storage is defined as a *double word*, which is four bytes or two 16-bit words.

DRAM   Acronym for *Dynamic Random-Access Memory*. DRAM memory is a very high-density form of data storage using charged capacitors instead of flip-flops. DRAM must be refreshed periodically or the charges in the capacitors will literally leak away.

Driver   Any device that can force a signal onto a net. See *Receiver*.

D-Shell Connectors   A style of connector often used for RS-232 serial connections, as well as other protocols. The connector is "D"-shaped to provide a method of polarizing the pins and ensuring that they are connected the correct way.

DSR   Abbreviation for the *Data Set Ready line* in a serial port. This line is asserted when the PC is ready to send data.

DTE Abbreviation for *Data Terminal Equipment*, the RS-232 standard that your PC's serial port is wired to. See *DCE*.

DTR Abbreviation for the *Data Terminal Ready line* of the serial port. This line is asserted by the terminal equipment to indicate that it can accept data.

Duty Cycle In a pulse-wave-modulated digital signal, the duty cycle is the fraction of time the signal is high over the total time of the repeating signal.

EBCDIC Abbreviation for IBM's *Extended Binary Coded Decimal Interchange Code*. This is IBM's equivalent to ASCII. It was surprising to many people when the PC was released and used ASCII and not EBCDIC.

ECC Abbreviation for *Error Correction Code*. A multibit extension put on a memory word to allow hardware to both detect failing bits, as well as "fix" them.

ECL Abbreviation for *Emitter-Coupled Logic*. This logic family is incompatible with TTL and most forms of CMOS. It is often used for very high speed circuits.

Edge Triggered Logic that changes, based on the change of a digital logic level. See *Level Sensitive*.

Editor Program located on your development system that is used to modify application source code.

EDO Abbreviation for *Enhanced Data Output*. This type of DRAM was introduced as a fast method of supplying data to a PC's processor. It is now largely superseded by SDRAM.

EEPROM Acronym for *Electrically Erasable Programmable Memory*. Nonvolatile memory that can be erased and reprogrammed electrically a byte at a time.

EGA Abbreviation for *Enhanced Graphics Adapter*.

EIDE Abbreviation for *Enhanced Integrated Drive Electronics*. An updated version of the PC/AT's IDE, which includes Plug'n'Play for different devices.

EMM Abbreviation for *Expanded Memory Manager*. This software tool is available in 80386 (and faster) processors running MS-DOS 3.0 and greater to provide access to more than 640 KB of memory in MS-DOS Real mode.

EMS Abbreviation for *Extended Memory Specification*. This is the hardware (386 and faster) Protect-mode capabilities of addressing more than the 640 KB available in the MS-DOS memory area.

Encapsulation Object-orientated programming term for keeping object's data separate or private from other objects.

Enumeration The process of identifying and loading device drivers for a hardware device that is available on a bus or detected through Plug'n'Play.

EOF Abbreviation for *end of file*. In MS-DOS files, *Ctrl-Z* (0x01A) is often used to indicate the end of a file.

EOL Abbreviation for *end of line*. At the end of all lines of data a CR (carriage return, 0x00D) is used to mark the end of the line. In many circumstances, a LF (line feed, 0x00A) character follows to move to the next line down.

EPROM Acronym for *Erasable Programmable Read-Only Memory*. Nonvolatile memory that can be electrically programmed and erased using ultraviolet light.

Event-Driven Programming A style of programming in which an application only executes when some external event occurs. These events can be hardware interrupts or user commands.

8

APPENDICES

FAT File format used in MS-DOS and Windows 16-bit operating systems. This format limits the filename to eight characters for the name and three characters for the extension. Later, 32-bit Windows kernel operating systems uses the high-performance file system format, which does not have this limitation and can support larger disk drives.

FF Abbreviation for the form-feed (0x00C) character. This character is used to move the paper in a printer to the next page. In CRT displays, the form-feed character is often used to clear the screen.

FPGA Abbreviation for *Field-Programmable Gate Array*. Semiconductor logic that can be customized outside of the chip factory.

FIFO Acronym for "First In First Out." Memory that will retrieve data in the order in which it was stored.

Firewire (Also known as *IEEE 1394.*) A high-speed serial bus protocol designed to eliminate the need for SCSI, PCI, and other high-speed bus protocols in the PC.

Flash A type of EEPROM that can be bulk erased, rather than erased one byte at a time. Often used for ROM in PCs.

Flip-flop A basic memory cell that can be loaded with a specific logic state and read back. The logic state will be stored as long as power is applied to the cell.

Floppy Drive Thin, flexible magnetic disks contained within a hard plastic shell and used to store and transfer data.

Focus The term used to describe the dialog box currently is "active" on the Windows desktop.

Folder When directories are displayed in Windows, they are called *folders*.

Frame An entire unit of data. A frame can be made up of multiple fields (in the case of NTSC composite video) or packets (in the case of serial communications).

Frequency The number of repetitions of a signal that can occur in a given period of time (typically one second). See *Period* and *Hertz*.

FTP Abbreviation for *File Transfer Protocol*. A method of transferring files to/from the Internet.

Functions A subroutine that returns a parameter to the caller.

Fuzzy Logic An extension of Boolean logic, which uses analog ranges of data from 0 to 1.

GAS Abbreviation for gallium arsenide semiconductor chips. Much faster than Silicon, they are significantly more difficult to work with.

Gate The lowest level of digital logic. The most common gate types are AND, OR, XOR, and NOT.

GB 1,073,741,824 bytes.

GFLOPS Loose acronym for *Billion of FLoating point Operations Per Second*. This is a primary measurement for supercomputer implementations.

.GIF A method of storing and displaying graphical data that has a reasonable amount of data compression at some loss of resolution.

Glue Logic The term used to describe simple gates and flip-flops used in a circuit to "glue" together larger functions.

GPF Abbreviation for *General-Protection Fault*. The precursor to the "blue screen of death" in 32-bit kernel Windows.

Ground Negative voltage to microcontroller/circuit. Also referred to as V_{ss}.

GUI   Acronym for *Graphical User Interface* (often pronounced "gooey"). A GUI is used, along with a Graphical Operating System (such as Microsoft Windows), to provide a simple, consistent interface for users that consists of a screen, keyboard and mouse.

GW-BASIC   A BASIC interpreter built into the original IBM PC's boot ROM. "GW" stands for "gee whiz."

Hard Drive   The device inside your PC that contains the operating system, applications, and some data. The hard drive is normally not removable (but might be in some types) and provides high-speed access to the programs and data.

Hertz   A unit of measurement of frequency. One Hertz (Hz) means that an incoming signal is oscillating once per second.

Hex Numbers   A value from 0 to 15 that is represented using four bits or the numbers *0* through *9* and *A* through *F*.

High-Level Language   A set of English (or other human language) statements that have been formatted for use as instructions for a computer. Some popular high-level languages used for microcontrollers include C, BASIC, Pascal, and Forth.

Horizontal Synch   A pulse used to indicate the start of a scan line in a video monitor or TV set.

HPFS   Abbreviation for the *High-Performance File System*. This disk format allows larger than FAT-specific file names (which can include blanks) and supports larger disk drives.

HTML   Abbreviation for *HyperText Markup Language*. The programming language used for Internet Web sites.

Hz   See Hertz.

IBM   Abbreviation for *International Business Machines*. The company that first designed the PC, PC/XT, and PC/AT.

IC   Abbreviation for *Integrated Circuit*. An IC consists of many (often millions) of transistors placed on a single chip.

IDE   Abbreviation for *Integrated Drive Electronics* or *Integrated Development Environment*. The hard drives used in the PC/AT were of the IDE format. An integrated development environment is a tool that combines an assembler/compiler, linker, and debugger all in one.

IEEE   Abbreviation/common name for the *Institute of Electrical and Electronic Engineers*. This organization provides methods of passing data between engineers, as well as publishing electrical and data standards.

Index Register   A 16-bit register that can have its contents used to point to a location in variable storage, control store, or the microcontroller's register space. See *Stack Pointer*.

Inductor   Wire wrapped around some kind of form (metal or plastic) to provide a magnetic method of storing energy. Inductors are often used in oscillator and filtering circuits.

Infrared   A wavelength of light (760 nm or longer) that is invisible to the human eye. Often used for short-distance communications.

Instantiation   Object-oriented programming term for creating an object of a specific class.

Intel   The company responsible for designing the processor and many of the peripheral interface chips used in the PC.

8
APPENDICES

Internet A series of computers linked together by a common, redundant set of wires. First developed in the 1960s as the ARPANet.

Interpreter A program that reads application source code and executes it directly, rather than compiling it.

Interrupt An event that causes the microprocessor's processor to stop what it is doing and respond.

Interrupt Controller The chip that arbitrates which interrupts are passed to the PC's processor and provides the processor with the requesting interrupt identification.

Instruction A series of bits which are executed by the microcontroller's processor to perform a basic function.

Instruction Cycle The minimum amount of time needed to execute a basic function in a microcontroller. One instruction cycle typically takes several clock cycles. See *Clock Cycles*.

I/O Abbreviation of *Input/Output*. I/O is the operation of passing data to and from the processor and memory to the "outside world."

I/O Space An address space totally devoted to providing access to I/O device control registers.

IRQ Abbreviation for *Interrupt ReQuest Line*. A bus line that is connected to the PC's interrupt controllers.

ISA Abbreviation for *Industry Standard Architecture*. This term is normally applied to the PC/AT's 16-bit I/O slots.

.JPG Another method of storing graphic data. This method provides modest compression with very little resolution loss.

K6 The AMD version of the Pentium processor. Currently, the K6-3 is the fastest AMD offering. Many inexpensive PCs use the AMD chips instead of those from Intel.

KB 1,024 bytes.

Kernel The core of the operating system, responsible for selecting which tasks should be executing.

Keyboard A matrix of buttons, arranged in a typewriter's QWERTY format, used to input text data into a PC.

kHz This is an abbreviation for measuring frequency in thousands of cycles per second.

Label An identifier used within a program to denote the address location of a control store or register address. See *Variable*.

Labview National Instruments hardware programming environment. Useful in connecting and controlling instruments to a PC.

LAN Acronym for *Local-Area Network*. A LAN consists of a hardware method of providing a method of communications between multiple PCs. Lately, LANs have included connections to printers, central files, and the Internet.

Laptop A portable PC, which normally has an internal battery for power and an integrated flat LCD display.

LCD Abbreviation for *Liquid Crystal Display*. A type of display that consists of a liquid suspended between two plates. When a voltage potential is placed on the plates, the liquid becomes opaque or transparent.

LED An abbreviation for *Light-Emitting Diode*. This diode (rectifier) device will emit light of a specific frequency when current is passed through it.

Level Conversion The process of converting logic signals from one family to another.

Level Sensitive Logic that changes based on the state of a digital logic signal. See *Edge Triggered*.

LF Abbreviation for the ASCII line feed (0x00A) character. This character is used with the carriage-return character to indicate the end of a line of ASCII text.

LIFO Acronym for *Last In First Out*. A type of memory in which the most recently stored data will be the first retrieved.

LIM The Lotus Intel Microsoft specification for providing extended memory in MS-DOS.

Linker A software product that combines object files into a final program file that can be loaded and executed in the PC.

List Server An Internet server used to distribute common-interest mail to a number of individuals.

Local Bus In the early 1980s, some PCs were provided with fast interfaces to the processors (bypassing the ISA bus) for disks and graphics adapters. The generic term for this interface is *local bus*, which includes the PCI bus—even though PCI is not interfaced to the processor or its address and data busses.

Logic Analyzer A tool that will graphically show the relationship of the waveforms of a number of different pins.

Logic Gate A circuit that outputs a logic signal, based on input logic conditions.

Logic Probe A simple device used to test a line for either being high, low, transitioning, or in a high-impedance state.

LRU Abbreviation for *Least Recently Used*, which is applicable in PC processors with cache memory (such as the Pentium). With the LRU algorithm, if the cache has to be updated, the memory that has not been accessed for the longest time is replaced.

LSB Abbreviation for *Least-Significant Bit* or *Least-Significant Byte*. The LSB is the smallest unit of a value.

Macro A programming construct that replaces a string of characters (and parameters) into a previously specified block of code or information.

Mask Programmable ROM A method of programming a memory that occurs at final assembly of a microcontroller. When the aluminum traces of a chip are laid down, a special photographic mask is made to create wiring that will result in a specific program being read from a microcontroller's control store.

Master The device which currently has control over a bus at a given time.

Matrix Keyboard A set of pushbutton switches wired in an X/Y pattern to allow button states to be read easily.

MB 1,048,576 bytes.

MCA Abbreviation for *MicroChannel Architecture*. MCA was a bus introduced with the PS/2 line of computers as a faster interface to adapters than ISA.

MCGA Abbreviation for *Monochrome/Color Graphics Adapter*. This device was introduced as a MDA and CGA register-compatible enhanced graphic adapter in low-end PS/2s.

MDA Abbreviation for *Monochrome Display Adapter*. Along with CGA, IBM introduced the MDA with the PC as a high-resolution text display. Special characters allow box graphics.

MDI Abbreviation for *Multiple Document Interface*. This is the default interface for Visual C++ applications.

Memory Circuits within a PC that provide code or data to the processor.

Memory Array A collection of flip-flops arranged in a matrix format that allows consistent addressing.

Memory Mapped I/O A method of placing peripheral registers in the same memory space as RAM or variable registers.

Memory Space The address space within the 8086 used for accessing operating system and application code and data.

Methods In object-orientated programming, a *method* is an interface to one particular aspect of an object.

MFC Abbreviation for *Microsoft Foundation Classes*. This is used to describe a set of classes in Microsoft's Visual C++ that carries out basic Windows API functions.

MFLOPS Abbreviation for *Millions of Floating point Operations Per Second*. This term is used to describe the computing power of a PC or workstation.

MHz An abbreviation for measuring frequency in millions of cycles per second.

Microsoft The company responsible for MS-DOS, Windows, and various applications and development tools (such as GW-BASIC, Visual Basic, and Visual C++).

MIDI Acronym for the *Musical Instrument Digital Interface* that is built into a PC's SoundBlaster card.

MIPS Abbreviation for *Millions of Instructions Per Second*. This acronym should be really be: *Misleading Indicator of Performance* and should not be a consideration when deciding, which PC to buy.

MMU Abbreviation for a PC's cache *Memory Management Unit*. This hardware is used to determine whether data is available from within the caches or from main memory.

MMX A hardware enhancement made to Pentium processors to allow matrix (parallel) arithmetic and bitwise operations, along with standard scalar operations.

Modal A description placed on a child dialog box. A dialog box is said to be modal if its parent cannot be accessed until the child operation has completed.

Modem A device used to allow PCs to communicate over telephone lines.

Monitor A program used to control the execution of an application inside a processor.

MOS Acronym for *Metal-Oxide Silicon*. A MOS transistor uses a metal Gate over a silicon channel, separated by a layer of silicon oxide for current control.

Mouse An input device used to allow a PC's user to select graphical data or controls within a Windows dialog box.

MPU Abbreviation for *microprocessor*.

MSB Abbreviation for *Most-Significant Bit* or *Most-Significant Byte*. The highest unit in a value.

MS-DOS Abbreviation for *MicroSoft-Disk Operating System*. A basic operating system that provides a consistent interface to PCs resources, such as disk drives, memory, and the CRT display.

MSDN Abbreviation for *MicroSoft Developer Network*. The development tool resources provided by Microsoft to aid in the development of Windows applications.

ms On thousandth of a second (0.001 seconds). See *nsec* and *μsec*.

Multi-Mastering The term used to describe a bus that can have different devices controlling the data transfer between devices.

Multi-Tasking   The term used to describe an operating system that allows multiple applications to run concurrently.

N/C   Abbreviation for *No Connect*. A pin that is left unconnected or "floating."

Negative Active Logic   A type of logic, where the digital signal is said to be asserted if it is at a low (0) value. See *Positive Active Logic*.

Nesting   Placing subroutine or interrupt execution within the execution of other subroutines or interrupts.

Net   A technical term for the connection of device pins in a circuit. Each net consists of all the connections to one device pin in a circuit.

Net, The   A colloquial term for the Internet (and a pretty bad movie starring Sandra Bullock).

Network   The medium used to connect multiple devices that are to communicate with one another.

NMI   Abbreviation for *Non-Maskable Interrupt*. The NMI will always interrupt the processor—even if interrupts are disabled or "masked."

NMOS Logic   Digital logic where only N-channel MOSFET transistors are used.

NOP   Abbreviation for the *No-OPeration instruction*. The NOP simply takes up space and processor cycles.

NOT   A logic gate that inverts the state of the input signal (1 NOT is 0).

ns   One billionth of a second (0.000000001 seconds). See *μsec* and *nsec*.

NTSC   Abbreviation for the *National Television Standards Committee*; the standards organization responsible for defining the TV signal format used in North America.

NVRAM   Abbreviation for *Non-Volatile Random Access Memory*. NVRAM is a generic term for any RAM memory that retains its contents after power has been taken away from the circuit. Although EEPROM and flash can be considered NVRAM, the typical use for the term is static RAM, which has an auxiliary (lithium) battery that powers the chip (and saves the data) when power is removed.

Object File   After assembly or high-level language compilation, a file is produced with the hex values (op codes) that make up a processor's instructions.

Object-Oriented Programming   A style of computer programming that represents both data and code as objects to make interfacing to different devices easier.

Octal Numbers   A method of representing numbers as the digits from 0 to 7. This method of representing numbers is not widely used, although some high-level languages, such as C, have made it available to programmers.

OE   Abbreviation for a chip's *Output Enable line*. Before a tri-state output on a chip can drive data out, the OE must be asserted, indicating that the receiver is ready for the data (and no other devices are driving on the nets).

Offset   An address within a specified segment.

OLE   Acronym for *Object Linking and Embedding*, which is normally pronounced "olé." Network database interface available to Windows.

One's Complement   The result of XORing a value with 0x0FF, which will invert each bit of a number. See *Two's Complement*.

Op Codes   The hex values that make up the processor instructions in an application.

Open Collector/Drain Output   An output circuit consisting of a single transistor that can pull the net which it is connected to ground.

Operating System   The control software within a PC that initiates program execution and controls access to system resources, such as the disk drives, memory, and CRT display.

OR   A basic logic gate, when any input is set to a *1*, a 1 is output.

OS/2   First introduced by IBM in 1987 along with the PS/2 as a full 32-bit Protect-mode operating system for the PC. Moderately successful, it has been overtaken by the Win32 kernel versions of Windows in recent years.

Oscilloscope   An instrument that is used to observe the waveform of an electrical signal. The two primary types of oscilloscopes in use today are the analog oscilloscope (which writes the current signal onto the phosphors of a CRT) and the digital storage oscilloscope (which saves the analog values of an incoming signal in RAM for replaying on either a built-in CRT or a computer connected to the device).

OTP   Abbreviation for *One-Time Programmable*. This term generally refers to a device with EPROM memory encased in a plastic package that does not allow the chip to be exposed to UV light. Notice that EEPROM devices in a plastic package can also be described as OTP when they can be electrically erased and reprogrammed.

Overloading   In Visual C++, multiple methods can be created for an object that all have the same name (although they have different parameters). These routines allow different ways of accessing class functions and data.

Packets   A unit of data that can be easily transmitted by a set piece of hardware.

Parallel   Passing data between devices with all the data bits being sent at the same time on multiple lines. This is typically much faster than sending data serially.

Parallel Port   The term used to describe the Centronics-compatible printer port built into the PC.

Parameter   A user-specified value for a subroutine or macro. A parameter can be a numeric value, a string, or a pointer, depending on the application.

Pascal   A programming language that has been used for PC application development programming. It became very popular with the introduction of Borland's Turbo Pascal.

Passive Components   Generally resistors, capacitors, inductors, and diodes, which do not require a power source to operate. The signal is modified within the device.

PC   Abbreviation and generic term for *Personal Computer* or *Program Counter*.

PCA   Abbreviation for *Printed Circuit Assembly*. A bare board with components (both active and passive) soldered onto it.

PC/AT   Abbreviation for *Personal Computer/Advanced Technology*. The PC/AT was introduced by IBM in 1984 as an enhancement to the original PC. The PC/AT provided 16-bit I/O slots (the original PC only contained eight-bit slots) along with an 80286 microprocessor and enhanced capabilities.

PC Board   Abbreviation *Printed Circuit Board*. See *Raw Card*.

PCCard   The new name for *PCMCIA*.

PCI   Abbreviation for *Peripheral Communication Interface*. A high-speed (33 or 66 MHz) bus used in modern PCs and workstations.

PCMCIA   Abbreviation for *Personal Computer Memory Card International Association Adapter cards*. Small, credit card-sized hardware adapter cards designed for PCs. Most often used with laptop PCs to provide networking and modem functions.

PC/XT   Abbreviation for *Personal Computer/Extended Technology*. The PC/XT was introduced by IBM after the PC as an enhancement with a hard drive and three additional eight-bit hardware adapter slots.

.PDF Files   Files suitable for viewing with Adobe Postscript.

Pentium The current Intel PC processor family used in PCs. The current high-speed device is the Pentium III.

Period The length of time that a repeating signal takes to go through one full cycle. The reciprocal of *frequency*.

PGA Abbreviation for *Pin Grid Array*. This chip in a package has an array of pins that are pushed into a PTH board or socket.

PIC Acronym for *Programmable Interrupt Controller*. *PIC* is the term normally used within Windows for the 8259A interrupt controllers built into the PC.

Ping The operation of sending a message to a device to see if it is operating properly.

PLD Abbreviation for *Programmable Logic Device*. This term encompasses both memory and logic chips, which are programmed outside of the device factory, but before being assembled on a PC board.

PLL Abbreviation for *Phased-Locked Loop*. Historically, these devices have most often been used for synching data to and from disk drives. More recently, these devices have been placed on processor chips to internally increase the speed of the device. For example, a 300-MHz Pentium II PC uses PLLs to multiply the processor's 100-MHz clock by three to get the actual operating speed.

Plug'n'Play Special circuitry built into adapter cards, disk drives, printers, and other peripherals, which can be uniquely polled by a PC to determine which adapters are built in and their operating characteristics.

PMOS Logic Digital logic where only P-channel MOSFET transistors are used.

Pointer A programming construct that is used to point to an arbitrary address in memory. Pointers can exist in assembly, as well as high-level languages.

Poll A programming technique in which a bit (or byte) is repeatedly checked until a specific value is found.

Polymorphism When methods are given the same label for different actions depending on the object it is applied to, they are described as being able to **morph** to different actions. The collective description for classes that have this ability is *polymorphism.*

Pop The operation of taking data off of a stack memory.

Port The term *port* is often used for I/O register addresses and communication methods. This term is often used to describe the operation of converting an application from one operating system to another or from one programming language to another.

Positive Active Logic Logic that becomes active when a signal becomes high (1). See *Negative Active Logic*.

PPM Measurement of something in *Parts Per Million*. An easy way of calculating the PPM of a value is to divide the value by the total number of samples or opportunities and multiplying by 1,000,000. 1% is equal to 10,000 PPM; 10% is equal to 100,000 PPM.

Printer Port The latches and input buffers used to provide an interface to printers and other TTL logic-level peripherals.

Process The label given to an application running under MS-DOS or Windows. "Processes" are designed to execute within the memory space of the processor. Multiple threads can run in each process.

Program Counter A counter within a computer processor that tracks the current program execution location. This counter can be updated by the counter and have its contents saved/restored on a stack.

8

APPENDICES

Programming Loading a program into a microcontroller control store. Also referred to as *burning*.

PROM Acronym for *Programmable Read-Only Memory*. Originally, an array of "fuses" that were "blown" to load in a program. Now, PROM can refer to EPROM memory in an OTP package.

Protect Mode When operating a PC in a multitasking, 32-bit flat memory model, the processor must be switched to Protect mode from Real mode. Applications running in Protect mode cannot access code or data outside the memory allocated for the application.

PS/2 Introduced by IBM in 1987 as an attempt to thwart clone manufacturers. The PS/2 line introduced the VGA and MCA features to the PC.

PTH Abbreviation for *Pin Through Hole*. Technology in which the pins of a chip are inserted into holes drilled into a FR4 PC card before soldering.

Pull Down A resistor (typically 100 to 500 Ohms) that is wired between a microcontroller pin and ground. See *Pull Up*.

Pull Up A resistor (typically 1 K to 10 K) that is wired between a microcontroller pin and V_{cc}. A switch pulling the signal at the microprocessor pin can be used to provide user input. See *Pull Down*.

Push The operation of putting data onto a stack memory.

PWB Abbreviation *Printed Wiring Board*. See *Raw Card*.

RAM Acronym for *Random-Access Memory*. Memory that you can write to and read from. In microcontrollers, virtually all RAM is static RAM (SRAM), which means that data is stored within it as long as power is supplied to the circuit. Dynamic RAM (DRAM) is very rarely used in microcontroller applications. EEPROM can be used for nonvolatile RAM storage.

RAS Acronym for *Row Address Strobe*. The RAS line on a DRAM is used to specify that the row address data is being driven on the multiplexed address bus.

Raw Card Fiberglass board with copper traces attached to it, which allows components to be interconnected. Also known as PC board, PWA, and bare board.

RC A resistor/capacitor network used to provide a specific delay for a built-in oscillator or reset circuit.

Real Mode Sixteen-bit operating mode used by the PC to run applications.

Receiver A device that senses the logic level in a circuit. A receiver cannot drive a signal.

Recursion A programming technique where a subroutine calls itself with modified parameters to carry out a task. This technique is not recommended for microcontrollers that can have a limited stack.

Register A memory address devoted to saving a value (such as RAM) or providing a hardware interface for the processor.

Relocatable Code written or compiled in such a way that it can be placed anywhere in the control store memory map after assembly and run without any problems.

Reset The act of stopping the execution of digital logic circuits and placing them in a state to be ready to start executing again. Also, a term used to describe a bit that has the value of 0.

Resistor   A device used to limit current in a circuit.

Resistor Ladder   A circuit consisting of a number of resistors that can be selected to provide varying voltage-divider circuits and output-differing analog voltages.

Reset   Placing a microcontroller in a known state before allowing it to execute.

RFI   Abbreviation for *Radio-Frequency Interference*. Electrical noise generated from a PC and external hardware can cause problems with local TVs and radios.

RI   Abbreviation for the *Ring Indicator line* on the serial port. This line is used with modems to indicate that the modem has called another device and is waiting for it to "pick up" the line.

RISC   Acronym for *Reduced Instruction Set Computer*. This is a philosophy in which the operation of a computer is sped up by reducing the operations performed by a processor to the absolute minimum for application execution and making all resources accessible by a consistent interface. The advantages of RISC include faster execution time and a smaller instruction set. See *CISC*.

ROM   Acronym for *Read-Only Memory*. This type of memory is typically used for control store because it cannot be changed by a processor during the execution of an application. Mask programmable ROM is specified by for the chip manufacturer to build devices with specific software as part of the device and cannot be programmed "in the field."

Rotate   A method of moving bits within a single or multiple registers. No matter how many times a "rotate" operation or instruction is carried out, the data in the registers will not be lost. See *Shift*.

RS-232   An asynchronous serial communications standard. Normal logic levels for a 1 is -12 V and for a 0 is +12 V.

RTC   Abbreviation for *Real-Time Clock*. This is the CMOS, battery-backed-up clock chip that is built into the PC.

SCSI   Acronym for *Small Computer Serial Interface*. This interface is often used for large, high-speed disk drives in PCs. SCSI is not limited by the speed nor size limitations of (E)IDE. Usually pronounced "Scuzzy".

SDRAM   Abbreviation for *Synchronous Dynamic Random-Access Memory*. SDRAM is capable of outputting data in adjacent memory locations very quickly (typically at a cycle time of 10 ns). This is very useful in high-speed PCs when instruction caches have to be loaded.

Segment   The starting address of a block of memory used for code or data.

Serial   Passing multiple bits using a serial line one at a time. See *Parallel*.

Serial Port   An I/O address that accesses hardware and converts data into serial information and transmits it in RS-232 format.

Set   The term used to describe a bit loaded with a 1.

Shift   A method of moving bits within a single or multiple registers. After a shift operation, bits are lost. See *Rotate*.

SIMM   Acronym for *Single Inline Memory Module*. This device is used to add memory to a PC using sockets on the motherboard.

SIPP   Acronym for *Single Inline Pinned Package*. This type of memory is different from SIMM and usually contains VRAM, which is soldered to the video display adapter's card.

Slave A device that is being controlled over a bus by a master.

SMD Abbreviation for *Surface-Mount Device*. An SMD chip differs from a PTH device because its pins are designed to be soldered to the surface of a card, as opposed to right through.

SMT Abbreviation for *Surface-Mount Technology*. A method of wiring circuits in which the pins of a chip are soldered to the surface of a PC card.

SOIC Abbreviation for *Small Outline Integrated Circuit*. This refers to a type of package, which is designed to be as "short" as possible on a card.

SoundBlaster A hardware standard created for outputting sounds (and music) from a PC.

Splat Asterisk (*). Easier to say, spell, and funnier than "asterisk."

SRAM Abbreviation for *Static Random-Access Memory*. A memory array that will not lose its contents while power is applied.

Stack LIFO memory used to store program counter and other context register information.

Stack Pointer An index register available within a processor that is used to store data and update itself to allow the next operation to be carried out with the index pointing to a new location.

State Analyzer A tool used to store and display state data on several lines. Rather than requiring a separate instrument, this option is often available in many logic analyzers.

State Machine A programming technique that uses external conditions and state variables to determine how a program is to execute.

String Series of ASCII characters saved sequentially in memory. When ended with 0x000 to note the end of the string, it is known as an *ASCIIZ string*.

Structure A programming construct used to describe data in a specific format.

Subdirectory See *Directory*.

Subroutines A small application program devoted to carrying out one task or operation. Usually called repeatedly by other subroutines or the application mainline.

Super VGA An enhancement to VGA that was originally based on IBM's 8514/A standard. Many manufacturers of high-performance display adapters use this term to describe any device that provides a "superset" of features to the VGA.

Synchronous Serial Data transmitted serially along with a clocking signal, which is used by the receiver to indicate when the incoming data is valid.

Task Another term used to describe a thread executing within a PC.

TCP/IP Abbreviation for *Transmission Control Protocol/Internet Protocol*. TCP/IP is the method in which processing devices connect to the Internet.

Thread The term used to describe a *task*, which is application code that can run either as part of a process or on its own.

.TIF A method to save and transmit graphical data. This method provides limited compression, but excellent resolution.

Timer A counter incremented by either an internal or external source. Often used to time events, rather than counting instruction cycles.

Traces Electrical signal paths etched in copper in a printed circuit card.

Transistor An electronic device by which current flow can be controlled.

TSR Abbreviation for *Terminate and Stay Resident*. A TSR application returns control to MS-DOS's COMMAND.COM user interface while keeping code active to enhance the operation of the PC.

TTL Abbreviation for *Transistor-to-Transistor Logic*. TTL was the basis for the glue functions in the original PC.

Two's Complement A method for representing positive and negative numbers in a digital system. To convert a number to a two's complement negative, it is complemented (converted to one's complement) and incremented.

UART Abbreviation for *Universal Asynchronous Receiver/Transmitter*. Peripheral hardware inside a microcontroller used to asynchronously communicate with external devices. See *USART* and *Asynchronous Serial*.

USART Abbreviation for *Universal Synchronous/Asynchronous Receiver/Transmitter*. Peripheral hardware inside a microcontroller used to synchronously (using a clock signal, either produced by the microcontroller or provided externally) or asynchronously communicate with external devices. See *UART* and *Synchronous Serial*.

USB Abbreviation for *Universal Serial Bus*. USB is a relatively low-speed serial bus designed to replace the keyboard, mouse, serial, parallel connectors, as well as many ISA slot functions in future PCs.

μsec One millionth of a second (0.000001 seconds). See *ns* and *ms*.

UV Light Abbreviation for *Ultra-Violet Light*. Light at shorter wavelengths than the human eye can see. UV light sources are often used with windowed microcontrollers with EPROM control store for erasing the contents of the control store.

V86 The label used to describe virtual 8086 processes in the Windows operating system. These V86 processes can execute MS-DOS applications as if they were running by themselves under MS-DOS while the processor was in Real mode.

Variable A label used in an application program that represents an address that contains the actual value to be used by the operation or instruction. Variables are normally located in RAM and can be read from or written to by a program.

V_{cc} Positive power voltage applied to a microcontroller/circuit. Generally, 2.0 V to 6.0 V, depending on the application. Also known as V_{dd}.

V_{dd} See V_{cc}.

Vertical Synch A signal used by a monitor or TV set to determine when to start displaying a new screen (field) of data.

VGA Abbreviation for *Video Graphics Adapter*. VGA was first introduced by IBM with the PS/2 line of computers. VGA provided enhanced graphics and text capabilities, along with increased pixel resolution.

Vias Holes in a printed circuit card.

Virtual Machine This term is used to describe the Windows method of operation with an application given a 4-GB virtual machine in which to execute in. Its acronym is VM.

Virtual Machine Manager The Windows function that loads and executes applications in their own virtual machine process.

Volatile RAM is considered to be volatile because, when power is removed, the contents are lost. EPROM, EEPROM, and PROM are considered to be nonvolatile because the values stored in the memory are saved—even if power is removed.

Voltage The amount of electrical force placed on a charge.

Voltage Regulators A circuit used to convert a supply voltage into a level useful for a circuit or microcontroller.

Volts Unit of voltage.

VRAM Abbreviation for *Video Random-Access Memory*. Data displayed on a PC's CRT is stored in specialized memory to be displayed by the display adapter without affecting the processor's performance.

V_{ss} See *Ground*.

VxD Abbreviation for *Virtual x Device driver*. This type of device driver is used in Windows to provide virtual access to a virtual machine application, giving it the appearance that it has the only access to the hardware that the device driver is accessing.

Wait States Extra time added to an external memory read or write.

Watchdog Timer Timer used to reset a microcontroller upon overflow. The purpose of the watchdog timer is to return the microcontroller to a known state if the program begins to run errantly (or "amok").

Wattage Measure of power consumed. If a device requires 1 A of current with a 1-V drop, 1 W of power is being consumed.

.WDMs Abbreviation and file type for *Windows Device Models*. WDMs are device drivers to be used in Windows 98 and Windows NT. WDMs are the only device drivers available for USB devices.

Windows The generic term for Microsoft Windows, which includes versions 3.1, 95, 98, NT, and 2000.

Wintel The term used to describe PCs, which run the Windows operating system with Intel processors and hardware.

Word The basic data size used by a processor. In the 8086, the word size is 16 bits.

WORM Acronym for *Write Once Read Many*. This term is often used to describe user-writeable CD-ROMs.

Write-Only Memory What you end up with when your home-built memory card isn't working properly.

XGA Abbreviation for *eXtended Graphics Adapter*. An IBM enhancement to the VGA standard.

XMS Abbreviation for *Extended Memory Specification*. Protect-mode memory, accessible outside of MS-DOS, is used to provide high memory to an application.

XOR A logic gate that outputs a 1 when the inputs are at different logic levels.

ZIF Abbreviation for *Zero Insertion Force*. ZIF sockets will allow the plugging/unplugging of devices without placing stress upon the device's pins.

ZIP Drive A disk drive that can save 100+ MB of data in a format similar to the floppy disk.

.ZIP Files Files combined together and compressed into a single file using the PKZIP program by PKWARE, Inc.

RESOURCES

This is a large book with a lot of information. I have tried to at least ensure that all the information needed to work through the sample applications can be found either within the book or on the accompanying CD-ROM. Despite this great amount of information, many questions still aren't answered in this book. If this is the case, I suggest that you look through the references and resources listed in this appendix.

Contacting the Author

I am always happy to hear from you if you have any questions or comments about the book. In my previous books (which have concerned microcontrollers), asked that you contact me through a relevant list server so that others can benefit from your question.

I can also be e-mailed directly at:

myke@passport.ca

I also have a Web page that contains additional information that I have learned since the book has been published, along with errata, answers to questions, information on the PC and microcontrollers, and a book room, from which you can order books online from Amazon.com:

http://www.myke.com

Useful Books

I have tried to list the best books that I have been able to find for programming the PC and explaining the hardware and how to interface to it. These are excellent references, many of which line my bookshelves and have become quite dog-eared with time. I have tried to categorize them under the headings that will allow you to find them most easily and I have made comments about them and what you can expect to find in them.

When you look for many of the books referenced in the following sections, you are probably going to be surprised to find that many of them are out of print. I have tried to find the best books possible and many of these can only be found from second-hand book stores or used book agents.

Some (especially IBM technical references) have been hoarded and probably are not available at any price. In this case, if you want a copy, I suggest that you find somebody who has a copy, become close friends, and ask them to leave the books to you in their will.

When looking for books on specific topics, you should check the Internet for reader's comments both on personal and commercial Web pages (such as Amazon.com). On my Web page, I will continue to maintain a list of books that I have found useful and are easily available. If you find anything you think should be included, please let me know and I will update my Web page with the information.

ENGINEERING REFERENCES

Even though I graduated from university almost 15 years ago, I keep a number of books on the shelf and refer to them continuously. These books are very nonspecific, but they do provide a great deal of useful information when developing PC interfaces. Along with references on electronic circuits, these books also provide background on how electronic devices work and information on specific devices.

For many of these books, I have two sets: one for work and one for home.

The Art of Electronics, 1989   The definitive book on electronics. It's a complete engineering course wrapped up in 1125 pages. Some people might find it to be a bit too complex, but just about any theoretical question you could have will be answered in this book.
   ISBN 0-521-37095-7

Bebop to the Boolean Boogie, 1995   Somewhat deeper in digital electronics (and less serious) than *The Art of Electronics*, Clive Maxwell's introduction to electronics stands out with clear and insightful explanations of how things work and why things are done the way they are. I bought my copy when it first became available in 1995 and still use it as a reference when I'm trying to explain how something works. It distinguishes itself from other books by explaining printed wiring assembly technology (both bare boards, and Components and soldering).
   ISBN 1-878707-22-1

The Encyclopedia of Electronic Circuits (Volumes 1 through 7)   Rudolf Graf's *Encyclopedia of Electronic Circuits* series is an excellent resource of circuits and ideas that have been cataloged according to circuit type. Each book contains more than 1000 circuits and can really make your life easier when you are trying to figure out how to do something. Each volume contains an index listing circuits for the current volume and the previous ones.
   Volume 1 ISBN   0-8306-1938-0
   Volume 2 ISBN   0-8306-3138-0
   Volume 3 ISBN   0-8306-3348-0
   Volume 4 ISBN   0-8306-3895-4
   Volume 5 ISBN   0-07-011077-8
   Volume 6 ISBN   0-07-011276-2

CMOS Cookbook, Revised 1988   In *CMOS Cookbook*, Don Lancaster introduces the reader to basic digital electronic theory. Also explaining the operation of CMOS gates, providing hints on soldering and prototyping, listing common CMOS parts (along with TTL pin out equivalents), and providing a number of example circuits (including a good basic definition of how NTSC video works). The update by Howard Berlin has ensured the chips presented in the book are still available. In the 1970s, Don Lancaster also wrote the *TTL Cookbook* (which was also updated in 1998), but I find the *CMOS Cookbook* to be the most complete and useful for modern applications.
   ISBN 0-7506-9943-4

The TTL Data Book for Design Engineers, Texas Instruments   I have a couple of 1981 printed copies of the second edition of this book and they are all falling apart from overuse. The Texas Instruments TTL data books have been used for years by hundreds of thousands of engineers to develop their circuits. Each datasheet is complete with pinouts, operating characteristics and internal circuit diagrams. Although the data books are not complete for the latest HC parts, they will give you just about everything you want to know about the operation of small-scale digital logic. The latest edition that I have ref-

8

APPENDICES

erences for was published in 1988 and is no longer in print, but you can pick them up in used book stores for relatively modest prices.

ISBN N/A

PC HARDWARE

Here are the best technical information books I have been able to find on the PC. Many of these books are out of print or hard to find, although you might have some luck with used book brokers and Amazon.com. Each of these books contains slightly different information and approaches things from a different perspective. I suggest that you try to find as many of them as possible to have as wide as possible viewpoint on the processors and hardware used in the PC.

Technical Reference for the Personal Computer AT, IBM, 1984 This PC/AT technical reference was published by IBM when the PC/AT first became available. This book provides a schematic for the motherboard and disk controller, prototype, serial/parallel, and SDLC adapters. Also included is a listing of the BIOS used in the PC/AT and runs on the 80286. This book is quite complete and will give you a good idea of how the functions are implemented in the PC (whereas today, the PC is made up of just a few ASICs). This book is very hard to find.

IBM Part Number 1502243

Personal System/2 Hardware Interface Technical Reference, IBM, 1988 This book was published by IBM when the PS/2 was released to show how the MicroChannel Architecture bus and the hardware for the different PS/2s worked. This book provides an excellent reference to the keyboard, serial/parallel, and VGA adapters. When new PS/2s were designed by IBM, reference inserts were produced. I suggest that you look for the PS/2 Model 30 80286 and PS/2 Model 55 inserts.

IBM Part Number 68X2330

The Programmer's PC Source Book, 2nd Edition, 1991 Thom Hogan's 850-page book is just about the best and most complete reference you can find anywhere on the PC. This book basically ends at the 386 (no 486, Pentiums of any flavor, PCI, Northbridge, Southbridge, or SuperIO, or any ASICs of any type), but if you need a basic PC reference that explains BIOS, all the standard I/O, DOS, and Windows 3.x interfaces, this is your book. Look for it at your local used book store. If they have a second copy, let me know; my copy is falling apart. The only problem with this book is that there are no later editions.

ISBN 1-55615-118-7

Microsystem Components Handbook:
Microprocessors, Volume 1, Intel, 1986

Microsystem Components, Handbook:
Microsystem Components, Volume 2, Intel, 1986 The 1980s *Intel Microsystem Components Handbooks* are a real treasure trove of information if you are planning on creating assembly-language applications, if you are going to interface to the DMA or in-

terrupt controller chips in the PC, or write applications that use the 8253/8254 timer. These books are primarily hardware references, so they are full of operating information and block diagrams for the different chips. Although the instruction set of the 8086, 80286, and 80386 are explained, you can find much better references in the other books listed here.
  ISBN N/A

Pentium Processor System Architecture, 1995   This book contains a very detailed description of how the Pentium processor works in the PC, along with a description of cache operation. This book does not explain such recent topics as the Pentium II and Celeron processors, or MMX technology.
  ISBN 0-201-40992-5

The Complete Guide to MMX Technology, 1997   *The Complete Guide to MMX Technology* will show you how exactly the new MMX instructions are used, as well as explaining how they can be integrated into your applications. A CD-ROM that comes with the book contains a large number of code examples and utilities to help you to develop programs that take advantage of the new features. This is not a book for the beginner, but if you are familiar with Protect-mode programming, this book will take you to the next step.
  ISBN 0-0700-6192-0

The Indispensable PC Hardware Book: Your Hardware Questions Answered, Third Edition, 1997   If you can't find the IBM, Intel, and Microsoft Press books listed previously (because they're out of print), *The Indispensable PC Hardware Book* is a good reference for you to have. In it, you will find a wealth of information on the PC and its hardware, BIOS, and MS-DOS. This book does not have a lot of practical information on interfacing devices to the PC, but it does provide you with all the reference information that you are going to need.
  ISBN 0-2014-0399-4

The Undocumented PC: A Programmer's Guide to I/O, CPUs and Fixed Memory Areas, 2nd Edition, 1996   Frank Van Gilluwe must have spent an unreasonable amount of time creating this book. Just about everything you would want to know about PCs, up to the Pentium II, and the latest advanced ASICs is covered here. I/O registers and bit functions, BIOS interfaces and more are available in this book. This book does not include interfacing hardware to the PC, but gives you a very solid background to the internals of the PC and enough information to screw it up in such a way that nobody could ever get it working again. The only complaint I have about this book is that the tone is a bit smug in places, but with the amount of work that went into this book and the utilities provided, maybe it's justified.
  ISBN 0-2014-7950-8

The Embedded PC's ISA Bus: Firmware, Gadgets and Practical Tricks, 1997   Ed Nisley's book is an almost complete opposite to the previous two books and *The Programmer's PC Sourcebook*. Where the other's books focus is on documenting the innards of the PC, Nisley's shows you how to practically interface to the PC's *Industry Standard Architecture (ISA)* bus and, if you follow through the book, you will end up with an LCD graphic display. Theory, register addresses and programming information is available in this book, but it is presented as Ed works through the projects. This book is a resource that you can go back to and look at actual oscilloscope photographs of bus accesses or discussions on how to decode bus signals. A lot of great tricks are in this book, which can be used for many different PC interfacing applications.

ISBN 1-5739-8017-X

Serial Port Complete: Programming and Circuits for RS-232 and RS-485 Links and Networks, 1998

Jan Axelson introduces asynchronous communications in the PC, along with the hardware (8250 port) and RS-232/RS-485 Electrical Standards in this book. Where this book really shines is in the 100 pages explaining RS-485 with sample circuits and applications (including a PC/Basic Stamp 2 network). Normally an understanding of RS-485 is gained from application notes and trial and error, but this book provides all of the information required to create your own applications. All of the code is written in Visual Basic with source code on an included diskette.

ISBN 0-9650-8192-3

Parallel Port Complete: Programming, Interfacing and Using the PC's Parallel Printer Port, 1997

Before this book, I shied away from interfacing to the PC's parallel port because I had many problems interfacing hardware to Windows applications and porting parallel port interfaces to different PCs. The example code is written in Visual Basic and is included on a diskette that comes with the book. The book is well written and can be easily worked through by technicians and students. After reading through the book, you'll probably be itching to start developing your own applications.

ISBN 0-9650-8191-5

Developing USB PC Peripherals, 1997

I am a bit amazed at how good this book is—especially because it was written before PCs were produced with USB ports built in and Windows was able to support it in native mode. This book is quite thin, but does contain a good explanation of how USB works, how it is implemented in a PC host and microcontroller, and it also provides a good explanation of .WDMs. Before embarking on a USB application design, you should read this book cover to cover.

ISBN 0-929392-38-8

8086 ASSEMBLY CODE

I have always felt that to truly understand a processor-based system, you have to understand how applications actually execute. I find the most efficient way of gaining this level of understanding is by learning the processor and its instruction set. In this book, I have tried to introduce you to the basic operation of the PC's processor, but to really be comfortable with it, you will have to load an assembler and linker onto your PC and start developing your own applications.

Intel 486 Microprocessor Family Programmer's Reference Manual, Intel, 1992

I have a number of Intel manuals that list the instructions and operating modes of the Protect-mode capable 8086 family members, but this book seems to be the best of them.

At 550 pages, it is pretty thick, but it explains all the instructions for both the 16-bit 8086 processor and 32-bit 80386, as well as how the various functions of Protect mode work.

ISBN N/A

Personal System/2 and Personal Computer BIOS Interface Technical Reference, IBM, 1988   This reference provides an excellent explanation of the different BIOS APIs. The text is concise and well written. The book, however, really shows its age in two areas. The first is in how IBM cross references the API functions to the IBM PCs of the 1980s. These PCs include the original PC, PC/XT, PC/AT, PC/Convertible, PS/2 Models 25 and 30, PS/2s with 80286s, and PS/2s with 80386s. This information is really of little use today. The second failing is IBM's inclusion of ABIOS, which was IBM's attempt at providing a Protect-mode BIOS interface (primarily for OS/2). Despite these problems, the book is an excellent and well-organized reference for the PC's BIOS APIs, along with hardware information, such as video modes and keyboard scan code information.

IBM Part Number 68X2341

The Programmer's PC Source Book, 2nd Edition, 1991   This book is probably the most useful hardware and software book available anywhere. This book contains a comprehensive listing of all the BIOS, MS-DOS, and (Win16 kernel) Windows APIs, along with I/O port addresses and hardware interrupt operation. Even though this book is approaching 10 years old, the hardware, BIOS and MS-DOS information provided in it is still accurate for modern PCs.

ISBN 1-55615-118-7

IBM PC and Assembly Language and Programming, 4th Edition, 1997 This is an excellent introduction to assembly-language programming with a fairly low-level approach concentrating on Microsoft's MASM and Borland's TASM. DEBUG.COM is used exclusively as a debug tool, which makes this book reasonably inexpensive to work with. I bought the first edition in 1983 when I first started working with the PC and I have kept up with the new editions over the years (largely because the older books fell apart from overuse).

ISBN 1-1375-6610-7

Assembly Language Master Class, 1995   This is not a starter-level book. It assumes quite a high level of understanding of the 8086 and 80386 Protect modes and describes how high-level language programming techniques can be implemented in assembly language, as well as focusing on creating hardware interface software in assembly language. This book should be treated as a compilation of 20 or so different assembly-language topics. The reason is that this book has 10 different authors (some of them Russian), so you might find that the writing changes style periodically and some concepts are not explained very clearly.

ISBN 1-8744-1634-6

Windows Assembly Language and Systems Programming: 16- and 32-Bit Low-Level Programming for the PC and Windows, 2nd Edition, 1997 Barry Kauler claims that he writes all his Windows applications in assembler. From this book, I would say that has the capabilities to create applications without the need of high-level languages. The book is clearly written and does give some excellent examples of how VxDs and DLLs are implemented. The one big problem with this book is that the example code will not assemble and link because it is provided on the diskette that comes with the book. Most of the problems can be resolved with a bit of work (especially if you are familiar with 8086 and MS-DOS assembly language), but it was not a process I enjoyed going through. My conclusion after working through this book is that I am richer for the practical knowledge I've gained and I never want to do any Windows programming in assembly language.

ISBN 0-8793-0474-X

HIGH-LEVEL LANGUAGE SOFTWARE DEVELOPMENT

In this book, I have tried to focus the applications on Assembler, BASIC, C, and C++. Previously, I presented a number of books that will help you learn assembly language and create applications in the PC using assembly language. For high-level languages, I have provided a list of introductory books on the different languages used for system programming of the PC both under MS-DOS and Windows.

For Visual Basic and Visual C++, you'll notice that I have not included any initial learning books (namely *Dummies* books) for the tools and that is because the CD-ROMs included in the "Learning Editions" of these programs are superior to virtually every beginner's book that is available. Once you have gone through the CD-ROMs, I suggest that you try your own applications and continue your education from there.

Microsoft GW-BASIC: User's Guide and Quick Reference, 1989 This is Microsoft's guide to GW-BASIC. Although out of print, it is an excellent introduction to the GW-BASIC language. GW-BASIC has been replaced by QuickBASIC (QBASIC) and Visual Basic, but the underlying statements in these two development languages use the syntax first developed for GW-BASIC.

ISBN 1-55615-260-4

A Brief Course in QBasic with an Introduction to Visual Basic 5.0, 1994 More than a book on QBasic, this is a good introductory text to structured programming and is a good secondary text after you have first gone through a language training tool. The concepts explained in the book will be valuable in times (and projects) to come.

ISBN 0-1397-3876-2

Advanced Visual Basic Techniques, 1997 Once you have completed the "Learning Edition" CD-ROM, this is an excellent book for you to learn more about Visual Basic and programming. Rod Stephens concentrates on aspects of Visual Basic that are not normally presented in beginning Visual Basic texts. These topics include advanced and custom control development, interfacing to networks and databases, and using ActiveX controls.

ISBN 0-471-18881-6

The C Programming Language, 2nd Edition, 1988   Brian W. Kernighan and Dennis M. Ritchie's classic text explaining the C programming language has not lost any of its usefulness since its introduction. This book has probably been used by more students in more colleges and universities than any other textbook. Despite the fact that the book was written originally for a programming course, the writing is crisp, sharp, and easily understandable. I've probably owned five copies of this book: a couple were worn out and a couple "grew legs" and walked out of my office.
   ISBN   0-13110-362-8

Inside Visual C++, 4th Edition, 1997   Once you have started working with Visual C++, you are going to need a few good texts for reference as you try to develop new and exciting applications. This book, by the late David Kruglinski, is probably the best that you will find. It provides similar examples as *Advanced Visual Basic Techniques*, along with an explanation of how multi-threaded applications are created under the Win32 kernel, as well as how DLLs can be created simply within the Visual C++ AppsWizard. This book focuses on Visual C++ 5.0 and the Microsoft Foundation Classes and is an excellent reference for both.
   ISBN   1-57231-565-2

Developing Professional Applications in Windows 95 and NT using MFC, 2nd Edition, 1997   This book is an excellent introduction to the Microsoft Foundation Classes and how they are structured and used. In this book, it is assumed that you are already familiar with C and C++ and are looking for information on creating Visual C++ applications with the MFC.
   ISBN   0-13-616343-2

WINDOWS SYSTEMS PROGRAMMING

Systems programming is not a topic with a wealth of good books. The three books I have presented here really are the best that I have been able to find. It probably shouldn't be a surprise for you to find out that two of them are from Microsoft Press. Much to the chagrin of my wife, I will continue to buy systems programming books for Windows (which tend to be large and expensive) and I will update my Web page with any good finds that I make.

Writing Windows VxDs and Device Drivers, 1997   Karen Hazzah's book about device drivers is an excellent practical introduction to VxDs and DLLs. This book provides a framework for understanding how the Win32 Windows kernel operates and how device drivers (both 16 and 32 bit) fit into this picture.
   ISBN   0-87930-438-3

Advanced Windows, 3rd Edition 1997   This book complements Karen Hazzah's excellently and provides a multitude of information about the Windows operating system and how to create hardware interfaces to it. This is my primary reference for developing hardware interface applications for Windows 95.
   ISBN   1-57231-548-2

8

APPENDICES

Systems Programming for Windows 95, 1996 Many people consider Walter Oney's tome about advanced programming in C/C++ to be the ultimate reference for creating VxDs and device drivers for Win32 kernel Windows. The book includes a very good, condensed explanation of the 32-bit operating system and how applications interface with them. There are some issues with some of the example applications, but they are covered and fixes for them are on the author's Web page.
  ISBN 1-55615-949-8

Part Suppliers

The following companies supplied components that are used in this book:

Digi-Key Digi-Key is an excellent source for a wide range of electronic parts. They are reasonably priced and most orders will be delivered the next day. They are real life savers when you're on a deadline.

> Digi-Key Corporation
> 701 Brooks Avenue South
> P.O. Box 677
> Thief River Falls, MN 56701-0677
> Phone: 1-800-344-4539 (1-800-DIGI-KEY)
> Fax: 1-218-681-3380
> **http://www.digi-key.com/**

AP Circuits AP Circuits will build prototype bare boards from your "Gerber" files. Boards are available within three days. I have been a customer of theirs for several years and they have always produced excellent quality and been helpful in providing direction to learning how to develop my own bare boards. Their Website contains all the tools necessary to develop your own Gerber files.

> Alberta Printed Circuits Ltd. #3,
> 1112-40th Avenue N.E.
> Calgary, Alberta
> T2E 5T8 Canada
> Phone: 1-403-250-3406
> BBS: 1-403-291-9342
> E-mail: staff@apcircuits.com
> **http://www.apcircuits.com/**

Wirz Electronics Wirz Electronics is a full-service microcontroller component and development system supplier. They are the main distributor for projects contained in my books. Wirz Electronics also carries the SimmStick prototyping systems, as well as their own line of motor and robot controllers.

Wirz Electonics
P.O. Box 457
Littleton, MA 01460-0457
Phone: 1-888-289-9479 (1-888-BUY-WIRZ)
E-mail: sales@wirz.com
http://www.wirz.com/

Tower Hobbies   Excellent source for servos and R/C parts useful in homebuilt robots.

Tower Hobbies
 P.O. Box 9078
Champaign, IL 61826-9078
Order Phone: 1-800-637-4989
Fax: 1(800)637-7303
Phone support: 1-800-637-6050
Phone: 1-217-398-3636
Worldwide fax: 1-217-356-6608
E-mail: orders@towerhobbies.com
http://www.towerhobbies.com/

JDR   Components, PC Parts/Accessories, and hard-to-find connectors.

JDR Microdevices
1850 South 10th Street
San Jose, CA 95112-4108
Toll Free in the USA & Canada: 1-800-538-5005
Toll Free Fax in the USA & Canada: 1-800-538-5005
Phone: 1-408-494-1400
E-mail: techsupport@jdr.com
BBS: 1-408-494-1430
Compuserve: 70007,1561
http://www.jdr.com/JDR

Newark   Components including the Dallas Line of semiconductors (the DS87C520 High
Speed and Microcontroller and DS275 is used for RS-232 level conversion in this book).

Phone: 1-800-463-9275 (1-800-4-NEWARK)
http://www.newark.com/

Marshall Industries   Marshall is a full-service distributor of Philips microcontrollers
as well as other parts.

Marshall Industries
9320 Telstar Avenue
El Monte, CA 91731
1-800-833-9910
http://www.marshall.com

Mondo-Tronics Robotics Store   Self-proclaimed as "The world's biggest collection of miniature robots and supplies" and I have to agree with them. This is a great source for servos, tracked vehicles, and robot arms.

Order Desk Mondo-tronics Inc.
524 San Anselmo Avenue #107-13
San Anselmo, CA 94960
Phone: 1-800-374-5764
Fax: 1-415-455-9333
http://www.robotstore.com/

Periodicals

Here are a number of magazines that provide a lot of information and projects on micro-controllers. Every month, each magazine has a better than 75% chance of presenting at least one device interface to a PC.

Circuit Cellar Ink

Subscription Department
P.O. Box 698
Holmes, PA 19043-9613
Phone: 1-800-269-6301
BBS: 1-860-871-1988
http://www.circellar.com/

Gernsback Publications:

Electronics Now Popular Electronics

Subscription Department
P.O. Box 51866
Boulder, CO 80323-1866
Phone: 1-800-999-7139
http://www.gernsback.com

Nuts & Volts

Subscription Department
430 Princeland Court
Corona, CA 91719
Phone: 1-800-783-4624
http://www.nutsvolts.com

Everyday Practical Electronics

Subscription Department
Allen House, East Borough
Wimborne, Dorset
BH21 1PF
United Kingdom
Phone: +44-0-1202-881749
http://www.epemag.wimborne.co.uk

Dr. Dobb's Software Journal

Subscription Department
P.O. Box 56188
Boulder, CO 80322-6188
Phone: 1-800-456-1215
Phone: 1-303-678-0439
Fax: 1-303-661-1885
http://www.ddj.com

Microsoft Systems Journal

Subscription Department
P.O. Box 56621
Boulder, CO 80322-6621
Phone: 1-800-666-1084
Phone: 1-303-678-0439
Fax: 1-303-661-1885
http://www.microsoft.com/msj/

Windows Developer's Journal

Subscription Department
P.O. Box 56565
Boulder, CO 80322
Phone: 1-800-365-1425
Phone: 1-303-678-0439
Fax: 1-303-661-1885
http://www.wdj.com

8
APPENDICES

Web Sites of Interest

The World Wide Web is becoming more pervasive in our society—especially for engineers and technicians, who rely upon the Web for data sheets, *FAQs (Frequently Asked Questions)*, and example applications. Unfortunately, because of the transitory nature of the Internet and the time between when I write this and when this book is published, some of these sites might no longer exist when you are looking for them.

Adobe PDF Viewers

http://www.adobe.com
Adobe .PDF file format is used for virtually all vendor data sheets, including the devices presented in this book (and their datasheets on the CD-ROM).

Altavista

http://www.altavista.com
This site is capable of accessing and searching literally millions of Web sites all over the world for your search parameters.

Amazon.com

http://www.amazon.com
The largest book seller on the Internet. I have been an associate of theirs for over a year (at **http://www.myke.com/Book_Room**) and I have been very pleased with the company's fast delivery and wide selection of books.

AMD

http://www.amd.com
AMD's Web site with information and data sheets on their processors.

Web Book on Batch Processing

http://gearbox.maem.umr.edu/~batch/index.html
This page contains an outstanding explanation of how batch files work and just how to get yourself in a great deal of trouble.

BIOS Survival Guide

http://www.lexology.co.uk/bios/bios_sg.htm
Information on how to interface with PC's BIOS.

CodeGuru

http://www.codeguru.com
Another good repository of PC programming information and samples for downloading.

Cypress Semiconductor

http://www.cypress.com
Information about Cypress's CY7C6xx microcontroller chip.

Experts Exchange

http://www.experts-exchange.com
Good reference for finding out more about PC hardware and software.

Fil's List of PC Hardware FAQs

http://paranoia.com/~filipg/HTML/LINK/LINK_IN.html
A set of FAQs about the PC and other hardware platforms that will come in useful when looking for PC specific information.

Filez PC Application Repository

http://www.filez.com
A huge repository of PC applications available for downloading.

Chris Hare's PC Hardware Links

http://www.erols.com/chare/hardware.htm
Links to PC hardware information pages.

IBM

http://www.pc.ibm.com
IBM's home page with technical information about the PC, as well as information on the products it sells in your country.

Intel

http://developer.intel.com/sites/developer/index.htm
Intel's developer site with chip information and data sheets.

Intel Secrets

http://www.x86.org
Interesting page detailing Intel (and AMD) PC processors.

I/O Port Definition

http://irb.cs.uni-magdeburg.de/~zbrog/asm/ports.html
Outstanding PC I/O Port Reference.

Steve Lawther's USB Page

http://ourworld.compuserve.com/homepages/steve_lawther/usbdev.htm
Good list of USB Web links and information.

8

APPENDICES

Linux Organization

http://www.linux.org
Primary resource for the Linux operating system.

List Of Stamp Applications (L.O.S.A)

http://www.hth.com/losa.htm
The list of parallax Basic stamp applications will give you an idea of what can be done with the Basic stamp (and other microcontrollers and the PC). The list contains projects ranging from using a Basic stamp to give a cat medication to providing a simple telemetry system for model rockets.

Lakeview Research

http://www.lvr.com
Jan Axelson's home page with ordering information for her books, as well as hardware interfacing information.

The Mining Company

http://www.miningco.com
Search page with recommended pages on a variety of different subjects. Good links to PC programming pages.

Motherboard World

http://www.motherboards.org
Everything you've ever wanted to know about PC motherboards.

The PC Guide

http://www.pcguide.com
Lots of good links and information about the PC.

PC Programming Languages Page

http://www.hut.fi/~then/programming.html
Lots of excellent links to PC programming reference pages.

PCI Bus Special Interest Group Home Page

http://www.pcisig.com
Information on the PCI bus, companies designing products for it, and information on joining the PCI special-interest group.

Philips Semiconductor Home Page

http://www-us2.semiconductors.philips.com
Philips Semiconductor home page with 8051-compatible USB microcontrollers.

Programming the SoundBlaster 16 DSP

http://www.ice-digga.com/programming/sb16.html
Good specification on the SoundBlaster and SoundBlaster 16 bit.

Seattle Robotics Society

http://www.hhhh.org/srs/
The Seattle Robotics Society has lots of information on interfacing digital devices to such "real-world" devices as motors, sensors, and servos. They also do a lot of neat things. Most of the applications use the Motorola 68HC11.

Software Developers Resources

http://home.sol.no/~jarlaase/devel.htm
Excellent links to PC and Windows programming resources.

TI's Firewire Home Page

http://www.ti.com/sc/1394
Links to TI Firewire products along with other companies.

Tom Pragnells's PC Reference Page

http://www.physiol.ox.ac.uk/~trp
Excellent PC programming reference information source.

USB Organization

http://www.usb.org
USB standards and information special interests group. List of available products.

Yahoo

http://www.yahoo.com
Probably the world's most famous Web site. Lots of Web sites sorted by different categories.

Compuware's Web Sites

http://www.compuware.com
Compuware is a manufacturer of many different Windows software application tools, including NuMega (formerly Vireo Software), which contains the VtoolsD, Driver::Works, and Soft-ICE Windows device driver development tools.
The NuMega home page can be found at:

http://www.vireo.com

8
APPENDICES

Useful Microsoft Web Sites

Despite being the premier supplier of PC operating systems and development tools, Microsoft does not have a Web site that is really easy to work through. Because of this, I have listed eight sites here that will help you find information on the development tools mentioned in this book, along with other helpful information.

The Microsoft Web pages contain a vast amount of useful information, but finding it sometimes can be difficult. Notice that some sites start with *msdn* instead of *www*.

http://www.microsoft.com

The entry point to Microsoft's Web page.

http://support.microsoft.com

This is the help search page.

http://www.microsoft.com/windows/default.asp

Windows operating system home page.

http://www.microsoft.com/developer

Microsoft's Developer Network (MSDN) home page.

http://www.microsoft.com/products/prodref/450-ov.htm

Product information for MASM 6.11.

http://msdn.microsoft.com/vbasic

Visual Basic's home page.

http://msdn.microsoft.com/visualc

Visual C++ home page.

http://msdn.microsoft.com/developer/sdk/default.htm

Software Development Kit ("SDK") home page.

http://www.pc.ibm.com/us/news/msinfo.html

Surprising as it seems, this page produced by IBM is an excellent reference to the Microsoft Web site and where to find specific information.

List Servers

If you're not familiar with list servers, I highly recommend that you join the ones that I have listed. A *list server* is an e-mail address which takes mail sent to it and redistributes it to a number of people. This means that a large amount of mail can be sent and received in a short period of time to a large number of people.

List servers are really wonderful things with it possible to get answers to questions within literally minutes after posing them (although hours afterward is probably more typical). A great deal of very knowledgeable people who can answer questions on a variety of subjects (and have opinions on more than just the subject at hand).

Having a great deal of people available makes the list essentially a community. This is a world-wide community and you have to try to be sensitive to different people's feelings and cultures. To this end, I have created the following set of guidelines for list servers. The genesis of these guidelines came about after MIT's PICList list server went through a period of time with problems with the same type of messages coming through over and over.

I think these are pretty good guidelines for any list server and I suggest that you try to follow them as much as possible to avoid getting into embarrassing situations (and having yourself berated or removed from a list because you made a gaff).

1 Don't subscribe to a List and then immediately start sending questions to the list. Instead, wait a day or so to get the hang of how messages are sent and replied to on the list and get a "feel" for the best way to ask questions.

2 Some lists resend a note sent to it (others do not). If you receive a copy of your first message, don't automatically think that it is a "bounce" (wrong address) and resend it. In this case, you might want to wait a day or so to see if any replies show up before trying to resend it. Once you've been on the list for a while, you should get an idea of how long it takes to show up on the list and how long it takes to get a reply.

3 If you don't get a reply to a request and don't see it referenced in the list, don't get angry or frustrated and send off a reply demanding help. There's a chance that nobody on the list knows exactly how to solve your problem or there's a problem with your mail system or the list's and your note didn't get distributed. In this case, try to break down the problem, ask the question a different way, and ask for somebody to send you a private note indicating that they have read your posting.

4 I've talked about being able to get replies within minutes in this appendix, please don't feel that this is something that you can count on. Nobody on any of the lists I've given in this book are paid to reply to your questions. The majority of people who reply are doing so to help others. Please respect that and don't badger. Help out in any way that you can.

5 If you are changing the Subject line of a post, please reference the previous topic (i.e., put in "was: '...'"). This will help others keep track of the conversation.

6 When replying to a previous post, try to minimize how much of the previous note is copied in your note and maximize the relevance to your reply. This is not to say that none of the message should be copied or referenced. There is a very fine balance between having too much and too little. The sender of the note you are replying to should be referenced (with their name or ID).

My rule is: if the original question is less than 10 lines, I copy it all; if it is longer, then I cut it down (identifying what was cut out with a "snip" Message), leaving just the question and any relevant information as quoted. Most mail programs will mark the quoted text with a > character, please use this convention to make it easier for others to follow your reply.

7 If you have a program that doesn't work, please don't copy the entire source into a note and then post it to a list. As soon as I see a note like this I just delete it and go on to the next one (and I suspect that I'm not the only one). Also, some lists might have a message size limit (anything above this limit is thrown out) and you will not receive any kind of confirmation.

If you are going to post source code: keep it short. People on the list are more than happy and willing to answer specific questions, but simply copying the complete source code in the note and asking a question like "Why won't the LCD display anything" really isn't useful for anybody. Instead, try to isolate the failing code and describe what is actually happening along with what you want to happen. If you do this, chances are you will get a helpful answer quickly.

When asking why something won't work, describe the hardware that you are using. If you are asking about support hardware (i.e., a programmer or emulator), be sure to describe your PC (or workstation) setup. If your application isn't working as expected, describe the hardware that you are using and what you have observed (i.e., if the clock lines are wiggling, or the application works normally when you put a scope probe on a pin).

8 You might find a totally awesome and appropriate Web page and want to share it with the list. Please make it easier on the people in the list to cut and paste the URL by putting it on a line all by itself in the format:

http://www.awesome-PC-page.com

9 If you have a new application, graphic, or whatever that requires more than 1 KB that you would like to share with everyone on the list, please don't send it as an attachment in a note to the list. Instead, either indicate you are have this amazing piece of work and tell people that you have it and where to request it (either to you directly or to a Web server address). Many list servers, if a large file is received may automatically delete (thrown into the "bit bucket") it and you might not get a message telling you what happened. If you don't have a Web page of your own or one you can access, requesting somebody to put it on their Web page or FTP server is a good alternative.

10 Many of these list servers are made available, maintained and/or moderated by the device's manufacturer. Keep this in mind if you are going to advertise your own product and understand what the company's policy on this is before sending out an advertisement.

11 Putting job postings or employment requests might be appropriate for a list (like the previous point, check with the list's maintainer). However, I don't recommend that the rate of pay or conditions of employment should be included in the note (unless you want to be characterized as "cheap," "greedy," "unreasonable," or "exploitive").

12 Spams are sent to every list server occasionally. Please do not reply to the note—even if the message says that to get off the spammer's mailing list just reply. This will send a message to everyone in the list. If you must send a note detailing your disgust, send it to the spam originator (although sending it to their ISP will probably get better results).

Note: A number of companies are sending out bogus spams to collect the originating addresses of replying messages and sell them to other companies or distributors of addresses on CD-ROM. When receiving a spam, see if it has been sent to you personally or the list before replying. Beware, if you are replying to the spam, you may be just sending your e-mail address to some company to sell to other spammers.

I know it's frustrating and, like everyone else, I'm sure you would like to have all spammers eviscerated and then taken out and shot, but if you want to minimize how much you are bothered by spams in the future, you just have to ignore all the spams that are sent to you. Eventually, if you don't reply, you will be dropped off from the lists that are bought, sold, and traded.

13 Off-topic messages, although tolerated, will probably bring lots of abuse upon yourself. If you feel it is appropriate to send an off-topic message, some lists request that you put *[OT]* in the subject line. Some members of the list use mail filters and this will allow them to ignore the off topic posts automatically.

Eventually a discussion (this usually happens with off-topic discussions) will get so strung out that there is only two people left arguing with each other. At this point, stop the discussion entirely or go private. You can obtain the other person's e-mail address from the header of the message. Send your message to him/her and not to the entire list. Everyone else on the list would have lost interest a long time ago and probably would like the discussion to just go away (so oblige them).

14 Posts referencing pirate sites and sources for "cracked" or "hacked" software is not appropriate in any case and might be illegal. If you are not sure if it is okay to post the latest software you've found on the 'Net, then don't until you have checked with the owners of the software and gotten their permission. It would also be a good idea to indicate in your post that you have the owner's permission to distribute cracked software.

Offering to read protected applications is also inappropriate for list servers. Many of the members of the list earn their livings from developing applications; few will favorably respond to offers of reading data from protected sources.

15 When you first subscribe to a list, you will get a reply telling you how to unsubscribe from the list. Don't lose this note. In the past in some lists, people having trouble unsubscribing have sent questions to the list asking how and sometimes getting angry when their requests go unheeded. If you are trying to unsubscribe from a list and need help from others on the list, explain what you are trying to do and how you've tried to accomplish it.

16 If you're like me and just log on once or twice a day, read all the notes regarding a specific thread before replying. When replying to a question that has already been answered look for what you can add to the discussion, not reiterate what's already been said.

17 Lastly, please try to be courteous to all on the list. Others might not have your knowledge and experience or they might be sensitive about different issues. There is a very high level of professionalism on all lists; please help maintain it.

Being insulting or rude will only get the same back and probably have your posts and legitimate questions ignored in the future by others on the list who don't want to have anything to do with you.

To put it succinctly: "Don't be offensive or easily offended."

To log onto the following listservers, send an e-mail note to the address specified with the message specified below the address:

8

APPENDICES

Beginner's Visual Basic
LISTSERV@PEACH.EASE.LSOFT.COM

```
SUBSCRIBE VISBAS-BEGINNERS
```

VISUAL BASIC HOW TO

LISTSERV@LISTSERV.XTRAS.COM

```
SUBSCRIBE VBHOWTO
```

Visual C++
LISTSERV@PEACH.EASE.LSOFT.COM

```
SUBSCRIBE MSVC
```

MFC and Advanced Visual C++
LISTSERV@LISTSERV.MSN.COM

```
SUBSCRIBE MFC
```

Software Development Kit (SDK) and Device Driver Development Kit (DDK)
LISTSERV@PEACH.EASE.LSOFT.COM

```
SUBSCRIBE DDK-L
```

Newsgroups

For some reason, newsgroups do not seem to follow the same high standards as established with the list servers. I tend to see a lot more arguments on the newsgroups than I do on the list servers, as well as significantly more insulting comments passed to new users.

For these reasons, I tend to avoid newsgroups, except when I have a question that can't be answered on the list servers or I want to advertise something (like updates to my Web page). Many people do, however, enjoy newsgroups and subscribe to them religiously.

For this reason, I have listed the newsgroups that I have found to be the most useful when I am designing PC hardware applications or software. Most of the topics of the various newsgroups are self explanatory from their names. You should use the same rules for VNews Groups as you would sending email to list servers.

alt.comp.hardware
alt.comp.hardware.overclocking

alt.windows95
comp.answers
comp.arch
comp.sys.ibm.pc.hardware.FAQ
comp.sys.ibm.pc.hardware.misc
comp.sys.ibm.pc.soundcard.misc
comp.sys.intel
microsoft.public.msdn
microsoft.public.win95
microsoft.public.win98
microsoft.public.winnt
comp.lang.basic.visual
sci.electronics.design
sci.electronics.repair

ASCII
CHARACTER TABLES

One of the most frustrating things in my life is trying to find an ASCII table for the PC. When IBM first developed the PC, they extended the seven-bit ASCII character set into an eight-bit character set with special characters (such as fractions and Greek letters) and graphics characters that allow you to create boxes for your text displays. This is known as the *IBM Extended ASCII Character* set and is available in MS-DOS. Microsoft further enhanced the character set with the latest versions of Windows. To avoid the perennial search for ASCII character sets, I have included these sets along with control characters used in the PC in this Appendix.

The MS-DOS (IBM Extended) and Windows character sets are basically the same for the standard ASCII characters, but do diverge quite a bit as you work with the enhanced characters. Never assume that a character is common between the two character sets. When developing applications, I recommend that you insert the desired character into the string instead of its hex representation. If the application is ported from MS-DOS to Windows or visa-versa, you should be able to quite easily see the differences and compensate for them.

ASCII Control Characters

The ASCII control characters were specified as a means of allowing one computer to communicate and control another. These characters are actually commands. If the BIOS or MS-DOS display or communications APIs are used with them, they will revert back to their original purpose. As noted when presented the IBM Extended ASCII characters, writing these values (all less than 0x020) to the display will display graphics characters.

For virtually all my applications, the only ASCII control characters that I use are carriage return/line feed to indicate the start of a line. *Null* is used to indicate the end of an ASCIIZ string. *Backspace* will move the cursor back one column to the start of the line. The *Bell* character, when sent to MS-DOS, will cause the PC's speaker to beep. *Horizontal Tab* is used to move the cursor to the start of the next column that is evenly distributed by eight. I will occasionally use *form feed* to clear the screen. I don't bother with any of the other control characters.

HEX	MNEMONIC	DEFINITION
00	NUL	Null. Used to indicate the end of a string
01	SOH	Message: "Start of Header"
02	STX	Message: "Start of Text"
03	ETX	Message: "End of Text"
04	EOT	End of Transmission
05	ENQ	Enquire for Identification or Information
06	ACK	Acknowledge the previous transmission
07	BEL	Ring the Bell
08	BS	Backspace. Move the Cursor on column to the left
09	HT	Horizontal Tab. Move the cursor to the Right to the next Tab Stop. (Normally a column evenly divisible by eight)
0A	LF	Line Feed. Move the Cursor down one line
0B	VT	Vertical tab. Move the Cursor down to the next Tab Line
0C	FF	Form Feed up to the start of the new page. For CRT displays, this is often used to clear the screen
0D	CR	Carriage Return. Move the Cursor to the leftmost column
0E	SO	The next group of characters do not follow ASCII Control conventions so they are "Shifted Out"
0F	SI	The following characters do follow the ASCII Control conventions and are "Shifted In"
10	DLE	Data Link Escape. The ASCII Control Character is the start of an Escape sequence. In most modern applications Escape (0x01B) is used for this function

8

APPENDICES

11	DC1	Not defined. Normally application specific
12	DC2	Not defined. Normally application specific
13	DC3	Not defined. Normally application specific
14	DC4	Not defined. Normally application specific
15	NAK	Negative Acknowledge. The previous transmission was not properly received
16	SYN	Synchronous Idle. If the serial transmission uses a synchronous protocol, this character is sent to ensure that the transmitter and receiver remain synched
17	ETB	End-of-Transmission Block
18	CAN	Cancel and disregard the previous transmission
19	EM	End of Medium. Indicates end of a file. For MS-DOS files, 0x01A is often used instead
1A	SUB	Substitute the following character with an incorrect one
1B	ESC	Escape. Used to temporarily halt execution or put an application into a mode to receive information
1C	FS	Marker for File Separation of data being sent
1D	GS	Marker for Group Separation of data being sent
1E	RS	Marker for Record Separation of data being sent
1F	US	Marker for Unit Separation of data being sent

IBM PC Extended ASCII Characters

ASCII, in its original form, is a seven-bit character set. When IBM designed the PC, it used the seven-bit ASCII codes as a base and extended it with additional characters. The seven bits gives a total number of 128 possible different characters (Figure C-1). Because the PC used a byte (eight bits) for data, when specifying the character font, IBM extended the ASCII character set to a full byte. An additional 128 characters were defined and "burned" into the character-generator ROMs.

These additional 128 characters are shown in Figure C-2 and can do a lot to enhance a character-mode application without having to resort to using graphics. These enhancements include special characters for languages other than English, engineering symbols, and simple graphics characters. These simple graphics characters allow you to draw lines and boxes on your display. Correctly used, they can add a lot to your application.

When you first write characters to the PC's display VRAM, you might be surprised to find that putting in a carriage return and line feed for the characters results in a note and a colored-in box being displayed on the screen. Normally writing to the MS-DOS or BIOS APIs would result in the cursor moving to the next line. If you are writing directly to VRAM, you have to track the cursor position manually. If you want to use an ASCII control character, then you will have to provide the actual functions.

Hex	0x	1x	2x	3x	4x	5x	6x	7x
x0	0	► 16	SP 32	0 48	@ 64	P 80	` 96	p 112
x1	☺ 1	◄ 17	! 33	1 49	A 65	Q 81	a 97	q 113
x2	● 2	↕ 18	" 34	2 50	B 66	R 82	b 98	r 114
x3	♥ 3	‼ 19	# 35	3 51	C 67	S 83	c 99	s 115
x4	♦ 4	¶ 20	$ 36	4 52	D 68	T 84	d 100	t 116
x5	♣ 5	§ 21	% 37	5 53	E 69	U 85	e 101	u 117
x6	♠ 6	▬ 22	& 38	6 54	F 70	V 86	f 102	v 118
x7	• 7	↨ 23	' 39	7 55	G 71	W 87	g 103	w 119
x8	◘ 8	↑ 24	(40	8 56	H 72	X 88	h 104	x 120
x9	◙ 9	↓ 25	) 41	9 57	I 73	Y 89	i 105	y 121
xA	◙ 10	→ 26	* 42	: 58	J 74	Z 90	j 106	z 122
xB	♂ 11	← 27	+ 43	; 59	K 75	[91	k 107	{ 123
xC	♀ 12	∟ 28	, 44	< 60	L 76	\ 92	l 108	¦ 124
xD	♪ 13	↔ 29	- 45	= 61	M 77	] 93	m 109	} 125
xE	♫ 14	▲ 30	. 46	> 62	N 78	^ 94	n 110	∼ 126
xF	☼ 15	▼ 31	/ 47	? 63	O 79	_ 95	o 111	Δ 127

FIGURE C-1   IBM PC "extended ASCII" set 0-0x07F.

8
APPENDICES

Hex	8x	9x	Ax	Bx	Cx	Dx	Ex	Fx
x0	Ç 128	É 144	á 160	▓ 176	└ 192	⊥ 208	α 224	≡ 240
x1	ü 129	æ 145	í 161	▓ 177	⊥ 193	╤ 209	β 225	± 241
x2	é 130	Æ 146	ó 162	█ 178	┬ 194	╥ 210	Γ 226	≥ 242
x3	â 131	ô 147	ú 163	│ 179	├ 195	╙ 211	π 227	≤ 243
x4	ä 132	ö 148	ñ 164	┤ 180	─ 196	╘ 212	Σ 228	⌠ 244
x5	à 133	ò 149	Ñ 165	╡ 181	┼ 197	╒ 213	σ 229	⌡ 245
x6	å 134	û 150	ª 166	╢ 182	╞ 198	╓ 214	µ 230	÷ 246
x7	ç 135	ù 151	º 167	╖ 183	╟ 199	╫ 215	τ 231	≈ 247
x8	ê 136	ÿ 152	¿ 168	╕ 184	╚ 200	╪ 216	Φ 232	° 248
x9	ë 137	Ö 153	⌐ 169	╣ 185	╔ 201	┘ 217	Θ 233	• 249
xA	è 138	Ü 154	¬ 170	║ 186	╩ 202	┌ 218	Ω 234	• 250
xB	ï 139	¢ 155	½ 171	╗ 187	╦ 203	█ 219	δ 235	√ 251
xC	î 140	£ 156	¼ 172	╝ 188	╠ 204	▄ 220	∞ 236	ⁿ 252
xD	ì 141	¥ 157	¡ 173	╜ 189	═ 205	█ 221	φ 237	2 253
xE	Ä 142	₧ 158	« 174	╛ 190	╬ 206	▌ 222	∈ 238	■ 254
xF	Å 143	ƒ 159	» 175	┐ 191	╧ 207	▐ 223	∩ 239	255

FIGURE C-2   IBM PC "extended ASCII" set 0x080-0x0FF.

The ASCII Control Characters, listed earlier in this appendix, will operate as you expect if you use the MS-DOS or BIOS APIs, but will put the characters listed in Figure C-1 if you write them to video RAM directly.

The PC's keyboard handler has a nice feature under MS-DOS—to convert keypad decimal values to a character while the *Alt* key is pressed. The decimal values are displayed in Figs. C-1 and C-2 as the lower right decimal number in each box. This feature allows you to enter in the special characters into your source without having to resort to entering decimal or hex values, which requires more space and are very difficult to see if a character has been entered incorrectly. All of the extended ASCII characters can be entered in this way, except for the Null (ASCII code 0x000) character.

ANSI Display Control Sequences

From MS-DOS applications, you can move the cursor or change the current display colors one of two ways. Normally, I use the BIOS functions and direct writes to VRAM. The second way is to load the ANSI.SYS device driver in the CONFigureSYS using the statement:

```
device = [d:][path]ANSI.SYS
```

When the escape sequences listed are output using the standard output device (using the MS-DOS APIs), the commands are executed.

Personally, I don't use this method a lot for two reasons. First, it is much slower than using the BIOS APIs and writing directly to VRAM. If you want an application that seems to change the screen in the blink of an eye, then the ANSI Display Control Sequences are not the way to do it. The second is, ANSI.SYS takes away 10 KB of memory that would normally be available for applications. This probably doesn't seem like a serious loss of memory in today's PCs, but in the early PCs, where 256 KB total memory was often the case, 10 KB was a big chunk of what was left over for applications.

The advantages of using the ANSI Display Control Sequences is that they will make your application very portable. By just passing the source to another system's compiler, you can move the application without worrying about the console interfacing. The second advantage is that if you are sending the data serially, then if the receiver is set up able to receive these sequences (set up as an ANSI or VT100-compatible Terminal), you can have simple graphic operations in your application.

In the following table, *ESC* is the ASCII Escape Character, 0x01B.

SEQUENCE	FUNCTION
Esc[=#h	Set the PC's Display mode. This is not available in "true" ANSI-compatible devices. # = 0 40 × 25 Monochrome # = 1 40 × 25 Color # = 2 80 × 25 Monochrome # = 3 80 × 25 Color

	# = 4 320 × 200 Color Graphics
	# = 5 320 × 200 Monochrome Graphics
	# = 6 640 × 200 Monochrome Graphics
	# = 7 Wrap to next line at line end
	# = 14 640 × 200 Color Graphics
	# = 15 640 × 350 Monochrome Graphics
	# = 16 640 × 480 Color Graphics
	# = 17 640 × 480 Color Graphics
	# = 18 640 × 480 Color Graphics
	# = 19 320 × 200 Color Graphics
Esc[=#l	Reset the PC's Display mode. This is not available in "true" ANSI compatible devices.
	# = 0 40 × 25 Monochrome
	# = 1 40 × 25 Color
	# = 2 80 × 25 Monochrome
	# = 3 80 × 25 Color
	# = 4 320 × 200 Color Graphics
	# = 5 320 × 200 Monochrome Graphics
	# = 6 640 × 200 Monochrome Graphics
	# = 7 Do not wrap at line end
Esc[#m	Set Character Attributes
	# = 0 Normal (gray on black)
	# = 1 Intensity Bit set for Foreground Colors
	# = 4 Underscore Characters in MDA
	# = 5 Blink Characters in MDA
	# = 7 Reverse the Character Foreground Color with the background
	# = 8 Make MDA Characters Invisible
	# = 30 Black Foreground
	# = 31 Red Foreground
	# = 32 Green Foreground
	# = 33 Yellow Foreground
	# = 34 Blue Foreground
	# = 35 Magenta Foreground
	# = 36 Cyan Foreground
	# = 37 White Foreground
	# = 40 Black Background
	# = 41 Red Background
	# = 42 Green Background
	# = 43 Yellow Background
	# = 44 Blue Background
	# = 45 Magenta Background
	# = 46 Cyan Background
	# = 47 White Background
Esc[2j	Clear the Display
Esc[K	Erases from the Current Cursor Position to the End of the Line
Esc[6n	Device Status Report. Request the current position to be returned in the "Standard Input" Device

Esc[#;%R	This is the Current Cursor Row (#) and Column (%) loaded into the Standard Input after a Device Status Report
Esc[#;%f	Move the Cursor to Row # and Column %
Esc[#;%F	Move the Cursor to Row # and Column %
Esc[#;%H	Move the Cursor to Row # and Column %
Esc[#A	Move the Cursor Up # Rows
Esc[#B	Move the Cursor Down # Rows
Esc[#C	Move the Cursor to the Right by # Columns
Esc[#D	Move the Cursor to the Left by # Columns
Esc[s	Saves the Current Cursor Position
Esc[u	Restores the Cursor Position to the saved position
Esc[F	Move the Cursor to the Home Position (Row = Column = 1)
Esc[H	Move the Cursor to the Home Position (Row = Column = 1)
Esc[#;%p	Reassign key # to %
Esc[#;STRp	Reassign key # to String *STR*

Windows ASCII Characters

Under Windows, characters are much more fluid than what you expect in MS-DOS and differ by being not being character-generator based. With the characters not being slaved to a ROM, the actual range of fonts is actually quite startling. As I looked at what was available, I realized that characters couldn't be used under Windows the same way they are used in MS-DOS. Under Windows, the character font used is specified from within the application and any graphics do not use special characters.

ASCII control characters do have meaning in Windows applications and do not have corresponding graphics characters for VRAM. For this reason, when you look at a Windows character set for a font, you will see that the characters start with the Blank (ASCII 0x020) and only have the 232 upper characters defined. This character set is based on ASCII with the upper 128 characters defined for special functions and "national languages."

To look at the different fonts installed in your Windows PC, from the Start toolbar invoke Help; from the Index, look for Character Map. The Character Map utility allows you to look at all the characters for a given font. For many traditional fonts, such as Arial, Courier New, and Times New Roman (the three that I use the most), the font information is quite traditional and looks like what you would expect. Figure C-3 shows the Arial font information.

, I remember reading an article some time ago saying that the advent of the PC has caused an explosion in the number of fonts being used. Before the PC, only five or six fonts were in common use. Today, there are literally thousands, as can be seen as you look through the Character Map function at some of the less traditional fonts. Figure C-4 shows the character map for the Harpoon font. I clicked on one of the characters (the *f*, if you can believe it) to have it magnified to show what it looks like. This font is almost illegible.

Another font, Kidnap, uses the cliché of cutting characters out of a magazine to provide a message that nobody can trace to provide a rather inventive font (Figure C-5). Notice that this font only has the basic letters and numbers and does not have any of the special characters evident in any of the more traditional fonts. In keeping with the theme of this font, it is disappointing to see that the *$* character is missing.

The available fonts can also degenerate to the point where they are completely illegible or only useful in very specific circumstances. A great example of this is the Semaphore font shown in Figure C-6. I guess it would be useful for a Boy Scout testing program, but I can't come up with many other applications that would use a font like this.

The point is: the Windows font used affects the character set that is displayed in the application. If I were to summarize my thoughts on using special characters in Windows, I could do it in two statements.

1 Stick to a traditional font (Figure C-3). Yes, lots of interesting fonts are available in Windows, but many of these do not have a full set of special characters. As well, many of these fonts are quite difficult for a casual user to decode. Avoid making them crazy by using something like the Harpoon font.

2 Windows is a graphical display system. If special characters or graphics are required, draw them yourself. This is very easy to do in either Visual Basic or Visual C++. In both cases, it can be done from the dialog box editor or from the application.

I would like to redirect your creativity from the character set font and more toward the actual application. Your users will be pleased if you just use straight ASCII alphanumeric characters and avoid using a font that can be described with such adjectives as "cool," "funky," or "gnarly."

If you would like to provide character graphics in Windows similar to MS-DOS, you should look for the "MS LineDraw" font on the Internet. This font is "monspace" which means each character is the same width. I use this font to display source code because I can inbed graphics as documentation.

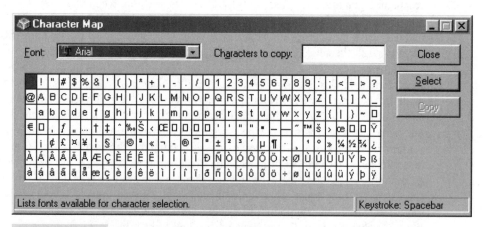

FIGURE C-3   Microsoft Windows "Arial" font.

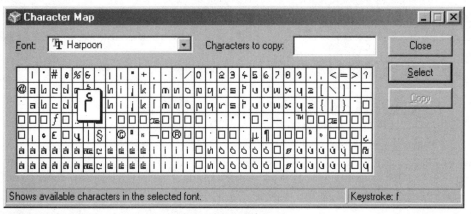

FIGURE C-4   Microsoft Windows "Harpoon" font.

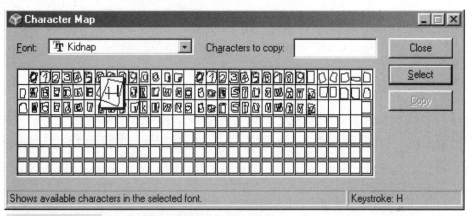

FIGURE C-5   Microsoft Windows "Kidnap" font.

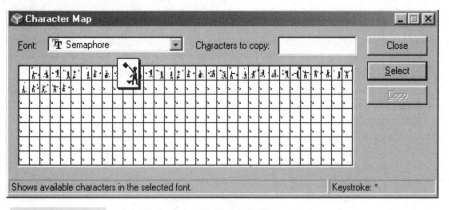

FIGURE C-6   Microsoft Windows "Semaphore" font.

8
APPENDICES

KEYBOARD
CODES

In MS-DOS, the keyboard codes are normally a combination of the keyboard scan code and appropriate ASCII code. The following table shows the different codes returned for keystrokes by themselves, and with a *Shift, Ctrl*, or *Alt* Modifier.

The table shows the codes in scan/ASCII configuration for the extended function keyboard characters. The standard function codes are the same, except that *F11*, *F12*, and the keypad *Center Key* do not return any codes and for the explicit arrow and explicit *Insert, Home, Page Up, Delete, End*, and *Page Down* keys, the 0x0E0 ASCII code is actually 0x000.

All values in the table are in hex and I have put in the keycodes as they appear on my PC. I have not made allowances for upper and lower case in this table. *KP* indicates the keypad and it, or a single *A* (which indicates alternate arrow and other keys), followed by *UA, DA, LA*, or *RA* indicates an Arrow. *I, D, H, PU, PD*, or *E* with *KP* or *A* indicates the *Insert, Delete, Home, Page Up, Page Down*, or *End* on the keypad, respectively.

The keypad numbers, when *Alt* is pressed is used to enter in specific ASCII codes in decimal. For example, *Alt, 6, 5* will enter in an ASCII *A* character. I have marked these keys in the table with #.

KEY	STANDARD CODES	*SHIFT* CODES	*CTRL* CODES	*ALT* CODES
Esc	01/1B	01/1B	01/1B	01/00
1	02/31	02/21	—	78/00
2	03/32	03/40	03/00	79/00
3	04/33	04/23	—	7A/00
4	05/34	05/24	—	7B/00
5	06/35	06/25	—	7C/00
6	07/36	07/5E	07/1E	7D/00
7	08/37	08/26	—	7E/00
8	09/38	09/2A	—	7F/00
9	0A/39	0A/28	—	80/00
0	0B/30	0B/29	—	81/00
-	0C/2D	0C/5F	0C/1F	82/00
=	0D/3D	9C/2B	—	83/00
BS	0E/08	0E/08	0E/7F	0E/00
Tab	0F/09	0F/00	94/00	A5/00
Q	10/71	10/51	10/11	10/00
W	11/77	11/57	11/17	11/00
E	12/65	12/45	12/05	12/00
R	13/72	13/52	13/12	13/00
T	14/74	14/54	14/14	14/00
Y	15/79	15/59	15/19	15/00
U	16/75	16/55	16/15	16/00
I	17/69	17/49	17/09	17/00
O	18/6F	18/4F	18/0F	18/00
P	19/70	19/50	19/10	19/00
[	1A/5B	1A/7B	1A/1B	1A/00
]	1B/5D	1B/7D	1B/1D	1B/00
Enter	1C/0D	1C/0D	1C/0A	1C/00
A	1D/61	1E/41	1E/01	1E/00
S	1F/73	1F/53	1F/13	1F/00
D	20/64	20/44	20/04	20/00
F	21/66	21/46	21/06	21/00
G	22/67	22/47	22/07	22/00

8

APPENDICES

KEY	STANDARD CODES	*SHIFT* CODES	*CTRL* CODES	*ALT* CODES
H	23/68	23/48	23/08	23/00
J	24/6A	24/4A	24/0A	24/00
K	25/6B	25/4B	25/0B	25/00
L	26/6C	26/4C	26/0C	26/00
;	27/3B	27/3A	—	27/00
'	28/27	28/22	—	28/00
`	29/60	29/7E	—	29/00
\	2B/5C	2B/7C	2B/1C	2B/00
Z	2C/7A	2C/5A	2C/1A	2C/00
X	2D/78	2D/58	2D/18	2D/00
C	2E/63	2E/43	2E/03	2E/00
V	2F/76	2F/56	2F/18	2F/00
B	30/62	30/42	30/02	30/00
N	31/6E	31/4E	31/0E	31/00
M	32/6D	32/4D	32/0D	32/00
,	33/2C	33/3C	—	33/00
.	34/2E	34/3E	—	34/00
/	35/2F	35/3F	—	35/00
KP *	37/2A	37/2A	96/00	37/00
SPACE	39/20	39/20	39/20	39/20
F1	3B/00	54/00	5E/00	68/00
F2	3C/00	55/00	5F/00	69/00
F3	3D/00	56/00	60/00	6A/00
F4	3E/00	57/00	61/00	6B/00
F5	3F/00	58/00	62/00	6C/00
F6	40/00	59/00	63/00	6D/00
F7	41/00	5A/00	64/00	6E/00
F8	42/00	5B/00	65/00	6F/00
F9	43/00	5C/00	66/00	70/00
F10	44/00	5D/00	67/00	71/00
F11	85/00	87/00	89/00	8B/00
F12	86/00	88/00	8A/00	8C/00
KP H	47/00	47/37	77/00	#

KEY	STANDARD CODES	*SHIFT* CODES	*CTRL* CODES	*ALT* CODES
KP UA	48/00	48/38	8D/00	#
KP PU	49/00	49/39	84/00	#
KP -	4A/2D	4A/2D	8E/00	4A/00
KP LA	4B/00	4B/34	73/00	#
KP C	4C/00	4C/35	8F/00	#
KP RA	4D/00	4D/36	74/00	#
KP +	4E/2B	4E/2B	90/00	4E/00
KP E	4F/00	4F/31	75/00	#
KP DA	50/00	50/32	91/00	#
KP PD	51/00	51/33	76/00	#
KP I	52/00	52/30	92/00	—
KP D	53/00	53/2E	93/00	—
KPEnter	E0/0D	E0/0D	E0/0A	—
KP /	E0/2F	E0/2F	95/00	—
PAUSE	—	—	72/00	—
BREAK	—	—	00/00	—
A H	47/E0	47/E0	77/E0	97/00
A UA	48/E0	48/E0	8D/E0	98/00
A PU	49/E0	49/E0	84/E0	99/00
A LA	4B/E0	4B/E0	73/E0	9B/00
A RA	4D/E0	4D/E0	74/E0	9D/00
A E	4F/E0	4F/E0	75/E0	9F/00
A DA	50/E0	50/E0	91/E0	A0/00
A PD	51/E0	51/E0	76/E0	A1/00
A I	52/E0	52/E0	92/E0	A2/00
A D	53/E0	53/E0	93/E0	A3/00

8

APPENDICES

STANDARD

DEVICE

ADDRESSES

The addresses provided here are general to the PC/AT, with some modern features included. The information provided here is adequate as a basic resource, but for work to be done with specific motherboards or cards, I recommend that you get the technical reference manuals.

Memory Map

I realize that throughout this book, I have described the PC's memory area several times, but for the appendices I wanted to include it one more time, just so that you have a fast reference to it (Figure E-1).

Register Input/Output Addresses

For the register I/O addresses, I have only included the addresses to 0x03FF (the lower 10 bits of the I/O space) for the PC/AT. Some PC/XT-specific registers have been omitted

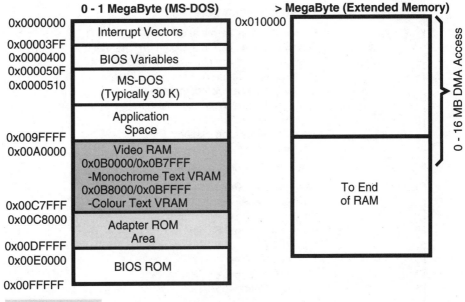

FIGURE E-1   PC memory map.

from this list. It is not obvious in the following table, but I/O port addresses 0x0000 to 0x00FF are on the motherboard, but the addresses above are on adapter cards.

For some motherboards, registers are accessed at addresses 0x0400 and above. To avoid problems, be sure that you only specify addresses below 0x0400.

ADDRESS	REGISTER DESCRIPTION
0000h	DMA channel 0 address (low addressed first, then high)
0001h	DMA channel 0 word count (low addressed first, then high)
0002h	DMA channel 1 address (low addressed first, then high)
0003h	DMA channel 1 word count (low addressed first, then high)
0004h	DMA channel 2 address (low addressed first, then high)
0005h	DMA channel 2 word count (low addressed first, then high)
0006h	DMA channel 3 address (low addressed first, then high)
0007h	DMA channel 3 word count (low addressed first, then high)
0008h	Read = DMA 1 channel 0–3 status register Bit 7 = Channel 3 Request Bit 6 = Channel 2 Request Bit 5 = Channel 1 Request Bit 4 = Channel 0 Request Bit 3 = Channel Terminal Count on Channel 3 Bit 2 = Channel Terminal Count on Channel 2

8

APPENDICES

ADDRESS	REGISTER DESCRIPTION
	Bit 1 = Channel Terminal Count on Channel 1
	Bit 0 = Channel Terminal Count on Channel 0
	Write = DMA 1 channel 0–3 command register
	Bit 7 = DACK Sense Active High
	Bit 6 = DREQ Sense Active High
	Bit 5 = Extended Write Selection
	Bit 4 = Rotating Priority
	Bit 3 = Compressed Timing
	Bit 2 = Enable Controller
0009h	DMA 1 write request register
000Ah	DMA 1 channel 0-3 mask register
	Bit 7–3 = Reserved
	Bit 2 = Mask bit
	Bit 1–0 = Channel Select
	- 00 Channel 0
	- 01 Channel 1
	- 10 Channel 2
	- 11 Channel 3
000Bh	DMA 1 channel 0–3 mode register
	Bit 7–6 = Operating Mode
	- 00 Demand mode
	- 01 Single mode
	- 10 Block mode
	- 11 Cascade mode
	Bit 5 = address increment select
	Bit 3–2 = Operation
	- 00 verify operation
	- 01 write to memory
	- 10 read from memory
	- 11 reserved
	Bit 1–0 = Channel Select
	- 00 Channel 0
	- 01 Channel 1
	- 10 Channel 2
	- 11 Channel 3
000Ch	DMA 1 Clear byte pointer flip-flop
000Dh	Read - DMA 1 read temporary register
	Write - DMA 1 master clear
000Eh	DMA 1 clear mask register
000Fh	DMA 1 write mask register
0020h	Interrupt Controller 1 initialization command word
	Bit 7–5 = 0 - Only used in 80/85 mode
	Bit 4 = ICW1 Request
	Bit 3 = Interrupt-Request Mode
	- 0 Edge-triggered mode

ADDRESS	REGISTER DESCRIPTION

                  - 1 Level-triggered mode
           Bit 2 = Interrupt Vector Size
             - 0 Eight-Byte interrupt vectors
             - 1 Four-Byte Interrupt Vectors
           Bit 1 = Operating Mode
             - 0 Cascade mode
             - 1 Single mode
           Bit 0 = IC4 Requirements
             - 0 not needed
             - 1 needed

0021h — Interrupt Controller 1 Interrupt Mask Register
    bit 7 = 0 enable parallel printer interrupt
    bit 6 = 0 enable diskette interrupt
    bit 5 = 0 enable fixed-disk interrupt
    bit 4 = 0 enable serial-port 1 interrupt
    bit 3 = 0 enable serial-port 2 interrupt
    bit 2 = 0 enable video interrupt
    bit 1 = 0 enable keyboard, mouse, RTC interrupt
    bit 0 = 0 enable timer interrupt

0040h — 8254 Timer Counter 0 & Counter Divisor Register

0041h — 8254 Timer Counter 1 & Counter Divisor Register

0042h — 8254 Timer Counter 2 & Counter Divisor Register

0043h — 8254 Timer Mode/Control port
    Bit 7–6 = Counter select
        - 00 Counter 0
        - 01 Counter 1
        - 10 Counter 2
    Bit 5–4 = Counter Read/Write Operation
        - 01 Read/Write Low Counter Byte
        - 10 Read/Write High Counter Byte
        - 11 Read/Write Low, then High Counter Bytes
    Bit 3–1 = Counter Mode Select
        - 000 Mode 0
        - 001 Mode 1/Programmable One Shot
        - x10 Mode 2/Rate Generator
        - x11 Mode 3/Square-Wave Generator
        - 100 Mode 4/Software-Triggered Strobe
        - 101 Mode 5/Hardware-Triggered Strobe
    Bit 0 = Counter Type
        - 0 Binary Counter
        - 1 BCD Counter

0060h — Read = Keyboard Controller
    Bit 7   = Keyboard Inhibit (Reset)
    Bit 6   = CGA (Reset)
    Bit 5   = Manufacturing Jumper Install
    Bit 4   = Reset if System RAM 512 KB
    Bit 3–0 = Reserved

8
APPENDICES

ADDRESS	REGISTER DESCRIPTION
	Write = Keyboard Controller
	Bit 7 = Keyboard Data Output
	Bit 6 = Keyboard Clock Output
	Bit 5 = Input Buffer Full (Reset)
	Bit 4 = Output Buffer Empty (Reset)
	Bit 3–2 = Reserved
	Bit 1 = Address line 20 gate
	Bit 0 = System reset
0061h	Read = Keyboard Controller Port B control register
	Bit 7 = Parity Check
	Bit 6 = Channel Check
	Bit 5 = Current Timer 2 Output
	Bit 4 = Toggles with each Refresh Request
	Bit 3 = Channel Check Status
	Bit 2 = Parity Check Status
	Bit 1 = Speaker Data Status
	Bit 0 = Timer 2 Gate-to-Speaker Status
	Write = 8255-Compatible Port
	Bit 7 = Clear Keyboard
	Bit 6 = Hold Keyboard Clock Low
	Bit 5 = I/O Check Enable
	Bit 4 = RAM Parity Check Enable
	Bit 3 = Read low/high switches
	Bit 2 = Reserved
	Bit 1 = Speaker Clock Enable
	Bit 0 = Timer 2 Gate-to-Speaker Enable
0064h	Read/Keyboard Controller Status
	Bit 7 = Parity Error on Keyboard Transmission
	Bit 6 = Receive Timeout
	Bit 5 = Transmit Timeout
	Bit 4 = Keyboard Inhibit
	Bit 3 = Input Register Type
	- 1 Data-in input register is command
	- 0 Data-in input register is data
	Bit 2 = System Flag Status
	Bit 1 = Input Buffer Status
	Bit 0 = Output Buffer Status
	Write Keyboard Controller Input Buffer
	20 = Read Byte Zero of Internal RAM, this is the last KB command send to 8042
	21–3F = Reads the Byte Specified in the Lower 5 Bits of the command in the 8042's internal RAM
	60–7F = Writes the Data Byte to the Address Specified in the 5 Lower Bits of the Command.
0065h	Address Line 20 Gate Control
	Bit 2 = A20 gate control
	1 = A20 enabled

ADDRESS	REGISTER DESCRIPTION
	0 = A20 disabled
0070h	CMOS RAM index register port
	Bit 7 = NMI Enable
	Bit 6–0 = CMOS RAM index
0071h	CMOS RAM data port
	00 = Current Second in BCD
	01 = Alarm Second in BCD
	02 = Current Minute in BCD
	03 = Alarm Minute in BCD
	04 = Current Hour in BCD
	05 = Alarm Hour in BCD
	06 = Day of Week in BCD
	07 = Day of Month in BCD
	08 = Month in BCD
	09 = Year in BCD (00–99)
	0A = Status Register A
	Bit 7 = Update Progress
	Bit 6–4 = Divider that Identifies the time-based Frequency
	Bit 3–0 = Rate Selection Output
	0B = Status Register B
	Bit 7 = Run/Halt Control
	Bit 6 = Periodic Interrupt Enable
	Bit 5 = Alarm Interrupt Enable
	Bit 4 = Update-Ended Interrupt Enable
	Bit 3 = Square-Wave Interrupt Enable
	Bit 2 = Calendar Format
	Bit 1 = Hour Mode
	Bit 0 = Daylight Savings time Enable
	0C = Status Register C
	Bit 7 = Interrupt Request Flag
	Bit 6 = Periodic Interrupt Flag
	Bit 5 = Alarm Interrupt Flag
	Bit 4 = Update Interrupt Flag
	Bit 3–0 = Reserved
	0D = Status Register D
	Bit 7 = Real-Time Clock Power
0080h	"MFG_PORT" Write Address
0080h	DMA Page Register (temporary storage)
0081h	DMA Channel 2 Page Address Byte 2
0082h	DMA Channel 3 Page Address Byte 2
0083h	DMA Channel 1 Page Address Byte 2
0084h	Extra Page Register
0085h	Extra Page Register
0086h	Extra Page Register

8

APPENDICES

ADDRESS	REGISTER DESCRIPTION
0087h	DMA Channel 0 Page Address Byte 2
0088h	Extra Page Register
0089h	DMA Channel 6 Page Address Byte 2
008Ah	DMA Channel 7 Page Address Byte 2
008Bh	DMA Channel 5 Page Address Byte 2
008Ch	Extra Page Register
008Dh	Extra Page Register
008Eh	Extra Page Register
008Fh	DMA Refresh Page Register

00A0h   Interrupt controller 2 Initialization Command Word
  Bit 7–5 = 0 - only used in 80/85 mode
  Bit 4   = ICW1 Request
  Bit 3   = Interrupt Request Mode
    - 0 Edge-triggered mode
    - 1 Level-triggered mode
  Bit 2   = Interrupt Vector Size
    - 0 Eight-Byte Interrupt Vectors
    - 1 Four-Byte Interrupt Vectors
  Bit 1   = Operating Mode
    - 0 Cascade mode
    - 1 Single mode
  Bit 0   = IC4 Requirements
    - 0 not needed
    - 1 needed

00A1h   Interrupt Controller 2 Mask Register
  Bit 7 = Reserved
  Bit 6 = Fixed Disk
  Bit 5 = Coprocessor exception
  Bit 4 = Mouse Interrupt
  Bit 3 = Reserved
  Bit 2 = Reserved
  Bit 1 = Redirect Cascade
  Bit 0 = Real-Time Clock

00D0h   Read - DMA Controller 2 Channel 4–7 status register
  Bit 7 = Channel 7 Request
  Bit 6 = Channel 6 Request
  Bit 5 = Channel 5 Request
  Bit 4 = Channel 4 Request
  Bit 3 = Channel 7 Terminal Count
  Bit 2 = Channel 6 Terminal Count
  Bit 1 = Channel 5 Terminal Count
  Bit 0 = Channel 4 Terminal Count
  Write DMA Controller 2 Channel 4–7 command register
  Bit 7 = DACK Sense Active High

ADDRESS	REGISTER DESCRIPTION
	Bit 6 = DREQ Sense Active High
	Bit 5 = Extended Write Selection
	Bit 4 = Rotating Priority
	Bit 3 = Compressed Timing
	Bit 2 = Enable Controller
00D2h	DMA Controller 2 Channel 4–7 Write Request Register
00D4h	DMA Controller 2 Channel 4–7 Write Single Mask Register
	Bit 7-3 = Reserved
	Bit 2 = Mask bit
	Bit 1–0 = Channel Select
	- 00 Channel 0
	- 01 Channel 1
	- 10 Channel 2
	- 11 Channel 3
00D6h	DMA Controller 2 Channel 4–7 Mode Register
	Bit 7–6 = Operating mode
	- 00 demand mode
	- 01 single mode
	- 10 block mode
	- 11 cascade mode
	Bit 5 = address increment select
	Bit 3–2 = Operation
	- 00 verify operation
	- 01 write to memory
	- 10 read from memory
	- 11 reserved
	Bit 1–0 = Channel select
	- 00 Channel 0
	- 01 Channel 1
	- 10 Channel 2
	- 11 Channel 3
00D8h	DMA Controller 2 Channel 4–7 Clear Byte Pointer
00Dah	Read = DMA Controller Channel 4–7 Read Temporary Register
	Write = DMA Controller Channel 4–7 Master Clear
00DCh	DMA Controller 2 Channel 4–7 Clear Mask Register
00DEh	DMA Controller 2 Channel 4–7 Write Mask Register
00F0h	Math Coprocessor Clear Busy Latch
00F1h	Math Coprocessor Reset
00F8h	Opcode Transfer Register
00FAh	Opcode Transfer Register
00FCh	Opcode Transfer Register
01F0h	Hard-Disk Controller Data Register
01F1h	Hard-Disk Controller Error Register

ADDRESS	REGISTER DESCRIPTION
	Bit 7 = Failing Drive
	Bit 6–3 = Reserved
	Bit 2–0 = Status
	- 001 No Error
	- 010 Formatter Device Error
	- 011 Sector Buffer Error
	- 100 ECC Circuitry Error
	- 101 Controlling Microprocessor Error
01F2h	Sector Count
01F3h	Sector Number
01F4h	Cylinder Low
01F5h	Cylinder High
01F6h	Drive/Head
01F7h	Read-Hard-Disk Controller Status Register
	Bit 7 = Controller execution status
	Bit 6 = Drive Status
	Bit 5 = Write Fault
	Bit 4 = Seek Complete
	Bit 3 = Sector Buffer Requires Servicing
	Bit 2 = Disk Data Read Successfully Corrected
	Bit 1 = Index
	Bit 0 = Previous Command Ended in Error
	Write = Hard Disk Controller Command Register
0201h	Read-Joystick Position and Status
	Bit 7 = Status B Joystick Button 2
	Bit 6 = Status B Joystick Button 1
	Bit 5 = Status A Joystick Button 2
	Bit 4 = Status A Joystick Button 1
	Bit 3 = B joystick Y coordinate
	Bit 2 = B joystick X coordinate
	Bit 1 = A joystick Y coordinate
	Bit 0 = A joystick X coordinate
	Write = Fire joystick's four one-shots
0220h	SoundBlaster-Left speaker Status/Address
	Address:
	01 = Enable waveform control
	02 = Timer #1 data
	03 = Timer #2 data
	04 = Timer control flags
	08 = Speech synthesis mode
	20–35 = Amplitude Modulation/Vibrato
	40–55 = Level key scaling/Total level
	60–75 = Attack/Decay rate
	80–95 = Sustain/Release rate
	A0–B8 = Octave/Frequency Number
	C0–C8 = Feedback/Algorithm

ADDRESS	REGISTER DESCRIPTION
	E0–F5 = Waveform Selection
0221h	SoundBlaster-Left speaker Data
0222h	SoundBlaster-Right speaker/Address Address: 01 = Enable waveform control 02 = Timer #1 data 03 = Timer #2 data 04 = Timer control flags 08 = Speech synthesis mode 20–35 = Amplitude modulation/vibrato 40–55 = Level key scaling/Total level 60–75 = Attack/Decay rate 80–95 = Sustain/Release rate A0–B8= Octave/Frequency Number C0–C8 = Feedback/Algorithm E0–F5 = Waveform Selection
0223h	Right speaker—data port
0278h	LPT2 data port
0279h	LPT2 Status Port Bit 7 = Busy Bit 6 = Acknowledge Bit 5 = Out of Paper Bit 4 = Printer Selected Bit 3 = Error Bit 2 = IRQ Occurred Bit 1–0 = Reserved
027Ah	LPT2 Control Port Bit 7–6 = Reserved Bit 5 = Data Output Control Bit 4 = IRQ Enable Bit 3 = Select Printer Bit 2 = Initialize Bit 1 = Line Feed Bit 0 = Strobe
02E8h	8514/A Display Status
02E8h	8514/A Horizontal Total
02EAh	8514/A DAC Mask
02EBh	8514/A DAC Read Index
02ECh	8514/A DAC Write Index
02EDh	8514/A DAC Data
02F8h	Serial Port 3 Transmitter/Receiver registers/Divisor Latch Low
02F9h	Serial Port 2 Interrupt Enable Register/Divisor Latch High

8

APPENDICES

ADDRESS	REGISTER DESCRIPTION
02FAh	Serial Port 2 Interrupt Identification Register
02FBh	Serial Port 2 Line Control Register
02FCh	Serial Port 2 Modem Control Register
02FDh	Serial Port 2 Line Status Register
02FFh	Serial Port 2 Scratchpad Register
0300h–031Fh	IBM Prototype Card Addresses
0360h–036Fh	Network Cards
0370h	Secondary Diskette Controller Status A
0371h	Secondary Diskette Controller Status B
0372h	Secondary Diskette Controller Digital Output Register
0374h	Read - Secondary Diskette Controller Main Status Register Secondary Diskette Controller Data Rate Select Register
0375h	Secondary Diskette Controller Command/Data Register
0377h	Read-Secondary Diskette Controller Digital Input Register Write-Select Register for Diskette Data Transfer Rate "STANDARD"
0378h	LPT1 Data port
0379h	LPT1 Status port 　Bit 7　 = Busy 　Bit 6　 = Acknowledge 　Bit 5　 = Out of Paper 　Bit 4　 = Printer Selected 　Bit 3　 = Error 　Bit 2　 = IRQ Occurred 　Bit 1–0 = Reserved
037Ah	LPT1 Control port 　Bit 7–6 = Reserved 　Bit 5　 = Data Output Control 　Bit 4　 = IRQ Enable 　Bit 3　 = Select Printer 　Bit 2　 = Initialize 　Bit 1　 = Line Feed 　Bit 0　 = Strobe
0380h–038Fh	Secondary SDLC Registers
0390h–039Fh	IBM Cluster adapter
03A0h–03AFh	Primary SDLC Registers
03B4h	MDA CRT Index Register
03B5h	MDA CRT Data Register

Address	Function
00	Horizontal Total
01	Horizontal Displayed
02	Horizontal Sync Position

ADDRESS	REGISTER DESCRIPTION
	03 Horizontal Sync Pulse Width
	04 Vertical Total
	05 Vertical Displayed
	06 Vertical Sync Position
	07 Vertical Sync Pulse Width
	08 Interlace Mode
	09 Maximum Scan Lines
	0A Cursor Start
	0B Cursor End
	0C Start Address High
	0D Start Address Low
	0E Cursor Location High
	0F Cursor Location Low
	10 Light Pen High
	11 Light Pen Low

03B8h   MDA Mode Control Register
bit 7–6 = Reserved
bit 5   = Blink Enable
bit 4   = Reserved
bit 3   = Video Enable
bit 2–1 = Reserved
bit 0   = High Resolution Mode

03B9h   EGA Color Select

03BAh   Read - EGA CRT Status Register
Write - EGA/VGA feature control register

03BBh   Reserved for EGA

03BCh   'MDA" LPT1 Data Port

03BDh   "MDA" LPT1 Status Port
Bit 7   = Busy
Bit 6   = Acknowledge
Bit 5   = Out of Paper
Bit 4   = Printer Selected
Bit 3   = Error
Bit 2   = IRQ Occurred
Bit 1–0 = Reserved

03BEh   "MDA" LPT 1 Control port
Bit 7–5 = Reserved
Bit 4   = IRQ Enable
Bit 3   = Select Printer
Bit 2   = Initialize
Bit 1   = Line Feed
Bit 0   = Strobe

03BFh   Hercules Configuration Switch Register
Bit 7–2 = Reserved
Bit 1   = Enable Upper 32-KB Graphic Buffer

8

APPENDICES

ADDRESS	REGISTER DESCRIPTION
	Bit 0 = Disable Graphics Mode
03C0h	EGA/VGA ATC Index/Data Register
03C1h	VGA Other Attribute Register
03C2h	Read-EGA/VGA Input Status 0 Register
	Write-VGA Miscellaneous Output Register
03C4h	VGA Sequencer Index Register
03C5h	VGA Other Sequencer Index Register
03C6h	VGA PEL Mask Register
03C7h	VGA PEL Address Read Mode/VGA DAC state register
03C8h	VGA PEL Address Write Mode
03C9h	VGA PEL Data Register
03CAh	VGA Feature Control Register
03CCh	VGA Miscellaneous Output Register
03CEh	VGA Graphics Address Register
03CFh	VGA Other Graphics Register
03D4h	CGA CRT Index Register
03D5h	CGA CRT (6845) data register
03D8h	CGA Mode Control Register
	Bit 7–6 = Reserved
	Bit 5 = Blink Enable
	Bit 4 = 640 × 200 Graphics Mode Select
	Bit 3 = Video Enable
	Bit 2 = Monochrome Signal Select
	Bit 1 = Text Mode Select
	Bit 0 = Text Mode Select
03D9h	CGA Palette Register
	Bit 7–6 = Reserved
	Bit 5 = Active Color Set Select
	Bit 4 = Intense Color Select
	Bit 3 = Intense Border Select
	Bit 2 = Red Border/Background/Foreground Select
	Bit 1 = Green Border/Background/Foreground Select
	Bit 0 = Blue Border/Background/Foreground Select
03DAh	CGA Status Register
	Bit 7–4 = Reserved
	Bit 3 = Vertical Retrace Status
	Bit 2 = Light Pen Status
	Bit 1 = Light Pen Trigger Set
	Bit 0 = Memory Select
03EAh	EGA/VGA Feature Control Register

ADDRESS	REGISTER DESCRIPTION
03EBh	Clear Light Pen Latch
03ECh	Preset Light Pen Latch
03E8h	Serial Port 3 Transmitter/Receiver Registers/Divisor Latch Low
03E9h	Serial Port 3 Interrupt Enable Register/Divisor Latch High
03EAh	Serial Port 3 Interrupt Identification Register
03EBh	Serial Port 3 Line Control Register
03ECh	Serial Port 3 Modem Control Register
03EDh	Serial Port 3 Line Status Register
03EFh	Serial Port 3 Scratchpad Register
03F0h	Primary Diskette Controller Status A
03F1h	Primary Diskette Controller Status B
03F2h	Primary Diskette Controller Digital Output Register
03F4h	Read-Primary Diskette Controller Main Status Register Primary Diskette Controller Data Rate Select Register
03F5h	Primary Diskette Controller Command/Data Register
03F7h	Read-Primary Diskette Controller Digital Input Register Write-Select Register for Diskette Data Transfer Rate
03F8h	Serial Port 3 Transmitter/Receiver Registers/Divisor Latch Low
03F9h	Serial Port 1 Interrupt Enable Register/Divisor Latch High
03FAh	Serial Port 1 Interrupt Identification Register
03FBh	Serial Port 1 Line Control Register
03FCh	Serial Port 1 Modem Control Register
03FDh	Serial Port 1 Line Status Register
03FFh	Serial Port 1 Scratchpad Register

8

APPENDICES

BIOS
VARIABLES

The BIOS variables are really the system variables for the PC and are available in the 0x00040 code segment. This segment is accessed within the BIOS functions by calling the DDS subroutine. As pointed out earlier in the book, you must never write to these variables and care must be taken before using the data in your application.

OFFSET	SIZE	BITS	DESCRIPTION
0	Word		COM1 Base Address
2	Word		COM2 Base Address
4	Word		COM3 Base Address
6	Word		COM4 Base Address (Not Conflict with SVGA Registers)
8	Word		LPT1 Base Address
A	Word		LPT2 Base Address
C	Word		LPT3 Base Address
E	Word		LPT4 Base Address (Only Available in Phoenix BIOS)
10	Byte		Installed Hardware
		7–6	Number of Floppy Drives (00=1 Drive, 01=2 Drives)
		5–4	Video Mode (00 = EGA/VGA Modes) (01 = 40x25 Color) (10 = 80x25 Color) (11 = 80x25 Monochrome)
		3	Reserved
		2	Set if Mouse Installed
		1	Set if Coprocessor Installed
		0	Floppy Drive Used for Booting
11	Byte		Installed Hardware
		7–6	Number of Printer Adapters (00=0 Printer Adapters) (01=1 Printer Adapter)
		5–4	Used for Specific IBM PCs
		3–1	Number of RS-232 Adapters (000=0 RS-232 Adapters) (001=1 RS-232 Adapter)
		0	Used for Specific IBM PCs
12	Byte		Used for Specific IBM PCs
13	Word		Memory size in KB (up to 640)
15	Word		Phoenix BIOS Test Port
17	Byte		Keyboard Control
		7	Set for *Insert Mode* Active
		6	Set for *Caps Lock* Active
		5	Set for *Num Lock* Active
		4	Set for *Scroll Lock* Active
		3	Set when *Alt* Pressed
		2	Set when *Ctrl* Pressed
		1	Set when *Left Shift* Pressed
		0	Set when *Right Shift* Pressed

8

APPENDICES

OFFSET	SIZE	BITS	DESCRIPTION
18	Byte		Keyboard Control
		7	Set when *Insert* Pressed
		6	Set when *Caps Lock Key* Pressed
		5	Set when *Num Lock* Key Pressed
		4	Set when *Scroll Lock* Key Pressed
		3	Set when Pause Mode Active
		2	Set when *SysReq* Key Pressed
		1	Set when Left *Alt* Key Pressed
		0	Set when Right *Alt* Key Pressed
19	Byte		Alternate Keyboard Entry
1A	Word		Pointer to Next Character to Process in Keyboard Buffer
1C	Word		Pointer to Next Available Character in Keyboard Buffer
1E	32 Bytes		Keyboard Buffer
3E	Byte		Floppy Recalibrate Status
		7	Interrupt Flag
		6–4	Reserved
		3	Recalibrate Drive 3
		2	Recalibrate Drive 2
		1	Recalibrate Drive 1
		0	Recalibrate Drive 0
3F	Byte		Floppy Motor Status
		7	Current Operation (0 = Read/Verify) (1 = Write)
		6	Reserved
		5–4	Drive Selected
		3	Drive Motor 3 On
		2	Drive Motor 2 On
		1	Drive Motor 1 On
		0	Drive Motor 0 On
40	Byte		Motor Off Counter
41	Byte		Previous Floppy Operation Status
		7	Drive Not Ready
		6	Seek Operation Failed
		5	Controller Failure
		4	CRC Error on Read
		3–0	Floppy Errors (1000 = DMA Overrun) (0100 = Sector Not Found) (0010 = Address Mark Not Found) (0001 = Invalid Drive Parameter) (0011 = Write Protect)

OFFSET	SIZE	BITS	DESCRIPTION
			(0110 = Door Open/Disk Change)
			(1001 = DMA Cross 64-KB Boundary)
			(1100 = Media Type Not Found)
42	7 Bytes		Floppy Controller Status
49	Byte		Display Mode
4A	Word		Number of Display Columns
4C	Word		Length of Regen Buffer in Bytes
			(Phoenix BIOS Current Page Size)
4E	Word		Address of Regen Buffer
			(Phoenix BIOS Current Page Addr)
50	Word		Page 1 Cursor Position (Column/Row)
52	Word		Page 2 Cursor Position (Column/Row)
54	Word		Page 3 Cursor Position (Column/Row)
56	Word		Page 4 Cursor Position (Column/Row)
58	Word		Page 5 Cursor Position (Column/Row)
5A	Word		Page 6 Cursor Position (Column/Row)
5C	Word		Page 7 Cursor Position (Column/Row)
5E	Word		Page 8 Cursor Position (Column/Row)
60	Word		Cursor Start/End
			(First Byte, Ending Line)
			(Second Byte, Starting Line)
62	Byte		Current Display Page
63	Word		Video Controller Base Address
65	Byte		Mode Select Register
66	Byte		Palette Value
67	Double Word		Pointer to Reset in SOME PCs
6B	Byte		Reserved
6C	Double Word		Timer Counter
			(Number of Ticks since Midnight)
70	Byte		Timer Overflow Flag
			(Number of Days PC has been Operating)
71	Byte		Break Key State
		7	Set if *Ctrl-Break* Pressed
		6–0	Reserved

8

APPENDICES

OFFSET	SIZE	BITS	DESCRIPTION
72	Word		Reset Operation Flag
			(0x01234 = Bypass Memory Test)
			(0x04321 = Save Memory Contents)
			(0x05678 = System Suspended)
			(0x09ABC = Manufacturing Test)
			(0x0ABCD = System Post Loop)
			(0x00064 = Phoenix BIOS Burn In)
74	Byte		Fixed Disk Previous Operation Status
			(0x000 = No Error)
			(0x001 = Invalid Parm/Bad Command)
			(0x002 = Address Mark Not Found)
			(0x003 = Write to Protected Disk)
			(0x004 = Sector Not Found)
			(0x005 = Reset Failed)
			(0x007 = Bad Parameter Table)
			(0x009 = DMA Cross 64-KB Boundary)
			(0x00A = Bad Sector Flag)
			(0x00B = Bad Cylinder Detected)
			(0x00D = Invalid Sector Format)
			(0x00E = Control Data Address Mark)
			(0x00F = DMA Arbitration Invalid)
			(0x010 = CRC or ECC on Disk Read)
			(0x011 = ECC Correct Data Error)
			(0x020 = Controller Failure)
			(0x040 = Seek Operation Failed)
			(0x080 = Drive Time Out/Not Ready)
			(0x0AA = Drive Not Ready)
			(0x0BB = Undefined Error)
			(0x0CC = Write Fault)
			(0x0E0 = Status Error)
			(0x0FF = Sense Operation Failed)
75	Byte		Number of Fixed Drives
76	Byte		Reserved for Fixed Drive Controller
77	Byte		Reserved for Fixed Drive Controller
78	Byte		Printer 1 Time Out Value
79	Byte		Printer 2 Time Out Value
7A	Byte		Printer 3 Time Out Value
7B	Byte		Printer 4 Time Out Value
7C	Byte		COM1 Time Out Value
7D	Byte		COM2 Time Out Value
7E	Byte		COM3 Time Out Value
7F	Byte		COM4 Time Out Value

OFFSET	SIZE	BITS	DESCRIPTION
80	Word		Keyboard Buffer Start Offset
82	Word		Keyboard Buffer End Offset
84	Byte		Video Rows (Zero Based)
85	Word		Character Height (Bytes/Character)
87	Byte		VGA Controller States
		7	Set for Clear RAM
		6–5	Memory in Adapter
			(00 = 64 KB)
			(01 = 128 KB)
			(10 = 192 KB)
			(11 = 256 KB)
		4	Reserved
		3	Set for VGA Adapter (0 = EGA)
		2	Set for Display Enable Wait
		1	Reset for VGA color adapter
		0	Set to Inhibit Cursor Translation
88	Byte		VGA Controller States
		7–4	Feature Connector
		3–0	EGA Option Switch Settings
89	Byte		VGA Control Bits
		7	Set for 200 Lines
		6–5	Reserved
		4	Set for 400 Lines
		3	Set for No Pallet Load
		2	Set for Monochrome Monitor
		1	Set for Grey Scaling On
		0	Reserved
8A	Byte		Index into VGA DCC Table
			(Phoenix VGA BIOS Only)
8B	Byte		Media Control Byte
		7–6	Last Floppy Drive Data Rate
			(00 = 500 KBps)
			(01 = 300 KBps)
			(10 = 250 KBps)
			(11 = Reserved)
		5–4	Last Floppy Drive Step Rate
		3–2	Start Floppy Drive Transfer
			(Phoenix BIOS Only)
		1–0	Reserved
8C	Byte		Fixed Disk Controller Status
8D	Byte		Fixed Disk Controller Error
8E	Byte		Fixed Disk Interrupt Control

8

APPENDICES

OFFSET	SIZE	BITS	DESCRIPTION
8F	Byte		Diskette Controller
			(Phoenix BIOS Only)
		7	Reserved
		6	Drive Determined for Drive 1
		5	Drive 1 is Multi-rate
		4	Drive 1 Supports Change Line
		3	Reserved
		2	Drive Determined for Drive 0
		1	Drive 0 is Multi-rate
		0	Drive 0 Supports Change Line
90	Byte		Drive 0 Media State
		7–6	Drive Data Rate
			(00 = 500 KBps)
			(01 = 300 KBps)
			(10 = 250 KBps)
			(11 = Reserved)
		5	Double Stepping Required
		4	Media Established
		3	Reserved
		2–0	Drive/Media State
			(000 = 360-KB Disk/360-KB Drive)
			(001 = 360-KB Disk/1.2-MB Drive)
			(010 = 1.2-MB Disk/1.2-MB Drive)
			(011 = 360-KB Disk/360-KB Drive)
			(100 = 360-KB Disk/1.2-MB Drive)
			(101 = 1.2-MB Disk/1.2-MB Drive)
			(110 = Reserved)
			(111 = None of the Above)
91	Byte		Drive 1 Media State
		7–6	Drive Data Rate
			(00 = 500 KBps)
			(01 = 300 KBps)
			(10 = 250 KBps)
			(11 = Reserved)
		5	Double Stepping Required
		4	Media Established
		3	Reserved
		2–0	Drive/Media State
			(000 = 360-KB Disk/360-KB Drive)
			(001 = 360-KB Disk/1.2-MB Drive)
			(010 = 1.2-MB Disk/1.2-MB Drive)
			(011 = 360-KB Disk/360-KB Drive)
			(100 = 360-KB Disk/1.2-MB Drive)
			(101 = 1.2-MB Disk/1.2-MB Drive)
			(110 = Reserved)
			(111 = None of the Above)
92	Word		Reserved

OFFSET	SIZE	BITS	DESCRIPTION
94	Byte		Floppy Drive 0 Cylinder
95	Byte		Floppy Drive 1 Cylinder
96	Byte		Keyboard Mode State
		7	Set when Read ID in Progress
		6	Set if Last Character was first ID Character
		5	Set when Force *Num Lock*
		4	Set if 101-/102-Key keyboard used
		3	Set if Right *Alt* Pressed
		2	Set if Right *Ctrl* Pressed
		1	Set if Last Code was E0
		0	Set if Last Code was E1
97	Byte		Keyboard LED Flags
		7	Keyboard Transmit Error Flag
		6	Mode Indicator Update
		5	Resend Receive Flag
		4	Acknowledgment Received
		3	Reserved (Must be Reset)
		2–0	LED State Bits
98	Double word		Pointer to User Wait Complete Flag
9C	Double word		User Wait Complete Flag (in μsecs)
A0	Byte		Wait Active Flag
		7	Wait Time has elapsed
		6–1	Reserved
		0	Int 15h Function 86h Executed
A1	7 bytes		Reserved
A8	Double Word		Video Parameter Table Pointer
AC	Double Word		Dynamic Save Area Pointer
B0	Double Word		Alpha Mode Auxilliary Character Generator Pointer
B4	Double Word		Graphics Mode Auxilliary Character Generator Pointer
B8	Double Word		Secondary Save Pointer
BC	68 Bytes		Reserved
100	Word		Print Screen Status Byte

8

APPENDICES

INTERRUPT

FUNCTION

BY NUMBER

How Interrupts have been allocated in the PC have been basically the same since 1981 when the PC was first introduced. The absolute address of the interrupt vector is four times the interrupt number. The following table, as well as identifying the interrupt, also identifies the chapter that I describe the function and characteristics of the interrupt.

As you go through this table, you'll see that I don't have references within the book for many of these interrupts, or many of them are marked *Reserved*. This does not mean the interrupt isn't potentially useful for your application. It means that no API, Pointer has been officially assigned to this interrupt number. As you work through your application, I suggest that if you might potentially want to use other interrupts that you look at the Intel or Microsoft Web pages for the most current specification for the different numbers.

For the most complete interrupt reference I've found, look up Ralf Brown's INTERRUP.LST file on the Internet. The reference that I have is dated March 26, 1995, but I have not found an error with the information, as of December 1998.

INTERRUPT	NAME AND COMMENTS	REFERENCE
00h	Divide by Zero Error	
01h	Single step	Interrupt Programming
02h	Nonmaskable	Interrupt Programming
03h	Breakpoint (Instruction 0x0CC)	Interrupt Programming
04h	Overflow	
05h	Print Screen	
06h–07h	Reserved	
08h	Time of Day Services	Precise Timing in PC
09h	Keyboard Interrupt	The Keyboard and Mouse Ports
0Ah	Slaved Second Interrupt Controller	
0Bh	COM1/COM3 Interrupt	RS-232—The Non-Standard
0Ch	COM2/COM3 Interrupt	RS-232—The Non-Standard
0Dh	Hard Disk Interrupt/LPT2 Interrupt	
0Eh	Diskette Interrupt	
0Fh	LPT1 Interrupt	The Centronics Parallel Port
10h	Video BIOS	The BIOS Interface, Appendix H
11h	BIOS Equipment Check	Appendix H
12h	BIOS Memory Size Determine	Appendix H
13h	Disk I/O BIOS	Appendix H
14h	Serial Communications BIOS	RS-232 The Non-Standard, Appendix H
15h	BIOS System Services	Appendix H
16h	Keyboard I/O BIOS	The Keyboard and Mouse, Appendix H
17h	Printer BIOS	The Centronics Parallel Port, Appendix H
18h	Resident BASIC Start Vector	MS-DOS Programming Languages and Application Development Tools
19h	Boot Strap Loader	The PC's Boot Process
1Ah	Time of Day BIOS Interrupt	Precise Timing in the PC, Appendix H
1Bh	Keyboard Break Vector	
1Ch	Timer Tick Vector	Precise Timing in the PC

8

APPENDICES

INTERRUPT	NAME AND COMMENTS	REFERENCE
1Dh	Table Address of Video Parameters	
1Eh	Table Address of Disk Parameters	
1Fh	Table Address of Graphic Characters	
20h	MS-DOS Program Terminate	Appendix I
21h	MS-DOS Function APIs	Appendix I
22h	MS-DOS Terminate Vector	Appendix I
23h	MS-DOS *Ctrl-C* vector	Appendix I
24h	MS-DOS Error Handler Vector	Appendix I
25h–26h	MS-DOS Absolute Disk I/O	Appendix I
27h	MS-DOS Terminate Stay Resident API	Appendix I
28h–2Eh	MS-DOS Reserved	Appendix I
2Fh	MS-DOS Multiplex interrupt	Appendix I
30h–32h	MS-DOS Reserved	Appendix I
33h	Mouse BIOS	Appendix H
34h–3Fh	MS-DOS Reserved	Appendix I
40h	Revectored Disk I/O BIOS Interrupt 13h	
41h	Table Address of Hard Drive 0 Parameters	
42h	Revectored EGA BIOS Interrupt 10h	
43h	Table Address of EGA Parameters	
44h–34h	Reserved	
46h	Table Address of Hard Drive 1 Parameters	
47h–49h	Reserved	
4Ah	ROM BIOS Alarm Handler	
4Bh–4Fh	Reserved	
50h	PC/AT Alarm BIOS Interrupt	
51h–59h	Reserved	
5Ah	NETBIOS Function APIs	
5Bh	NETBIOS Remap of Vector 19h	
5Ch	NETBIOS Entry Point	
5Dh–66h	Reserved	
67h	LIM EMS Memory Function APIs	MS-DOS
68h–6Fh	Reserved	
70h	RTC Interrupt	Precise Timing in the PC

INTERRUPT	NAME AND COMMENTS	REFERENCE
71h	Slave Interrupt Controller Redirect	Interrupt Programming
72h	IRQ10	Interrupt Programming
73h	IRQ11	Interrupt Programming
74h	IRQ12	Interrupt Programming
75h	IRQ13	Interrupt Programming
76h	IRQ14	Interrupt Programming
77h	IRQ15	Interrupt Programming
78h–7Fh	Not Allocated/Available for Use	
80h–85h	Reserved for Cassette BASIC	MS-Dos Programming Languages and Application Development Tools
86h–F0h	Used by BASIC	MS-Dos Programming Languages and Application Development Tools
F1h–FFh	Used during PC Boot as a Temporary Stack Area. Should NOT be used for Interrupts or Variables	

8

APPENDICES

BIOS
INTERRUPT
FUNCTIONS

The BIOS Interrupt Functions were introduced with the PC in 1980 as a standard method of interfacing with console and disk Input/Output and has remained largely unchanged since then. The BIOS functions or "APIs" can only be accessed from MS-DOS command line programming using the interrupts and registers I have listed below.

Accessing BIOS functions directly from your application can be a somewhat risky proposition with incorrect accesses resulting in the PC locking up or trashing the current diskette or hard drive. Before using the BIOS APIs in your application instead of language or operating system functions, I recommend that you read through "The BIOS Interface" and "Practical PC Programming," earlier in the book.

Interrupt 10h: Video

The video BIOS Interrupt (10h) provides a basic level of control over the screen that should only be used from the MS-DOS command line programs. This level of control is useful for setting specific colors or screen operations that are not normally available in high-level language libraries. Attempting to modify the video hardware while executing in Windows will either fail or cause the PC to stop working.

Instead of using the Video BIOS (or the MS-DOS Int 21h functions) to write to Video RAM ("VRAM"), I normally write directly to memory using the code that I show in "The BIOS Interface Chapter." It is quite easy to write to VRAM and accessing it directly allows much faster updates than would be possible using the BIOS or MS-DOS functions.

The normal Display modes for a color Display are:

MODE	TYPE	COLORS	TEXT FORMAT	PAGES	BUFFER START
00h	Text	16	40×25	8	0B8000h
01h	Text	16	40×25	8	0B8000h
02h	Text	16	80×25	8	0B8000h
03h	Text	16	80×25	8	0B8000h
04h	Graphics	4	40×25	1	0B8000h
05h	Graphics	4	40×25	1	0B8000h
06h	Graphics	2	80×25	1	0B8000h
07h	Text	Mono	80×25	4	0B0000h
08h	Graphics	16	20×25	1	0B0000h
09h	Graphics	16	40×25	1	0B0000h
0Ah	Graphics	4	80×25	1	0B0000h
0Dh	Graphics	16	40×25	8	0A0000h
0Eh	Graphics	16	80×25	4	0A0000h
0Fh	Graphics	Mono	80×25	2	0A0000h
10h	Graphics	16	80×25	2	0A0000h
11h	Graphics	2	80×30	1	0A0000h
12h	Graphics	16	80×30	1	0A0000h
13h	Graphics	256	40×25	1	0A0000h

For the graphics modes, a character is 8×8 pixels across and the processor draws each character (it does not use the built in font memory).

The Video BIOS Functions are as follows:

8
APPENDICES

FUNCTION	INPUT	OUTPUT	COMMENTS
Set Display Mode	AH = 00h AL = Video Mode	None	Set the Display to the Mode Specified in the Table above.
Set Cursor Type	AH = 01h CH = Start Scan Line CL = End Scan Line	None	Set the height of the hardware Cursor. If bits 6 and 7 are set in CH, then the Cursor will be turned off.
Set Cursor Position	AH = 02h BH = Display Page DH = Row DL = Column	None	Move the Hardware Cursor to the Specified Position on the Specified Page.
Read Cursor Position	AH = 03h BH = Display Page	CH = Starting Scan Line CL = Ending Scan Line DH = Row DL = Column	This Function Reads both the Cursor Position, but the Hardware Cursor Type as well.
Read Light Pen Position	AH = 04h	AH = Pen trigger (1 = Pen pressed) BX = Pixel column CX = Pixel row DH = Character row DL = Character column	The light pen was a feature in early display adapters, but the feature can be emulated by the mouse.
Select Display Page Number	AH = 05h AL = Page number	None	Set a new display Page (zero based).
Initialize Window, Scroll Up	AH = 06h AL = Lines to scroll up BH = 0 for blank Window CH = Upper row	None	Create a text window on the current display page and, optionally, scroll up the contents by a set number of lines.

Function	Input	Output	Description
	CL = Left column DH = Lower row DL = Right column		
Initialize Window, Scroll Down	AH = 07h AL = Lines to scroll down BH = 0 for blank window CH = Upper row CL = Left column DH = Lower row DL = Right column	None	Create a text window on the current display page and, optionally, scroll down the contents by a set number of lines.
Read Character And Attribute	AH = 08h BH = Page number	AH = Attribute AL = Character	Read the current character and its attribute byte at the current hardware cursor position for the page. The cursor position is also incremented.
Write Character And Attribute	AH = 09h AL = Character BH = Page number CX = Number of characters to write	None	Write the character and attribute CX times on the specified page. Writing will stop at the end of the display page. The cursor is incremented by CX.
Write Character Only At Cursor	AH = 0Ah AL = Character BH = Page number CX = Number of characters to write	None	Write the character CX times on the specified page. Writing will stop at the end of the display page. The cursor is incremented by CX.
Set Color Palette	AH = 0Bh BH = Palette ID BL = Color ID	None	If BH = 0 set the Red/Green/Brown palette, if BH = 1, set the Cyan/Magenta/White palette. Palettes are largely obsolete since the introduction of the EGA/VGA.
Write Pixel	AH = 0Ch AL = Color	None	Write the pixel at the specified location. If bit 7 of AL is set, then the pixel value is XOR'd with the contents of

FUNCTION	INPUT	OUTPUT	COMMENTS
			the pixel.
Read Pixel	AH = 0Dh BH = Page number CX = Pixel column DX = Pixel row	AL = Color	Return the pixel color.
Write Text in Teletype Mode	AH = 0Eh AL = Character BH = Page number BL = Foreground color	None	Write the character as if on a teletype. CR/LF/BS/Tab/ Bell are treated as commands and not as characters. The page cursor is updated appropriately. I often use this BIOS command to produce a "beep" from the PC's speaker, rather than accessing the hardware directly.
Get Current Display Mode	AH = 0Fh	AH = Columns AL = Display mode BH = Active page number	Return the display mode currently displayed.

Set Palette Registers	AH = 10h
	AL = Command
	  0 = Set one palette
	    register
	BH = Register
	BL = Value
	  1 = Set overscan
	    register
	BH = Value
	  2 = Set all palette
	    registers
	ES:DX = Pointer to
	    table
	  3 = Toggle intensity or
	    blinking bit
		See "Input"	This function was originally used for the CGA, but has been enhanced for the VGA. This BIOS function is most useful for changing the VGA DAC values.

BL = 0 enable
    Intensity/1
    enable blinking
7 = Read one palette
    register
BL = Register
BH = Returned value
8 = Read overscan
    register
BH = Returned value
9 = Read all palette
    registers and
    overscan
ES:DX = returned
        table
10h = Set one color
      register
BH = Register
DH = Red
CH = Green
CL = Blue
12h = set block of color
      registers
ES:DX = pointer
        to color table
BX = First color register
CX = Number of
     registers
13h = Select color
      register
BL = 0 Select paging
     mode

FUNCTION	INPUT	OUTPUT	COMMENTS
	1 Select page		
	15h = Read single DAC color register		
	BX = Color register		
	DH = Red		
	CH = Green		
	CL = Blue		
	17h = Read block of color registers		
	BX = Start register		
	CX = Number To Read		
	EX:DX = Pointer to buffer		
	1Ah = Read color paging status		
	BH = Current page		
	BL = Paging mode		
	1Bh = Sum color values to grey		
	BX = Start register		
	CX = Number of registers		
Character Generator	AH = 11h	See "Input"	This BIOS function allows you to change the current font for your application. I often find it useful to add one or two of my own characters to the font for special operations. Most of these functions are only available in EGA/VGA display adapters.
	AL = Command		
	0 = Load user text font		
	BH = Number of bytes per character		
	BL = Block		
	CX = Number of characters		
	DX = First character		

ES:BP = Pointer to font table

1 = Load ROM 8×14 text font

    BL = Block to load

2 = Load ROM 8×8 text font

    BL = Block to load

3 = Set block specifier

    BL = Select character block

4 = Load ROM 8×16 text font

    BL = Block to load

10h = Load user text font

    BH = Number of bytes per character

    BL = Block

    CX = Number of characters

    DX = ID of the first character

    ES:BP = Pointer to font table

1h = Load ROM 8×14 text font

    BL = Block to load

12h = Load ROM 8×8 text font

    BL = Block to load

14h = Load ROM 8×16

FUNCTION	INPUT	OUTPUT	COMMENTS
	text font		
	BL = Block to load		
	20h = Set user graphics character pointer to interrupt 1Fh		
	ES:BP = pointer to user graphic font		
	21h = Set user graphics character pointer to interrupt 43h		
	BL = Rows		
	CX = Bytes per character		
	DL = Rows per screen		
	ES:BP = pointer to font table		
	22h = use ROM 8×14 text font for graphics		
	BL = Rows		
	DL = Rows/Screen		
	23h = Use ROM 8×8 text font for graphics		
	BL = Rows		
	DL = Rows/Screen		
	24h = Use ROM 8×16 text font for graphics		
	BL = Rows		

DL = Rows/Screen
30h = Get font pointer information
   BH = Font pointer (coded)
   CX = bytes per character
   DL = Rows
   ES:BP = pointer to font

Alternate Select   AH = 12h   See "Input"

   This function allows control over the VGA hardware. For most applications this function should not be accessed.

   BL = Command
   10h = Return configuration information
      BH = Color or monochrome
      BL = Memory available
      CH = Adapter bits
      CL = Switch settings
   20h = Switch to alternate print screen routine
   30h = Select VGA text scan lines
      AL = Scan lines (0 – 200, 1 – 350, 2 – 400)
   31h = Mode set palette loading
      AL = 0 for disable, 1 for enable
   32h = Enable VGA

FUNCTION	INPUT	OUTPUT	COMMENTS
	output	AL = 0 for enable, 1 for disable	
	33h = Enable grey shades	AL = Enable summing, 1 for disable	
	34h = Enable cursor scaling	AL = 0 for enable, 1 for disable	
	35h = Switch display	AL = Code for switch ES:DX = Pointer to 128 byte save buffer	
	36h = Video screen	AL = 0 for On, 1 for Off	
Write String	AH = 13h AL = Mode BH = Page number BL = Attribute CX = Character count DX = Start cursor position ES:BP = Pointer to string	None	Write the string to the display with the attribute byte if bit 1 of AL is reset.
Read Display Codes	AH = 1Ah AL = 0	AL = 1Ah BH = Alternate display code BL = Active Display code:	This function will allow you to check to see what the PC is actually running.

0 = No display
1 = MDA with monitor
2 = CGA with monitor
4 = EGA with color monitor
5 = EGA with monochrome monitor
6 = PGS with color monitor
7 = VGA with monochrome monitor
8 = VGA with color monitor
0FFh = Unknown monitor type

AL = 1Ah

This function is used to "force" a specific monitor type to the system.

Write Display Codes

AH = 1Ah
AL = 1
BH = Alternate display code
BL = Active display code:
0 = No display
1 = MDA with monitor
2 = CGA with monitor
4 = EGA with color monitor
5 = EGA with monochrome monitor
6 = PGS with color monitor

FUNCTION	INPUT	OUTPUT	COMMENTS
	7 = VGA with monochrome monitor 8 = VGA with color monitor 0FFh = Unknown monitor type		
Return Video State Buffer	AH = 1Bh BX = 0 ES:LDI = pointer to video state buffer	AL = 1Bh	This function returns the video state buffer. The video state buffer data format is shown below.
Return Save/Restore	AH = 1Ch AL = 0 CX = Requested states Bit 0 = Save or restore video hardware state Bit 1 = Save or restore video BIOS state Bit 2 = Save or restore BIOS data area Bit 3 to 15 = Always Set to zero	AL = 1Ch BX = Number of 64-byte blocks for state	This function is used to save or restore the different video state buffers.
Save Video State	AH = 1Ch AL = 1 ES:BX = Pointer to video state buffer CX = Requested states Bit 0 = Save or restore video hardware state	AL = 1Ch	This function writes a video state buffer from the specified memory area.

Bit 1 = Save or restore
video BIOS state

Bit 2 = Save or restore
BIOS data area

Bit 3 to 15 = Always Set
to zero

Restore Video   AL = 1Ch   This function writes a video state buffer from the
State   specified memory area.

AH = 1Ch
AL = 2
ES:BX = Pointer to video
state buffer

CX = Requested states

Bit 0 = Save or restore
video hardware
state

Bit 1 = Save or restore
video BIOS state

Bit 2 = Save or restore
BIOS data area

Bit 3 to 15 = Always
Set to zero

The Video State Buffer contains all the information used by the video subsystem. This data can be read from the video subsystem and restored using the BIOS Video State Functions.

BUFFER OFFSET	SIZE	FUNCTION
0	4 Bytes	Pointer to static functionality information
4	Byte	Video mode
5	Word	Character columns in display
7	Word	Length of regenerator buffer
9	Word	Start address in regeneration buffer
0Bh	Word	Cursor position for page 0
0Dh	Word	Cursor position for page 1
0Fh	Word	Cursor position for page 2
11h	Word	Cursor position for page 3
13h	Word	Cursor position for page 4
15h	Word	Cursor position for page 5
17h	Word	Cursor position for page 6
19h	Word	Cursor position for page 7
1Bh	Word	Cursor type
1Dh	Byte	Active display page
1Eh	Word	CRT controller address
20h	Byte	3x8 register setting
21h	Byte	3x9 register setting
22h	Byte	Character rows in display
23h	Word	Character height
25h	Byte	Active display combination code
26h	Byte	Alternate display combination code
27h	Word	Number of color supported in current Display mode
29h	Byte	Number of pages supported in current Display mode
2Ah	Byte	Number of scan lines supported in current display mode
2Bh	Byte	Primary character block
2Ch	Byte	Secondary character block
2Dh	Byte	Miscellaneous information: Bit 5 = 0 Background intensity, 1 Blinking Bit 4 = 0 No emulation, 1 Emulated Cursor

		Bit 3 = 1 Mode set default palette loading disabled
		Bit 2 = 1 Monochrome display attached
		Bit 1 = 1 Summing is active
		Bit 0 = 1 All modes on all displays are active
2Eh	3 Bytes	Reserved
31h	Byte	Amount of VGA memory available 0 = 64 KB, 1 = 128 KB, 2 = 192 KB, 3 = 256 KB
32h	Byte	Save pointer state information
		Bit 5 = 1 DCC extension active
		Bit 4 = 1 Palette override active
		Bit 3 = 1 Graphics font override active
		Bit 2 = 1 Alpha font override active
		Bit 1 = 1 Dynamic save area active
		Bit 0 = 0 512-Character set active
33h	13 Bytes	Reserved

Interrupt 11h: Equipment Determination

A BIOS interrupt that can provide useful information to your application is the Equipment Determination interrupt, which can give you an idea of whether or not your application will be able to run on the current PC.

After executing an Int 11h instruction, AX is set with the following information:

BIT	MEANING
14–15	Number of printers
13	Internal modem installed
12	Game port installed
9–11	Number of RS-232 ports
8	DMA present
6–7	Number of floppy drives
4–5	Current video mode (01 = 40 × 35 color, 10 = 80 × 25 color, 11 = 8 × 25 mono)
3	Not used
2	Pointing device (mouse) installed
1	Math co-processor installed
0	Floppy drive installed

Obviously, much of this information is irrelevant in modern PCs (which have built-in math processors or DMA as a matter of course), but much of the other information can be useful before attempting to execute an application that requires specific hardware to run correctly.

Interrupt 12: Get Memory Size

Executing an Int 12h instruction will set AX with the number of KB of RAM that are available in the PC between 0 and 640 KB. The normal value to be returned is 280h (640).

Interrupt 13h: Disk BIOS

Few things can screw up a PC as quickly and as completely as incorrect disk BIOS calls. I debated on whether or not I should include the BIOS information in this book because of the danger of someone writing incorrect data to a hard drive.

I decided to include this information because the BIOS diskette read APIs can be called for implementing an OSLess boot as well as using the disk subsystem for storing data in a nonstandard format. Nonstandard (i.e., non-MS-DOS) storage of data has the advantages of providing a reasonable level of security, as well as a denser method of storing data than would be available with MS-DOS. Also, it has the added advantage of being faster to retrieve data.

Care should be taken that no disk BIOS operations are ever directed toward the hard file containing the boot operating system information.

After almost every disk BIOS function, AH contains a Status byte, the values returned are defined as:

VALUE	FLOPPY/HARD	DESCRIPTION
00h	Both	No error
01h	Both	Invalid disk parameter (bad command)
02h	Both	Address mark not found
03h	Both	Attempted write on protected disk
04h	Both	Sector not found
05h	Fixed	Reset failed
06h	Floppy	Diskette not in drive
07h	Fixed	Bad parameter table
08h	Floppy	DMA overrun on previous operation
09h	Both	Attempt to cross 65-KB segment on DMA operation
0Ah	Fixed	Bad sector flag

0Bh	Fixed	Bad cylinder detected
0Ch	Floppy	Media type not found
0Dh	Fixed	Invalid of sectors in format
0Eh	Fixed	Control data address mark detected
0Fh	Fixed	DMA arbitration level out of valid range
10h	Both	CRC or ECC error on disk read
11h	Fixed	ECC corrected data error
20h	Both	Controller error
40h	Both	Seek operation failed
80h	Both	Drive timed out/not ready
0AAh	Fixed	Drive not ready
0BBh	Fixed	Undefined error
0CCh	Fixed	Write error
0E0h	Fixed	Status error
0FFh	Fixed	Sense operation failed

Along with the Status byte, the carry flag is used to indicate if an error has occurred.

The Disk BIOS APIs are as follows. As a couple of notes, for every time *DL* is specified as the Drive, if Bit 7 is set, then the drive referred to is a hard drive. Also I have taken out two APIs that were specific to the PC/XT under the assumption that they will not be required for any kind of modern application.

8

APPENDICES

FUNCTION	INPUT	OUTPUT	COMMENTS
Reset Disk System	AH = 00h DL = Drive	AH = Status	Reset the specified drive. If Bit 7 of DL is set, then reset hard drive, else floppy.
Get Disk System Status	AH = 01h DL = Drive	AH = Status AL = Previous status Carry = Set on error	Return the status information for the drive. If Bit 7 of DL is set then hard drive specified, else floppy.
Read Disk	AH = 02h AL = Number of sectors to read CH = Cylinder number CL = Sector number DH = Head number DL = Drive number ES:BX = Pointer to read buffer	AH = Status AL = Sectors read Carry = Set on error	Read the specified number of sectors from the disk. If Bit 7 of DL is set then hard drive selected, else floppy.
Write Disk	AH = 03h AL = Number of sectors to write CH = Cylinder number CL = Sector number DH = Head number DL = Drive number ES:BX = Pointer to data to write	AH = Status AL = Number of sectors written Carry = Set on error	Write the specified number of sectors to the disk from the buffer pointed to by ES:BX. If Bit 7 of DL is set then hard drive selected, else floppy.
Verify Sectors	AH = 04h AL = Number of sectors to read CH = Cylinder number	AH = Status AL = Sectors read Carry = Set on error	Compare the data in the specified sectors to the buffer. If Bit 7 of DL is set then hard drive selected, else floppy.

		Description
	CL = Sector number DH = Head number DL = Drive number ES:BX = Pointer to read buffer	
Format Cylinder	AH = 05h AL = Number of sectors CH = Cylinder number CL = Sector number DH = Head number DL = Drive number	AH = Status Carry = Set on Error	Format the sectors in the specified cylinder. Normally the first sector is zero and the number to format is the number of sectors per track.
Format Cylinder And Set Bad Sector Flags	AH = 06h AL = Interleave Ratio CH = Cylinder number CL = Sector number DH = Head number DL = Drive number	AH = Status Carry = Set on Error	Format the sectors in the specified cylinder. This function is normally only used with hard drives with the parameters known.
Format Drive Starting at Cylinder	AH = 06h AL = Interleave ratio CH = Cylinder number CL = Sector number DH = Head number DL = Drive number	AH = Status Carry = Set on error	Format the Drive starting at the specified cylinder. This Function is normally only used with hard drives with the parameters known.
Read the Drive Parameters	AH = 08h DL = Drive number	AX = 0 BH = 0 BL = Drive type (0 = 360 KB 1 = 1.2 MB 2 = 720 KB 3 = 1.44 MB	Return the Information on the specified drive. If bit 7 of DL is set, then hard drive else floppy.

FUNCTION	INPUT	OUTPUT	COMMENTS
		CH = Maximum cylinders CL = Maximum sectors/track DH = Maximum heads DL = Number of drives Carry = Set on error ES:DI = Pointer to parameter table	
Initialize Drive Pair Characteristics	AH = 09h DL = Drive number	AH = Status Carry = Set on error	Initialize drives on single disk bus.
Read Long Sectors	AH = 0Ah AL = Number of sectors CX = Cylinder number DH = Head number DL = Drive number ES:BX = Pointer to read buffer	AH = Status Carry = Set on error	Read the full track of the drive.
Write Long Sectors	AH = 0Bh All = Number of sectors CX = Cylinder number DH = Head number DL = Drive number ES:BX = Pointer to write buffer	AH = Status Carry = Set on error	Write the full track of the drive.
Seek	AH = 0Ch AL = Number of sectors CX = Cylinder number DH = Head number	AH = Status Carry = Set on error	Move the current drive pointer to a new position.

Function	Input	Output	Description
	DL = Drive number		
Alternate Disk	AH = 0Dh DL = Drive number	AH = Status Carry = Set on error	Reset the disk drive.
Test Drive Ready	AH = 10h DL = Drive number	AH = Status Carry = Set on error	Test drive's current state.
Recalibrate Drive	AH = 11h DL = Drive	AH = Status Carry = Set on error	Reset the drive to specified parameters.
Controller RAM Diagnostic	AH = 12h AL = Number of sectors CH = Cylinder CL = Sector DH = Head DL = Drive	AH = Status AL = 0 Carry = Set on error	Test the disk controller for specified location of the disk.
Controller Drive Diagnostic	AH = 13h AL = Number of sectors CH = Cylinder CL = Sector DH = Head DL = Drive	AH = Status AL = 0 Carry = Set on error	Test the controller's ability to write to the disk.
Controller Internal Diagnostic	AH = 14h AL = Number of sectors CH = Cylinder CL = Sector DH = Head DL = Drive	AH = Status AL = 0 Carry = Set on error	Run internal drive diagnostics
Read DASDType	AH = 15h DL = Drive	AH = DASD type 0 = Drive not present 1 = No change line supported	Return the disk type with number of blocks available if a hard drive.

FUNCTION	INPUT	OUTPUT	COMMENTS
		2 = Change line supported 3 = Fixed disk CX:DX = Number of 512-byte blocks Carry = Set on error	
Read Diskette Change Line Status	AH = 16h DL = Drive	AH = Status Carry = Set on error	Check if diskette has been removed/changed.
Set Diskette Type For Format	AH = 17h AL = DASD Tgype 1 = 360-KB disk/drive 2 = 360-KB disk in 1.2-MB drive 3 = 1.2-MB disk/drive 4 = 70-KB disk/drive DL = Drive	AH = Status Carry = Set on error	Set the drive controller to the correct type of diskette media before format.
Set Hard Disk Type for Format	AH = 18h CH = Number of tracks CL = Number of sectors DL = Drive	AH = Status ES:DI = Pointer to parameter table Carry = Set on error	Set the drive controller with the correct hard-disk parameters before format.

Interrupt 14h: RS-232 Communications

The RS-232 Communications BIOS APIs are actually some of the least-usable functions in the PC's ROM. The RS-232 handshaking lines must be properly wired between the PC and the device it is to be communicating with. If these lines are not properly connected, data will not be transferred and the BIOS functions will not return for a number of seconds before the function times out. It is easy to fake this out by shorting the DSR/DTR and CTS/RTS lines together, but I find it much easier to interface directly with the 8250 serial port.

The modem and line status register bits are defined as:

BIT	MODEM STATUS REGISTER
7	Received line signal detect
6	Ring indicator (RI)
5	Data set ready (DSR)
4	Clear to send (CTS)
3	Delta receive signal detect
2	Trailing edge ring detector
1	Delta data set ready (DSR)
0	Delta clear to send (CTS)

BIT	MODEM CONTROL REGISTER
5–7	Reserved
4	Loop TX to RX internally
3	Out2
2	Out1 (When set, serial interrupts enabled)
1	Request to send (RTS)
0	Data terminal ready (DTR)

BIT	LINE STATUS BYTE
7	Time out
6	TX shift register empty
5	TX holding register empty
4	Break detect
3	Framing error
2	Parity error
1	Overrun error
0	Data ready

8

APPENDICES

The COM port Initialization Parameter is defined as:

BIT	FUNCTION	
5–7	Baud rate specification:	000 to 110 bps 001 to 150 bps 010 to 300 bps 011 to 600 bps 100 to 1200 bps (default) 101 to 2400 bps 110 to 4800 bps 111 to 9600 bps
3–4	Parity:	00 to no parity 01 to odd parity 10 to no parity 11 to even parity
2	Stop Bits	0 to 1 stop bit 1 to 2 stop bits
0–1	Word Length	10 to 7 bits 11 to 9 bits

The RS-232 Communications APIs are:

FUNCTION	INPUT	OUTPUT	COMMENTS
Initialize Communications Port	AH = 00h AL = Init parameter DX = Port number	AH = Line status AL = Modem status	Initialize the serial port. Note, AH = 004h provides extended capabilities
Write Character	AH = 01h AL = Character DX = Port	AH = Line status AL = Modem status	Send the character when the modem handshake allows or time out.
Read Character	AH = 02h DX = Port	AH = Line status AL = Character	Wait for the character to be received when the modem handshake allows or time out.
Status Request	AH = 03h DX = Port	AH = Line status AL = Modem status	Return the current serial port status.
Extended Port Initialize	AH = 04h AL = 0 for no break, 1 for sending break BH = Parity 0 = No parity 1 = Odd parity 2 = Even parity 3 = Odd stick parity 4 = Even stick parity BL = Stop Bits 0 = One 1 = Two CH = Word Length 0 = 5 bits 1 = 6 bits 2 = 7 bits 3 = 8 bits	AH = Line status AL = Modem status	This is a more complete serial port initialize.

FUNCTION	INPUT	OUTPUT	COMMENTS
	CL = Data Rate		
	0 = 110 bps		
	1 = 150 bps		
	2 = 300 bps		
	3 = 600 bps		
	4 = 1200 bps		
	5 = 2400 bps		
	6 = 4800 bps		
	7 = 9600 bps		
	8 = 19200 bps		
	DX = Port		
Read Modem Control Register	AH = 05h AL = 0 DX = Port	BL = Modem-control register	Return the contents of the modem-control register
Write to Modem Control Register	AH = 05h AL = 1 BL = New modem-control register value	AH = Line status AL = Modem status	Set the modem-control register to a new state.

Interrupt 15h: System Services

BIOS Interrupt 15h was originally used for the cassette interface in the PC to turn on and off the motor and pass data between a cassette recorder and the PC. This hardware has not been included on a PC's motherboard for more than 15 years (as I write this), so I have not included the BIOS calls in this summary.

This really leaves Interrupt 15 available for other BIOS services, which have been used to provide an interface to advanced hardware features within the PC and processor. The APIs allow control of specific devices, access to Protect-mode memory in the PC, and a hardware interface to a built-in pointing device.

To access Protect-mode memory (also known as *Extended Memory*), a *descriptor table* is defined as 48 bytes that could be declared in the assembler format:

```
GDT:                          ; Global Descriptor Table
Dummy        db    0 rep 8    ; Eight Bytes Initialized to
                              ; Zero for the "Dummy" value
Location     db    0 rep 8    ; Eight Bytes Initialized to
                              ; Zero for BIOS GDT Reference
Source       dw    ?          ; Segment Limit (1 to 65535 Bytes)
             db    ?, ?, ?    ; 24 Bit Physical Address
             db    093h       ; Access Rights (Read/Write)
             dw    0
Destination  dw    ?          ; Segment Limit (1 to 65535 Bytes)
             db    ?, ?, ?    ; 24 Bit Physical Address
             db    093h       ; Access Rights (Read/Write
             dw    0
BIOS         db    0 rep 8    ; BIOS Protected Mode Segment
SS           db    0 rep 8    ; Protected mode Stack Area
```

The System configuration parameters are defined as the nine-byte table:

OFFSET	SIZE	DESCRIPTION
0	Word	Number of bytes in table (minimum 10)
2	Byte	System model number
3	Byte	System submodel number
4	Byte	BIOS revision level
5	Byte	Features information Bit 7 Set for hard disk using DMA 3 Bit 6 Set for second interrupt chip present Bit 5 Set for real-time clock enabled Bit 4 Keyboard intercept enabled Bit 3 Set for external event supported Bit 2 Set for extended BIOS area allocation Bit 0–1 Reserved
6	Byte	Feature information
7	Byte	Feature information
8	Byte	Feature information
9	Byte	Feature information

The Mouse Port Status Byte is defined as:

VALUE	DESCRIPTION
0	No error
1	Invalid function call
2	Invalid input to function call
3	Interface error
4	Resend
5	No far call installed for device

FUNCTION	INPUT	OUTPUT	COMMENTS
Open Device	AH = 80h BX = Device ID CX = Process ID Carry = 0	AH = 0 AL = 80h	Open a device driver for an application
Close Device	AH = 81h BX = Device ID CX = Process ID Carry = 0	AH = 0 AL = 81h	Close the device driver
Program Terminate	AH = 82h BX = Device ID Carry = 0	AH = 0 AL = 82h	Terminate the process
Event Wait Set	AH = 83h AL = 0 ES:BX = Pointer to flag byte CX:DX = Number of μS to setting Bit 7 of flag byte	AH = 83h	Bit 7 of the flag byte will be set after the number of usecs in CX:DX have passed. The timing has a granularity of 976 ms.

Function	Input	Output	Description
Event Wait Cancel	AH = 83h AL = 1	AH = 83h	Turn off the event wait operation
Joystick Switch Read	AH = 084h DX = 0	AL = Switches in bits 4 to 7	Read the four joystick switches (two in each joystick). Normally, hardware is accessed directly.
Joystick Potentiometer Read	AH = 084h DX = 1	AH = A(x) BX = A(y) CX = B(x) DX = B(y)	Read the four joystick potentiometers (two in each joystick). Normally hardware is accessed directly.
"SysReq" Key Press Status	AH = 85h Carry = 0	AL = Key Status (0 for pressed)	This API gives the capability of polling the SysReq key.
Wait	AH = 86h CX:DX = Wait in μs	Carry = Set if wait operation already initiated	This API does not return until the set number of microseconds has passed. The timer has a granularity of 976 μs.
Move Block	AH = 87 h ES:SI = Pointer to the global descriptor block CX = Number of words to move	Ahh = Status 0 = Successful, 1 = RAM Parity, 2 = Error 3 = Gate address fail	Move the block data in or out of real to extended memory. The use of this API is not recommended because of the opportunity to damage the contents of memory outside the current 1-MB memory space.
Get Extended Memory Size	AH = 88h	AX = Number of 1-BK blocks	Return the memory above 1 MB installed in the PC.
Switch to Protected Mode	AH = 89h BH = Index to level 1 BL = Index to level 2 ES:DI = Pointer to global desciptor table	AX = Status (0 if successful, 0FFh if unsuccessful) All other registers destroyed	This API is not recommended because protected mode is usually used by Windows or other operating systems or applications and execution within this area will cause problems with the other program's execution.

FUNCTION	INPUT	OUTPUT	COMMENTS

Device Busy	AH = 90h
	AL = Type Code
	  0 = Hard disk
	  1 = Floppy disk
	  2 = Keyboard
	  3 = Mouse
	  80h = network time out
	  FCh = Hard disk time out
	  FDh = Floppy disk motor time out
	  FEh = Printer time out
		Carry = Set if Wait Time
		  Requirements Satisfied
			This API will allow an application to force an error in the specified hardware.

Interrupt Complete	AH = 91h	AL = Type Code
		  (0 = Hard disk time out
		  (1 = Floppy disk time out
		  (2 = Keyboard
		  (3 = Mouse
		  (80h = Network
		  (FCh = Hard disk time out
		  (FDh = Floppy disk time out
		  (FEh = Printer Time out
			Indicate to BIOS that the pending interrupt has completed.

Return System Configuration Information	AH = C0h	ES:BX = Pointer to system descriptor table	Return a pointer to the system information.
Return External BIOS Segment Address	AH = C1h	ES = Segment of extended BIOS data area	Return a pointer to any extended BIOS code.
Enable Pointing Device	AH = C2h AL = 0 BH = 1	AH = Status Carry = Set on error	Enable the Built-n Mouse hardware.
Disable Pointing	AH = C2h	AH = Status	Disable the built-in mouse hardware.

Command	Input	Output	Description
Device	AL = 0 BH = 0	Carry = Set on error	
Reset Pointing Device	AH = C2h AL = 1	AH = Status BH = Device ID BL = Destroyed Carry = Set on error	Reset the built-in mouse hardware.
Set Pointing Device Sample Rate	AH = C2h AL = 2 BH = Sample Rate (0 to 10 /sec, 1 to 20 /sec, 2 to 40 /sec, 3 to 60 /sec)	AH = Status Carry = Set on error	Specify the Rate in which Data is Sampled.
Set Pointing Device Resolution	AH = C2h AL = 3 BH = Resolution (0 to 1 /mm, 1 to 2 /mm, 2 to 4 /mm, 3 to 6 /mm)	AH = Status BH = Device ID BL = Destroyed Carry = Set on error	Specify the built-in mouse hardware pointing resolution.
Read Pointing Device Type	AH = C2h AL = 4	AH = Status BH = Device ID Carry = Set on error	Read device type. If successful, AH = 0.
Initialize Pointing Device	AH = C2h AL = 5 BH = Bytes in data package	AH = Status BH = Device ID Carry = Set on error	Initialize the mouse hardware.
Extended Pointing Device Commands	AH = C2h AL = 6	AH = Status BL = Status byte 1	These commands provide the current mouse hardware status information.

FUNCTION	INPUT	OUTPUT	COMMENTS

	BH = Command
	(0 = Get status
	(1 = Set scaling to 1 to 1
	(2 = Set scaling to 2 to 1
		Bit 6 to 0 Stream mode
		1 = Remote mode
		Bit 5 = 0 disabled
		Bit 4 = 0 1-to-1 scaling
		Bit 2 Set for left button
		Bit 0 Set for right button
		CL = Status Byte 2
		0 - 1 /mm,
		1 - 2 /mm,
		2 - 4 /mm,
		3 - 6 //m)
		DL = Status
		Byte 3
		0Ah = 10 /sec,
		14h = 20 /sec,
		28h = 40 /sec,
		3Ch = 60 /sec,
		50h = 80 /sec,
		64h = 100 /sec,
		C8h = 200 /sec	

Device Driver Initialize Call	AH = C2h AL = 7 ES:BX = Pointer to device driver	AH = Status Carry = Set on error	Initialize the device driver

Interrupt 16h: Keyboard Interface

The keyboard BIOS APIs simply read the keyboard buffer and converts the scan codes read from the buffer into ASCII characters or control characters as explained in Appendix C. The keyboard system variables keep track of the *Shift*, *Ctrl*, and *Alt* keys, as well to ensure that the correct key state is returned.

For event-driven applications, you should use the Read Status APIs before the read character to see if the keyboard buffer has anything ready to read. If nothing unread is in the keyboard buffer, then the API will wait indefinitely for a key to be pressed.

Typically, I only use the Extended keyboard APIs because they support modern keyboards with 12 function keys (the original PC and PC/AT keyboards had only 10 function keys). In the Status APIs, up to two flags bytes are returned and are in the following formats.

Keyboard flags byte:

BIT	FUNCTION
7	Set when Insert state active
6	Set when Caps Lock active
5	Set when Num Lock active
4	Set when Scroll Lock active
3	Set when a *Alt* key held down
2	Set when a *Ctrl* key held down
1	Set when the *Left Shift* key held down
0	Set when the *Right Shift* key held down

Extended keyboard flags byte:

BIT	FUNCTION
7	Set when "SysReq" Key Pressed
6	Set when "Caps Lock" Key Pressed
5	Set when "Num Lock" Key Pressed
4	Set when "Scroll Lock" Key Pressed
3	Set when Right "Alt" Key Pressed
2	Set when Right "Ctrl" Key Pressed
1	Set when Left "Alt" Key Pressed
0	Set when Left "Ctrl" Key Pressed

The keyboard BIOS APIs follow.

FUNCTION	INPUT	OUTPUT	COMMENTS
Read Character	AH = 00h	AH = Scan code AL = ASCII character	This command returns the next unread key from the buffer or waits for a key to return.
Read Status	AH = 01h	AH = Scan code AL = ASCII character Zero = Set if no character available	Poll the keyboard buffer and return the next keystroke or set the zero flag.
Read Flags	AH = 02h	AH = 00 AL = Keyboard flags byte	Return the keyboard flags byte

Set Typematic Rate and Delay	AH = 03h
	AL = 5
	BH = Delay
	  0 to 250 ms
	  1 to 500 ms
	  2 to 750 ms
	  3 to 1000 ms
	BL = Rate
	  0 to 30 cps
	  4 to 20 cps
	  8 to 15 cps
	  12 to 10 cps
	  16 to 7.5 cps
	  20 to 5 cps
	  24 to 3.75 cps
	  28 to 2.5 cps
		None	Set the keyboard delay before resending the held-down character and then the rate at which they are set. This function should be set by the operating system utilities, rather than from an appciiation. I have not put in the intermediate values.

Read Typematic Rate and Delay	AH = 03h AL = 6	BH = Delay BL = Rate	Read the current delay and rate set into the keyboard.

Keyboard Write	AH = 05h BH = Scan code BL = ASCII character	AL = 0 if buffer written successfully	This command writes a new character into the keyboard buffer (and not to the keyboard or other external device as the name would imply).
Keyboard Functionality Determination	AH = 09h	AL = Function code Bit 3 Set if can read delay/rate Bit 2 Set if can set delay/rate Bit 1 Set if cannot set delay/rate Bit 0 Set if return to default delay/rate supported	This API returns the capabilities of the keyboard and hardware to change the typematic rate and delay.
Extended Keyboard Read	AH = 10h	AH = Scan code AL = ASCII code	Return the full keyboard code if keyboard buffer has an unread key or wait for a key to return.
Extended Keyboard Status	AH = 11h	AH = Scan code AL = ASCII code Zero = Set if No character to return	Check the keyboard buffer and return the next key to process or set the zero flag.
Extended Shift Status	AH = 12h	AH = Extended keyboard flags AL = Keyboard flags byte	Return the extended keyboard Shift/Ctrl/Alt status.

8 APPENDICES

Interrupt 17h: Printer Interface

The printer interface is designed for a Centronics-compatible ASCII parallel printer. The API interface is strictly designed for this application and is not suited for using as part of an interface to your own hardware.

The printer status byte passes back information from the printer port (along with program status information) directly:

BIT	FUNCTION
7	Not busy
6	Acknowledge
5	Out of paper
4	Selected
3	Error
0	Time out

The printer APIs follow. The printer number is defined as 0 for LPT1, 1 for LPT2, 2 for LPT3, and 3 for LPT4.

FUNCTION	INPUT	OUTPUT	COMMENTS
Write Character	AH = 00h AL = Character DX = Printer number	AH = Status	Send the specified character. If the printer is not present or not working, the Time-Out bit will be set.
Initialize Printer Port	AH = 01h DX = Printer number	AH = Status	Initialize the printer port and printer connected to it.
Status Request	AH = 02h DX = Printer number	AH = Status	Return the current printer status.

Interrupt 19h: Bootstrap Loader

Once the POST has finished executing, an *Int 19h* instruction is executed to load the operating system. The handler at this vector checks the primary boot drive (normally set in the RTC/CMOS information to diskette drive *A:* or a network card) and attempts to load Cylinder 0, Sector 1 into address 0x00000:0x07C00. If it is successful, execution is passed to this address.

If the read is not successful, then there is an attempt to check the secondary boot drive (normally hard drive *C:*) and tries to load address 0x0000:0x07C00 from each drive with the boot sector. If the attempts to load a boot sector are unsuccessful, then an *Int 18h* instruction is executed to attempt a cassette BASIC boot. In most PCs, an error message is displayed.

The *Int 19h* instruction should not be used as a method to reset or reboot a PC. Executing an *Int 19h* instruction will reset the disk hardware without regard to the current disk status. If a file is left open, then there will be a chance for it to be corrupted and will prevent the PC from booting again later.

Interrupt 1Ah: System Timer and RTC Services

The system timer and RTC APIs were introduced with the PC/AT as a standard method of accessing a *Real-Time Clock (RTC)* chip built onto the PC's motherboard. The information passed between the APIs and an application can be somewhat unusual, so be sure that you check to see what is specified as the data.

8

APPENDICES

FUNCTION	INPUT	OUTPUT	COMMENTS
Read Clock Count	AH = 00h	AH = 00h AL = 24 hour CX:DX = Number of 55-ms periods since the day the PC was started	This API returns the number of 18.2 intervals per second clock interrupts since the PC was booted up with AL recording the number of days the PC has been running.
Set Clock Count	AH = 01h CX:DX = Number of 55-ms periods since the day the PC was started	AH = 0 Carry = Set on error	Set the Number of 19.2 intervals per second clock interrups since the PC was booted up (change the PC's time). This function should be accessed using the operating system utilities.
Read Real-Time Clock Time	AH = 02h	AH = 00h AL = BCD hours CH = BCD hours CL = BCD minutes DH = BCD seconds DL = Set if operative	Read the battery-backed-up RTC contents.
Set Real-Time Clock Time	AH = 03h CH = BCD hours CL = BCD minutes DH = BCD seconds DL = DST option if set to 1	AH = 0	Set the battery-backed-up RTC contents. This API should only be used by the operating system utilities.
Read Real-time Clock Date	AH = 04h	AH = 0 CH = BCD century (only 19 or 20 valid)	Read the current date from the RTC chip.

Function	Input	Output	Description
Set Real-Time Clock Date	AH = 05h CH = BCD century (Only 19 or 20 valid) CL = BCD year DH = BCD month DL = BCD day	CL = BCD year DH = BCD month DL = BCD day AH = 0	Set the current Date into the RTC Chip. This API should only be used by operating system utilities.
Set Real Time Clock Alarm	AH = 06h CH = BCD hours CL = BCD minutes CH = BCD sections	Carry = Set if alarm already set or if no RTC.	Setup RTC hardware to request an interrupt number 70h.
Turn Off Real Time Clock Alarm	AH = 07h	Carry = Set if alarm not set or if no RTC.	Turn off the RTC alarm.
Read Real Time Clock Alarm	AH = 09h	CH = BCD hours CL = BCD minutes DH = BCD seconds DL = Alarm status 0 = Alarm disabled 1 = Alarm enabled	Read the current RTC alarm settings.
Read System Timer Day Count	AH = 0Ah	CX = Number of days since Jan. 1, 1980.	Get the date information in a non-BCD format.
Set System Timer Day Count	AH = 0Bh CX = Number of days since Jan. 1, 1980	None	Set the current date. Note that this API should only be called by the operating-system API.

Interrupt 33: Mouse Interrupt

Normally, interrupt 33h (for the mouse or pointing device) is lumped in with the MS-DOS operating system functions because it is loaded in with the operating system before any applications are run (but after the regular BIOS functions and hardware are set up). I tend to think of it as a BIOS API because it interfaces to device hardware.

The mouse BIOS interrupt functions do require an operating system to work, however. If a mouse or other pointing device is going to be used in an operating systemless environment (i.e., from boot ROM or OSless disk boot), then the mouse hardware will have to be interfaced with directly by the application.

Normally, a program such as MOUSE.COM is run from AUTOEXEC.BAT to load the mouse-control software and BIOS APIs.

I have broken with this convention and put the mouse interrupt functions in with the BIOS functions because it seems to bit better in this category. The mouse has become a standard device in the PC and, even with different "pointing devices" (the PC that I am writing this on has a touchpad and my laptop has a trackpoint that looks like a pencil eraser), the same functions are used to interface to the application.

One difference to note between the mouse and other interrupt functions is their use of all of the AX register (and not just AH) for specifying the function. Many of the functions are quite complex and are required for advanced functions; I recommend that only the simple position and button state functions be used.

FUNCTION	INPUT	OUTPUT	COMMENTS
Mouse Reset and Status	AX = 00h	AX = Status BX = Buttons	For the reset and status function, if a mouse and software has been installed, upon return AX will equal 1 (otherwise 0) and BX will contain the number of buttons on the mouse (normally 2).
Show Cursor	AX = 01h	None	The cursor flag is incremented. If the result is equal to 0 then the cursor will be displayed.
Hide Cursor	AX = 02h	None	The cursor flag is decremented and the cursor is not displayed on the screen.
Get Button Status and Mouse Position	AX = 03h	BX = Pressed flags CX = Horizontal position DX = Vertical position	In BX, if Bit 0 is set, then the left button is pressed and Bit 1 represents the right button. For three-button mice, Bit 2 is the middle button.
Set Mouse Cursor Position	AX = 04h CX = Horizontal position DX = Vertical position	None	Move the mouse to the specified position.
Get Button Press Information	AX = 05h BX = Button	AX = Status BX = Count CX = Horizontal position of last press. DX = Vertical position of last press	Bit 0 of AX is the left button and Bit 1 of AX is the right button. *Count* is the number of times the button has been pressed. The cursor position returned is the last position that the button was in when it was pressed.
Get Button Release Information	AX = 06h BX = Button	AX = Status BX = Count CX = Horizontal position of last release DX = Vertical position of last release	This function works like *AX = 5*, but returns the cursor position when the button was released. This function should only be used after checking that the Button is no longer pressed.

FUNCTION	INPUT	OUTPUT	COMMENTS
Set Min/Max Horizontal Cursor Position	AX = 07h CX = Minimum position DX = Maximum position	None	Cursor movement is restricted to the max./min.set.
Set Min/Max Vertical Cursor Position	AX = 08h CX = Minimum position DX = Maximum position	None	Cursor movement is restricted to the max./min. set.
Set Graphics Cursor Block	AX = 009h BX = Horizontal "hot spot" CX = Vertical "hot spot" ES:DX = Pointer to screen/cursor masks	None	This function changes the mouse cursor to the specified graphic.
Set Text Cursor	AX = 0Ah BX = Cursor type CX = Screen mask or cursor start DX = Cursor mask or cursor end	None	This function sets the cursor type in text Windows or screens. If a built-in hardware cursor is to be used then the *cursor start* and *cursor end* are the same values as specified in the video BIOS (Int 10h).
Read Mouse Motion Counters	AX = 0Bh	CX = Horizontal count DX = Vertical count	CX/DX have the distance from last call to function. Units are "mickeys" that are specific to the mouse.

Set Interrupt Call Mask and Address	AX = 0Ch
	CX = Mask
	  Bit 0 = Cursor move
	  Bit 1 = Left button pressed
	  Bit 2 = Left button release
	  Bit 3 = Right button pressed
	  Bit 4 = Right button released
		None	This function sets an address of an interrupt handler to jump to if the Mask conditions in CX are met. Upon entry into interrupt handler, the following registers are set:
			AX = Mask bit, which triggered interrupt
			BX = Button state (Bit 0 = left, Bit 1 = right)
			CX = Horizontal cursor position
			DX = Vertical cursor position
			DI = Vertical cursor position
			SI = Horizontal mouse counts

Function	Input	Output	Description
	ES:DX = Interrupt handler address		
Set Light Pen Emulation ON	AX = 0Dh	None	In this mode, the pen is down when both buttons are pressed and up when both buttons are released.
Set Light Pen Emulation off	AX = 0Eh	None	This function disables the light pen emulation.
Set the Mickey/Pixel Ratio	AX = 0Fh CX = Horizontal ratio DX = Vertical ratio		This function sets how far on the screen a "mickey" will move the mouse's cursor. This function should only be used in the operating system's setting the mouse sensitivity utility.
Conditional Mouse Cursor off	AX = 10h CX = Left Screen boundary SI = Right screen boundary DX = Upper screen boundary DI = Lower screen boundary	None	The mouse will be turned off if the specified window is entered. Int 33h AX = 01h is used to turn it back on.
Set Double Speed Threshold	AX = 13h DX = Threshold speed	None	Set the maximum mouse movement speed. This function should never be used; the maximum mouse movement speed should be set by operating system utilities.
Swap Interrupt Subroutines	AX = 14h BX:DX = Pointer to the new handler CX = New call mask Bit 0 = Cursor move Bit 1 = Left button	BX:DX = Pointer to the old interrupt handler CX = Old interrupt handler's mask	Change which handler is going to respond to the specific mouse interrupt requests.

FUNCTION	INPUT	OUTPUT	COMMENTS
	pressed Bit 2 = Left button release Bit 3 = Right button pressed Bit 4 = Right button released		
Get Mouse Drive State Storage Requirements	AX = 15h	BX = Buffer size	Find out how much memory (in bytes) is required for the mouse driver.
Save Mouse Driver State	AX = 16h ES:DX = Pointer to buffer	None	Save the current mouse driver. The size required is found using interrupt 33h, AX = 15h.
Restore Mouse Driver State	AX = 17h ES:DX = Pointer to buffer	None	Copy buffer into the mouse driver.
Set Alternate Call mask Subroutine	AX = 18h ES:DX = Pointer to interrupt handler CX = New call mask Bit 0 = Cursor move Bit 1 = Left button pressed Bit 2 = Left button release Bit 3 = Right button pressed Bit 4 = Right button released Bit 5 = *Shift* pressed with button press or release	None	Add another interrupt handler for mask bits

Function	Parameters	Returns	Description
	Bit 6 = *Ctrl* pressed with button press or release		
	Bit 7 = *Alt* pressed with button press or release		
Get User Alternate Call mask Subroutine	AX = 19h ES:DX = Pointer to interrupt handler CX = New call mask Bit 0 = Cursor move Bit 1 = Left button pressed Bit 2 = Left button release Bit 3 = Right button pressed Bit 4 = Right button released Bit 5 = *Shift* pressed with button press or release Bit 6 = *Ctrl* pressed with button press or release Bit 7 = *Alt* pressed with button press or release	AX = Status BX:DX = Pointer to interrupt handler CX = User interrupt handler mask	Return a pointer to user's interrupt handler. If status = –1, then BX, CX, and DX are all equal to zero.
Set Mouse Sensitivity	AX = 1Ah BX = Horizontal "mickey"	None	Specify how the mouse is to operate. This function should only be used by the operating system utilities.

FUNCTION	INPUT	OUTPUT	COMMENTS
	sensitivity number CX = Vertical "mickey" sensitivity number DX = Threshold for double speed		
Get Mouse Sensitivity	AX = 1Bh	BX = Horizontal "mickey" sensitivity number CX = Vertical "mickey" sensitivity number DX = Threshold for double speed	Read the current mouse/pointing device sensitivity values
Set Mouse Interrupt Rate	AX = 1Ch AX = Interrupt rate	None	Set the interrupt rate as: 0 = No interrupts allowed 1 = 30 interrupts per second 2 = 50 interrupts per second 3 = 100 interrupts per second 4 = 200 interrupts per second
Set CRT Page Number	AX = 1Dh BX = CRT page	None	Set a new current display page. Int 10h, AH = 05h should be used instead.
Get CRT Page Number	AX = 1Eh	BX = CRT page	Get the current display page.
Disable Mouse Driver	AX = 1Fh	AX = Status ES:BX = Original interrupt 33h vector	Stop the mouse driver from requesting interrupts
Enable Mouse Driver	AX = 20h	None	Enable the mouse driver.
Mouse Driver Software	AX = 21h	AX = Status BX = 2	Reset the mouse driver software. Status = –1 if the mouse driver is installed, 21h otherwise.

Reset		

Set System Languages	AX = 22h
	BX = Language number
	  0 = English
	  1 = French
	  2 = Dutch
	  3 = German
	  4 = Swedish
	  5 = Finnish
	  6 = Spanish
	  7 = Portuguese
	  8 = Italian
		None	This function should never be used, instead the operating system utilities should be used.

Get System Language Number	AX = 23h	BX = Language number
		  0 = English
		  1 = French
		  2 = Dutch
		  3 = German
		  4 = Swedish
		  5 = Finnish
		  6 = Spanish
		  7 = Portuguese
		  8 = Italian
			Return the current language the operating system is using.

Get Mouse Type, Driver Version and IRQ Number	AX = 24h	BX = Mouse driver version
		CH = Mouse type
		  1 = Bus mouse
		  2 = Serial mouse
		  3 = InPort mouse
		  4 = PS/2 mouse
			Return the operating information for the mouse used.

FUNCTION	INPUT	OUTPUT	COMMENTS
Get General Mouse Driver Information	AX = 25h	5 = HP mouse CL = IRQ number AH = Status Bit 7 = Driver Type (1 = sys, 0 = com) Bit 6 (1 = integrated) Bit 4–5 = Cursor type (00 = Software, 01 = Hardware text, 1x = Graphics) Bit 0–3 = Int 33h, AX = 1Ch interrupt rate AL = Driver version BX = fCursor lock CX = FinMouse code DX = fMouse busy	Return driver information. This information should not be used in an application.
Get Maximum Virtual Co-ordinates Information	AX = 26h	BX = Mouse disabled flag CX = X maximum DX = Y maximum	This information is used to determine the maximum size available in an application screen. Mouse disabled flag = 1 when the mouse is disabled.
Get Screen/Cursor Masks and Mickey Count	AX = 27h	AX = Screen mask value or cursor line start BX = Cursor mask value or cursor line end CX = Horizontal "mickey" count	Return cursor information

Function	Registers	Description
	DX = Vertical "mickey" count	
Set Video Mode	AX = 28h CX = Requested video mode DX = Font size	Set the video parameters for current screen. Int 10h AH = 00h can also be used.
	CX = 0 (if successful)	
Get Cursor Hot Spot	AX = 30h	Return the mouse hot spot information and Mouse type
	AX = fCursor BX = Horizontal cursor hot spot CX = Vertical cursor hot spot DX = Type of mouse 0 = None 1 = Bus 2 = Serial 3 = InPort 4 = IBM 5 = HP	
Load Acceleration Curve Array	AX = 31h BX = Curve number ES:SI = Pointer to curve array	Load mouse acceleration curve values for a specific curve.
	AX = 0 (if successful)	
Read Acceleration Curve Array	AX = 32h	Read the acceleration curve out of memory.
	AX = 0 (if successful) BX = Current active curve ES:SI = Pointer to currently active curve	
Set/Get The	AX = 33h	Set a specific acceleration curve to be the active one
	AX = 0 (if successful)	

FUNCTION	INPUT	OUTPUT	COMMENTS
Active Acceleration Curve Array	BX = New active curve	BX = Current active curve ES:SI = Pointer to the currently active curve information.	and return its array information.
Mouse Hardware Reset	AX = 35h	AX = −1 (if successful)	Reset the mouse hardware.
Get Min/Max Virtual Coordinates	AX = 37h	AX = Current virtual X minimum CX = Current virtual X maximum BX = Current virtual Y minimum DX = Current virtual Y maximum	Return the virtual window minimum and maximum coordinates
Get MOUSE.INI Location	AX = 40h	ES:DX = Pointer to MOUSE.INI in memory.	Return a pointer to the mouse parameters in memory.

878

MS-DOS

INTERRUPT FUNCTIONS

CONTENTS AT A GLANCE

The MS-DOS APIs are actually quite straightforward and have become much easier to work with over the years. When MS-DOS was first introduced in 1981, many of the standard functions that are available in the DOS Function API ("Int 21h") were spread out around a number of other interrupts and were actually harder to work with. This has actually changed over the years to the point where MS-DOS has become a consistent and easy to work with interface.

As I go through the different interrupts, remember that the primary BIOS interrupt is Interrupt 21h and this will be the single interrupt API that you will have to work with in your applications.

Interrupt 20h–Program Terminate

The "Program Terminate" interrupt instruction ("Int 20h") can be executed to end the current program, but the Interrupt 21h function 4Ch ("End Program") is considered to be the "correct" way to do it in modern systems. The reason why Interrupt 21h, AH = 4Ch is preferred is because an error code can be passed to the executing program.

Invoking "Int 20h" will cause the memory currently allocated to the program to be freed (returned to the MS-DOS memory pool) and execution returned to the executing program with an error status of zero ("good").

Interrupt 21h–Function Request

It will probably be surprising to you, but to find a complete set of documentation for the MS-DOS interrupt 21h function is just about impossible. For the list below, I had over seven hundred pages to draw from. The reason for this large number of choices is based on the enhancements made to MS-DOS over the years, the different versions and the third parties adding APIs to interface with their devices.

The list below consists of what I consider to be the "baseline" MS-DOS APIs, which are essentially MS-DOS 3.3 API functions with a limited number of network functions. As well, I have included references to third party APIs, to give you an idea of what's available.

The list below is in a "Quick Reference" format. The list is fairly complete with most of the MS-DOS APIs that you will need when developing simple MS-DOS applications, but for Device Drivers and Network Operations, I suggest that you consult an MS-DOS Technical Reference or Device Driver specification.

FUNCTION	INPUT	OUTPUT	COMMENTS
Program Terminate	AH = 00h CS = PSP segment	N/A	End the application. If CS is not pointing to the application's CS, then the reset will not free the application's memory.
Keyboard Input With Echo	AH = 01h	AL = Keystroke	Wait for a keystroke, return it, and display it. If a function key (extended codes that start with 0×000 or 0×0E0), then execute this API twice.
Display Character	AH = 02h DL = Character	AL = Character	Send and display a character to the standard display.
Auxilliary Input	AH = 03h	AL = Character	Read a character from an auxilliary console (such as COM1').
Auxilliary Output	AH = 04h DL = Character	None	Write a character to the auxilliary console.
Printer Output	AH = 05h DL = Character	None	Write a character to the printer. If the printer is busy or unconnected, MS-DOS can take over and buffer the character or provide an error message external to the application.
Direct Console Input	AH = 06h DL = 0FFh	AL = Keyboard status (0 = nothing buffered, else character)	This API is similar to AH = 01h and requires a second read for a function key scan code. *Ctrl-Break* is not checked in this API.
Direct Console Output	AH = 06h DL != 0FFh	None	Output character to the console.
Direct Console Input without Echo	AH = 07h	AL = Character	Wait for buffered keystroke. If a function key, a second read is required. *Ctrl-Break* is not checked in this API.
Console Input Without Echo	AH = 08h	AL = Character	Wait for buffered keystroke. If a function key, a second read is required.

FUNCTION	INPUT	OUTPUT	COMMENTS
Write String to Standard Output (Print String)	AH = 09h DS:DX = Pointer to string to display.	None	Send the specified string (ending with $) To the primary printer device. This command will always return, but MS-DOS may buffer or provide an error external to the application.
Buffered Keyboard Input	AH = 0Ah DS:DX = Pointer to buffer	None	Keyboard data is saved in the buffer until enter (CR – 0xOD) is pressed. The first byte of the buffer is the size while the second byte is the number of characters actually read. If the buffer-size limit is reached, all subsequent characters until enter results in beeps.
Check Standard Input Status	AH = 0Bh	AL = Status (0FFh = Character waiting)	Check keyboard buffer status.
Clear Keyboard Buffer and Invoke Keyboard Function	AH = 0Ch AL = Function number (01h, 06h, 07h, 08h, 0Ah are valid)	AL = Character	Clear the keyboard buffer and wait for a keystroke using one of the key input APIs.
Disk Reset	AH = 0Dh	None	Write all modified FCBs to disk.
Select New Default Drive	AH = 0Eh DL = Drive number (A = 0, B = 1, etc.)	AL = Total number of drives.	Specify a new default drive.
Open File using FCB	AH = 0Fh DS:DX = Pointer to unopened FCB	AL = Status (00 = File opened)	This API opens a predefined file.
Close File using FCB	AH = 10h DS:DX = Pointer to opened FCB	AL = Status (00 = Operation successful)	Close an FCB that was opened for writing after saving changed buffers.
Search for File using FCB	AH = 11h DS:DX = Pointer to unopened FCB	AL = Status (00 = File found)	Check the current default disk and path for the file specified in the FCB. ? is allowed as a wild card.

Function	Call	Returns	Description
Search for Next Entry using FCB	AH = 12h DS:DX = Pointer to unopened FCB	AL = Status (00 = File found)	Look for the next instance of the search filename.
Delete File using FCB	AH = 13h DS:DX = Pointer to unopened FCB	AL = Status (00 = File deleted)	Deletes all files in the current directory that match the filename in the FCB.
Sequential Read using FCB	AH = 14h DS:DX = Pointer to opened FCB	AL = Status (00 = Read successful, 01 = EOF; no data read, 02h = DTA too small, 03h = Partial DTA read to EOF)	Reads from the current file the size of the DTA in the FCB.
Sequential Write Using FCB	AH = 15h DS:DX = Pointer to opened FCB	AL = Status (00 = Write successful, 01 = Disk full, 02h = Write cancelled)	Write data from the FCB's DTA buffer onto the disk file.
Create File Using FCB	AH = 16h DS:DX = Pointer to unopened FCB	AL = Status (00 = File created)	Create a file for writing and open it.
Rename File Using FCB	AH = 17h DS:DX = Pointer to unopened FCB	AL = Status (00 = File renamed)	Rename the file.
Null Function	AH = 18h	None	
Return Current Default Disk	AH = 19h	AL = Current default drive (0 = A, 1 = B ...)	This API corresponds to CP/M's BDOS function.

FUNCTION	INPUT	OUTPUT	COMMENTS
Set Disk Transfer Address (DTA)	AH = 1Ah DS:DX = DTA	None	Specify a new DTA for the application. If no DTA set, the default is offset 080h of the PSP.
Return Default Drive Allocation Table Information	AH = 1Bh	DS:BX = Pointer to media descriptor byte DX = Number of allocation units AL = Number of sectors per allocation unit CX = Size of physical sector	Return information about the current default disk.
Return Allocation Table Information For the Default Drive	AH = 1Ch DL = Drive number (0 =- A, 1 = B ...)	DS:BX = Pointer to media descriptor byte AL = Number of sectors per allocation unit CX = Size of physical sector	Same as AH = 1Bh except drive is specified.
Null Function	AH = 1Dh	None	This API corresponds to get drive bit map function.
Null Function	AH = 1Eh	None	This API corresponds to CP/M's set file attributes function.
Get Default Drive Parameter Block	AH h= 1Fh	AL = Status (00 = Operation successful) DS:BX = Drive parameter block	This undocumented function returns the current default drive's parameter block.
Null Function	AH = 20h	None	This API corresponds to CP/M's get/set default user number function.
Random Read From Opened FCB	AH = 21h DS:DX = Pointer to opened FCB	AL = Status (00 = Successful, 01 = EOF, 02 = DTA too small, 03 = Partial read)	Move the file pointer and perform a read.

Function	Input	Output	Description
Random Write To Opened FCB	AH = 22h DS:DX = Pointer to opened FCB	AL = Status (00 = Successful, 01 = Disk full, 02 = write unsuccessful)	Move the file pointer and perform a write.
Get Unopened FCB File Size	AH = 23h DS:DX = Pointer to unopened FCB	AL = Status (00 = File found)	Return the size of the specified file (with wild cards).
Set Random Record Number For FCB	AH = 24h DS:DX = Pointer to opened FCB	None	Set the file pointers value. This is often used to switch from sequential reads to random ones.
Set Interrupt Vector	AH = 25h AL = Interrupt number DS:DX = Pointer to new handler	None	Set the specified interrupt vector pointer to the specified interrupt handler.
Create a New Program Segment Prefix	H = 26h DX = Segment number f or the new PSP	None	Copy 256 bytes of current PSP into a new location. This function is used to start a subprogram from the current application. AH = 4Bh should be used instead.
Random Block Read using FCB	AH = 27h CX = Number of records to read DS:DX = Pointer to opened FCB	AL = Status (0 = Successful, 1 = No data read (EOF) 2 = DTA too small, 3 = Partial read) CX = Actual number of records read	Read the specified number of records from a file.
Random Block Write Using FCB	AH = 28h CX = Number of records to write	AL = Status (0 = successful, 1 = Disk full,	Write the specified number of records to a file.

FUNCTION	INPUT	OUTPUT	COMMENTS
	DS:DX = Pointer to opened FCB	2 = write not Complete) CX = Actual number of records read	
Parse Filename Into a FCB	AH = 29h AL = Bit value for parsing control (Bit 4–7 = Reversed Bit 3 = Use existing FCB extension Bit 2 = Use existing FCB filename Bit 1 = Use existing FCB default drive Bit 0 = Skip leading separators) DS: SI = Pointer to filename to parse ES:DI = Pointer to unopened FCB	AL = Status (0 = No filename to parse, 1 = invalid filename, 2 = Invalid drive) DS:SI = Pointer to first character after filename ES:DI = Pointer to first byte of formatted FCB	Convert a filename (with command-line wild-card characters) into FCB-compatible format.
Get System Date	AH = 2Ah	AL = Day of the week CX = Year 0 = Sun) DH = Month 1 = January) DL = Day (1 to 31)	Return the current date.
Set System Date	AH = 2Bh CX = Year DH = Month (1 = January) DL = Day (1 to 31)	AL = Status (0 = Valid Date)	Set the system date.
Get System Time	AH = 2Ch	CH = Hour (0 to 23) CL = Minutes (0 to 59)	When reading back the system time, do not rely on hundredths to be accurate because they are based on

Function	Call registers	Return registers	Description
		DH = Seconds (0 to 59) DL = Hundredths of seconds (0 to 99)	18.2-Hz system clock.
Set System Time	AH = 2Dh CH = hour (0 to 23) CL = Minutes (0 to 59) DH = Seconds (0 to 59) DL = Hundredths of seconds (0 to 99)	AL = Status (0 = Valid time)	Set the current system time.
Set Verify Switch	AH = 2Eh AL = 1	None	Carry out a verify operation after every disk write.
Reset Verify Switch	AH = 2Eh AL = 0	None	Do not verify after every disk write.
Get Current Disk Transfer Address (DTA)	AH = 2Fh	ES:BX = Pointer to current DTA	Return address of the current DTA.
Get MS-DOS Version Number	AH = 30h	AL = Major version number AH = minor version number BX = 0 CX = 0	Return the version of MS-DOS currently executing.
Terminate Process and Stay Resident (TSR)	AH = 31h AL = Return code DX = Saved memory size in paragraphs	N/A	Return execution to the process' caller, but leave the specified number of paragraphs unchanged in memory.
Get MS-DOS Drive	AH = 32h	AL = Status	Return pointer to the specified Drive parameter block.

FUNCTION	INPUT	OUTPUT	COMMENTS
Parameter Block	DL = Drive Number (0 = A, 1 = B …)	(0 = Successful) DS:BX = Pointer to drive parameter block	Similar to AH = 1Fh, except that drive is specified.
Get Extended Ctrl-Break Checking	AH = 33h AL = 0	DL = Current state (0 = Off)	Return the Current State of Ctrl-Break Check.
Set Extended Ctrl-Break Checking	AH = 33h AL = 1 DL = State (0 = Off, 1 = On)	DL = Current state (0 = Off)	Change the current state of the *Ctrl-Break* check.
Get INDOS Address Flag	AH = 34h	ES:BX = Pointer to byte	Return address of the INDOS flag. This API should only be accessed at the start of an application.
Get Interrupt Vector	AH = 35h AL = Interrupt vector number	ES:BX = Pointer to vector	Return the address for the interrupt number's vector.
Get Disk Free Space	AH = 36h DL = Drive number (0 = Default, 1 = A, 2 = B …)	AX = 0FFFFh if drive is invalid else number of sectors per cluster BX = Available clusters CX = Bytes per sector DX = Clusters per drive	Find the amount of available space on the specified drive.
Reserved	AH = 37h	N/A	This API is used by many third-party vendors. Do not use it in your own applications.
Return Country Dependant Information	AH = 38h AL = Function code (0) DS:DX = Pointer to the 32-byte memory area	Carry = Set if error AX = Error if carry set DS:DX = Country data	Return the country-specific information. Can also be used to set the country-specific information (Although setting information should be done by MS-DOS utilities).

Create a Subdirectory	AH = 39h DS:DX = Pointer to ASCIIZ string	Carry = Set if error AX = Error if carry set	Create the specified subdirectory (md = MS-DOS command).
Remove a Subdirectory	AH = 3Ah DS:DX = Pointer to ASCIIZ string	Carry = Set if error AX = Error if carry set	Delete the specified subdirectory (rd = MS-DOS command).
Specify the Current Subdirectory	AH = 3Bh DS:DX = Pointer to ASCIIZ string	Carry = Set if error AX = Error if carry set	Set a new default subdirectory (cd = MS-DOS command).
Create the File and Open It	AH = 3Ch DS:DX = Pointer to ASCIIZ string CX = Attributes of file. (Bit 15 -7 reserved (0), Bit 6 = 0 Archive, Bit 5 = Bit 4 = 0 Bit 3 = 0 Bit 2 = System Bit 1 = Hidden Bit 0 = Read only)	Carry = Set if error AX = Handle or error if carry set	Create the directory entry and open the file.
Open the File	AH = 3Dh DS:DX = Pointer to ASCIIZ string AL = Access Code (Bit 7 = Private, Bit 6–4 = Sharing mode 000 = Compatibility, 001 = DENYALL 010 = DENYWRITE	Carry = Set if error AX = Handle or error if carry set	Open the file for reading/writing.

FUNCTION	INPUT	OUTPUT	COMMENTS
	011 = DENYREAD 100 = DENYNONE 111 = Network FCB, Bit 3 = Reserved Bit 2–0 = Access 000 = Read only 001 = Write only 010 = Read/write)		
Close the File Handle	AH = 3Eh BX = Handle	Carry = Set if error AX = Handle or error if carry set	Close the open file.
Read from File Handle	AH = 3Fh BX = File handle CX = Number of bytes to read DS:DX = Buffer address	Carry = Set if error AX = Number of bytes read or error if carry set	Read the specified number of bytes from the file.
Write to File Handle	AH = 40h BX = File handle CX = Number of bytes to write DS:DX = Buffer Address	Carry = Set if error AX = Number of bytes written or error if carry set	Write the specified number of bytes to the file.
Delete File	AH = 41h DS:DX = Pointer to ASCIIZ filename	Carry = Set if error AX = Number of bytes written or error if carry set	Delete the file from the disk. Normal MS-DOS command-line rules are used.
Move File Pointer (LSEEK)	AH = 42h AL = Method of moving (0 = Move from file start, 1 = Move from current	Carry = Set if error DX:AX = New offset in file or, if carry set, AX is the error code	Move the MS-DOS file pointer to a new offset.

2 = Move to end of file)

BX = File handle

CX:DX = Number of bytes to move

Get File Mode	AH = 43h
	AL = 0
	DS:DX = Pointer to
	    ASCIIZ filename
		Carry = Set on error
		AX = Error code
		CX = File attribute if
		    carry reset
		    (Bit 5 = Archive,
		    Bit 4 = Directory,
		    Bit 3 = Reserved,
		    Bit 2 = System,
		    Bit 1 = Hidden,
		    Bit 0 = Read only)
			Read the file directory information.

Set File Mode	AH = 43h
	AL = 1
	DS:DX = Pointer to
	    ASCIIZ filename
	
	CX = File attribute
	    (Bit 5 = Archive,
	    Bit 4 = Directory,
	    Bit 3 = Reserved,
	    Bit 2 = System,
	    Bit 1 = Hidden,
	    Bit 0 = Read only)
		Carry = Set on error
		AX = Error code if carry
		    set
			Change the file directory information.

Get Device
Information
(IOCTL)
	AH = 44h
	AL = 0
	BX = Handle
		Carry = Set on error
		    code
		AX = Error code if carry
		    set
		DX = Device information
		    word if carry reset
		    character:
			Get device information

FUNCTION	INPUT	OUTPUT	COMMENTS
		(Bit 14 = device driver can process IOCTL,	
		Bit 13 = Output until busy support,	
		Bit 11 = Driver support for open/close,	
		Bit 7 = Set device,	
		Bit 6 = EOF on input,	
		Bit 5 = Raw (binary) mode,	
		Bit 4 = Device is special (uses Int 29h),	
		Bit 3 = Clock device,	
		Bit 2 = Null device,	
		Bit 1 = standard output,	
		Bit 0 = standard input)	
		Disk:	
		(Bit 15 = File is remote,	
		Bit 14 = File date/time not set on close,	
		Bit 11 = Media is not removable,	
		Bit 8 = Request Int 24 h if past EOF,	
		Bit 7 = File clear,	
		Bit 6 = File updated	
		Bit 0–5 = File number A = 0 …)	

Set Device
Information
(IOCTL)

AH = 44h
AL = 1
BX = Handle
DX = Device character:
(Bit 14 = Device driver
can process
IOCTL,
Bit 13 = Output until
busy support,
Bit 11 = driver support
for open/close,
Bit 7 = Set device,
Bit 6 = EOF on input,
Bit 5 = Raw (binary)
mode,
Bit 4 = Device is special
(uses Int 29h),
Bit 3 = Clock device,
Bit 2 = Null device,
Bit 1 = Standard output,
Bit 0 = Standard input)
Disk:
(Bit 15 = File is remote,
Bit 14 = File date/time
not set on
close,
Bit 11 = Media is not
removable,
Bit 8 = Request Int 24h
if past EOF,
Bit 7 = File clear,
Bit 6 = File updated

Carry = Set on error code   Set device information
AX = Error code if carry
set

FUNCTION	INPUT	OUTPUT	COMMENTS
	Bit 0–5 = File number, A = 0 …)		
Read from IOCTL Device	AH = 44h AL = 2 BX = File handle CX = Number of bytes to read DS:DX = Pointer to Buffer	Carry = Set on error AX = Error code if carry set, else number of bytes read	Read from IOCTL device like file-handle device.
Write to IOCTL Device	AH = 44h AL = 3 BX = File handle CX = Number of bytes to write DS:DX = Pointer to buffer	Carry = Set on error AX = Error code if carry set, else number of bytes written	Write to IOCTL device like file-handle device.
Read from Block IOCTL Device	AH = 44h AL = 4 BL = Drive number (0 = Default, A = 1 …) CX = Number of bytes to read DS:DX = Pointer to buffer	Carry = Set on error AX = Error code if carry set, else number of bytes read	Read data from an IOCTL block device.
Write to Block IOCTL Device	AH = 44h AL = 5 BL = Drive number (0 = Default, A = 1 …) CX = Number of bytes to write DS:DX = Pointer to buffer	Carry = Set on error AX = Error code if carry set, else number of bytes written	Write data to an IOCTL block device.

Function	Input	Output	Description
Get IOCTL Device Input Status	AH = 44h AL = 6 BX = File handle	Carry = Set on error AX = Error code if carry set, else For files: AL = 0FFh if not EOF or AL = 0 if EOF For devices: AL = 0 = Not ready AL = 0Fh = Ready	Get the status of the device's input.
Get IOCTL Device Output Status	AH = 44h AL = 7 BX = File handle	Carry = Set on error AX = Error code if carry set, else For files: AL = 0FFh if not EOF or AL = 0 if EOF For devices: AL = 0 = Not ready AL = 0Fh = Ready	Get the status of the device's output.
IOCTL Media Type	AH = 44h AL = 9 BL = Drive number (0 - Default, 1 - A ...)	AX = Status (0 = Removable 1 = Fixed 0Fh = If BL is invalid)	Return the type of media for device.
Check if IOCTL Block Device is Remote	AH = 44h AL = 9 BL = Drive number (0 = Default, 1 = A...)	Carry = Set if error DX = Attribute word (Bit 12 = Set for remote)	Set attribute bit if the device is remote to the PC (i.e., on a network).
Check if Handle is for	AH = 44h AL = 0Ah	Carry = Set if error	Set attribute bit if the device is remote to the PC (i.e., on a network).

FUNCTION	INPUT	OUTPUT	COMMENTS
a Remote IOCTL	BX = File handle	DX = Attribute word (Bit 15 = Set for remote)	
Set Sharing Retry Count for IOCTL Device	AH = 44h AL = 0Bh CX = Number of times to run the delay loop DX = Number of retries	Carry = Set if error AX = Error code if carry set	Set the number of retries and delay for device-sharing problems.
Generic IOCTL Device Request	AH = 44h AL = 0Ch BX = File Handle CH = Device category (01h = COMn, 03h = Console, 05h = LPTn, 00–7Fh = Reserved, 80h–FFh = Available for applications) CL = Function number (40h = Set device Parameters, 41h = Write track on logical device, 42h = Format and verify track on logical device,	Carry = Set on error AX = Error code if carry set	Perform basic file operations on the device.

60h = Get device
parameters,

61h = Get device
parameters,

61h = Read track
on logical
device,

62h = Verify track
on logical
device)

Generic IOCTL
Device Request

AH = 44h

AL = 0Dh

BL = Drive number
(0 = Default,
1 = A ...)

CH = Device category
(01h = COMn,
03h = Console,
05h = LPTn,
00–7Fh = Reserved,
80h–FFh = Available
for applications)

CL = Function number
(40h = Set device
parameters,

41h = Write track on
logical device,

42h = Format and
verify track on
logical device,

Carry = Set on error

AX = Error code if carry
set

Perform basic file operations on the device.

FUNCTION	INPUT	OUTPUT	COMMENTS
	60h = Get device parameters, 61h = Read track on logical device, 62h = Verify track on logical device)		
Get Logical IOCTL Drive Map	AH = 44h AL = 0Eh BL = Drive number (0 = Default, 1 = A . . .)	Carry = Set if error AX = Error code if carry set AL = Number of last drive assigned to this drive number	If a logical drive is assigned to a physical one, return the last drive number.
Set logical IOCTL Drive	AH = 44h AL = 0Fh BL = Drive number (0 = Default, 1 = A . . .)	Carry = Set if error AX = Error code if carry set. AL = Number of new logical drive	This operation sets a new logical drive to the device. This is useful for avoiding "swap diskette" messages in applications.
Duplicate a File Handle	AH = 45h BX = File handle	Carry = Set if error AX = Error code if carry set else new file handle	Create a second handle to access a file. Note, if one handle's file pointer is changed, then both are changed.
Force a Duplicate File Handle handles.	AH = 46h AH = 46h BX = File handle CX = New duplicate file handle	Carry = Set if error AX = Error code if carry set	Force a specific handle number to be set to an open file. This API can be dangerous to use with poorly chosen handles.

Function	Input	Output	Description
Get Current Directory	AH = 47h DL = Drive number (0 = Default, 1 = A ....) DS:SI = Pointer to 64-byte memory area	Carry = Set if error AX = Error code if carry set	Returns the current subdirectory path for the specified drive.
Allocate Memory	AH = 49h BX = Number of paragraphs required.	Carry = Set if error AX = Error code if carry set, else segment of allocated memory BX = Number of free paragraphs available if carry set	Attempt to allocate a specified number of paragraphs. Note: Be sure to check the carry flag before writing to the segment returned in AX (which might be an error code).
Free Allocated Memory	AH = 49h ES = Segment of memory to free	Carry = Set if error AX = Error code if carry set	When finished with allocated memory, you must free it. This includes ending applications that have allocated memory.
Modify Allocated Memory (SETBLOCK)	AH = 4Ah ES = Segment of memory to resize BX = Number of paragraphs for resized memory block	Carry = Set if error AX = Error code if carry set BX = Maximum number of paragraphs if request is to "grow" block	Resize the allocated block. This API is most useful for freeing memory after an application has started executing and has all available memory devoted to it.
Execute a Program (EXEC)	AH = 4Bh AL = 0 DS:DX = File to start Executing	Carry = Set if error AX = error code if carry set	This API loads and starts execution of a "child" process. Note, AH = 4Bh is often used by viruses to load.

FUNCTION	INPUT	OUTPUT	COMMENTS
	ES:BX = Pointer to parameter block (Offset 0 = segment of environment, Offset 2 = pointer to command-line parameters, Offset 6 = pointer to first FCB, Offset 0Ah = pointer to second FCB)		
Load a Program Overlay	AH = 4Bh AL = 3 DS:DX = File to load ES:BX = Pointer to parameter block (Offset 0 = Segment address to load file, Offset 2 = Relocation factor, normally 0)	Carry = Set if error AX = Error code if carry set	Load a file, but do not create a PSP. This is used to load "overlays" for multiple applications. This API can be used as a quick and dirty way to load files into RAM. Note: AH = 4Bh is often used by viruses to load.
Terminate the Process (EXIT)	AH = 4Ch AL = Return code	N/A	End the current application and pass an error code back to the parent process (the one that initiated the application).
Get Return Code of Subprocess (WAIT)	AH = 4Dh	AL = Return code AH = Exit code Type (0 = Normal, 1 = Ctrl-Break)	After a child process has finished, get the termination reason/status.

Function	Registers (Input)	Output	Description
		2 = Device error, 3 = TSR)	
Find First Matching File	AH = 4Eh DS:DX = Pointer to filename CX = File attribute (Bit 5 = Archive Bit, Bit 4 = Subdirectory, Bit 3 = Volume in first 11 bytes, Bit 2 = System file, Bit 1 = Hidden file)	Carry = Set on error, error to filename AX = Error code if carry set.	Look through the default or specified path for the file name (which can MS-DOS wildcards). If found, place information in the current DTA. If no file can be found meeting the criteria, the carry flag is set.
Find Next Matching File	AH = 4Fh	Carry = Set if error AX = Error code if carry set	Using the DTA set up by previous file matching APIs, the DTA is updated with a new file. If no file is to be found, then the carry flag is set.
Internal MS-DOS APIs	AH = 50h–53h	N/A	These functions are internal to APIs MS-DOS and cannot be used by applications.
Get the Verify Flag Value	AH = 54h	AL = Verify flag (0 = off, 1 = on)	Return the state of the verify flag.
Internal MS-DOS API	AH = 55h	N/A	This functions is internal to MS-DOS and cannot be used by applications.
Rename a File	AH = 56h DS:DX = Pointer to ASCIIZ file to be renamed ES:DI = Pointer to new ASCIIZ filename	Carry = Set if error AX = Error code if carry set	Rename a file or move it (the paths can be different).
Get File Last Update Date	AH = 57h AL = 0	Carry = Set if error AX = Error code if carry	Return the date/time information for the file handle.

FUNCTION	INPUT	OUTPUT	COMMENTS
And Time	BX = File handle	set CX = Time from file's table (Bit 15–11 = Hours, Bit 10–5 = Minutes, Bit 4–0 = Seconds/2) DX = Date from file's table (Bit 15–9 = year from 1980, Bit 8–5 = Month, 1–12, Bit 4–0 = Day, 1–31)	
Set File Last Update Date And Time	AH = 57h AL = 1 BX = File handle CX = Time from file's table (Bit 15–11 = Hours, Bit 10–5 = Minutes, Bit 4–0 = Seconds/2) DX = Date from file's table (Bit 15–9 = Year from 1980, Bit 8–5 = Month, 1–12, Bit 4–0 = Day, 1–31)	Carry = Set if error AX = Error code if carry set	Change the date/time information for the file handle.
Get Memory Allocation Strategy	AH = 58h AL = 0	Carry = Set if error AX = Error code if carry set AH = 0	Return the current memory allocation strategy. The codes listed are for DOS 5.0+. Earlier versions use different codes.

		AL = Allocation strategy (40h = High memory first fit, 41h = High memory best fit, 42h = High memory last fit, 80h = First fit, try high then low, 81h = Best fit, try high then low, 82h = Last fit, try high then low)	
		Carry = Set if error AX = Error code if carry set	Change the current memory allocation strategy. The codes listed are for DOS 5.0+. Earlier versions use different codes. This is parameter should only be changed if there is a specific problem to be solved in the application.
Set Memory Allocation Strategy	AH = 58h BH = 0 BL = Allocation strategy (40h = High memory first fit, 41h = High memory best fit, 42h = High memory last fit, 80h = First fit, try high then low, 81h = Best fit, try high then low, 82h = Last fit, try high then low)		
Get Extended Error Information	AH = 59h BX = 0	AX = Extended error code	If an error is returned from an MS-DOS API. Additional, more specific information can be requested from

FUNCTION	INPUT	OUTPUT	COMMENTS
Create an Unique file	AH = 5Ah DS:DX = Pointer to ASCIIZ path string ending in a backslash (\) CX = File attributes (Bit 5 = archive bit, Bit 4 = Subdirectory, Bit 3 = Volume in first 11 bytes, Bit 2 = System file, Bit 1 = Hidden file)	BH = Error class BL = Suggested action CH = Suggested "locus" Carry = Set if error AX = Error code if carry set DS:DX = Full path with new filename	MS-DOS. This API is primarily used by compilers to generate temporary data storage files.
Create a New file	AH = 5Bh DS:DX = Pointer to ASCIIZ file name string CX = File attributes (Bit 5 = Archive bit, Bit 4 = Subdirectory, Bit 3 = Volume in first 11 bytes, Bit 2 = System file, Bit 1 = Hidden file)	Carry = Set if error AX = Error code if carry set AX = Handle	This API will create a new file and open it for the application.
Lock File Access	AH = 5Ch AL = 0 BX = File handle CX:DX = Offset within file SI:DI = Length of locked	Carry = Set if error AX = Error code if carry set	This API prevents other processes from accessing specific portions of a file being used by the current process.

Function	Parameters	Return	Description
Unlock File Access	AH = 5Ch AL = 1 BX = File handle CX:DX = Offset within file SI:DI = Length of locked range	Carry = Set if error AX = Error code if carry set	This API allows other processes access to the current file. the CX:DX and SI:DI parameters must be the same as "lock file access" used.
Internal MS-DOS API	AH = 5Dh	N/A	This functions is internal to MS-DOS and cannot be used by applications.
Get Network Machine Name	AH = 5Eh AL = 0 DS:DX = Pointer to 15-byte buffer	Carry = Set if error AX = Error code if carry set AX = Error code if carry set CH = Name/number (0 = Not defined) CL = NETBIOS name number for the name	Load the buffer pointed to by DS:DX with the NETBIOS name. This function will only work with a machine on a NETBIOS network.
NETBIOS APIs	AH = 5Eh–5Fh	N/A	These functions are used bye NETBIOS to provide file sharing and printer control for network applications.
Internal MS-DOS API	AH = 60h	N/A	This function is internal to MS-DOS and cannot be used by applications.
Unused MS-DOS API	AH = 61h	N/A	This API is not used by MS-DOS and simply returns to the caller.
Return Current PSPO Segment	AH = 62h	BX = Segment of current PSP	Upon return, BX:0 points to the application's PSP.
Remaining MS-DOS APIs	AH = 63h–FFh	N/A	All remaining API numbers are allocated to OS/2 or used by virus' as a method of operation. None of these APIs should be used by an application.

Interrupt 22h–Terminate Address

The Terminate Address Vector (at Interrupt 22h's vector or address 0:0x088) is executed during program terminate before control is returned to "command.com". This "hook" provides you with a method of executing your own code before the memory used by the program is cleaned up.

The Interrupt 22h vector can be "captured", using the techniques for sharing a vector that I showed earlier in the book, with the original Interrupt 22h jumped to after the application Interrupt 22h code has executed. In this case you don't have to worry about saving or restoring context information (although you should make sure the stack is at the same value as when your code was entered).

The reason why I don't think this interrupt vector should be captured and used to clean up the application's resources is because it seems to be "sloppy" using the operating system to notify the application when it has ended. Normally, I like to perform clean up of open files and allocated memory before indicating that the application has finished.

This interrupt can not be invoked by your application; to end the application, an "Int 21h" instruction should be executed with AH equal to 4Ch.

Interrupt 23h–Ctrl-Break Exit Address

The "Ctrl-Break" vector works similarly to the "Terminate Address" for Interrupt 22h. The Interrupt 23h vector is executed when the user presses the "Ctrl-Break" key combination while an MS-DOS function is being executed or a standard I/O operation is taking place.

The Application Interrupt 23h handler is exactly the same as any other software interrupt handler, at the start of the handler, the context registers that are changed are pushed onto the stack, the handler function is executed, and the context registers are restored. At the end of the Interrupt 23h handler, an "iret" instruction is executed and control returns to the currently executing MS-DOS function.

The "Ctrl-Break" software interrupt 23h can be useful for many applications, but console I/O has to use the MS-DOS functions which may restrict the operation of the application somewhat (as compared to the BIOS keyboard and screen I/O functions).

Interrupt 24h–Critical Error Handler Vector

The Critical Error Handler Vector is actually quite an interesting and potentially powerful feature of MS-DOS. This vector can be captured by an application and be used to provide a custom response to a DOS error (instead of the standard one-line MS-DOS responses). If you have created a game or an application which uses a graphical screen instead of just MS-DOS console I/O, this vector will allow the error to be processed without having to switch modes, having your screen overwritten by MS-DOS or loosing the error.

Most of the errors you will experience with MS-DOS revolve around the disk subsystems and errors with the media (such as not having a diskette in the drive or the diskette is unformatted) or the printer is not working. Simply inserting a valid diskette or checking the printer's connection and having the user check if the power switch is "on" can rectify most of these errors. Custom error messages or instructions for fixing the problem can be added to the application.

After this vector has been captured, the new handler will execute when an error occurs in an MS-DOS API. The device causing the error is passed in AH and will have bit seven set if the error was caused in the disk sub-system. If AH bit seven is set, then the operation information and valid responses are also passed in AH with the following bits:

BITS	DESCRIPTION
5	Set if IGNORE is allowed
4	Set if RETRY is allowed
3	Set if FAIL Is allowed
2–1	Affected Disk Area: 00 – DOS area 01 – File allocation table 10 – Directory 11 – Data area
0	Set if Write Operation Reset if Read Operation

The lower eight bits of DI contains the error number and the errors consist of:

NUMBER	DESCRIPTION
0h	Attempt to write on write-protected diskette
1h	Unknown unit
2h	Drive not ready (may be diskette not in drive)
3h	Unknown command
4h	Data error (CRC)
5h	Bad request structure
6h	Seek error
7h	Unknown media type
8h	Sector not found
9h	Printer out of paper
Ah	Write fault
Bh	Read fault
Ch	General failure

The final data passed to handler at the start of the Critical Error Handler is the "Device Header Control Block", which is pointed to by BP:SI. This block consists of:

OFFSET	DATA TYPE	DESCRIPTION
0h	Double Word	Pointer to the next device

4h	Word	Device Type parameters:
		  Bit 15 – 1 = Character Device
		         0 = Block Device
		  Bit 14 – IOCTL Bit
		  If Bit 15 = 1
		    Bit 3 – Set if current CLOCK Device
		    Bit 2 – Set if current NULL Device
		    Bit 1 – Set if current standard Output
		    Bit 0 – Set if current standard Input.

6h	Word	Pointer to Device Driver Strategy Entry Point
8h	Word	Pointer to Device Driver Interrupt Entry Point
Ah	8 Bytes	Character Device Named Field Device For Block devices. The first byte is the number of units.

If this information is processed within the handler and the handler returns execution to MS-DOS (using an "iret" instruction), then AL must be set with a command code for MS-DOS to respond to the error. The valid commands are:

VALUE	COMMAND
0	Ignore the Error
1	Retry the Operation
2	Terminate the Program through Interrupt 23h
3	Fail the System Call in Progress

Another option to process the error is to return execution to the calling location with a custom error. When the Interrupt 24h vector executes, the application's stack is passed to the handler, with the following information:

REGISTER	COMMENTS
IP CS	Registers from MS-DOS issuing the Int 24h instruction

FLAGS	
AX	Registers saved by MS-DOS with the Application's Registers at the time of the Int 21h instruction
BX	
CX	
DX	
SI	
DI	
BP	
DS	
ES	
IP	Registers from the original Int 21h Instruction
CX	
FLAGS	

To return an error to the application from the Interrupt 24h vector, the following code should be used:

```
add SP, 8            ;  Move the Stack to "BX"
mov AX, ErrorNumber  ;  Load AX with the Error Number

pop BX               ;  Restore the Registers
pop CX
pop DX
pop SI
pop DI
pop BP
pop DS
pop ES
stc                  ;  Set the Carry Flag to indicate the error
ret 2                ;   Flag set
```

Interrupt 25h & 26h–Absolute Disk Accesses

I like to think of Interrupts 25h and 26h as another way you can trash your system's hard files although I can see them as a useful way of copying floppy diskettes. These two MS-DOS interrupts are used to read and write directly to the drives without accessing the MS-

DOS file system. If you are going to write directly to the disk, I suppose using this interrupt API is preferable to using BIOS APIs.

For Interrupts 25h and 26h, the disk is laid out with "logical sectors" which use a numbering scheme that is based on the head, track and sector of the disk. Using this scheme, I have created the table below showing how the logical tracks work for a diskette with 2 sides (heads), 80 tracks per side and 18 sectors per track (this is the normal configuration of a 1.44 MByte diskette).

LOGICAL SECTOR	HEAD	TRACK	SECTOR
0	0	0	0
1	0	0	1
2	0	0	2
18	0	1	0
19	0	1	1
20	0	1	2
720	0	40	0
721	0	40	1
1440	1	0	0
1441	1	0	1

This scheme actually works reasonably well for hard files, but there is a problem; as hard files have gotten larger, the maximum size supported by this scheme becomes a problem. In the PC, each sector is 512 bytes, this means that the maximum size disk supported by the Interrupt 25h and 26h "logical Sectors" is 33,553,920 bytes which is about a half a percent of the total capacity of a modern hard disk drive. You should note that this was the maximum size of the PC/AT's hard file.

For this reason, I feel that Interrupt 25h and 26h are only useable for diskette drives.

The actual interrupt functions are quite straightforward, the codes listed below are for IBM and non-IBM BIOS with the error codes returned in AL and AH, respectively

CODE	IBM ERROR	NON-IBM ERROR
00h		Write Protect Error
01h	Bad Command	Unknown Unit
02h	Address Mark Not Found	Drive Not Ready
03h	Write Protect Error	
04h	Sector Not Found	Data CRC Error
06h		Seek Error
07h		Unknown Media
08h		Sector Not Found

0Ah		Write Fault
0Bh		Read Fault
0Ch		General Disk Failure
0Fh		Invalid Media Change
10h	Data CRC Error	
20h	Controller Failure	
40h	Seek Error	
80h	No Response from Drive Controller	

The Interrupt APIs are defined as follows with all register contents changed from when the APIs were invoked:

INTERRUPT	INPUT	OUTPUT	COMMENTS
Int 25h	AL = Drive Number ES:BX = Pointer to data buffer CX = Number of sectors to read DX = First logical sector	Carry = Reset if operation successful if error then AH/AL contains the error code all other register contents lost	Read the specified number of sectors starting at the specified logical sector.
Int 26h	AL = Drive number ES:BX = Pointer to data buffer CX = Number of sectors to write DX = First logical sector	Carry = Reset if operation successful if error then AH/AL contains the error code. All other register contents lost	Write data from the buffer starting at the specified logical sector for the specified number of sectors.

8
APPENDICES

Interrupt 27h–Terminate but Stay Resident

Interrupt 27h provides a single interrupt interface to allow an MS-DOS program to "Terminate and Stay Resident", which means that after a program is loaded, it can return execution to the MS-DOS command line program while still leaving part of the program in memory. This allows advanced functions to be added to an MS-DOS based PC without having to upgrade the operating system or add complex features.

After a program has executed its TSR set up code, it will set DX to the last address plus one that it wants to save and then executes an "Int 27h" instruction. Upon execution of this instruction, the memory above the offset at DX will be returned to the system and execution will return to "command.com".

Interrupt 27h is similar to Interrupt 20h in that a much more capable function has been provided in Interrupt 21h. Actually, I would recommend that in the Interrupt 21h API call, AH is equal to 31h ("Terminate and Stay Resident") be used exclusively instead because it can return error codes to the caller and is the "more standard" way of carrying out a Terminate and Stay Resident program.

Interrupt 2Fh–Multiplex Interrupt

The "Multiplex Interrupt" is a method built into MS-DOS for different processes to communicate with one another using a shared interrupt (2Fh) and as an interface to device drivers added to the system software. The Multiplex Interrupt has very specific requirements for the interface so that the APIs of the device drivers can be processed properly without any problems with "upsteam" or "downstream" drivers or shared interrupts.

In most MS-DOS/Windows PCs, there are already a number of built in "processes" that are loaded into the Multiplex Interrupt before you can load any device drivers, TSRs or applications.

These processes include:

PROCESS NUMBER	PROCESS
01h	Print.exe
10h	Share.exe
11h	Network
14h	National Language Support (Nlsfunc.exe)
16h	MS-DOS Idle
1Ah	Ansi.sys
43h	Himem.sys
48h	Doskey.com
4Bh	Build Notification Chain
ADh	Keyb.com
B0h	Graftable.com
B7h	Append.exe

The "Process Numbers" of the new multiplex Interrupt installation. The process number should be between 080h and 0FFh because MS-DOS has reserved 000h to 07Fh. For determining whether or not a process number can be used, the Multiplex Interrupt has to be issued with the proposed process number in AH and AL set to Zero (which is the "Get Installed State" Multiplex Interrupt request).

The "Standard" Multiplex Interrupt requests (which are put in AL) with parameters and possible returned information is as follows:

FUNCTION	INPUT	OUTPUT	COMMENTS
Get Installed State	AH = Process number AL = 0	AL = 0, Not used, OK to install AL = 1, Not used, not OK to install AL = 0FFh, used	This function checks to see if the specified process number can be used for the multiplex interrupt.
Submit File	AH = Process number AL = 1 DS:DX = Pointer to ASCIIZ file name	AL = Operation Status	Pass an MS-DOS drive, path and filename to the multiplex interrupt.
Cancel File	AH = Process number AL = 2 DS:DX = Pointer to ASCIIZ file name	AL = Operation status	The MS-DOS drive, path and filename are passed to the multiplex interrupt in order for the handler to delete the file from the application's queue.
Cancel All Files	AH = Process number AL = 3	AL = Operation status	Instruct the handler to delete all files in the application's queue.
Status	AH = Process number AL = 4	DX = Error count	Return the number of errors encountered by the process.
End of Status	AH = Process number AL = 5	AX = Error codes	Return the error codes encountered by the multiplex interrupt handler.

To determine whether or not a process number can be used, you would probably want to use the code:

```
mov BX, 080h
                    ;  Start at Process 080h and go to 0FFh
```

```
Loop:                        ;  Loop Here until BX contains Valid process #
  mov AH, BL                 ;  Load the Process Number to Test
  mov AL, 0                  ;  Get the Process Number's Status
  int 2Fh                    ;  Request the Status
  or  AL, AL                 ;  If Zero, Okay to Install
  jz  Skip
  inc BL                     ;  Try the Next Process Number
  jmp Loop
Skip:                        ;  BL contains a Valid Process Number
```

Along with the standard functions listed above, each Multiplex Interrupt can have it's own specific functions that are specified in AL by the caller. The restriction on the function number is that it cannot be 00h to 05h or 0F8h to 0FFh. Any other code can be used and is really up to the application developer.

For each standard function, there are the standard Multiplex Interrupt error codes that should be returned. If the error doesn't match any of the standard ones, then you are free to specify your own.

ERROR CODE	DESCRIPTION
01h	Invalid Function
02h	File Not Found
03h	Path Not Found
04h	Too Many Open Files
05h	Access Denied
08h	Queue Full
09h	Busy
0Ch	Name too long
0Fh	Invalid Drive

A typical Multiplex Interrupt Handler will look like:

```
Mint_Num    db    ?        ;  Multiplex Interrupt Handler Process Number

Mint_Old    dd    ?        ;  Previous Multiplex Interrupt Handler Vector

Mint:                      ;  Multiplex Interrupt Handler
  cmp AH,  CS:Mint_Num     ;  Is the request directed toward this Handler?
  jz  Mint_Start
  jmp CS:Mint_Old          ;  No, Jump to the Previous Vector
```

```
Mint_Start:                 ; Now, can start processing Multiplex Int.

   or   AL, AL              ; Is this the Install Check?
   jz   Mint_Handler

     mov AL,  0FFh          ; Indicate the Handler is used

   iret                     ; Return to code that Invoked the Int 2Fh

Mint_Handler:               ; Now, Handle the Multiplex Interrupt Request
```

The two variables are set before the Multiplex Interrupt is determined to be active. The "Mint_Num" variable is the process number (that I showed how to determine above). "Mint_Old" is the previous vector to the Multiplex Interrupt and it is determined, along with installing the vector using the code:

```
   Mov AH,  035h                ; Get Current Multiplex Interrupt Vector
   Mov AL,  02Fh
   Int 021h

   Mov CS:Mint_Old.PtrSeg, ES   ; Save the Old Vector
   Mov CS:Mint_Old.PtrOff, BX
   Mov   AH,  025h              ; Load the Multiplex Interrupt with the
   Mov AL, 02Fh                 ;  New Vector
   Push CS
   Pop DS
   Lea DX, Mint
```

The Multiplex Interrupt is the preferable method of adding BIOS functions to your PC instead of trying to figure out which interrupts are available within the PC.

Interrupts 28h–2Eh, 30h–32h & 34h–3h

MS-DOS has been assigned interrupts 20h to 3Fh. I have described the operation of the primary API interrupts but I am going to avoid describing the operation of the secondary interrupts and just describe them as "Reserved". Over the Internet, you can probably find information describing how these interrupts are used, but I just want to say that this information should be ignored and the interrupts are never accessed or initiated using the "int xxh" instruction.

With different versions of MS-DOS (including the versions available with Windows), these interrupts can execute provide APIs or be used as vectors for different functions. You may find that your application is easier to write using the reserved interrupts, but I have to caution you against attempting to use them because these APIs are "reserved", Microsoft (and IBM for "DOS 2000") may change the execution of these interrupts in different versions of MS-DOS.

8

APPENDICES

WINDOWS EXTENSIONS
AND DPMI INTERRUPT
FUNCTION BY NUMBER

The "Dos Protect Mode Interrupts" are a set of 0x02F and 0x031 interrupt APIs that give an MS-DOS application running in "V86" mode access to the Windows sixteen bit protect mode functions. As you look through them, note that the parameter values are not consistent (along with registers changed upon return) for the different APIS.

These functions are largely obsolete, but many applications have been written that use them. I don't recommend their use for new applications, but it is useful to have a list of them for maintaining older applications.

INPUT PARAMETERS	OUTPUT PARAMETERS	NAME AND COMMENTS
Int 2Fh AX = 01600h	AL = 0 or 080h if 386 Enhanced Mode is not Running	Get Enhanced Mode Windows Installed State.
Int 2Fh AX = 01602h	ES:DI = Pointer to Windows Enhanced Mode Entry Point	Get Pointer to the Windows Enhanced Mode Entry Point.
Int 2Fh AX = 01605h CX = 0 ES:BX = 0:0 DS:SI = 0:0	DX = Windows Type Bit 0 - Set if "Standard Mode" Windows Initializing DI = Version Number of Windows	Windows Initilization Notification for MS-DOS Device Drivers and TSRs.
Int 2Fh AX = 01606h DX = Specify Standard or Enhanced Mode 386 Services Bit 0 = 0 for Enhanced Mode Services	No Return Value	Windows Termination Notification
Int 2Fh AX = 01607h BX = Virtual Device Identifier Others Specific To Action	Specific to Action	Device Call out–Used to pass Parameters to a Device Driver.
Int 2Fh AX = 01608h	No Return Value	Windows Initialization Notification.
Int 2Fh AX = 01609h	No Return Value	Windows Begin Exit– Notify Device Drivers and TSRs that Windows is about to end.
Int 2 Fh AX = 01608h	Al = 0 if function Supported (else left) As 080h	Release Current Virtual Machine Time-Slice-Force Windows to Swap Processing to another VM.

INPUT PARAMETERS	OUTPUT PARAMETERS	NAME AND COMMENTS
Int 2Fh AX = 01681h	No Return Value	Begin Critical Section– Notify Device Drivers and TSRs that Task Switching Cannot occur.
Int 2Fh AX = 01682h	No Return Value	End Critical Section– Notify Device Drivers and TSRs that Task Switching can take Place.
Int 2Fh AX = 01683h	BX = Vritual Machine Identifier	Get Current Virtual Machine Identifier–Return the VM Identifier for the Current Process.
Int 2Fh AX = 01684h BX = Device Identifier Identifier	ES:DI = 0 if function is not Supported ES:DI = Entry Point if Function Supported	Get Device Entry Point Address.
Int 2Fh AX = 01685h BX = Virtual Machine Identifier CX = Flags Bit 0 - Set to Wait for Interrupts Enabled Bit 1 - Set to Wait for Critical Section Released DX:SI = Priority ES:DI = Callback Function Address	CF = Set if Request Fails AX = 00001h, 00002h or 00003h if Request Fails	Switch Virtual Machine and Callback Addresses.
Int 2Fh AX = 01686h	AX == 0 if in Protect Mode AX ! = 0 if not in Protect Mode	Get CPU Mode - Indicate whether or not Executing in Protect Mode.
Int 2Fh AX = 01687h	AX ! = 0 if DPMI Not Available/No Other Registers Changed AX == 0 if DPMI Present BX = Flags Bit 0 - Set if 32 bit Mode is supported Bit 1–15 = Not Used	Get Protected Mode Switch Entry Point - Used as a Test for the Capabilities of the PC the application is running in.

INPUT PARAMETERS	OUTPUT PARAMETERS	NAME AND COMMENTS
	CL = Processor Type 2 - 80286 3 - 80386 4 - 80486 5 - Pentium 6+ - Reserved for Future Processors DH = DPMI Major Version Number (Normally 1) DL = DPMI Minor Version Number (Normally 0) SI = Number of Paragraphs Used for DPMI Host Functions ES:DI = Pointer to Address to Enter Protected Mode	
Int 2Fh AX = 04000h	AL = Return Value	Enable Virtual Machine Assisted Save/Restore – Primarily used to capture Virtual Machine updates of The Video RAM.
Int 2Fh AX = 04001h	No Return Value	Notify Background Switch– Notify Virtual Machine that It no longer has the "Focus" of Windows.
Int 2F AX = 04002h	No Return Value	Notify Foreground Switch– Notify Virtual Machine that It now has the "Focus" of Windows.
Int 2F AX = 04003h	No Return Value	Notify Enter Critical Section - Notify Virtual Display Device that the Critical Section has started executing.
Int 2F AX = 04004h	No Return Value	Notify End Critical Section - Notify Virtual Display Device that the Critical Section has completed Executing.

8

APPENDICES

INPUT PARAMETERS	OUTPUT PARAMETERS	NAME AND COMMENTS
Int 2Fh AX = 04005h	No Return Value	Save Video Register State - Notify Virtual Machines that The Virtual Display Device Requires access to the Hardware registers.
Int 2Fh AX = 04006h	No Return Value	Restore Video Register State - Notify Virtual Machines that the Virtual Display Device No longer Requires Access to the Hardware Registers.
Int 2Fh AX = 04007h	No Return Value	Disable Virtual Machine Assisted Save/Restore - Direct the Virtual Display Driver to Stop Notifying the Virtual Machines When it Needs to Access the Hardware Registers.
Int 31h AX = 00000h CX = Number of LDT Descriptors To Allocate	CF = Set if Request Fails AX = Error Code if Request Fails AX = Base Selector if Request Completes	Allocate LDT Descriptors– Allocate one or more descriptors which must be Initialized by the Applications.
Int 31h AX = 00001h BX = LDT Descriptor to Free	CF = Set if Request Fails AX = 08022h if invalid Descriptor	Free the Specified LDT Descriptor.
Int 31h AX = 00002h BX = Real Mode Segment Address	CF = Set if Request Fails AX = 08011h if Descriptor Unavailable AX = Selector for Real Mode Segment	Map a real mode segment to an LDT Descriptor that can be used in Protect Mode.
Int 31h AX = 00003h	CF = Clear AX = Selector Increment Value	Get Selector Increment Value–ncrement the Number of Descriptors for an application.
Int 31h AX = 00006h BX = Selector	CF = SEt if Request Fails AX = 08022h if invalid Selector	Get Segment Base Address–Returns the physical address for the

INPUT PARAMETERS	OUTPUT PARAMETERS	NAME AND COMMENTS
	AX = 32-bit physical base Address of segment	specified selector.
Int 31h AX = 00007h BX = Selector CX:DX = 32-bit Physical Segment Address	CF = Set if Request Fails AX = 08022h or 08025h if Request Fails	Set Segment Base Address–Set the Specified Physical Address for the Selector.
Int 31h AX = 00008h BX = Selector CX:DX = 32-bit Segment Limit	CF = Set if Request Fails AX = 08021h, 08022h or 08025h if Request Fails	Set Segment Limit –Set the maximum size of Selector.
Int 31h AX = 00009h BX = Selector CH = 80386 Extended access Rights/Type Byte CL = Access Rights/Type Byte	CF = Set if Request Fails AX = 08021h, 08022h, 08025h if Request Fails	Set Descriptor Access Rights–Modify the Access rights for the specified Selector.
Int 31h AX = 0000Ah BX = Selector	CF = Set if Request Fails AX = New Selector if Request Completes AX = 08011h or 8022h if Request Fails	Create Alias Descriptor– Create a new LDT data descriptor that has the same physical address and Size limit as Specified Selector.
Int 31h AX = 0000Bh BX = Selector ES:DI = Pointer to 8 Byte Buffer	CF = Set if Request Fails AX = 08022h if Request Fails	Copy Descriptor into 8 Byte Buffer.
Int 31h AX = 0000Ch BX = Selector ES:DI = Pointer to 8 Byte Buffer	CF = Set if Request Fails AX = 08021h, 08022h, 08025h if Request Fails	Set the Descriptor with the Buffer Value.
Int 31h AX = 0000Dh BX = Selector	CF = Set if Request Fails AX = 08011h or 08012h if Request Fails	Allocate Specific LDT Descriptor.
Int 31h AX = 00100h BX = Number of Paragraphs to Allocate	CF = Set if Request Fails AX = Segment Base Address of Allocated Block if Request Completes	Allocate DOS Memory Block–Allocate memory in Protect Mode as if in Real (MS-DOS) Mode.

8

APPENDICES

INPUT PARAMETERS	OUTPUT PARAMETERS	NAME AND COMMENTS
	DX = Selector for Allocated Block if Request Completes AX = 00007h or 00008h if Request Fails BX = Size of largest number Of Paragraphs available if Request Fails	
Int 31h AX = 00101h DX = Selector	CF = Set if Request Fails AX = 00007h, 00009h, 08022h If Request Fails	Free DOS Memory Block.
Int 31h AX = 00102h BX = New Block Size in Paragraphs DX = Selector	CF = Set if Request Fails AX = 00007h or 00008h if Request Fails	Resize a specific DOS Memory Block.
Int 31h AX = 00200h BL = Interrupt Number	CF = Reset CX:DX = Segment: Offset of Real Mode Interrupt Vector	Return the Real Mode Interrupt Vector Address.
Int 31h AX = 00201h BL = Interrupt Number CX:DX = Segment: Offset Of Real Mode Interrupt Vector	CF = Reset	Set a New Real Mode Interrupt Vector Address.
Int 31h AX = 00202h BL = Exception Number	CF = Set if Request Fails AX = 08021h if Request Fails CX:DX = Selector:Offset of Exception Handler	Return the Address of the Protect Mode Exception Handler in the range of 0 to 01Fh.
Int 31h AX = 00203h BL = Exception Number CX:DX = Selector:Offset Of Exception Handler	CF = Set if Request Fails AX = 08022h	Set the Address of the Protect Mode Exception Handler in the Range of 0 to 01Fh.
Int 31h AX = 00204h BL = Interrupt Number	CF = Reset CX:DX = Selector: Offset of Interrupt Handler	Return the Address of the Protect Mode Interrupt Handler.

INPUT PARAMETERS	OUTPUT PARAMETERS	NAME AND COMMENTS

Int 31h
AX = 00205h
BL = Interrupt Number
CX:DX = Selector: Offset
       Of Interrupt
       Handler
	CF = Set if Request Fails
	AX = 08022h if Request
	    Fails
		Set the Address of the
		Protected Mode Interrupt
		Handler.

INPUT PARAMETERS	OUTPUT PARAMETERS	NAME AND COMMENTS

Int 31h
AX = 00300h
BL = Interrupt Number
BH = Flags
 Bit 0 - Zero
CX = Number of Words
    to Copy
ES:DI = Selector:Offset
       Of Real Mode
       Register Data
	CF = Set if Request Fails
	ES:DI = Selector : Offset
	     of Modified Real
	     Mode Register
	     Data Structure
	AX = 08012h, 08013h,
	    08014h or 08021h if
	    Request Fails
		Simulate a Real Mode
		Interrupt–Execution
		passed to Real Mode
		Interrupt Handler.

Register Data in Format:

Offset	Length	Contents
0×000	4	DI/EDI
0×004	4	SI/ESI
0×008	4	BP/EBP
0×00C	4	Reserved
0×010	4	BX/EBX
0×014	4	DX/EDX
0×018	4	CX/ECX
0×01C	4	AX/EAX
0×020	2	CPU Flags
0×022	2	ES
0×025	2	DS
0×026	2	FS
0×028	2	GS
0×02A	2	IP (Rsvd)
0×02C	2	CS(Rsvd)
0×02E	2	SP
0×030	2	SS
(Rsvd)		Reserved/Not Used

INPUT PARAMETERS	OUTPUT PARAMETERS	NAME AND COMMENTS

Int 31h
AX = 00301h
 	
BH = Flags
 Bit 0 - Zero
CX = Number of Words
    to Copy
ES:DI = Selector:Offset
       Of Real Mode
       Register Data
	CF = Set if Request Fails
	ES:DI = Selector:Offset
	     of Modified Real
	     Mode Register
	     Data Structure
	AX = 08012h, 08013h,
	    08014h or 08021h if
	    Request Fails
		Simulate a Real Mode
		Far Call Execution
		passed to Real Mode
		Subroutine. Return uses.
		"ret".

Register Data in Format:

Offset	Length	Contents
0×000	4	DI/EDI
0×004	4	SI/ESI
0×008	4	BP/EBP
0×00C	4	Reserved
0×010	4	BX/EBX
0×014	4	DX/EDX
0×018	4	CX/ECX

8

APPENDICES

INPUT PARAMETERS	OUTPUT PARAMETERS	NAME AND COMMENTS
		0×01C 4 AX/EAX
		0×020 2 CPU Flags
		0×022 2 ES
		0×025 2 DS
		0×026 2 FS
		0×028 2 GS
		0×02A 2 IP
		0×02C 2 CS
		0×02E 2 SP
		0×030 2 SS

Int 31h
AX = 00302h
 	
BH = Flags
  Bit 0 - Zero
CX = Number of Words
    to Copy
ES:DI = Selector:Offset
    Of Real Mode
    Register Data
	CF = Set if Request Fails
	ES:DI = Selector : Offset
	    of Modified Real
	    Mode Register
	    Data Structure
	AX = 08012h, 08013h,
	    08014h or 08021h if
	    Request Fails
		Simulate a Real Mode
		Far Call - Execution
		passed to Real Mode
		Subroutine. Return uses.
		"iret"
		
		  Register Data in Format:
		Offset Length Contents
		0×000 4 DI/EDI
		0×004 4 SI/ESI
		0×008 4 BP/EBP
		0×00C 4 Reserved
		0×010 4 BX/EBX
		0×014 4 DX/EDX
		0×018 4 CX/ECX
		0×01C 4 AX/EAX
		0×020 2 CPU Flags
		0×022 2 ES
		0×025 2 DS
		0×026 2 FS
		0×028 2 GS
		0×02A 2 IP
		0×02C 2 CS
		0×02E 2 SP
		0×030 2 SS

Int 31h
AX = 00303h
DS:SI = Selector : Offset
    Of Protect
    Mode
    Subroutine
ES:DI = Selector : Offset
    Of Real Mode
    Register Data
	CF = Set if Request Fails
	AX = 08015h if Request
	    Fails
	CX:DX = Segment:Offset
	    of Real Mode
	    Callback
		Allocate Real Mode
		Callback Address–
		Transfer Control from Real
		Mode to Protected Mode.

Int 31h
AX = 00304h
CX:DX = Real Mode
    Callback Address
	CF = Set if Request Fails
	AX = 08024h if Request
	    Fails
		Free Real Mode Callback
		Address

INPUT PARAMETERS	OUTPUT PARAMETERS	NAME AND COMMENTS

Int 31h
AX = 00305h
	CF = Reset
	AX = Buffer Size in Bytes
	BX:CX = Real Mode
	       Address
	SI:DI = Protected Mode
	       Address
		Get State Save/Restore
		Addresses - Return
		Address of routines used
		to save and restore task's
		Registers.

Int 31h
Mode
 	
AX = 00306h
	Sitch
	
	CF = Reset
	BX:CX = Real to
	       Protected
	SI:DI = Protected to
	       Real Mode Switch
	       Address
		Address
		
		Get Raw Mode Switch
		Address for low-level
		Switching.

Int 31h
AX = 00400h
	CF = Reset
	AH = DPMI Major Version
	       Number
	AL = DPMI Minor Version
	       Number
	BX = Flags
	  Bit 0 Set if Host is 32 bit
	    BPMI
	  Bit 1 Set if execution
	    Returned to Real Mode
	    for "Reflected" interrupts
	  Bit 2 Set if VM Supported
	  Bit 3 Reserved
	CL = Processor Type
	  2 = 80286
	  3 = 80386
	  4 = 80486
	  5 = Pentium
	DH = Current Virtual PIC2
	    Base Interrupt Value
	DL = Current Virtual Slave
	    PIC Base Interrupt
	    Value
		Get DPMI Version
		Information.

Int 31h
AX = 00500h
ES:DI = Selector : Offset
      Of 48 Byte
      Buffer
	CF = Reset	Get Free Memory
		Information–Load Buffer
		with Information about the
		Current Memory Status.
		Offset Length Contents
		0×000 4 Largest

INPUT PARAMETERS	OUTPUT PARAMETERS	NAME AND COMMENTS		
		0×004	4	Free Block Available Maximum Unlocked Page Available
		0×008	4	Maximum Locked Page Available
		0×00C	4	Linear Address Space Size in Pages
		0×010	4	Total Number of Unlocked Pages
		0×014	4	Total Number of Free Pages
		0×018	4	Total Number of Physical Pages
		0×01C	4	Free Linear Address Space in Pages
		0×020	4	Size of Paging File in Pages
		0×024	12	Reserved

Int 31h
AX = 00501h
BX:DX = Size of Block in
    Bytes
	CF = Set if Request Fails
	AX = 08012, 08013,
	    08014, 08016h or
	    08021h if Request
	    Fails
	BX:CX = Linear Address of
	    Allocated
	    Memory Block
		Allocate Memory Block.		

INPUT PARAMETERS	OUTPUT PARAMETERS	NAME AND COMMENTS
	SI:DI = Memory Block Handle	
Int 31h AX = 00502h SI:DI = Memory Block Handle	CF = Set if Request Fails AX = 08023h if Request Fails	Free Allocated Memory Block.
Int 31h AX = 00503h BX:CX = New Size Of Block SI:DI = Memory Block Handle	CF = Set if Request Fails AX = 08012, 08013h, 08014h, 08016h, or 08021h or 08023h if Request Fails	Resize the Allocated Memory Block.
Int 31h AX = 00600h BX:CX = Starting Segment : Offset Of Real Memory SI:DI = Size of Block to Lock	CF = Set if Request Fails AX = 08013h, 08017h, 08025h if Request Fails	Lock the Specified Linear Region.
Int 31h AX = 00601h BX:CX = Starting Segment : Offset Of Locked Real Memory SI:DI = Size of Block to Unlock	CF = Set if Request Fails AX = 08002h or 08025h if Request Fails	Unlock the Specified Linear Address.
Int 31h AX = 00602h BX:CX = Starting Segment : Offset Of Real Memory SI:DI = Size of Block	CF = Set if Request Fails AX = 08002h or 08025h if Request Fails	Mark the Real Mode Memory Region as Pageable.
Int 31h AX = 00603h BX:CX = Starting Segment : Offset Of Real Memory SI:DI = Size of Block	CF = Set if Request Fails AX = 08002h, 08013h or 08025h if Request Fails	Relock Real Mode Memory Region as No Longer Pageable.
Int 31h AX = 00604h	CF = Set if Request Fails AX = 08001h if Request	Get the Page Size.

8

APPENDICES

INPUT PARAMETERS	OUTPUT PARAMETERS	NAME AND COMMENTS
	Fails BX:CX = Page Size in Bytes	

Int 31h
AX = 00702h
BX:CX = Starting
      Segment : Offset
      Of Real Memory
SI:DI = Size of Block
	CF = Set if Request Fails
	AX = 08025h if Request
	      Fails
		Mark Page as Demand
		Paging Candidate.

Int 31h
AX = 00703h
BX:CX = Starting
      Segment : Offset
      Of Real Memory
SI:DI = Size of Block
	CF = Set if Request Fails
	AX = 08025h if Request
	      Fails
		Discard Page Contents–
		Block will no longer be
		paged to disk.

Int 31h
AX = 00800h
BX:CX = Starting
      Segment : Offset
      Of Real Memory
SI:DI = Size of Block
	CF = Set if Request Fails
	AX = 08003h or 08021h if
	      Request Fails
	BX:CX = Linear Address
	      of Physical
	      Memory
		Physical Address
		Mapping - Converts
		Physical Address to
		Linear Address.

Int 31h
AX = 00900h
	CF = Reset
	AL = 1 if Virtual Interrupts
	      Were previously
	      Enabled
		Get and Disable Virtual
		Interrupts.

Int 31h
AX = 00901h
	CF = Reset
	AL = 1 if Virtual Interrupts
	      Were Previously
	      Enabled
		Get and Enable Virtual
		Interrupts.

Int 31h AX = 00902h	CF = Reset AL = 1 if Virtual Interrupts Are Enabled	Get the Virtual Interrupt State.

Int 31h
AX = 00A00h
DS:SI = Selector : Offset
      Of ASCIIZ
      String
	CF = Set if Request Fails
	AX = 08001h if Request
	      Fails
	ES:DI = Selector : Offset of
	      Extended API Entry
	      Point.
		Get Vendor Specified API
		Entry Point. The DX, GS,
		EAX, ECX, EDX, ESI and
		EBP may be Modified.

INPUT PARAMETERS	OUTPUT PARAMETERS	NAME AND COMMENTS

Int 31h
AX = 00B00h
BX:CX = Linear Address
      Watchpoint
DH = Type of Watchpoint
 0 - Execute
 1 - Write
 2 - Read/Write
DL = Size of Watchpoint
    in Bytes (up to 4)
	CF = Set if Request Fails
	AX = 08016h, 08021h or
	    08035h if Request
	    Fails
	BX = Watchpoint Handle
		Set a Debug Watchpoint.

Int 31h AX = 00B01h BX = Watchpoint Handle	CF = Set if Request Fails AX = 08023h if Request Fails	Clear a Debug Watchpoint.

Int 31h
AX = 00B02h
BX = Watchpoint Handle
	CF = Set if Request Fails
	AX = 08023h if Request
	    Fails
	AX = 1 if Request
	    Completes And
	    Watchpoint
	    Encountered
		Poll the State of the
		Watchpoint.

Int 31h AX = 00B03h BX = Watchpoint Handle	CF = Set if Request Fails AX = 08023h if Request Fails	Reset the Debug Watchpoint.

8

APPENDICES

MICROSOFT
FOUNDATION CLASS
HIERARCHY CHART

The *Microsoft Foundation Classes (MFC)* is the basis for the Microsoft Windows interface. These classes provide access to wide variety of different objects and data structures. The classes can be used to derive new ones for new data structures and dialog-box controls.

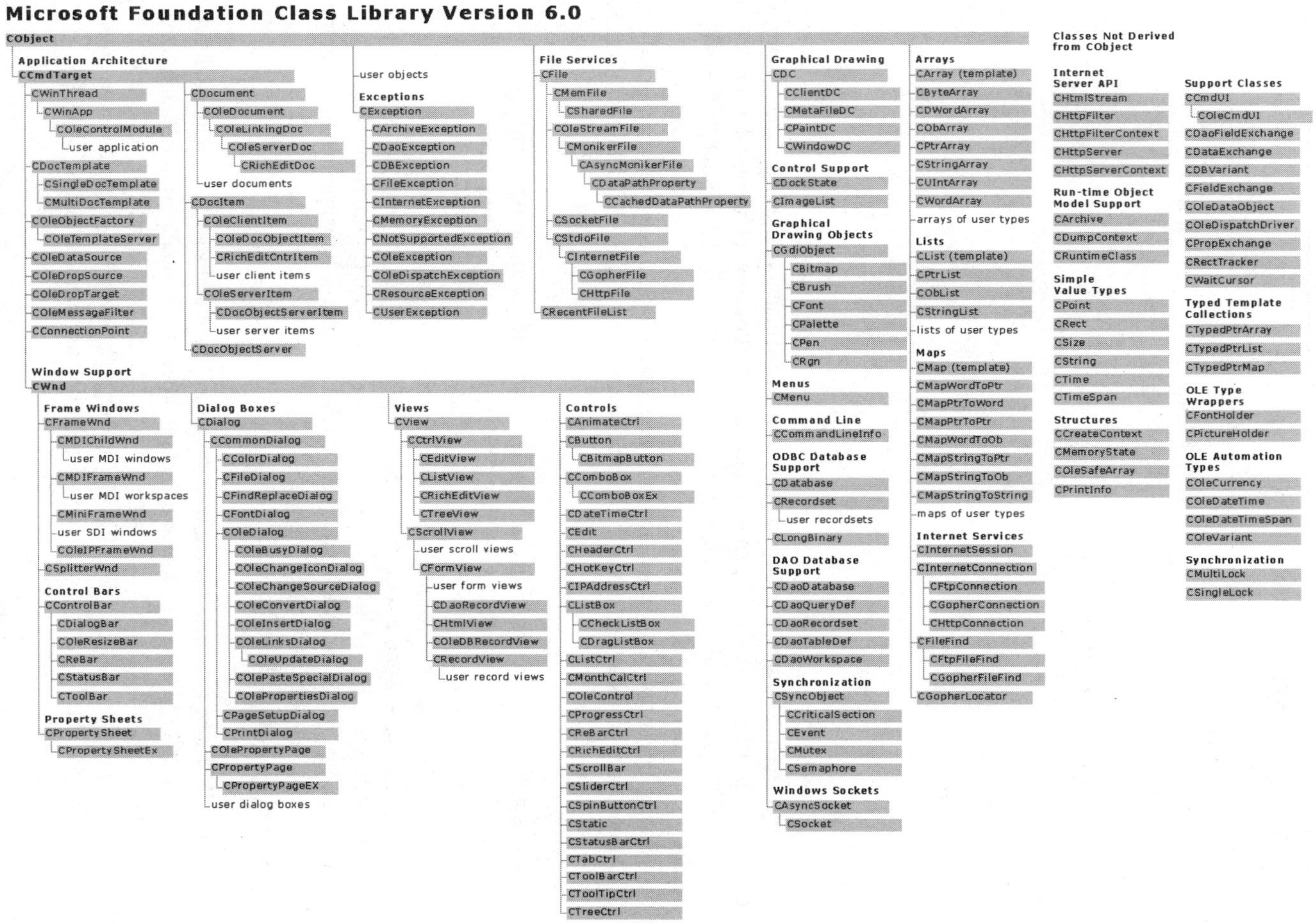

Microsoft Foundation Class Library Version 6.0

CObject

Application Architecture

CCmdTarget
- CWinThread
  - CWinApp
    - COleControlModule
    - -user application
- CDocTemplate
  - CSingleDocTemplate
  - CMultiDocTemplate
- COleObjectFactory
  - COleTemplateServer
- COleDataSource
- COleDropSource
- COleDropTarget
- COleMessageFilter
- CConnectionPoint

CDocument
- COleDocument
  - COleLinkingDoc
    - COleServerDoc
    - CRichEditDoc
- -user documents
- CDocItem
  - COleClientItem
    - COleDocObjectItem
    - CRichEditCntrItem
  - COleServerItem
    - CDocObjectServerItem
  - -user client items
  - -user server items
- CDocObjectServer

-user objects

Exceptions

CException
- CArchiveException
- CDaoException
- CDBException
- CFileException
  - CInternetException
- CMemoryException
- CNotSupportedException
- COleException
  - COleDispatchException
- CResourceException
- CUserException

File Services

CFile
- CMemFile
  - CSharedFile
- COleStreamFile
- CMonikerFile
  - CAsyncMonikerFile
    - CDataPathProperty
      - CCachedDataPathProperty
- CSocketFile
- CStdioFile
  - CInternetFile
    - CGopherFile
    - CHttpFile
- CRecentFileList

Graphical Drawing

CDC
- CClientDC
- CMetaFileDC
- CPaintDC
- CWindowDC

Control Support

CDockState
CImageList

Graphical Drawing Objects

CGdiObject
- CBitmap
- CBrush
- CFont
- CPalette
- CPen
- CRgn

Arrays

CArray (template)
- CByteArray
- CWordArray
- CDWordArray
- CPtrArray
- CStringArray
- CUIntArray
- CWordArray
- -arrays of user types

Lists

CList (template)
- CPtrList
- CObList
- CStringList
- -lists of user types

Maps

CMap (template)
- CMapWordToPtr
- CMapPtrToWord
- CMapPtrToPtr
- CMapWordToOb
- CMapStringToPtr
- CMapStringToOb
- CMapStringToString
- -maps of user types

Classes Not Derived from CObject

Internet Server API
- CHtmlStream
- CHttpFilter
- CHttpFilterContext
- CHttpServer
- CHttpServerContext

Run-time Object Model Support
- CArchive
- CDumpContext
- CRuntimeClass

Simple Value Types
- CPoint
- CRect
- CSize
- CString
- CTime
- CTimeSpan

Structures
- CCreateContext
- CMemoryState
- COleSafeArray
- CPrintInfo

Support Classes
- CCmdUI
- COleCmdUI
- CDaoFieldExchange
- CDataExchange
- CDBVariant
- CFieldExchange
- COleDataObject
- COleDispatchDriver
- CPropExchange
- CRectTracker
- CWaitCursor

Typed Template Collections
- CTypedPtrArray
- CTypedPtrList
- CTypedPtrMap

OLE Type Wrappers
- CFontHolder
- CPictureHolder

OLE Automation Types
- COleCurrency
- COleDateTime
- COleDateTimeSpan
- COleVariant

Synchronization
- CMultiLock
- CSingleLock

Menus

CMenu

Command Line

CCommandLineInfo

ODBC Database Support

CDatabase
CRecordset
-user recordsets

DAO Database Support

CDaoDatabase
CDaoQueryDef
CDaoRecordset
CDaoTableDef
CDaoWorkspace

Synchronization

CSyncObject
- CCriticalSection
- CEvent
- CMutex
- CSemaphore

Windows Sockets

CAsyncSocket
- CSocket

Internet Services

CInternetSession
CInternetConnection
- CFtpConnection
- CGopherConnection
- CHttpConnection
CFileFind
- CFtpFileFind
- CGopherFileFind
CGopherLocator

CLongBinary

Controls

- CAnimateCtrl
- CButton
  - CBitmapButton
- CComboBox
  - CComboBoxEx
- CDateTimeCtrl
- CEdit
- CHeaderCtrl
- CHotKeyCtrl
- CIPAddressCtrl
- CListBox
  - CCheckListBox
  - CDragListBox
- CListCtrl
- COleControl
- CMonthCalCtrl
- CProgressCtrl
- CReBarCtrl
- CRichEditCtrl
- CScrollBar
- CSliderCtrl
- CSpinButtonCtrl
- CStatic
- CStatusBarCtrl
- CTabCtrl
- CToolBarCtrl
- CToolTipCtrl
- CTreeCtrl

Views

CView
- CCtrlView
  - CEditView
  - CListView
  - CRichEditView
  - CTreeView
- CScrollView
  - -user scroll views
  - CFormView
    - CHtmlView
    - CDaoRecordView
    - CRecordView
  - -user form views
  - -user record views

Window Support

CWnd

Frame Windows

CFrameWnd
- CMDIChildWnd
- -user MDI windows
- CMDIFrameWnd
- -user MDI workspaces
- CMiniFrameWnd
- -user SDI windows
- COleIPFrameWnd
CSplitterWnd

Control Bars

CControlBar
- CDialogBar
- COleResizeBar
- CReBar
- CStatusBar
- CToolBar

Property Sheets

CPropertySheet
- CPropertySheetEx

Dialog Boxes

CDialog
- CCommonDialog
  - CColorDialog
  - CFileDialog
  - CFindReplaceDialog
  - CFontDialog
- COleDialog
  - COleBusyDialog
  - COleChangeIconDialog
  - COleChangeSourceDialog
  - COleConvertDialog
  - COleInsertDialog
  - COleLinksDialog
  - COleUpdateDialog
  - COlePasteSpecialDialog
  - COlePropertiesDialog
- CPageSetupDialog
- CPrintDialog
CPropertyPage
- CPropertyPageEx
-user dialog boxes

FIGURE K-1 "Microsoft Foundation Library" classes.

THE

CD-ROM

I am pleased to be able to give you the source and executable files from the book on a CD-ROM. The CD-ROM also has an *html* interface to allow you to browse the contents of the CD-ROM quickly and easily and link to my web page for updates, errata and the latest PC links that I have been able to find.

Rather than provide a "page" for each application or project, I have broken the applications and projects presented in this book into the following subdirectories on the CD-ROM:

- assembler—the Assembly Language Template and Example Applications
- utilities—Utility Program for finding out more about the PC and helping you with your own Applications
- projects—Source code and Executables for the Projects
- soundblaster—Source code and Executables for Operating your "SoundBlaster" card
- VisualBasic—Example Visual Basic Applications with Control Enhancements
- games—some of the Applications which not only show how application programming is done, but you can waste time with
- html—The html Interface code

The CD-ROM has been created with "autorun" code and should bring up an html interface on your web browser. To access the html interface manually, start a Web browser (for this appendix, I have used Microsoft's "Internet Explorer"). Under "Files", select "Open" as is shown in Fig. L-1. After clicking on "Open", you will get a request to enter a file specification (Fig. L-2) from which you will click on "Browse . . ." (Fig. L-3).

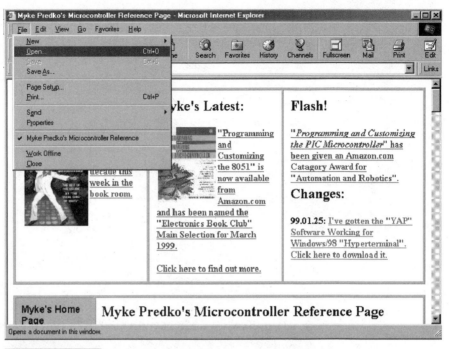

FIGURE L-1   Opening a file from Internet Explorer.

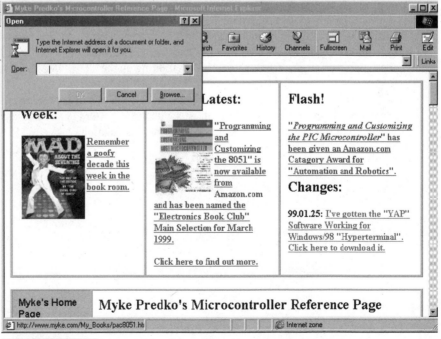

FIGURE L-2   Specifying a file to open in Internet Explorer.

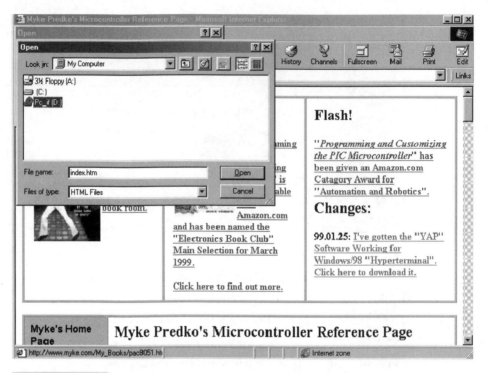

FIGURE L-3   Selecting the CD-ROM as the .html source.

From the Disk selection under "My Computer", select your CD-ROM drive (which, in my PC is "D:") and then double click on "index.html" (Fig. L-4). The browser will return you to the "Open" dialog box, which is the same as Fig. L-2 except that the file to open has been entered for you. Clicking on "OK" will bring up the CD-ROM's html Interface (Fig. L-5).

Every effort has been made to ensure that the CD-ROM works properly and all the files on it are correct. If you have any problems with the CD-ROM at all, please contact me via email and I will get you the missing or corrected information.

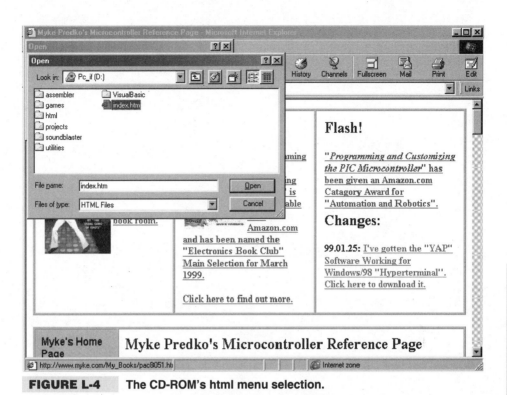

FIGURE L-4   The CD-ROM's html menu selection.

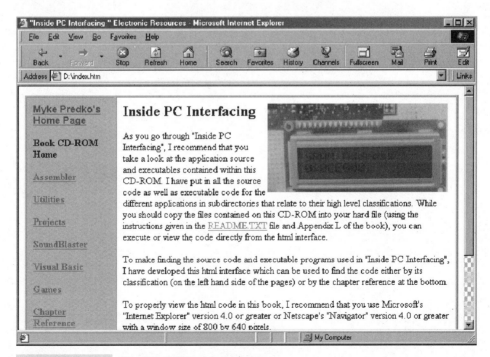

FIGURE L-5   The CD-ROM's html interface.

INDEX

Note: **Boldface** numbers indicate illustrations.

ABOUT THE AUTHOR

Myke Predko is the author of *Programming & Customizing the 8051™ Microcontroller*, *The Microcontroller Handbook*, and *Programming & Customizing the PIC Microcontroller*, also from TAB Books, and New Product Test Engineer at Celestica in Toronto, Ontario, Canada, where he works with new electronic product designers. He has also served as a test engineer, product engineer, and manufacturing manager for some of the world's largest computer manufacturers. Mr. Predko has a patent pending on an automated test for PC motherboards as well as patents pending on microcontroller architecture design. He is a graduate of the University of Waterloo in electrical engineering.

SOFTWARE AND INFORMATION LICENSE